ALFRED · A · KNOPF · NEW YORK

CHARLES
UNIVERSITY
OF CALIFORNIA,
BERKELEY
MUSCATINE
& MARLENE
GRIFFITH
LANEY COLLEGE

THE SECOND EDITION

BORZOI

COLLEGE

READER

Acknowledgments

W. H. AUDEN, "September 1, 1939" from *The Collected Poetry of W. H. Auden.* Copyright 1940 and renewed 1968 by W. H. Auden. Reprinted by permission of Random House, Inc., and Faber and Faber, Ltd. "Moon Landing" from *The New Yorker.* Copyright © 1968 by The New Yorker Magazine, Inc. Reprinted by permission of Curtis Brown, Ltd.

JAMES BALDWIN, from *The Fire Next Time.* Copyright © 1963, 1962 by James Baldwin. Reprinted by permission of the publisher, The Dial Press. "Notes of a Native Son" from *Notes of a Native Son* by James Baldwin. Copyright © 1955 by James Baldwin. Reprinted by permission of Beacon Press.

RUTH BENEDICT, "Racism: The *ism* of the Modern World" from *Race: Science and Politics* by Ruth Benedict. Copyright 1940 by Ruth Benedict. Reprinted by permission of The Viking Press, Inc., and Routledge & Kegan Paul, Ltd.

BRUNO BETTELHEIM, "The Anatomy of Academic Discontent" from *Change in Higher Education* (May–June 1969), pp. 18–26. Reprinted by permission of the author and *Change* Magazine.

HAIG A. BOSMAJIAN, "The Language of White Racism" from *College English,* Vol. 31, no. 3 (December 1969). Reprinted by permission of the author and the National Council of Teachers of English.

NORMAN O. BROWN, "Apocalypse" from *Harper's,* 222 (May 1961), 47–49. Reprinted by permission of the author.

ROBERT BRUSTEIN, "The Case for Professionalism" from *The New Republic* (April 26, 1969). © 1969, Harrison-Blaine of New Jersey, Inc. Reprinted by permission of *The New Republic.*

ALBERT CAMUS, "The Artist and His Time" from *The Myth of Sisphyus and Other Essays* by Albert Camus, translated by Justin O'Brien. Retitled "What Can the Artist Do in the World of Today?" in this edition. Copyright © 1955 by Alfred A. Knopf, Inc. Reprinted by permission of Alfred A. Knopf, Inc.

NICOLA CHIAROMONTE, "Letter from Rome" from *Encounter* (July 1968). Reprinted by permission of the author and publisher.

KENNETH B. CLARK, "The Cry of the Ghetto" from *Dark Ghetto* by Kenneth B. Clark. Copyright © 1965 by Kenneth B. Clark. Reprinted by permission of Harper & Row, Publishers, Inc.

ELDRIDGE CLEAVER, "A Religious Conversion, More or Less" and " 'The Christ' and His Teachings" from *Soul on Ice* by Eldridge Cleaver. Copy-

ERICH FROMM, from *The Revolution of Hope,* pp. 25–46, 133–140. Copyright © 1968 by Erich Fromm. Reprinted by permission of Harper & Row, Publishers, Inc.

ROBERT FROST, "For Once, Then, Something" from *The Poetry of Robert Frost* edited by Edward Connery Lathem. Copyright 1923, © 1969 by Holt, Rinehart and Winston, Inc. Copyright 1951 by Robert Frost. Reprinted by permission of Holt, Rinehart and Winston, Inc.

RICHARD GILMAN, "White Standards and Black Writing" from *The Confusion of Realms* by Richard Gilman. Copyright © 1963, 1966, 1967, 1968, 1969 by Richard Gilman. Reprinted by permission of Random House, Inc.

ALLEN GINSBERG, "A Letter to Secretary McNamara" from *Allen Ginsberg in America* by Jane Kramer. Copyright © 1968, 1969 by Jane Kramer. Reprinted by permission of Random House, Inc. Part of the material in this book originally appeared in *The New Yorker* in somewhat different form. "A Supermarket in California" from *Howl and Other Poems* by Allen Ginsberg. Copyright © 1956, 1959 by Allen Ginsberg. Reprinted by permission of City Lights Books.

WILLIAM GOLDING, from "Party of One—Thinking as a Hobby," first published in *Holiday.* © 1961 The Curtis Publishing Company. Reprinted by permission of the author.

RICHARD HOFSTADTER, "Commencement Address" from *The American Scholar,* Vol. 37 (Autumn 1969). Copyright © 1968 by the United Chapters of Phi Beta Kappa. Reprinted by permission of the publisher.

JOHN HOLT, "Introduction" to *Teaching the Unteachable* by Herbert Kohl. Copyright © 1967 The New York Review. Reprinted by permission of *The New York Review of Books.* "Letter from Berkeley" from *Yale Alumni Magazine* (November 1969). Copyright © 1969 by John Holt. Reprinted by permission of Robert Lescher, Literary Agent.

GERARD MANLEY HOPKINS, "God's Grandeur" from *Poems of Gerard Manley Hopkins,* Third Edition, edited by W. H. Gardner. Copyright 1948 by Oxford University Press, Inc. Reprinted by permission of Oxford University Press, Inc.

ALDOUS HUXLEY, "The Arts of Selling" and "Propaganda Under a Dictatorship" from *Brave New World Revisited* by Aldous Huxley. Copyright © 1958 by Aldous Huxley. Reprinted by permission of Harper & Row, Publishers, Inc., and Chatto and Windus, Ltd.

JANE JACOBS, "Violence in the City Streets" (title of version in *Harper's* [September 1961], pp. 37–43) by Jane Jacobs. This material appears in another version in *The Death and Life of Great American Cities* by Jane Jacobs. Reprinted by permission of Random House, Inc. "How City Planners Hurt Cities" from *Saturday Evening Post* (October 14, 1961), pp. 12, 14. © 1961 by Jane Jacobs. Reprinted by permission of the author.

PAUL JACOBS, "The Most Cheerful Graveyard in the World" from *The Reporter* (September 18, 1958), pp. 26–30. Copyright © 1958 by Paul Jacobs. Reprinted by permission of Cyrilly Abels.

DAN JACOBSON, "The Severed Tendon" from *No Further West* by Dan Jacobson. Copyright © 1957, 1958, 1959 by Dan Jacobson. Reprinted by permission of The Macmillan Company and Weidenfeld and Nicolson, Ltd.

LEROI JONES, "Young Soul" from *Black Magic: Poetry 1961–1967* by LeRoi Jones. Copyright © 1969 by LeRoi Jones. Reprinted by permission of the publisher, The Bobbs-Merrill Company, Inc. "The Myth of a 'Negro Literature'" from *Home: Social Essays* by LeRoi Jones. Copyright © 1962, 1966 by LeRoi Jones. Reprinted by permission of William Morrow and Company, Inc. "The Revolutionary Theatre" from *Liberator*, Vol. 5 (July 1965). Copyright © 1965 by *Liberator*. Reprinted by permission of the publisher.

MARTIN LUTHER KING, JR., "Letter from Birmingham Jail, April 16, 1963" from *Why We Can't Wait* by Martin Luther King, Jr. Copyright © 1963 by Martin Luther King, Jr. Reprinted by permission of Harper & Row, Publishers, Inc.

JAMES SIMON KUNEN, from *The Strawberry Statement*. Copyright © 1968, 1969 by James S. Kunen. Reprinted by permission of Random House, Inc.

SUSANNE K. LANGER, "The Prince of Creation" from *Fortune* (January 1944), pp. 127–128, 130, 132, 134, 136, 139–140, 142, 144, 146, 148, 150, 152, 154. Reprinted by permission of the author. Originally entitled "The Lord of Creation." "The Cultural Importance of Art" from *Philosophical Sketches* by Susanne K. Langer, Baltimore, The Johns Hopkins Press, 1962. Reprinted by permission.

WALTER LAQUEUR, "Reflections on Youth Movements" from *Commentary* (June 1969). Copyright © 1969 by the American Jewish Committee. Reprinted by permission of the author and publisher.

WALTER LIPPMANN, "The Indispensable Opposition" from *The Atlantic Monthly* (August 1939). Copyright © 1939, 1967, The Atlantic Monthly Company, Boston, Mass. Reprinted by permission of the author and publisher.

ARCHIBALD MACLEISH, "Ars Poetica" from *Collected Poems 1917–1952* by Archibald MacLeish. Reprinted by permission of Houghton Mifflin Company.

NORMAN MAILER, "Why Are We in New York?" from *The New York*

ACKNOWLEDGMENTS

Times Magazine (May 18, 1969). © 1969 by The New York Times Company. Reprinted by permission of the author, the publisher, and the author's agent, Scott Meredith Literary Agent, Inc., 580 Fifth Avenue, New York, N.Y. 10036.

MALCOLM X, "The Ballot or the Bullet" from *Malcolm X Speaks* edited by George Breitman. Copyright © 1965 by Merit Publishers and Betty Shabazz. Reprinted by permission of Pathfinder Press, Inc.

MARYA MANNES, "How Do You Know It's Good?" from *But Will It Sell?* by Marya Mannes. Copyright, ©, 1964 by Marya Mannes. Reprinted by permission of J. B. Lippincott Company.

HENRI MATISSE, "Notes of a Painter" from *Matisse: His Art and His Public* by Alfred H. Barr, Jr. Copyright 1951 by The Museum of Modern Art, New York. Reprinted with its permission. "Notes d'un peintre" was originally published in *La Grande Revue*, Paris, December 25, 1908. The first complete English translation by Margaret Scolari Barr was published in *Henri-Matisse*, The Museum of Modern Art, 1931, and then again in *Matisse: His Art and His Public*, together with paragraph headings which were added by the editor for the convenience of the reader.

THOMAS MERTON, "Day of a Stranger." Copyright © 1967 by the Trustees of the Merton Legacy Trust. Reprinted by permission of New Directions Publishing Corporation for the Trustees of the Merton Legacy Trust. First published in *The Hudson Review*, Vol. XX (Summer 1967).

MARIANNE MOORE, "Poetry" from *Collected Poems* by Marianne Moore. Copyright 1935 by Marianne Moore, renewed 1963 by Marianne Moore and T. S. Eliot. Reprinted by permission of The Macmillan Company.

PERRY MORGAN, "The Case for the White Southerner" from *Esquire* (January 1962), pp. 41, 43, 45, 134. © 1961 by Esquire, Inc. Reprinted by permission of Esquire, Inc.

LEWIS MUMFORD, "The Disappearing City" from *The Urban Prospect* by Lewis Mumford. © 1962 by Lewis Mumford. Reprinted by permission of Harcourt Brace Jovanovich, Inc.

GEORGE ORWELL, "Politics and the English Language" and "Shooting an Elephant" from *Shooting an Elephant and Other Essays* by George Orwell. Copyright, 1945, 1946, 1949, 1950, by Sonia Brownell Orwell. "Marrakech" and "Why I Write" from *Such, Such Were the Joys* by George Orwell. Copyright, 1945, 1952, 1953, by Sonia Brownell Orwell. Reprinted by permission of Harcourt Brace Jovanovich, Inc., Sonia Brownell, and Secker & Warburg, Ltd.

NORMAN PODHORETZ, "My Negro Problem—and Ours" from *Doings and Undoings* by Norman Podhoretz. Copyright © 1963 by Norman Podhoretz. Reprinted by permission of Farrar, Straus & Giroux, Inc.

"Public Statement of Eight Alabama Clergymen" issued April 12, 1963, Pamphlet No. 589A of the American Friends Service Committee. Reprinted by permission of the Protestant Episcopal Church in the Diocese of Alabama, a corporation.

MARY CAROLINE RICHARDS, from *Centering.* Copyright © 1964 by Mary Caroline Richards. Reprinted by permission of Wesleyan University Press.

JAMES HARVEY ROBINSON, "On Various Kinds of Thinking" from *The Mind in the Making* by James Harvey Robinson. Copyright 1921 by Harper & Brothers; renewed 1949 by Bankers Trust Company. Reprinted by permission of Harper & Row, Publishers, Inc.

JOHN A. T. ROBINSON, "Our Image of God Must Go" from *The Observer, London* (March 17, 1963), p. 1. Reprinted by permission of The Observer, London.

THEODORE ROSZAK, from *The Making of a Counter Culture,* pp. 205–209, 269–289. Copyright © 1968, 1969 by Theodore Roszak. Reprinted by permission of Doubleday & Company, Inc.

CARL SANDBURG, "Chicago" from *Chicago Poems* by Carl Sandburg. Copyright 1916 by Holt, Rinehart and Winston, Inc. Copyright 1944 by Carl Sandburg. Reprinted by permission of Holt, Rinehart and Winston, Inc.

W. T. STACE, "Man Against Darkness" from *The Atlantic Monthly,* 182 (September 1948), 53–58. Reprinted by permission of Mrs. W. T. Stace.

DYLAN THOMAS, "In My Craft or Sullen Art" from *Collected Poems* by Dylan Thomas. Copyright 1946 by New Directions Publishing Corporation. Reprinted by permission of New Directions Publishing Corporation and J. M. Dent & Sons, Ltd., Literary Executors of the Dylan Thomas Estate.

JAMES THURBER, "The Greatest Man in the World," from *The Thurber Carnival,* published by Harper & Row. Copr. © 1945 James Thurber. Reprinted by permission of Mrs. James Thurber. Originally appeared in *The New Yorker.*

PAUL TILLICH, "The Lost Dimension in Religion" from *The Saturday Evening Post* (June 14, 1958). Copyright © 1958 by the Curtis Publishing Company. Reprinted by permission of *The Saturday Evening Post.*

MAO TSE-TUNG, "Talks at the Yenan Forum on Art and Literature" from *Selected Works* (1941–1945), Vol. IV. Copyright © 1956 by International Publishers Co., Inc. Reprinted by permission of International Publishers Co., Inc.

BARBARA W. TUCHMAN, "The Missing Element: Moral Courage" from *In Search of Leaders: Current Issues in Higher Education* edited by G. Kerry Smith. Reprinted by permission of the National Education Association.

RICHARD M. WEAVER, "Ultimate Terms in Contemporary Rhetoric" from Chapter 9 of *The Ethics of Rhetoric* by Richard M. Weaver. Copyright 1953 by Henry Regnery Company. Reprinted by permission of Henry Regnery Company.

EUDORA WELTY, "Must the Novelist Crusade?" Copyright © 1965 by Eudora Welty. Reprinted by permission of Random House, Inc. This essay will appear in a collection of Miss Welty's literary essays, to be published by Random House, Inc. Originally appeared in *The Atlantic Monthly* (October 1965).

E. B. WHITE, "The Morning of the Day They Did It (February 25, 1950)" from *The Second Tree from the Corner* by E. B. White. Copyright 1950 by E. B. White. Reprinted by permission of Harper & Row, Publishers, Inc. Originally appeared in *The New Yorker*.

LYNN WHITE, JR., "The Historical Roots of Our Ecologic Crisis," from *Science*, 155 (March 10, 1967), 1203–1207. Copyright 1967 by the American Association for the Advancement of Science. Reprinted by permission of the author and publisher.

TOM WOLFE, "O Rotten Gotham" from *The Pump House Gang* by Tom Wolfe. Copyright © 1968 by Tom Wolfe, copyright © 1966 by the World Journal Tribune Corporation, copyright © 1964, 1965, 1966 by the New York Herald Tribune, Inc. Reprinted by permission of Farrar, Straus & Giroux, Inc.

WILLIAM BUTLER YEATS, "Sailing to Byzantium" from *Collected Poems* by William Butler Yeats. Copyright 1928 by The Macmillan Company, renewed 1956 by Georgie Yeats. Reprinted by permission of The Macmillan Company, M. B. Yeats, and the Macmillan Co. of Canada.

We remain indebted to the colleagues and friends who helped us with the first edition of this book. Now others, including many teachers and students, have given valuable criticisms and suggestions for this revised edition. For their particular pains we should like to mention Rosemary Fayerwether, David Fogel, Robert J. Griffin, Virgil Grillo, Myrna Harrison, Hilda Johnston, Richard L. Larson, David Littlejohn, Emily Meyer, John M. Murphy, and Roger E. Wiehe. Mike Mehlman, Joan Berman and John McPherson helped us with bibliographical problems; Sandra Hudson and Alison Muscatine worked with us to prepare the manuscript; June Fischbein has seen the book through the press. To all, our grateful thanks!

Berkeley, California   C.M.
1971   M.G.

Contents

Introduction   xxi

THINKING AND FEELING   1

FULKE GREVILLE, LORD BROOKE *Chorus of Priests,
from* Mustapha [*poem*]   3

E. E. CUMMINGS *since feeling is first* [*poem*]   4

LEROI JONES *Young Soul* [*poem*]   5

WILLIAM GOLDING *Thinking as a Hobby*   5

JAMES HARVEY ROBINSON *On Various Kinds of Thinking*   12

ALDOUS HUXLEY *Propaganda Under a Dictatorship*   27

MARY CAROLINE RICHARDS *Centering as Dialogue*   33

RALPH WALDO EMERSON *The American Scholar*   42

NORMAN O. BROWN *Apocalypse*   54

THE RIGHT USE OF LANGUAGE   61

SUSANNE K. LANGER *The Prince of Creation*   63

GEORGE ORWELL *Politics and the English Language*   79

RICHARD M. WEAVER *Ultimate Terms in Contemporary Rhetoric*   90

ALLEN GINSBERG *A Letter to Secretary McNamara*   107

JOHN HOLT Introduction *to Herbert Kohl's "Teaching the
Unteachable"*   111

HAIG A. BOSMAJIAN *The Language of White Racism*   116

ALDOUS HUXLEY *The Arts of Selling*   127

PAUL JACOBS *The Most Cheerful Graveyard in the World*   134

THE AMERICAN CRISIS   143

WALT WHITMAN *I Hear America Singing* [*poem*]   145

ALLEN GINSBERG *A Supermarket in California* [*poem*]   145

ALEXIS DE TOCQUEVILLE   *Four Essays from* Democracy in America   146

Of the Principal Source of Belief Among Democratic Nations   147

*Why the Americans Are More Addicted to Practical Than to
   Theoretical Science*   151

What Sort of Despotism Democratic Nations Have to Fear   157

General Survey of the Subject   162

JOHN FITZGERALD KENNEDY   *Inaugural Address*   166

BENJAMIN DEMOTT   *America the Unimagining*   169

JOAN DIDION   *Some Dreamers of the Golden Dream*   178

HENRY STEELE COMMAGER   *A Historian Looks at
   Our Political Morality*   193

JAMES BALDWIN   *from* The Fire Next Time   199

RACE AND RACISM

211

RUTH BENEDICT   *Racism: The* ism *of the Modern World*   213

GEORGE ORWELL   *Shooting an Elephant*   215

GEORGE ORWELL   *Marrakech*   222

ROBERT COLES   *The Last Ditch*   227

PERRY MORGAN   *The Case for the White Southerner*   242

JAMES BALDWIN   *Notes of a Native Son*   251

NORMAN PODHORETZ   *My Negro Problem—and Ours*   269

FRANTZ FANON   *By Way of Conclusion*   281

DISSENT AND CIVIL DISOBEDIENCE

289

THOMAS JEFFERSON   *Declaration of Independence*   291

THE FIRST CONGRESS OF THE UNITED STATES   *The Bill of Rights*   295

WALTER LIPPMANN   *The Indispensable Opposition*   297

PLATO   *from* The Crito   304

HENRY DAVID THOREAU   *Civil Disobedience*   309

MARTIN LUTHER KING, JR.   *Letter from Birmingham Jail*   328

MALCOLM X *The Ballot or the Bullet* 345

ERWIN N. GRISWOLD *Dissent—1968 Style* 363

THE STUDENT AND THE UNIVERSITY 379

JAMES SIMON KUNEN *from* The Strawberry Statement 381

NICOLA CHIAROMONTE *Letter from Rome* 394

JOHN HOLT *Letter from Berkeley* 399

BRUNO BETTELHEIM *The Anatomy of Academic Discontent* 415

WALTER LAQUEUR *Reflections on Youth Movements* 428

ROBERT BRUSTEIN *The Case for Professionalism* 445

RICHARD HOFSTADTER *Commencement Address* 450

GEORGE W. WETHERILL *University Research at Livermore and Los Alamos* 456

TECHNOLOGY AND HUMAN VALUES 467

W. H. AUDEN *Moon Landing* [poem] 469

ERICH FROMM *Where Are We Now and Where Are We Headed?* 470

LYNN WHITE, JR. *The Historical Roots of Our Ecologic Crisis* 486

THEODORE ROSZAK *from* The Myth of Objective Consciousness 497

THEODORE ROSZAK *Objectivity Unlimited* 500

F. M. ESFANDIARY *The Mystical West Puzzles the Practical East* 515

JONATHAN SWIFT *The Grand Academy of Lagado* 521

E. B. WHITE *The Morning of the Day They Did It* [story] 529

THE FATE OF THE CITY 543

CARL SANDBURG *Chicago* [poem] 545

LEWIS MUMFORD *The Disappearing City* 546

DAN JACOBSON *The Severed Tendon* 552

JANE JACOBS *Violence in the City Streets* 556

JANE JACOBS *How City Planners Hurt Cities* 567

HARVEY COX *Anonymity*   572

TOM WOLFE *O Rotten Gotham*   581

KENNETH B. CLARK *The Cry of the Ghetto*   591

NORMAN MAILER *Why Are We in New York?*   599

THE FUTURE OF RELIGION   613

GERARD MANLEY HOPKINS *God's Grandeur* [poem]   615

MATTHEW ARNOLD *Dover Beach* [poem]   615

CLARENCE DARROW *Why I Am an Agnostic*   616

W. T. STACE *Man Against Darkness*   623

PAUL TILLICH *The Lost Dimension in Religion*   634

JOHN A. T. ROBINSON *Our Image of God Must Go*   642

ERICH FROMM *Toward Radical Humanism*   648

ELDRIDGE CLEAVER *A Religious Conversion, More or Less*   654

ELDRIDGE CLEAVER *"The Christ" and His Teachings*   655

THOMAS MERTON *Day of a Stranger*   660

THE FUNCTION OF ART   669

SUSANNE K. LANGER *The Cultural Importance of Art*   671

HENRI MATISSE *Notes of a Painter*   678

GEORGE ORWELL *Why I Write*   685

ALBERT CAMUS *What Can the Artist Do in the World of Today?* 691

MAO TSE-TUNG *from* Talks at the Yenan Forum on Art
and Literature   694

EUDORA WELTY *Must the Novelist Crusade?*   700

LEROI JONES *The Myth of a "Negro Literature"*   710

LEROI JONES *The Revolutionary Theatre*   717

SEVEN POEMS ON ART

JOHN KEATS, *Ode on a Grecian Urn*   721

WILLIAM BUTLER YEATS, *Sailing to Byzantium*   722

ROBERT FROST, *For Once, Then, Something*   724

MARIANNE MOORE, *Poetry*   724

W. H. AUDEN, *September 1, 1939*   725

DYLAN THOMAS, *In My Craft or Sullen Art*   728

ARCHIBALD MACLEISH, *Ars Poetica*   729

ON THE STANDARDS OF JUDGMENT   731

BARBARA W. TUCHMAN   *The Missing Element: Moral Courage*   733

JAMES THURBER   *The Greatest Man in the World* [story]   740

RICHARD GILMAN   *White Standards and Black Writing*   746

MARYA MANNES   *How Do You Know It's Good?*   753

Author and Title Index   } follows page 759
Rhetorical Index

Introduction

Most of the pieces in this book were written by the kind of person who thinks, feels, and cares. We present it in the hope that it will help the reader to discover his own thoughts and feelings, to test them actively among the thoughts and feelings of others, and to develop attitudes based on rational insight and human sympathy. We can think of few better means to this end than honest reading and honest writing, and no better time and place than a beginning college course.

In the first edition of this book our emphasis was squarely on the prose of thought. This revised edition is different in that although expository prose is still our main concern, we have opened the book out in the direction of feeling. The addition of such authors as Norman O. Brown, John Holt, Benjamin DeMott, Mary Caroline Richards, Allen Ginsberg, and Theodore Roszak give feeling more room as a subject for consideration. These authors and others—as Joan Didion, Frantz Fanon, Malcolm X, Tom Wolfe, Thomas Merton, and Norman Mailer —additionally bring more feeling into the book in their styles. We have added some more poems. This aspect of the revision, then, is intended to correct a certain dryness in the first edition and also to respond to a conviction growing in our culture—and debated in the first section of the book—that thinking by itself is not enough.

A second aspect of the revision simply brings it up to date. We have found that while the issues raised by each section remain comfortably permanent, the arguments in some have changed remarkably in recent years. Thus the sections entitled Thinking and Feeling, The American Crisis, The Future of Religion, Dissent and Civil Disobedience, and Technology and Human Values have been substantially reconceived, and there is something new in each section. A new section, The Student and the University, has been added. The section Race and Racism not only includes more recent pieces, but we have given new attention to the impact of the race problem in other sections: The Right Use of Language, The American Crisis, Dissent and Civil Disobedience, The Fate of the City, The Function of Art, On the Standards of Judgment.

These changes, and the desire to produce a smaller book, more accessible and more manageable, have made it necessary to exclude some sections that we thought less lively than the present ones. But some teachers will find old favorites missing, and for this we apologize.

Otherwise, the book's organization is the same. We have collected under each topic pieces representing a variety of attitudes, often in direct conflict with each other. The reading presents, then, a wide range of ideas and assumptions, and at the same time a continuous dialogue or debate among them. We hope that the reading, in raising issues, will help the reader to see that he has something to think about. Suggesting comparison at every point, giving ready occasion to take sides and to criticize, the book is directly suited to generating discussion and writing.

This second edition is richer in styles and genres than the first edition. Although it is still primarily organized to set off the exposition of ideas, it can be well studied for the way in which all of the major rhetorical categories—description, narration, definition, comparison, and the like— can be used to express or support ideas. Since all but a few of the essays are English originals, they can be studied as authentic examples of English style. Since all but a few are either complete works in themselves or are coherent, unabridged sections (usually chapters) of longer works, they can be studied as compositional wholes. We have made no silent omissions, preferring to present the essays as they were written, with the occasional peculiarities of their time and place. We preface each selection with a headnote about its author and its original publication.

THINKING
AND FEELING

Almost all of the pieces in this book are records of men and women deliberately using their capacities to think and to feel in an effort to comprehend experience—either their own experience or that of other people and other times. In this first section we present some works which deal directly with thought and feeling themselves. This section and the one following, on the right use of language, thus serve as preface and justification to the whole collection.

Our need for thought is clear. The eminent biochemist Albert Szent-Gyorgyi, thinking of the possibility of atomic war, has put the dilemma plainly: "If it is our intelligence which led us into trouble it may be our intelligence which can lead us out of it." The essay by Aldous Huxley printed in this section similarly suggests forcible, topical, practical arguments—in this case for thought as necessary protection against political annihilation.

But thinking is a discipline and an art, and often it is subverted rather than energized by feeling. What we accept rationally we often find hard to put into practice. Within us, what we think we think may be in unsettling and sometimes unconscious conflict with what we really feel. It is the recognition of this that adds to the persuasiveness of the first two essays. Golding's essay arises out of his awareness of the problem of distinguishing thought and feeling and is developed by a witty account of three different kinds of thinking. Robinson's fuller and more philosophical treatment of kinds of thinking is similarly based on his recognition of the unconscious and his wish to distinguish real thinking from emotional prejudice.

But even for trained thinkers, thinking is not enough. Threatened as we seem to be today by a mechanistic, alienating life style, we need more and more to be concerned with wholeness, with the self come together in equilibrium, the integration of thought and feeling in total experience. Thus Mary Caroline Richards argues that "wisdom is not the product of mental effort," but "a state of the total being." Emerson's famous essay also insists on the validity of total experience—"Only so much do I know, as I have lived"—and leads to the challenging distinction between "Man Thinking," characterized by self-trust, and man as "mere thinker" or parroter or bookworm. Norman O. Brown's Phi Beta Kappa address, delivered 123 years after Emerson's, also focuses on mind and feeling, but here mind "at the end of its tether," with our only hope in the rejection of rationality and the rediscovery of mysteries and magic.

Fulke Greville, Lord Brooke
(1554–1628)

CHORUS OF PRIESTS, FROM MUSTAPHA

Oh wearisome Condition of Humanity!
Borne under one Law, to another bound:
Vainely begot, and yet forbidden vanity:
Created sicke, commanded to be sound:
What meaneth Nature by these diverse Lawes?
Passion and Reason, Selfe-division cause:

Is it the marke, or Maiesty of Power
To make offences that it may forgive?
Nature herselfe, doth her owne selfe defloure,
To hate those errors She her selfe doth give.
For how should man thinke that, he may not doe
If Nature did not faile, and punish too?

Tyrant to others, to her selfe unjust,
Onely commands things difficult and hard.
Forbids us all things, which it knowes is lust,
Makes easy paines, unpossible reward.
If Nature did not take delight in blood,
She would have made more easie waies to good.

We that are bound by vowes, and by Promotion,
With pompe of holy Sacrifice and rites,
To teach beleefe in good and still devotion,
To preach of Heavens wonders, and delights:
Yet when each of us, in his owne heart lookes,
He findes the God there, farre unlike his Bookes.

                                        (1609)

3

E. E. Cummings (1894–1962)

SINCE FEELING IS FIRST

since feeling is first
who pays any attention
to the syntax of things
will never wholly kiss you;

wholly to be a fool
while Spring is in the world

my blood approves,
and kisses are a better fate
than wisdom
lady i swear by all flowers. Don't cry
—the best gesture of my brain is less than
your eyelids' flutter which says

we are for each other: then
laugh, leaning back in my arms
for life's not a paragraph

And death i think is no parenthesis

(1926)

LeRoi Jones (1934-)

YOUNG SOUL

First, feel, then feel, then
read, or read, then feel, then
fall, or stand, where you
already are. Think
of your self, and the other
selves . . . think
of your parents, your mothers
and sisters, your bentslick
father, then feel, or
fall, on your knees
if nothing else will move you,

then read
and look deeply
into all matters
come close to you
city boys—
country men

Make some muscle
in your head, but
use the muscle
in yr heart

William Golding

*William Gerald Golding, a British author, was born in 1911 and
educated at Marlborough grammar school and at Oxford. At
first destined for a scientific career, he shifted his attention to
literature after two years in the University and published a volume*

of poems. During World War II he served in the Royal Navy,
rising to the command of a rocket-launching ship. Since the war he
has devoted himself to teaching and writing, and to his hobbies,
which he once described as "thinking, classical Greek, sailing,
and archaeology." He is widely known for his strikingly original
novels, especially Pincher Martin *(1956), describing the feelings*
of a shipwrecked sailor on an isolated rock in mid-ocean, and
Lord of the Flies *(1954), a deeply symbolic account of a group of*
schoolboys who revert to savagery when marooned on an island.
The present essay first appeared in the August 1961 issue of
Holiday.

THINKING AS A HOBBY

While I was still a boy, I came to the conclusion that there were three grades of thinking; and since I was later to claim thinking as my hobby, I came to an even stranger conclusion—namely, that I myself could not think at all.

I must have been an unsatisfactory child for grownups to deal with. I remember how incomprehensible they appeared to me at first, but not, of course, how I appeared to them. It was the headmaster of my grammar school who first brought the subject of thinking before me—though neither in the way, nor with the result he intended. He had some statuettes in his study. They stood on a high cupboard behind his desk. One was a lady wearing nothing but a bath towel. She seemed frozen in an eternal panic lest the bath towel slip down any farther; and since she had no arms, she was in an unfortunate position to pull the towel up again. Next to her, crouched the statuette of a leopard, ready to spring down at the top drawer of a filing cabinet labeled A–AH. My innocence interpreted this as the victim's last, despairing cry. Beyond the leopard was a naked, muscular gentleman, who sat, looking down, with his chin on his fist and his elbow on his knee. He seemed utterly miserable.

Some time later, I learned about these statuettes. The headmaster had placed them where they would face delinquent children, because they symbolized to him the whole of life. The naked lady was the Venus of Milo. She was Love. She was not worried about the towel. She was just busy being beautiful. The leopard was Nature, and he was being natural. The naked, muscular gentleman was not miserable.

He was Rodin's Thinker, an image of pure thought. It is easy to buy small plaster models of what you think life is like.

I had better explain that I was a frequent visitor to the headmaster's study, because of the latest thing I had done or left undone. As we now say, I was not integrated. I was, if anything, disintegrated; and I was puzzled. Grownups never made sense. Whenever I found myself in a penal position before the headmaster's desk, with the statuettes glimmering whitely above him, I would sink my head, clasp my hands behind my back and writhe one shoe over the other.

The headmaster would look opaquely at me through flashing spectacles.

"What are we going to do with you?"

Well, what *were* they going to do with me? I would writhe my shoe some more and stare down at the worn rug.

"Look up, boy! Can't you look up?"

Then I would look up at the cupboard, where the naked lady was frozen in her panic and the muscular gentleman contemplated the hindquarters of the leopard in endless gloom. I had nothing to say to the headmaster. His spectacles caught the light so that you could see nothing human behind them. There was no possibility of communication.

"Don't you ever think at all?"

No, I didn't think, wasn't thinking, couldn't think—I was simply waiting in anguish for the interview to stop.

"Then you'd better learn—hadn't you?"

On one occasion the headmaster leaped to his feet, reached up and plonked Rodin's masterpiece on the desk before me.

"That's what a man looks like when he's really thinking."

I surveyed the gentleman without interest or comprehension.

"Go back to your class."

Clearly there was something missing in me. Nature had endowed the rest of the human race with a sixth sense and left me out. This must be so, I mused, on my way back to the class, since whether I had broken a window, or failed to remember Boyle's Law, or been late for school, my teachers produced me one, adult answer: "Why can't you think?"

As I saw the case, I had broken the window because I had tried to hit Jack Arney with a cricket ball and missed him; I could not remember Boyle's Law because I had never bothered to learn it; and I was late for school because I preferred looking over the bridge into the river. In fact, I was wicked. Were my teachers, perhaps, so good that they could not understand the depths of my depravity? Were they clear, untormented people who could direct their every action by

7

this mysterious business of thinking? The whole thing was incomprehensible. In my earlier years, I found even the statuette of the Thinker confusing. I did not believe any of my teachers were naked, ever. Like someone born deaf, but bitterly determined to find out about sound, I watched my teachers to find out about thought.

There was Mr. Houghton. He was always telling me to think. With a modest satisfaction, he would tell me that he had thought a bit himself. Then why did he spend so much time drinking? Or was there more sense in drinking than there appeared to be? But if not, and if drinking were in fact ruinous to health—and Mr. Houghton was ruined, there was no doubt about that—why was he always talking about the clean life and the virtues of fresh air? He would spread his arms wide with the action of a man who habitually spent his time striding along mountain ridges.

"Open air does me good, boys—I know it!"

Sometimes, exalted by his own oratory, he would leap from his desk and hustle us outside into a hideous wind.

"Now, boys! Deep breaths! Feel it right down inside you—huge draughts of God's good air!"

He would stand before us, rejoicing in his perfect health, an open-air man. He would put his hands on his waist and take a tremendous breath. You could hear the wind, trapped in the cavern of his chest and struggling with all the unnatural impediments. His body would reel with shock and his ruined face go white at the unaccustomed visitation. He would stagger back to his desk and collapse there, useless for the rest of the morning.

Mr. Houghton was given to high-minded monologues about the good life, sexless and full of duty. Yet in the middle of one of these monologues, if a girl passed the window, tapping along on her neat little feet, he would interrupt his discourse, his neck would turn of itself and he would watch her out of sight. In this instance, he seemed to me ruled not by thought but by an invisible and irresistible spring in his nape.

His neck was an object of great interest to me. Normally it bulged a bit over his collar. But Mr. Houghton had fought in the First World War alongside both Americans and French, and had come—by who knows what illogic?—to a settled detestation of both countries. If either country happened to be prominent in current affairs, no argument could make Mr. Houghton think well of it. He would bang the desk, his neck would bulge still further and go red. "You can say what you like," he would cry, "but I've thought about this—and I know what I think!"

Mr. Houghton thought with his neck.

There was Miss Parsons. She assured us that her dearest wish was

8

our welfare, but I knew even then, with the mysterious clairvoyance of childhood, that what she wanted most was the husband she never got. There was Mr. Hands—and so on.

I have dealt at length with my teachers because this was my introduction to the nature of what is commonly called thought. Through them I discovered that thought is often full of unconscious prejudice, ignorance and hypocrisy. It will lecture on disinterested purity while its neck is being remorselessly twisted toward a skirt. Technically, it is about as proficient as most businessmen's golf, as honest as most politicians' intentions, or—to come near my own preoccupation—as coherent as most books that get written. It is what I came to call grade-three thinking, though more properly, it is feeling, rather than thought.

True, often there is a kind of innocence in prejudices, but in those days I viewed grade-three thinking with an intolerant contempt and an incautious mockery. I delighted to confront a pious lady who hated the Germans with the proposition that we should love our enemies. She taught me a great truth in dealing with grade-three thinkers; because of her, I no longer dismiss lightly a mental process which for nine-tenths of the population is the nearest they will ever get to thought. They have immense solidarity. We had better respect them, for we are outnumbered and surrounded. A crowd of grade-three thinkers, all shouting the same thing, all warming their hands at the fire of their own prejudices, will not thank you for pointing out the contradictions in their beliefs. Man is a gregarious animal, and enjoys agreement as cows will graze all the same way on the side of a hill.

Grade-two thinking is the detection of contradictions. I reached grade two when I trapped the poor, pious lady. Grade-two thinkers do not stampede easily, though often they fall into the other fault and lag behind. Grade-two thinking is a withdrawal, with eyes and ears open. It became my hobby and brought satisfaction and loneliness in either hand. For grade-two thinking destroys without having the power to create. It set me watching the crowds cheering His Majesty the King and asking myself what all the fuss was about, without giving me anything positive to put in the place of that heady patriotism. But there were compensations. To hear people justify their habit of hunting foxes and tearing them to pieces by claiming that the foxes liked it. To hear our Prime Minister talk about the great benefit we conferred on India by jailing people like Pandit Nehru and Gandhi. To hear American politicians talk about peace in one sentence and refuse to join the League of Nations in the next. Yes, there were moments of delight.

But I was growing toward adolescence and had to admit that Mr. Houghton was not the only one with an irresistible spring in his neck.

I, too, felt the compulsive hand of nature and began to find that pointing out contradiction could be costly as well as fun. There was Ruth, for example, a serious and attractive girl. I was an atheist at the time. Grade-two thinking is a menace to religion and knocks down sects like skittles. I put myself in a position to be converted by her with an hypocrisy worthy of grade three. She was a Methodist—or at least, her parents were, and Ruth had to follow suit. But, alas, instead of relying on the Holy Spirit to convert me, Ruth was foolish enough to open her pretty mouth in argument. She claimed that the Bible (King James Version) was literally inspired. I countered by saying that the Catholics believed in the literal inspiration of Saint Jerome's *Vulgate*, and the two books were different. Argument flagged.

At last she remarked that there were an awful lot of Methodists, and they couldn't be wrong, could they—not all those millions? That was too easy, said I restively (for the nearer you were to Ruth, the nicer she was to be near to) since there were more Roman Catholics than Methodists anyway; and they couldn't be wrong, could they—not all those hundreds of millions? An awful flicker of doubt appeared in her eyes. I slid my arm round her waist and murmured breathlessly that if we were counting heads, the Buddhists were the boys for my money. But Ruth had *really* wanted to do me good, because I was so nice. She fled. The combination of my arm and those countless Buddhists was too much for her.

That night her father visited my father and left, red-cheeked and indignant. I was given the third degree to find out what had happened. It was lucky we were both of us only fourteen. I lost Ruth and gained an undeserved reputation as a potential libertine.

So grade-two thinking could be dangerous. It was in this knowledge, at the age of fifteen, that I remember making a comment from the heights of grade two, on the limitations of grade three. One evening I found myself alone in the school hall, preparing it for a party. The door of the headmaster's study was open. I went in. The headmaster had ceased to thump Rodin's Thinker down on the desk as an example to the young. Perhaps he had not found any more candidates, but the statuettes were still there, glimmering and gathering dust on top of the cupboard. I stood on a chair and rearranged them. I stood Venus in her bath towel on the filing cabinet, so that now the top drawer caught its breath in a gasp of sexy excitement. "A-ah!" The portentous Thinker I placed on the edge of the cupboard so that he looked down at the bath towel and waited for it to slip.

Grade-two thinking, though it filled life with fun and excitement, did not make for content. To find out the deficiencies of our elders bolsters the young ego but does not make for personal security. I found that grade two was not only the power to point out contradictions. It took the swimmer some distance from the shore and left him there, out of his depth. I decided that Pontius Pilate was a typical grade-two thinker. "What is truth?" he said, a very common grade-two thought, but one that is used always as the end of an argument instead of the beginning. There is a still higher grade of thought which says, "What is truth?" and sets out to find it.

But these grade-one thinkers were few and far between. They did not visit my grammar school in the flesh though they were there in books. I aspired to them, partly because I was ambitious and partly because I now saw my hobby as an unsatisfactory thing if it went no further. If you set out to climb a mountain, however high you climb, you have failed if you cannot reach the top.

I *did* meet an undeniably grade-one thinker in my first year at Oxford. I was looking over a small bridge in Magdalen Deer Park, and a tiny mustached and hatted figure came and stood by my side. He was a German who had just fled from the Nazis to Oxford as a temporary refuge. His name was Einstein.

But Professor Einstein knew no English at that time and I knew only two words of German. I beamed at him, trying wordlessly to convey by my bearing all the affection and respect that the English felt for him. It is possible—and I have to make the admission—that I felt here were two grade-one thinkers standing side by side; yet I doubt if my face conveyed more than a formless awe. I would have given my Greek and Latin and French and a good slice of my English for enough German to communicate. But we were divided; he was as inscrutable as my headmaster. For perhaps five minutes we stood together on the bridge, undeniable grade-one thinker and breathless aspirant. With true greatness, Professor Einstein realized that any contact was better than none. He pointed to a trout wavering in midstream.

He spoke: *"Fisch."*

My brain reeled. Here I was, mingling with the great, and yet helpless as the veriest grade-three thinker. Desperately I sought for some sign by which I might convey that I, too, revered pure reason. I nodded vehemently. In a brilliant flash I used up half of my German vocabulary. *"Fisch. Ja. Ja."*

For perhaps another five minutes we stood side by side. Then Professor Einstein, his whole figure still conveying good will and amiability, drifted away out of sight.

I, too, would be a grade-one thinker. I was irreverent at the best of times. Political and religious systems, social customs, loyalties and traditions, they all came tumbling down like so many rotten apples off a tree. This was a fine hobby and a sensible substitute for cricket, since you could play it all the year round. I came up in the end with what must always remain the justification for grade-one thinking, its sign, seal and charter. I devised a coherent system for living. It was a moral system, which was wholly logical. Of course, as I readily admitted, conversion of the world to my way of thinking might be difficult, since my system did away with a number of trifles, such as big business, centralized government, armies, marriage. . . .

It was Ruth all over again. I had some very good friends who stood by me, and still do. But my acquaintances vanished, taking the girls with them. Young women seemed oddly contented with the world as it was. They valued the meaningless ceremony with a ring. Young men, while willing to concede the chaining sordidness of marriage, were hesitant about abandoning the organizations which they hoped would give them a career. A young man on the first rung of the Royal Navy, while perfectly agreeable to doing away with big business and marriage, got as red-necked as Mr. Houghton when I proposed a world without any battleships in it.

Had the game gone too far? Was it a game any longer? In those prewar days, I stood to lose a great deal, for the sake of a hobby.

Now you are expecting me to describe how I saw the folly of my ways and came back to the warm nest, where prejudices are so often called loyalties, where pointless actions are hallowed into custom by repetition, where we are content to say we think when all we do is feel.

But you would be wrong. I dropped my hobby and turned professional.

If I were to go back to the headmaster's study and find the dusty statuettes still there, I would arrange them differently. I would dust Venus and put her aside, for I have come to love her and know her for the fair thing she is. But I would put the Thinker, sunk in his desperate thought, where there were shadows before him—and at his back, I would put the leopard, crouched and ready to spring.

James Harvey Robinson

James Harvey Robinson (1863–1936), American historian and university professor, was educated at Harvard and Freiburg. He taught history at the University of Pennsylvania and from 1895 to 1919 at Columbia. Resigning in 1919 in protest against the expulsion of a group of professors for their opposition to World

*War I, he attacked Columbia president Nicholas Murray Butler
for his alleged attempts to suppress freedom of expression at the
University. Robinson then helped to found the New School for
Social Research in New York City, and he taught there until 1921,
when he retired to devote the rest of his life to writing. Among
his dozen volumes of historical and philosophical writing, perhaps
the best known to the general public is* The Mind in the Making
(1921), subtitled The Relation of Intelligence to Social Reform.
*Chapter 2 of this book has been excerpted and reprinted so often
that it has itself been the subject of an amusing article by
Professor David Novarr ("OVKOT," AAUP Bulletin, vol. 37,
1951). But familiarity has not reduced its value. We reprint the
chapter here in full, using the heading of the first section as title
for the whole.*

ON VARIOUS KINDS OF THINKING

*Good sense is, of all things among men, the most equally distributed; for everyone
thinks himself so abundantly provided with it that those even who are the most
difficult to satisfy in everything else do not usually desire a larger measure of
this quality than they already possess.*

—DESCARTES

*We see man to-day, instead of the frank and courageous recognition of his status,
the docile attention to his biological history, the determination to let nothing stand
in the way of the security and permanence of his future, which alone can establish
the safety and happiness of the race, substituting blind confidence in his destiny,
unclouded faith in the essentially respectful attitude of the universe toward his moral
code, and a belief no less firm that his traditions and laws and institutions necessarily contain permanent qualities of reality.*

—WILLIAM TROTTER

1. ON VARIOUS KINDS OF THINKING

The truest and most profound observations on Intelligence have in the
past been made by the poets and, in recent times, by story-writers.
They have been keen observers and recorders and reckoned freely
with the emotions and sentiments. Most philosophers, on the other
hand, have exhibited a grotesque ignorance of man's life and have
built up systems that are elaborate and imposing, but quite unrelated

to actual human affairs. They have almost consistently neglected the actual process of thought and have set the mind off as something apart to be studied by itself. *But no such mind, exempt from bodily processes, animal impulses, savage traditions, infantile impressions, conventional reactions, and traditional knowledge, ever existed,* even in the case of the most abstract of metaphysicians. Kant entitled his great work *A Critique of Pure Reason.* But to the modern student of mind pure reason seems as mythical as the pure gold, transparent as glass, with which the celestial city is paved.

Formerly philosophers thought of mind as having to do exclusively with conscious thought. It was that within man which perceived, remembered, judged, reasoned, understood, believed, willed. But of late it has been shown that we are unaware of a great part of what we perceive, remember, will, and infer; and that a great part of the thinking of which we are aware is determined by that of which we are not conscious. It has indeed been demonstrated that our unconscious psychic life far outruns our conscious. This seems perfectly natural to anyone who considers the following facts:

The sharp distinction between the mind and the body is, as we shall find, a very ancient and spontaneous uncritical savage prepossession. What we think of as "mind" is so intimately associated with what we call "body" that we are coming to realize that the one cannot be understood without the other. Every thought reverberates through the body, and, on the other hand, alterations in our physical condition affect our whole attitude of mind. The insufficient elimination of the foul and decaying products of digestion may plunge us into deep melancholy, whereas a few whiffs of nitrous monoxide may exalt us to the seventh heaven of supernal knowledge and godlike complacency. And *vice versa,* a sudden word or thought may cause our heart to jump, check our breathing, or make our knees as water. There is a whole new literature growing up which studies the effects of our bodily secretions and our muscular tensions and their relation to our emotions and our thinking.

Then there are hidden impulses and desires and secret longings of which we can only with the greatest difficulty take account. They influence our conscious thought in the most bewildering fashion. Many of these unconscious influences appear to originate in our very early years. The older philosophers seem to have forgotten that even they were infants and children at their most impressionable age and never could by any possibility get over it.

The term "unconscious," now so familiar to all readers of modern works on psychology, gives offense to some adherents of the past. There should, however, be no special mystery about it. It is not a new animistic abstraction, but simply a collective word to include all

14

the physiological changes which escape our notice, all the forgotten experiences and impressions of the past which continue to influence our desires and reflections and conduct, even if we cannot remember them. What we can remember at any time is indeed an infinitesimal part of what has happened to us. We could not remember anything unless we forgot almost everything. As Bergson says, the brain is the organ of forgetfulness as well as of memory. Moreover, we tend, of course, to become oblivious to things to which we are thoroughly accustomed, for habit blinds us to their existence. So the forgotten and the habitual make up a great part of the so-called "unconscious."

If we are ever to understand man, his conduct and reasoning, and if we aspire to learn to guide his life and his relations with his fellows more happily than heretofore, we cannot neglect the great discoveries briefly noted above. We must reconcile ourselves to novel and revolutionary conceptions of the mind, for it is clear that the older philosophers, whose works still determine our current views, had a very superficial notion of the subject with which they dealt. But for our purposes, with due regard to what has just been said and to much that has necessarily been left unsaid (and with the indulgence of those who will at first be inclined to dissent), *we shall consider mind chiefly as conscious knowledge and intelligence, as what we know and our attitude toward it—our disposition to increase our information, classify it, criticize it, and apply it.*

We do not think enough about thinking, and much of our confusion is the result of current illusions in regard to it. Let us forget for the moment any impressions we may have derived from the philosophers, and see what seems to happen in ourselves. The first thing that we notice is that our thought moves with such incredible rapidity that it is almost impossible to arrest any specimen of it long enough to have a look at it. When we are offered a penny for our thoughts we always find that we have recently had so many things in mind that we can easily make a selection which will not compromise us too nakedly. On inspection we shall find that even if we are not downright ashamed of a great part of our spontaneous thinking it is far too intimate, personal, ignoble or trivial to permit us to reveal more than a small part of it. I believe this must be true of everyone. We do not, of course, know what goes on in other people's heads. They tell us very little and we tell them very little. The spigot of speech, rarely fully opened, could never emit more than driblets of the ever renewed hogshead of thought—*noch grösser wie's Heidelberger Fass.* We find it hard to believe that other people's thoughts are as silly as our own, but they probably are.

We all appear to ourselves to be thinking all the time during our waking hours, and most of us are aware that we go on thinking while

15

we are asleep, even more foolishly than when awake. When uninterrupted by some practical issue we are engaged in what is now known as a *reverie*. This is our spontaneous and favorite kind of thinking. We allow our ideas to take their own course and this course is determined by our hopes and fears, our spontaneous desires, their fulfillment or frustration; by our likes and dislikes, our loves and hates and resentments. There is nothing else anything like so interesting to ourselves as ourselves. All thought that is not more or less laboriously controlled and directed will inevitably circle about the beloved Ego. It is amusing and pathetic to observe this tendency in ourselves and in others. We learn politely and generously to overlook this truth, but if we dare to think of it, it blazes forth like the noontide sun.

The reverie or "free association of ideas" has of late become the subject of scientific research. While investigators are not yet agreed on the results, or at least on the proper interpretation to be given to them, there can be no doubt that our reveries form the chief index to our fundamental character. They are a reflection of our nature as modified by often hidden and forgotten experiences. We need not go into the matter further here, for it is only necessary to observe that the reverie is at all times a potent and in many cases an omnipotent rival to every other kind of thinking. It doubtless influences all our speculations in its persistent tendency to self-magnification and self-justification, which are its chief preoccupations, but it is the last thing to make directly or indirectly for honest increase of knowledge.[1] Philosophers usually talk as if such thinking did not exist or were in some way negligible. This is what makes their speculations so unreal and often worthless.

The reverie, as any of us can see for himself, is frequently broken and interrupted by the necessity of a second kind of thinking. We have to make practical decisions. Shall we write a letter or no? Shall we take the subway or a bus? Shall we have dinner at seven or half past? Shall we buy U.S. Rubber or a Liberty Bond? Decisions are easily distinguishable from the free flow of the reverie. Sometimes they demand a good deal of careful pondering and the recollection of

---

[1] The poet-clergyman, John Donne, who lived in the time of James I, has given a beautifully honest picture of the doings of a saint's mind: "I throw myself down in my chamber and call in and invite God and His angels thither, and when they are there I neglect God and His angels for the noise of a fly, for the rattling of a coach, for the whining of a door. I talk on in the same posture of praying, eyes lifted up, knees bowed down, as though I prayed to God, and if God or His angels should ask me when I thought last of God in that prayer I cannot tell. Sometimes I find that I had forgot what I was about, but when I began to forget it I cannot tell. A memory of yesterday's pleasures, a fear of to-morrow's dangers, a straw under my knee, a noise in mine ear, a light in mine eye, an anything, a nothing, a fancy, a chimera in my brain troubles me in my prayer."—Quoted by Robert Lynd, *The Art of Letters*, pp. 46–47.

pertinent facts; often, however, they are made impulsively. They are a more difficult and laborious thing than the reverie, and we resent having to "make up our mind" when we are tired, or absorbed in a congenial reverie. Weighing a decision, it should be noted, does not necessarily add anything to our knowledge, although we may, of course, seek further information before making it.

2. RATIONALIZING

A third kind of thinking is stimulated when anyone questions our belief and opinions. We sometimes find ourselves changing our minds without any resistance or heavy emotion, but if we are told that we are wrong we resent the imputation and harden our hearts. We are incredibly heedless in the formation of our beliefs, but find ourselves filled with an illicit passion for them when anyone proposes to rob us of their companionship. It is obviously not the ideas themselves that are dear to us, but our self-esteem, which is threatened. We are by nature stubbornly pledged to defend our own from attack, whether it be our person, our family, our property, or our opinion. A United States Senator once remarked to a friend of mine that God Almighty could not make him change his mind on our Latin-America policy. We may surrender, but rarely confess ourselves vanquished. In the intellectual world at least peace is without victory.

Few of us take the pains to study the origin of our cherished convictions; indeed, we have a natural repugnance to so doing. We like to continue to believe what we have been accustomed to accept as true, and the resentment aroused when doubt is cast upon any of our assumptions leads us to seek every manner of excuse for clinging to them. *The result is that most of our so-called reasoning consists in finding arguments for going on believing as we already do.*

I remember years ago attending a public dinner to which the Governor of the state was bidden. The chairman explained that His Excellency could not be present for certain "good" reasons; what the "real" reasons were the presiding officer said he would leave us to conjecture. This distinction between "good" and "real" reasons is one of the most clarifying and essential in the whole realm of thought. We can readily give what seem to us "good" reasons for being a Catholic or a Mason, a Republican or a Democrat, an adherent or opponent of the League of Nations. But the "real" reasons are usually on quite a different plane. Of course the importance of this distinction is popularly, if somewhat obscurely, recognized. The Baptist missionary is ready enough to see that the Buddhist is not such because his doctrines would bear careful inspection, but because he happened to be born in a Buddhist family in Tokio. But it would be treason to his faith

17

to acknowledge that his own partiality for certain doctrines is due to the fact that his mother was a member of the First Baptist church of Oak Ridge. A savage can give all sorts of reasons for his belief that it is dangerous to step on a man's shadow, and a newspaper editor can advance plenty of arguments against the Bolsheviki. But neither of them may realize why he happens to be defending his particular opinion.

The "real" reasons for our beliefs are concealed from ourselves as well as from others. As we grow up we simply adopt the ideas presented to us in regard to such matters as religion, family relations, property, business, our country, and the state. We unconsciously absorb them from our environment. They are persistently whispered in our ear by the group in which we happen to live. Moreover, as Mr. Trotter has pointed out, these judgments, being the product of suggestion and not of reasoning, have the quality of perfect obviousness, so that to question them

. . . is to the believer to carry skepticism to an insane degree, and will be met by contempt, disapproval, or condemnation, according to the nature of the belief in question. When, therefore, we find ourselves entertaining an opinion about the basis of which there is a quality of feeling which tells us that to inquire into it would be absurd, obviously unnecessary, unprofitable, undesirable, bad form, or wicked, we may know that that opinion is a nonrational one, and probably, therefore, founded upon inadequate evidence.[2]

Opinions, on the other hand, which are the result of experience or of honest reasoning do not have this quality of "primary certitude." I remember when as a youth I heard a group of business men discussing the question of the immortality of the soul, I was outraged by the sentiment of doubt expressed by one of the party. As I look back now I see that I had at the time no interest in the matter, and certainly no least argument to urge in favor of the belief in which I had been reared. But neither my personal indifference to the issue, nor the fact that I had previously given it no attention, served to prevent an angry resentment when I heard *my* ideas questioned.

This spontaneous and loyal support of our preconceptions—this process of finding "good" reasons to justify our routine beliefs—is known to modern psychologists as "rationalizing"—clearly only a new name for a very ancient thing. Our "good" reasons ordinarily have no value in promoting honest enlightenment, because, no matter how solemnly they may be marshaled, they are at bottom the result of personal preference or prejudice, and not of an honest desire to seek or accept new knowledge.

---

[2] *Instincts of the Herd*, p. 44.

In our reveries we are frequently engaged in self-justification, for we cannot bear to think ourselves wrong, and yet have constant illustrations of our weaknesses and mistakes. So we spend much time finding fault with circumstances and the conduct of others, and shifting on to them with great ingenuity the onus of our own failures and disappointments. *Rationalizing is the self-exculpation which occurs when we feel ourselves, or our group, accused of misapprehension or error.*

The little word *my* is the most important one in all human affairs, and properly to reckon with it is the beginning of wisdom. It has the same force whether it is *my* dinner, *my* dog, and *my* house, or *my* faith, *my* country, and *my* God. We not only resent the imputation that our watch is wrong, or our car shabby, but that our conception of the canals of Mars, of the pronunciation of "Epictetus," of the medicinal value of salicine, or the date of Sargon I, are subject to revision.

Philosophers, scholars, and men of science exhibit a common sensitiveness in all decisions in which their *amour propre* is involved. Thousands of argumentative works have been written to vent a grudge. However stately their reasoning, it may be nothing but rationalizing, stimulated by the most commonplace of all motives. A history of philosophy and theology could be written in terms of grouches, wounded pride, and aversions, and it would be far more instructive than the usual treatments of these themes. Sometimes, under Providence, the lowly impulse of resentment leads to great achievements. Milton wrote his treatise on divorce as a result of his troubles with his seventeen-year-old wife, and when he was accused of being the leading spirit in a new sect, the Divorcers, he wrote his noble *Areopagitica* to prove his right to say what he thought fit, and incidentally to establish the advantage of a free press in the promotion of Truth.

All mankind, high and low, thinks in all the ways which have been described. The reverie goes on all the time not only in the mind of the mill hand and the Broadway flapper, but equally in weighty judges and godly bishops. It has gone on in all the philosophers, scientists, poets, and theologians that have ever lived. Aristotle's most abstruse speculations were doubtless tempered by highly irrelevant reflections. He is reported to have had very thin legs and small eyes, for which he doubtless had to find excuses, and he was wont to indulge in very conspicuous dress and rings and was accustomed to arrange his hair carefully.[3] Diogenes the Cynic exhibited the impudence of a touchy soul. His tub was his distinction. Tennyson in beginning his "Maud" could not forget his chagrin over losing his patrimony years before as the result of an unhappy investment in the Patent Decorative Carving

---

[3] Diogenes Laertius, book v.

Company. These facts are not recalled here as a gratuitous disparagement of the truly great, but to insure a full realization of the tremendous competition which all really exacting thought has to face, even in the minds of the most highly endowed mortals.

And now the astonishing and perturbing suspicion emerges that perhaps almost all that had passed for social science, political economy, politics, and ethics in the past may be brushed aside by future generations as mainly rationalizing. John Dewey has already reached this conclusion in regard to philosophy.[4] Veblen[5] and other writers have revealed the various unperceived presuppositions of the traditional political economy, and now comes an Italian sociologist, Vilfredo Pareto, who, in his huge treatise on general sociology, devotes hundreds of pages to substantiating a similar thesis affecting all the social sciences.[6] This conclusion may be ranked by students of a hundred years hence as one of the several great discoveries of our age. It is by no means fully worked out, and it is so opposed to nature that it will be very slowly accepted by the great mass of those who consider themselves thoughtful. As a historical student I am personally fully reconciled to this newer view. Indeed, it seems to me inevitable that just as the various sciences of nature were, before the opening of the seventeenth century, largely masses of rationalizations to suit the religious sentiments of the period, so the social sciences have continued even to our own day to be rationalizations of uncritically accepted beliefs and customs.

It will become apparent as we proceed that the fact that an idea is ancient and that it has been widely received is no argument in its favor, but should immediately suggest the necessity of carefully testing it as a probable instance of rationalization.

3. HOW CREATIVE THOUGHT TRANSFORMS THE WORLD

This brings us to another kind of thought which can fairly easily be distinguished from the three kinds described above. It has not the usual qualities of the reverie, for it does not hover about our personal complacencies and humiliations. It is not made up of the homely decisions forced upon us by everyday needs, when we review our little stock of existing information, consult our conventional preferences and

---

[4] *Reconstruction in Philosophy.*
[5] *The Place of Science in Modern Civilization.*
[6] *Traité de Sociologie Générale, passim.* The author's term *"derivations"* seems to be his precise way of expressing what we have called the "good" reasons, and his *"residus"* correspond to the "real" reasons. He well says, *"L'homme éprouve le besoin de raisonner, et en outre d'étendre un voile sur ses instincts et sur ses sentiments"*—hence, rationalization. (P. 788.) His aim is to reduce sociology to the "real" reasons. (P. 791.)

obligations, and make a choice of action. It is not the defense of our own cherished beliefs and prejudices just because they are our own—mere plausible excuses for remaining of the same mind. On the contrary, it is that peculiar species of thought which leads us to *change* our mind.

It is this kind of thought that has raised man from his pristine, subsavage ignorance and squalor to the degree of knowledge and comfort which he now possesses. On his capacity to continue and greatly extend this kind of thinking depends his chance of groping his way out of the plight in which the most highly civilized peoples of the world now find themselves. In the past this type of thinking has been called Reason. But so many misapprehensions have grown up around the word that some of us have become very suspicious of it. I suggest, therefore, that we substitute a recent name and speak of "creative thought" rather than of Reason. *For this kind of meditation begets knowledge, and knowledge is really creative inasmuch as it makes things look different from what they seemed before and may indeed work for their reconstruction.*

In certain moods some of us realize that we are observing things or making reflections with a seeming disregard of our personal preoccupations. We are not preening or defending ourselves; we are not faced by the necessity of any practical decision, nor are we apologizing for believing this or that. We are just wondering and looking and mayhap seeing what we never perceived before.

Curiosity is as clear and definite as any of our urges. We wonder what is in a sealed telegram or in a letter in which some one else is absorbed, or what is being said in the telephone booth or in low conversation. This inquisitiveness is vastly stimulated by jealousy, suspicion, or any hint that we ourselves are directly or indirectly involved. But there appears to be a fair amount of personal interest in other people's affairs even when they do not concern us except as a mystery to be unraveled or a tale to be told. The reports of a divorce suit will have "news value" for many weeks. They constitute a story, like a novel or play or moving picture. This is not an example of pure curiosity, however, since we readily identify ourselves with others, and their joys and despair then become our own.

We also take note of, or "observe," as Sherlock Holmes says, things which have nothing to do with our personal interests and make no personal appeal either direct or by way of sympathy. This is what Veblen so well calls "idle curiosity." And it is usually idle enough. Some of us when we face the line of people opposite us in a subway train impulsively consider them in detail and engage in rapid inferences and form theories in regard to them. On entering a room there are those who will perceive at a glance the degree of preciousness of the rugs, the character of the pictures, and the personality revealed by the books. But there are many, it would seem, who are so absorbed in their personal reverie or in some definite purpose that they have no bright-eyed energy for idle curiosity. The tendency to miscellaneous observation we come by honestly enough, for we note it in many of our animal relatives.

Veblen, however, uses the term "idle curiosity" somewhat ironically, as is his wont. It is idle only to those who fail to realize that it may be a very rare and indispensable thing from which almost all distinguished human achievement proceeds, since it may lead to systematic examination and seeking for things hitherto undiscovered. For research is but diligent search which enjoys the high flavor of primitive hunting. Occasionally and fitfully idle curiosity thus leads to creative thought, which alters and broadens our own views and aspirations and may in turn, under highly favorable circumstances, affect the views and lives of others, even for generations to follow. An example or two will make this unique human process clear.

Galileo was a thoughtful youth and doubtless carried on a rich and varied reverie. He had artistic ability and might have turned out to be a musician or painter. When he had dwelt among the monks at Valambrosa he had been tempted to lead the life of a religious. As a boy he busied himself with toy machines and he inherited a fondness for mathematics. All these facts are of record. We may safely assume also that, along with many other subjects of contemplation, the Pisan maidens found a vivid place in his thoughts.

One day when seventeen years old he wandered into the cathedral of his native town. In the midst of his reverie he looked up at the lamps hanging by long chains from the high ceiling of the church. Then something very difficult to explain occurred. He found himself no longer thinking of the building, worshipers, or the services; of his artistic or religious interests; of his reluctance to become a physician as his father wished. He forgot the question of a career and even the *graziosissime donne*. As he watched the swinging lamps he was suddenly wondering if mayhap their oscillations, whether long or short, did not occupy the same time. Then he tested this hypothesis by counting his pulse, for that was the only timepiece he had with him.

This observation, however remarkable in itself, was not enough to produce a really creative thought. Others may have noticed the same thing and yet nothing came of it. Most of our observations have no assignable results. Galileo may have seen that the warts on a peasant's face formed a perfect isosceles triangle, or he may have noticed with boyish glee that just as the officiating priest was uttering the solemn words, *ecce agnus Dei*, a fly lit on the end of his nose. To be really creative, ideas have to be worked up and then "put over," so that they become a part of man's social heritage. The highly accurate pendulum clock was one of the later results of Galileo's discovery. He himself was led to reconsider and successfully to refute the old notions of falling bodies. It remained for Newton to prove that the moon was falling, and presumably all the heavenly bodies. This quite upset all the consecrated views of the heavens as managed by angelic engineers. The universality of the laws of gravitation stimulated the attempt to seek other and equally important natural laws and cast grave doubts on the miracles in which mankind had hitherto believed. In short, those who dared to include in their thought the discoveries of Galileo and his successors found themselves in a new earth surrounded by new heavens.

On the 28th of October, 1831, two hundred and fifty years after Galileo had noticed the isochronous vibrations of the lamps, creative thought and its currency had so far increased that Faraday was wondering what would happen if he mounted a disk of copper between the poles of a horseshoe magnet. As the disk revolved an electric current was produced. This would doubtless have seemed the idlest kind of an experiment to the stanch business men of the time, who, it happened, were just then denouncing the child-labor bills in their anxiety to avail themselves to the full of the results of earlier idle curiosity. But should the dynamos and motors which have come into being as the outcome of Faraday's experiment be stopped this evening, the business man of to-day, agitated over labor troubles, might, as he trudged home past lines of "dead" cars, through dark streets to an unlighted house, engage in a little creative thought of his own and perceive that he and his laborers would have no modern factories and mines to quarrel about had it not been for the strange practical effects of the idle curiosity of scientists, inventors, and engineers.

The examples of creative intelligence given above belong to the realm of modern scientific achievement, which furnishes the most striking instances of the effects of scrupulous, objective thinking. But there are, of course, other great realms in which the recording and embodiment of acute observation and insight have wrought themselves into the higher life of man. The great poets and dramatists and our modern story-tellers have found themselves engaged in productive reveries, noting and artistically presenting their discoveries for the delight and instruction of those who have the ability to appreciate them.

The process by which a fresh and original poem or drama comes into being is doubtless analogous to that which originates and elaborates so-called scientific discoveries; but there is clearly a temperamental difference. The genesis and advance of painting, sculpture, and music offer still other problems. We really as yet know shockingly little about these matters, and indeed very few people have the least curiosity about them.[7] Nevertheless, creative intelligence in its various forms and activities is what makes man. Were it not for its slow, painful, and constantly discouraged operations through the ages man would be no more than a species of primate living on seeds, fruit, roots, and uncooked flesh, and wandering naked through the woods and over the plains like a chimpanzee.

The origin and progress and future promotion of civilization are ill understood and misconceived. These should be made the chief theme of education, but much hard work is necessary before we can reconstruct our ideas of man and his capacities and free ourselves from innumerable persistent misapprehensions. There have been obstructionists in all times, not merely the lethargic masses, but the moralists, the rationalizing theologians, and most of the philosophers, all busily if unconsciously engaged in ratifying existing ignorance and mistakes and discouraging creative thought. Naturally, those who reassure us seem worthy of honor and respect. Equally naturally those who puzzle us with disturbing criticisms and invite us to change our ways are objects of suspicion and readily discredited. Our personal discontent does not ordinarily extend to any critical questioning of the general situation in which we find ourselves. In every age the prevailing conditions of civilization have appeared quite natural and inevitable to those who grew up in them. The cow asks no questions as to how it happens to have a dry stall and a supply of hay. The kitten laps its warm milk from a china saucer, without knowing anything about porcelain; the dog nestles in the corner of a divan with no sense of obligation to the inventors of upholstery and the manufacturers of down pillows. So we humans accept our breakfasts, our trains and telephones and orchestras and movies, our national Constitution, our moral code and standards of manners, with the simplicity and innocence of a pet rabbit. We have absolutely inexhaustible capacities for appropriating what others do for us with no thought of a "thank you." We do not feel called upon to make any least contribution to the merry game ourselves. Indeed, we are usually quite unaware that a game is being played at all.

We have now examined the various classes of thinking which we can readily observe in ourselves and which we have plenty of reasons

---

[7] Recently a re-examination of creative thought has begun as a result of new knowledge which discredits many of the notions formerly held about "reason." See, for example, *Creative Intelligence*, by a group of American philosophic thinkers; John Dewey, *Essays in Experimental Logic* (both pretty hard books); and Veblen, *The Place of Science in Modern Civilization.* Easier than these and very stimulating are Dewey, *Reconstruction in Philosophy*, and Woodworth, *Dynamic Psychology.*

to believe go on, and always have been going on, in our fellow-men. We can sometimes get quite pure and sparkling examples of all four kinds, but commonly they are so confused and intermingled in our reverie as not to be readily distinguishable. The reverie is a reflection of our longings, exultations, and complacencies, our fears, suspicions, and disappointments. We are chiefly engaged in struggling to maintain our self-respect and in asserting that supremacy which we all crave and which seems to us our natural prerogative. It is not strange, but rather quite inevitable, that our beliefs about what is true and false, good and bad, right and wrong, should be mixed up with the reverie and be influenced by the same considerations which determine its character and course. We resent criticisms of our views exactly as we do of anything else connected with ourselves. Our notions of life and its ideals seem to us to be *our own* and as such necessarily true and right, to be defended at all costs.

We very rarely consider, however, the process by which we gained our convictions. If we did so, we could hardly fail to see that there was usually little ground for our confidence in them. Here and there, in this department of knowledge or that, some one of us might make a fair claim to have taken some trouble to get correct ideas of, let us say, the situation in Russia, the sources of our food supply, the origin of the Constitution, the revision of the tariff, the policy of the Holy Roman Apostolic Church, modern business organization, trade unions, birth control, socialism, the League of Nations, the excess-profits tax, preparedness, advertising in its social bearings; but only a very exceptional person would be entitled to opinions on all of even these few matters. And yet most of us have opinions on all these, and on many other questions of equal importance, of which we may know even less. We feel compelled, as self-respecting persons, to take sides when they come up for discussion. We even surprise ourselves by our omniscience. Without taking thought we see in a flash that it is most righteous and expedient to discourage birth control by legislative enactment, or that one who decries intervention in Mexico is clearly wrong, or that big advertising is essential to big business and that big business is the pride of the land. As godlike beings why should we not rejoice in our omniscience?

It is clear, in any case, that our convictions on important matters are not the result of knowledge or critical thought, nor, it may be added, are they often dictated by supposed self-interest. Most of them are *pure prejudices* in the proper sense of that word. We do not form them ourselves. They are the whisperings of "the voice of the herd." We have in the last analysis no responsibility for them and need assume none. They are not really our own ideas, but those of others no more well informed or inspired than ourselves, who have got them in the

25

same careless and humiliating manner as we. It should be our pride to revise our ideas and not to adhere to what passes for respectable opinion, for such opinion can frequently be shown to be not respectable at all. We should, in view of the considerations that have been mentioned, resent our supine credulity. As an English writer has remarked:

"If we feared the entertaining of an unverifiable opinion with the warmth with which we fear using the wrong implement at the dinner table, if the thought of holding a prejudice disgusted us as does a foul disease, then the dangers of man's suggestibility would be turned into advantages."[8]

The purpose of this essay is to set forth briefly the way in which the notions of the herd have been accumulated. This seems to me the best, easiest, and least invidious educational device for cultivating a proper distrust for the older notions on which we still continue to rely.

The "real" reasons, which explain how it is we happen to hold a particular belief, are chiefly historical. Our most important opinions —those, for example, having to do with traditional, religious, and moral convictions, property rights, patriotism, national honor, the state, and indeed all the assumed foundations of society—are, as I have already suggested, rarely the result of reasoned consideration, but of unthinking absorption from the social environment in which we live. Consequently, they have about them a quality of "elemental certitude," and we especially resent doubt or criticism cast upon them. So long, however, as we revere the whisperings of the herd, we are obviously unable to examine them dispassionately and to consider to what extent they are suited to the novel conditions and social exigencies in which we find ourselves to-day.

The "real" reasons for our beliefs, by making clear their origins and history, can do much to dissipate this emotional blockade and rid us of our prejudices and preconceptions. Once this is done and we come critically to examine our traditional beliefs, we may well find some of them sustained by experience and honest reasoning, while others must be revised to meet new conditions and our more extended knowledge. But only after we have undertaken such a critical examination in the light of experience and modern knowledge, freed from any feeling of "primary certitude," can we claim that the "good" are also the "real" reasons for our opinions.

I do not flatter myself that this general show-up of man's thought through the ages will cure myself or others of carelessness in adopting ideas, or of unseemly heat in defending them just because we have

---

[8] Trotter, *op. cit.*, p. 45. The first part of this little volume is excellent.

adopted them. But if the considerations which I propose to recall are really incorporated into our thinking and are permitted to establish our general outlook on human affairs, they will do much to relieve the imaginary obligation we feel in regard to traditional sentiments and ideals. Few of us are capable of engaging in creative thought, but some of us can at least come to distinguish it from other and inferior kinds of thought and accord to it the esteem that it merits as the greatest treasure of the past and the only hope of the future.

Aldous Huxley

Aldous Leonard Huxley (1894–1963), one of the most well-known of modern English novelists and essayists, came from a family celebrated for intellectual achievement. He was the son of Leonard Huxley, author and editor; grandson of the naturalist Thomas Huxley; and grandnephew of Matthew Arnold. His brother Sir Julian is a distinguished biologist and his half-brother David won the 1963 Nobel Prize in physiology. Huxley studied at Eton and Oxford, despite a serious eye disease which made him almost totally blind for three years. Reading with the aid of a magnifying glass, he graduated from Oxford in 1915 with honors in English literature. In 1919 he joined the staff of Athenaeum, *a London literary magazine, and then followed a steady production of writings in all genres.*

The success of his early novels allowed Huxley to move to Italy in 1923 and thence to France; in 1934 he traveled in the United States and finally settled in southern California, near Los Angeles. Here he continued to write books, articles, and an occasional movie scenario. He studied Vedanta and other Eastern religions and became interested in the effect of drugs on the mind.

Huxley wrote eleven novels, the best known being Antic Hay *(1923),* Point Counter Point *(1928),* Brave New World *(1932), and* After Many a Summer Dies the Swan *(1939). Huxley's reputation rests equally on his over twenty volumes of essays and belles-lettres, including* On the Margin *(1923),* Jesting Pilate *(1926),* Vulgarity in Literature *(1930),* Ends and Means *(1937),* The Perennial Philosophy *(1945),* Science, Liberty, and Peace *(1946),* The Doors of Perception *(1954), and* Literature and Science *(1963).*

Huxley's Brave New World *(1932) has turned out to be devastatingly accurate both as a piece of futuristic science fiction and as a satire on modern technological mass-produced civilization. It has become so widely known that in 1958 Huxley could safely give the title* Brave New World Revisited *to a study of the progress of dehumanization and mental tyranny in the intervening quarter century. Both Huxley essays in the present volume are taken from* Brave New World Revisited. *The following is Chapter 5.*

PROPAGANDA UNDER A DICTATORSHIP

At his trial after the Second World War, Hitler's Minister for Armaments, Albert Speer, delivered a long speech in which, with remarkable acuteness, he described the Nazi tyranny and analyzed its methods. "Hitler's dictatorship," he said, "differed in one fundamental point from all its predecessors in history. It was the first dictatorship in the present period of modern technical development, a dictatorship which made complete use of all technical means for the domination of its own country. Through technical devices like the radio and the loud-speaker, eighty million people were deprived of independent thought. It was thereby possible to subject them to the will of one man. . . . Earlier dictators needed highly qualified assistants even at the lowest level—men who could think and act independently. The totalitarian system in the period of modern technical development can dispense with such men; thanks to modern methods of communication, it is possible to mechanize the lower leadership. As a result of this there has arisen the new type of the uncritical recipient of orders."

In the Brave New World of my prophetic fable technology had advanced far beyond the point it had reached in Hitler's day; consequently the recipients of orders were far less critical than their Nazi counterparts, far more obedient to the order-giving elite. Moreover, they had been genetically standardized and postnatally conditioned to perform their subordinate functions, and could therefore be depended upon to behave almost as predictably as machines. As we shall see in a later chapter, this conditioning of "the lower leadership" is already going on under the Communist dictatorships. The Chinese and the Russians are not relying merely on the indirect effects of advancing technology; they are working directly on the psychophysical organisms of their lower leaders, subjecting minds and bodies to a system of ruthless and, from all accounts, highly effective conditioning. "Many a man," said Speer, "has been haunted by the nightmare that one day nations might be dominated by technical means. That nightmare was almost realized in Hitler's totalitarian system." Almost, but not quite. The Nazis did not have time—and perhaps did not have the intelligence and the necessary knowledge—to brainwash and condition their lower leadership. This, it may be, is one of the reasons why they failed.

Since Hitler's day the armory of technical devices at the disposal of the would-be dictator has been considerably enlarged. As well as the radio, the loud-speaker, the moving picture camera and the rotary press, the contemporary propagandist can make use of television to broadcast the image as well as the voice of his client, and can record both image and voice on spools of magnetic tape. Thanks to technological progress, Big Brother can now be almost as omnipresent as God. Nor is it only on the technical front that the hand of the would-be dictator has been strengthened. Since Hitler's day a great deal of work has been carried out in those fields of applied psychology and neurology which are the special province of the propagandist, the indoctrinator and the brainwasher. In the past these specialists in the art of changing people's minds were empiricists. By a method of trial and error they had worked out a number of techniques and procedures, which they used very effectively without, however, knowing precisely why they were effective. Today the art of mind-control is in process of becoming a science. The practitioners of this science know what they are doing and why. They are guided in their work by theories and hypotheses solidly established on a massive foundation of experimental evidence. Thanks to the new insights and the new techniques made possible by these insights, the nightmare that was "all but realized in Hitler's totalitarian system" may soon be completely realizable.

But before we discuss these new insights and techniques let us take a look at the nightmare that so nearly came true in Nazi Germany. What were the methods used by Hitler and Goebbels for "depriving eighty million people of independent thought and subjecting them to the will of one man"? And what was the theory of human nature upon which those terrifyingly successful methods were based? These questions can be answered, for the most part, in Hitler's own words. And what remarkably clear and astute words they are! When he writes about such vast abstractions as Race and History and Providence, Hitler is strictly unreadable. But when he writes about the German masses and the methods he used for dominating and directing them, his style changes. Nonsense gives place to sense, bombast to a hard-

29

boiled and cynical lucidity. In his philosophical lucubrations Hitler was either cloudily daydreaming or reproducing other people's half-baked notions. In his comments on crowds and propaganda he was writing of things he knew by firsthand experience. In the words of his ablest biographer, Mr. Alan Bullock, "Hitler was the greatest demagogue in history." Those who add, "only a demagogue," fail to appreciate the nature of political power in an age of mass politics. As he himself said, "To be a leader means to be able to move the masses." Hitler's aim was first to move the masses and then, having pried them loose from their traditional loyalties and moralities, to impose upon them (with the hypnotized consent of the majority) a new authoritarian order of his own devising. "Hitler," wrote Hermann Rauschning in 1939, "has a deep respect for the Catholic church and the Jesuit order; not because of their Christian doctrine, but because of the 'machinery' they have elaborated and controlled, their hierarchical system, their extremely clever tactics, their knowledge of human nature and their wise use of human weaknesses in ruling over believers." Ecclesiasticism without Christianity, the discipline of a monastic rule, not for God's sake or in order to achieve personal salvation, but for the sake of the State and for the greater glory and power of the demagogue turned Leader—this was the goal toward which the systematic moving of the masses was to lead.

Let us see what Hitler thought of the masses he moved and how he did the moving. The first principle from which he started was a value judgment: the masses are utterly contemptible. They are incapable of abstract thinking and uninterested in any fact outside the circle of their immediate experience. Their behavior is determined, not by knowledge and reason, but by feelings and unconscious drives. It is in these drives and feelings that "the roots of their positive as well as their negative attitudes are implanted." To be successful a propagandist must learn how to manipulate these instincts and emotions. "The driving force which has brought about the most tremendous revolutions on this earth has never been a body of scientific teaching which has gained power over the masses, but always a devotion which has inspired them, and often a kind of hysteria which has urged them into action. Whoever wishes to win over the masses must know the key that will open the door of their hearts." . . . In post-Freudian jargon, of their unconscious.

Hitler made his strongest appeal to those members of the lower middle classes who had been ruined by the inflation of 1923, and then ruined all over again by the depression of 1929 and the following years. "The masses" of whom he speaks were these bewildered, frustrated and chronically anxious millions. To make them more mass-like, more homogeneously subhuman, he assembled them, by the thousands and the tens of thousands, in vast halls and arenas, where individuals could lose their personal identity, even their elementary humanity, and be merged with the crowd. A man or woman makes direct contact with society in two ways: as a member of some familial, professional or religious group, or as a member of a crowd. Groups are capable of being as moral and intelligent as the individuals who form them; a crowd is chaotic, has no purpose of its own and is capable of anything except intelligent action and realistic thinking. Assembled in a crowd, people lose their powers of reasoning and their capacity for moral choice. Their suggestibility is increased to the point where they cease to have any judgment or will of their own. They become very excitable, they lose all sense of individual or collective responsibility, they are subject to sudden accesses of rage, enthusiasm and panic. In a word, a man in a crowd behaves as though he had swallowed a large dose of some powerful intoxicant. He is a victim of what I have called "herd-poisoning." Like alcohol, herd-poison is an active, extraverted drug. The crowd-intoxicated individual escapes from responsibility, intelligence and morality into a kind of frantic, animal mindlessness.

During his long career as an agitator, Hitler had studied the effects of herd-poison and had learned how to exploit them for his own purposes. He had discovered that the orator can appeal to those "hidden forces" which motivate men's actions, much more effectively than can the writer. Reading is a private, not a collective activity. The writer speaks only to individuals, sitting by themselves in a state of normal sobriety. The orator speaks to masses of individuals, already well primed with herd-poison. They are at his mercy and, if he knows his business, he can do what he likes with them. As an orator, Hitler knew his business supremely well. He was able, in his own words, "to follow the lead of the great mass in such a way that from the living emotion of his hearers the apt word which he needed would be suggested to him and in its turn this would go straight to the heart of his hearers." Otto Strasser called him a "loud-speaker, proclaiming the most secret desires, the least admissible instincts, the sufferings and personal revolts of a whole nation." Twenty years before Madison Avenue embarked upon "Motivational Research," Hitler was systematically exploring and exploiting the secret fears and hopes, the cravings, anxieties and frustrations of the German masses. It is by manipulating "hidden forces" that the advertising experts induce us to buy their wares—a toothpaste, a brand of cigarettes, a political candidate. And it is by appealing to the same hidden forces—and to others too dangerous for Madison Avenue to meddle with—that Hitler induced the German masses to buy themselves a Fuehrer, an insane philosophy and the Second World War.

Unlike the masses, intellectuals have a taste for rationality and an interest in facts. Their critical habit of mind makes them resistant to the kind of propaganda that works so well on the majority. Among the masses "instinct is supreme, and from instinct comes faith. . . . While the healthy common folk instinctively close their ranks to form a community of the people" (under a Leader, it goes without saying) "intellectuals run this way and that, like hens in a poultry yard. With them one cannot make history; they cannot be used as elements composing a community." Intellectuals are the kind of people who demand evidence and are shocked by logical inconsistencies and fallacies. They regard over-simplification as the original sin of the mind and have no use for the slogans, the unqualified assertions and sweeping generalizations which are the propagandist's stock in trade. "All effective propaganda," Hitler wrote, "must be confined to a few bare necessities and then must be expressed in a few stereotyped formulas." These stereotyped formulas must be constantly repeated, for "only constant repetition will finally succeed in imprinting an idea upon the memory of a crowd." Philosophy teaches us to feel uncertain about the things that seem to us self-evident. Propaganda, on the other hand, teaches us to accept as self-evident matters about which it would be reasonable to suspend our judgment or to feel doubt. The aim of the demagogue is to create social coherence under his own leadership. But, as Bertrand Russell has pointed out, "systems of dogma without empirical foundations, such as scholasticism, Marxism and fascism, have the advantage of producing a great deal of social coherence among their disciples." The demagogic propagandist must therefore be consistently dogmatic. All his statements are made without qualification. There are no grays in his picture of the world; everything is either diabolically black or celestially white. In Hitler's words, the propagandist should adopt "a systematically one-sided attitude towards every problem that has to be dealt with." He must never admit that he might be wrong or that people with a different point of view might be even partially right. Opponents should not be argued with; they should be attacked, shouted down, or, if they become too much of a nuisance, liquidated. The morally squeamish intellectual may be shocked by this kind of thing. But the masses are always convinced that "right is on the side of the active aggressor."

Such, then, was Hitler's opinion of humanity in the mass. It was a very low opinion. Was it also an incorrect opinion? The tree is known by its fruits, and a theory of human nature which inspired the kind of techniques that proved so horribly effective must contain at least an element of truth. Virtue and intelligence belong to human beings as individuals freely associating with other individuals in small groups. So do sin and stupidity. But the subhuman mindlessness to

32

which the demagogue makes his appeal, the moral imbecility on which he relies when he goads his victims into action, are characteristic not of men and women as individuals, but of men and women in masses. Mindlessness and moral idiocy are not characteristically human attributes; they are symptoms of herd-poisoning. In all the world's higher religions, salvation and enlightenment are for individuals. The kingdom of heaven is within the mind of a person, not within the collective mindlessness of a crowd. Christ promised to be present where two or three are gathered together. He did not say anything about being present where thousands are intoxicating one another with herd-poison. Under the Nazis enormous numbers of people were compelled to spend an enormous amount of time marching in serried ranks from point A to point B and back again to point A. "This keeping of the whole population on the march seemed to be a senseless waste of time and energy. Only much later," adds Hermann Rauschning, "was there revealed in it a subtle intention based on a well-judged adjustment of ends and means. Marching diverts men's thoughts. Marching kills thought. Marching makes an end of individuality. Marching is the indispensable magic stroke performed in order to accustom the people to a mechanical, quasi-ritualistic activity until it becomes second nature."

From his point of view and at the level where he had chosen to do his dreadful work, Hitler was perfectly correct in his estimate of human nature. To those of us who look at men and women as individuals rather than as members of crowds, or of regimented collectives, he seems hideously wrong. In an age of accelerating over-population, of accelerating over-organization and ever more efficient means of mass communication, how can we preserve the integrity and reassert the value of the human individual? This is a question that can still be asked and perhaps effectively answered. A generation from now it may be too late to find an answer and perhaps impossible, in the stifling collective climate of that future time, even to ask the question.

Mary Caroline Richards

Mary Caroline Richards was educated at Reed College and the University of California at Berkeley, where she received a Ph.D. in English in 1942. It was only then that "instead of taking up a college professorship," she turned to the art of pottery. She

has been potter, poet, and teacher, and in Centering: In Pottery,
Poetry and the Person *(1964), a provocative spiritual auto-*
biography, she chronicles her need to think, to feel, and to make
in order to be. "As we come into touch with other beings," she
concludes, "we discover ourselves. This is precise. As I
experience the presence of a tree or a field or a stream or another
person or a tremor that runs through me with a force of its own,
I know myself through that experience;" and at the same time
"It is important to let the reins hang loose . . . to be well
enough seated not to fall in the energetic release . . . to have a
good balance, on center."

CENTERING AS DIALOGUE

Centering: that act which precedes all others on the potter's wheel.
The bringing of the clay into a spinning, unwobbling pivot, which
will then be free to take innumerable shapes as potter and clay press
against each other. The firm, tender, sensitive pressure which yields
as much as it asserts. It is like a handclasp between two living hands,
receiving the greeting at the very moment that they give it. It is this
speech between the hand and the clay that makes me think of dialogue. And it is a language far more interesting than the spoken
vocabulary which tries to describe it, for it is spoken not by the
tongue and lips but by the whole body, by the whole person, speaking
and listening. And with listening too, it seems to me, it is not the
ear that hears, it is not the physical organ that performs that act of
inner receptivity. It is the total person who hears. Sometimes the
skin seems to be the best listener, as it prickles and thrills, say to a
sound or a silence; or the fantasy, the imagination: how it bursts into
inner pictures as it listens and then responds by pressing its language,
its forms, into the listening clay. To be open to what we hear, to be
open in what we say . . .

.   .   .

I am a question-asker and a truth-seeker. I do not have much in the
way of status in my life, nor security. I have been on quest, as it
were, from the beginning. For a long time I thought there was something wrong with me: no ambition, no interest in tenure, always on
the march, changing every seven years, from landscape to landscape.
Certain elements were constant: the poetry, the desire for relationship,

34

the sense of voyage. But lately I have developed also a sense of destination, or destiny. And a sense that if I am to be on quest, I must expect to live like a pilgrim; I must keep to the inner path. I must be able to be whoever I am.

For example, it seemed strange to me, as to others, that, having taken my Ph.D. in English, I should then in the middle of my life, instead of taking up a college professorship, turn to the art of pottery. During one period, when people asked me what I did, I was uncertain what to answer; I guessed I could say I taught English, wrote poetry, and made pottery. What was my occupation? I finally gave up and said "Person."

Having been imbued with the ordinary superstitions of American higher education, among which is the belief that something known as the life of the mind is more apt to take you where you want to go than any other kind of life, I busied myself with learning to practice logic, grammar, analysis, summary, generalization; I learned to make distinctions, to speculate, to purvey information. I was educated to be an intellectual of the verbal type. I might have been a philosophy major, a literature major, a language major. I was always a kind of oddball even in undergraduate circles, as I played kick-goal on the Reed College campus with President Dexter Keezer. And in graduate school, even more so. Examinations tended to make me merry, often seeming to me to be some kind of private game, some secret ritual compulsively played by the professors and the institution. I invariably became facetious in all the critical hours. All that solemnity for a few facts! I couldn't believe they were serious. But they were. I never quite understood it. But I loved the dream and the reality that lay behind those texts and in the souls of my teachers. I often felt like a kind of fraud, because I suspected that the knowledge I was acquiring and being rewarded for by academic diploma was wide wide of the truth I sensed to live somewhere, somewhere. I felt that I knew little of real importance; and when would the day come that others would realize it too, and I would be exposed? I have had dream after dream in which it turns out that I have not really completed my examinations for the doctorate and have them still to pass. And I sweat with anxiety. A sense of occupying a certain position without possessing the real thing: the deeper qualifications of wisdom and prophecy. But of course it was not the world who exposed me, it was my dreams. I do not know if I am a philosopher, but if philosophy is the love of wisdom, then I am a philosopher, because I love wisdom and that is why I love the crafts, because they are wise.

I became a teacher quite by chance. Liked it, found in education an image through which I could examine the possibilities of growth, of nourishment, of the experiences that lead to knowledge of nature

35

and of self. It was a good trade to be in if you were a question-asker.

But the trouble was that though the work absorbed my mind, it used very little else. And I am by now convinced that wisdom is not the product of mental effort. Wisdom is a state of the total being, in which capacities for knowledge and for love, for survival and for death, for imagination, inspiration, intuition, for all the fabulous functioning of this human being who we are, come into a center with their forces, come into an experience of meaning that can voice itself as wise action. It is not enough to belong to a Society of Friends who believe in non-violence if, when frustrated, your body spontaneously contracts and shoots out its fist to knock another man down. It is in our bodies that redemption takes place. It is the physicality of the crafts that pleases me: I learn through my hands and my eyes and my skin what I could never learn through my brain. I develop a sense of life, of the world of earth, air, fire, and water—and wood, to add the fifth element according to Oriental alchemy—which could be developed in no other way. And if it is life I am fostering, I must maintain a kind of dialogue with the clay, listening, serving, interpreting as well as mastering. The union of our wills, like a marriage, it is a beautiful act, the act of centering and turning a pot on the potter's wheel; and the sexual images implicit in the forming of the cone and opening of the vessel are archetypal; likewise the give-and-take in the forming of a pot out of slabs, out of raw shards, out of coils; the union of natural intelligences: the intelligence of the clay, my intelligence, the intelligence of the tools, the intelligence of the fire.

You don't need me to tell you what education is. Everybody really knows that education goes on all the time everywhere all through our lives, and that it is the process of waking up to life. Jean Henri Fabre said something just about like that, I think. He said that to be educated was not to be taught but to wake up. It takes a heap of resolve to keep from going to sleep in the middle of the show. It's not that we want to sleep our lives away. It's that it requires certain kinds of energy, certain capacities for taking the world into our consciousness, certain real powers of body and soul to be a match for reality. That's why knowledge and consciousness are two quite different things. Knowledge is like a product we consume and store. All we need are good closets. By consciousness I mean a state of being "awake" to the world throughout our organism. This kind of consciousness requires not closets but an organism attuned to the finest perceptions and responses. It allows experience to breathe through it as light enters and changes a room. When knowledge is transformed into consciousness and into will, ah then we are on the high road indeed . . .

That which we consume, with a certain passivity, accepting it for the most part from our teachers, who in turn have accepted it from theirs, is like the food we eat. And food, in order to become energy, or will, is transformed entirely by the processes of metabolism. We do not become the food we eat. Rather the food turns into us. Similarly with knowledge, at best. Hopefully, we do not turn into encyclopedias or propaganda machines or electric brains. Our knowledge, if we allow it to be transformed within us, turns into capacity for life-serving human deeds. If knowledge does not turn into life, it makes cripples and madmen and dunces. It poisons just as food would if it stayed in the stomach and was never digested, and the waste products never thrown off.

It is dangerous to seek to possess knowledge, as if it could be stored. For one thing, it tends to make one impatient with ignorance, as people busy with money-seeking tend to be impatient with idlers. Though ignorance is the prime prerequisite for education, many teachers appear offended by it—or worse, contemptuous. Perhaps it is partly for this reason that many prefer to give advanced courses to select or "gifted" groups.

The possession of knowledge may create a materialism of its own. Knowledge becomes property. Teachers compete with each other for status, wealth, influence. A professor of education was speaking to friends of education in the county where I live, and she was urging pay raises as bait for hiring good teachers, "for after all, the standard of success is the salary check." Naturally in this climate professional educators are apt to quarrel over tactics and to engage in pressure politics, motivated by a desire to protect their security and to establish their views as ruling policy. In other words, education may be sacrificed to knowledge-as-commodity. Just as life is sometimes sacrificed to art-as-arrangement. The quest is abandoned. Instead, property is bought at the site of the last dragon killed, and a ruling class is formed out of the heroes. The knights grow fat and lazy and conceited and petulant. They parade in their armor on special occasions to bedazzle the populace. But in their hearts are terror and duplicity. And when difficult times come, they fall upon each other with their rusty axes and try to divide the world into those who know and those who don't. There is nothing to equal in bitterness and gall, childishness and spite, the intramural warfare of the academic community. Where is honor? Where is devotion? Where is responsibility of soul?

Such an atmosphere brought me gradually to imagine possible shortcomings in the educational system I had docilely trusted. Initiative and imagination seemed sorely lacking. Teachers seemed to apply to their students the same pressures that had crippled them. Most of us have been brain-washed to think that knowledge and security make the world go round. And if the world seems to be going round very

37

poorly, we do not think of questioning deeply its education. The need for creative imagination in the intellectually trained person is drastic. Also the need for spontaneous human feeling.

Fashionable thinking may dominate the scientist and artist and scholar alike. For them, knowledge is the body of facts currently in fashion. Art is the image and compositional practice now in fashion. Since it is difficult to test the truth of most facts, faculty and students alike settle for "interesting," "original," and "self-consistent" theories. An ability to marshal and interpret "evidence" is highly esteemed, though evidence is often no more than opinions strongly held or secondary research. Very little stress is placed on developing powers of observation or on intuition. Thus, with primary experience held so at a distance, sensory life in particular, I find that my principal task in teaching adults is to win their trust. They tend to be overwhelmingly oriented to manipulation and to effect. It rarely occurs to them to work in a direct way with what they know and are. Their primary motivations are to please, to make a strong impression, to do either what is expected (if they are docile) or what is unexpected (if they are hostile). They assume that pretense and falsity are virtues. The whole thing sometimes seems like a massive confidence game.

Like other men, teachers tend to withhold themselves from naked personal contact. They tend to pin their hopes on jargon and style. And this, I have observed, is what many students learn from them: afraid to reveal themselves, burdened with shame and dismay and hopelessness, or expertise and cunning.

A theory much in vogue is that Western man is sick with sexual repression and pleasure anxiety. I believe that the squelching of the "person" and his spontaneous intuitive response to experience is as much at the root of our timidity, our falseness. Teachers and students who in the great school markets barter their learning for salaries and grades are hungry for respect, for personal relationship, for warmth. Unfortunately, they have the impression that these are extracurricular (like Newton's secondary qualities of color and so on)—and their capacity for balance between the life within and the world without shrinks or falters, or their desperation turns rank.

It is a sensitive matter, of course. I am not going to all these words merely to insult the spirit of true research. But my life as a teacher and as a member of the human community advises me that education may estrange us from life-commitment as well as bind us firmly within it. There are all kinds of things to learn, and we had best learn them all. One of the reasons formal education is in danger today is that a sense of work is split off from human earnestness. How may this split be healed? Working with our materials as artist-craftsmen may help to engender a new health here.

An act of the self, that's what one must make. An act of the self, from me to you. From center to center. We must mean what we say, from our innermost heart to the outermost galaxy. Otherwise we are lost and dizzy in a maze of reflections. We carry light within us. There is no need merely to reflect. Others carry light within them. These lights must wake to each other. My face is real. Yours is. Let us find our way to our initiative.

For must we not show ourselves to each other, and will we not know then who are the teachers and who are the students? Do we not all learn from one another? My students at City College are worldly-wise and naïve as lambs. I am sophisticated and uninformed. We make a good combination. They have never heard of e. e. cummings, who lived in their city, nor of the New York painters. They do not know that there are free art galleries where they may see the latest works of modern artists. They do not know very much about contemporary "culture." But they know well the life of the subway, the office, the factory, the union hall, the hassle for employment; they know what they did in the war or in their escape from Hungary or Germany, or in occupied France, or Israel. They know what it is like to be black in America. They are patient with my obtuseness, they check my too quick judgments, my sarcasm which is unperceptive. I help them to unmask, to be openly as tender and hopeful and generous as they inwardly are. I help them to open themselves to knowledge. They help me to open myself to life. We are equal in courage.

Must weakness be concealed in order that respect be won? Must love and fervor be concealed? Must we pretend to fearlessness? and certainty? Surely education should equip us to know what to fear and what to be uncertain of. Surely it should equip us in personal honor.

Must. Should. Convenient words! Exhortations meant to loosen the grip of congealed behavior . . . Perhaps these perceptions are not the proper work of intellect, but of some other faculty deeply neglected in our education. In any case, at a critical moment in life my hunger for nakedness and realism and nobility turned to the clay of earth itself, and to water and fire.

I took up pottery also, in a sense, by chance. Unforeseen opportunity joined with interest and readiness. Like teaching, not a consciously sought but surely a destined union. For the materials and processes of pottery spoke to me of cosmic presences and transformations quite as surely as the pots themselves enchanted me. Experiences of the plastic clay and the firing of the ware carried more than commonplace values. Joy resonated deep within me, and it has stirred these thoughts only slowly to the surface. I have come to feel that we live in a universe of spirit, which materializes and de-materializes

39

grandly; all things seem to me to live, and all acts to contain meaning deeper than matter-of-fact; and the things we do with deepest love and interest compel us by the spiritual forces which dwell in them. This seems to me to be a dialogue of the visible and the invisible to which our ears are attuned.

There was, first of all, something in the nature of the clay itself. You can do very many things with it, push this way and pull that, squeeze and roll and attach and pinch and hollow and pile. But you can't do everything with it. You can go only so far, and then the clay resists. To know ourselves by our resistances—this is a thought first expressed to me by the poet Charles Olson.

And so it is with persons. You can do very many things with us: push us together and pull us apart and squeeze us and roll us flat, empty us out and fill us up. You can surround us with influences, but there comes a point when you can do no more. The person resists, in one way or another (if it is only by collapsing, like the clay). His own will becomes active.

This is a wonderful moment, when one feels his will become active, come as a force into the total assemblage and dynamic intercourse and interpenetration of will impulses. When one stands like a natural substance, plastic but with one's own character written into the formula, ah then one feels oneself part of the world, taking one's shape with its help—but a shape only one's own freedom can create.

And the centering of the clay, of which I have spoken. The opening of the form. And the firing of the pot. This experience has deep psychic reverberations: how the pot, which was originally plastic, sets into dry clay, brittle and fragile, and then by being heated to a certain temperature hardens into stone. By natural law as it were, it takes its final form. Ordeal by fire. Then, the form once taken, the pot may not last, the body may perish; but the inner form has been taken, and it cannot break in the same sense.

I, like everyone I know, am instinctively motivated toward symbols of wholeness. What is a simpler, more natural one than the pot fired? Wholeness may be thought of as a kind of inner equilibrium, in which all our capacities have been brought into functioning as an organism. The potencies of the whole organism flow into the gestures of any part. And the sensation in any part reverberates throughout the soul. The unconscious and conscious levels of being can work together at the tasks of life, conveying messages to each other, assimilating one another. In wholeness I sense an integration of those characteristics which are uniquely ME and those interests which I share with the rest of mankind. As for example any bowl is symbolic of an archetypal circular form, which I share with all, but which *I* make and which therefore contains those very qualities of myself which are active in

40

the making. I believe that pots have the smell of the person who makes them: a smell of tenderness, of vanity or ambition, of ease and naturalness, of petulance, uncertainty, callousness, fussiness, playfulness, solemnity, exuberance, absent-mindedness. The pot gives off something. It gives off its innerness, that which it holds but which cannot be seen.

In pottery, by developing sensitivity in manipulating natural materials by hand, I found a wisdom which had died out of the concepts I learned in the university: abstractions, mineralized and dead; while the minerals themselves were alive with energy and meaning. The life I found in the craft helped to bring to a new birth my ideals in education. Some secret center became vitalized in those hours of silent practice in the arts of transformation.

The experience of centering was one I particularly sought because I thought of myself as dispersed, interested in too many things. I envied people who were "single-minded," who had one powerful talent and who knew when they got up in the morning what it was they had to do. Whereas I, wherever I turned, felt the enchantment: to the window for the sweetness of the air; to the door for the passing figures; to the teapot, the typewriter, the knitting needles, the pets, the pottery, the newspaper, the telephone. Wherever I looked, I could have lived.

It took me half my life to come to believe I was OK even if I did love experience in a loose and undiscriminating way and did not know for sure the difference between good and bad. My struggles to accept my nature were the struggles of centering. I found myself at odds with the propaganda of our times. One is supposed to be either an artist or a homemaker, by one popular superstition. Either a teacher or a poet, by a theory which says that poetry must not sermonize. Either a craftsman or an intellectual, by a snobbism which claims either hand or head as the seat of true power. One is supposed to concentrate and not to spread oneself thin, as the jargon goes. And this is a jargon spoken by a cultural leadership from which it takes time to win one's freedom, if one is not lucky enough to have been born free. Finally, I hit upon an image: a seed-sower. Not to worry about which seeds sprout. But to give them as my gift in good faith.

But in spite of my self-acceptance, I still clung to a concept of purity which was chaste and aloof from the fellowship of man, and had yet to center the image of a pure heart in whose bright warm streams the world is invited to bathe. A heart who can be touched and who stirs in response, bringing the whole body into an act of greeting.

Well then, I became a potter.

Ralph Waldo Emerson

*Emerson (1803–1882) is one of the greatest figures in American
thought and letters. He spent his childhood in Boston and was
trained at Harvard to be a Unitarian minister in the family
tradition. Beset by doubts, he resigned from the ministry in
1832 and took up a career of writing and lecturing, during which
he continued to work out his transcendentalist philosophy and his
ethical doctrine of self-reliance. The present essay was an address
delivered to the Phi Beta Kappa chapter at Harvard on August 31,
1837. Its vehement oratorical quality, the memorableness of single
phrases, are typical of Emerson, whose style inherits much from
the tradition of the New England sermon. Oliver Wendell
Holmes called this essay "our intellectual Declaration of
Independence." Its appeal to "literary nationalism" (here somewhat
muffled by our omission of the final fifth of the essay) is perhaps
less important than its recording of a stage in the struggle of a
first-class man and thinker to find a way of life that could be
pursued with self-reliance and integrity.*

THE AMERICAN SCHOLAR

MR. PRESIDENT AND GENTLEMEN:

I greet you on the recommencement of our literary year. Our anniversary is one of hope, and, perhaps, not enough of labor. We do
not meet for games of strength or skill, for the recitation of histories,
tragedies, and odes, like the ancient Greeks; for parliaments of love
and poesy, like the Troubadours; nor for the advancement of science,
like our contemporaries in the British and European capitals. Thus
far, our holiday has been simply a friendly sign of the survival of the
love of letters amongst a people too busy to give to letters any more.
As such it is precious as the sign of an indestructible instinct. Perhaps
the time is already come when it ought to be, and will be, something
else; when the sluggard intellect of this continent will look from under
its iron lids and fill the postponed expectation of the world with something better than the exertions of mechanical skill. Our day of dependence, our long apprenticeship to the learning of other lands, draws
to a close. The millions that around us are rushing into life, cannot

always be fed on the sere remains of foreign harvests. Events, actions arise, that must be sung, that will sing themselves. Who can doubt that poetry will revive and lead in a new age, as the star in the constellation Harp, which now flames in our zenith, astronomers announce, shall one day be the pole-star for a thousand years?

In this hope I accept the topic which not only usage but the nature of our association seem to prescribe to this day,—the AMERICAN SCHOLAR. Year by year we come up hither to read one more chapter of his biography. Let us inquire what light new days and events have thrown on his character and his hopes.

It is one of those fables which out of an unknown antiquity convey an unlooked-for wisdom, that the gods, in the beginning, divided Man into men, that he might be more helpful to himself; just as the hand was divided into fingers, the better to answer its end.

The old fable covers a doctrine ever new and sublime; that there is One Man,—present to all particular men only partially, or through one faculty; and that you must take the whole society to find the whole man. Man is not a farmer, or a professor, or an engineer, but he is all. Man is priest, and scholar, and statesman, and producer, and soldier. In the *divided* or social state these functions are parcelled out to individuals, each of whom aims to do his stint of the joint work, whilst each other performs his. The fable implies that the individual, to possess himself, must sometimes return from his own labor to embrace all the other laborers. But, unfortunately, this original unit, this fountain of power, has been so distributed to multitudes, has been so minutely subdivided and peddled out, that it is spilled into drops, and cannot be gathered. The state of society is one in which the members have suffered amputation from the trunk, and strut about so many walking monsters,—a good finger, a neck, a stomach, an elbow, but never a man.

Man is thus metamorphosed into a thing, into many things. The planter, who is Man sent out into the field to gather food, is seldom cheered by any idea of the true dignity of his ministry. He sees his bushel and his cart, and nothing beyond, and sinks into the farmer, instead of Man on the farm. The tradesman scarcely ever gives an ideal worth to his work, but is ridden by the routine of his craft, and the soul is subject to dollars. The priest becomes a form; the attorney a statute-book; the mechanic a machine; the sailor a rope of the ship.

In this distribution of functions the scholar is the delegated intellect. In the right state he is *Man Thinking.* In the degenerate state, when the victim of society, he tends to become a mere thinker, or still worse, the parrot of other men's thinking.

In this view of him, as Man Thinking, the theory of his office is contained. Him Nature solicits with all her placid, all her monitory pictures; him the past instructs; him the future invites. Is not indeed every man a student, and do not all things exist for the student's behoof? And, finally, is not the true scholar the only true master? But the old oracle said, "All things have two handles: beware of the wrong one." In life, too often, the scholar errs with mankind and forfeits his privilege. Let us see him in his school, and consider him in reference to the main influences he receives.

I. The first in time and the first in importance of the influences upon the mind is that of nature. Every day, the sun; and, after sunset, Night and her stars. Ever the winds blow, ever the grass grows. Every day, men and women, conversing—beholding and beholden. The scholar is he of all men whom this spectacle most engages. He must settle its value in his mind. What is nature to him? There is never a beginning, there is never an end, to the inexplicable continuity of this web of God, but always circular power returning into itself. Therein it resembles his own spirit, whose beginning, whose ending, he never can find,—so entire, so boundless. Far too as her splendors shine, system on system shooting like rays, upward, downward, without centre, without circumference,—in the mass and in the particle, Nature hastens to render account of herself to the mind. Classification begins. To the young mind every thing is individual, stands by itself. By and by, it finds how to join two things and see in them one nature; then three, then three thousand; and so, tyrannized over by its own unifying instinct, it goes on tying things together, diminishing anomalies, discovering roots running under ground whereby contrary and remote things cohere and flower out from one stem. It presently learns that since the dawn of history there has been a constant accumulation and classifying of facts. But what is classification but the perceiving that these objects are not chaotic, and are not foreign, but have a law which is also a law of the human mind? The astronomer discovers that geometry, a pure abstraction of the human mind, is the measure of planetary motion. The chemist finds proportions and intelligible method throughout matter; and science is nothing but the finding of analogy, identity, in the most remote parts. The ambitious soul sits down before each refractory fact; one after another reduces all strange constitutions, all new powers, to their class and their law, and goes on forever to animate the last fibre of organization, the outskirts of nature, by insight.

Thus to him, to this schoolboy under the bending dome of day, is suggested that he and it proceed from one root; one is leaf and one is flower; relation, sympathy, stirring in every vein. And what is that root? Is not that the soul of his soul? A thought too bold; a dream too wild. Yet when this spiritual light shall have revealed the law of more earthly natures,—when he has learned to worship the soul, and to see that the natural philosophy that now is, is only the first gropings of its gigantic hand, he shall look forward to an ever expanding knowledge as to a becoming creator. He shall see that nature is the opposite of the soul, answering to it part for part. One is seal and one is print. Its beauty is the beauty of his own mind. Its laws are the laws of his own mind. Nature then becomes to him the measure of his attainments. So much of nature as he is ignorant of, so much of his own mind does he not yet possess. And, in fine, the ancient precept, "Know thyself," and the modern precept, "Study nature," become at last one maxim.

II. The next great influence into the spirit of the scholar is the mind of the Past,—in whatever form, whether of literature, of art, of institutions, that mind is inscribed. Books are the best type of the influence of the past, and perhaps we shall get at the truth,—learn the amount of this influence more conveniently,—by considering their value alone.

The theory of books is noble. The scholar of the first age received into him the world around; brooded thereon; gave it the new arrangement of his own mind, and uttered it again. It came into him life; it went out from him truth. It came to him short-lived actions; it went out from him immortal thoughts. It came to him business; it went from him poetry. It was dead fact; now, it is quick thought. It can stand, and it can go. It now endures, it now flies, it now inspires. Precisely in proportion to the depth of mind from which it issued, so high does it soar, so long does it sing.

Or, I might say, it depends on how far the process had gone, of transmuting life into truth. In proportion to the completeness of the distillation, so will the purity and imperishableness of the product be. But none is quite perfect. As no air-pump can by any means make a perfect vacuum, so neither can any artist entirely exclude the conventional, the local, the perishable from his book, or write a book of pure thought, that shall be as efficient, in all respects, to a remote posterity, as to contemporaries, or rather to the second age. Each age, it is found, must write its own books; or rather, each generation for the next succeeding. The books of an older period will not fit this.

Yet hence arises a grave mischief. The sacredness which attaches to the act of creation, the act of thought, is transferred to the record. The poet chanting was felt to be a divine man: henceforth the chant is divine also. The writer was a just and wise spirit: henceforward it is settled the book is perfect; as love of the hero corrupts into worship of his statue. Instantly the book becomes noxious: the guide is a tyrant. The sluggish and perverted mind of the multitude, slow to open to the incursions of Reason, having once so opened, having once received this book, stands upon it, and makes an outcry if it is disparaged. Colleges are built on it. Books are written on it by thinkers, not by Man Thinking; by men of talent, that is, who start wrong, who set out from accepted dogmas, not from their own sight of principles. Meek young men grow up in libraries, believing it their duty to accept the views which Cicero, which Locke, which Bacon, have given; forgetful that Cicero, Locke, and Bacon were only young men in libraries when they wrote these books.

Hence, instead of Man Thinking, we have the bookworm. Hence the book-learned class, who value books, as such; not as related to nature and the human constitution, but as making a sort of Third Estate with the world and the soul. Hence the restorers of readings, the emendators, the bibliomaniacs of all degrees.

Books are the best of things, well used; abused, among the worst. What is the right use? What is the one end which all means go to effect? They are for nothing but to inspire. I had better never see a book than to be warped by its attraction clean out of my own orbit, and made a satellite instead of a system. The one thing in the world, of value, is the active soul. This every man is entitled to; this every man contains within him, although in almost all men obstructed and as yet unborn. The soul active sees absolute truth and utters truth, or creates. In this action it is genius; not the privilege of here and there a favorite, but the sound estate of every man. In its essence it is progressive. The book, the college, the school of art, the institution of any kind, stop with some past utterance of genius. This is good, say they,—let us hold by this. They pin me down. They look backward and not forward. But genius looks forward: the eyes of man are set in his forehead, not in his hindhead: man hopes: genius creates. Whatever talents may be, if the man create not, the pure efflux of the Deity is not his;—cinders and smoke there may be, but not yet flame. There are creative manners, there are creative actions, and creative words; manners, actions, words, that is, indicative of no custom or authority, but springing spontaneous from the mind's own sense of good and fair.

On the other part, instead of being its own seer, let it receive from another mind its truth, though it were in torrents of light, without periods of solitude, inquest, and self-recovery, and a fatal disservice is done. Genius is always sufficiently the enemy of genius by overinfluence. The literature of every nation bears me witness. The English dramatic poets have Shakspearized now for two hundred years.

Undoubtedly there is a right way of reading, so it be sternly subordinated. Man Thinking must not be subdued by his instruments.

Books are for the scholar's idle times. When he can read God directly, the hour is too precious to be wasted in other men's transcripts of their readings. But when the intervals of darkness come, as come they must,—when the sun is hid and the stars withdraw their shining, —we repair to the lamps which were kindled by their ray, to guide our steps to the East again, where the dawn is. We hear, that we may speak. The Arabian proverb says, "A fig tree, looking on a fig tree, becometh fruitful."

It is remarkable, the character of the pleasure we derive from the best books. They impress us with the conviction that one nature wrote and the same reads. We read the verses of one of the great English poets, of Chaucer, of Marvell, of Dryden, with the most modern joy,—with a pleasure, I mean, which is in great part caused by the abstraction of all *time* from their verses. There is some awe mixed with the joy of our surprise, when this poet, who lived in some past world, two or three hundred years ago, says that which lies close to my own soul, that which I also had well-nigh thought and said. But for the evidence thence afforded to the philosophical doctrine of the identity of all minds, we should suppose some preëstablished harmony, some foresight of souls that were to be, and some preparation of stores for their future wants, like the fact observed in insects, who lay up food before death for the young grub they shall never see.

I would not be hurried by any love of system, by any exaggeration of instincts, to underrate the Book. We all know, that as the human body can be nourished on any food, though it were boiled grass and the broth of shoes, so the human mind can be fed by any knowledge. And great and heroic men have existed who had almost no other information than by the printed page. I only would say that it needs a strong head to bear that diet. One must be an inventor to read well. As the proverb says, "He that would bring home the wealth of the Indies, must carry out the wealth of the Indies." There is then creative reading as well as creative writing. When the mind is braced by labor and invention, the page of whatever book we read becomes luminous with manifold allusion. Every sentence is doubly significant, and the sense of our author is as broad as the world. We then see, what is always true, that as the seer's hour of vision is short and rare among heavy days and months, so is its record, perchance, the least part of his volume. The discerning will read, in his Plato or Shakspeare, only that least part,—only the authentic utterances of the oracle; —all the rest he rejects, were it never so many times Plato's and Shakspeare's.

Of course there is a portion of reading quite indispensable to a wise man. History and exact science he must learn by laborious reading.

Colleges, in like manner, have their indispensable office,—to teach elements. But they can only highly serve us when they aim not to drill, but to create; when they gather from far every ray of various genius to their hospitable halls, and by the concentrated fires, set the hearts of their youth on flame. Thought and knowledge are natures in which apparatus and pretension avail nothing. Gowns and pecuniary foundations, though of towns of gold, can never countervail the least sentence or syllable of wit. Forget this, and our American colleges will recede in their public importance, whilst they grow richer every year.

III. There goes in the world a notion that the scholar should be a recluse, a valetudinarian,—as unfit for any handiwork or public labor as a penknife for an axe. The so-called "practical men" sneer at speculative men, as if, because they speculate or *see*, they could do nothing. I have heard it said that the clergy,—who are always, more universally than any other class, the scholars of their day,—are addressed as women; that the rough, spontaneous conversation of men they do not hear, but only a mincing and diluted speech. They are often virtually disfranchised; and indeed there are advocates for their celibacy. As far as this is true of the studious classes, it is not just and wise. Action is with the scholar subordinate, but it is essential. Without it he is not yet man. Without it thought can never ripen into truth. Whilst the world hangs before the eye as a cloud of beauty, we cannot even see its beauty. Inaction is cowardice, but there can be no scholar without the heroic mind. The preamble of thought, the transition through which it passes from the unconscious to the conscious, is action. Only so much do I know, as I have lived. Instantly we know whose words are loaded with life, and whose not.

The world,—this shadow of the soul, or *other me*,—lies wide around. Its attractions are the keys which unlock my thoughts and make me acquainted with myself. I run eagerly into this resounding tumult. I grasp the hands of those next me, and take my place in the ring to suffer and to work, taught by an instinct that so shall the dumb abyss be vocal with speech. I pierce its order; I dissipate its fear; I dispose of it within the circuit of my expanding life. So much only of life as I know by experience, so much of the wilderness have I vanquished and planted, or so far have I extended my being, my dominion. I do not see how any man can afford, for the sake of his nerves and his nap, to spare any action in which he can partake. It is pearls and rubies to his discourse. Drudgery, calamity, exasperation, want, are instructors in eloquence and wisdom. The true scholar grudges every opportunity of action past by, as a loss of power. It is the raw material out of which the intellect moulds her splendid products. A strange process too, this by which experience is converted into thought, as a mulberry leaf is converted into satin. The manufacture goes forward at all hours.

The actions and events of our childhood and youth are now matters of calmest observation. They lie like fair pictures in the air. Not so with our recent actions,—with the business which we now have in hand. On this we are quite unable to speculate. Our affections as yet circulate through it. We no more feel or know it than we feel the feet, or the hand, or the brain of our body. The new deed is yet a part of life,—remains for a time immersed in our unconscious life. In some contemplative hour it detaches itself from the life like a ripe fruit, to become a thought of the mind. Instantly it is raised, transfigured; the corruptible has put on incorruption. Henceforth it is an object of beauty, however base its origin and neighborhood. Observe too the impossibility of antedating this act. In its grub state, it cannot fly, it cannot shine, it is a dull grub. But suddenly, without observation, the selfsame thing unfurls beautiful wings, and is an angel of wisdom. So is there no fact, no event, in our private history, which shall not, sooner or later, lose its adhesive, inert form, and astonish us by soaring from our body into the empyrean. Cradle and infancy, school and playground, the fear of boys, and dogs, and ferules, the love of little maids and berries, and many another fact that once filled the whole sky, are gone already; friend and relative, profession and party, town and country, nation and world, must also soar and sing.

Of course, he who has put forth his total strength in fit actions has the richest return of wisdom. I will not shut myself out of this globe of action, and transplant an oak into a flowerpot, there to hunger and pine; nor trust the revenue of some single faculty, and exhaust one vein of thought, much like those Savoyards, who, getting their livelihood by carving shepherds, shepherdesses, and smoking Dutchmen, for all Europe, went out one day to the mountain to find stock, and discovered that they had whittled up the last of their pine trees. Authors we have, in numbers, who have written out their vein, and who, moved by a commendable prudence, sail for Greece or Palestine, follow the trapper into the prairie, or ramble round Algiers, to replenish their merchantable stock.

If it were only for a vocabulary, the scholar would be covetous of action. Life is our dictionary. Years are well spent in country labors; in town; in the insight into trades and manufactures; in frank intercourse with many men and women; in science; in art; to the one end of mastering in all their facts a language by which to illustrate and embody our perceptions. I learn immediately from any speaker how much he has already lived, through the poverty or the splendor of his speech. Life lies behind us as the quarry from whence we get tiles and copestones for the masonry of to-day. This is the way to learn grammar. Colleges and books only copy the language which the field and the work-yard made.

But the final value of action, like that of books, and better than books, is that it is a resource. The great principle of Undulation in nature, that shows itself in the inspiring and expiring of the breath; in desire and satiety; in the ebb and flow of the sea; in day and night; in heat and cold; and, as yet more deeply ingrained in every atom and every fluid, is known to us under the name of Polarity,—these "fits of easy transmission and reflection," as Newton called them, are the law of nature because they are the law of spirit.

The mind now thinks, now acts, and each fit reproduces the other. When the artist has exhausted his materials, when the fancy no longer paints, when thoughts are no longer apprehended and books are a weariness,—he has always the resource *to live*. Character is higher than intellect. Thinking is the function. Living is the functionary. The stream retreats to its source. A great soul will be strong to live, as well as strong to think. Does he lack organ or medium to impart his truths? He can still fall back on this elemental force of living them. This is a total act. Thinking is a partial act. Let the grandeur of justice shine in his affairs. Let the beauty of affection cheer his lowly roof. Those "far from fame," who dwell and act with him, will feel the force of his constitution in the doings and passages of the day better than it can be measured by any public and designed display. Time shall teach him that the scholar loses no hour which the man lives. Herein he unfolds the sacred germ of his instinct, screened from influence. What is lost in seemliness is gained in strength. Not out of those on whom systems of education have exhausted their culture, comes the helpful giant to destroy the old or to build the new, but out of unhandselled savage nature; out of terrible Druids and Berserkers come at last Alfred and Shakspeare.

I hear therefore with joy whatever is beginning to be said of the dignity and necessity of labor to every citizen. There is virtue yet in the hoe and the spade, for learned as well as for unlearned hands. And labor is everywhere welcome; always we are invited to work; only be this limitation observed, that a man shall not for the sake of wider activity sacrifice any opinion to the popular judgments and modes of action.

I have now spoken of the education of the scholar by nature, by books, and by action. It remains to say somewhat of his duties.

They are such as become Man Thinking. They may all be comprised in self-trust. The office of the scholar is to cheer, to raise, and to guide men by showing them facts amidst appearances. He plies the slow, unhonored, and unpaid task of observation. Flamsteed and Herschel, in their glazed observatories, may catalogue the stars with the praise of all men, and the results being splendid and useful, honor is sure. But he, in his private observatory, cataloguing obscure and nebulous stars of the human mind, which as yet no man has thought of as such,—watching days and months sometimes for a few facts; correcting still his old records;—must relinquish display and immediate fame. In the long period of his preparation he must betray often an ignorance and shiftlessness in popular arts, incurring the disdain of the able who shoulder him aside. Long he must stammer in his speech; often forego the living for the dead. Worse yet, he must accept—how often!—poverty and solitude. For the ease and pleasure of treading the old road, accepting the fashions, the education, the religion of society, he takes the cross of making his own, and, of course, the self-accusation, the faint heart, the frequent uncertainty and loss of time, which are the nettles and tangling vines in the way of the self-relying and self-directed; and the state of virtual hostility in which he seems to stand to society, and especially to educated society. For all this loss and scorn, what offset? He is to find consolation in exercising the highest functions of human nature. He is one who raises himself from private considerations and breathes and lives on public and illustrious thoughts. He is the world's eye. He is the world's heart. He is to resist the vulgar prosperity that retrogrades ever to barbarism, by preserving and communicating heroic sentiments, noble biographies, melodious verse, and the conclusions of history. Whatsoever oracles the human heart, in all emergencies, in all solemn hours, has uttered as its commentary on the world of actions,—these he shall receive and impart. And whatsoever new verdict Reason from her inviolable seat pronounces on the passing men and events of to-day,—this he shall hear and promulgate.

These being his functions, it becomes him to feel all confidence in himself, and to defer never to the popular cry. He and he only knows the world. The world of any moment is the merest appearance. Some great decorum, some fetish of a government, some ephemeral trade, or war, or man, is cried up by half mankind and cried down by the other half, as if all depended on this particular up or down. The odds are that the whole question is not worth the poorest thought which the scholar has lost in listening to the controversy. Let him not quit his belief that a popgun is a popgun, though the ancient and honorable of the earth affirm it to be the crack of doom. In silence, in steadiness, in severe abstraction, let him hold by himself; add observation to observation, patient of neglect, patient of reproach, and bide his own time,—happy enough if he can satisfy himself alone that this day he has seen something truly. Success treads on every right step. For the instinct is sure, that prompts him to tell his brother what he thinks. He then learns that in going down into the secrets of his own mind he has descended into the secrets of all minds. He learns that he who has mastered any law in his private thoughts, is master to that extent of all men whose language he speaks, and of all into whose language his own can be translated. The poet, in utter solitude remembering his spontaneous thoughts and recording them, is found to have recorded that which men in crowded cities find true for them also. The orator distrusts at first the fitness of his frank confessions, his want of knowledge of the persons he addresses, until he finds that he is the complement of his hearers;—that they drink his words because he fulfils for them their own nature; the deeper he dives into his privatest, secretest presentiment, to his wonder he finds this is the most acceptable, most public, and universally true. The people delight in it; the better part of every man feels, This is my music; this is myself.

In self-trust all the virtues are comprehended. Free should the scholar be,—free and brave. Free even to the definition of freedom, "without any hindrance that does not arise out of his own constitution." Brave; for fear is a thing which a scholar by his very function puts behind him. Fear always springs from ignorance. It is a shame to him if his tranquillity, amid dangerous times, arise from the presumption that like children and women his is a protected class; or if he seek a temporary peace by the diversion of his thoughts from politics or vexed questions, hiding his head like an ostrich in the flowering bushes, peeping into microscopes, and turning rhymes, as a boy whistles to keep his courage up. So is the danger a danger still; so is the fear worse. Manlike let him turn and face it. Let him look into its eye and search its nature, inspect its origin,—see the whelping of this lion,—which lies no great way back; he will then find in himself a perfect comprehension of its nature and extent; he will have made his hands meet on the other side, and can henceforth defy it and pass on superior. The world is his who can see through its pretension. What deafness, what stone-blind custom, what overgrown error you behold is there only by sufferance,—by your sufferance. See it to be a lie, and you have already dealt it its mortal blow.

Yes, we are the cowed,—we the trustless. It is a mischievous notion that we are come late into nature; that the world was finished a long time ago. As the world was plastic and fluid in the hands of God, so it is ever to so much of his attributes as we bring to it. To ignorance and sin, it is flint. They adapt themselves to it as they may; but in proportion as a man has any thing in him divine, the firmament flows before him and takes his signet and form. Not he is great who can alter matter, but he who can alter my state of mind. They are the kings of the world who give the color of their present thought to all nature and all art, and persuade men by the cheerful serenity of their carrying the matter, that this thing which they do is the apple which the ages have desired to pluck, now at last ripe, and inviting nations to the harvest. The great man makes the great thing. Wherever Macdonald sits, there is the head of the table. Linnæus makes botany the most alluring of studies, and wins it from the farmer and the herb-woman; Davy, chemistry; and Cuvier, fossils. The day is always his who works in it with serenity and great aims. The unstable estimates of men crowd to him whose mind is filled with a truth, as the heaped waves of the Atlantic follow the moon.

For this self-trust, the reason is deeper than can be fathomed,—darker than can be enlightened. I might not carry with me the feeling of my audience in stating my own belief. But I have already shown the ground of my hope, in adverting to the doctrine that man is one. I believe man has been wronged; he has wronged himself. He has almost lost the light that can lead him back to his prerogatives. Men are become of no account. Men in history, men in the world of to-day, are bugs, are spawn, and are called "the mass" and "the herd." In a century, in a millennium, one or two men; that is to say, one or two approximations to the right state of every man. All the rest behold in the hero or the poet their own green and crude being,—ripened; yes, and are content to be less, so that may attain to its full stature. What a testimony, full of grandeur, full of pity, is borne to the demands of his own nature, by the poor clansman, the poor partisan, who rejoices in the glory of his chief. The poor and the low find some amends to their immense moral capacity, for their acquiescence in a political and social inferiority. They are content to be brushed like flies from the path of a great person, so that justice shall be done by him to that common nature which it is the dearest desire of all to see enlarged and glorified. They sun themselves in the great man's light, and feel it to be their own element. They cast the dignity of man from their downtrod selves upon the shoulders of a hero, and will perish to add one drop of blood to make that great heart beat, those giant sinews combat and conquer. He lives for us, and we live in him.

Men, such as they are, very naturally seek money or power; and power because it is as good as money,—the "spoils," so called, "of office." And why not? for they aspire to the highest, and this, in their sleep-walking, they dream is highest. Wake them and they shall quit the false good and leap to the true, and leave governments to clerks and desks. This revolution is to be wrought by the gradual domestication of the idea of Culture. The main enterprise of the world for splendor, for extent, is the upbuilding of a man. Here are the materials strewn along the ground. The private life of one man shall be a more illustrious monarchy, more formidable to its enemy, more sweet and serene in its influence to its friend, than any kingdom in history. For a man, rightly viewed, comprehendeth the particular natures of all men. Each philosopher, each bard, each actor has only done for me, as by a delegate, what one day I can do for myself. The books which once we valued more than the apple of the eye, we have quite exhausted. What is that but saying that we have come up with the point of view which the universal mind took through the eyes of one scribe; we have been that man, and have passed on. First, one, then another, we drain all cisterns, and waxing greater by all these supplies, we crave a better and more abundant food. The man has never lived that can feed us ever. The human mind cannot be enshrined in a person who shall set a barrier on any one side to this unbounded, unboundable empire. It is one central fire, which, flaming now out of the lips of Etna, lightens the capes of Sicily, and now out of the throat of Vesuvius, illuminates the towers and vineyards of Naples. It is one light which beams out of a thousand stars. It is one soul which animates all men.

• • •

Norman O. Brown

Norman O. Brown was born in Mexico, of British parents, in 1913. He received the B.A. from Balliol College, Oxford, in 1936, and the Ph.D. from the University of Wisconsin in 1942. He served with the O.S.S. during World War II and was for many years thereafter a professor at Wesleyan University. He has subsequently taught at Rochester and at the University of California at Santa Cruz. Brown was trained as a classicist and is the author of several works on Greek mythology, but he has always had very broad intellectual interests, and a deep study of Freud in the 1950s led to the publication of his psychoanalytic interpretation of history, Life Against Death *(1959), which made him world famous as a moral and political thinker. The gnomic*

Love's Body (1966) confirms his passage from historian and
philosopher to mystic and prophet. "Apocalypse: The Place of
Mystery in the Life of the Mind" is the title of the Phi Beta
Kappa oration delivered at Columbia in 1960.

APOCALYPSE

I didn't know whether I should appear before you—there is a time to
show and a time to hide; there is a time to speak, and also a time
to be silent. What time is it? It is fifteen years since H. G. Wells
said Mind was at the End of its Tether—with a frightful queerness
come into life: there is no way out or around or through, he said; it
is the end. It is because I think mind is at the end of its tether that
I would be silent. It is because I think there is a way out—a way
down and out—the title of Mr. John Senior's new book on the occult
tradition in literature—that I will speak.

Mind at the end of its tether: I can guess what some of you are
thinking—*his* mind is at the end of its tether—and this could be; it
scares me but it deters me not. The alternative to mind is certainly
madness. Our greatest blessings, says Socrates in the *Phaedrus*, come
to us by way of madness—provided, he adds, that the madness comes
from the god. Our real choice is between holy and unholy madness:
open your eyes and look around you—madness is in the saddle any-
how. Freud is the measure of our unholy madness, as Nietzsche is
the prophet of the holy madness, of Dionysus, the mad truth. Dionysus has returned to his native Thebes; mind—at the end of its
tether—is another Pentheus, up a tree. Resisting madness can be the
maddest way of being mad.

And there is a way out—the blessed madness of the maenad and
the bacchant: "Blessed is he who has the good fortune to know the
mysteries of the gods, who sanctifies his life and initiates his soul, a
bacchant on the mountains, in holy purifications." It is possible to be
mad and to be unblest; but it is not possible to get the blessing without the madness; it is not possible to get the illuminations without
the derangement. Derangement is disorder: the Dionysian faith is that
order as we have known it is crippling, and for cripples; that what is
past is prologue; that we can throw away our crutches and discover
the supernatural power of walking; that human history goes from man
to superman.

No superman I; I come to you not as one who has supernatural powers, but as one who seeks for them, and who has some notions which way to go to find them.

Sometimes—most times—I think that the way down and out leads out of the university, out of the academy. But perhaps it is rather that we should recover the academy of earlier days—the Academy of Plato in Athens, the Academy of Ficino in Florence, Ficino who says, "The spirit of the god Dionysus was believed by the ancient theologians and Platonists to be the ecstasy and abandon of disencumbered minds, when partly by innate love, partly at the instigation of the god, they transgress the natural limits of intelligence and are miraculously transformed into the beloved god himself: where, inebriated by a certain new draft of nectar and by an immeasurable joy, they rage, as it were, in a bacchic frenzy. In the drunkenness of this Dionysian wine, our Dionysius (the Areopagite) expresses his exultation. He pours forth enigmas, he sings in dithyrambs. To penetrate the profundity of his meanings, to imitate his quasi-Orphic manner of speech, we too require the divine fury."

At any rate the point is first of all to find again the mysteries. By which I do not mean simply the sense of wonder—that sense of wonder which is indeed the source of all true philosophy—by mystery I mean secret and occult; therefore unpublishable; therefore outside the university as we know it; but not outside Plato's Academy, or Ficino's.

Why are mysteries unpublishable? First because they cannot be put into words, at least not the kind of words which earned you your Phi Beta Kappa keys. Mysteries display themselves in words only if they can remain concealed; this is poetry, isn't it? We must return to the old doctrine of the Platonists and Neo-Platonists, that poetry is veiled truth; as Dionysus is the god who is both manifest and hidden; and as John Donne declared, with the Pillar of Fire goes the Pillar of Cloud. This is also the new doctrine of Ezra Pound, who says: "Prose is not education but the outer courts of the same. Beyond its doors are the mysteries. Eleusis. Things not to be spoken of save in secret. The mysteries self-defended, the mysteries that cannot be revealed. Fools can only profane them. The dull can neither penetrate the secretum nor divulge it to others." The mystic academies, whether Plato's or Ficino's, knew the limitations of words and drove us on beyond them, to go over, to go under, to the learned ignorance, in which God is better honored and loved by silence than by words, and better seen by closing the eyes to images than by opening them.

And second, mysteries are unpublishable because only some can see them, not all. Mysteries are intrinsically esoteric, and as such an offense to democracy: is not publicity a democratic principle? Publication makes it republican—a thing of the people. The pristine academies were esoteric and aristocratic, self-consciously separate from the profane vulgar. Democratic resentment denies that there can be any-thing that can't be seen by everybody; in the democratic academy truth is subject to public verification; truth is what any fool can see. This is what is meant by the so-called scientific method: so-called science is the attempt to democratize knowledge—the attempt to substitute method for insight, mediocrity for genius, by getting a standard oper-ating procedure. The great equalizers dispensed by the scientific method are the tools, those analytical tools. The miracle of genius is replaced by the standardized mechanism. But fools with tools are still fools, and don't let your Phi Beta Kappa key fool you. Tibetan prayer wheels are another way of arriving at the same result: the degeneration of mysticism into mechanism—so that any fool can do it. Perhaps the advantage is with Tibet: for there the mechanism is external while the mind is left vacant; and vacancy is not the worst condition of the mind. And the resultant prayers make no futile claim to originality or immortality; being nonexistent, they do not have to be catalogued or stored.

The sociologist Simmel sees showing and hiding, secrecy and pub-licity, as two poles, like Yin and Yang, between which societies oscil-late in their historical development. I sometimes think I see that civilizations originate in the disclosure of some mystery, some secret; and expand with the progressive publication of their secret; and end in exhaustion when there is no longer any secret, when the mystery has been divulged, that is to say profaned. The whole story is illus-trated in the difference between ideogram and alphabet. The alphabet is indeed a democratic triumph; and the enigmatic ideogram, as Ezra Pound has taught us, is a piece of mystery, a piece of poetry, not yet profaned. And so there comes a time—I believe we are in such a time—when civilization has to be renewed by the discovery of new mysteries, by the undemocratic but sovereign power of the imagina-tion, by the undemocratic power which makes poets the unacknowl-edged legislators of mankind, the power which makes all things new.

The power which makes all things new is magic. What our time needs is mystery: what our time needs is magic. Who would not say that only a miracle can save us? In Tibet the degree-granting insti-tution is, or used to be, the College of Magic Ritual. It offers courses in such fields as clairvoyance and telepathy; also (attention physics majors) internal heat: internal heat is a yoga bestowing supernatural control over body temperature. Let me succumb for a moment to the fascination of the mysterious East and tell you of the examination procedure for the course in internal heat. Candidates assemble naked, in midwinter, at night, on a frozen Himalayan lake. Beside each one is placed a pile of wet frozen undershirts; the assignment is to wear, until they are dry, as many as possible of these undershirts before dawn. Where the power is real, the test is real, and the grading system dumfoundingly objective. I say no more. I say no more; Eastern Yoga does indeed demonstrate the existence of supernatural powers, but it does not have the particular power our Western society needs; or rather I think that each society has access only to its own proper powers; or rather each society will only get the kind of power it knows how to ask for.

The Western consciousness has always asked for freedom: the human mind was born free, or at any rate born to be free, but everywhere it is in chains; and now at the end of its tether. It will take a miracle to free the human mind: because the chains are magical in the first place. We are in bondage to authority outside ourselves: most obviously—here in a great university it must be said—in bondage to the authority of books. There is a Transcendentalist anticipation of what I want to say in Emerson's Phi Beta Kappa address on the American scholar:

"The books of an older period will not fit this. Yet hence arises a grave mischief. The sacredness which attaches to the act of creation, the act of thought, is transferred to the record. Instantly the book becomes noxious: the guide is a tyrant. The sluggish and perverted mind of the multitude having once received this book, stands upon it, and makes an outcry if it is destroyed. Colleges are built on it. Meek young men grow up in libraries. Hence, instead of Man Thinking, we have the bookworm. I had better never see a book than to be warped by its attraction clean out of my own orbit, and make a satellite instead of a system. The one thing in the world, of value, is the active soul."

How far this university is from that ideal is the measure of the defeat of our American dream.

This bondage to books compels us not to see with our own eyes; compels us to see with the eyes of the dead, with dead eyes. Whitman, likewise in a Transcendentalist sermon, says, "You shall no longer take things at second or third hand, nor look through the eyes of the dead, nor feed on the specters in books." There is a hex on us, the specters in books, the authority of the past; and to exorcise these ghosts is the great work of magical self-liberation. Then the eyes of the spirit would become one with the eyes of the body, and god would be in us, not outside. God in us: *entheos:* enthusiasm; this is the essence of the holy madness. In the fire of the holy madness even books lose their gravity, and let themselves go up into the flame: "Properly," says Ezra Pound, "we should read for power. Man reading should be man intensely alive. The book should be a ball of light in one's hand."

58

I began with the name of Dionysus; let me be permitted to end with the name of Christ: for the power I seek is also Christian. Nietzsche indeed said the whole question was Dionysus versus Christ; but only the fool will take these as mutually exclusive opposites. There is a Dionysian Christianity, an apocalyptic Christianity, a Christianity of miracles and revelations. And there always have been some Christians for whom the age of miracle and revelation is not over; Christians who claim the spirit; enthusiasts. The power I look for is the power of enthusiasm; as condemned by John Locke; as possessed by George Fox, the Quaker; through whom the houses were shaken; who saw the channel of blood running down the streets of the city of Litchfield; to whom, as a matter of fact, was even given the magic internal heat—"The fire of the Lord was so in my feet, and all around me, that I did not matter to put on my shoes any more."

Read again the controversies of the seventeenth century and discover our choice: we are either in an age of miracles, says Hobbes, miracles which authenticate fresh revelations; or else we are in an age of reasoning from already received Scripture. Either miracle or Scripture. George Fox, who came up in spirit through the flaming sword into the paradise of God, so that all things were new, he being renewed to the state of Adam which he was in before he fell, sees that none can read Moses aright without Moses' spirit; none can read John's words aright, and with a true understanding of them, but in and with the same divine spirit by which John spake them, and by his burning shining light which is sent from God. Thus the authority of the past is swallowed up in new creation; the word is made flesh. We see with our own eyes and to see with our own eyes is second sight. To see with our own eyes is second sight.

> Twofold Always. May God us keep
> From single vision and Newton's sleep.

THE RIGHT USE OF LANGUAGE

The subject we propose in this section is an ancient one, going back at least to the first rhetoricians and sophists—Plato and Aristotle among them—who were deeply concerned with the distinction between eloquence devoted to good ends and eloquence devoted to bad. This distinction was crucial in a culture in which direct speech was the main mode of communication, and a capacity to speak, argue, and answer well was the sole protection of a man's rights.

In the intervening centuries, the ethics of rhetoric has lost none of its importance. If anything, readers, writers, listeners, and viewers in an age of mass communications, of public relations, advertising, and image-manufacturing, need to be especially aware of the difference between honest language and deceit. Beneath "the right use of language" lie the profoundest matters of our political and moral welfare. Mrs. Langer's essay begins the section with a clear and powerful description of symbolism, the means by which language and thought are related. Her stress on the uniquely human capacity to manipulate symbols (with its paradoxical gifts of both reason and lunacy) opens the political and moral question in the broadest terms: "The envisagements of good and evil, which make man a moral agent, make him also a conscript, a prisoner, and a slave. His constant problem is to escape the tyrannies he has created." Orwell's famous essay takes up the question of language and politics very specifically, showing how bad writing and bad thinking propagate each other, and how they are related to badness in our political life. Both of these essays were written with the horrors of World War II vividly in mind; unfortunately neither has lost a bit of its relevance since.

Weaver's focus on a few key terms in modern American usage has a similarly moral concern, moving from a study of the terms themselves to showing how the same terms, if accepted unreflectedly, "lure us down the roads of hatred and tragedy." Ginsberg's letter is based on the same dark assumption: "Whoever controls the language, the images, controls the race." But in his attempt to write "about reality" to Mr. McNamara, he produces a refreshing, if unconventional, exercise in the rhetoric of goodness.

John Holt's essay is concerned with how to teach students "to use words better," and with the difference it makes to our society whether "the children of our poor, and notably our Negro poor, learn to speak and write well or not." Haig Bosmajian shows how language reflects racism and suggests that whites need "to discard their racist terms, phrases, and clichés . . . before blacks and whites can discuss seriously the eradication of white racism." The section ends with essays by Huxley and Jacobs, who respectively analyze and illustrate in varying tones the problem of language and values in commercial life.

Susanne K. Langer

Mrs. Langer (born 1895) was educated at Radcliffe College,
where she received the Ph.D. in 1926. She has taught philosophy
at Radcliffe, Wellesley, Smith, and Columbia, and in 1954
became chairman of the Philosophy Department at Connecticut
College. She is now professor emeritus and research scholar,
pursuing investigations in the philosophy of art, expression, and
meaning. One of the few notable women in a field traditionally
dominated by men, Mrs. Langer has reached a large audience and
has had great influence on recent thinking, especially about the
arts. Her best-known book is Philosophy in a New Key *(1942),*
in which, taking her cue from the researches of Ernst Cassirer, she
investigates "the symbolism of reason, rite, and art." She has
also written An Introduction to Symbolic Logic *(1937),* Feeling
and Form *(1953),* The Problem of Art *(1957), and* Mind: An
Essay on Human Feeling, *vol. 1 (1967). The present essay,*
clearly deriving from her interest in symbolism, appeared in
Fortune *in January 1944, at the height of World War II.*

THE PRINCE OF CREATION

The world is aflame with man-made public disasters, artificial rains of brimstone and fire, planned earthquakes, cleverly staged famines and floods. The Prince of Creation is destroying himself. He is throwing down the cities he has built, the works of his own hand, the wealth of many thousand years in his frenzy of destruction, as a child knocks down its own handiwork, the whole day's achievement, in a tantrum of tears and rage.

What has displeased the royal child? What has incurred his world-shattering tantrum?

The bafflement of the magnificent game he is playing. Its rules and its symbols, his divine toys, have taken possession of the player. For this global war is not the old, hard, personal fight for the means of life, *bellum omnium contra omnes,* which animals perpetually wage; this is a war of monsters. Not mere men but great superpersonal giants, the national states, are met in combat. They do not hate and attack and wrestle as injured physical creatures do; they move heavily, inexorably, by strategy and necessity, to each other's destruction. The game of national states has come to this pass, and the desperate players ride their careening animated toys to a furious suicide.

These moloch gods, these monstrous states, are not natural beings; they are man's own work, products of the power that makes him lord over all other living things—his mind. They are not of the earth, earthy, as families and herds, hives and colonies are, whose members move and fight as one by instinct and habit until a physical disturbance splits them and the severed parts reconstitute themselves as new organized groups. The national states are not physical groups; they are social symbols, profound and terrible.

They are symbols of the new way of life, which the past two centuries have given us. For thousands of years, the pattern of daily life —working, praying, building, fighting, and raising new generations— repeated itself with only slow or unessential changes. The social symbols expressive of this life were ancient and familiar. Tribal gods or local saints, patriarchs, squires, or feudal lords, princes and bishops, raised to the highest power in the persons of emperors and popes— they were all expressions of needs and duties and opinions grounded in an immemorial way of life. The average man's horizon was not much greater than his valley, his town, or whatever geographical ramparts bounded his community. Economic areas were small, and economic problems essentially local. Naturally in his conception the powers governing the world were local, patriarchal, and reverently familiar.

Then suddenly, within some two hundred years, and for many places far less than that, the whole world has been transformed. Communities of different tongues and faiths and physiognomies have mingled; not as of old in wars of conquest, invading lords and conquered population gradually mixing their two stocks, but by a new process of foot-loose travel and trade, dominated by great centers of activity that bring individuals from near and far promiscuously together as a magnet draws filings from many heaps into close but quite accidental contact. Technology has made old horizons meaningless and localities indefinite. For goods and their destinies determine the structure of human societies. This is a new world, a world of persons, not of families and clans, or parishes and manors. The proletarian order is not founded on a hearth and its history. It does not express itself in a dialect, a local costume, a rite, a patron saint. All such traditions by mingling have canceled each other, and disappeared.

Most of us feel that since the old controlling ideas of faith and custom are gone, mankind is left without anchorage of any sort. None of the old social symbols fit this modern reality, this shrunken and undifferentiated world in which we lead a purely economic, secular, essentially homeless life.

But mankind is never without its social symbols; when old ones die, new ones are already in process of birth; and the new gods that have superseded all faiths are the great national states. The conception of them is mystical and moral, personal and devotional; they conjure with names and emblems, and demand our constant profession and practice of the new orthodoxy called "Patriotism."

Of all born creatures, man is the only one that cannot live by bread alone. He lives as much by symbols as by sense report, in a realm compounded of tangible things and virtual images, of actual events and ominous portents, always between fact and fiction. For he sees not only actualities but meanings. He has, indeed, all the impulses and interests of animal nature; he eats, sleeps, mates, seeks comfort and safety, flees pain, falls sick and dies, just as cats and bears and fishes and butterflies do. But he has something more in his repertoire, too—he has laws and religions, theories and dogmas, because he lives not only through sense but through symbols. That is the special asset of his mind, which makes him the master of earth and all its progeny.

By the agency of symbols—marks, words, mental images, and icons of all sorts—he can hold his ideas for contemplation long after their original causes have passed away. Therefore, he can think of things that are not presented or even suggested by his actual environment. By associating symbols in his mind, he combines things and events that were never together in the real world. This gives him the power we call imagination. Further, he can symbolize only part of an idea and let the rest go out of consciousness; this gives him the faculty that has been his pride throughout the ages—the power of abstraction. The combined effect of these two powers is inestimable. They are the roots of his supreme talent, the gift of reason.

In the war of each against all, which is the course of nature, man has an unfair advantage over his animal brethren; for he can see what is not yet there to be seen, know events that happened before his birth, and take possession of more than he actually eats; he can kill at a distance; and by rational design he can enslave other creatures to live and act for him instead of for themselves.

Yet this mastermind has strange aberrations. For in the whole animal kingdom there is no such unreason, no such folly and impracticality as man displays. He alone is hounded by imaginary fears, beset by ghosts and devils, frightened by mere images of things. No other creature wastes time in unprofitable ritual or builds nests for dead specimens of its race. Animals are always realists. They have intelligence in varying degrees—chickens are stupid, elephants are said to be very clever—but, bright or foolish, animals react only to reality. They may be fooled by appearance, by pictures or reflections, but once they know them as such, they promptly lose interest. Distance and darkness and silence are not fearful to them, filled with voices or forms, or invisible presences. Sheep in the pasture do not seem to fear phantom sheep beyond the fence, mice don't look for mouse goblins in the clock, birds do not worship a divine thunderbird.

But oddly enough, men do. They think of all these things and guard against them, worshiping animals and monsters even before they conceive of divinities in their own image. Men are essentially unrealistic. With all their extraordinary intelligence, they alone go in for patently impractical actions—magic and exorcism and holocausts—rites that have no connection with common-sense methods of self-preservation, such as a highly intelligent animal might use. In fact, the rites and sacrifices by which primitive man claims to control nature are sometimes fatal to the performers. Indian puberty rites are almost always intensely painful, and African natives have sometimes died during initiations into honorary societies.

We usually assume that very primitive tribes of men are closer to animal estate than highly civilized races; but in respect of practical attitudes, this is not true. The more primitive man's mind, the more fantastic it seems to be; only with high intellectual discipline do we gradually approach the realistic outlook of intelligent animals.

Yet this human mind, so beclouded by phantoms and superstitions, is probably the only mind on earth that can reach out to an awareness of things beyond its practical environment and can also conceive of such notions as truth, beauty, justice, majesty, space and time and creation.

There is another paradox in man's relationship with other creatures: namely, that those very qualities he calls animalian—"brutal," "bestial," "inhuman"—are peculiarly his own. No other animal is so deliberately cruel as man. No other creature intentionally imprisons its own kind, or invents special instruments of torture such as racks and thumbscrews for the sole purpose of punishment. No other animal keeps its own brethren in slavery; so far as we know, the lower animals do not commit anything like the acts of pure sadism that figure rather largely in our newspapers. There is no torment, spite, or cruelty for its own sake among beasts, as there is among men. A cat plays with its prey, but does not conquer and torture smaller cats. But man, who knows good and evil, is cruel for cruelty's sake; he who has a moral law is more brutal than the brutes, who have none; he alone inflicts suffering on his fellows with malice aforethought.

If man's mind is really a higher form of the animal mind, his morality a specialized form of herd instinct, then where in the course of evolution did he lose the realism of a clever animal and fall prey to subjective fears? And why should he take pleasure in torturing helpless members of his own race?

The answer is, I think, that man's mind is *not* a direct evolution from the beast's mind, but is a unique variant and therefore has had a meteoric and startling career very different from any other animal history. The trait that sets human mentality apart from every other is its preoccupation with symbols, with images and names that *mean* things, rather than with things themselves. This trait may have been a mere sport of nature once upon a time. Certain creatures do develop tricks and interests that seem biologically unimportant. Pack rats, for instance, and some birds of the crow family take a capricious pleasure in bright objects and carry away such things for which they have, presumably, no earthly use. Perhaps man's tendency to see certain forms as *images*, to hear certain sounds not only as signals but as expressive tones, and to be excited by sunset colors or starlight, was originally just a peculiar sensitivity in a rather highly developed brain. But whatever its cause, the ultimate destiny of this trait was momentous; for all human activity is based on the appreciation and use of symbols. Language, religion, mathematics, all learning, all science and superstition, even right and wrong, are products of symbolic expression rather than direct experience. Our commonest words, such as "house" and "red" and "walking," are symbols; the pyramids of Egypt and the mysterious circles of Stonehenge are symbols; so are dominions and empires and astronomical universes. We live in a mind-made world, where the things of prime importance are images or words that embody ideas and feelings and attitudes.

The animal mind is like a telephone exchange; it receives stimuli from outside through the sense organs and sends out appropriate responses through the nerves that govern muscles, glands, and other parts of the body. The organism is constantly interacting with its surroundings, receiving messages and acting on the new state of affairs that the messages signify.

But the human mind is not a simple transmitter like a telephone exchange. It is more like a great projector; for instead of merely

67

mediating between an event in the outer world and a creature's responsive action, it transforms or, if you will, distorts the event into an image to be looked at, retained, and contemplated. For the images of things that we remember are not exact and faithful transcriptions even of our actual sense impressions. They are made as much by what we think as by what we see. It is a well-known fact that if you ask several people the size of the moon's disk as they look at it, their estimates will vary from the area of a dime to that of a barrel top. Like a magic lantern, the mind projects its ideas of things on the screen of what we call "memory"; but like all projections, these ideas are transformations of actual things. They are, in fact, *symbols* of reality, not pieces of it.

A symbol is not the same thing as a sign; that is a fact that psychologists and philosophers often overlook. All intelligent animals use signs; so do we. To them as well as to us sounds and smells and motions are signs of food, danger, the presence of other beings, or of rain or storm. Furthermore, some animals not only attend to signs but produce them for the benefit of others. Dogs bark at the door to be let in; rabbits thump to call each other; the cooing of doves and the growl of a wolf defending his kill are unequivocal signs of feelings and intentions to be reckoned with by other creatures.

We use signs just as animals do, though with considerably more elaboration. We stop at red lights and go on green; we answer calls and bells, watch the sky for coming storms, read trouble or promise or anger in each other's eyes. That is animal intelligence raised to the human level. Those of us who are dog lovers can probably all tell wonderful stories of how high our dogs have sometimes risen in the scale of clever sign interpretation and sign using.

A sign is anything that announces the existence or the imminence of some event, the presence of a thing or a person, or a change in a state of affairs. There are signs of the weather, signs of danger, signs of future good or evil, signs of what the past has been. In every case a sign is closely bound up with something to be noted or expected in experience. It is always a part of the situation to which it refers, though the reference may be remote in space and time. In so far as we are led to note or expect the signified event we are making correct use of a sign. This is the essence of rational behavior, which animals show in varying degrees. It is entirely realistic, being closely bound up with the actual objective course of history—learned by experience, and cashed in or voided by further experience.

If man had kept to the straight and narrow path of sign using, he would be like the other animals, though perhaps a little brighter. He would not talk, but grunt and gesticulate and point. He would make his wishes known, give warnings, perhaps develop a social system like that of bees and ants, with such a wonderful efficiency of communal enterprise that all men would have plenty to eat, warm apartments—all exactly alike and perfectly convenient—to live in, and everybody could and would sit in the sun or by the fire, as the climate demanded, not talking but just basking, with every want satisfied, most of his life. The young would romp and make love, the old would sleep, the middle-aged would do the routine work almost unconsciously and eat a great deal. But that would be the life of a social, superintelligent, purely sign-using animal.

To us who are human, it does not sound very glorious. We want to go places and do things, own all sorts of gadgets that we do not absolutely need, and when we sit down to take it easy we want to talk. Rights and property, social position, special talents and virtues, and above all our ideas, are what we live for. We have gone off on a tangent that takes us far away from the mere biological cycle that animal generations accomplish; and that is because we can use not only signs but symbols.

A symbol differs from a sign in that it does not announce the presence of the object, the being, condition, or whatnot, which is its meaning, but merely *brings this thing to mind.* It is not a mere "substitute sign" to which we react as though it were the object itself. The fact is that our reaction to hearing a person's name is quite different from our reaction to the person himself. There are certain rare cases where a symbol stands directly for its meaning: in religious experience, for instance, the Host is not only a symbol but a Presence. But symbols in the ordinary sense are not mystic. They are the same sort of thing that ordinary signs are; only they do not call our attention to something necessarily present or to be physically dealt with—they call up merely a conception of the thing they "mean."

The difference between a sign and a symbol is, in brief, that a sign causes us to think or act *in face of* the thing signified, whereas a symbol causes us to think *about* the thing symbolized. Therein lies the great importance of symbolism for human life, its power to make this life so different from any other animal biography that generations of men have found it incredible to suppose that they were of purely zoological origin. A sign is always embedded in reality, in a present that emerges from the actual past and stretches to the future; but a symbol may be divorced from reality altogether. It may refer to what is *not* the case, to a mere idea, a figment, a dream. It serves, therefore, to liberate thought from the immediate stimuli of a physically present world; and that liberation marks the essential difference between human and non-human mentality. Animals think, but they think *of* and *at* things; men think primarily *about* things. Words, pictures, and memory images are symbols that may be combined and varied in a thousand ways. The result is a symbolic structure whose meaning is a complex of all their respective meanings, and this kaleidoscope of *ideas* is the typical product of the human brain that we call the "stream of thought."

The process of transforming all direct experience into imagery or into that supreme mode of symbolic expression, language, has so completely taken possession of the human mind that it is not only a special talent but a dominant, organic need. All our sense impressions leave their traces in our memory not only as signs disposing our practical reactions in the future but also as symbols, images representing our *ideas* of things; and the tendency to manipulate ideas, to combine and abstract, mix and extend them by playing with symbols, is man's outstanding characteristic. It seems to be what his brain most naturally and spontaneously does. Therefore his primitive mental function is not judging reality, but *dreaming his desires.*

Dreaming is apparently a basic function of human brains, for it is free and unexhausting like our metabolism, heartbeat, and breath. It is easier to dream than not to dream, as it is easier to breathe than to refrain from breathing. The symbolic character of dreams is fairly well established. Symbol mongering, on this ineffectual, uncritical level, seems to be instinctive, the fulfillment of an elementary need rather than the purposeful exercise of a high and difficult talent.

The special power of man's mind rests on the evolution of this special activity, not on any transcendently high development of animal intelligence. We are not immeasurably higher than other animals; we are different. We have a biological need and with it a biological gift that they do not share.

Because man has not only the ability but the constant need of *conceiving* what has happened to him, what surrounds him, what is demanded of him—in short, of symbolizing nature, himself, and his hopes and fears—he has a constant and crying need of *expression.* What he cannot express, he cannot conceive; what he cannot conceive is chaos, and fills him with terror.

If we bear in mind this all-important craving for expression we get a new picture of man's behavior; for from this trait spring his powers and his weaknesses. The process of symbolic transformation that all our experiences undergo is nothing more nor less than the process of *conception,* which underlies the human faculties of abstraction and imagination.

When we are faced with a strange or difficult situation, we cannot react directly, as other creatures do, with flight, aggression, or any such simple instinctive pattern. Our whole reaction depends on how we manage to conceive the situation—whether we cast it in a definite dramatic form, whether we see it as a disaster, a challenge, a fulfillment of doom, or a fiat of the Divine Will. In words or dreamlike images,

70

in artistic or religious or even in cynical form, we must *construe* the events of life. There is great virtue in the figure of speech, "I can *make* nothing of it," to express a failure to understand something. Thought and memory are processes of *making* the thought content and the memory image; the pattern of our ideas is given by the symbols through which we express them. And in the course of manipulating those symbols we inevitably distort the original experience, as we abstract certain features of it, embroider and reinforce those features with other ideas, until the conception we project on the screen of memory is quite different from anything in our real history.

Conception is a necessary and elementary process; what we do with our conceptions is another story. That is the entire history of human culture—of intelligence and morality, folly and superstition, ritual, language, and the arts—all the phenomena that set man apart from, and above, the rest of the animal kingdom. As the religious mind has to make all human history a drama of sin and salvation in order to define its own moral attitudes, so a scientist wrestles with the mere presentation of "the facts" before he can reason about them. The process of *envisaging* facts, values, hopes, and fears underlies our whole behavior pattern; and this process is reflected in the evolution of an extraordinary phenomenon found always, and only, in human societies—the phenomenon of language.

Language is the highest and most amazing achievement of the symbolistic human mind. The power it bestows is almost inestimable, for without it anything properly called "thought" is impossible. The birth of language is the dawn of humanity. The line between man and beast—between the highest ape and the lowest savage—is the language line. Whether the primitive Neanderthal man was anthropoid or human depends less on his cranial capacity, his upright posture, or even his use of tools and fire, than on one issue we shall probably never be able to settle—whether or not he spoke.

In all physical traits and practical responses, such as skills and visual judgments, we can find a certain continuity between animal and human mentality. Sign using is an ever evolving, ever improving function throughout the whole animal kingdom, from the lowly worm that shrinks into his hole at the sound of an approaching foot, to the dog obeying his master's command, and even to the learned scientist who watches the movements of an index needle.

This continuity of the sign-using talent has led psychologists to the belief that language is evolved from the vocal expressions, grunts and coos and cries, whereby animals vent their feelings or signal their fellows; that man has elaborated this sort of communion to the point where it makes a perfect exchange of ideas possible.

I do not believe that this doctrine of the origin of language is correct.

71

The essence of language is symbolic, not signific; we use it first and most vitally to formulate and hold ideas in our own minds. Conception, not social control, is its first and foremost benefit.

Watch a young child that is just learning to speak play with a toy; he says the name of the object, e.g.: "Horsey! horsey! horsey!" over and over again, looks at the object, moves it, always saying the name to himself or to the world at large. It is quite a time before he talks to anyone in particular; he talks first of all to himself. This is his way of forming and fixing the *conception* of the object in his mind, and around this conception all his knowledge of it grows. *Names* are the essence of language; for the *name* is what abstracts the conception of the horse from the horse itself, and lets the mere idea recur at the speaking of the name. This permits the conception gathered from one horse experience to be exemplified again by another instance of a horse, so that the notion embodied in the name is a general notion.

To this end, the baby uses a word long before he *asks for* the object; when he wants his horsey he is likely to cry and fret, because he is reacting to an actual environment, not forming ideas. He uses the animal language of *signs* for his wants; talking is still a purely symbolic process—its practical value has not really impressed him yet.

Language need not be vocal; it may be purely visual, like written language, or even tactual, like the deaf-mute system of speech; but it *must be denotative*. The sounds, intended or unintended, whereby animals communicate do not constitute a language, because they are signs, not names. They never fall into an organic pattern, a meaningful syntax of even the most rudimentary sort, as all language seems to do with a sort of driving necessity. That is because signs refer to actual situations, in which things have obvious relations to each other that require only to be noted; but symbols refer to ideas, which are not physically there for inspection, so their connections and features have to be represented. This gives all true language a natural tendency toward growth and development, which seems almost like a life of its own. Languages are not invented; they grow with our need for expression.

In contrast, animal "speech" never has a structure. It is merely an emotional response. Apes may greet their ration of yams with a shout of "Nga!" But they do not say "Nga" between meals. If they could *talk about* their yams instead of just saluting them, they would be the most primitive men instead of the most anthropoid of beasts. They would have ideas, and tell each other things true or false, rational or irrational; they would make plans and invent laws and sing their own praises, as men do.

The history of speech is the history of our human descent. Yet the habit of transforming reality into symbols, of contemplating and combining and distorting symbols, goes beyond the confines of language. All *images* are symbols, which make us think about the things they mean.

This is the source of man's great interest in "graven images," and in *mere appearances* like the face of the moon or the human profiles he sees in rocks and trees. There is no limit to the meanings he can read into natural phenomena. As long as this power is undisciplined, the sheer enjoyment of finding meanings in everything, the elaboration of concepts without any regard to truth and usefulness, seems to run riot; superstition and ritual in their pristine strength go through what some anthropologists have called a "vegetative" stage, when dreamlike symbols, gods and ghouls and rites, multiply like the overgrown masses of life in a jungle. From this welter of symbolic forms emerge the images that finally govern a civilization; the great symbols of religion, society, and selfhood.

What does an image "mean?" Anything it is thought to resemble. It is only because we can abstract quite unobvious forms from the actual appearance of things that we see line drawings in two dimensions as images of colored, three-dimensional objects, find the likeness of a dipper in a constellation of seven stars, or see a face on a pansy. Any circle may represent the sun or moon; an upright monolith may be a man.

Wherever we can fancy a similarity we tend to see something represented. The first thing we do, upon seeing a new shape, is to assimilate it to our own idea of something that it resembles, something that is known and important to us. Our most elementary concepts are of our own actions, and the limbs or organs that perform them; other things are named by comparison with them. The opening of a cave is its mouth, the divisions of a river its arms. Language, and with it all articulate thought, grows by this process of unconscious metaphor. Every new idea urgently demands a word; if we lack a name for it, we call it after the first namable thing seen to bear even a remote analogy to it. Thus all the subtle and variegated vocabulary of a living language grows up from a few roots of very general application; words as various in meaning as "gentle" and "ingenious" and "general" spring from the one root "ge" meaning "to give life."

Yet there are conceptions that language is constitutionally unfit to express. The reason for this limitation of our verbal powers is a subject for logicians and need not concern us here. The point of interest to us is that, just as rational, discursive thought is bound up with language, so the life of feeling, of direct personal and social consciousness, the emotional stability of man and his sense of orientation in the world are bound up with images directly given to his senses: fire and water, noise and silence, high mountains and deep caverns, the brief beauty of flowers, the persistent grin of a skull. There seem to be irresistible parallels between the expressive forms we find in nature and the forms of our inner life; thus the use of light to represent all things good, joyful, comforting, and of darkness to express all sorts of sorrow, despair, or horror, is so primitive as to be well-nigh unconscious.

A flame is a soul; a star is a hope; the silence of winter is death. All such images, which serve the purpose of metaphorical thinking, are *natural symbols*. They have not conventionally assigned meanings, like words, but recommend themselves even to a perfectly untutored mind, a child's or a savage's, because they are definitely articulated *forms*, and to see something expressed in such forms is a universal human talent. We do not have to learn to use natural symbols; it is one of our primitive activities.

The fact that sensuous forms of natural processes have a significance beyond themselves makes the range of our symbolism, and with it the horizon of our consciousness, much wider and deeper than language. This is the source of ritual, mythology, and art. Ritual is a symbolic rendering of certain emotional *attitudes*, which have become articulate and fixed by being constantly expressed. Mythology is man's image of his world, and of himself in the world. Art is the exposition of his own subjective history, the life of feeling, the human spirit in all its adventures.

Yet this power of envisagement, which natural symbolism bestows, is a dangerous one; for human beings can envisage things that do not exist, and create horrible worlds, insupportable duties, monstrous gods and ancestors. The mind that can see past and future, the poles and the antipodes, and guess at obscure mechanisms of nature, is ever in danger of seeing what is not there, imagining false and fantastic causes, and courting death instead of life. Because man can play with ideas, he is unrealistic; he is inclined to neglect the all-important interpretation of signs for a rapt contemplation of symbols.

Some twenty years ago, Ernst Cassirer set forth a theory of human mentality that goes far toward explaining the vagaries of savage religions and the ineradicable presence of superstition even in civilized societies: a symbol, he observed, is the embodiment of an idea; it is at once an abstract and a physical fact. Now its great emotive value lies in the concept it conveys; this inspires our reverent attitude, the attention and awe with which we view it. But man's untutored thought always tends to lose its way between the symbol and the fact. A skull represents death; but to a primitive mind the skull *is* death. To have it in the house is not unpleasant but dangerous. Even in civilized societies, symbolic objects—figures of saints, relics, crucifixes—are revered for their supposed efficacy. Their actual power is a power of *expression,* of embodying and thus revealing the greatest concepts humanity has reached; these concepts are the commanding forces that change our estate from a brute existence to the transcendent life of the spirit. But the symbol-loving mind of man reveres the meaning not *through* the articulating form but *in* the form so that the image appears to be the actual object of love and fear, supplication and praise.

Because of this constant identification of concepts with their expressions, our world is crowded with unreal beings. Some societies have actually realized that these beings do not belong to nature, and have postulated a so-called "other world" where they have their normal existence and from which they are said to descend, or arise, into our physical realm. For savages it is chiefly a nether world that sends up spooks; for more advanced cults it is from the heavens that supernatural beings, the embodiments of human ideas—of virtue, triumph, immortality—descend to the mundane realm. But from this source emanates also a terrible world government, with heavy commands and sanctions. Strange worship and terrible sacrifices may be the tithes exacted by the beings that embody our knowledge of nonanimalian human nature.

So the gift of symbolism, which is the gift of reason, is at the same time the seat of man's peculiar weakness—the danger of lunacy. Animals go mad with hydrophobia or head injuries, but purely mental aberrations are rare; beasts are not generally subject to insanity except through a confusion of signs, such as the experimentally produced "nervous breakdown" in rats. It is man who hears voices and sees ghosts in the dark, feels irrational compulsions and holds fixed ideas. All these phantasms are symbolic forms that have acquired a false factual status. It has been truly said that everybody has some streak of insanity; i.e., the threat of madness is the price of reason.

Because we can think of things potential as well as actual, we can be held in nonphysical bondage by laws and prohibitions and commands and by images of a governing power. This makes men tyrants over their own kind. Animals control each other's actions by immediate threats, growls and snarls and passes; but when the bully is roving elsewhere, his former domain is free of him. We control our inferiors by setting up symbols of our power, and the mere idea that words or images convey stands there to hold our fellows in subjection even when we cannot lay our hands on them. There is no flag over the country where a wolf is king; he is king where he happens to prowl, so long as he is there. But men, who can embody ideas and set them up to view, oppress each other by symbols of might.

The envisagements of good and evil, which make man a moral agent, make him also a conscript, a prisoner, and a slave. His constant problem is to escape the tyrannies he has created. Primitive societies are almost entirely tyrannical, symbol-bound, coercive organizations; civilized governments are so many conscious schemes to justify or else to disguise man's inevitable bondage to law and conscience.

Slowly, through ages and centuries, we have evolved a picture of the world we live in; we have made a drama of the earth's history and enhanced it with a backdrop of divinely ordered, star-filled space. And all this structure of infinity and eternity against which we watch the pageant of life and death, and all the moral melodrama itself, we have wrought by a gradual articulation of such vast ideas in symbols—symbols of good and evil, triumph and failure, birth and maturity and death. Long before the beginning of any known history, people saw in the heavenly bodies, in the changes of day and night or of the seasons, and in great beasts, symbolic forms to express those ultimate concepts that are the very frame of human existence. So gods, fates, the cohorts of good and evil were conceived. Their myths were the first formulations of cosmic ideas. Gradually the figures and traditions of religion emerged; ritual, the overt expression of our mental attitudes, became more and more intimately bound to definite and elaborate concepts of the creative and destructive powers that seem to control our lives.

Such beings and stories and rites are sacred because they are the great symbols by which the human mind orients itself in the world. To a creature that lives by reason, nothing is more terrible than what is formless and meaningless; one of our primary fears is fear of chaos. And it is the fight against chaos that has produced our most profound and indispensable images—the myths of light and darkness, of creation and passion, the symbols of the altar flame, the daystar, and the cross.

For thousands of years people lived by the symbols that nature presented to them. Close contact with earth and its seasons, intimate knowledge of stars and tides, made them feel the significance of natural phenomena and gave them a poetic, unquestioning sense of orientation. Generations of erudite and pious men elaborated the picture of the temporal and spiritual realms in which each individual was a pilgrim soul.

Then came the unprecedented change, the almost instantaneous leap of history from the immemorial tradition of the plow and the anvil to the new age of the machine, the factory, and the ticker tape. Often in no more than the length of a life-time the shift from handwork to mass production, and with it from poetry to science and from faith to nihilism, has taken place. The old nature symbols have become remote and have lost their meanings; in the clatter of gears and the confusion of gadgets that fill the new world, there will not be any obvious and rich and sacred meanings for centuries to come. All the accumulated creeds and rites of men are suddenly in the melting pot. There is no fixed community, no dynasty, no family inheritance—only the one huge world of men, vast millions of men, still looking on each other in hostile amazement.

A sane, intelligent animal should have invented, in the course of ten thousand years or more, some sure and obvious way of accommodating indefinite numbers of its own kind on the face of a fairly spacious earth. Modern civilization has achieved the highest triumphs of knowledge, skill, ingenuity, theory; yet all around its citadels, engulfing and demolishing them, rages the maddest war and confusion, inspired by symbols and slogans as riotous and irrational as anything the "vegetative" stage of savage phantasy could provide. How shall we reconcile this primitive nightmare excitement with the achievements of our high, rational, scientific culture?

The answer is, I think, that we are no longer in possession of a definite, established culture; we live in a period between an exhausted age—the European civilization of the white race—and an age still unborn, of which we can say nothing as yet. We do not know what races shall inherit the earth. We do not know what even the next few centuries may bring. But it is quite evident, I think, that we live in an age of transition, and that before many more generations have passed, mankind will make a new beginning and build itself a different world. Whether it will be a "brave, new world," or whether it will start all over with an unchronicled "state of nature" such as Thomas Hobbes described, wherein the individual's life is "nasty, brutish, and short," we simply cannot tell. All we know is that every tradition, every institution, every tribe is gradually becoming uprooted and upset, and we are waiting in a sort of theatrical darkness between the acts.

Because we are at a new beginning, our imaginations tend to a wild, "vegetative" overgrowth. The political upheavals of our time are marked, therefore, by a veritable devil dance of mystical ideologies, vaguely conceived, passionately declared, holding out fanatic hopes of mass redemption and mass beatitudes. Governments vie with each other in proclaiming social plans, social aims, social enterprises, and demanding bloody sacrifices in the name of social achievements.

New conceptions are always clothed in an extravagant metaphorical form, for there is no language to express genuinely new ideas. And in their pristine strength they imbue the symbols that express them with their own mystery and power and holiness. It is impossible to disengage the welter of ideas embodied in a swastika, a secret sign, or a conjuring word from the physical presence of the symbol itself; hence the apparently nonsensical symbol worship and mysticism that go with new movements and visions. This identification of symbolic form and half-articulate meaning is the essence of all mythmaking.

Of course the emotive value is incomprehensible to anyone who does not see such figments as expressive forms. So an age of vigorous new conception and incomplete formulation always has a certain air of madness about it. But it is really a fecund and exciting period in the life of reason. Such is our present age. Its apparent unreason is a tremendous unbalance and headiness of the human spirit, a conflict not only of selfish wills but of vast ideas in the metaphorical state of emergence.

The change from fixed community life and ancient local custom to the mass of unpedigreed human specimens that actually constitutes the world in our industrial and commercial age has been too sudden for the mind of man to negotiate. Some transitional form of life had to mediate between those extremes. And so the idol of nationality arose from the wreckage of tribal organization. The concept of the national state is really the old tribe concept applied to millions of persons, unrelated and different creatures gathered under the banner of a government. Neither birth nor language nor even religion holds such masses together, but a mystic bond is postulated even where no actual bond of race, creed, or color may ever have existed.

At first glance it seems odd that the concept of nationality should reach its highest development just as all actual marks of national origins—language, dress, physiognomy, and religion—are becoming mixed and obliterated by our new mobility and cosmopolitan traffic. But it is just the loss of these things that inspires this hungry seeking for something like the old egocentric pattern in the vast and formless brotherhood of the whole earth. While mass production and universal communication clearly portend a culture of world citizenship, we cling desperately to our nationalism, a more and more attenuated version of the old clan civilization. We fight passionate and horrible wars for the symbols of our nations, we make a virtue of self-glorification and exclusiveness and invent strange anthropologies to keep us at least theoretically set apart from other men.

Nationalism is a transition between an old and a new human order. But even now we are not really fighting a war of nations; we are fighting a war of fictions, from which a new vision of the order of nature will someday emerge. The future, just now, lies wide open—open and dark, like interstellar space; but in that emptiness there is room for new gods, new cultures, mysterious now and nameless as an unborn child.

George Orwell

Orwell's reputation has shown no sign of decline since his death at forty-six in 1950. He is likely to be ranked permanently among the great English essayists. On presenting him an award in 1949, the editors of Partisan Review *commented that his writing "has been marked by a singular directness and honesty, a scrupulous fidelity to his experience that has placed him in that valuable class of the writer who is a witness to his time."*

His real name was Eric Arthur Blair, and he was born in 1903 in Bengal, a province of British India. His first school experience is vividly described in the essay "Such, Such Were the Joys." He attended Eton on a King's Scholarship from 1917 to 1921, then served for five years in the Imperial Police in Burma. Returning to Europe, he spent some poverty-stricken years doing odd jobs, from teaching to dishwashing, while he wrote novels and short stories that did not sell. His Down and Out in Paris and London *(1933) is a vivid record of those years. In 1936 Orwell went to Spain to take part in the Civil War and reported his experiences in* Homage to Catalonia *(1938). Among his other books are the celebrated* Nineteen Eighty-Four *(1949), a terrifying novel picturing the complete victory of totalitarianism,* Animal Farm: A Fairy Story *(1945), and the essay collections* Shooting an Elephant and Other Essays *(1950),* Such, Such Were the Joys *(1953), and* Collected Essays *(1966). The present essay first appeared in the London monthly* Horizon *in 1946 and was reprinted in the 1950 collection.*

POLITICS AND THE ENGLISH LANGUAGE

Most people who bother with the matter at all would admit that the English language is in a bad way, but it is generally assumed that we cannot by conscious action do anything about it. Our civilization is decadent and our language—so the argument runs—must inevitably share in the general collapse. It follows that any struggle against the abuse of language is a sentimental archaism, like preferring candles to electric light or hansom cabs to aeroplanes. Underneath this lies the half-conscious belief that language is a natural growth and not an instrument which we shape for our own purposes.

Now, it is clear that the decline of a language must ultimately have political and economic causes: it is not due simply to the bad influence of this or that individual writer. But an effect can become a cause, reinforcing the original cause and producing the same effect in an intensified form, and so on indefinitely. A man may take to drink because he feels himself to be a failure, and then fail all the more completely because he drinks. It is rather the same thing that is happening to the English language. It becomes ugly and inaccurate because our thoughts are foolish, but the slovenliness of our language makes it easier for us to have foolish thoughts. The point is that the process is reversible. Modern English, especially written English, is full of bad habits which spread by imitation and which can be avoided if one is willing to take the necessary trouble. If one gets rid of these habits one can think more clearly, and to think clearly is a necessary first step towards political regeneration: so that the fight against bad English is not frivolous and is not the exclusive concern of professional writers. I will come back to this presently, and I hope that by that time the meaning of what I have said here will have become clearer. Meanwhile, here are five specimens of the English language as it is now habitually written.

These five passages have not been picked out because they are especially bad—I could have quoted far worse if I had chosen—but because they illustrate various of the mental vices from which we now suffer. They are a little below the average, but are fairly representative samples. I number them so that I can refer back to them when necessary:

(1) I am not, indeed, sure whether it is not true to say that the Milton who once seemed not unlike a seventeenth-century Shelley had not become, out of an experience ever more bitter in each year, more alien [sic] to the founder of that Jesuit sect which nothing could induce him to tolerate.

PROFESSOR HAROLD LASKI
(ESSAY IN *Freedom of Expression*).

(2) Above all, we cannot play ducks and drakes with a native battery of idioms which prescribes such egregious collocations of vocables as the Basic *put up with* for *tolerate* or *put at a loss* for *bewilder*.

PROFESSOR LANCELOT HOGBEN
(*Interglossa*).

(3) On the one side we have the free personality: by definition it is not neurotic, for it has neither conflict nor dream. Its desires, such as they are, are transparent, for they are just what institutional approval keeps in the forefront of consciousness; another institu-

tional pattern would alter their number and intensity; there is little in them that is natural, irreducible, or culturally dangerous. But *on the other side*, the social bond itself is nothing but the mutual reflection of these self-secure integrities. Recall the definition of love. Is not this the very picture of a small academic? Where is there a place in this hall of mirrors for either personality or fraternity?

ESSAY ON PSYCHOLOGY IN Politics (NEW YORK).

(4) All the "best people" from the gentlemen's clubs, and all the frantic fascist captains, united in common hatred of Socialism and bestial horror of the rising tide of the mass revolutionary movement, have turned to acts of provocation, to foul incendiarism, to medieval legends of poisoned wells, to legalize their own destruction of proletarian organizations, and rouse the agitated petty-bourgeoisie to chauvinistic fervor on behalf of the fight against the revolutionary way out of the crisis.

COMMUNIST PAMPHLET.

(5) If a new spirit *is* to be infused into this old country, there is one thorny and contentious reform which must be tackled, and that is the humanization and galvanization of the B.B.C. Timidity here will bespeak canker and atrophy of the soul. The heart of Britain may be sound and of strong beat, for instance, but the British lion's roar at present is like that of Bottom in Shakespeare's *Midsummer Night's Dream*—as gentle as any sucking dove. A virile new Britain cannot continue indefinitely to be traduced in the eyes or rather ears, of the world by the effete languors of Langham Place, brazenly masquerading as "standard English." When the voice of Britain is heard at nine o'clock, better far and infinitely less ludicrous to hear aitches honestly dropped than the present priggish, inflated, inhibited, schoolma'amish arch braying of blameless bashful mewing maidens!

LETTER IN Tribune.

Each of these passages has faults of its own, but, quite apart from avoidable ugliness, two qualities are common to all of them. The first is staleness of imagery; the other is lack of precision. The writer either has a meaning and cannot express it, or he inadvertently says something else, or he is almost indifferent as to whether his words mean anything or not. This mixture of vagueness and sheer incompetence is the most marked characteristic of modern English prose, and especially of any kind of political writing. As soon as certain topics are raised, the concrete melts into the abstract and no one seems able to think of turns of speech that are not hackneyed: prose consists less and less of *words* chosen for the sake of their meaning, and more and more of *phrases* tacked together like the sections of a prefabricated hen-house. I list below, with notes and examples, various of the tricks by means of which the work of prose-construction is habitually dodged:

Dying metaphors. A newly invented metaphor assists thought by evoking a visual image, while on the other hand a metaphor which is technically "dead" (e.g. *iron resolution*) has in effect reverted to being an ordinary word and can generally be used without loss of vividness. But in between these two classes there is a huge dump of worn-out metaphors which have lost all evocative power and are merely used because they save people the trouble of inventing phrases for themselves. Examples are: *Ring the changes on, take up the cudgels for, toe the line, ride roughshod over, stand shoulder to shoulder with, play into the hands of, no axe to grind, grist to the mill, fishing in troubled waters, on the order of the day, Achilles' heel, swan song, hotbed.* Many of these are used without knowledge of their meaning (what is a "rift," for instance?), and incompatible metaphors are frequently mixed, a sure sign that the writer is not interested in what he is saying. Some metaphors now current have been twisted out of their original meaning without those who use them even being aware of the fact. For example, *toe the line* is sometimes written *tow the line.* Another example is *the hammer and the anvil,* now always used with the implication that the anvil gets the worst of it. In real life it is always the anvil that breaks the hammer, never the other way about: a writer who stopped to think what he was saying would be aware of this, and would avoid perverting the original phrase.

Operators or *verbal false limbs.* These save the trouble of picking out appropriate verbs and nouns, and at the same time pad each sentence with extra syllables which give it an appearance of symmetry. Characteristic phrases are *render inoperative, militate against, make contact with, be subjected to, give rise to, give grounds for, have the effect of, play a leading part (role) in, make itself felt, take effect, exhibit a tendency to, serve the purpose of, etc., etc.* The keynote is the elimination of simple verbs. Instead of being a single word, such as *break, stop, spoil, mend, kill,* a verb becomes a *phrase,* made up of a noun or adjective tacked on to some general-purpose verb such as *prove, serve, form, play, render.* In addition, the passive voice is wherever possible used in preference to the active, and noun constructions are used instead of gerunds (*by examination of* instead of *by examining*). The range of verbs is further cut down by means of the *-ize* and *de-* formations, and the banal statements are given an appearance of profundity by means of the *not un-* formation. Simple conjunctions and prepositions are replaced by such phrases as *with respect to, having regard to, the fact that, by dint of, in view of, in the interests of, on the hypothesis that;* and the ends of sentences are saved from anticlimax by such resounding common-places as *greatly to be de-*

sired, cannot be left out of account, a development to be expected in the near future, deserving of serious consideration, brought to a satisfactory conclusion, and so on and so forth.

Pretentious diction. Words like *phenomenon, element, individual* (as noun), *objective, categorical, effective, virtual, basic, primary, promote, constitute, exhibit, exploit, utilize, eliminate, liquidate,* are used to dress up simple statements and give an air of scientific impartiality to biased judgments. Adjectives like *epoch-making, epic, historic, unforgettable, triumphant, age-old, inevitable, inexorable, veritable,* are used to dignify the sordid processes of international politics, while writing that aims at glorifying war usually takes on an archaic color, its characteristic words being: *realm, throne, chariot, mailed fist, trident, sword, shield, buckler, banner, jackboot, clarion.* Foreign words and expressions such as *cul de sac, ancien régime, deus ex machina, mutatis mutandis, status quo, gleichschaltung, weltanschauung,* are used to give an air of culture and elegance. Except for the useful abbreviations *i.e., e.g.,* and *etc.,* there is no real need for any of the hundreds of foreign phrases now current in English. Bad writers, and especially scientific, political and sociological writers, are nearly always haunted by the notion that Latin or Greek words are grander than Saxon ones, and unnecessary words like *expedite, ameliorate, predict, extraneous, deracinated, clandestine, subaqueous* and hundreds of others constantly gain ground from their Anglo-Saxon opposite numbers.[1] The jargon peculiar to Marxist writing (*hyena, hangman, cannibal, petty bourgeois, these gentry, lacquey, flunkey, mad dog, White Guard,* etc.) consists largely of words and phrases translated from Russian, German or French; but the normal way of coining a new word is to use a Latin or Greek root with the appropriate affix and, where necessary, the *-ize* formation. It is often easier to make up words of this kind (*deregionalize, impermissible, extramarital, non-fragmentary* and so forth) than to think up the English words that will cover one's meaning. The result, in general, is an increase in slovenliness and vagueness.

Meaningless words. In certain kinds of writing, particularly in art criticism and literary criticism, it is normal to come across long passages which are almost completely lacking in meaning.[2] Words like

---

[1] An interesting illustration of this is the way in which the English flower names which were in use till very recently are being ousted by Greek ones, *snapdragon* becoming *antirrhinum, forget-me-not* becoming *myosotis,* etc. It is hard to see any practical reason for this change of fashion: it is probably due to an instinctive turning-away from the more homely word and a vague feeling that the Greek word is scientific.

[2] Example: "Comfort's catholicity of perception and image, strangely Whitmanesque in range, almost the exact opposite in aesthetic compulsion, continues to evoke that trembling atmospheric accumulative hinting at a cruel, an inexorably serene timelessness. . . . Wrey Gardiner scores by aiming at simple bull's-eyes with precision. Only they are not so simple, and through this contented sadness runs more than the surface bittersweet of resignation." (*Poetry Quarterly.*)

romantic, plastic, values, human, dead, sentimental, natural, vitality, as used in art criticism, are strictly meaningless, in the sense that they not only do not point to any discoverable object, but are hardly ever expected to do so by the reader. When one critic writes, "The outstanding feature of Mr. X's work is its living quality," while another writes, "The immediately striking thing about Mr. X's work is its peculiar deadness," the reader accepts this as a simple difference of opinion. If words like *black* and *white* were involved, instead of the jargon words *dead* and *living,* he would see at once that language was being used in an improper way. Many political words are similarly abused. The word *Fascism* has now no meaning except in so far as it signifies "something not desirable." The words *democracy, socialism, freedom, patriotic, realistic, justice,* have each of them several different meanings which cannot be reconciled with one another. In the case of a word like *democracy,* not only is there no agreed definition, but the attempt to make one is resisted from all sides. It is almost universally felt that when we call a country democratic we are praising it: consequently the defenders of every kind of régime claim that it is a democracy, and fear that they might have to stop using the word if it were tied down to any one meaning. Words of this kind are often used in a consciously dishonest way. That is, the person who uses them has his own private definition, but allows his hearer to think he means something quite different. Statements like *Marshal Pétain was a true patriot, The Soviet Press is the freest in the world, The Catholic Church is opposed to persecution,* are almost always made with intent to deceive. Other words used in variable meanings, in most cases more or less dishonestly, are: *class, totalitarian, science, progressive, reactionary, bourgeois, equality.*

Now that I have made this catalogue of swindles and perversions, let me give another example of the kind of writing that they lead to. This time it must of its nature be an imaginary one. I am going to translate a passage of good English into modern English of the worst sort. Here is a well-known verse from *Ecclesiastes:*

"I returned and saw under the sun, that the race is not to the swift, nor the battle to the strong, neither yet bread to the wise, nor yet riches to men of understanding, nor yet favour to men of skill; but time and chance happeneth to them all."

Here it is in modern English:

"Objective consideration of contemporary phenomena compels the conclusion that success or failure in competitive activities exhibits no tendency to be commensurate with innate capacity, but that a considerable element of the unpredictable must invariably be taken into account."

This is a parody, but not a very gross one. Exhibit (3), above, for instance, contains several patches of the same kind of English. It will be seen that I have not made a full translation. The beginning and ending of the sentence follow the original meaning fairly closely, but in the middle the concrete illustrations—race, battle, bread—dissolve into the vague phrase "success or failure in competitive activities." This had to be so, because no modern writer of the kind I am discussing—no one capable of using phrases like "objective consideration of contemporary phenomena"—would ever tabulate his thoughts in that precise and detailed way. The whole tendency of modern prose is away from concreteness. Now analyse these two sentences a little more closely. The first contains forty-nine words but only sixty syllables, and all its words are those of everyday life. The second contains thirty-eight words of ninety syllables: eighteen of its words are from Latin roots, and one from Greek. The first sentence contains six vivid images, and only one phrase ("time and chance") that could be called vague. The second contains not a single fresh, arresting phrase, and in spite of its ninety syllables it gives only a shortened version of the meaning contained in the first. Yet without a doubt it is the second kind of sentence that is gaining ground in modern English. I do not want to exaggerate. This kind of writing is not yet universal, and outcrops of simplicity will occur here and there in the worst-written page. Still, if you or I were told to write a few lines on the uncertainty of human fort nes, we should probably come much nearer to my imaginary sentence than to the one from *Ecclesiastes*.

As I have tried to show, modern writing at its worst does not consist in picking out words for the sake of their meaning and inventing images in order to make the meaning clearer. It consists in gumming together long strips of words which have already been set in order by someone else, and making the results presentable by sheer humbug. The attraction of this way of writing is that it is easy. It is easier—even quicker, once you have the habit—to say *In my opinion it is not an unjustifiable assumption that* than to say *I think*. If you use ready-made phrases, you not only don't have to hunt about for words; you also don't have to bother with the rhythms of your sentences, since these phrases are generally so arranged as to be more or less euphonious. When you are composing in a hurry—when you are dictating to a stenographer, for instance, or making a public speech—it is natural to fall into a pretentious, Latinized style. Tags like *a consideration which we should do well to bear in mind* or *a conclusion to which all of us would readily assent* will save many a sentence from coming down with a bump. By using stale metaphors, similes and idioms, you save much mental effort, at the cost of leaving your meaning vague, not only for your reader but for yourself. This is the significance of mixed metaphors. The sole aim of a metaphor is to call up a visual image. When these images clash—as in *The Fascist octopus has sung its swan song, the jackboot is thrown into the melting pot*—it can be taken as certain that the writer is not seeing a mental image of the objects he is naming; in other words he is not really thinking. Look again at the examples I gave at the beginning of this essay. Professor Laski (1) uses five negatives in fifty-three words. One of these is superfluous, making nonsense of the whole passage, and in addition there is the slip *alien* for akin, making further nonsense, and several avoidable pieces of clumsiness which increase the general vagueness. Professor Hogben (2) plays ducks and drakes with a battery which is able to write pre-scriptions, and, while disapproving of the everyday phrase *put up with*, is unwilling to look *egregious* up in the dictionary and see what it means; (3), if one takes an uncharitable attitude towards it, is simply meaningless: probably one could work out its intended meaning by reading the whole of the article in which it occurs. In (4), the writer knows more or less what he wants to say, but an accumulation of stale phrases chokes him like tea leaves blocking a sink. In (5), words and meaning have almost parted company. People who write in this man-ner usually have a general emotional meaning—they dislike one thing and want to express solidarity with another—but they are not inter-ested in the detail of what they are saying. A scrupulous writer, in every sentence that he writes, will ask himself at least four questions, thus: What am I trying to say? What words will express it? What image or idiom will make it clearer? Is this image fresh enough to have an effect? And he will probably ask himself two more: Could I put it more shortly? Have I said anything that is avoidably ugly? But you are not obliged to go to all this trouble. You can shirk it by simply throwing your mind open and letting the ready-made phrases come crowding in. They will construct your sentences for you—even think your thoughts for you, to a certain extent—and at need they will perform the important service of partially concealing your mean-ing even from yourself. It is at this point that the special connection between politics and the debasement of language becomes clear.

In our time it is broadly true that political writing is bad writing. Where it is not true, it will generally be found that the writer is some kind of rebel, expressing his private opinions and not a "party line." Orthodoxy, of whatever color, seems to demand a lifeless, imitative style. The political dialects to be found in pamphlets, leading articles, manifestos, White Papers and the speeches of under-secretaries do, of course, vary from party to party, but they are all alike in that one almost never finds in them a fresh, vivid, home-made turn of speech. When one watches some tired hack on the platform mechanically re-peating the familiar phrases—*bestial atrocities, iron heel, bloodstained tyranny, free peoples of the world, stand shoulder to shoulder*—one often has a curious feeling that one is not watching a live human being but some kind of dummy: a feeling which suddenly becomes stronger at moments when the light catches the speaker's spectacles and turns them into blank discs which seem to have no eyes behind them. And this is not altogether fanciful. A speaker who uses that kind of phraseology has gone some distance towards turning himself into a machine. The appropriate noises are coming out of his larynx, but his brain is not involved as it would be if he were choosing his words for himself. If the speech he is making is one that he is accustomed to make over and over again, he may be almost unconscious of what he is saying, as one is when one utters the responses in church. And this reduced state of consciousness, if not indispensable, is at any rate favorable to political conformity.

In our time, political speech and writing are largely the defence of the indefensible. Things like the continuance of British rule in India, the Russian purges and deportations, the dropping of the atom bombs on Japan, can indeed be defended, but only by arguments which are too brutal for most people to face, and which do not square with the professed aims of political parties. Thus political language has to consist largely of euphemism, question-begging and sheer cloudy vagueness. Defenceless villages are bombarded from the air, the inhabitants driven out into the countryside, the cattle machine-gunned, the huts set on fire with incendiary bullets: this is called *pacification*. Millions of peasants are robbed of their farms and sent trudging along the roads with no more than they can carry: this is called *transfer of population* or *rectification of frontiers*. People are imprisoned for years without trial, or shot in the back of the neck or sent to die of scurvy in Arctic lumber camps: this is called *elimination of unreliable elements*. Such phraseology is needed if one wants to name things without calling up mental pictures of them. Consider for instance some comfortable English professor defending Russian totalitarianism. He cannot say outright, "I believe in killing off your opponents when you can get good results by doing so." Probably, therefore, he will say something like this:

"While freely conceding that the Soviet régime exhibits certain features which the humanitarian may be inclined to deplore, we must, I think, agree that a certain curtailment of the right to political opposition is an unavoidable concomitant of transitional periods, and that the rigors which the Russian people have been called upon to undergo have been amply justified in the sphere of concrete achievement."

The inflated style is itself a kind of euphemism. A mass of Latin words falls upon the facts like soft snow, blurring the outlines and covering up all the details. The great enemy of clear language is insincerity. When there is a gap between one's real and one's declared aims, one turns as it were instinctively to long words and exhausted idioms, like a cuttlefish squirting out ink. In our age there is no such thing as "keeping out of politics." All issues are political issues, and politics itself is a mass of lies, evasions, folly, hatred and schizophrenia. When the general atmosphere is bad, language must suffer. I should expect to find—this is a guess which I have not sufficient knowledge to verify—that the German, Russian and Italian languages have all deteriorated in the last ten or fifteen years, as a result of dictatorship.

But if thought corrupts language, language can also corrupt thought. A bad usage can spread by tradition and imitation, even among people who should and do know better. The debased language that I have been discussing is in some ways very convenient. Phrases like *a not unjustifiable assumption, leaves much to be desired, would serve no good purpose, a consideration which we should do well to bear in mind,* are a continuous temptation, a packet of aspirins always at one's elbow. Look back through this essay, and for certain you will find that I have again and again committed the very faults I am protesting against. By this morning's post I have received a pamphlet dealing with conditions in Germany. The author tells me that he "felt impelled" to write it. I open it at random, and here is almost the first sentence that I see: "[The Allies] have an opportunity not only of achieving a radical transformation of Germany's social and political structure in such a way as to avoid a nationalistic reaction in Germany itself, but at the same time of laying the foundations of a cooperative and unified Europe." You see, he "feels impelled" to write—feels, presumably, that he has something new to say—and yet his words, like cavalry horses answering the bugle, group themselves automatically into the familiar dreary pattern. This invasion of one's mind by ready-made phrases (*lay the foundations, achieve a radical transformation*) can only be prevented if one is constantly on guard against them, and every such phrase anaesthetizes a portion of one's brain.

I said earlier that the decadence of our language is probably curable. Those who deny this would argue, if they produced an argument at all, that language merely reflects existing social conditions, and that we cannot influence its development by any direct tinkering with words and constructions. So far as the general tone or spirit of a language goes, this may be true, but it is not true in detail. Silly words and expressions have often disappeared, not through any evolutionary process but owing to the conscious action of a minority. Two recent examples were *explore every avenue* and *leave no stone unturned,* which were killed by the jeers of a few journalists. There is a long list of flyblown metaphors which could similarly be got rid of if enough people would interest themselves in the job; and it should also be possible to laugh the *not un-* formation out of existence,[3] to reduce the amount of Latin and Greek in the average sentence, to drive out foreign phrases and strayed scientific words, and, in general, to make pretentiousness unfashionable. But all these are minor points. The defence of the English language implies more than this, and perhaps it is best to start by saying what it does *not* imply.

To begin with it has nothing to do with archaism, with the salvaging of obsolete words and turns of speech, or with the setting up of a "standard English" which must never be departed from. On the contrary, it is especially concerned with the scrapping of every word or idiom which has outworn its usefulness. It has nothing to do with correct grammar and syntax, which are of no importance so long as one makes one's meaning clear, or with the avoidance of Americanisms, or with having what is called a "good prose style." On the other hand it is not concerned with fake simplicity and the attempt to make written English colloquial. Nor does it even imply in every case preferring the Saxon word to the Latin one, though it does imply using the fewest and shortest words that will cover one's meaning. What is above all needed is to let the meaning choose the word, and not the other way about. In prose, the worst thing one can do with words is to surrender to them. When you think of a concrete object, you think wordlessly, and then, if you want to describe the thing you have been visualizing you probably hunt about till you find the exact words that seem to fit it. When you think of something abstract you are more inclined to use words from the start, and unless you make a conscious effort to prevent it, the existing dialect will come rushing in and do the job for you, at the expense of blurring or even changing your meaning. Probably it is better to put off using words as long as possible and get one's meaning as clear as one can through pictures or sensations. Afterwards one can choose—not simply *accept*—the phrases that will best cover the meaning, and then switch round and decide what impression one's words are likely to make on another person. This last effort of the mind cuts out all stale or mixed images, all prefabricated phrases, needless repetitions, and humbug and vagueness generally. But one can often be in doubt about the effect of a word or a phrase, and one needs rules that one can rely on when instinct fails. I think the following rules will cover most cases:

(i) Never use a metaphor, simile or other figure of speech which you are used to seeing in print.

(ii) Never use a long word where a short one will do.

---

[3] One can cure oneself of the *not un-* formation by memorizing this sentence: *A not unblack dog was chasing a not unsmall rabbit across a not ungreen field.*

(iii) If it is possible to cut a word out, always cut it out.

(iv) Never use the passive where you can use the active.

(v) Never use a foreign phrase, a scientific word or a jargon word if you can think of an everyday English equivalent.

(vi) Break any of these rules sooner than say anything outright barbarous.

These rules sound elementary, and so they are, but they demand a deep change of attitude in anyone who has grown used to writing in the style now fashionable. One could keep all of them and still write bad English, but one could not write the kind of stuff that I quoted in those five specimens at the beginning of this article.

I have not here been considering the literary use of language, but merely language as an instrument for expressing and not for concealing or preventing thought. Stuart Chase and others have come near to claiming that all abstract words are meaningless, and have used this as a pretext for advocating a kind of political quietism. Since you don't know what Fascism is, how can you struggle against Fascism? One need not swallow such absurdities as this, but one ought to recognize that the present political chaos is connected with the decay of language, and that one can probably bring about some improvement by starting at the verbal end. If you simplify your English, you are freed from the worst follies of orthodoxy. You cannot speak any of the necessary dialects, and when you make a stupid remark its stupidity will be obvious, even to yourself. Political language—and with variations this is true of all political parties, from Conservatives to Anarchists—is designed to make lies sound truthful and murder respectable, and to give an appearance of solidity to pure wind. One cannot change this all in a moment, but one can at least change one's own habits, and from time to time one can even, if one jeers loudly enough, send some worn-out and useless phrase—some *jackboot, Achilles' heel, hotbed, melting pot, acid test, veritable inferno* or other lump of verbal refuse—into the dustbin where it belongs.

Richard M. Weaver

Professor Weaver was born in Asheville, North Carolina, in 1910, and educated at Kentucky, Vanderbilt, and Louisiana State, where he received the doctorate in 1943. He soon joined the Department of English in the College of the University of Chicago

*and remained there until his death in 1963. An intense, tough-
minded man, he was profoundly displeased with the "pseudoscientific"
direction of modern thought. In most of his writings he attempts
to redirect our attention to the ideas of form, order, and human
worth that he feels we have lost in the course of our "progress."
Some of his books are* Ideas Have Consequences *(1948),* Visions
of Order: The Cultural Crisis of Our Time *(1957),* Life
Without Prejudice and Other Essays *(published posthumously
in 1966), and* The Ethics of Rhetoric *(1957), from which we
print here the final chapter. The reader should not allow himself
to be put off by the rather technical first two paragraphs; a full
understanding of them depends on a knowledge of earlier chapters
but is not essential to an appreciation of the rest of the essay.*

ULTIMATE TERMS IN CONTEMPORARY RHETORIC

We have shown that rhetorical force must be conceived as a power transmitted through the links of a chain that extends upward toward some ultimate source. The higher links of that chain must always be of unique interest to the student of rhetoric, pointing, as they do, to some prime mover of human impulse. Here I propose to turn away from general considerations and to make an empirical study of the terms on these higher levels of force which are seen to be operating in our age.

We shall define term simply here as a name capable of entering into a proposition. In our treatment of rhetorical sources, we have regarded the full predication consisting of a proposition as the true validator. But a single term is an incipient proposition, awaiting only the necessary coupling with another term; and it cannot be denied that single names set up expectancies of propositional embodiment. This causes everyone to realize the critical nature of the process of naming. Given the name "patriot," for example, we might expect to see coupled with it "Brutus," or "Washington," or "Parnell"; given the term "hot," we might expect to see "sun," "stove," and so on. In sum, single terms have their potencies, this being part of the phenomenon of names, and we shall here present a few of the most noteworthy in our time, with some remarks upon their etiology.

Naturally this survey will include the "bad" terms as well as the "good" terms, since we are interested to record historically those expressions to which the populace, in its actual usage and response, appears to attribute the greatest sanction. A prescriptive rhetoric may specify those terms which, in all seasons, ought to carry the greatest potency, but since the affections of one age are frequently a source of wonder to another, the most we can do under the caption "contemporary rhetoric" is to give a descriptive account and withhold the moral until the end. For despite the variations of fashion, an age which is not simply distraught manages to achieve some system of relationship among the attractive and among the repulsive terms, so that we can work out an order of weight and precedence in the prevailing rhetoric once we have discerned the "rhetorical absolutes"— the terms to which the very highest respect is paid.

It is best to begin boldly by asking ourselves, what is the "god term" of the present age? By "god term" we mean that expression about which all other expressions are ranked as subordinate and serving dominations and powers. Its force imparts to the others their lesser degree of force, and fixes the scale by which degrees of comparison are understood. In the absence of a strong and evenly diffused religion, there may be several terms competing for this primacy, so that the question is not always capable of definite answer. Yet if one has to select the one term which in our day carries the greatest blessing, and—to apply a useful test—whose antonym carries the greatest rebuke, one will not go far wrong in naming "progress." This seems to be the ultimate generator of force flowing down through many links of ancillary terms. If one can "make it stick," it will validate almost anything. It would be difficult to think of any type of person or of any institution which could not be recommended to the public through the enhancing power of this word. A politician is urged upon the voters as a "progressive leader"; a community is proud to style itself "progressive"; technologies and methodologies claim to the "progressive"; a peculiar kind of emphasis in modern education calls itself "progressive," and so on without limit. There is no word whose power to move is more implicitly trusted than "progressive." But unlike some other words we shall examine in the course of this chapter, its rise to supreme position is not obscure, and it possesses some intelligible referents.

Before going into the story of its elevation, we must prepare ground by noting that it is the nature of the conscious life of man to revolve around some concept of value. So true is this that when the concept is withdrawn, or when it is forced into competition with another concept, the human being suffers an almost intolerable sense of being lost. He has to know where he is in the ideological cosmos in order to coordinate his activities. Probably the greatest cruelty which can be inflicted upon the psychic man is this deprivation of a sense of tendency. Accordingly every age, including those of rudest cultivation, sets up some kind of sign post. In highly cultivated ages, with individuals of exceptional intellectual strength, this may take the form of a metaphysic. But with the ordinary man, even in such advanced ages, it is likely to be some idea abstracted from religion or historical speculation, and made to inhere in a few sensible and immediate examples.

Since the sixteenth century we have tended to accept as inevitable an historical development that takes the form of a changing relationship between ourselves and nature, in which we pass increasingly into the role of master of nature. When I say that this seems inevitable to us, I mean that it seems something so close to what our more religious forebears considered the working of providence that we regard as impiety any disposition to challenge or even suspect it. By a transposition of terms, "progress" becomes the salvation man is placed on earth to work out; and just as there can be no achievement more important than salvation, so there can be no activity more justified in enlisting our sympathy and support than "progress." As our historical sketch would imply, the term began to be used in the sixteenth century in the sense of continuous development or improvement; it reached an apogee in the nineteenth century, amid noisy demonstrations of man's mastery of nature, and now in the twentieth century it keeps its place as one of the least assailable of the "uncontested terms," despite critical doubts in certain philosophic quarters. It is probably the only term which gives to the average American or West European of today a concept of something bigger than himself, which he is socially impelled to accept and even to sacrifice for. This capacity to demand sacrifice is probably the surest indicator of the "god term," for when a term is so sacrosanct that the material goods of this life must be mysteriously rendered up for it, then we feel justified in saying that it is in some sense ultimate. Today no one is startled to hear of a man's sacrificing health or wealth for the "progress" of the community, whereas such sacrifices for other ends may be regarded as self-indulgent or even treasonable. And this is just because "progress" is the coordinator of all socially respectable effort.

Perhaps these observations will help the speaker who would speak against the stream of "progress," or who, on the other hand, would parry some blow aimed at him through the potency of the word, to realize what a momentum he is opposing.

Another word of great rhetorical force which owes its origin to the same historical transformation is "fact." Today's speaker says "It is a fact" with all the gravity and air of finality with which his less secular-minded ancestor would have said "It is the truth."[1] "These are

---

[1] It is surely worth observing that nowhere in the King James Version of the Bible does the word "fact" occur.

facts"; "Facts tend to show"; and "He knows the facts" will be recognized as common locutions drawing upon the rhetorical resource of this word. The word "fact" went into the ascendent when our system of verification changed during the Renaissance. Prior to that time, the type of conclusion that men felt obligated to accept came either through divine revelation, or through dialectic, which obeys logical law. But these were displaced by the system of verification through correspondence with physical reality. Since then things have been true only when measurably true, or when susceptible to some kind of quantification. Quite simply, "fact" came to be the touchstone after the truth of speculative inquiry had been replaced by the truth of empirical investigation. Today when the average citizen says "It is a fact" or says that he "knows the facts in the case," he means that he has the kind of knowledge to which all other knowledges must defer. Possibly it should be pointed out that his "facts" are frequently not facts at all in the etymological sense; often they will be deductions several steps removed from simply factual data. Yet the "facts" of his case carry with them this aura of scientific irrefragability, and he will likely regard any questioning of them as sophistry. In his vocabulary a fact is a fact, and all evidence so denominated has the prestige of science.

These last remarks will remind us at once of the strongly rhetorical character of the word "science" itself. If there is good reason for placing "progress" rather than "science" at the top of our series, it is only that the former has more scope, "science" being the methodological tool of "progress." It seems clear, moreover, that "science" owes its present status to an hypostatization. The hypostatized term is one which treats as a substance or a concrete reality that which has only conceptual existence; and every reader will be able to supply numberless illustrations of how "science" is used without any specific referent. Any utterance beginning "Science says" provides one: "Science says there is no difference in brain capacity between the races"; "Science now knows the cause of encephalitis"; "Science says that smoking does not harm the throat." Science is not, as here it would seem to be, a single concrete entity speaking with one authoritative voice. Behind these large abstractions (and this is not an argument against abstractions as such) there are many scientists holding many different theories and employing many different methods of investigation. The whole force of the word nevertheless depends upon a bland assumption that all scientists meet periodically in synod and there decide and publish what science believes. Yet anyone with the slightest scientific training knows that this is very far from a possibility. Let us consider therefore the changed quality of the utterance when it is amended to read "A majority of scientists say"; or "Many scientists believe"; or "Some scientific experiments have indicated." The change will not do. There has to be a creature called "science"; and its creation has as a matter of practice been easy, because modern man has been conditioned to believe that the powers and processes which have transformed his material world represent a very sure form of knowledge, and that there must be a way of identifying that knowledge. Obviously the rhetorical aggrandizement of "science" here parallels that of "fact," the one representing generally and the other specifically the whole subject matter of trustworthy perception.

Furthermore, the term "science" like "progress" seems to satisfy a primal need. Man feels lost without a touchstone of knowledge just as he feels lost without the direction-finder provided by progress. It is curious to note that actually the word is only another name for knowledge (L. *scientia*), so that if we should go by strict etymology, we should insist that the expression "science shows" (*i.e.*, "knowledge knows") is pure tautology. But our rhetoric seems to get around this by implying that science is *the* knowledge. Other knowledges may contain elements of quackery, and may reflect the selfish aims of the knower; but "science," once we have given the word its incorporation, is the undiluted essence of knowledge. The word as it comes to us then is a little pathetic in its appeal, inasmuch as it reflects the deeply human feeling that somewhere somehow there must be people who know things "as they are." Once God or his ministry was the depository of such knowledge, but now, with the general decay of religious faith, it is the scientists who must speak *ex cathedra*, whether they wish to or not.

The term "modern" shares in the rhetorical forces of the others thus far discussed, and stands not far below the top. Its place in the general ordering is intelligible through the same history. Where progress is real, there is a natural presumption that the latest will be the best. Hence it is generally thought that to describe anything as "modern" is to credit it with all the improvements which have been made up to now. Then by a transference the term is applied to realms where valuation is, or ought to be, of a different source. In consequence, we have "modern living" urged upon us as an ideal; "the modern mind" is mentioned as something superior to previous minds; sometimes the modifier stands alone as an epithet of approval: "to become modern" or "to sound modern" are expressions that carry valuation. It is of course idle not to expect an age to feel that some of its ways and habits of mind are the best; but the extensive transformations of the past hundred years seem to have given "modern" a much more decisive meaning. It is as if a difference of degree had changed into a difference of kind. But the very fact that a word is not used very analytically may increase its rhetorical potency, as we shall see later in connection with a special group of terms.

Another word definitely high up in the hierarchy we have outlined is "efficient." It seems to have acquired its force through a kind of no-nonsense connotation. If a thing is efficient, it is a good adaptation of means to ends, with small loss through friction. Thus as a word expressing a good understanding and management of cause and effect, it may have a fairly definite referent; but when it is lifted above this and made to serve as a term of general endorsement, we have to be on our guard against the stratagems of evil rhetoric. When we find, to cite a familiar example, the phrase "efficiency apartments" used to give an attractive aspect to inadequate dwellings, we may suspect the motive behind such juxtaposition. In many similar cases, "efficient," which is a term above reproach in engineering and physics, is made to hold our attention where ethical and aesthetic considerations are entitled to priority. Certain notorious forms of government and certain brutal forms of warfare are undeniably efficient; but here the featuring of efficiency unfairly narrows the question.

Another term which might seem to have a different provenance but which participates in the impulse we have been studying is "American." One must first recognize the element of national egotism which makes this a word of approval with us, but there are reasons for saying that the force of "American" is much more broadly based than this. "This is the American way" or "It is the American thing to do" are expressions whose intent will not seem at all curious to the average American. Now the peculiar effect that is intended here comes from the circumstance that "American" and "progressive" have an area of synonymity. The Western World has long stood as a symbol for the future; and accordingly there has been a very wide tendency in this country, and also I believe among many people in Europe, to identify that which is American with that which is destined to be. And this is much the same as identifying it with the achievements of "progress." The typical American is quite fatuous in this regard: to him America is the goal toward which all creation moves; and he judges a country's civilization by its resemblance to the American model. The matter of changing nationalities brings out this point very well. For a citizen of a European country to become a citizen of the United States is considered natural and right, and I have known those so transferring their nationality to be congratulated upon their good sense and their anticipated good fortune. On the contrary, when an American takes out British citizenship (French or German would be worse), this transference is felt to be a little scandalous. It is regarded as somehow perverse, or as going against the stream of things. Even some of our intellectuals grow uneasy over the action of Henry James and T. S. Eliot, and the masses cannot comprehend it at all. Their adoption of British citizenship is not mere defection from a country; it is treason to history. If Americans wish to become Europeans, what has happened to the hope of the world? is, I imagine, the question at the back of their minds. The tremendous spread of American fashions in behavior and entertainment must add something to the impetus, but I believe the original source to be this prior idea that America, typifying "progress," is what the remainder of the world is trying to be like.

It follows naturally that in the popular consciousness of this country, "un-American" is the ultimate in negation. An anecdote will serve to illustrate this. Several years ago a leading cigarette manufacturer in this country had reason to believe that very damaging reports were being circulated about his product. The reports were such that had they not been stopped, the sale of this brand of cigarettes might have been reduced. The company thereupon inaugurated an extensive advertising campaign, the object of which was to halt these rumors in the most effective way possible. The concocters of the advertising copy evidently concluded after due deliberation that the strongest term of condemnation which could be conceived was "un-American," for this was the term employed in the campaign. Soon the newspapers were filled with advertising rebuking this "un-American" type of depreciation which had injured their sales. From examples such as this we may infer that "American" stands not only for what is forward in history, but also for what is ethically superior, or at least for a standard of fairness not matched by other nations.

And as long as the popular mind carries this impression, it will be futile to protest against such titles as "The Committee on un-American activities." While "American" and "un-American" continue to stand for these polar distinctions, the average citizen is not going to find much wrong with a group set up to investigate what is "un-American" and therefore reprehensible. At the same time, however, it would strike him as most droll if the British were to set up a "Committee on un-British Activities" or the French a "Committee on un-French Activities." The American, like other nationals, is not apt to be much better than he has been taught, and he has been taught systematically that his country is a special creation. That is why some of his ultimate terms seem to the general view provincial, and why he may be moved to polarities which represent only local poles.

If we look within the area covered by "American," however, we find significant changes in the position of terms which are reflections of cultural and ideological changes. Among the once powerful but now waning terms are those expressive of the pioneer ideal of ruggedness and self-sufficiency. In the space of fifty years or less we have seen

97

the phrase "two-fisted American" pass from the category of highly effective images to that of comic anachronisms. Generally, whoever talks the older language of strenuosity is regarded as a reactionary, it being assumed by social democrats that a socially organized world is one in which cooperation removes the necessity for struggle. Even the rhetorical trump cards of the 1920's, which Sinclair Lewis treated with such satire, are comparatively impotent today, as the new social consciousness causes terms of centrally planned living to move toward the head of the series.

Other terms not necessarily connected with the American story have passed a zenith of influence and are in decline; of these perhaps the once effective "history" is the most interesting example. It is still to be met in such expressions as "History proves" and "History teaches"; yet one feels that it has lost the force it possessed in the previous century. Then it was easy for Byron—"the orator in poetry"—to write, "History with all her volumes vast has but one page"; or for the commemorative speaker to deduce profound lessons from history. But people today seem not to find history so eloquent. A likely explanation is that history, taken as whole, is conceptual rather than factual, and therefore a skepticism has developed as to what it teaches. Moreover, since the teachings of history are principally moral, ethical, or religious, they must encounter today that threshold resentment of anything which savors of the prescriptive. Since "history" is inseparable from judgment of historical fact, there has to be a considerable community of mind before history can be allowed to have a voice. Did the overthrow of Napoleon represent "progress" in history or the reverse? I should say that the most common rhetorical uses of "history" at the present are by intellectuals, whose personal philosophy can provide it with some kind of definition, and by journalists, who seem to use it unreflectively. For the contemporary masses it is substantially true that "history is bunk."

An instructive example of how a coveted term can be monopolized may be seen in "allies." Three times within the memory of those still young, "allies" (often capitalized) has been used to distinguish those fighting on our side from the enemy. During the First World War it was a supreme term; during the Second World War it was again used with effect; and at the time of the present writing it is being used to designate that nondescript combination fighting in the name of the United Nations in Korea. The curious fact about the use of this term is that in each case the enemy also has been constituted of "allies." In the First World War Germany, Austria-Hungary, and Turkey were "allies"; in the Second, Germany and Italy; and in the present conflict the North Koreans and the Chinese and perhaps the Russians are "allies." But in the rhetorical situation it is not possible to refer to them as "allies," since we reserve that term for the alliance representing our side. The reason for such restriction is that when men or nations are "allied," it is implied that they are united on some sound principle or for some good cause. Lying at the source of this feeling is the principle discussed by Plato, that friendship can exist only among the good, since good is an integrating force and evil a disintegrating one. We do not, for example, refer to a band of thieves as "the allies" because that term would impute laudable motives. By confining the term to our side we make an evaluation in our favor. We thus style ourselves the group joined for purposes of good. If we should allow it to be felt for a moment that the opposed combination is also made up of allies, we should concede that they are united by a principle, which in war is never done. So as the usage goes, we are always allies in war and the enemy is just the enemy, regardless of how many nations he has been able to confederate. Here is clearly another instance of how tendencies may exist in even the most innocent-seeming language.

Now let us turn to the terms of repulsion. Some terms of repulsion are also ultimate in the sense of standing at the end of the series, and no survey of the vocabulary can ignore these prime repellants. The counterpart of the "god term" is the "devil term," and it has already been suggested that with us "un-American" comes nearest to filling that role. Sometimes, however, currents of politics and popular feeling cause something more specific to be placed in that position. There seems indeed to be some obscure psychic law which compels every nation to have in its national imagination an enemy. Perhaps this is but a version of the tribal need for a scapegoat, or for something which will personify "the adversary." If a nation did not have an enemy, an enemy would have to be invented to take care of those expressions of scorn and hatred to which peoples must give vent. When another political state is not available to receive the discharge of such emotions, then a class will be chosen, or a race, or a type, or a political faction, and this will be held up to a practically standardized form of repudiation. Perhaps the truth is that we need the enemy in order to define ourselves, but I will not here venture further into psychological complexities. In this type of study it will be enough to recall that during the first half century of our nation's existence, "Tory" was such a devil term. In the period following our Civil War, "rebel" took its place in the Northern section and "Yankee" in the Southern, although in the previous epoch both of these had been terms of esteem. Most readers will remember that during the First World War "pro-German" was a term of destructive force. During the Second World War "Nazi" and "Fascist" carried about equal power to condemn, and then, following the breach with

Russia, "Communist" displaced them both. Now "Communist" is beyond any rival the devil term, and as such it is employed even by the American president when he feels the need of a strong rhetorical point.

A singular truth about these terms is that, unlike several which were examined in our favorable list, they defy any real analysis. That is to say, one cannot explain how they generate their peculiar force of repudiation. One only recognizes them as publicly-agreed-upon devil terms. It is the same with all. "Tory" persists in use, though it has long lost any connection with redcoats and British domination. Analysis of "rebel" and "Yankee" only turns up embarrassing contradictions of position. Similarly we have all seen "Nazi" and "Fascist" used without rational perception; and we see this now, in even greater degree, with "Communist." However one might like to reject such usage as mere ignorance, to do so would only evade a very important problem. Most likely these are instances of the "charismatic term," which will be discussed in detail presently.

No student of contemporary usage can be unmindful of the curious reprobative force which has been acquired by the term "prejudice." Etymologically it signifies nothing more than a prejudgment, or a judgment before all the facts are in; and since all of us have to proceed to a great extent on judgments of that kind, the word should not be any more exciting than "hypothesis." But in its rhetorical applications "prejudice" presumes far beyond that. It is used, as a matter of fact, to characterize unfavorably any value judgment whatever. If "blue" is said to be a better color than "red," that is prejudice. If people of outstanding cultural achievement are praised through contrast with another people, that is prejudice. If one mode of life is presented as superior to another, that is prejudice. And behind all is the implication, if not the declaration, that it is un-American to be prejudiced.

I suspect that what the users of this term are attempting, whether consciously or not, is to sneak "prejudiced" forward as an uncontested term, and in this way to disarm the opposition by making all positional judgments reprehensible. It must be observed in passing that no people are so prejudiced in the sense of being committed to valuations as those who are engaged in castigating others for prejudice. What they expect is that they can nullify the prejudices of those who oppose them, and then get their own installed in the guise of the *sensus communis*. Mark Twain's statement, "I know that I am prejudiced in this matter, but I would be ashamed of myself if I weren't" is a therapeutic insight into the process; but it will take more than a witticism to make headway against the repulsive force gathered behind "prejudice."

If the rhetorical use of the term has any rational content, this probably comes through a chain of deductions from the nature of democracy; and we know that in controversies centered about the meaning of democracy, the air is usually filled with cries of "prejudice." If democracy is taken crudely to mean equality, as it very frequently is, it is then a contradiction of democracy to assign inferiority and superiority on whatever grounds. But since the whole process of evaluation is a process of such assignment, the various inequalities which are left when it has done its work are contradictions of this root notion and hence are "prejudice"—the assumption of course being that when all the facts are in, these inequalities will be found illusory. The man who dislikes a certain class or race or style has merely not taken pains to learn that it is just as good as any other. If all inequality is deception, then superiorities must be accounted the products of immature judgment. This affords plausible ground, as we have suggested, for the coupling of "prejudice" and "ignorance."

Before leaving the subject of the ordered series of good and bad terms, one feels obliged to say something about the way in which hierarchies can be inverted. Under the impulse of strong frustration there is a natural tendency to institute a pretense that the best is the worst and the worst is the best—an inversion sometimes encountered in literature and in social deportment. The best illustration for purpose of study here comes from a department of speech which I shall call "GI rhetoric." The average American youth, put into uniform, translated to a new and usually barren environment, and imbued from many sources with a mission of killing, has undergone a pretty severe dislocation. All of this runs counter to the benevolent platitudes on which he was brought up, and there is little ground for wonder if he adopts the inverted pose. This is made doubly likely by the facts that he is at a passionate age and that he is thrust into an atmosphere of superinduced excitement. It would be unnatural for him not to acquire a rhetoric of strong impulse and of contumacious tendency.

What he does is to make an almost complete inversion. In this special world of his he recoils from those terms used by politicians and other civilians and by the "top brass" when they are enunciating public sentiments. Dropping the conventional terms of attraction, this uprooted and specially focussed young man puts in their place terms of repulsion. To be more specific, where the others use terms reflecting love, hope, and charity, he uses almost exclusively terms connected with excretory and reproductive functions. Such terms comprise what Kenneth Burke has ingeniously called "the imagery of killing." By an apparently universal psychological law, faeces and the act of defecation are linked with the idea of killing, of destruction, of total repudiation—perhaps the word "elimination" would comprise the whole body of notions. The reproductive act is associated especially with the idea of aggressive exploitation. Consequently when the GI feels that he must give his speech a proper show of spirit, he places the symbols for these things in places which would normally be filled by prestige terms from the "regular" list. For specimens of such language presented in literature, the reader is referred to the fiction of Ernest Hemingway and Norman Mailer.

Anyone who has been compelled to listen to such rhetoric will recall the monotony of the vocabulary and the vehemence of the delivery. From these two characteristics we may infer a great need and a narrow means of satisfaction, together with the tension which must result from maintaining so arduous an inversion. Whereas previously the aim had been to love (in the broad sense) it is now to kill; whereas it had been freedom and individuality, it is now restriction and brutalization. In taking revenge for a change which so contradicts his upbringing he is quite capable, as the evidence has already proved, of defiantly placing the lower level above the higher. Sometimes a clever GI will invent combinations and will effect metaphorical departures, but the ordinary ones are limited to a reiteration of the stock terms—to a reiteration, with emphasis of intonation, upon "the imagery of killing."[2] Taken as a whole, this rhetoric is a clear if limited example of how the machine may be put in reverse—of how, consequently, a sort of devil worship may get into language.

A similar inversion of hierarchy is to be seen in the world of competitive sports, although to a lesser extent. The great majority of us in the Western world have been brought up under the influence, direct or indirect, of Christianity, which is a religion of extreme altruism. Its terms of value all derive from a law of self-effacement and of consideration for others, and these terms tend to appear whenever we try to rationalize or vindicate our conduct. But in the world of competitive sports, the direction is opposite: there one is applauded for egotistic display and for success at the expense of others—should one mention in particular American professional baseball? Thus the terms with which an athlete is commended will generally point away from the direction of Christian passivity, although when an athlete's character is described for the benefit of the general public, some way is usually found to place him in the other ethos, as by calling attention

---

[2] Compare Sherwood Anderson's analysis of the same phenomenon in *A Story Teller's Story* (New York, 1928), p. 198: "There was in the factories where I worked and where the efficient Ford type of man was just beginning his dull reign this strange and futile outpouring of men's lives in vileness through their lips. Ennui was at work. The talk of the men about me was not Rabelaisian. In old Rabelais there was the salt of infinite wit and I have no doubt that the Rabelaisian flashes that came from our own Lincoln, Washington, and others had point and a flare to them.
But in the factories and in army camps!"

to his natural kindness, his interest in children, or his readiness to share his money.

Certainly many of the contradictions of our conduct may be explained through the presence of these small inverted hierarchies. When, to cite one familiar example, the acquisitive, hard-driving local capitalist is made the chief lay official of a Christian church, one knows that in a definite area there has been a transvaluation of values.

Earlier in the chapter we referred to terms of considerable potency whose referents it is virtually impossible to discover or to construct through imagination. I shall approach this group by calling them "charismatic terms." It is the nature of the charismatic term to have a power which is not derived, but which is in some mysterious way given. By this I mean to say that we cannot explain their compulsiveness through referents of objectively known character and tendency. We normally "understand" a rhetorical term's appeal through its connection with something we apprehend, even when we object morally to the source of the impulse. Now "progress" is an understandable term in this sense, since it rests upon certain observable if not always commendable aspects of our world. Likewise the referential support of "fact" needs no demonstrating. These derive their force from a reading of palpable circumstance. But in charismatic terms we are confronted with a different creation: these terms seem to have broken loose somehow and to operate independently of referential connections (although in some instances an earlier history of referential connection may be made out). Their meaning seems inexplicable unless we accept the hypothesis that their content proceeds out of a popular will that they *shall* mean something. In effect, they are rhetorical by common consent, or by "charisma." As is the case with charismatic authority, where the populace gives the leader a power which can by no means be explained through his personal attributes, and permits him to use it effectively and even arrogantly, the charismatic term is given its load of impulsion without reference, and it functions by convention. The number of such terms is small in any one period, but they are perhaps the most efficacious terms of all.

Such rhetorical sensibility as I have leads me to believe that one of the principal charismatic terms of our age is "freedom." The greatest sacrifices that contemporary man is called upon to make are demanded in the name of "freedom"; yet the referent which the average man attaches to this word is most obscure. Burke's dictum that "freedom inheres in something sensible" has not prevented its breaking loose from all anchorages. And the evident truth that the average man, given a choice between exemption from responsibility and responsibility, will choose the latter, makes no impression against its power. The fact, moreover, that the most extensive use of the term is made by modern politicians and statesmen in an effort to get men to assume more responsibility (in the form of military service, increased taxes, abridgement of rights, etc.) seems to carry no weight either.[3] The fact that what the American pioneer considered freedom has become wholly impossible to the modern apartment-dwelling metropolitan seems not to have damaged its potency. Unless we accept some philosophical interpretation, such as the proposition that freedom consists only in the discharge of responsibility, there seems no possibility of a correlation between the use of the word and circumstantial reality. Yet "freedom" remains an ultimate term, for which people are asked to yield up their first-born.

There is plenty of evidence that "democracy" is becoming the same kind of term. The variety of things it is used to symbolize is too weird and too contradictory for one to find even a core meaning in present-day usages. More important than this for us is the fact, noted by George Orwell, that people resist any attempt to define democracy, as if to connect it with a clear and fixed referent were to vitiate it. It may well be that such resistance to definition of democracy arises from a subconscious fear that a term defined in the usual manner has its charisma taken away. The situation then is that "democracy" means "be democratic," and that means exhibit a certain attitude which you can learn by imitating your fellows.

If rationality is measured by correlations and by analyzable content, then these terms are irrational; and there is one further modern development in the creation of such terms which is strongly suggestive of irrational impulse. This is the increasing tendency to employ in the place of the term itself an abbreviated or telescoped form—which form is nearly always used with even more reckless assumption of authority. I seldom read the abbreviation "U S" in the newspapers without wincing at the complete arrogance of its rhetorical tone. Daily we see "U S Cracks Down on Communists"; "U S Gives OK to Atomic Weapons"; "U S Shocked by Death of Official." Who or what is this "U S"? It is clear that "U S" does not suggest a union of forty-eight states having republican forms of government and held together by a constitution of expressly delimited authority. It suggests rather an abstract force out of a new world of forces, whose will is law and whom the individual citizen has no way to placate. Consider the individual citizen confronted by "U S" or "FBI." As long as terms stand for identifiable organs of government, the citizen feels that he knows the world he moves around in, but when the forces of government are referred to by these bloodless

---

[3] One is inevitably reminded of the slogan of Oceania in Orwell's *Nineteen Eighty-four:* "Freedom is Slavery."

abstractions, he cannot avoid feeling that they are one thing and he another. Let us note while dealing with this subject the enormous proliferation of such forms during the past twenty years or so. If "U S" is the most powerful and prepossessing of the group, it drags behind it in train the previously mentioned "FBI," and "NPA," "ERP," "FDIC," "WPA," "HOLC," and "OSS," to take a few at random. It is a fact of ominous significance that this use of foreshortened forms is preferred by totalitarians, both the professed and the disguised. Americans were hearing the terms "OGPU," "AMTORG" and "NEP" before their own government turned to large-scale state planning. Since then we have spawned them ourselves, and, it is to be feared, out of similar impulse. George Orwell, one of the truest humanists of our age, has described the phenomenon thus: "Even in the early decades of the twentieth century, telescoped words and phrases had been one of the characteristic features of political language; and it had been noticed that the tendency to use abbreviations of this kind was most marked in totalitarian countries and totalitarian organizations. Examples were such words as Nazi, Gestapo, Comintern, Inprecor, Agitprop."[4]

I venture to suggest that what this whole trend indicates is an attempt by the government, as distinguished from the people, to confer charismatic authority. In the earlier specimens of charismatic terms we were examining, we beheld something like the creation of a spontaneous general will. But these later ones of truncated form are handed down from above, and their potency is by fiat of whatever group is administering in the name of democracy. Actually the process is no more anomalous than the issuing of pamphlets to soldiers telling them whom they shall hate and whom they shall like (or try to like), but the whole business of switching impulse on and off from a central headquarters has very much the meaning of *Gleichschaltung* as that word has been interpreted for me by a native German. Yet it is a disturbing fact that such process should increase in times of peace, because the persistent use of such abbreviations can only mean a serious divorce between rhetorical impulse and rational thought. When the ultimate terms become a series of bare abstractions, the understanding of power is supplanted by a worship of power, and in our condition this can mean only state worship.

It is easy to see, however, that a group determined upon control will have as one of its first objectives the appropriation of sources of charismatic authority. Probably the surest way to detect the fabricated charismatic term is to identify those terms ordinarily of limited power which are being moved up to the front line. That is to say, we may suspect the act of fabrication when terms of secondary or even tertiary

---

[4] "Principles of Newspeak," *Nineteen Eighty-four* (New York, 1949), p. 310.

rhetorical rank are pushed forward by unnatural pressure into ultimate positions. This process can nearly always be observed in times of crisis. During the last war, for example, "defense" and "war effort" were certainly regarded as culminative terms. We may say this because almost no one thinks of these terms as the natural sanctions of his mode of life. He may think thus of "progress" or "happiness" or even "freedom"; but "defense" and "war effort" are ultimate sanctions only when measured against an emergency situation. When the United States was preparing for entry into that conflict, every departure from our normal way of life could be justified as a "defense" measure. Plants making bombs to be dropped on other continents were called "defense" plants. Correspondingly, once the conflict had been entered, everything that was done in military or civilian areas was judged by its contribution to the "war effort." This last became for a period of years the supreme term: not God or Heaven or happiness, but successful effort in the war. It was a term to end all other terms or a rhetoric to silence all other rhetoric. No one was able to make his claim heard against "the war effort."

It is most important to realize, therefore, that under the stress of feeling or preoccupation, quite secondary terms can be moved up to the position of ultimate terms, where they will remain until reflection is allowed to resume sway. There are many signs to show that the term "aggressor" is now undergoing such manipulation. Despite the fact that almost no term is more difficult to correlate with objective phenomena, it is being rapidly promoted to ultimate "bad" term. The likelihood is that "aggressor" will soon become a depository for all the resentments and fears which naturally arise in a people. As such, it will function as did "infidel" in the mediaeval period and as "reactionary" has functioned in the recent past. Manifestly it is of great advantage to a nation bent upon organizing its power to be able to stigmatize some neighbor as "aggressor," so that the term's capacity for irrational assumption is a great temptation for those who are not moral in their use of rhetoric. This passage from natural or popular to state-engendered charisma produces one of the most dangerous lesions of modern society.

An ethics of rhetoric requires that ultimate terms be ultimate in some rational sense. The only way to achieve that objective is through an ordering of our own minds and our own passions. Every one of psychological sophistication knows that there is a pleasure in willed perversity, and the setting up of perverse shibboleths is a fairly common source of that pleasure. War cries, school slogans, coterie passwords, and all similar expressions are examples of such creation. There may be areas of play in which these are nothing more than a diversion; but there are other areas in which such expressions lure us down the roads of hatred and tragedy. That is the tendency of all words of false or "engineered" charisma. They often sound like the very gospel of one's society, but in fact they betray us; they get us to do what the adversary of the human being wants us to do. It is worth considering whether the real civil disobedience must not begin with our language.

Lastly, the student of rhetoric must realize that in the contemporary world he is confronted not only by evil practitioners, but also, and probably to an unprecedented degree, by men who are conditioned by the evil created by others. The machinery of propagation and inculcation is today so immense that no one avoids entirely the assimilation and use of some terms which have a downward tendency. It is especially easy to pick up a tone without realizing its trend. Perhaps the best that any of us can do is to hold a dialectic with himself to see what the wider circumferences of his terms of persuasion are. This process will not only improve the consistency of one's thinking but it will also, if the foregoing analysis is sound, prevent his becoming a creature of evil public forces and a victim of his own thoughtless rhetoric.

Allen Ginsberg

Allen Ginsberg might narrowly be identified as a controversial American poet, but at the present writing he seems to be emerging as something larger, perhaps a world-wide symbol, vastly unconventional and benevolent of personal freedom, peace, love, and doing one's own thing. He was born in Newark, N. J., in 1926 and graduated from Columbia in 1948. After beginning at a highly conventional job in the early 1950s as a market-research consultant, he underwent a species of conversion, or mental crisis, from which his present role has evolved. The publication of Howl and Other Poems *(1956) established his reputation as a poet, and he has habitually offered poetry readings and advice at colleges, art galleries, coffee shops, and mass meetings all over the world. In 1962–1963 he traveled in the Far East, principally India; in 1965 he visited Cuba and Central Europe. He was expelled from Cuba for denouncing Cuban treatment of homosexuals, and from Czechoslovakia after being crowned King of May by Prague students. Ginsberg's continuing*

career as a poet is recorded in such volumes as Kaddish and
Other Poems *(1961),* Reality Sandwiches *(1963), and* Planet
News: Poems 1961–1967 *(1968). He contributed to* The
Marijuana Papers *(1966), and in 1970 published his* Indian
Journals. *He has been translated into nine languages and was
awarded a Guggenheim Fellowship in 1965–1966 and an
American Academy of Arts and Letters grant in 1969.*

*He has long been active in the antiwar movement. In 1966
Robert McNamara, ex-president of the Ford Motor Company,
was President Johnson's Secretary of Defense, in charge of
prosecuting the Vietnam War. Ginsberg's letter to him, with its
context, is provided by Jane Kramer's* Allen Ginsberg in America
*(1969), here reporting a conversation between Ginsberg and a
student in Berkeley in the winter of 1967.*

A LETTER TO SECRETARY McNAMARA

The boy with the orange tapped him on the shoulder. "Allen, I don't
want to interrupt or anything," he said, "but what did you mean a
while ago about hippies having a new kind of human experience?"

"I was talking about a mutation of the race," Ginsberg replied,
tipping back in his blue patio chair.

"I know *that,* but I still don't know what you *meant,*" the boy with
the orange said.

"What I meant," Ginsberg said, "is that the past is bunk for people
now. All past consciousness is bunk. History is bunk. Like Henry
Ford said about technology—there's nothing to be learned from history
any more. We're in science fiction now. All the revolutions and the
old methods and techniques for changing consciousness are bankrupt.
We're back to magic, to psychic life. Like the civil rights movement
hasn't succeeded in altering the fear-consciousness of the white
Southern middle class, but the hippies might."

"But the civil rights movement's got power," the boy with the
orange said. "The hippies, they haven't got any power."

Ginsberg groaned. "Don't you know that power's a hallucination?"
he said. "The civil rights movement, Sheriff Rainey, *Time Magazine,*
McNamara, Mao—it's all a hallucination. No one can get away with
saying that's real. All public reality's a script, and anybody can write

the script the way he wants. The warfare's psychic now. Whoever controls the language, the images, controls the race. Power all boils down to whether McNamara gets up on the right side of the bed. And who's McNamara anyway? He's a lot of TV dots. *That's* public reality. Like imagine what would happen if McNamara got on television and started saying, 'Some of the fellows, some of the human beings we've been fighting with' instead of 'some of the Communists.' Words like 'Communist,' 'capitalist'—they're language as hypnosis, as an outrage against feeling. They're not the reality we know in the bedroom; they're comic-strip reality. They ought to be printed in the papers in those little balloons."

"Yeah, man, but that's life, that's where it's at," the boy from the drama department remarked, helping himself to the remainder of Orlovsky's cornflakes.

"Look, do you want to roll back the darkness or sit there complaining?" Ginsberg said. He told the boy to start writing letters about reality to the public people. *He* had been writing letters like that when *he* was in college, he said. Harry Truman had got quite a few of them then. And last year, after the Berkeley peace march, he had even been moved to sit down and try communicating with Robert McNamara. His letter read:

Dear Mr. McNamara, I am not sure you will respect my advice, but anyway, you cannot help but be interested if I can reach you with this message, so let us try.

The first thing is, be calm, there is no essential threat to anybody's ultimate being. Not yours, you also are safe, as is one supposed to be your or our enemy. He is also safe.

The reason for this is, as the old Chinese sages recognized earlier in time, that the very flesh universe we find ourselves trapped in is, in its nature, unthreatening because it is empty—illusory—Shakespeare & the Chinese agree—Prospero the Wise Man agrees—everything's all right because we are inhabiting a very special realm of pure Dream.

But as I get excited as Mao Tse-tung (whoever he is) gets frightened, as you take things so seriously, the dream turns to a kind of physical nightmare, with apparent conflict and—ugh—suffering death—well, death is built into it in any case—but the anxiety and paranoia—fear of a cosmic ENEMY is the stricken-feeling anxiety chord that runs thru.

Everybody's heart in America right now tonight—and in Vietnam or China we can only imagine &—try to calm that panic.

Now, are you doing things to calm that panic, or are you now, generally in fantasy or manifest thought (orders for more bomb), seized by that panic and acting it out? and so creating material conditions for it (the panic-fear-paranoia of Invasion by alien forces from some Outside) to flourish in everybody's mind—our own mind as well as the minds of China?

I do not know directly personally from contact with you what your sub-jective attitude is, but from what I read in the reduplicated Images of the mass media, you yourself are sending out waves of anxiety and fear.

Now given your material prominence and TV centrality and known and unknown governmental power-centralization, you must realize that it is your Will, your Fantasy, that dominates the mind-screen images of vast— not all—regions of the populace.

But there are large regions of age and youth whose consciousness oper-ates independently of the sense of fear you manifest. If not fear, the sense of conflict.

A question of staying calm, sitting in the room, the war will end, no-body ultimately wants it, a small area of consciousness living in fear of the shattering of its own Imagery—may prefer that & pain & death to realization —that the war does not actually exist, except in your mind and the mind of your corresponding Powers on the "Other Side."

Both sides are an illusion—you must by now have read basic Buddhist or Bob Dylan heard, texts & advices how to escape from the trap.

Unfortunately both you and Johnson—seem to me—surrounded by men who have not actually controlled their own Passions—simply, angryness, tendencies toward self-righteous exclusion of other forms of consciousness. The waves of emotional hysteria—both sides—not any material struggle for space in the universe—are the problem. In Other words the cold war all along has been an Emotional problem of those panicked by power and leadership—they have not been calm & tranquil—They—and you—have separated yourself out, away, from the Communists and other life forms, and have not made sufficient effort to provide conditions for these life forms to "co."—Yes—"exist." Coexistence—unless you anticipate a Wag-nerian battle for control of the Universe—Dualities and ultimate conflict— do you dream of such a thing necessary—many do. Many posit their whole consciousness on early fear that it's kill or be devoured—Anyway—Coexis-tence is the only mode of consciousness which will allow space for both you and the Chinese to exist on the planet. Unless that space is provided and made way for, paid for with cooperation and COMMUNICATION on basic psychic levels—reassurance, etc., such as I am giving you now— has to be given the Chinese—Unless as I say that is given—a straight two-handed calm show of amiability—free joy even—Naturally the Chinese are going to feel persecuted and paranoid. And if they feel that—in response to what is basically the Ill-Will of Americans toward their supposed Threat —then they will act unstable and hostile and we—beginning with what was a fixed white Image, and an artificial Moral image—superiority—will also act hostile.

So we have two life forms—both brothers in their desire for life, both trapped in the dream that it is somehow "Real," both in separate universes of mental suspicion.

Naturally you'll have a conflict that way.

If you can find the imagination to break thru that—even if it involves the bankruptcy of your whole phenomenal Purpose, your whole concluded idea system, your SELF and its apparent sensory impressions—yea yea yes— we & you too share in the madness, you are not more Sane than my appeal to you after all, dear—I mean with your vast Armada you're going to think *I'm* unbalanced or don't understand the pith experience of the TRAP? Well, we're all desperate, myself the most, so certainly you'll suffer no more in change than me, or Mao Tse-tung—

But the change must begin inside you, not Outside.

I have specific suggestions how to manifest this change—but it would mean a healthy change for America, and China, and be happy and not frightened to see you and talk to you or anyone else you think hath focal Hand in the balances of phantasy & thought.

No war is necessary, it never was outside of our fear contaminating the Chinese and their fear contaminating us—it's all hysteria—only solution is literally to cut thru the hysteria to a ground—our own natural lucidity and wrinkled eyes and flesh feel—where we can all exist together, such as this strange existence is, without the tremor and tightening of body and fantasy agitation of mind—into uncontrolled isolation-fear and wrath army consequent.

That's where "it all is," no place else, neither in a preordained dialectic or some logical imperative of "History."

Poets now say History is over; what they mean is that the reality approaching and the possible Doom or liberation from encroaching serpent-fear is a purely subjective matter. It's already time for you, & Leaders, to take on that subjective responsibility and not set it outside yourself. I'm taking it on by writing you this letter and offering you my Self to come and if need be calm your fear that anyone need be "conquered" any more.

Please reply if you have read and understood this with your own eyes. Thank you,

ALLEN GINSBERG

John Holt

John Holt (born 1923) is a teacher. He is also an eloquent and influential contemporary spokesman for educational reform. Born in New York City, educated at Yale University, he has taught on all levels of the educational ladder; beginning reading, experimental math, and general fifth grade in elementary school; English, French, math, and soccer in high school; composition for teachers at the University of California, Berkeley; education at Harvard Graduate School. His experiences as a teacher led to his two quietly revolutionary books, How Children Fail *(1964) and* How Children

*Learn (1967). Both derive from Holt's remarkable powers of
observation and reflect his painstaking attention to and respect for
the response of his pupils. His most recent book is* What Do I Do
Monday? *(1970), and he is a frequent contributor to such journals
as* New York Review *and* The Saturday Review. *The
essay we present here was first printed as the Introduction to
Herbert Kohl's* Teaching the Unteachable *(1967), the account
of an experiment in teaching writing to ghetto children.*

INTRODUCTION TO HERBERT KOHL'S
TEACHING THE UNTEACHABLE

A few years ago, when the poverty program got under way, and we
began to rediscover our poor, there was a rush of articles about the
children growing up in our city slums. They proved to be strange,
silent creatures indeed. We were told that they didn't know the names
of things, didn't know that things had names, didn't even know their
own names. We were told that, having never heard any real speech,
they could hardly speak more than occasional monosyllables themselves. The people who reported these things were serious, and sympathetic, and sincerely believed every word they said—and I, like many
other people, believed them.

How do you find out, anyway, whether a child knows his own name?
Smiling kindly at him, and speaking in a gentle and reassuring tone
of voice, you ask him, "What's your name?" If he doesn't answer,
it presumably shows that he doesn't know. Or perhaps, knowing his
name, you call him by it. If, hearing his name, he makes no move or
reply, again it shows that he doesn't know it. Simple.

Only, as Mr. Kohl has shown, and by now some others as well, it
may not be so simple. It makes a certain kind of sense to try to
judge what a child knows by seeing what he can do, but it leaves out
the possibility that he may choose not to show what he can do, that
he may decide that at school the safest course is to say and do as
little as possible—at least until he knows what and who this strange
place and these strange people are.

I am suddenly reminded of Submarine Officers Training School in
New London in the fall of 1943. Here we sat, 270 student officers,
and there up in front were our teachers, ex-sub skippers yanked away
from the Pacific and their chances for heroism, fame, and advance-

ment. "We want to know who you are," they told us. "If you see us in the bar at the Officer's Club come up, and introduce yourselves, and we'll have some talk." Some students took this advice. How friendly and welcoming was the submarine service! How pleasant and salty and exciting were these veteran skippers! Yes; but they were also, to a man, sore as hell about being in New London instead of the Pacific, and when, in class or on a training ship or wherever, their anger and impatience could not be contained, the students who got it in the neck were very likely to be the ones whose names they knew. They never knew mine; when I graduated, 13th in the class, the only officer who knew me by name was the school Exec, from whom I had had to get permission to leave on weekends. My caution paid off handsomely. It should not surprise us if slum children, finding themselves in a place where most of the grown-ups neither look nor sound like anyone they know, are equally cautious.

There is no need to set forth here the many ways in which the schools of our city slums are in most cases an environment fiercely and unrelievedly hostile and destructive to the children who attend them. That story has been told in part by Mr. Kohl, and will be told many times again. I would like to stress here a somewhat different point. From Mr. Kohl's book we could easily get the impression that he is talking about a special problem—how to make disadvantaged children articulate and literate. In fact the problem is much wider. Our so-called best schools are turning out students most of whom, in any real and important sense, are as inarticulate as the most deprived children of the ghettos, as little able to speak or write simply and directly about things of importance to them, what they know, want, and care about. The training in writing that they get, unless they are very lucky, is largely training in bullslinging and snowjobbery. Every year students at all levels write millions of papers. It is a safe bet that most of the time—I would guess over 95 percent—the writers of these papers do not care about and in fact have no honest and genuine opinions about what they are writing, and would not write it if they were not made to. I once asked a very able high school senior, a straight A student in English, if she ever kept any of her old English papers. She looked at me amazed. "For heaven's sake," she said, "What for?"

What for, indeed? And a senior, soon to graduate cum laude from one of the leading Ivy League colleges, told me not long ago—and I have to add that he was no radical or troublemaker—that he and everyone he knew were wholly convinced that their surest chance of getting an A on their papers and in their courses was to repeat the professor's ideas back to him, though of course in somewhat altered language.

It would be easy to compile a bookful of horror stories about schools and classrooms where neatness, mechanical accuracy, and orthodoxy of opinion—i.e., agreeing with the teacher's spoken or even unspoken notions of what is right and proper for children to believe and say—count for far more than honest, independent, original expression. It is still common in a great many schools to fail papers that have more than a very few errors in grammar, punctuation, or spelling, regardless of any other merit they might have. Not long ago I talked to the mother of an eight- or nine-year-old whose most recent paper, entirely free of any mechanical errors and otherwise (as the teacher admitted) well written, was failed because he wrote it in three colors of ink. And this was in a "good" school system. But the real reason why our schools do not turn out people who can use language simply and strongly, let alone beautifully, lies deeper. It is that with very few exceptions the schools, from kindergarten through graduate school, do not give a damn what the students think. Think, care about, or want to know. What counts is what the system has decided they shall be made to learn. Teachers' manuals for the elementary and even secondary grades instruct teachers to have "discussions" in which they "bring out the following points." What kind of a discussion is this? And at my alma mater, Yale, when the sensible and overdue suggestion was recently made that the resident colleges institute non-credit seminars on matters of current interest and concern to the students, there was a howl of protest from many leading members of the faculty. They insisted that all courses must be instituted and controlled by the departments. One man spoke of the danger of "academic bull-sessions." Another said, hard as it may be to believe, that such issues as the war in Vietnam were too recent to be discussed "in depth" or "dispassionately," and that to try to discuss it would only lead to "sloppy and disorganized thinking." A shameful business; but probably all too typical. Easy to see why Paul Goodman speaks of "academic monks."

If we are to make real progress in improving student writing, the first lesson we have to learn is this. A student will only be concerned with his own use of language, will only care about its effectiveness, and therefore try to judge its effectiveness—and therefore be able to improve its effectiveness—when he is talking to an audience, not just one that allows him to say what he wants as he wants, but one that takes him and his ideas seriously. This does not mean letting him take a shot at expressing his thoughts so that we teachers can then demolish them or show how much better are our own. In this respect the so-called and perhaps misnamed Socratic method is not only dishonest but destructive. It is easy for even half-smart adults to win arguments with children who are unskilled at arguing, or to lead them into logical traps and pitfalls. Children so outplayed at the word game will after a while simply stop playing it, or will concentrate on playing it our way. What we have to recognize is something quite different, that it is the effort to use words well, to say what he wants to say, to people whom he trusts, and wants to reach and move, that alone will teach a young person to use words better. No doubt, given this starting point, some technical advice and help may at times be useful; but we must begin from here or we will make no progress at all.

A final question. What difference does it make? Above all, what difference does it make whether the children of our poor, and notably our Negro poor, learn to speak and write well or not? Should we not bend all our efforts to giving them the kind of training that will enable them to get jobs and do work that will lift them, at least a little, out of their poverty? The answer is that this is nowhere near enough. It is of the greatest importance to our society that the children of our poor, particularly if they are Negroes, shall be skillful in the use of words. Not just skillful enough to be able to read signs and instructions, but skillful enough to be able to reach, instruct, and move other men. For our society faces a choice. Either we become a genuinely integrated society, in which the color of a man's skin has no more to do with the way other men treat him and feel about him than, say, the color of his eyes or his hair, or we will become a genuinely, wholeheartedly, unashamedly racist society, like that of Nazi Germany or present South Africa—with perhaps our own Final Solution waiting at the end. In short, either we whites get cured of our racism, and fairly soon, or it will kill all of whatever decent is left in our society. One thing that might help cure us is a Negro population articulate enough to make us feel what racism is like for those who suffer under it. No doubt we have some Negro spokesmen today, but they are so few—too few, and too remote. What a few Baldwins, Kings, and Carmichaels now tell us, we need to be told by thousands, hundreds of thousands. Enough Negroes, with enough words, might break down our often unspoken and even unconscious feeling that they are different, inferior, despicable, even terrifying, and awaken instead in us an awareness of our common humanity, and their pain, and our responsibility for it. And while they are doing that, they might at the same time organize and educate themselves, and their allies among the other poor and dispossessed, into a political force strong and effective enough to make some of the changes we need to make our society, in Paul Goodman's words, not Great but only decent, a society in which all men can live without hate, fear, or guilt.

Haig A. Bosmajian

Haig A. Bosmajian (born 1928) studied at the University of California and received the Ph.D. from Stanford in 1960. He has taught at the Universities of Idaho and Connecticut and is presently Associate Professor of Speech at the University of Washington. Professor Bosmajian's principal interests are in the areas of dissent, freedom of speech, and rhetorical strategies. He recently became editor of Free Speech, *the newsletter of the Freedom of Speech Committee of the Speech Association of America. Among his books are* The Rhetoric of the Civil Rights Movement *(1969) and the forthcoming* Dissent: Symbolic Behavior and Rhetorical Strategies. *He has also published many essays, on such subjects as the rhetoric of Nazism and Communism, and on nonverbal communication. The present essay is from* College English, *December 1969. The issue of May 1970 contains some interesting comments on it.*

THE LANGUAGE OF WHITE RACISM

The attempts to eradicate racism in the United States have been focused notably on the blacks of America, not the whites. What is striking is that while we are inundated with TV programs portraying the plight of black Americans, and with panel discussions focusing on black Americans, we very seldom hear or see any extensive public discussion, literature or programs directly related to the source of the racism, the white American. We continually see on our TV sets and in our periodicals pictures and descriptions of undernourished black children, but we seldom see pictures or get analyses of the millions of school-age white suburban children being taught racism in their white classrooms; we see pictures of unemployed blacks aimlessly walking the streets in their black communities, but seldom do we ever see the whites who have been largely responsible, directly or indirectly, for this unemployment and segregation; we continually hear panelists discussing and diagnosing the blacks in America, but seldom do we hear panelists diagnosing the whites and their subtle and not so subtle racism.

Gunnar Myrdal, in the Introduction to his classic *An American Dilemma*, wrote that as he "proceeded in his studies into the Negro

116

problem [an unfortunate phrase], it became increasingly evident that little, if anything, could be scientifically explained in terms of the peculiarities of the Negroes themselves." It is the white majority group, said Myrdal, "that naturally determines the Negro's 'place.' All our attempts to reach scientific explanations of why the Negroes are what they are and why they live as they do have regularly led to determinants on the white side of the race line." As the July 1966 editorial in *Ebony* put it, "for too long now, we have focused on the symptoms of the disease rather than the disease itself. It is time now for us to face the fact that Negroes are oppressed in America not by 'the pathology of the ghetto,' as some experts contend, but by the pathology of the white community." In calling for a White House Conference on Whites, the *Ebony* editorial made the important point that "we need to know more about the pathology of the white community. We need conferences in which white leaders will talk not about us [Negroes] but about themselves."

White Americans, through the mass media and individually, must begin to focus their attention not on the condition of the victimized, but on the victimizer. Whitey must begin to take the advice of various black spokesmen who suggest that white Americans start solving the racial strife in this country by eradicating white racism in white communities, instead of going into black communities or joining black organizations or working for legislation to "give" the blacks political and social rights. This suggestion has come from Floyd McKissick, Malcolm X, and Stokely Carmichael. McKissick, when asked what the role of the white man was in the black man's struggle, answered: "If there are whites who are not racists, and I believe there are a few, a *very* few, let them go to their own communities and teach; teach white people the truth about the black man." Malcolm X wrote in his autobiography: "The Negroes aren't the racists. Where the really sincere white people have to do their 'proving' of themselves is not among the black *victims*, but on the battle lines of where America's racism really *is*—and that's in their own home communities; America's racism is among their own fellow whites. That's where the sincere whites who really mean to accomplish something have to work." Stokely Carmichael, writing in the September 22, 1966, issue of *The New York Review of Books*, said: "One of the most disturbing things about almost all white supporters of the movement has been that they are afraid to go into their own communities—which is where the racism exists— and work to get rid of it."

A step in that direction which most whites can take is to clean up their language to rid it of words and phrases which connote racism to the blacks. Whereas many blacks have demonstrated an increased sensitivity to language and an awareness of the impact of words and

117

phrases upon both black and white listeners, the whites of this nation have demonstrated little sensitivity to the language of racial strife. Whitey has been for too long speaking and writing in terminology which, often being offensive to the blacks, creates hostility and suspicions and breaks down communication.

The increased awareness and sensitivity of the black American to the impact of language is being reflected in various ways. Within the past two years, there have been an increasing number of references by Negro writers and speakers to the "Through the Looking Glass" episode where Humpty Dumpty says: "When I use a word it means just what I choose it to mean—neither more nor less." "The question is," said Alice, "whether you can make words mean so many different things." "The question is," said Humpty Dumpty, "which is to be master—that's all." The "Through the Looking Glass" episode was used by Lerone Bennett, Jr., in the November 1967 issue of *Ebony* to introduce his article dealing with whether black Americans should call themselves "Negroes," "Blacks," or "Afro-Americans." In a speech delivered January 16, 1967, to the students at Morgan State College, Stokely Carmichael prefaced a retelling of the above Lewis Carroll tale with: "It [definition] is very, very important because I believe that people who can define are masters." Carmichael went on to say: "So I say 'black power' and someone says 'you mean violence.' And they expect me to say, 'no, no. I don't mean violence, I don't mean that.' Later for you; I am master of my own terms. If black power means violence to you, that is your problem. . . . I know what it means in my mind. I will stand clear and you must understand that because the first need of a free people is to be able to define their own terms and have those terms recognized by their oppressors. . . . Camus says that when a slave says 'no' he begins to exist."

This concern for words and their implications in race relations was voiced also by Martin Luther King who pointed out that "even semantics have conspired to make that which is black seem ugly and degrading." Writing in his last book before his death, *Where Do We Go From Here: Chaos or Community?*, King said: "In Roget's Thesaurus there are some 120 synonyms for 'blackness' and at least 60 of them are offensive—such words as 'blot,' 'soot,' 'grime,' 'devil,' and 'foul.' There are some 134 synonyms for 'whiteness,' and all are favorable, expressed in such words as 'purity,' 'cleanliness,' 'chastity,' and 'innocence.' A white lie is better than a black lie. The most degenerate member of the family is the 'black sheep,' not the 'white sheep.' "

In March 1962, *The Negro History Bulletin* published an article by L. Eldridge Cleaver, then imprisoned in San Quentin, who devoted several pages to a discussion of the black American's acceptance of a white society's standards for beauty and to an analysis of the negative connotations of the term "black" and the positive connotations of the term "white." Cleaver tells black Americans that "what we must do is stop associating the Caucasian with these exalted connotations of the word *white* when we think or speak of him. At the same time, we must cease associating ourselves with the unsavory connotations of the word black." Cleaver makes an interesting point when he brings to our attention the term "non-white." He writes: "The very words that we use indicate that we have set a premium on the Caucasian ideal of beauty. When discussing inter-racial relations, we speak of 'white people' and 'non-white people.' Notice that that particular choice of words gives precedence to 'white people' by making them a center—a standard—to which 'non-white' bears a negative relation. Notice the different connotations when we turn around and say 'colored' and 'non-colored,' or 'black' or 'non-black.' "

Simon Podair, writing in the Fourth Quarter issue, 1956, of *Phylon* examines the connotations of such words as "blackmail," "blacklist," "blackbook," "blacksheep," and "blackball." The assertion made by Podair that it has been white civilization which has attributed to the word "black" things undesirable and evil warrants brief examination. He is correct when he asserts that "language as a potent force in our society goes beyond being merely a communicative device. Language not only expresses ideas and concepts but it may actually shape them. Often the process is completely unconscious, with the individual concerned unaware of the influence of the spoken or written expressions upon his thought processes. Language can thus become an instrument of both propaganda and indoctrination for a given idea." Further, Podair is correct in saying that "so powerful is the role of language in its imprint upon the human mind that even the minority group may begin to accept the very expressions that aid in its stereotyping. Thus, even Negroes may develop speech patterns filled with expressions leading to the strengthening of stereotypes." Podair's point is illustrated by the comments made by a Negro state official in Washington upon hearing of the shooting of Robert Kennedy. The Director of the Washington State Board Against Discrimination said: "This is a black day in our country's history." Immediately after uttering this statement with the negative connotation of "black," he declared that Robert Kennedy "is a hero in the eyes of black people—a champion of the oppressed—and we all pray for his complete recovery."

Although King, Cleaver, and Podair, and others who are concerned with the negative connotations of "black" in the white society are partially correct in their analysis, they have omitted in their discussions two points which by their omission effect an incomplete analysis. First, it is not quite accurate to say, as Podair has asserted, that the concepts of black as hostile, foreboding, wicked, and gloomy "cannot be considered accidental and undoubtedly would not exist in a society wherein whites were a minority. Historically, these concepts have evolved as a result of the need of the dominant group to maintain social and economic relationships on the basis of inequality if its hegemony was to survive." This is inaccurate because the terms "blackball," "blacklist," "blackbook," and "blackmail" did not evolve as "a result of the need of the dominant group to maintain social and economic relationships on the basis of inequality if its hegemony was to survive." The origins of these terms are to be found in the sixteenth and seventeenth centuries in England where the terms were mostly based on the color of the book cover, the color of printing, or the color of the object from which the word got its meaning, as for instance the term "to blackball" coming from "the black ball" which centuries ago was a small black ball used as a vote against a person or thing. A "black-letter day" had its origin in the eighteenth century to designate an inauspicious day, as distinguished from a "red-letter day," the reference being to the old custom of marking the saint's days in the calendar with red letters.

More important, the assertion that the negative connotations of "black" and the positive connotations of "white" would not exist in a society wherein whites were a minority is not accurate. Centuries ago, before black societies ever saw white men, "black" often had negative connotations and "white" positive in those societies. T. O. Beidelman has made quite clear in his article "Swazi Royal Ritual," which appeared in the October 1966 issue of *Africa*, that black societies in southeast Africa, while attributing to black positive qualities, can at the same time attribute to black negative qualities; the same applies to the color white. Beidelman writes that for the Swazi "darkness, as the 'covered' moon, is an ambiguous quality. Black symbolizes 'impenetrability of the future,' but also the 'sins and evils of the past year. . . .'" Black beads may symbolize marriage and wealth in cattle, but at the same time they can symbolize evil, disappointment, and misfortune. "The word *mnyama* means black and dark, but also means deep, profound, unfathomable, and even confused, dizzy, angry." To the Swazi, "that which is dark is unknown and ambiguous and dangerous, but it is also profound, latent with unknown meanings and possibilities." As for "white," *mhlophe* means to the Swazi "white, pale, pure, innocent, perfect, but this may also mean destitute and empty. The whiteness of the full moon, *inyanga isidindile*, relates to fullness; but this term *dinda* can also mean to be useless, simply because it refers to that which is fully exposed and having no further unknown potentialities."

What King, Cleaver, and Podair have failed to do in their discussions of the negative connotations of "black" and the positive connotations

120

of "white" is to point out that in black societies "black" often connotes that which is hostile, foreboding, and gloomy and "white" has symbolized purity and divinity. Furthermore, in white societies, "white" has numerous negative connotations: white livered (cowardly), white flag (surrender), white elephant (useless), white plague (tuberculosis), white wash (conceal), white feather (cowardice), *et cetera*. The ugliness and terror associated with the color white are portrayed by Melville in the chapter "The Whiteness of the Whale" in *Moby Dick*. At the beginning of the chapter, Melville says: "It was the whiteness of the whale that above all things appalled me."

What I am suggesting here is that the Negro writers, while legitimately concerned with the words and phrases which perpetuate racism in the United States have, at least in their analysis of the term "black," presented a partial analysis. This is not to say, however, that most of the analysis is not valid as far as it goes. Podair is entirely correct when he writes: "In modern American life language has become a fulcrum of prejudice as regards Negro-white relationships. Its effect has been equally potent upon the overt bigot as well as the confused member of the public who is struggling to overcome conscious or unconscious hostility towards minority groups. In the case of the Negro, language concepts have supported misconceptions and disoriented the thinking of many on the question of race and culture." Not only has the Negro become trapped by these "language concepts," but so too have the whites who, unlike the blacks, have demonstrated very little insight into the language of white racism and whose "language concepts" have "supported misconceptions and disoriented the thinking of many on the question of race and culture."

The Negroes' increased understanding and sensitivity to language as it is related to them demands that white Americans follow suit with a similar understanding and sensitivity which they have not yet demonstrated too well. During the 1960's, at a time when black Americans have been attempting more than ever to communicate with whites, through speeches, marches, sit-ins, demonstrations, through violence and non-violence, the barriers of communication between blacks and whites seem to be almost as divisive as they have been in the past one hundred years, no thanks to the whites. One has only to watch the TV panelists, blacks and whites, discussing the black American's protest and his aspirations, to see the facial expressions of the black panelists when a white on the panel speaks of "our colored boys in Vietnam." The black panelists knowingly smile at the racist phrasing and it is not difficult to understand the skepticism and suspicion which the blacks henceforth will maintain toward the white panelist who offends with "our colored boys in Vietnam." "Our colored boys in Vietnam" is a close relation to "our colored people" and "our colored," phrases which communicate more to the black American listener than intended by the white speaker. John Howard Griffin has pointed out something that applies not only to Southern whites, but to white Americans generally: "A great many of us Southern whites have grown up using an expression that Negroes can hardly bear to hear and yet tragically enough we use it because we believe it. It's an expression that we use when we say how much we love, what we patronizingly call 'our Negroes.'" The white American who talks of "our colored boys in Vietnam" offends the Negro triply; first, by referring to the black American men as "our" which is, as Griffin points out, patronizing; second, by using the nineteenth century term "colored"; third, by referring to the black American men as "boys."

Most whites, if not all, know that "nigger" and "boy" are offensive to the Negro; in fact, such language could be classified as "fighting words." But the insensitive and offensive whites continue today to indulge in expressing their overt and covert prejudices by using these obviously derogatory terms. Running a series of articles on racism in athletics, *Sports Illustrated* quoted a Negro football player as saying: "The word was never given bluntly; usually it took the form of a friendly, oblique talk with one of the assistant coaches. I remember one time one of the coaches came to me and said, '[Head Coach] Jim Owens loves you boys. We know you get a lot of publicity, but don't let it go to your head.' Hell, when he said 'Jim Owens loves you boys,' I just shut him off. That did it. I knew what he was talking about." An athletic director at one of the larger Southwestern Universities, discussing how much sports have done for the Negro, declared: "In general, the nigger athlete is a little hungrier and we have been blessed with having some real outstanding ones. We think they've done a lot for us, and we think we've done a lot for them" (*Sports Illustrated*, July 1, 1968). One of the Negro athletes said of the coaching personnel at the same university: "They can pronounce Negro if they want to. *They can pronounce it.* But I think it seems like such a little thing to them. The trouble with them is they're not thinking of the Negro and how he feels. Wouldn't you suppose that if there was one word these guys that live off Negroes would get rid of, one single word in the whole vocabulary, it would be *nigger?*" (*Sports Illustrated*, July 15, 1968). When a newspaperman tried to get the attention of Elvin Hayes, star basketball player at the University of Houston, the reporter shouted, "Hey, boy!" Hayes turned to the reporter and said: "Boy's on *Tarzan*. Boy plays on *Tarzan*. I'm no boy. I'm 22 years old. I worked hard to become a man. I don't call you boy." The reporter apologized and said: "I didn't mean anything by it" (*Sports Illustrated*, July 1, 1968).

Whites who would never think of referring to Negroes as "boy" or

122

"nigger" do, however, reveal themselves through less obviously racist language. A day does not go by without one hearing, from people who should know better, about "the Negro problem," a phrase which carries with it the implication that the Negro is a problem. One is reminded of the Nazis talking about "the Jewish problem." There was no Jewish problem! Yet the phrase carried the implication that the Jews were a problem in Germany and hence being a problem invited a solution and the solution Hitler proposed and carried out was the "final solution." Even the most competent writers fall into the "Negro problem" trap; James Reston of the *New York Times* wrote on April 7, 1968: "When Gunnar Myrdal, the Swedish social philosopher who has followed the Negro problem in America for forty years, came back recently, he felt that a great deal had changed for the better, but concluded that we have greatly underestimated the scope of the Negro problem." Myrdal himself titled his 1944 classic work *The American Dilemma: The Negro Problem and Modern Democracy.* A book published in 1967, *The Negro in 20th Century America,* by John Hope Franklin and Isidore Starr, starts off in the Table of Contents with "Book One: *The Negro Problem*"; the foreword begins, "The Negro problem was selected because it is one of the great case studies in man's never-ending fight for equal rights." One of the selections in the book, a debate in which James Baldwin participates, has Baldwin's debate opponent saying that "the Negro problem is a very complicated one." There are several indications that from here on out the black American is no longer going to accept the phrase "the Negro problem." As Lerone Bennett, Jr., said in the August 1965 issue of *Ebony,* "there is no Negro problem in America. The problem of race in America, insofar as that problem is related to packets of melanin in men's skins, is a white problem." In 1966, the editors of *Ebony* published a book of essays dealing with American black-white relations entitled *The WHITE Problem in America.* It is difficult to imagine Negroes sitting around during the next decade talking about "the Negro problem," just as it is difficult to imagine Jews in 1939 referring to themselves as "the Jewish problem."

The racial brainwashing of whites in the United States leads them to utter such statements as "You don't sound like a Negro" or "Well, he didn't sound like a Negro to me." John Howard Griffin, who changed the color of his skin from white to black to find out what it meant to be black in America, was ashamed to admit that he thought he could not pass for a Negro because he "didn't know how to speak Negro." "There is an illusion in this land," said Griffin, "that unless you sound as though you are reading Uncle Remus you couldn't possibly have an authentic Negro dialect. But I don't know what we've been using for ears because you don't have to be in the Negro community five minutes before the truth strikes and the truth is that there are just as many speech patterns in the Negro community as there are in any other, particularly in areas of rigid segregation where your right shoulder may be touching the shoulder of a Negro PhD and your left shoulder the shoulder of the disadvantaged." A black American, when told that he does not "sound like a Negro," legitimately can ask his white conversationalist, "What does a Negro sound like?" This will probably place the white in a dilemma for he will either have to admit that sounding like a Negro means sounding like Prissy in *Gone With the Wind* ("Who dat say who dat when you say dat?") or that perhaps there is no such thing as "sounding like a Negro." Goodman Ace, writing in the July 27, 1968, issue of the *Saturday Review* points out that years ago radio program planners attempted to write Negroes into the radio scripts, portraying the Negro as something else besides janitors, household maids, and train porters. Someone suggested that in the comedy radio show *Henry Aldrich* Henry might have among his friends a young Negro boy, without belaboring the point that the boy was Negro. As Mr. Ace observes, "just how it would be indicated on radio that the boy is black was not mentioned. Unless he was to be named Rufus or Rastus." Unless, it might be added, he was to be made to "sound like a Negro."

Psychiatrist Frantz Fanon, who begins his *Black Skin, White Masks* with a chapter titled "The Negro and Language," explains the manner of many whites when talking to Negroes and the effects of this manner. Although he is writing about white Europeans, what Fanon says applies equally to white Americans. He points out that most whites "talk down" to the Negro, and this "talking down" is, in effect, telling the Negro, "You'd better keep your place." Fanon writes: "A white man addressing a Negro behaves exactly like an adult with a child and starts smirking, whispering, patronizing, cozening." The effect of the whites' manner of speaking to the Negro "makes him angry, because he himself is a pidgin-nigger-talker." "But I will be told," says Fanon, "there is no wish, no intention to anger him. I grant this; but it is just this absence of wish, this lack of interest, this indifference, this automatic manner of classifying him, imprisoning him, primitivizing him, decivilizing him, that makes him angry." If a doctor greets his Negro patient with "You not feel good, no?" or "G'morning pal. Where's it hurt? Huh? Lemme see—belly ache? Heart pain?" the doctor feels perfectly justified in speaking that way, writes Fanon, when in return the patient answers in the same fashion; the doctor can then say to himself, "You see? I wasn't kidding you. That's just the way they are." To make the Negro talk pidgin, as Fanon observes, "is to fasten him to the effigy of him, to snare him, to imprison him, the eternal victim of an essence, of an *appearance* for which he is not

124

responsible. And naturally, just as a Jew who spends money without thinking about it is suspect, a black man who quotes Montesquieu had better be watched." The whites, in effect, encourage the stereotype of the Negro; they perpetuate the stereotype through the manner in which they speak about and speak to Negroes. And if Fanon is correct, the whites by "talking down" to the Negro are telling that black American citizen to "remember where you come from!"

Another facet of the racism of the whites' language is reflected in their habit of referring to talented and great writers, athletes, entertainers, and clergymen as "a great Negro singer" or "a great black poet" or "a great Negro ball player." What need is there for whites to designate the color or race of the person who has excelled? Paul Robeson and Marian Anderson are great and talented singers. James Baldwin and LeRoi Jones are talented writers. Why must the whites qualify the greatness of these individuals with "black" or "colored" or "Negro"? Fanon briefly refers to this predilection of whites to speak with this qualification:

. . . Charles-André Julien introducing Aimé Césaire as "a Negro poet with a university degree," or again, quite simply, the expression, "a great black poet."

These ready-made phrases, which seem in a common-sense way to fill a need—for Aimé Césaire is really black and a poet—have a hidden subtlety, a permanent rub. I know nothing of Jean Paulhan except that he writes very interesting books; I have no idea how old Roger Caillois is, since the only evidence I have of his existence are the books of his that streak across my horizon. And let no one accuse me of affective allergies; what I am trying to say is that there is no reason why André Breton should say of Césaire, "Here is a black man who handles the French language as no white man today can."

The tendency to designate and identify a person as a Negro when the designation is not necessary carries over into newspaper and magazine reporting of crimes. There was no need for *Time* magazine (July 19, 1968) to designate the race of the individual concerned in the following *Time* report: "In New York City, slum dwellers were sent skidding for cover when Bobby Rogers, 31, Negro superintendent of a grubby South Bronx tenement, sprayed the street with bullets from a sawed-off .30 cal. semiautomatic carbine, killing three men and wounding a fourth." *Time*, for whatever reason, designated the race of the person involved in this instance, but the reports on other criminal offences cited by *Time*, on the same page, did not indicate the race of the "suspects." As a label of primary potency, "Negro" stands out over "superintendent." The assumption that whites can understand and sympathize with the Negro's dismay when black "suspects" are identified by race and white "suspects" are not, is apparently an unwarranted assumption; or it may be possible that the whites *do* understand the dismay and precisely for that reason continue to designate the race of the black criminal suspect. To argue that if the race is not designated in the news story then the reader can assume that the suspected criminal is white, is not acceptable for it makes all the difference if the suspect is identified as "a Negro superintendent," "a white superintendent," or "a superintendent." If we were told, day in and day out, that "a *white* bank clerk embezzled" or "a *white* service station operator stole" or "a *white* unemployed laborer attacked," it would make a difference in the same sense that it makes a difference to identify the criminal suspect as "Negro" or "black."

If many Negroes find it hard to understand why whites have to designate a great writer or a great artist or a common criminal as "colored" or "Negro," so too do many Negroes find it difficult to understand why whites must designate a Negro woman as a "Negress." Offensive as "Negress" is to most blacks, many whites still insist on using the term. In a July 28, 1968, *New York Times Magazine* article, the writer, discussing the 1968 campaigning of Rockefeller and Nixon, wrote: "A fat Negress on the street says, passionately, 'Rocky! Rocky!' " As Gordon Allport has written in *The Nature of Prejudice*, "members of minority groups are often understandably sensitive to names given them. Not only do they object to deliberately insulting epithets, but sometimes see evil intent where none exists." Allport gives two examples to make his point: one example is the spelling of the word "Negro" with a small "n" and the other example is the word "Negress." "Sex differentiations are objectionable," writes Allport, "since they seem doubly to emphasize ethnic differences: why speak of Jewess and not of Protestantess, or of Negress, and not of whitess?" Just as "Jewess" is offensive to the Jews, so too is "Negress" offensive to the Negroes. "A Negro woman" does not carry the same connotations as "Negress," the latter conveying an emotional emphasis on both the color and sex of the individual. *Webster's New World Dictionary of the American Language* says of "Negress": "A Negro woman or girl: often a patronizing or contemptuous term."

When the newspaper reporter tried to get the attention of twenty two year old basketball star Elvin Hayes by shouting, "Hey, boy!" and Hayes vigorously objected to being called "boy," the reporter apologized and said: "I didn't mean anything by it." In a few cases, a very few cases, white Americans indeed "didn't mean anything by it." That excuse, however, will no longer do. The whites must make a serious conscious effort to discard the racist clichés of the past, the overt and covert language of racism. "Free, white, and 21" or "That's white of you" are phrases whites can no longer indulge in. Asking white Americans to change their language, to give up some of their clichés, is disturbing enough since the request implies a deficiency in the past use of that language; asking that they discard the language of racism is also disturbing because the people being asked to make the change, in effect, are being told that they have been the perpetrators and perpetuators of racism. Finally, and most important, calling the Negro "nigger" or "boy," or "speaking down" to the Negro, gives Whitey a linguistic power over the victimized black American, a power most whites are unwilling or afraid to give up. A person's language is an extension of himself and to attack his use of language is to attack him. With the language of racism, this is exactly the point, for the language of white racism and the racism of the whites are almost one and the same. Difficult and painful as it may be for whites to discard their racist terms, phrases, and clichés, it must be done before blacks and whites can discuss seriously the eradication of white racism.

Aldous Huxley

This is Chapter 6 of Huxley's Brave New World Revisited *(1958). For information on the author and his writings, see page 27.*

THE ARTS OF SELLING

The survival of democracy depends on the ability of large numbers of people to make realistic choices in the light of adequate information. A dictatorship, on the other hand, maintains itself by censoring or distorting the facts, and by appealing, not to reason, not to enlightened self-interest, but to passion and prejudice, to the powerful "hidden forces," as Hitler called them, present in the unconscious depths of every human mind.

In the West, democratic principles are proclaimed and many able and conscientious publicists do their best to supply electors with adequate information and to persuade them, by rational argument, to make realistic choices in the light of that information. All this is greatly to the good. But unfortunately propaganda in the Western democracies, above all in America, has two faces and a divided personality. In charge of the editorial department there is often a democratic Dr. Jekyll—a propagandist who would be very happy to prove that John Dewey had been right about the ability of human nature to respond to truth and reason. But this worthy man controls only a part of the machinery of mass communication. In charge of advertising we find an anti-democratic, because anti-rational, Mr. Hyde—or rather a Dr. Hyde, for Hyde is now a Ph.D. in psychology and has a master's degree as well in the social sciences. This Dr. Hyde would be very unhappy indeed if everybody always lived up to John Dewey's faith in human nature. Truth and reason are Jekyll's affair, not his. Hyde is a motivation analyst, and his business is to study human weaknesses and failings, to investigate those unconscious desires and fears by which so much of men's conscious thinking and overt doing is determined. And he does this, not in the spirit of the moralist who would like to make people better, or of the physician who would like to improve their health, but simply in order to find out the best way to take advantage of their ignorance and to exploit their irrationality for the pecuniary benefit of his employers. But after all, it may be argued, "capitalism is dead, consumerism is king"—and consumerism requires the services of expert salesmen versed in all the arts (including the more insidious arts) of persuasion. Under a free enterprise system commercial propaganda by any and every means is absolutely indispensable. But the indispensable is not necessarily the desirable. What is demonstrably good in the sphere of economics may be far from good for men and women as voters or even as human beings. An earlier, more moralistic generation would have been profoundly shocked by the bland cynicism of the motivation analysts. Today we read a book like Mr. Vance Packard's *The Hidden Persuaders,* and are more amused than horrified, more resigned than indignant. Given Freud, given Behaviorism, given the mass producer's chronically desperate need for mass consumption, this is the sort of thing that is only to be expected. But what, we may ask, is the sort of thing that is to be expected in the future? Are Hyde's activities compatible in the long run with Jekyll's? Can a campaign in favor of rationality be successful in the teeth of another and even more vigorous campaign in favor of irrationality? These are questions which, for the moment, I shall not attempt to answer, but shall leave hanging, so to speak, as a backdrop to our discussion of the methods of mass persuasion in a technologically advanced democratic society.

The task of the commercial propagandist in a democracy is in some ways easier and in some ways more difficult than that of a political propagandist employed by an established dictator or a dictator in the making. It is easier inasmuch as almost everyone starts out with a prejudice in favor of beer, cigarettes and iceboxes, whereas almost nobody starts out with a prejudice in favor of tyrants. It is more difficult inasmuch as the commercial propagandist is not permitted, by the rules of his particular game, to appeal to the more savage instincts of his public. The advertiser of dairy products would dearly love to tell his readers and listeners that all their troubles are caused by the machinations of a gang of godless international margarine manufacturers, and that it is their patriotic duty to march out and burn the oppressors' factories. This sort of thing, however, is ruled out, and he must be content with a milder approach. But the mild approach is less exciting than the approach through verbal or physical violence. In the long run, anger and hatred are self-defeating emotions. But in the short run they pay high dividends in the form of psychological and even (since they release large quantities of adrenalin and noradrenalin) physiological satisfaction. People may start out with an initial prejudice against tyrants; but when tyrants or would-be tyrants treat them to adrenalin-releasing propaganda about the wickedness of their enemies —particularly of enemies weak enough to be persecuted—they are ready to follow him with enthusiasm. In his speeches Hitler kept repeating such words as "hatred," "force," "ruthless," "crush," "smash"; and he would accompany these violent words with even more violent gestures. He would yell, he would scream, his veins would swell, his face would turn purple. Strong emotion (as every actor and dramatist knows) is in the highest degree contagious. Infected by the malignant frenzy of the orator, the audience would groan and sob and scream in an orgy of uninhibited passion. And these orgies were so enjoyable that most of those who had experienced them eagerly came back for more. Almost all of us long for peace and freedom; but very few of us have much enthusiasm for the thoughts, feelings and actions that make for peace and freedom. Conversely almost nobody wants war or tyranny; but a great many people find an intense pleasure in the thoughts, feelings and actions that make for war and tyranny. These thoughts, feelings and actions are too dangerous to be exploited for commercial purposes. Accepting this handicap, the advertising man must do the best he can with the less intoxicating emotions, the quieter forms of irrationality.

Effective rational propaganda becomes possible only when there is a clear understanding, on the part of all concerned, of the nature of symbols and of their relations to the things and events symbolized. Irrational propaganda depends for its effectiveness on a general failure to understand the nature of symbols. Simple-minded people tend to equate the symbol with what it stands for, to attribute to things and events some of the qualities expressed by the words in terms of which the propagandist has chosen, for his own purposes, to talk about them. Consider a simple example. Most cosmetics are made of lanolin, which is a mixture of purified wool fat and water beaten up into an emulsion. This emulsion has many valuable properties: it penetrates the skin, it does not become rancid, it is mildly antiseptic and so forth. But the commercial propagandists do not speak about the genuine virtues of the emulsion. They give it some picturesquely voluptuous name, talk ecstatically and misleadingly about feminine beauty and show pictures of gorgeous blondes nourishing their tissues with skin food. "The cosmetic manufacturers," one of their number has written, "are not selling lanolin, they are selling hope." For this hope, this fraudulent implication of a promise that they will be transfigured, women will pay ten or twenty times the value of the emulsion which the propagandists have so skilfully related, by means of misleading symbols, to a deep-seated and almost universal feminine wish—the wish to be more attractive to members of the opposite sex. The principles underlying this kind of propaganda are extremely simple. Find some common desire, some widespread unconscious fear or anxiety; think out some way to relate this wish or fear to the product you have to sell; then build a bridge of verbal or pictorial symbols over which your customer can pass from fact to compensatory dream, and from the dream to the illusion that your product, when purchased, will make the dream come true. "We no longer buy oranges, we buy vitality. We do not buy just an auto, we buy prestige." And so with all the rest. In toothpaste, for example, we buy, not a mere cleanser and antiseptic, but release from the fear of being sexually repulsive. In vodka and whisky we are not buying a protoplasmic poison which, in small doses, may depress the nervous system in a psychologically valuable way; we are buying friendliness and good fellowship, the warmth of Dingley Dell and the brilliance of the Mermaid Tavern. With our laxatives we buy the health of a Greek god, the radiance of one of Diana's nymphs. With the monthly best seller we acquire culture, the envy of our less literate neighbors and the respect of the sophisticated. In every case the motivation analyst has found some deep-seated wish or fear, whose energy can be used to move the consumer to part with cash and so, indirectly, to turn the wheels of industry. Stored in the minds and bodies of countless individuals, this potential energy is released by, and transmitted along, a line of symbols carefully laid out so as to bypass rationality and obscure the real issue.

Sometimes the symbols take effect by being disproportionately impressive, haunting and fascinating in their own right. Of this kind are the rites and pomps of religion. These "beauties of holiness" strengthen faith where it already exists and, where there is no faith, contribute to conversion. Appealing, as they do, only to the aesthetic sense, they guarantee neither the truth nor the ethical value of the doctrines with which they have been, quite arbitrarily, associated. As a matter of plain historical fact, the beauties of holiness have often been matched and indeed surpassed by the beauties of unholiness. Under Hitler, for example, the yearly Nuremberg rallies were masterpieces of ritual and theatrical art. "I had spent six years in St. Petersburg before the war in the best days of the old Russian ballet," writes Sir Nevile Henderson, the British ambassador to Hitler's Germany, "but for grandiose beauty I have never seen any ballet to compare with the Nuremberg rally." One thinks of Keats—"beauty is truth, truth beauty." Alas, the identity exists only on some ultimate, supramundane level. On the levels of politics and theology, beauty is perfectly compatible with nonsense and tyranny. Which is very fortunate; for if beauty were incompatible with nonsense and tyranny, there would be precious little art in the world. The masterpieces of painting, sculpture and architecture were produced as religious or political propaganda, for the greater glory of a god, a government or a priesthood. But most kings and priests have been despotic and all religions have been riddled with superstition. Genius has been the servant of tyranny and art has advertised the merits of the local cult. Time, as it passes, separates the good art from the bad metaphysics. Can we learn to make this separation, not after the event, but while it is actually taking place? That is the question.

In commercial propaganda the principle of the disproportionately fascinating symbol is clearly understood. Every propagandist has his Art Department, and attempts are constantly being made to beautify the billboards with striking posters, the advertising pages of magazines with lively drawings and photographs. There are no masterpieces; for masterpieces appeal only to a limited audience, and the commercial propagandist is out to captivate the majority. For him, the ideal is a moderate excellence. Those who like this not too good, but sufficiently striking, art may be expected to like the products with which it has been associated and for which it symbolically stands.

Another disproportionately fascinating symbol is the Singing Commercial. Singing Commercials are a recent invention; but the Singing Theological and the Singing Devotional—the hymn and the psalm—are as old as religion itself. Singing Militaries, or marching songs, are coeval with war, and Singing Patriotics, the precursors of our national anthems, were doubtless used to promote group solidarity, to emphasize the distinction between "us" and "them," by the wandering bands of paleolithic hunters and food gatherers. To most people music is intrinsically attractive. Moreover, melodies tend to ingrain themselves in the listener's mind. A tune will haunt the memory during the whole of a lifetime. Here, for example, is a quite uninteresting statement or value judgment. As it stands nobody will pay attention to it. But now set the words to a catchy and easily remembered tune. Immediately they become words of power. Moreover, the words will tend automatically to repeat themselves every time the melody is heard or spontaneously remembered. Orpheus has entered into an alliance with Pavlov—the power of sound with the conditioned reflex. For the commercial propagandist, as for his colleagues in the fields of politics and religion, music possesses yet another advantage. Nonsense which it would be shameful for a reasonable being to write, speak or hear spoken can be sung or listened to by that same rational being with pleasure and even with a kind of intellectual conviction. Can we learn to separate the pleasure of singing or of listening to song from the all too human tendency to believe in the propaganda which the song is putting over? That again is the question.

Thanks to compulsory education and the rotary press, the propagandist has been able, for many years past, to convey his messages to virtually every adult in every civilized country. Today, thanks to radio and television, he is in the happy position of being able to communicate even with unschooled adults and not yet literate children.

Children, as might be expected, are highly susceptible to propaganda. They are ignorant of the world and its ways, and therefore completely unsuspecting. Their critical faculties are undeveloped. The youngest of them have not yet reached the age of reason and the older ones lack the experience on which their new-found rationality can effectively work. In Europe, conscripts used to be playfully referred to as "cannon fodder." Their little brothers and sisters have now become radio fodder and television fodder. In my childhood we were taught to sing nursery rhymes and, in pious households, hymns. Today the little ones warble the Singing Commercials. Which is better—"Rheingold is my beer, the dry beer," or "Hey diddle-diddle, the cat and the fiddle"? "Abide with me" or "You'll wonder where the yellow went, when you brush your teeth with Pepsodent"? Who knows?

"I don't say that children should be forced to harass their parents into buying products they've seen advertised on television, but at the same time I cannot close my eyes to the fact that it's being done every day." So writes the star of one of the many programs beamed to a juvenile audience. "Children," he adds, "are living, talking records of what we tell them every day." And in due course these living, talking records of television commercials will grow up, earn money and buy the products of industry. "Think," writes Mr. Clyde Miller ecstatically, "think of what it can mean to your firm in profits if you can condition a million or ten million children, who will grow up into adults trained to buy your product, as soldiers are trained in advance when they hear the trigger words, Forward March!" Yes, just think of it! And at the same time remember that the dictators and the would-be dictators have been thinking about this sort of thing for years, and that millions, tens of millions, hundreds of millions of children are in process of growing up to buy the local despot's ideological product and, like well-trained soldiers, to respond with appropriate behavior to the trigger words implanted in those young minds by the despot's propagandists.

Self-government is in inverse ratio to numbers. The larger the constituency, the less the value of any particular vote. When he is merely one of millions, the individual elector feels himself to be impotent, a negligible quantity. The candidates he has voted into office are far away, at the top of the pyramid of power. Theoretically they are the servants of the people; but in fact it is the servants who give orders and the people, far off at the base of the great pyramid, who must obey. Increasing population and advancing technology have resulted in an increase in the number and complexity of organizations, an increase in the amount of power concentrated in the hands of officials and a corresponding decrease in the amount of control exercised by electors, coupled with a decrease in the public's regard for democratic procedures. Already weakened by the vast impersonal forces at work in the modern world, democratic institutions are now being undermined from within by the politicians and their propagandists.

Human beings act in a great variety of irrational ways, but all of them seem to be capable, if given a fair chance, of making a reasonable choice in the light of available evidence. Democratic institutions can be made to work only if all concerned do their best to impart knowledge and to encourage rationality. But today, in the world's most powerful democracy, the politicians and their propagandists prefer to make nonsense of democratic procedures by appealing almost exclusively to the ignorance and irrationality of the electors. "Both parties," we were told in 1956 by the editor of a leading business journal, "will merchandize their candidates and issues by the same methods that business has developed to sell goods. These include scientific selection of appeals and planned repetition. . . . Radio spot announcements and ads will repeat phrases with a planned intensity. Billboards will push slogans of proven power. . . . Candidates need, in addition to rich voices and good diction, to be able to look 'sincerely' at the TV camera."

The political merchandisers appeal only to the weaknesses of voters, never to their potential strength. They make no attempt to educate the masses into becoming fit for self-government; they are content merely to manipulate and exploit them. For this purpose all the resources of psychology and the social sciences are mobilized and set to work. Carefully selected samples of the electorate are given "interviews in depth." These interviews in depth reveal the unconscious fears and wishes most prevalent in a given society at the time of an election. Phrases and images aimed at allaying or, if necessary, enhancing these fears, at satisfying these wishes, at least symbolically, are then chosen by the experts, tried out on readers and audiences, changed or improved in the light of the information thus obtained. After which the political campaign is ready for the mass communicators. All that is now needed is money and a candidate who can be coached to look "sincere." Under the new dispensation, political principles and plans for specific action have come to lose most of their importance. The personality of the candidate and the way he is projected by the advertising experts are the things that really matter.

In one way or another, as vigorous he-man or kindly father, the candidate must be glamorous. He must also be an entertainer who never bores his audience. Inured to television and radio, that audience is accustomed to being distracted and does not like to be asked to concentrate or make a prolonged intellectual effort. All speeches by the entertainer-candidate must therefore be short and snappy. The great issues of the day must be dealt with in five minutes at the most —and preferably (since the audience will be eager to pass on to something a little livelier than inflation or the H-bomb) in sixty seconds flat. The nature of oratory is such that there has always been a tendency among politicians and clergymen to over-simplify complex issues. From a pulpit or a platform even the most conscientious of speakers finds it very difficult to tell the whole truth. The methods now being used to merchandise the political candidate as though he were a deodorant positively guarantee the electorate against ever hearing the truth about anything.

Paul Jacobs

Paul Jacobs, social scientist and writer, was born in New York City in 1918 and attended C.C.N.Y. and the University of Minnesota. He first became active in the union movement as an organizer and later became a labor consultant and copublisher of a labor paper. More recently he has been a consultant to the Peace

Corps and the War on Poverty program and has conducted
research and taught journalism at the University of California.
He contributes regularly to the Economist *of London and has*
written for The Reporter, Commentary, Commonweal,
Atlantic, *and* Harper's. *He is joint editor of* Labor in a Free
Society *(1959) and author of* The State of the Unions *(1963),*
The New Radicals *(with S. Landau, 1966),* Prelude to Riot:
A View of Urban America from the Bottom *(1967), and*
Between the Rock and the Hard Place *(1970). The present*
essay first appeared in The Reporter, *September 18, 1958.*

THE MOST CHEERFUL GRAVEYARD IN THE WORLD

Along with amassing a comfortable fortune by convincing Los Angelenos that the only fitting way to begin a "happy Eternal Life" is by being laid to rest, in one way or another, at Forest Lawn Memorial Park, the cemetery he founded in 1917, Dr. Hubert Eaton, or "Digger" as he is known in the trade, has also succeeded in almost completely revising the dying industry.

The Digger, whose official title of "Doctor" is purely honorary, accomplished this revision by the simple but profound device of converting the hitherto prosaic art of dying into a gloriously exciting, well-advertised event, somehow intimately and patriotically connected with the American way of life.

Today, thanks to Eaton, dying in Los Angeles is something to be eagerly anticipated, because it is only after death that one can gain permanent tenure at Forest Lawn. Eaton, in one of his earlier roles—that of "the Builder"—described Forest Lawn as "a place where lovers new and old shall love to stroll and watch the sunset's glow, planning for the future or reminiscing of the past; a place where artists study and sketch; where school teachers bring happy children to see the things they read of in books; where little churches invite, triumphant in the knowledge that from their pulpits only words of Love can be spoken; where memorialization of loved ones in sculptured marble and pictorial glass shall be encouraged but controlled by acknowledged artists; a place where the sorrowing will be soothed and strengthened because it will be God's garden. A place that shall be protected by an immense Endowment Care Fund, the principal of which can never be expended—only the income therefrom used to care for and perpetuate this Garden of Memory.

135

"This is the Builder's Dream; this is the Builder's Creed."

The Builder's Creed is chiseled into a huge, upright stone slab on Forest Lawn's Cathedral Drive, just outside the Great Mausoleum and hard by the Shrine of Love. Viewed, usually in reverent awe, by more than a million visitors each year, Forest Lawn is, along with Disneyland, a favorite tourist attraction in Southern California, far outdrawing the concrete footprints in front of Grauman's Chinese Theatre.

A smaller inscription underneath the Creed points out that on New Year's Day, 1917, Eaton stood on a hilltop overlooking the small country cemetery which had just been placed in his charge. An un-employed mining engineer, Eaton had gone into the cemetery business after a vein of gold in his mine had suddenly vanished.

"A vision came to the man of what this tiny 'God's Acre' might become; and standing there, he made a promise to The Infinite. When he reached home, he put this promise into words and called it 'The Builder's Creed.' Today, Forest Lawn's almost three hundred acres are eloquent witness that The Builder kept faith with his soul."

Indeed, yes. The "almost three hundred acres" also bear eloquent witness to the fact that Eaton, still digging holes in the ground, worked a vein of gold infinitely more reliable than the one that vanished from his mine—the "Science and Art," as he describes it, "of Persuasion." So strongly does Eaton believe the "profession of salesmanship is the greatest of all professions" that he has established The Foundation for the Science and Art of Persuasion at his alma mater, William Jewell College, Liberty, Missouri.

Forest Lawn reflects Eaton's skill in the "Science." The "country cemetery" with only a "scant dozen acres of developed ground" has grown into Forest Lawn Memorial Park, with a permanent "population" of more than 170,000, increasing at the rate of approximately 6,500 a year.

In fact, business has been so good that there are now two additional Forest Lawn "Memorial Parks" in Los Angeles: Forest Lawn-Hollywood Hills, the focus of a bitter political struggle in the city, and adjacent to it Mount Sinai, designed to attract the growing Jewish population of Los Angeles.

Forest Lawn offers the largest religious painting in the United States, displayed in a building, the Hall of the Crucifixion, specially designed for it. There, for a voluntary contribution of twenty-five cents, the visitor sits comfortably in a large theatre, in one of a "broad sweep of seats, richly upholstered in burgundy, rising tier above tier, matching the splendor of the architecture," and watches the three-thousand-pound curtain open on Jesus at Calvary, forty-five feet high and 195 feet long. A lecture about the painting, supplemented with a moving arrow, is delivered by a tape recording in the special kind of rich, organ-tone voice used throughout Forest Lawn.

There are also hundreds of statues, both originals and reproductions, scattered throughout the three hundred acres. Typical of these is an eighteen-figure group depicting Forest Lawn's solution to the "Mystery of Life." Interpretations of the eighteen figures are supplied: "(17) the atheist, the fool, who grinningly cares not at all; while (18) the stoic sits in silent awe and contemplation of that which he believes he knows but cannot explain with any satisfaction."

At the Court of David there is a huge reproduction of Michelangelo's "David"—with a large fig leaf added by Forest Lawn. An exact copy of the sculptor's "Moses" is displayed at the entrance to the Cathedral Corridor in Memorial Terrace, "the only one," according to Forest Lawn, "cast from clay masks placed directly on the original statue in the Church of Saint Peter in Chains at Rome, Italy."

So that the masks could be made, the Church of Saint Peter had to be closed for a day, something that had not happened before. "I gave a lot of dinners and I bought a lot of wine and I sent a lot of cables and St. Peter's was closed," Eaton modestly explains.

Color photos and post cards of the "Moses" statue can be purchased, along with thousands of other items, at Forest Lawn's souvenir shop. There, browsing visitors can choose from showcases displaying money clips, cocktail napkins, book matches, jigsaw puzzles, and charm brace-lets—all decorated with Forest Lawn motifs. Prices range from a modest twenty-nine cents for a key chain to $125 for a glass vase etched with a Forest Lawn scene.

There are brown plastic nutshells containing little photos of Forest Lawn, ladies' compacts, cigarette lighters, cufflinks, salt and pepper shakers, picture frames, demitasse spoons, bookmarks, cups and saucers, pen and pencil sets, glass bells, wooden plaques, ashtrays, place mats and doilies, perfume and powder sets, jackknives, and a great variety of other goodies, all with an appropriate Forest Lawn theme. Books like *The Loved One*, Evelyn Waugh's satire of Forest Lawn, are not on sale in the souvenir shop. (Eaton occasionally expresses resentment over the treatment given the cemetery by novelists—especially by one writer to whom he extended free run of the park only to be parodied later. But Eaton also understands that such novels have brought world-wide publicity to Forest Lawn and have not adversely affected his sales, which come not from England but from Los Angeles.)

Among the most popular items at the souvenir shop are those showing reproductions of Forest Lawn's three churches, the Church of the Recessional, the Little Church of the Flowers, and the Wee Kirk o' the Heather.

"Providing a dignified setting for final tribute," the three churches "serve also for the joyous and memorable ceremonies of christening and the exchange of marriage vows." Since the churches have opened, more than 43,000 persons have had "memorable" marriages in them. But Forest Lawn makes no money directly from marrying people, and the profits from the souvenir shop are used for the upkeep of the Hall of the Crucifixion. Forest Lawn's real business is burying people.

"The hardest thing in the world to sell," states one of the organization's top officials, "are 'spaces.'" ("Space" is the euphemism used at Forest Lawn for "grave plot.") The reason for the difficulty is that Forest Lawn's sales organization, which comprises about 175 people, concentrates on sales made "Before Need," another phrase in Forest Lawn's own peculiar language of the flowers. Selling cemetery plots "Before Need" rather than "At Time of Need" or "Post Need," although difficult, is very profitable, since under California law a cemetery pays taxes only on its unsold plots. Once a "space" has been sold, it is removed from the tax rolls. Thus it is to the obvious advantage of Forest Lawn to sell off its land as quickly as possible, without waiting for "Need."

There are approximately fifteen hundred individual "spaces" to the acre in Forest Lawn. Prices average $300 per space. There are also rather more elegant neighborhoods at Forest Lawn which are less crowded and therefore more expensive. In the Gardens of Memory, entered only with a special key, there are "memorial sanctuaries designed for families who desire the privacy and protection of crypt interment, but who at the same time long for the open skies and the natural beauty of a verdant garden bathed in sunlight. Under the lawns in the Gardens of Memory have been created a number of monolithically constructed crypts of steel-reinforced concrete."

In the area of ground burial, Forest Lawn has contributed a pleasant innovation. No tombstones are permitted, only markers, set flush with the ground so that there is in fact the pleasant appearance of a park with sweeping green lawns.

But one does not have to be interred to take up permanent residence at Forest Lawn. A number of other arrangements can be made, including being inurned after cremation in the columbarium for as little as $145 or entombed in a mausoleum crypt—which can cost as much as $800,000, as in the case of the Irving Thalberg mausoleum. One can also be placed in a large wall out in the open air. Families may be interred, inurned, or entombed as a unit to maintain "togetherness." Should one feel the need for fresh air while spending the "happy Eternal Life" in a crypt, it is possible, at added cost naturally, to have a ventilating system installed. In the mausoleum, tape-recorded music is played as well.

Inurnment is not restricted to a single form of urn. The law in

California, which has a strong undertakers' lobby, provides that after cremation ashes must be buried or placed in a columbarium. A wide variety of urn designs can be seen, ranging from books and loving cups to miniature coffins.

The price for the casket or urn sets the approximate amount paid for the funeral itself, but here the range is far greater than for the "space." The least expensive casket, with the metal screw heads showing, is $115; the most expensive goes for $17,500.

Forest Lawn's rich, creamy advertising presentations combine the hard and the soft sell. On radio and television, the same institutional approach is as manifest as at the cemetery itself. Programs of church services and organ music are announced in deep, sonorous tones, and practically no mention is made of the company's product. The institutional approach is also used on billboards picturing stained-glass windows or the "Moses" statue. However, many of Forest Lawn's billboards are given over to the hard, competitive sell, featuring what is Hubert Eaton's original contribution to the American way of death: the concept of combining in one place mortuary functions, such as embalming, with funeral services and burial, thus obviating the necessity for outside undertakers, florists, funeral chapels, and long processions to the cemetery. Forest Lawn successfully undertook the elimination of the undertaking middleman.

Today, Forest Lawn's hard-sell slogans of "Everything In One Beautiful Place" and "Just One Phone Call" are widely copied, as are the ads which usually feature back or side views, sometimes in color, of two dry-eyed, well-groomed people talking to a distinguished-looking, gray-mustached bank-president or diplomat-type man, identified by a discreet sign on his desk as a "Funeral Counselor." Sometimes only the "Counselor" is shown, answering the "Just One Phone Call" with the dedicated air of a statesman. It is clear from the ads that at Forest Lawn, where the concept of death has been abolished, the standards of accepted behavior demand no vulgar signs of outward grief.

But even though its competitors copy Forest Lawn today, Eaton faced a bitter battle when he first attempted to bring a mortuary into the cemetery. Forest Lawn's permit to operate a mortuary was given only after a determined struggle waged against him by some of the undertakers who foresaw disaster for themselves in the new trend of combined services. It was during this period that Forest Lawn began to build up its own political operations, which today make it the most powerful spokesman for the industry in the state.

There have been a number of occasions when, in its self-interest, Forest Lawn has had to do battle, sometimes in ways that might have been frowned on by the dignified gentlemen in their ads. From the

1930's to the early 1950's, Forest Lawn was in a running argument with the county assessor's office over the tax assessments made on its property, with Forest Lawn always claiming that the assessments were too high and almost always getting them reduced, even as much as fifty per cent, by the county board of supervisors. Some supervisors did consistently oppose Forest Lawn's plea for tax reduction and supported the assessor, but when the votes were taken a majority always supported Forest Lawn.

In 1938, in one of its early appearances before the board of supervisors, Forest Lawn requested a tax reduction, claiming that the vacant property in the land it then owned would remain unsold until 1973. At the time, the county assessor pointed out that Forest Lawn had "acquired additional property when they said it was going to take thirty-five years to sell out what they now have, yet they go to work and buy seventy-five acres adjoining at a big price."

Ten years later, in 1948, the issue of how long it would take to fill Forest Lawn's vacant "spaces" became one of the central points in a bitter political hassle within the Los Angeles City Council, and the cemetery completely reversed its argument of ten years earlier. At issue was Forest Lawn's request for a zoning change to permit the use, as a cemetery, of 480 acres of land adjoining Griffith Park, a public park and playground in the Hollywood area.

Forest Lawn's first request to develop this new cemetery was submitted to and rejected by the city planning commission in 1946. When the request was again rejected in 1948, Forest Lawn appealed, claiming, in contrast to its 1938 plea of unsold land, that "by the year 1965 all of the available grave spaces in existing cemeteries will have been exhausted."

The odds against Forest Lawn's gaining approval for its plan to open a new cemetery seemed formidable. The planning commission opposed it, the park department opposed it, the board of health commissioners opposed it, the water and power commission opposed it, the board of public works opposed it, the Hollywood chamber of commerce opposed it, and a variety of community groups opposed it. But the "Builder's Dream" triumphed, and on March 9, 1948, the city council voted 11–3 to permit the opening of the cemetery.

Never an organization to leave stones unturned, within a few hours Forest Lawn had hastily dug six holes in the ground and buried six bodies in them; a move which, under state law, immediately qualified the area as a commercial graveyard that could not then be disturbed or moved except under very specific circumstances.

"We got the bodies we buried through the county hospital or from their next of kin in advance," states Ugene Blalock, vice-president and general counsel of Forest Lawn, "and we made no charge for our

140

services. If the vote in the council had gone against us, we would have given them a free burial elsewhere."

In fact, however, the council vote has rarely gone against Forest Lawn, even when the city fathers were voting on whether to give Beverly Hills the street where Eaton lives, thus providing the Digger with a more distinguished address. Although he hasn't moved, Eaton now lives in Beverly Hills.

No one is quite sure about the exact basis for Eaton's influence; or if they are, they're not willing to talk about it for the record. Blalock states that Forest Lawn as an institution has not made, as far as he knows, any campaign contribution in eighteen years, although he adds, "Individuals may make political contributions." But politics aside, it is Hubert Eaton, master salesman, who is chiefly responsible for Forest Lawn's success.

It is from Eaton's mind that has come the creation of the Council of Regents of Memorial Court of Honor, twenty-two "outstanding business and professional men" who advise "on all matters concerning the growth of the Memorial Park as a cultural center of religion and fine arts."

Its members, who include the president of Occidental College and the chancellor of the University of Southern California, wear a handsome, flowing red robe, trimmed with velvet, and an elegant round red hat, also trimmed daintily with velvet, while around their necks hangs a kind of Maltese Cross decoration, perhaps the Order of Forest Lawn.

Such touches as these distinguish the imaginative Eaton from his colleagues. Eaton's devotion to salesmanship, as evidenced by his creating special heart-shaped children's sections at Forest Lawn, named Babyland and Lullabyland, began early in life, according to "The Forest Lawn Story," his biography sold at the souvenir shop.

The son of a college professor, Eaton, states the biography, "sat in his little cubbyhole behind his father's bookshelves ostensibly studying but actually eavesdropping on his father's conversations with callers. Invariably they came for advice on one thing or another but more often than not, it was advice on matters affecting money. From these conversations he learned the word salesmanship and what it meant."

It was Eaton, too, who initiated many Forest Lawn public-service activities—the inspirational speaker made available to service clubs, the thirteen half-hour Bible films, and the giving of the Forest Lawn Awards for Persuasive Writing as a "practical service to students and Christian liberal arts colleges."

Long interested in "small, independent, liberal arts colleges" as being "America's last bulwark against the march of Socialism . . ." Eaton believes that "most" college professors are "semi-socialists at heart" who teach young people that salesmanship "smacks of chicanery, demagoguery, of influencing people against their wills . . ."

But Eaton isn't always so serious. Even when he was at college himself, he always had a "good sense of humor." His biography relates that one of his favorite tricks was to persuade a visitor to allow a funnel to be inserted into the top of his trousers and then to make him balance a penny on his chin and try to drop it into the funnel. While the visitor was in this position, young Hubert "or one of his cronies would pour a cup of cold water into the funnel."

Eaton's "good sense of humor changed little in succeeding years," states his biographer, and it certainly hadn't changed much the night when Eaton gave one of his usual huge, lavish parties for a group of friends and guests. It was called "An Enchanted Evening in the South Pacific," of which "Trader" Hubert Eaton was the master of ceremonies. Elaborate Hawaiian acts were presented, and guests received a large, beautifully printed eight-page souvenir program in color, in which Eaton had himself depicted as "Your Happy Planter," jumping from page to page on a golden-shovel pogo stick.

On the cultural level, the printed program carried a large reproduction of the "David" statue, with a fig leaf, a Hawaiian lei, and a girl curled around its neck, all illustrating a poem, "The Secret of Hubie's David," which described just how it was decided to add a fig leaf to Forest Lawn's copy of Michelangelo's "David" in order not to shock "the ladies of L.A."

But surely the greatest of all the improvements that Eaton has made on the past is Forest Lawn itself. Here, what might have been just an ordinary "country cemetery" has been parlayed into a solemn institution, profitable and widely imitated, looking like Edgar Guest's idea of Heaven brought to earth, while representing a social level to which all people can aspire after death. And in the future, says Hubert Eaton, "When the place is all filled up, my idea, from a financial standpoint, has always been to make Forest Lawn into a museum and charge admission."

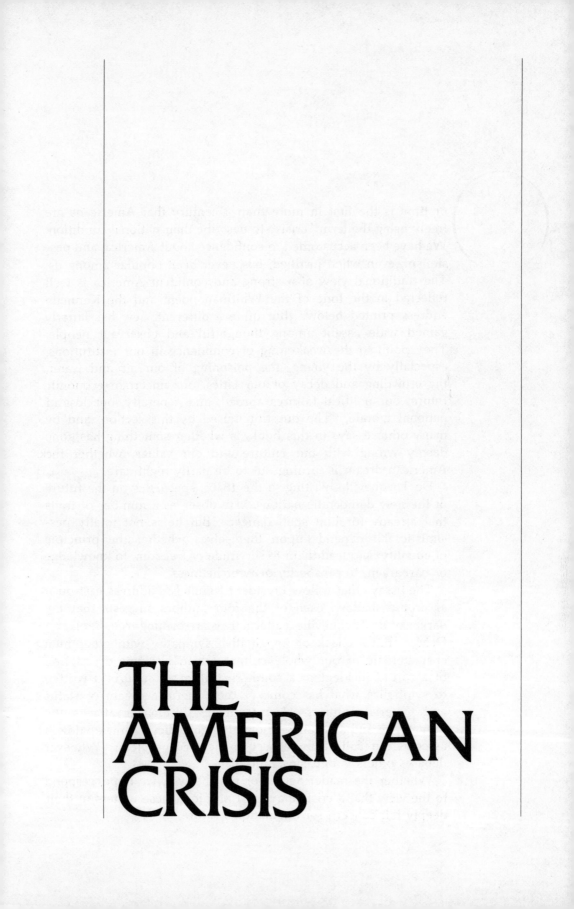

THE
AMERICAN
CRISIS

Our time is the first in more than a century that Americans are freely using the term "crisis" to describe their national condition. We have been accustomed to confidence about America, and pessimism, even when justified, has never been popular among us. The traditional view of a strong and confident America is well reflected in the tone of the Whitman poem and the Kennedy address printed below. But quite a different view has latterly gained wide assent among thoughtful and observant people. They point to the weakening of confidence in our institutions, especially by the young, the poisoning of our air and water, the crowding and decay of our cities, our uncertain economic future, our political failures abroad, and generally, our loss of national morale. The question raised by this section, and by many other essays in this book, is whether something has gone deeply wrong with our culture and our values, whether the American dream is turning out to be partly nightmare.

De Tocqueville, writing in the 1840s, speculates on the future of the new democratic nations. He observes a number of traits that already for him spell danger. But he is not totally pessimistic: "it depends upon themselves whether the principle of equality is to lead them to servitude or freedom, to knowledge or barbarism, to prosperity or wretchedness."

The essays that follow President Kennedy's address cast on it an ironic shadow; each of the four authors suggests that the darker of de Tocqueville's alternatives are coming true. Benjamin DeMott finds a lack of imaginative sympathy with other men characteristic of our whole culture. Joan Didion's description of a sordid incident in a southern California suburb is written to symbolize what has come of the American dream of status and material comfort. Henry Steele Commager attacks the immaturity and arrogance of our foreign policy. James Baldwin assesses our culture in respect to the race problem: "Whoever debases others is debasing himself."

Whether the reader agrees or not, he will, we hope, respond to the view that a crisis may exist and join these writers in their deeply felt concern for our nation's future.

Walt Whitman (1819–1892)

I HEAR AMERICA SINGING

I hear America singing, the varied carols I hear,
Those of mechanics, each one singing his as it should be blithe
    and strong,
The carpenter singing his as he measures his plank or beam,
The mason singing his as he makes ready for work, or leaves off
    work,
The boatman singing what belongs to him in his boat, the deckhand
    singing on the steamboat deck,
The shoemaker singing as he sits on his bench, the hatter singing
    as he stands,
The wood-cutter's song, the ploughboy's on his way in the morn-
    ing, or at noon intermission or at sundown,
The delicious singing of the mother, or of the young wife at work,
    or of the girl sewing or washing,
Each singing what belongs to him or her and to none else,
The day what belongs to the day—at night the party of young
    fellows, robust, friendly,
Singing with open mouths their strong melodious songs.

                                              (1860)

Allen Ginsberg (1926–)

A SUPERMARKET IN CALIFORNIA

What thoughts I have of you tonight, Walt Whitman, for I walked
down the sidestreets under the trees with a headache self-conscious
looking at the full moon.

In my hungry fatigue, and shopping for images, I went into the neon fruit supermarket, dreaming of your enumerations!

What peaches and what penumbras! Whole families shopping at night! Aisles full of husbands! Wives in the avocados, babies in the tomatoes!—and you, Garcia Lorca, what were you doing down by the watermelons?

I saw you, Walt Whitman, childless, lonely old grubber, poking among the meats in the refrigerator and eyeing the grocery boys.

I heard you asking questions of each: Who killed the pork chops? What price bananas? Are you my Angel?

I wandered in and out of the brilliant stacks of cans following you, and followed in my imagination by the store detective.

We strode down the open corridors together in our solitary fancy tasting artichokes, possessing every frozen delicacy, and never passing the cashier.

Where are we going, Walt Whitman? The doors close in an hour. Which way does your beard point tonight?

(I touch your book and dream of our odyssey in the supermarket and feel absurd.)

Will we walk all night through solitary streets? The trees add shade to shade, lights out in the houses, we'll both be lonely.

Will we stroll dreaming of the lost America of love past blue automobiles in driveways, home to our silent cottage?

Ah, dear father, graybeard, lonely old courage-teacher, what America did you have when Charon quit poling his ferry and you got out on a smoking bank and stood watching the boat disappear on the black waters of Lethe?

Berkeley 1955

(1956)

Alexis de Tocqueville

Alexis Charles Henri Clérel de Tocqueville was born in Paris in 1805. He studied law and, as the son of an influential aristocratic family, he was given a judicial post in the court at Versailles. After the July Revolution of 1830, de Tocqueville felt increasingly uncertain of his allegiance to the new government, and he succeeded in securing a commission to go to America to study the prison system. Even closer to his heart was the opportunity to study a democratic system of government at first hand and to judge the possibilities of its application in Europe. For nine months in 1831 and 1832 de Tocqueville and his friend and fellow-magistrate Gustave de Beaumont traveled widely in America, visiting prisons, taking notes, writing letters, interviewing prominent people, requesting memoranda on special subjects, and collecting books and documents. On their return, the two young Frenchmen soon completed their prison report; then each turned to his own study of America. De Tocqueville published his book, De la démocratie en Amérique, *in two parts. The first, a description and critical analysis of the American government in the age of Jackson, was published in 1835. The second, a more philosophical study, with greater regard to the general applicability of American traits, came out in 1840.*

De Tocqueville was elected to the French Chamber of Deputies in 1837 and briefly held the post of Minister for Foreign Affairs under Napoleon III, but his major energies were devoted to political thought rather than to politics. He published L'Ancien régime et la revolution *three years before his death in 1859.*

Democracy in America *was quickly recognized as an important book, and was translated into many languages. The first English translation was made by Henry Reeve, an Englishman, in 1838. This was retranslated by the American scholar Francis Bowen in 1862. The text of the chapters from Part II that we present below is taken from Phillips Bradley's excellent modern edition (with corrections) of the Bowen translation.*

FOUR ESSAYS FROM **DEMOCRACY IN AMERICA**

OF THE PRINCIPAL SOURCE OF BELIEF AMONG DEMOCRATIC NATIONS

At different periods dogmatic belief is more or less common. It arises in different ways, and it may change its object and its form; but under no circumstances will dogmatic belief cease to exist, or, in other words, men will never cease to entertain some opinions on trust and without discussion. If everyone undertook to form all his own opinions and to seek for truth by isolated paths struck out by himself alone, it would follow that no considerable number of men would ever unite in any common belief.

But obviously without such common belief no society can prosper; say, rather, no society can exist; for without ideas held in common there is no common action, and without common action there may still be men, but there is no social body. In order that society should exist and, *a fortiori*, that a society should prosper, it is necessary that the minds of all the citizens should be rallied and held together by certain predominant ideas; and this cannot be the case unless each of them sometimes draws his opinions from the common source and consents to accept certain matters of belief already formed.

If I now consider man in his isolated capacity, I find that dogmatic belief is not less indispensable to him in order to live alone than it is to enable him to co-operate with his fellows. If man were forced to demonstrate for himself all the truths of which he makes daily use, his task would never end. He would exhaust his strength in preparatory demonstrations without ever advancing beyond them. As, from the shortness of his life, he has not the time, nor, from the limits of his intelligence, the capacity, to act in this way, he is reduced to take on trust a host of facts and opinions which he has not had either the time or the power to verify for himself, but which men of greater ability have found out, or which the crowd adopts. On this groundwork he raises for himself the structure of his own thoughts; he is not led to proceed in this manner by choice, but is constrained by the inflexible law of his condition. There is no philosopher in the world so great but that he believes a million things on the faith of other people and accepts a great many more truths than he demonstrates.

This is not only necessary but desirable. A man who should undertake to inquire into everything for himself could devote to each thing but little time and attention. His task would keep his mind in perpetual unrest, which would prevent him from penetrating to the depth of any truth or of making his mind adhere firmly to any conviction. His intellect would be at once independent and powerless. He must therefore make his choice from among the various objects of human belief and adopt many opinions without discussion in order to search the better into that smaller number which he sets apart for investigation. It is true that whoever receives an opinion on the word of another does so far enslave his mind, but it is a salutary servitude, which allows him to make a good use of freedom.

A principle of authority must then always occur, under all circumstances, in some part or other of the moral and intellectual world. Its place is variable, but a place it necessarily has. The independence of individual minds may be greater or it may be less; it cannot be unbounded. Thus the question is, not to know whether any intellectual authority exists in an age of democracy, but simply where it resides and by what standard it is to be measured.

I have shown in the preceding chapter how equality of conditions leads men to entertain a sort of instinctive incredulity of the supernatural and a very lofty and often exaggerated opinion of human understanding. The men who live at a period of social equality are not therefore easily led to place that intellectual authority to which they bow either beyond or above humanity. They commonly seek for the sources of truth in themselves or in those who are like themselves. This would be enough to prove that at such periods no new religion could be established, and that all schemes for such a purpose would be not only impious, but absurd and irrational. It may be foreseen that a democratic people will not easily give credence to divine missions; that they will laugh at modern prophets; and that they will seek to discover the chief arbiter of their belief within, and not beyond, the limits of their kind.

When the ranks of society are unequal, and men unlike one another in condition, there are some individuals wielding the power of superior intelligence, learning, and enlightenment, while the multitude are sunk in ignorance and prejudice. Men living at these aristocratic periods are therefore naturally induced to shape their opinions by the standard of a superior person, or a superior class of persons, while they are averse to recognizing the infallibility of the mass of the people.

The contrary takes place in ages of equality. The nearer the people are drawn to the common level of an equal and similar condition, the less prone does each man become to place implicit faith in a certain man or a certain class of men. But his readiness to believe the multitude increases, and opinion is more than ever mistress of the world. Not only is common opinion the only guide which private judgment retains among a democratic people, but among such a people it possesses a power infinitely beyond what it has elsewhere. At periods of equality men have no faith in one another, by reason of their common resemblance; but this very resemblance gives them almost unbounded confidence in the judgment of the public; for it would seem probable that, as they are all endowed with equal means of judging, the greater truth should go with the greater number.

When the inhabitant of a democratic country compares himself individually with all those about him, he feels with pride that he is the equal of any one of them; but when he comes to survey the totality of his fellows and to place himself in contrast with so huge a body, he is instantly overwhelmed by the sense of his own insignificance and weakness. The same equality that renders him independent of each of his fellow citizens, taken severally, exposes him alone and unprotected to the influence of the greater number. The public, therefore, among a democratic people, has a singular power, which aristocratic nations cannot conceive; for it does not persuade others to its beliefs, but it imposes them and makes them permeate the thinking of everyone by a sort of enormous pressure of the mind of all upon the individual intelligence.

In the United States the majority undertakes to supply a multitude of ready-made opinions for the use of individuals, who are thus relieved from the necessity of forming opinions of their own. Everybody there adopts great numbers of theories, on philosophy, morals, and politics, without inquiry, upon public trust; and if we examine it very closely, it will be perceived that religion itself holds sway there much less as a doctrine of revelation than as a commonly received opinion.

The fact that the political laws of the Americans are such that the majority rules the community with sovereign sway materially increases the power which that majority naturally exercises over the mind. For nothing is more customary in man than to recognize superior wisdom in the person of his oppressor. This political omnipotence of the majority in the United States doubtless augments the influence that public opinion would obtain without it over the minds of each member of the community; but the foundations of that influence do not rest upon it. They must be sought for in the principle of equality itself, not in the more or less popular institutions which men living under that condition may give themselves. The intellectual dominion of the greater number would probably be less absolute among a democratic people governed by a king than in the sphere of a pure democracy, but it will always be extremely absolute; and by whatever political laws men are governed in the ages of equality, it may be foreseen that faith in public opinion will become for them a species of religion, and the majority its ministering prophet.

Thus intellectual authority will be different, but it will not be diminished; and far from thinking that it will disappear, I augur that it may readily acquire too much preponderance and confine the action of private judgment within narrower limits than are suited to either the greatness or the happiness of the human race. In the principle of equality I very clearly discern two tendencies; one leading the mind of every man to untried thoughts, the other prohibiting him from thinking at all. And I perceive how, under the dominion of certain laws, democracy would extinguish that liberty of the mind to which a democratic social condition is favorable; so that, after having broken all the bondage once imposed on it by ranks or by men, the human mind would be closely fettered to the general will of the greatest number.

If the absolute power of a majority were to be substituted by democratic nations for all the different powers that checked or retarded overmuch the energy of individual minds, the evil would only have changed character. Men would not have found the means of independent life; they would simply have discovered (no easy task) a new physiognomy of servitude. There is, and I cannot repeat it too often, there is here matter for profound reflection to those who look on freedom of thought as a holy thing and who hate not only the despot, but despotism. For myself, when I feel the hand of power lie heavy on my brow, I care but little to know who oppresses me; and I am not the more disposed to pass beneath the yoke because it is held out to me by the arms of a million men.

WHY THE AMERICANS ARE MORE ADDICTED TO PRACTICAL THAN TO THEORETICAL SCIENCE

If a democratic state of society and democratic institutions do not retard the onward course of the human mind, they incontestably guide it in one direction in preference to another. Their efforts, thus circumscribed, are still exceedingly great, and I may be pardoned if I pause for a moment to contemplate them.

I had occasion, in speaking of the philosophical method of the American people, to make several remarks that it is necessary to make use of here.

Equality begets in man the desire of judging of everything for himself; it gives him in all things a taste for the tangible and the real, a contempt for tradition and for forms. These general tendencies are principally discernible in the peculiar subject of this chapter.

Those who cultivate the sciences among a democratic people are always afraid of losing their way in visionary speculation. They mistrust systems; they adhere closely to facts and study facts with their own senses. As they do not easily defer to the mere name of any fellow man, they are never inclined to rest upon any man's authority; but, on the contrary, they are unremitting in their efforts to find out the weaker points of their neighbor's doctrine. Scientific precedents have little weight with them; they are never long detained by the subtlety of the schools nor ready to accept big words for sterling coin; they penetrate, as far as they can, into the principal parts of the subject that occupies them, and they like to expound them in the popular language. Scientific pursuits then follow a freer and safer course, but a less lofty one.

The mind, it appears to me, may divide science into three parts.

The first comprises the most theoretical principles and those more abstract notions whose application is either unknown or very remote.

The second is composed of those general truths that still belong to pure theory, but lead nevertheless by a straight and short road to practical results.

Methods of application and means of execution make up the third.

Each of these different portions of science may be separately cultivated, although reason and experience prove that no one of them can prosper long if it is absolutely cut off from the two others.

In America the purely practical part of science is admirably understood, and careful attention is paid to the theoretical portion which is immediately requisite to application. On this head the Americans always display a clear, free, original, and inventive power of mind. But hardly anyone in the United States devotes himself to the essentially theoretical and abstract portion of human knowledge. In this respect the Americans carry to excess a tendency that is, I think, discernible, though in a less degree, among all democratic nations.

Nothing is more necessary to the culture of the higher sciences or of the more elevated departments of science than meditation; and nothing is less suited to meditation than the structure of democratic society. We do not find there, as among an aristocratic people, one class that keeps quiet because it is well off; and another that does not venture to stir because it despairs of improving its condition. Everyone is in motion, some in quest of power, others of gain. In the midst of this universal tumult, this incessant conflict of jarring interests, this continual striving of men after fortune, where is that calm to be found which is necessary for the deeper combinations of the intellect? How can the mind dwell upon any single point when everything whirls around it, and man himself is swept and beaten onwards by the heady current that rolls all things in its course?

You must make the distinction between the sort of permanent agitation that is characteristic of a peaceful democracy and the tumultuous and revolutionary movements that almost always attend the birth and growth of democratic society. When a violent revolution occurs among a highly civilized people, it cannot fail to give a sudden impulse to their feelings and ideas. This is more particularly true of democratic revolutions, which stir up at once all the classes of which a people is composed and beget at the same time inordinate ambition in the breast of every member of the community. The French made surprising advances in the exact sciences at the very time at which they were finishing the destruction of the remains of their former feudal society; yet this sudden fecundity is not to be attributed to democracy, but to the unexampled revolution that attended its growth. What happened at that period was a special incident, and it would be unwise to regard it as the test of a general principle.

Great revolutions are not more common among democratic than

among other nations; I am even inclined to believe that they are less so. But there prevails among those populations a small, distressing motion, a sort of incessant jostling of men, which annoys and disturbs the mind without exciting or elevating it.

Men who live in democratic communities not only seldom indulge in meditation, but they naturally entertain very little esteem for it. A democratic state of society and democratic institutions keep the greater part of men in constant activity; and the habits of mind that are suited to an active life are not always suited to a contemplative one. The man of action is frequently obliged to content himself with the best he can get because he would never accomplish his purpose if he chose to carry every detail to perfection. He has occasion perpetually to rely on ideas that he has not had leisure to search to the bottom; for he is much more frequently aided by the seasonableness of an idea than by its strict accuracy; and in the long run he risks less in making use of some false principles than in spending his time in establishing all his principles on the basis of truth. The world is not led by long or learned demonstrations; a rapid glance at particular incidents, the daily study of the fleeting passions of the multitude, the accidents of the moment, and the art of turning them to account decide all its affairs.

In the ages in which active life is the condition of almost everyone, men are generally led to attach an excessive value to the rapid bursts and superficial conceptions of the intellect, and on the other hand to undervalue unduly its slower and deeper labors. This opinion of the public influences the judgment of the men who cultivate the sciences; they are persuaded that they may succeed in those pursuits without meditation, or are deterred from such pursuits as demand it.

There are several methods of studying the sciences. Among a multitude of men you will find a selfish, mercantile, and trading taste for the discoveries of the mind, which must not be confounded with that disinterested passion which is kindled in the heart of a few. A desire to utilize knowledge is one thing; the pure desire to know is another. I do not doubt that in a few minds and at long intervals an ardent, inexhaustible love of truth springs up, self-supported and living in ceaseless fruition, without ever attaining full satisfaction. It is this ardent love, this proud, disinterested love of what is true, that raises men to the abstract sources of truth, to draw their mother knowledge thence.

If Pascal had had nothing in view but some large gain, or even if he had been stimulated by the love of fame alone, I cannot conceive that he would ever have been able to rally all the powers of his mind, as he did, for the better discovery of the most hidden things of the Creator. When I see him, as it were, tear his soul from all the cares of life to devote it wholly to these researches and, prematurely snapping the links that bind the body to life, die of old age before forty, I stand amazed and perceive that no ordinary cause is at work to produce efforts so extraordinary.

The future will prove whether these passions, at once so rare and so productive, come into being and into growth as easily in the midst of democratic as in aristocratic communities. For myself, I confess that I am slow to believe it.

In aristocratic societies the class that gives the tone to opinion and has the guidance of affairs, being permanently and hereditarily placed above the multitude, naturally conceives a lofty idea of itself and of man. It loves to invent for him noble pleasures, to carve out splendid objects for his ambition. Aristocracies often commit very tyrannical and inhuman actions, but they rarely entertain groveling thoughts; and they show a kind of haughty contempt of little pleasures, even while they indulge in them. The effect is to raise greatly the general pitch of society. In aristocratic ages vast ideas are commonly entertained of the dignity, the power, and the greatness of man. These opinions exert their influence on those who cultivate the sciences as well as on the rest of the community. They facilitate the natural impulse of the mind to the highest regions of thought, and they naturally prepare it to conceive a sublime, almost a divine love of truth.

Men of science at such periods are consequently carried away towards theory; and it even happens that they frequently conceive an inconsiderate contempt for practice. "Archimedes," says Plutarch, "was of so lofty a spirit that he never condescended to write any treatise on the manner of constructing all these engines of war. And as he held this science of inventing and putting together engines, and all arts generally speaking which tended to any useful end in practice, to be vile, low, and mercenary, he spent his talents and his studious hours in writing only of those things whose beauty and subtlety had in them no admixture of necessity." Such is the aristocratic aim of science; it cannot be the same in democratic nations.

The greater part of the men who constitute these nations are extremely eager in the pursuit of actual and physical gratification. As they are always dissatisfied with the position that they occupy and are always free to leave it, they think of nothing but the means of changing their fortune or increasing it. To minds thus predisposed, every new method that leads by a shorter road to wealth, every machine that spares labor, every instrument that diminishes the cost of production, every discovery that facilitates pleasures or augments them, seems to be the grandest effort of the human intellect. It is chiefly from these motives that a democratic people addicts itself to scientific pursuits, that it understands and respects them. In aristocratic ages

154

science is more particularly called upon to furnish gratification to the mind; in democracies, to the body.

You may be sure that the more democratic, enlightened, and free a nation is, the greater will be the number of these interested promoters of scientific genius and the more will discoveries immediately applicable to productive industry confer on their authors gain, fame, and even power. For in democracies the working class take a part in public affairs; and public honors as well as pecuniary remuneration may be awarded to those who deserve them.

In a community thus organized, it may easily be conceived that the human mind may be led insensibly to the neglect of theory; and that it is urged, on the contrary, with unparalleled energy, to the applications of science, or at least to that portion of theoretical science which is necessary to those who make such applications. In vain will some instinctive inclination raise the mind towards the loftier spheres of the intellect; interest draws it down to the middle zone. There it may develop all its energy and restless activity and bring forth wonders. These very Americans who have not discovered one of the general laws of mechanics have introduced into navigation an instrument that changes the aspect of the world.

Assuredly I do not contend that the democratic nations of our time are destined to witness the extinction of the great luminaries of man's intelligence, or even that they will never bring new lights into existence. At the age at which the world has now arrived, and among so many cultivated nations perpetually excited by the fever of productive industry, the bonds that connect the different parts of science cannot fail to strike the observer; and the taste for practical science itself, if it is enlightened, ought to lead men not to neglect theory. In the midst of so many attempted applications of so many experiments repeated every day, it is almost impossible that general laws should not frequently be brought to light; so that great discoveries would be frequent, though great inventors may be few.

I believe, moreover, in high scientific vocations. If the democratic principle does not, on the one hand, induce men to cultivate science for its own sake, on the other it enormously increases the number of those who do cultivate it. Nor is it credible that among so great a multitude a speculative genius should not from time to time arise inflamed by the love of truth alone. Such a one, we may be sure, would dive into the deepest mysteries of nature, whatever the spirit of his country and his age. He requires no assistance in his course; it is enough that he is not checked in it. All that I mean to say is this: permanent inequality of conditions leads men to confine themselves to the arrogant and sterile research for abstract truths, while the social condition and the institutions of democracy prepare them to seek the

155

immediate and useful practical results of the sciences. This tendency is natural and inevitable; it is curious to be acquainted with it, and it may be necessary to point it out.

If those who are called upon to guide the nations of our time clearly discerned from afar off these new tendencies, which will soon be irresistible, they would understand that, possessing education and freedom, men living in democratic ages cannot fail to improve the industrial part of science, and that henceforward all the efforts of the constituted authorities ought to be directed to support the highest branches of learning and to foster the nobler passion for science itself. In the present age the human mind must be coerced into theoretical studies; it runs of its own accord to practical applications; and, instead of perpetually referring it to the minute examination of secondary effects, it is well to divert it from them sometimes, in order to raise it up to the contemplation of primary causes.

Because the civilization of ancient Rome perished in consequence of the invasion of the Barbarians, we are perhaps too apt to think that civilization cannot perish in any other manner. If the light by which we are guided is ever extinguished, it will dwindle by degrees and expire of itself. By dint of close adherence to mere applications, principles would be lost sight of; and when the principles were wholly forgotten, the methods derived from them would be ill pursued. New methods could no longer be invented, and men would continue, without intelligence and without art, to apply scientific processes no longer understood.

When Europeans first arrived in China, three hundred years ago, they found that almost all the arts had reached a certain degree of perfection there, and they were surprised that a people which had attained this point should not have gone beyond it. At a later period they discovered traces of some higher branches of science that had been lost. The nation was absorbed in productive industry; the greater part of its scientific processes had been preserved, but science itself no longer existed there. This served to explain the strange immobility in which they found the minds of this people. The Chinese, in following the track of their forefathers, had forgotten the reasons by which the latter had been guided. They still used the formula without asking for its meaning; they retained the instrument, but they no longer possessed the art of altering or renewing it. The Chinese, then, had lost the power of change; for them improvement was impossible. They were compelled at all times and in all points to imitate their predecessors lest they should stray into utter darkness by deviating for an instant from the path already laid down for them. The source of human knowledge was all but dry; and though the stream still ran on, it could neither swell its waters nor alter its course.

Notwithstanding this, China had existed peaceably for centuries. The invaders who had conquered the country assumed the manners of the inhabitants, and order prevailed there. A sort of physical prosperity was everywhere discernible; revolutions were rare, and war was, so to speak, unknown.

It is then a fallacy to flatter ourselves with the reflection that the barbarians are still far from us; for if there are some nations that allow civilization to be torn from their grasp, there are others who themselves trample it underfoot.

WHAT SORT OF DESPOTISM DEMOCRATIC NATIONS HAVE TO FEAR

I had remarked during my stay in the United States that a democratic state of society, similar to that of the Americans, might offer singular facilities for the establishment of despotism; and I perceived, upon my return to Europe, how much use had already been made, by most of our rulers, of the notions, the sentiments, and the wants created by this same social condition, for the purpose of extending the circle of their power. This led me to think that the nations of Christendom would perhaps eventually undergo some oppression like that which hung over several of the nations of the ancient world.

A more accurate examination of the subject, and five years of further meditation, have not diminished my fears, but have changed their object.

No sovereign ever lived in former ages so absolute or so powerful as to undertake to administer by his own agency, and without the assistance of intermediate powers, all the parts of a great empire; none ever attempted to subject all his subjects indiscriminately to strict uniformity of regulation and personally to tutor and direct every member of the community. The notion of such an undertaking never occurred to the human mind; and if any man had conceived it, the want of information, the imperfection of the administrative system, and, above all, the natural obstacles caused by the inequality of conditions would speedily have checked the execution of so vast a design.

When the Roman emperors were at the height of their power, the different nations of the empire still preserved usages and customs of great diversity; although they were subject to the same monarch, most of the provinces were separately administered; they abounded in powerful and active municipalities; and although the whole government of the empire was centered in the hands of the Emperor alone and he always remained, in case of need, the supreme arbiter in all matters, yet the details of social life and private occupations lay for the most part beyond his control. The emperors possessed, it is true, an immense and unchecked power, which allowed them to gratify all their whimsical tastes and to employ for that purpose the whole strength of the state. They frequently abused that power arbitrarily to deprive their subjects of property or of life; their tyranny was extremely onerous to the few, but it did not reach the many; it was confined to some few main objects and neglected the rest; it was violent, but its range was limited.

It would seem that if despotism were to be established among the democratic nations of our days, it might assume a different character; it would be more extensive and more mild; it would degrade men without tormenting them. I do not question that, in an age of instruction and equality like our own, sovereigns might more easily succeed in collecting all political power into their own hands and might interfere more habitually and decidedly with the circle of private interests than any sovereign of antiquity could ever do. But this same principle of equality which facilitates despotism tempers its rigor. We have seen how the customs of society become more humane and gentle in proportion as men become more equal and alike. When no member of the community has much power or much wealth, tyranny is, as it were, without opportunities and a field of action. As all fortunes are scanty, the passions of men are naturally circumscribed, their imagination limited, their pleasures simple. This universal moderation moderates the sovereign himself and checks within certain limits the inordinate stretch of his desires.

Independently of these reasons, drawn from the nature of the state of society itself, I might add many others arising from causes beyond my subject; but I shall keep within the limits I have laid down.

Democratic governments may become violent and even cruel at certain periods of extreme effervescence or of great danger, but these crises will be rare and brief. When I consider the petty passions of our contemporaries, the mildness of their manners, the extent of their education, the purity of their religion, the gentleness of their morality, their regular and industrious habits, and the restraint which they almost all observe in their vices no less than in their virtues, I have no fear that they will meet with tyranny in their rules, but rather with guardians.[1]

I think, then, that the species of oppression by which democratic nations are menaced is unlike anything that ever before existed in the world; our contemporaries will find no prototype of it in their memories. I seek in vain for an expression that will accurately convey the whole of the idea I have formed of it; the old words *despotism* and

---

[1] See Appendix A, page 162.

tyranny are inappropriate: the thing itself is new, and since I cannot name, I must attempt to define it.

I seek to trace the novel features under which despotism may appear in the world. The first thing that strikes the observation is an innumerable multitude of men, all equal and alike, incessantly endeavoring to procure the petty and paltry pleasures with which they glut their lives. Each of them, living apart, is as a stranger to the fate of all the rest; his children and his private friends constitute to him the whole of mankind. As for the rest of his fellow citizens, he is close to them, but does not see them; he touches them, but he does not feel them; he exists only in himself and for himself alone; and if his kindred still remain to him, he may be said at any rate to have lost his country.

Above this race of men stands an immense and tutelary power, which takes upon itself alone to secure their gratifications and to watch over their fate. That power is absolute, minute, regular, provident, and mild. It would be like the authority of a parent if, like that authority, its object was to prepare men for manhood; but it seeks, on the contrary, to keep them in perpetual childhood: it is well content that the people should rejoice, provided they think of nothing but rejoicing. For their happiness such a government willingly labors, but it chooses to be the sole agent and the only arbiter of that happiness; it provides for their security, foresees and supplies their necessities, facilitates their pleasures, manages their principal concerns, directs their industry, regulates the descent of property, and subdivides their inheritances: what remains, but to spare them all the care of thinking and all the trouble of living?

Thus it every day renders the exercise of the free agency of man less useful and less frequent; it circumscribes the will within a narrower range and gradually robs a man of all the uses of himself. The principle of equality has prepared men for these things; it has predisposed men to endure them and often to look on them as benefits.

After having thus successively taken each member of the community in its powerful grasp and fashioned him at will, the supreme power then extends its arm over the whole community. It covers the surface of society with a network of small complicated rules, minute and uniform, through which the most original minds and the most energetic characters cannot penetrate, to rise above the crowd. The will of man is not shattered, but softened, bent, and guided; men are seldom forced by it to act, but they are constantly restrained from acting. Such a power does not destroy, but it prevents existence; it does not tyrannize, but it compresses, enervates, extinguishes, and stupefies a people, till each nation is reduced to nothing better than a flock of timid and industrious animals, of which the government is the shepherd.

I have always thought that servitude of the regular, quiet, and gentle kind which I have just described might be combined more easily than is commonly believed with some of the outward forms of freedom, and that it might even establish itself under the wing of the sovereignty of the people.

Our contemporaries are constantly excited by two conflicting passions: they want to be led, and they wish to remain free. As they cannot destroy either the one or the other of these contrary propensities, they strive to satisfy them both at once. They devise a sole, tutelary, and all-powerful form of government, but elected by the people. They combine the principle oi centralization and that of popular sovereignty; this gives them a respite: they console themselves for being in tutelage by the reflection that they have chosen their own guardians. Every man allows himself to be put in leading-strings, because he sees that it is not a person or a class of persons, but the people at large who hold the end of his chain.

By this system the people shake off their state of dependence just long enough to select their master and then relapse into it again. A great many persons at the present day are quite contented with this sort of compromise between administrative despotism and the sovereignty of the people; and they think they have done enough for the protection of individual freedom when they have surrendered it to the power of the nation at large. This does not satisfy me: the nature of him I am to obey signifies less to me than the fact of extorted obedience.

I do not deny, however, that a constitution of this kind appears to me to be infinitely preferable to one which, after having concentrated all the powers of government, should vest them in the hands of an irresponsible person or body of persons. Of all the forms that democratic despotism could assume, the latter would assuredly be the worst.

When the sovereign is elective, or narrowly watched by a legislature which is really elective and independent, the oppression that he exercises over individuals is sometimes greater, but it is always less degrading; because every man, when he is oppressed and disarmed, may still imagine that, while he yields obedience, it is to himself he yields it, and that it is to one of his own inclinations that all the rest give way. In like manner, I can understand that when the sovereign represents the nation and is dependent upon the people, the rights and the power of which every citizen is deprived serve not only the head of the state, but the state itself; and that private persons derive some return from the sacrifice of their independence which they have made to the public. To create a representation of the people in every centralized country is, therefore, to diminish the evil that extreme centralization may produce, but not to get rid of it.

I admit that, by this means, room is left for the intervention of individuals in the more important affairs; but it is not the less suppressed in the smaller and more private ones. It must not be forgotten that it is especially dangerous to enslave men in the minor details of life. For my own part, I should be inclined to think freedom less necessary in great things than in little ones, if it were possible to be secure of the one without possessing the other.

Subjection in minor affairs breaks out every day and is felt by the whole community indiscriminately. It does not drive men to resistance, but it crosses them at every turn, till they are led to surrender the exercise of their own will. Thus their spirit is gradually broken and their character enervated; whereas that obedience which is exacted on a few important but rare occasions only exhibits servitude at certain intervals and throws the burden of it upon a small number of men. It is in vain to summon a people who have been rendered so dependent on the central power to choose from time to time the representatives of that power; this rare and brief exercise of their free choice, however important it may be, will not prevent them from gradually losing the faculties of thinking, feeling, and acting for themselves, and thus gradually falling below the level of humanity.

I add that they will soon become incapable of exercising the great and only privilege which remains to them. The democratic nations that have introduced freedom into their political constitution at the very time when they were augmenting the despotism of their administrative constitution have been led into strange paradoxes. To manage those minor affairs in which good sense is all that is wanted, the people are held to be unequal to the task; but when the government of the country is at stake, the people are invested with immense powers; they are alternately made the playthings of their ruler, and his masters, more than kings and less than men. After having exhausted all the different modes of election without finding one to suit their purpose, they are still amazed and still bent on seeking further; as if the evil they notice did not originate in the constitution of the country far more than in that of the electoral body.

It is indeed difficult to conceive how men who have entirely given up the habit of self-government should succeed in making a proper choice of those by whom they are to be governed; and no one will ever believe that a liberal, wise, and energetic government can spring from the suffrages of a subservient people.[2]

A constitution republican in its head and ultra-monarchical in all its other parts has always appeared to me to be a shortlived monster. The vices of rulers and the ineptitude of the people would speedily

---

[2] See Appendix B, page 162.

bring about its ruin; and the nation, weary of its representatives and of itself, would create freer institutions or soon return to stretch itself at the feet of a single master.

APPENDIX A

I have often asked myself what would happen if, amid the laxity of democratic customs, and as a consequence of the restless spirit of the army, a military government were ever to be established among any of the nations of our times. I think that such a government would not differ much from the outline I have drawn in the chapter to which this note refers, and that it would retain none of the fierce characteristics of a military oligarchy. I am persuaded that in such a case a sort of fusion would take place between the practices of civil officials and those of the military service. The administration would assume something of a military character, and the army some of the practices of the civil administration. The result would be a regular, clear, exact, and absolute system of government; the people would become the reflection of the army, and the community be regimented like a garrison.

APPENDIX B

It cannot be absolutely or generally affirmed that the greatest danger of the present age is license or tyranny, anarchy or despotism. Both are equally to be feared; and the one may proceed as easily as the other from one and the same cause: namely, that *general apathy* which is the consequence of individualism. It is because this apathy exists that the executive government, having mustered a few troops, is able to commit acts of oppression one day; and the next day a party which has mustered some thirty men in its ranks can also commit acts of oppression. Neither the one nor the other can establish anything which will last; and the causes which enable them to succeed easily prevent them from succeeding for long; they rise because nothing opposes them, and they sink because nothing supports them. The proper object, therefore, of our most strenuous resistance is far less either anarchy or despotism than that apathy which may almost indifferently beget either the one or the other.

GENERAL SURVEY OF THE SUBJECT

Before finally closing the subject that I have now discussed, I should like to take a parting survey of all the different characteristics of modern society and appreciate at last the general influence to be exercised by the principle of equality upon the fate of mankind; but I am stopped by the difficulty of the task, and, in presence of so great a theme, my sight is troubled and my reason fails.

The society of the modern world, which I have sought to delineate and which I seek to judge, has but just come into existence. Time has not yet shaped it into perfect form; the great revolution by which it has been created is not yet over; and amid the occurrences of our time it is almost impossible to discern what will pass away with the revolution itself and what will survive its close. The world that is rising into existence is still half encumbered by the remains of the world that is waning into decay; and amid the vast perplexity of human affairs none can say how much of ancient institutions and former customs will remain or how much will completely disappear.

Although the revolution that is taking place in the social condition, the laws, the opinions, and the feelings of men is still very far from being terminated, yet its results already admit of no comparison with anything that the world has ever before witnessed. I go back from age to age up to the remotest antiquity, but I find no parallel to what is occurring before my eyes; as the past has ceased to throw its light upon the future, the mind of man wanders in obscurity.

Nevertheless, in the midst of a prospect so wide, so novel, and so confused, some of the more prominent characteristics may already be discerned and pointed out. The good things and the evils of life are more equally distributed in the world: great wealth tends to disappear, the number of small fortunes to increase; desires and gratifications are multiplied, but extraordinary prosperity and irremediable penury are alike unknown. The sentiment of ambition is universal, but the scope of ambition is seldom vast. Each individual stands apart in solitary weakness, but society at large is active, provident, and powerful; the performances of private persons are insignificant, those of the state immense.

There is little energy of character, but customs are mild and laws humane. If there are few instances of exalted heroism or of virtues of the highest, brightest, and purest temper, men's habits are regular, violence is rare, and cruelty almost unknown. Human existence becomes longer and property more secure; life is not adorned with brilliant trophies, but it is extremely easy and tranquil. Few pleasures are either very refined or very coarse, and highly polished manners are as uncommon as great brutality of tastes. Neither men of great learning nor extremely ignorant communities are to be met with; genius becomes more rare, information more diffused. The human mind is impelled by the small efforts of all mankind combined together, not by the strenuous activity of a few men. There is less perfection, but more abundance, in all the productions of the arts.

The ties of race, of rank, and of country are relaxed; the great bond of humanity is strengthened.

If I endeavor to find out the most general and most prominent of all these different characteristics, I perceive that what is taking place in men's fortunes manifests itself under a thousand other forms. Almost all extremes are softened or blunted: all that was most prominent is superseded by some middle term, at once less lofty and less low, less brilliant and less obscure, than what before existed in the world.

When I survey this countless multitude of beings, shaped in each other's likeness, amid whom nothing rises and nothing falls, the sight of such universal uniformity saddens and chills me and I am tempted to regret that state of society which has ceased to be. When the world was full of men of great importance and extreme insignificance, of great wealth and extreme poverty, of great learning and extreme ignorance, I turned aside from the latter to fix my observation on the former alone, who gratified my sympathies. But I admit that this gratification arose from my own weakness; it is because I am unable to see at once all that is around me that I am allowed thus to select and separate the objects of my predilection from among so many others. Such is not the case with that Almighty and Eternal Being whose gaze necessarily includes the whole of created things and who surveys distinctly, though all at once, mankind and man.

We may naturally believe that it is not the singular prosperity of the few, but the greater well-being of all that is most pleasing in the sight of the Creator and Preserver of men. What appears to me to be man's decline is, to His eye, advancement; what afflicts me is acceptable to Him. A state of equality is perhaps less elevated, but it is more just: and its justice constitutes its greatness and its beauty. I would strive, then, to raise myself to this point of the divine contemplation and thence to view and to judge the concerns of men.

No man on the earth can as yet affirm, absolutely and generally, that the new state of the world is better than its former one; but it is already easy to perceive that this state is different. Some vices and some virtues were so inherent in the constitution of an aristocratic nation and are so opposite to the character of a modern people that they can never be infused into it; some good tendencies and some bad propensities which were unknown to the former are natural to the latter; some ideas suggest themselves spontaneously to the imagination of the one which are utterly repugnant to the mind of the other. They are like two distinct orders of human beings, each of which has its own merits and defects, its own advantages and its own evils. Care must therefore be taken not to judge the state of society that is now coming into existence by notions derived from a state of society that no longer exists; for as these states of society are exceedingly different

164

in their structure, they cannot be submitted to a just or fair comparison. It would be scarcely more reasonable to require of our contemporaries the peculiar virtues which originated in the social condition of their forefathers, since that social condition is itself fallen and has drawn into one promiscuous ruin the good and evil that belonged to it.

But as yet these things are imperfectly understood. I find that a great number of my contemporaries undertake to make a selection from among the institutions, the opinions, and the ideas that originated in the aristocratic constitution of society as it was; a portion of these elements they would willingly relinquish, but they would keep the remainder and transplant them into their new world. I fear that such men are wasting their time and their strength in virtuous but unprofitable efforts. The object is, not to retain the peculiar advantages which the inequality of conditions bestows upon mankind, but to secure the new benefits which equality may supply. We have not to seek to make ourselves like our progenitors, but to strive to work out that species of greatness and happiness which is our own.

For myself, who now look back from this extreme limit of my task and discover from afar, but at once, the various objects which have attracted my more attentive investigation upon my way, I am full of apprehensions and of hopes. I perceive mighty dangers which it is possible to ward off, mighty evils which may be avoided or alleviated; and I cling with a firmer hold to the belief that for democratic nations to be virtuous and prosperous, they require but to will it.

I am aware that many of my contemporaries maintain that nations are never their own masters here below, and that they necessarily obey some insurmountable and unintelligent power, arising from anterior events, from their race, or from the soil and climate of their country. Such principles are false and cowardly; such principles can never produce aught but feeble men and pusillanimous nations. Providence has not created mankind entirely independent or entirely free. It is true that around every man a fatal circle is traced beyond which he cannot pass; but within the wide verge of that circle he is powerful and free; as it is with man, so with communities. The nations of our time cannot prevent the conditions of men from becoming equal, but it depends upon themselves whether the principle of equality is to lead them to servitude or freedom, to knowledge or barbarism, to prosperity or wretchedness.

John Fitzgerald Kennedy

The thirty-fifth President of the United States was born in Massachusetts in 1917. He studied at the London School of Economics under Harold Laski in 1935 and briefly at Princeton. He then enrolled at Harvard and received a B.S. in 1940. In World War II he served in the Navy as a PT boat commander and was decorated with the Navy and Marine Corps medal. He ran for Congress in 1946 and served two terms as representative from the eleventh Massachusetts district. He was senator from 1953 to 1961 and President from 1961 until his assassination in Dallas, Texas, on November 22, 1963. His published writings include Why England Slept *(1940),* Profiles in Courage *(1956), which won a Pulitzer Prize for biography,* The Strategy of Peace *(1960),* To Turn the Tide *(1962), and* A Nation of Immigrants *(1964). His inaugural address was delivered at the Capitol, January 20, 1961.*

INAUGURAL ADDRESS

VICE PRESIDENT JOHNSON, MR. SPEAKER, MR. CHIEF JUSTICE, PRESIDENT EISEN-HOWER, VICE PRESIDENT NIXON, PRESIDENT TRUMAN, REVEREND CLERGY, FELLOW CITIZENS:

We observe today not a victory of party but a celebration of freedom —symbolizing an end as well as a beginning—signifying renewal as well as change. For I have sworn before you and Almighty God the same solemn oath our forebears prescribed nearly a century and three quarters ago.

The world is very different now. For man holds in his mortal hands the power to abolish all forms of human poverty and all forms of human life. And yet the same revolutionary beliefs for which our forebears fought are still at issue around the globe—the belief that the rights of man come not from the generosity of the state but from the hand of God.

We dare not forget today that we are the heirs of that first revolution. Let the word go forth from this time and place, to friend and foe alike, that the torch has been passed to a new generation of

Americans—born in this century, tempered by war, disciplined by a hard and bitter peace, proud of our ancient heritage—and unwilling to witness or permit the slow undoing of those human rights to which this Nation has always been committed, and to which we are committed today at home and around the world.

Let every nation know, whether it wishes us well or ill, that we shall pay any price, bear any burden, meet any hardship, support any friend, oppose any foe to assure the survival and the success of liberty.

This much we pledge—and more.

To those old allies whose cultural and spiritual origins we share, we pledge the loyalty of faithful friends. United, there is little we cannot do in a host of cooperative ventures. Divided, there is little we can do—for we dare not meet a powerful challenge at odds and split asunder.

To those new states whom we welcome to the ranks of the free, we pledge our word that one form of colonial control shall not have passed away merely to be replaced by a far more iron tyranny. We shall not always expect to find them supporting our view. But we shall always hope to find them strongly supporting their own freedom —and to remember that, in the past, those who foolishly sought power by riding the back of the tiger ended up inside.

To those peoples in the huts and villages of half the globe struggling to break the bonds of mass misery, we pledge our best efforts to help them help themselves, for whatever period is required—not because the Communists may be doing it, not because we seek their votes, but because it is right. If a free society cannot help the many who are poor, it cannot save the few who are rich.

To our sister republics south of our border, we offer a special pledge—to convert our good words into good deeds—in a new alliance for progress—to assist free men and free governments in casting off the chains of poverty. But this peaceful revolution of hope cannot become the prey of hostile powers. Let all our neighbors know that we shall join with them to oppose aggression or subversion anywhere in the Americas. And let every other power know that this hemisphere intends to remain the master of its own house.

To that world assembly of sovereign states, the United Nations, our last best hope in an age where the instruments of war have far outpaced the instruments of peace, we renew our pledge of support—to prevent it from becoming merely a forum for invective—to strengthen its shield of the new and the weak—and to enlarge the area in which its writ may run.

Finally, to those nations who would make themselves our adversary, we offer not a pledge but a request: that both sides begin anew the quest for peace, before the dark powers of destruction unleashed by science engulf all humanity in planned or accidental self-destruction.

We dare not tempt them with weakness. For only when our arms are sufficient beyond doubt can we be certain beyond doubt that they will never be employed.

But neither can two great and powerful groups of nations take comfort from our present course—both sides overburdened by the cost of modern weapons, both rightly alarmed by the steady spread of the deadly atom, yet both racing to alter that uncertain balance of terror that stays the hand of mankind's final war.

So let us begin anew—remembering on both sides that civility is not a sign of weakness, and sincerity is always subject to proof. Let us never negotiate out of fear. But let us never fear to negotiate.

Let both sides explore what problems unite us instead of belaboring those problems which divide us.

Let both sides, for the first time, formulate serious and precise proposals for the inspection and control of arms—and bring the absolute power to destroy other nations under the absolute control of all nations.

Let both sides seek to invoke the wonders of science instead of its terrors. Together let us explore the stars, conquer the deserts, eradicate disease, tap the ocean depths, and encourage the arts and commerce.

Let both sides unite to heed in all corners of the earth the command of Isaiah—to "undo the heavy burdens . . . [and] let the oppressed go free."

And if a beachhead of cooperation may push back the jungle of suspicion, let both sides join in creating a new endeavor, not a new balance of power, but a new world of law, where the strong are just and the weak secure and the peace preserved.

All this will not be finished in the first one hundred days. Nor will it be finished in the first one thousand days, nor in the life of this Administration, nor even perhaps in our lifetime on this planet. But let us begin.

In your hands, my fellow citizens, more than mine, will rest the final success or failure of our course. Since this country was founded, each generation of Americans has been summoned to give testimony to its national loyalty. The graves of young Americans who answered the call to service surround the globe.

Now the trumpet summons us again—not as a call to bear arms, though arms we need—not as a call to battle, though embattled we are—but a call to bear the burden of a long twilight struggle, year in and year out, "rejoicing in hope, patient in tribulation"—a struggle against the common enemies of man: tyranny, poverty, disease, and war itself.

Can we forge against these enemies a grand and global alliance, North and South, East and West, that can assure a more fruitful life for all mankind? Will you join in that historic effort?

In the long history of the world, only a few generations have been granted the role of defending freedom in its hour of maximum danger. I do not shrink from this responsibility—I welcome it. I do not believe that any of us would exchange places with any other people or any other generation. The energy, the faith, the devotion which we bring to this endeavor will light our country and all who serve it—and the glow from that fire can truly light the world.

And so, my fellow Americans: ask not what your country can do for you—ask what you can do for your country.

My fellow citizens of the world: ask not what America will do for you, but what together we can do for the freedom of man.

Finally, whether you are citizens of America or citizens of the world, ask of us here the same high standards of strength and sacrifice which we ask of you. With a good conscience our only sure reward, with history the final judge of our deeds, let us go forth to lead the land we love, asking His blessing and His help, but knowing that here on earth God's work must truly be our own.

Benjamin DeMott

Benjamin DeMott (born 1924) was educated at George Washington University and at Harvard, where he received the Ph.D. in 1953. He is now Professor of English at Amherst. Professor DeMott received the Harbison Award for distinguished teaching from the Danforth Foundation in 1969 and has twice been a Guggenheim Fellow. In addition to being a scholar, he is a novelist and an extremely productive literary and social critic. He writes regularly for Harper's, American Scholar, Esquire, *and* Saturday Review, *and has often spoken to educational conferences. His favorite subject is American popular culture, and his highly individual style is of a piece with his sharp, uncompromising views. Among his books are the novels* The Body's Cage

(1959) and A Married Man (1968), and three essay collections:
Hells and Benefits (1962), You Don't Say (1966), and
Supergrow (1969). The present essay is from the 1968 American
Scholar.

AMERICA THE UNIMAGINING

A man in his early fifties, vigorous, strong faced, well liked in his
town. Family man, business success (small-city merchandising operation). No reader but a great keeper-up—business papers, hard news,
world events, facts that matter. Pleasures? He "gets a kick out of"
gadgets and machines—wild stereo layout in the cathedral living room,
complicated ship-to-shore gear on his boat, a genuine systems approach
for stock control in the stores. Further pleasures: he's outdoorsy,
handy at home, a Dartmouth man, skier, active in business and community clubs, nonchurchgoer, nonpolitical arguefier—

At parties he doesn't talk much to women. Also he stands back
a little from his kids. Pleasant-tentative with his bright daughter,,
straightarrowish "Dad" with his teen-aged boys. Stands back, too,
from the "creative" phases of the business—buying side, advertising,
display, et cetera—leaving this to a younger brother. (Let something
"real sticky" turn up anywhere, though, and nobody but he can deal.
Who else, for instance, would be up to a face-off with the old family
friend, one of his store managers, when the detective service reports
the man is robbing them blind?) As for a personality profile—

—I am more interested in a man's behavior than in his inner life,
Check. In shaping character, externals are more important than inner
tendencies, Check. I sometimes have trouble figuring out the behavior
of people who are emotionally unstable, Check. Math is one of my
best subjects, Check. I think I'm practical and efficient when there's
something that has to be done, Check. I don't have the temperament
for the "romantic" point of view, Check. I have few emotional problems, Check. A first principle with me is that it's a man's duty to
adjust himself to his environment, Check. I am a fairly conventional
person, Check. My relations with other people are usually uncomplicated, Check. My ideas are more often sound and sensible than
unusual or imaginative, Check. I say what I have to say in a few
simple words so that I'm easily understood, Check. There's a lot in
the economic interpretation of history, Check. I find it easier to deal
with concrete facts in one special field than with general ideas about

man or nature, Check. I think science offers as good a guide as any to the future, Check. When I'm working out a problem I try to stick as close as possible to the facts, Check. I enjoy an intimate conversation with one person more than general conversation with several, No. When I hear a person talk, I think more about his personality than I do about what he's saying, No. I think I have a good understanding of women, No. I love to talk about my innermost feelings to a sympathetic friend, Nah. I often think I can feel my way into the innermost being of another person, No. It takes a good deal to make me angry, Check. Unselfishness and sympathy are more desirable than high ideals and ambitions, False. I'm apt to make up stories by myself about the private thoughts and experiences of the people I meet, No. I believe the world may be well lost for love, No. I live in my imagination as much as I do in the external world, No. I dislike everything that has to do with money—buying, selling, bargaining, Oh, sure. I like being in the thick of the action, Yes, emphatically. I like to have people about me most of the time, Yes, emphatically. . . .

Other items worth noting about this man? One: inclined to treat characters as functions, he regularly "explains" people by telling you what they do (a parenthetical phrase—Harry's a doctor, Hank's a cop, Lucille's had a couple of pairs of twins). Another point: the fellow is good to tie up by, any sloppy night in any Maine harbor, and makes, in general, a fine summer neighbor—fun outings to the island, family picnics, softball on the sand, sun's over the yardarm, *et cetera*. Further point: when you step away from him, sit in judgment, dwell on his limits, you not only feel like a heel: you discover again that one of the several reasons for not judging is that the minute it's done, the judge is judged, stands fully visible in his own fatuity and self-congratulation, beyond sympathy, ripe for sentence himself. Yet another item: the man is representative. Tens of millions are excluded from his place, just at this moment: going from the middle up in society is where you're likely to find him, not from the middle down. But the excluded millions can't forever escape; even now they are being graded "up" on his curve. Every year the movement of economic life shoots tens of thousands toward him—into his set of mind, his style, his inward truth. He's no "middle-class stereotype," in short; he is an American destination or finish line, the possible end of the race.

Finally, last point about the man: he is in trouble. There's a withering in him, a metaphorical arm gone, some limb, some key part missing, something stunted. The present judge speaks quickly, on the run, hoping to hide himself from the next judge: the man just described is in one flat word, *unfulfilled*.

To say as much is, by instant extension, to discount the seriousness of the famous American commitment to the ideal of individual self-fulfillment. And while such discounting is standard practice among the knowing, it isn't at first glance easy to defend. Granted, the language in which national commitments and values are usually spelled out—the language of Civics classes and Scouting Award nights—does beg to be mocked. "The social organization of America is compatible with its free political institutions . . ." "America is a society in which equality of opportunity is supported by specific social mechanisms, including classlessness, a wide spectrum of inviolable and equal individual rights guaranteed to all individuals, guarantees of minimum welfare for all and special assistance to any that are at unusual economic disadvantage . . ." "Enhancing the dignity of the individual citizen, developing his capabilities for self-fulfillment, is a prime concern of the American government . . . The environments which help to shape the character of the individual—his home life, education, religious training, occupation, etc.—are in varying degrees matters of public concern. The object of this concern is to develop typical traits of character—independence of spirit, respect for the rights of others, cooperativeness, sense of civic responsibility—and others which will make the individual a better, more constructive citizen." —Formulations like these cry out for qualification, amendment, hints of stylish self-restraint. Some humility, please.

But the cry for humility can itself become cant. Live abroad in a middle-class community—leafy Edgbaston in England, say, or on the Lisbon-Cascais line, and you turn up only ambiguous testimony on the matter of the American versus the European sense of civic responsibility. But in the area of attitudes and policies concerning education, those ambiguities disappear. The cause of "trained excellence" is Everyman's cause here; my right to as much education as I can bear goes relatively unchallenged. No events, no crisis, seemingly, can interrupt this national dream—self-realization through mental development. And no taxpayer protest ever badly smutches this piety. A day or so after the fearful October 1967 Peace Demonstration at the Pentagon the President, meeting with a group of teachers at the White House, turned eloquent, some might have said moving, on the subject of self-realization and the school. Appointments this morning, he explained, with the National Security Council, and with the president of Mexico—but you, you teachers, you are more important. Whatever else they said about him, the President went on, they would have to say that because of programs he instituted, a million people were in college this year who would not otherwise have had a chance to go. And how much more remained to be done! Four men out of ten on earth could not read or write! He himself hoped to return to teaching when his political career was over.

The books on the Cabinet Room shelf suggested an absence of a passion for the higher literary culture—O. Henry, a high-school physics text, a high-school chemistry text and the like. The few institutions in the country where the idea of standards was well rooted were meritocratic in assumption—which meant not only antiaristocratic but antidemocratic as well. By far the larger part of the huge federal expenditures in the field of education supported phases of the defense program. And, more important than any of this, profound inequities still existed in the system of public education. But from none of this did it follow that the cause or dream in question was a sham. The old programs and the new—Headstart, the regional educational laboratories, the tuition loan bank—had flaws, could not meet every need. But the motive behind them was, in essence, no more suspect than the motive behind the foundation of the first free public education system on earth. That motive was the nurture of a citizen both useful to the community at large and decently developed for himself—gifts realized, mind awake, wholeness intact. An unmockable aim, in sum: dignity for man.

And yet, and yet: the Product of It All looks out from the mirror and reveals himself to be stunted. Somewhere—not simply in the stereotype of himself but in his actuality—he is locked in himself; somewhere he is fixed in an inhuman rigidity; somewhere there is a "malfunction." How to account for this? Has the nation from the start been the captive of theories about the formation and nurture of individual selfhood that are wrongheaded—theories that are in themselves obstacles to self-realization? Is there a uniquely American muddle about fulfillment? If so, what is its nature? How is it to be solved?

Stupidity alone answers confidently—but several relevant observations come to mind. Chief among them is that, for complex social, historical and cultural reasons, the nature of human growth—in particular, the central role of the imagination in determining its rate and quality—has not often been placed clearly before the national view.

Commentators by the hundred score the country off for garishness, gross materialism, unspirituality; few focus on the poverty of its conception of growth. Yet that is the fairer target. The nation prates of self-realization, and rests in near obliviousness that my humanness depends upon my capacity and my desire to make real to myself the inward life, the subjective reality, of the lives that are lived beyond me. The nation feeds itself on rhetoric about "individual rates of progress"—and yet possesses little knowledge, if any, of the steps by which the human being becomes itself, the acts of the imagination on which the achievement of personhood depends.

And, to repeat, this ignorance or obliviousness is no mystery. Human growth stems from the exercise of our power to grasp another being's difference from within: how can that argument maintain itself among a people convinced of the fundamental sameness of men? As Tocqueville long ago pointed out, the myth of sameness is a keystone in the deep structure of American belief. (Tocqueville's specific point was that the American protest on behalf of "the individual" was rooted in the assumption that all individuals, once free "to be themselves," would desire the same things and feel in the same ways.) And it is a fact that the moral imperative of the imaginative act is rarely proclaimed in American public or cultural life. A black singer invited to a White House conference bursts out in condemnation of the guests for the unreality of their proposals, when the latter are seen in the light of her experience. The First Lady's eyes moisten. Shaken but proud, she responds that she "cannot understand" the outburst, she has not had the same experience. And in the morning the country's leading newspaper, the New York *Times,* salutes the First Lady for her "candor," agrees that the feelings and sense of life of the black community are beyond our imagining, and consigns us to a blank, abstract, useless, uncomprehending pity.

And the story is roughly the same on the contemporary intellectual scene. It is a French voice, Jean Paul Sartre's—not an American voice —that defines my attempts to mechanize others, to "see" them as functions, as destructive of my own growth, a permanent barrier to the creation both of my being-in-itself and my being-for-others. (". . . there are men who die without—save for brief and terrifying flashes of illumination—ever having suspected what the *Other* is.") And among recent philosophers it is a German voice, Max Scheler's—not an American one—that dares to formulate an equation setting out relations of identity between individual growth, the perfection of love, and the grasp of the full distinctness and separateness of another human being. ("Love calls explicitly for an understanding entry into the individuality of *another* person *distinct in character* from the entering self . . . a warm and whole-hearted endorsement of 'his' reality as an individual, and 'his' being what he is . . . In love . . . there is built up, within the phenomenon itself, a clear-cut consciousness of two *distinct* persons. This consciousness is not merely a starting point; it reaches full maturity only as love pursues its course.")

What is more, a backward glance at the American cultural heritage confirms that the most powerful voices of American literary culture have been precisely those which, in one manner or another, have been most committedly hostile to the enterprise of attentive imaginative concentration on the fathoming of individual differences. D. H. Lawrence, in his *Studies,* broods hard on the stunted quality of the selves created in the writing of Poe and Whitman, and attributes it in the end to their incapacity to imagine and value a *separate* otherness. Love was a theme for both, but for neither was it a possibility; each man was drawn by fantasies of merging, total engrossment, loss of awareness of the other as separate—fantasies that teased him into confusing "understanding" with the act of sinking one's soul in another. And wherever the engrosser or merger disappears from American letters, an even more frightening figure—the self-bound man (Captain Ahab is the Prince)—stands forth in his place. In Emerson, for example, self-fulfillment appears to require an absolute denial of others, a massive, unrelenting independence, a readiness for isolation. Responding to a culture of conformity, this sage declared that a man bent on realizing himself must learn to carry himself in separation from otherness—"as if everything were titular and ephemeral but he." Widen the gulf, Emerson cries:

We must go alone. I like the silent church before the service begins, better than any preaching. How far off, how cool, how chaste the persons look, begirt each with a precinct or sanctuary! So let us always sit.

Or again:

At times the whole world seems to be in conspiracy to importune you with emphatic trifles. Friend, client, child, sickness, fear, want, charity, all knock at once at the closet door, and say, "Come out unto us." But keep thy state; come not into their confusion.

Or yet again:

Live no longer to the expectation of these deceived and deceiving people with whom we converse. Say to them, O Father, O mother, O wife, O brother, O friend, I have lived with you after appearances hitherto. Henceforward I am the truth's . . . If you are noble, I will love you; if you are not, I will not hurt you and myself by hypocritical attentions.

Emerson does allow that he could love another, if the person were noble, but it is separateness, not love, that rouses him to lyricism: in his view, to say it once more, becoming a fulfilled man means drawing oneself more tightly, consciously, firmly back within the limits of the primal, existent self.

And the Emersonian stance turns up repeatedly in American literature, in popular culture (the art Western), everywhere in American society. (It may even whisper to us in the writings of David Riesman and Nathan Glazer; the utopian archetype of self-realized man described by them as "autonomous" has a definite taste for Emersonian gestures against otherness.) Over and over we are enjoined to find "our own thing," our own bag, in the hippie phrase. And again and again the success of our search is presumed to depend upon our power to cut ourselves off, to harden the wall around us, not only to march to the beat of our own drum, but seemingly to hear no other sound.

There are, of course, counter voices here and there. Although his message did not cut through, smothered in clichés of life adjustment, John Dewey frequently dwelt on connections between human growth and sound education of the imagination—that instrument by which people gain in "flexibility, in scope, and in sympathy, till the life which the individual lives is informed with the life of nature and society." More than one American research psychologist has convinced himself of the centrality of imagination in the course of human development, and has attempted inquiries into the nurture of the imaginative man—witness the labors of Henry Murray and his associates at Harvard in the late 1930's. "Self-Other" theories of growth, which stress self-dramatization and imaginative role-playing, have a place in the history of American philosophy, owing chiefly to the writings of George Herbert Mead. ("The self by its reflexive form announces itself as a conscious organism which is what it is only so far as it can pass from its own system into those of others, and can thus, in passing, occupy both its own system and that into which it is passing . . . Shut up within his own world . . . he would have no entrance into possibilities other than those which his own organized act involved . . . It is here that mental life arises—")

And there is one, great, almost forgotten American voice that put the case for fulfillment as dependent upon imaginative growth in utterly unambiguous terms—I speak of Charles Horton Cooley, a founder of American sociology. In *Human Nature and the Social Order*, Cooley laid it down that:

> . . . the imaginations which people have of one another are the *solid facts* of society . . . I do not mean merely that society must be studied *by* the imagination—that is true of all investigations in their higher reaches—but that the *object* of study is primarily an imaginative idea or group of ideas in the mind, that we have to imagine imaginations. The intimate grasp of any social fact will be found to require that we divine what men think of one another. Charity, for instance, is not understood without imagining what ideas the giver and recipient have of each other; to grasp homicide we must, for one thing, conceive how the offender thinks of his victim and of the administrators of the law; the relation between the employing and hand-laboring classes is first of all a matter of personal attitude which we must apprehend by sympathy with both, and so on . . .

Nor did Cooley stop here—with a mere definition of an appropriate area of inquiry for his field. He went on to assert that the quality of imaginative sympathies is the surest measure of the degree of human growth and fulfillment:

One's range of sympathy is a measure of his personality, indicating how much or how little of a man he is.

And he was certain beyond doubt that those who deprecated this sympathy, shrugged it off with prattle about *sensitivity*, missed its richly complicated nature and meaning:

[Sympathy] is in no way a special faculty but a function of the whole mind to which every special faculty contributes, so that what a person is and what he can understand or enter into through the life of others are very much the same thing. We often hear people described as sympathetic who have little mental power, but are of a sensitive, impressionable, quickly responsive type of mind. The sympathy of such a mind always has some defect corresponding to its lack of character and of constructive force. A strong, deep understanding of other people implies mental energy and stability; it is a work of persistent, cumulative imagination . . .

But if there is a native tradition that understands the nurture of the imagination to be a key to general human growth, it is, by all odds, a minority tradition, far away from the center of popular belief. The weight of the general culture presses continually toward feats of objectification—objectification of labor (the assembly line, time study), of love (sex research), of desire (image making, consumer research). At the center stands the conviction that fulfillment is deliverance into a function—a job, a title, a carpet, an income, a pool, somebody else's respect. I, the free American, am free to "find my own place," my "social niche," my "professional slot." I go forth from myself, I *go places*, ranchhouse to White House, dropout to Ph.D., $12 weekly to $100 a day. And up the line, where I have it made, I "am more interested in a man's behavior than in his inner life," I believe man's first duty is to "adjust himself to his environment," I doubt that anyone can "feel his way into the innermost being of another person," I don't seek inward truths . . .

Is mockery in order? The objectifying American culture can be damned for having only once in its history concerned itself intensely with the matter of precisely what this or that individual man felt in this or that instant of time (the occasion was the period of witch trials in the seventeenth century, when it was found useful to know the inward workings of the devil). It can be damned as well for having consistently refused to introduce into its elementary educational system those "studies"—improvisation, mime, dance, "dramatics"—that elsewhere in the West are accepted as the basic human efforts at developing an imagination of otherness. It can be damned, more fiercely, for its incalculable failures of imagination—as for example its incapacity to make real to itself the inward life, man by man, woman by woman, child by child, of its black people. But there are, here as always in life, qualifications to be entered: if there is no imagination of deprivation among us, there is guilt at good fortune, and this sufficed to rebuild a world and feed a dozen famines. And in any event it is not seemly for a professing humanist to lay down accusations here, for the American humanist—the teacher and scholar whose texts and knowledge should have been the greatest resources of those in pursuit of the truth of "the other subject"—has himself been a cop-out, an objectifier, a character madly eager to turn art itself into a "body of objective knowledge" to be mastered for "career examinations."

The point of substance, in fine, lies beyond accusations or "cultural critiques." It is a matter simply of a general, culture-wide dimming of the lights of inward life, a matter of failed encounters, missed meetings, hands that do not reach out, minds that hear the lock turn in their prison doors. —It is night time, the Maine harbor again. A lantern in the rain, motion of shore waters, a welcome, a beginning . . . But we don't go on, neither he nor she nor I. "My ideas are more often sound and sensible . . ." "I say what I have to say in a few simple words . . ." No hardrock, an occasional pot putterer, we would nevertheless prefer that people "not get ideas about us." And as for the famous still sad music of humanity, we don't hear it much. We don't flow, we hold on tight inside, we do the generous thing over and over and invariably do it ungenerously, we see and feel and imagine ourselves to be highly responsible, competent, the solid people of the earth, the independents, the resilients, the unwhiners. And for that idea cr vision of ourselves we pay terribly—gouge out our innerness—become less than men.

Joan Didion

A native Californian, Joan Didion was born in Sacramento in 1934 and educated at the University of California, Berkeley. She received Vogue's *Prix de Paris the year of her graduation in 1956 and in 1963 was awarded the Bread Loaf Fellowship in fiction. A frequent contributor of articles and reviews to the now extinct* Saturday Evening Post, *to* Mademoiselle, *and to other magazines, she has been associate feature editor of* Vogue *and is a contributing editor to the* National Review. *Her books*

include two novels, Run River *(1963) and* Play It as It Lays
(1970), and Slouching Towards Bethlehem *(1968), a collection
from which we print the essay below.*

SOME DREAMERS OF THE GOLDEN DREAM

This is a story about love and death in the golden land, and begins
with the country. The San Bernardino Valley lies only an hour east
of Los Angeles by the San Bernardino Freeway but is in certain ways
an alien place: not the coastal California of the subtropical twilights
and the soft westerlies off the Pacific but a harsher California, haunted
by the Mojave just beyond the mountains, devastated by the hot dry
Santa Ana wind that comes down through the passes at 100 miles an
hour and whines through the eucalyptus windbreaks and works on the
nerves. October is the bad month for the wind, the month when
breathing is difficult and the hills blaze up spontaneously. There
has been no rain since April. Every voice seems a scream. It is the
season of suicide and divorce and prickly dread, wherever the wind
blows.

The Mormons settled this ominous country, and then they abandoned
it, but by the time they left the first orange tree had been planted and
for the next hundred years the San Bernardino Valley would draw a
kind of people who imagined they might live among the talismanic
fruit and prosper in the dry air, people who brought with them Midwestern ways of building and cooking and praying and who tried to
graft those ways upon the land. The graft took in curious ways. This
is the California where it is possible to live and die without ever eating
an artichoke, without ever meeting a Catholic or a Jew. This is the
California where it is easy to Dial-A-Devotion, but hard to buy a
book. This is the country in which a belief in the literal interpretation
of Genesis has slipped imperceptibly into a belief in the literal interpretation of *Double Indemnity,* the country of the teased hair and the
Capris and the girls for whom all life's promise comes down to a
waltz-length white wedding dress and the birth of a Kimberly or a
Sherry or a Debbi and a Tijuana divorce and a return to hairdressers'
school. "We were just crazy kids," they say without regret, and look
to the future. The future always looks good in the golden land,
because no one remembers the past. Here is where the hot wind
blows and the old ways do not seem relevant, where the divorce rate
is double the national average and where one person in every thirty-

eight lives in a trailer. Here is the last stop for all those who come from somewhere else, for all those who drifted away from the cold and the past and the old ways. Here is where they are trying to find a new life style, trying to find it in the only places they know to look: the movies and the newspapers. The case of Lucille Marie Maxwell Miller is a tabloid monument to that new life style.

Imagine Banyan Street first, because Banyan is where it happened. The way to Banyan is to drive west from San Bernardino out Foothill Boulevard, Route 66: past the Santa Fe switching yards, the Forty Winks Motel. Past the motel that is nineteen stucco tepees: "SLEEP IN A WIGWAM—GET MORE FOR YOUR WAMPUM." Past Fontana Drag City and the Fontana Church of the Nazarene and the Pit Stop A Go-Go; past Kaiser Steel, through Cucamonga, out to the Kapu Kai Restaurant-Bar and Coffee Shop, at the corner of Route 66 and Carnelian Avenue. Up Carnelian Avenue from the Kapu Kai, which means "Forbidden Seas," the subdivision flags whip in the harsh wind. "HALF-ACRE RANCHES! SNACK BARS! TRAVERTINE ENTRIES! $95 DOWN." It is the trail of an intention gone haywire, the flotsam of the New California. But after a while the signs thin out on Carnelian Avenue, and the houses are no longer the bright pastels of the Springtime Home owners but the faded bungalows of the people who grow a few grapes and keep a few chickens out here, and then the hill gets steeper and the road climbs and even the bungalows are few, and here—desolate, roughly surfaced, lined with eucalyptus and lemon groves—is Banyan Street.

Like so much of this country, Banyan suggests something curious and unnatural. The lemon groves are sunken, down a three- or four-foot retaining wall, so that one looks directly into their dense foliage, too lush, unsettlingly glossy, the greenery of nightmare; the fallen eucalyptus bark is too dusty, a place for snakes to breed. The stones look not like natural stones but like the rubble of some unmentioned upheaval. There are smudge pots, and a closed cistern. To one side of Banyan there is the flat valley, and to the other the San Bernardino Mountains, a dark mass looming too high, too fast, nine, ten, eleven thousand feet, right there above the lemon groves. At midnight on Banyan Street there is no light at all, and no sound except the wind in the eucalyptus and a muffled barking of dogs. There may be a kennel somewhere, or the dogs may be coyotes.

Banyan Street was the route Lucille Miller took home from the twenty-four-hour Mayfair Market on the night of October 7, 1964, a night when the moon was dark and the wind was blowing and she was out of milk, and Banyan Street was where, at about 12:30 a.m., her 1964 Volkswagen came to a sudden stop, caught fire, and began to burn. For an hour and fifteen minutes Lucille Miller ran up and down Banyan calling for help, but no cars passed and no help came.

At three o'clock that morning, when the fire had been put out and the California Highway Patrol officers were completing their report, Lucille Miller was still sobbing and incoherent, for her husband had been asleep in the Volkswagen. "What will I tell the children, when there's nothing left, nothing left in the casket," she cried to the friend called to comfort her. "How can I tell them there's nothing left?"

In fact there was something left, and a week later it lay in the Draper Mortuary Chapel in a closed bronze coffin blanketed with pink carnations. Some 200 mourners heard Elder Robert E. Denton of the Seventh-Day Adventist Church of Ontario speak of "the temper of fury that has broken out among us." For Gordon Miller, he said, there would be "no more death, no more heartaches, no more mis-understandings." Elder Ansel Bristol mentioned the "peculiar" grief of the hour. Elder Fred Jensen asked "what shall it profit a man, if he shall gain the whole world, and lose his own soul?" A light rain fell, a blessing in a dry season, and a female vocalist sang "Safe in the Arms of Jesus." A tape recording of the service was made for the widow, who was being held without bail in the San Bernardino County Jail on a charge of first-degree murder.

Of course she came from somewhere else, came off the prairie in search of something she had seen in a movie or heard on the radio, for this is a Southern California story. She was born on January 17, 1930, in Winnipeg, Manitoba, the only child of Gordon and Lily Max-well, both schoolteachers and both dedicated to the Seventh-Day Adventist Church, whose members observe the Sabbath on Saturday, believe in an apocalyptic Second Coming, have a strong missionary tendency, and, if they are strict, do not smoke, drink, eat meat, use makeup, or wear jewelry, including wedding rings. By the time Lucille Maxwell enrolled at Walla Walla College in College Place, Washington, the Adventist school where her parents then taught, she was an eighteen-year-old possessed of unremarkable good looks and remark-able high spirits. "Lucille wanted to see the world," her father would say in retrospect, "and I guess she found out."

The high spirits did not seem to lend themselves to an extended course of study at Walla Walla College, and in the spring of 1949 Lucille Maxwell met and married Gordon ("Cork") Miller, a twenty-four-year-old graduate of Walla Walla and of the University of Oregon dental school, then stationed at Fort Lewis as a medical officer. "Maybe you could say it was love at first sight," Mr. Maxwell recalls. "Before they were ever formally introduced, he sent Lucille a dozen and a half roses with a card that said even if she didn't come out on a date with him, he hoped she'd find the roses pretty anyway." The Maxwells remember their daughter as a "radiant" bride.

Unhappy marriages so resemble one another that we do not need to know too much about the course of this one. There may or may not have been trouble on Guam, where Cork and Lucille Miller lived while he finished his Army duty. There may or may not have been problems in the small Oregon town where he first set up private practice. There appears to have been some disappointment about their move to California: Cork Miller had told friends that he wanted to become a doctor, that he was unhappy as a dentist and planned to enter the Seventh-Day Adventist College of Medical Evangelists at Loma Linda, a few miles south of San Bernardino. Instead he bought a dental practice in the west end of San Bernardino County, and the family settled there, in a modest house on the kind of street where there are always tricycles and revolving credit and dreams about bigger houses, better streets. That was 1957. By the summer of 1964 they had achieved the bigger house on the better street and the familiar accouterments of a family on its way up: the $30,000 a year, the three children for the Christmas card, the picture window, the family room, the newspaper photographs that showed "Mrs. Gordon Miller, Ontario Heart Fund Chairman. . . ." They were paying the familiar price for it. And they had reached the familiar season of divorce.

It might have been anyone's bad summer, anyone's siege of heat and nerves and migraine and money worries, but this one began particularly early and particularly badly. On April 24 an old friend, Elaine Hayton, died suddenly; Lucille Miller had seen her only the night before. During the month of May, Cork Miller was hospitalized briefly with a bleeding ulcer, and his usual reserve deepened into depression. He told his accountant that he was "sick of looking at open mouths," and threatened suicide. By July 8, the conventional tensions of love and money had reached the conventional impasse in the new house on the acre lot at 8488 Bella Vista, and Lucille Miller filed for divorce. Within a month, however, the Millers seemed reconciled. They saw a marriage counselor. They talked about a fourth child. It seemed that the marriage had reached the traditional truce, the point at which so many resign themselves to cutting both their losses and their hopes.

But the Millers' season of trouble was not to end that easily. October 7 began as a commonplace enough day, one of those days that sets the teeth on edge with its tedium, its small frustrations. The temperature reached 102° in San Bernardino that afternoon, and the Miller children were home from school because of Teachers' Institute. There was ironing to be dropped off. There was a trip to pick up a prescription for Nembutal, a trip to a self-service dry cleaner. In the early evening, an unpleasant accident with the Volkswagen: Cork Miller hit and killed a German shepherd, and afterward said that his head felt "like it had a Mack truck on it." It was something he often said. As of that evening Cork Miller was $63,479 in debt, including the $29,637 mortgage on the new house, a debt load which seemed oppressive to him. He was a man who wore his responsibilities uneasily, and complained of migraine headaches almost constantly.

He ate alone that night, from a TV tray in the living room. Later the Millers watched John Forsythe and Senta Berger in *See How They Run,* and when the movie ended, about eleven, Cork Miller suggested that they go out for milk. He wanted some hot chocolate. He took a blanket and pillow from the couch and climbed into the passenger seat of the Volkswagen. Lucille Miller remembers reaching over to lock his door as she backed down the driveway. By the time she left the Mayfair Market, and long before they reached Banyan Street, Cork Miller appeared to be asleep.

There is some confusion in Lucille Miller's mind about what happened between 12:30 a.m., when the fire broke out, and 1:50 a.m., when it was reported. She says that she was driving east on Banyan Street at about 35 m.p.h. when she felt the Volkswagen pull sharply to the right. The next thing she knew the car was on the embankment, quite near the edge of the retaining wall, and flames were shooting up behind her. She does not remember jumping out. She does remember prying up a stone with which she broke the window next to her husband, and then scrambling down the retaining wall to try to find a stick. "I don't know how I was going to push him out," she says. "I just thought if I had a stick, I'd push him out." She could not, and after a while she ran to the intersection of Banyan and Carnelian Avenue. There are no houses at that corner, and almost no traffic. After one car had passed without stopping, Lucille Miller ran back down Banyan toward the burning Volkswagen. She did not stop, but she slowed down, and in the flames she could see her husband. He was, she said, "just black."

At the first house up Sapphire Avenue, half a mile from the Volkswagen, Lucille Miller finally found help. There Mrs. Robert Swenson called the sheriff, and then, at Lucille Miller's request, she called Harold Lance, the Millers' lawyer and their close friend. When Harold Lance arrived he took Lucille Miller home to his wife, Joan. Twice Harold Lance and Lucille Miller returned to Banyan Street and talked to the Highway Patrol officers. A third time Harold Lance returned alone, and when he came back he said to Lucille Miller, "O.K. . . . you don't talk any more."

When Lucille Miller was arrested the next afternoon, Sandy Slagle was with her. Sandy Slagle was the intense, relentlessly loyal medical student who used to baby-sit for the Millers, and had been living as a member of the family since she graduated from high school in 1959.

The Millers took her away from a difficult home situation, and she thinks of Lucille Miller not only as "more or less a mother or a sister" but as "the most wonderful character" she has ever known. On the night of the accident, Sandy Slagle was in her dormitory at Loma Linda University, but Lucille Miller called her early in the morning and asked her to come home. The doctor was there when Sandy Slagle arrived, giving Lucille Miller an injection of Nembutal. "She was crying as she was going under," Sandy Slagle recalls. "Over and over she'd say, 'Sandy, all the hours I spent trying to save him and now what are they trying to *do* to me?' "

At 1:30 that afternoon, Sergeant William Paterson and Detectives Charles Callahan and Joseph Karr of the Central Homicide Division arrived at 8488 Bella Vista. "One of them appeared at the bedroom door," Sandy Slagle remembers, "and said to Lucille, 'You've got ten minutes to get dressed or we'll take you as you are.' She was in her nightgown, you know, so I tried to get her dressed."

Sandy Slagle tells the story now as if by rote, and her eyes do not waver. "So I had her panties and bra on her and they opened the door again, so I got some Capris on her, you know, and a scarf." Her voice drops. "And then they just took her."

The arrest took place just twelve hours after the first report that there had been an accident on Banyan Street, a rapidity which would later prompt Lucille Miller's attorney to say that the entire case was an instance of trying to justify a reckless arrest. Actually what first caused the detectives who arrived on Banyan Street toward dawn that morning to give the accident more than routine attention were certain apparent physical inconsistencies. While Lucille Miller had said that she was driving about 35 m.p.h. when the car swerved to a stop, an examination of the cooling Volkswagen showed that it was in low gear, and that the parking rather than the driving lights were on. The front wheels, moreover, did not seem to be in exactly the position that Lucille Miller's description of the accident would suggest, and the right rear wheel was dug in deep, as if it had been spun in place. It seemed curious to the detectives, too, that a sudden stop from 35 m.p.h.—the same jolt which was presumed to have knocked over a gasoline can in the back seat and somehow started the fire—should have left two milk cartons upright on the back floorboard, and the remains of a Polaroid camera box lying apparently undisturbed on the back seat.

No one, however, could be expected to give a precise account of what did and did not happen in a moment of terror, and none of these inconsistencies seemed in themselves incontrovertible evidence of criminal intent. But they did interest the Sheriff's Office, as did Gordon Miller's apparent unconsciousness at the time of the accident, and the length of time it had taken Lucille Miller to get help. Something, moreover, struck the investigators as wrong about Harold Lance's attitude when he came back to Banyan Street the third time and found the investigation by no means over. "The way Lance was acting," the prosecuting attorney said later, "they thought maybe they'd hit a nerve."

And so it was that on the morning of October 8, even before the doctor had come to give Lucille Miller an injection to calm her, the San Bernardino County Sheriff's Office was trying to construct another version of what might have happened between 12:30 and 1:50 a.m. The hypothesis they would eventually present was based on the somewhat tortuous premise that Lucille Miller had undertaken a plan which failed: a plan to stop the car on the lonely road, spread gasoline over her presumably drugged husband, and, with a stick on the accelerator, gently "walk" the Volkswagen over the embankment, where it would tumble four feet down the retaining wall into the lemon grove and almost certainly explode. If this happened, Lucille Miller might then have somehow negotiated the two miles up Carnelian to Bella Vista in time to be home when the accident was discovered. This plan went awry, according to the Sheriff's Office hypothesis, when the car would not go over the rise of the embankment. Lucille Miller might have panicked then—after she had killed the engine the third or fourth time, say, out there on the dark road with the gasoline already spread and the dogs baying and the wind blowing and the unspeakable apprehension that a pair of headlights would suddenly light up Banyan Street and expose her there—and set the fire herself.

Although this version accounted for some of the physical evidence —the car in low because it had been started from a dead stop, the parking lights on because she could not do what needed doing without some light, a rear wheel spun in repeated attempts to get the car over the embankment, the milk cartons upright because there had been no sudden stop—it did not seem on its own any more or less credible than Lucille Miller's own story. Moreover, some of the physical evidence did seem to support her story: a nail in a front tire, a nine-pound rock found in the car, presumably the one with which she had broken the window in an attempt to save her husband. Within a few days an autopsy had established that Gordon Miller was alive when he burned, which did not particularly help the State's case, and that he had enough Nembutal and Sandoptal in his blood to put the average person to sleep, which did: on the other hand Gordon Miller habitually took both Nembutal and Fiorinal (a common headache prescription which contains Sandoptal), and had been ill besides.

It was a spotty case, and to make it work at all the State was going to have to find a motive. There was talk of unhappiness, talk of another man. That kind of motive, during the next few weeks, was what they set out to establish. They set out to find it in accountants' ledgers and double-indemnity clauses and motel registers, set out to determine what might move a woman who believed in all the promises of the middle class—a woman who had been chairman of the Heart Fund and who always knew a reasonable little dressmaker and who had come out of the bleak wild of prairie fundamentalism to find what she imagined to be the good life—what should drive such a woman to sit on a street called Bella Vista and look out her new picture window into the empty California sun and calculate how to burn her husband alive in a Volkswagen. They found the wedge they wanted closer at hand than they might have at first expected, for, as testimony would reveal later at the trial, it seemed that in December of 1963 Lucille Miller had begun an affair with the husband of one of her friends, a man whose daughter called her "Auntie Lucille," a man who might have seemed to have the gift for people and money and the good life that Cork Miller so noticeably lacked. The man was Arthwell Hayton, a well-known San Bernardino attorney and at one time a member of the district attorney's staff.

In some ways it was the conventional clandestine affair in a place like San Bernardino, a place where little is bright or graceful, where it is routine to misplace the future and easy to start looking for it in bed. Over the seven weeks that it would take to try Lucille Miller for murder, Assistant District Attorney Don A. Turner and defense attorney Edward P. Foley would between them unfold a curiously predictable story. There were the falsified motel registrations. There were the lunch dates, the afternoon drives in Arthwell Hayton's red Cadillac convertible. There were the interminable discussions of the wronged partners. There were the confidantes ("I knew everything," Sandy Slagle would insist fiercely later. "I knew every time, places, everything") and there were the words remembered from bad magazine stories ("Don't kiss me, it will trigger things," Lucille Miller remembered telling Arthwell Hayton in the parking lot of Harold's Club in Fontana after lunch one day) and there were the notes, the sweet exchanges: "Hi Sweetie Pie! You are my cup of tea!! Happy Birthday—you don't look a day over 29!! Your baby, Arthwell."

And, toward the end, there was the acrimony. It was April 24, 1964, when Arthwell Hayton's wife, Elaine, died suddenly, and nothing good happened after that. Arthwell Hayton had taken his cruiser, *Captain's Lady*, over to Catalina that weekend; he called home at nine o'clock Friday night, but did not talk to his wife because Lucille Miller answered the telephone and said that Elaine was showering. The next morning the Haytons' daughter found her mother in bed, dead. The newspapers reported the death as accidental, perhaps the result of an allergy to hair spray. When Arthwell Hayton flew home from Catalina that weekend, Lucille Miller met him at the airport, but the finish had already been written.

It was in the breakup that the affair ceased to be in the conventional mode and began to resemble instead the novels of James M. Cain, the movies of the late 1930's, all the dreams in which violence and threats and blackmail are made to seem commonplaces of middle-class life. What was most startling about the case that the State of California was preparing against Lucille Miller was something that had nothing to do with law at all, something that never appeared in the eight-column afternoon headlines but was always there between them: the revelation that the dream was teaching the dreamers how to live. Here is Lucille Miller talking to her lover sometime in the early summer of 1964, after he had indicated that, on the advice of his minister, he did not intend to see her any more: "First, I'm going to go to that dear pastor of yours and tell him a few things. . . . When I do tell him that, you won't be in the Redlands Church any more. . . . Look, Sonny Boy, if you think your reputation is going to be ruined, your life won't be worth two cents." Here is Arthwell Hayton, to Lucille Miller: "I'll go to Sheriff Frank Bland and tell him some things that I know about you until you'll wish you'd never heard of Arthwell Hayton." For an affair between a Seventh-Day Adventist dentist's wife and a Seventh-Day Adventist personal-injury lawyer, it seems a curious kind of dialogue.

"Boy, I could get that little boy coming and going," Lucille Miller later confided to Erwin Sprengle, a Riverside contractor who was a business partner of Arthwell Hayton's and a friend to both the lovers. (Friend or no, on this occasion he happened to have an induction coil attached to his telephone in order to tape Lucille Miller's call.) "And he hasn't got one thing on me that he can prove. I mean, I've got concrete—he has nothing concrete." In the same taped conversation with Erwin Sprengle, Lucille Miller mentioned a tape that she herself had surreptitiously made, months before, in Arthwell Hayton's car.

"I said to him, I said 'Arthwell, I just feel like I'm being used.' . . . He started sucking his thumb and he said 'I love you. . . . This isn't something that happened yesterday. I'd marry you tomorrow if I could. I don't love Elaine.' He'd love to hear that played back, wouldn't he?"

"Yeah," drawled Sprengle's voice on the tape. "That would be just a little incriminating, wouldn't it?"

"Just a *little* incriminating," Lucille Miller agreed. "It really *is*."

Later on the tape, Sprengle asked where Cork Miller was.

"He took the children down to the church."

"You didn't go?"

"No."

"You're naughty."

It was all, moreover, in the name of "love"; everyone involved placed a magical faith in the efficacy of the very word. There was the significance that Lucille Miller saw in Arthwell's saying that he "loved" her, that he did not "love" Elaine. There was Arthwell insisting, later, at the trial, that he had never said it, that he may have "whispered sweet nothings in her ear" (as her defense hinted that he had whispered in many ears), but he did not remember bestowing upon her the special seal, saying the word, declaring "love." There was the summer evening when Lucille Miller and Sandy Slagle followed Arthwell Hayton down to his new boat in its mooring at Newport Beach and untied the lines with Arthwell aboard, Arthwell and a girl with whom he later testified he was drinking hot chocolate and watching television. "I did that on purpose," Lucille Miller told Erwin Sprengle later, "to save myself from letting my heart do something crazy."

January 11, 1965, was a bright warm day in Southern California, the kind of day when Catalina floats on the Pacific horizon and the air smells of orange blossoms and it is a long way from the bleak and difficult East, a long way from the cold, a long way from the past. A woman in Hollywood staged an all-night sit-in on the hood of her car to prevent repossession by a finance company. A seventy-year-old pensioner drove his station wagon at five miles an hour past three Gardena poker parlors and emptied three pistols and a twelve-gauge shotgun through their windows, wounding twenty-nine people. "Many young women become prostitutes just to have enough money to play cards," he explained in a note. Mrs. Nick Adams said that she was "not surprised" to hear her husband announce his divorce plans on the Les Crane Show, and, farther north, a sixteen-year-old jumped off the Golden Gate Bridge and lived.

And, in the San Bernardino County Courthouse, the Miller trial opened. The crowds were so bad that the glass courtroom doors were shattered in the crush, and from then on identification disks were issued to the first forty-three spectators in line. The line began forming at 6 a.m., and college girls camped at the courthouse all night, with stores of graham crackers and No-Cal.

All they were doing was picking a jury, those first few days, but the sensational nature of the case had already suggested itself. Early in December there had been an abortive first trial, a trial at which no evidence was ever presented because on the day the jury was seated the San Bernardino *Sun-Telegram* ran an "inside" story quoting Assistant District Attorney Don Turner, the prosecutor, as saying, "We are looking into the circumstances of Mrs. Hayton's death. In view of the current trial concerning the death of Dr. Miller, I do not feel I should comment on Mrs. Hayton's death." It seemed that there had been barbiturates in Elaine Hayton's blood, and there had seemed some irregularity about the way she was dressed on that morning when she was found under the covers, dead. Any doubts about the death at the time, however, had never gotten as far as the Sheriff's Office. "I guess somebody didn't want to rock the boat," Turner said later. "These were prominent people."

Although all of that had not been in the *Sun-Telegram*'s story, an immediate mistrial had been declared. Almost as immediately, there had been another development: Arthwell Hayton had asked news-papermen to an 11 a.m. Sunday morning press conference in his office. There had been television cameras, and flash bulbs popping. "As you gentlemen may know," Hayton had said, striking a note of stiff bon-homie, "there are very often women who become amorous toward their doctor or lawyer. This does not mean on the physician's or lawyer's part that there is any romance toward the patient or client."

"Would you deny that you were having an affair with Mrs. Miller?" a reporter had asked.

"I would deny that there was any romance on my part whatsoever."

It was a distinction he would maintain through all the wearing weeks to come.

So they had come to see Arthwell, these crowds who now milled beneath the dusty palms outside the courthouse, and they had also come to see Lucille, who appeared as a slight, intermittently pretty woman, already pale from lack of sun, a woman who would turn thirty-five before the trial was over and whose tendency toward hag-gardness was beginning to show, a meticulous woman who insisted, against her lawyer's advice, on coming to court with her hair piled high and lacquered. "I would've been happy if she'd come in with it hanging loose, but Lucille wouldn't do that," her lawyer said. He was Edward P. Foley, a small, emotional Irish Catholic who several times wept in the courtroom. "She has a great honesty, this woman," he added, "but this honesty about her appearance always worked against her."

By the time the trial opened, Lucille Miller's appearance included maternity clothes, for an official examination on December 18 had revealed that she was then three and a half months pregnant, a fact which made picking a jury even more difficult than usual, for Turner was asking the death penalty. "It's unfortunate but there it is," he would say of the pregnancy to each juror in turn, and finally twelve were seated, seven of them women, the youngest forty-one, an assembly of the very peers—housewives, a machinist, a truck driver, a grocery-store manager, a filing clerk—above whom Lucille Miller had wanted so badly to rise.

That was the sin, more than the adultery, which tended to reinforce the one for which she was being tried. It was implicit in both the defense and the prosecution that Lucille Miller was an erring woman, a woman who perhaps wanted too much. But to the prosecution she was not merely a woman who would want a new house and want to go to parties and run up high telephone bills ($1,152 in ten months), but a woman who would go so far as to murder her husband for his $80,000 in insurance, making it appear an accident in order to collect another $40,000 in double indemnity and straight accident policies. To Turner she was a woman who did not want simply her freedom and a reasonable alimony (she could have had that, the defense contended, by going through with her divorce suit), but wanted everything, a woman motivated by "love and greed." She was a "manipulator." She was a "user of people."

To Edward Foley, on the other hand, she was an impulsive woman who "couldn't control her foolish little heart." Where Turner skirted the pregnancy, Foley dwelt upon it, even calling the dead man's mother down from Washington to testify that her son had told her they were going to have another baby because Lucille felt that it would "do much to weld our home again in the pleasant relations that we used to have." Where the prosecution saw a "calculator," the defense saw a "blabbermouth," and in fact Lucille Miller did emerge as an ingenuous conversationalist. Just as, before her husband's death, she had confided in her friends about her love affair, so she chatted about it after his death, with the arresting sergeant. "Of course Cork lived with it for years, you know," her voice was heard to tell Sergeant Paterson on a tape made the morning after her arrest. "After Elaine died, he pushed the panic button one night and just asked me right out, and that, I think, was when he really—the first time he really faced it." When the sergeant asked why she had agreed to talk to him, against the specific instructions of her lawyers, Lucille Miller said airily, "Oh, I've always been basically quite an honest person. . . . I mean I can put a hat in the cupboard and say it cost ten dollars less, but basically I've always kind of just lived my life the way I wanted to, and if you don't like it you can take off."

The prosecution hinted at men other than Arthwell, and even, over Foley's objections, managed to name one. The defense called Miller suicidal. The prosecution produced experts who said that the Volkswagen fire could not have been accidental. Foley produced witnesses who said that it could have been. Lucille's father, now a junior-highschool teacher in Oregon, quoted Isaiah to reporters: "*Every tongue that shall rise against thee in judgment thou shalt condemn.*" "Lucille did wrong, her affair," her mother said judiciously. "With her it was love. But with some I guess it's just passion." There was Debbie, the Millers' fourteen-year-old, testifying in a steady voice about how she and her mother had gone to a supermarket to buy the gasoline can the week before the accident. There was Sandy Slagle, in the courtroom every day, declaring that on at least one occasion Lucille Miller had prevented her husband not only from committing suicide but from committing suicide in such a way that it would appear an accident and ensure the double-indemnity payment. There was Wenche Berg, the pretty twenty-seven-year-old Norwegian governess to Arthwell Hayton's children, testifying that Arthwell had instructed her not to allow Lucille Miller to see or talk to the children.

Two months dragged by, and the headlines never stopped. Southern California's crime reporters were headquartered in San Bernardino for the duration: Howard Hertel from the *Times*, Jim Bennett and Eddy Jo Bernal from the *Herald-Examiner*. Two months in which the Miller trial was pushed off the *Examiner*'s front page only by the Academy Award nominations and Stan Laurel's death. And finally, on March 2, after Turner had reiterated that it was a case of "love and greed," and Foley had protested that his client was being tried for adultery, the case went to the jury.

They brought in the verdict, guilty of murder in the first degree, at 4:50 p.m. on March 5. "She didn't do it," Debbie Miller cried, jumping up from the spectators' section. "She didn't *do* it." Sandy Slagle collapsed in her seat and began to scream. "Sandy, for God's sake please *don't*," Lucille Miller said in a voice that carried across the courtroom, and Sandy Slagle was momentarily subdued. But as the jurors left the courtroom she screamed again: "You're murderers. . . . Every last one of you is a *murderer*." Sheriff's deputies moved in then, each wearing a string tie that read "1965 SHERIFF'S RODEO," and Lucille Miller's father, that sad-faced junior-high-school teacher who believed in the word of Christ and the dangers of wanting to see the world, blew her a kiss off his fingertips.

The California Institution for Women at Frontera, where Lucille Miller is now, lies down where Euclid Avenue turns into country road, not too many miles from where she once lived and shopped and organized the Heart Fund Ball. Cattle graze across the road, and Rainbirds sprinkle the alfalfa. Frontera has a softball field and tennis courts, and looks as if it might be a California junior college, except that the trees are not yet high enough to conceal the concertina wire around the top of the Cyclone fence. On visitors' day there are big cars in the parking area, big Buicks and Pontiacs that belong to grandparents and sisters and fathers (not many of them belong to husbands), and some of them have bumper stickers that say "SUPPORT YOUR LOCAL POLICE."

A lot of California murderesses live here, a lot of girls who somehow misunderstood the promise. Don Turner put Sandra Garner here (and her husband in the gas chamber at San Quentin) after the 1959 desert killings known to crime reporters as "the soda-pop murders." Carole Tregoff is here, and has been ever since she was convicted of conspiring to murder Dr. Finch's wife in West Covina, which is not too far from San Bernardino. Carole Tregoff is in fact a nurse's aide in the prison hospital, and might have attended Lucille Miller had her baby been born at Frontera; Lucille Miller chose instead to have it outside, and paid for the guard who stood outside the delivery room in St. Bernardine's Hospital. Debbie Miller came to take the baby home from the hospital, in a white dress with pink ribbons, and Debbie was allowed to choose a name. She named the baby Kimi Kai. The children live with Harold and Joan Lance now, because Lucille Miller will probably spend ten years at Frontera. Don Turner waived his original request for the death penalty (it was generally agreed that he had demanded it only, in Edward Foley's words, "to get anybody with the slightest trace of human kindness in their veins off the jury"), and settled for life imprisonment with the possibility of parole. Lucille Miller does not like it at Frontera, and has had trouble adjusting. "She's going to have to learn humility," Turner says. "She's going to have to use her ability to charm, to manipulate."

The new house is empty now, the house on the street with the sign that says

PRIVATE ROAD

BELLA VISTA

DEAD END

The Millers never did get it landscaped, and weeds grow up around the fieldstone siding. The television aerial has toppled on the roof, and a trash can is stuffed with the debris of family life: a cheap suitcase, a child's game called "Lie Detector." There is a sign on what would have been the lawn, and the sign reads "ESTATE SALE." Edward Foley is trying to get Lucille Miller's case appealed, but there have been delays. "A trial always comes down to a matter of sympathy," Foley says wearily now. "I couldn't create sympathy for her." Everyone is a little weary now, weary and resigned, everyone except Sandy Slagle, whose bitterness is still raw. She lives in an apartment near the medical school in Loma Linda, and studies reports of the case in *True Police Cases* and *Official Detective Stories*. "I'd much rather we not talk about the Hayton business too much," she tells visitors, and she keeps a tape recorder running. "I'd rather talk about Lucille and what a wonderful person she is and how her rights were violated." Harold Lance does not talk to visitors at all. "We don't want to give away what we can sell," he explains pleasantly; an attempt was made to sell Lucille Miller's personal story to *Life*, but *Life* did not want to buy it. In the district attorney's offices they are prosecuting other murders now, and do not see why the Miller trial attracted so much attention. "It wasn't a very interesting murder as murders go," Don Turner says laconically. Elaine Hayton's death is no longer under investigation. "We know everything we want to know," Turner says.

Arthwell Hayton's office is directly below Edward Foley's. Some people around San Bernardino say that Arthwell Hayton suffered; others say that he did not suffer at all. Perhaps he did not, for time past is not believed to have any bearing upon time present or future, out in the golden land where every day the world is born anew. In any case, on October 17, 1965, Arthwell Hayton married again, married his children's pretty governess, Wenche Berg, at a service in the Chapel of the Roses at a retirement village near Riverside. Later the newlyweds were feted at a reception for seventy-five in the dining room of Rose Garden Village. The bridegroom was in black tie, with a white carnation in his buttonhole. The bride wore a long white *peau de soie* dress and carried a shower bouquet of sweetheart roses with stephanotis streamers. A coronet of seed pearls held her illusion veil.

1966

Henry Steele Commager

Henry Steele Commager (born 1902) is one of the most prominent and most prolific historians of America. Educated at the University of Chicago, he has taught principally at N.Y.U., Columbia, and Amherst, where he has been Professor of History since 1956. Dr. Commager has lectured widely in the United States and abroad and has received many honorary degrees. As author, editor, and collaborator he has produced more than a score of books, among them Documents of American History *(1934),* Theodore Parker *(1936),* The American Mind *(1951),* Freedom, Loyalty and Dissent *(1954), and* The Commonwealth of Learning *(1968).* The Growth of the American Republic *(with S. E. Morison, 1931) has remained in successive*

editions an influential general history widely used as a college
text. The present essay first appeared in The Saturday Review,
July 10, 1965.

A HISTORIAN LOOKS AT OUR POLITICAL MORALITY

"Every philosophy," wrote Alfred North Whitehead, "is tinged with
the coloring of some secret, imaginative background, which never
emerges explicitly in its train of reasoning." True enough—though
never is a pretty strong word here. What is the secret, or perhaps the
inarticulate imaginative background, that colors American thinking
about relations with other peoples and nations in the past and today?
Is it not the once explicit and openly avowed, but now implicit assumption of American superiority, both material and moral, especially to
lesser breeds without our law? Is it not the assumption that America
is somehow outside the workings of history, above the processes of
history, exempt from such laws as may govern history?

The origin of this attitude traces back to the generation that created
the new nation and came to think of that nation as a people apart. It
is rooted in the long-popular notion of New World innocence and Old
World corruption, New World virtue and Old World vice, a notion
that runs like a red thread through the whole of our literature from
Benjamin Franklin to Henry James, and through our politics and diplomacy as well. It is connected with the convulsive fact of physical
removal—the uprooting and transplanting to new and more fertile soil,
with the phenomenon of a continuous westward emigration from the
Old World, while so few went eastward across the ocean. It is related
to the American priority in independence and in nation-making, with
the glowing achievements of the new nation—religious freedom, for
example, the end to colonialism, the classless society—and over the
years it was strengthened by the argument of special destiny, and by
the experience of abundance and freedom from Old World wars, and
of growth even beyond the dreams of the Founding Fathers. No wonder the notion of a special providence and a special destiny caught
the American imagination.

Something was to be said for all this in the early years of the Republic, when the American world was not only new but brave. Rather
less was to be said for it as the nineteenth century wore on—the century that saw the new nation indulge in so many of the follies of the

older nations: slavery, racial and religious intolerance, the disparity between rich and poor, civil war, imperialism, and foreign wars.

But even in the nineteenth century, perhaps especially in the nineteenth century, Americans developed the habit of brushing aside whatever was embarrassing that still characterizes them, the habit of taking for granted a double standard of history and morality. There were, to be sure, awkward things in our history, but somehow they were not to be held against us, somehow they didn't count. The conquest and decimation of the Indian didn't count—after all, the Indians were heathens—and when that argument lost its force, there was the undeniable charge that they got in the way of progress. The students of my own college celebrate Lord Jeffrey Amherst on all ceremonial occasions, but few of them remember that Lord Amherst's solution to the Indian problem was to send the Indians blankets infected with smallpox! How many of us, after all, remember what Helen Hunt Jackson called a "Century of Dishonor"? Or there was slavery; it was pervasive and flourishing, and slaveholders defended it as a moral good. Somehow slavery didn't count, either, because it was nature's way of bringing the African to Western civilization, or because it was all so romantic (only recently have we developed a sense of guilt here).

The Industrial Revolution, too, brought in its train most of the evils that afflicted Europe in these same stormy years, but that could all be put down as the price of progress, which is just what Herbert Spencer and his infatuated American followers did. And surely no one could assert that the price was too high. So, too, with what, in other nations, would be called imperialism, but with us was called "westward expansion"—manifest destiny working itself out in some foreordained fashion. The Mexicans do not take quite this view of the matter, but that has not troubled us. Even now we do not inquire quite as closely into the war-guilt question for the Mexican War, or the war with Spain, or the Filipino war, as we do for the Franco-Prussian War or World War I. Poets like William Vaughn Moody raised their voices in vain against the Philippine War:

Alas, what sounds are these that come
Sullenly over the Pacific Seas—
Sounds of ignoble battle, striking dumb
The season's half awakened ecstasies? . . .
Was it for this our fathers kept the law?
This crown shall crown their struggle and their truth?
Are we the eagle nation Milton saw
Mewing its mighty youth,
Soon to possess the mountain winds of Truth
And be a swift familiar of the sun . . .
Or have we but the talons and the maw . . . ?

But who now remembers William Vaughn Moody?

We are no longer quite so sure of the New World innocence and Old World corruption as in the past—sometimes we suspect it may be the other way around—but the older notions of American superiority, and of the exemption of America from the familiar processes of history persist. They were very much in the mind of Woodrow Wilson when he prepared to make the world safe for democracy. But then the world we made did not suit us at all; clearly we had been betrayed by the wicked diplomats of the Old World. We cut our losses and withdrew into isolation and watched the Old World destroy itself with a kind of malign satisfaction, meanwhile congratulating ourselves that we were not involved and that our irresponsibility was really a form of moral superiority.

For we were very sure of our own virtue, and we read history to discover that we were a peculiar people. Our history books exalted everything American. They contrasted our Indian policy with the wicked policy of the Spaniards—that was part of the black legend—conveniently overlooking the elementary fact that the Indian survived in Mexico and South America but not in the United States. They painted slavery as a romantic institution, or perhaps as a kind of fortunate accident for the Africans. They even ascribed the exceeding bounty of nature not to providence or to luck but to our own virtue. In recent years many of our spokesmen commit the vulgar error of identifying an economy based on unrestricted exploitation of natural abundance as "the American way of life," and of scorning less fortunate people for having fewer resources and a different, and obviously inferior, way of life. We forget Reinhold Niebuhr's admonishment that "The more we indulge in uncritical reverence for the supposed wisdom of the American way of life, the more odious we make it in the eyes of the world, and the more we destroy our moral authority. . . ."

During the great war we responded, generously and unselfishly, to the challenge that confronted us; this was, in a sense, our finest hour, too: Lend-Lease, the alliance with Britain, the acceptance of the Soviet as an ally in the struggle against tyranny, the Atlantic Charter and the United Nations and the far-sighted Marshall Plan, the response to the challenge of aggression in Korea. But the rising threat of Communism did what the actual attack by Nazi and Fascist powers had been unable to do. The prolonged struggle with Communism, which we sometimes call the Cold War, accentuated our innate sense of superiority. To vast numbers of Americans it justified—and apparently still does justify—resort to almost any weapons or conduct. For years now we have heard, and not from extremists alone, that the struggle between democracy and Communism is the struggle between Light and Darkness, Good and Evil, and that the moral distinction is an absolute one.

The arguments that were invoked to justify religious wars and religious persecution in past centuries are invoked now to justify sleepless hostility to Communism—even preventive war. Happily, the extremists have not had their way in the conduct of foreign policy, but we know how effective they have been on the domestic scene, how they have denounced as traitors those who do not agree with them and persecuted them with relentless venom, how they have poisoned public life, and private, too, preaching hatred of Russia, hatred of Cuba, hatred of China—hatred directed toward all those who do not agree with them and with their easy remedies. Those hatemongers, sure of themselves and of their moral superiority, have not hesitated to ignore law and the Constitution when it suited their book or to lie and cheat and betray in what they complacently assumed was a good cause because they espoused it. In 1801 Jefferson warned against suspicion and hatred in public life: "Let us," he said in his first inaugural address:

. . . restore to social intercourse that harmony and affection without which liberty and even life itself are but dreary things. And let us reflect that, having banished from our land that religious intolerance under which mankind so long bled and suffered, we have yet gained little if we countenance a political intolerance as despotic and wicked, and capable of as bitter and bloody persecutions.

Not since the fateful decade of the 1850s has that warning been more relevant than in this generation. Those who cultivate and spread the gospel of hatred throughout our society bear a heavy responsibility. They do not really weaken Communism; they weaken democracy and liberty. By their conduct and their philosophy they lower the moral standards of the society they pretend to defend. Eager to put down imagined subversion, they are themselves the most subversive of all the elements in our society, for they subvert "that harmony and affection" without which a society cannot be a commonwealth.

Much of our current foreign policy takes once again the form of indulgence in a double standard of morality. Thus it is contrary to international law to make reconnaissance flights over the territory of another nation—the Soviet reminded us of that a few years back—but we boast that we make such flights over Cuba and over China: if Cuban planes flew over Florida or Chinese over Hawaii we might take a less easygoing view of the matter. We justly condemn Nazi destruction of Rotterdam and Warsaw, cities that were not military objectives, but we conveniently forget that we were chiefly responsible for the senseless destruction of Dresden—not a military object—within a few weeks of the end of the war, with a loss of 135,000 lives. It is a matter for rejoicing that *we* have the nuclear bomb, but when China detonated her first bomb our President told us that "this is a dark day in history." Perhaps so, though so far we are the only nation that has ever used the bomb—a fact which the Asians remember a bit better than we do. And even now Senator Russell assures us that he would favor using it again if our soldiers in Vietnam got into trouble. Even the present war in Vietnam—the President has now used the word *war* for it, so perhaps we can abandon the hypocritical vocabulary with which we have heretofore bemused ourselves—tempts us constantly to indulge in a double standard. The Vietcong engages in "terror attacks" but our bombings do not presumably hurt anybody. When we use gas it is not really gas but just something our own police use here at home. Our airmen and marines are "observers" but the enemy's soldiers are terrorists. Guerrilla warfare—is it from the North?—justifies bombing at the source: if Castro accepted that theory and bombed those bases in Florida and Guatemala that launched guerrilla attacks on his island, we might take a different view of the matter. When the Russians announced that they would not tolerate an unfriendly government in Hungary, and sent their troops and tanks crashing into that country in 1956, we were rightly outraged, but we think it quite right for us to announce that we will not tolerate an unfriendly regime in Santo Domingo and to send 20,000 Marines to "restore order" in that island. We complain, and rightly, that other countries do not abide by their international agreements, but we are ready to forgive ourselves for brushing aside international agreements when we face something we regard as an "emergency."

We have always criticized secret diplomacy—remember President Wilson's crusade—but when the CIA operates with such secrecy that even our own government is apparently taken by surprise, that just shows how clever we are. For the Russians or the Chinese to stir up revolution in other lands is subversive of international order, but when we encourage a coup d'etat or a revolution—from Iran to Brazil to Vietnam—it is all in a good cause.

We have not of late heard quite so much as some months back of what must surely be counted the ultimate arrogance—the cry of the "better dead than Red" crusaders. Those highly vocal martyrs are so sure that they speak for God that they are quite ready to condemn to extinction not only themselves and their fellow citizens, but the rest of the world and all potential posterity.

It is three-quarters of a century now since Lord Acton made the famous pronouncement that all power tends to corrupt and that absolute power corrupts absolutely. We had thought, and hoped, that we were exempt from this rule, but it is clear that we are not. Power exposes us to the same temptation to ruthlessness, lawlessness, hypocrisy, and vanity to which all great powers were exposed in the past.

In a simpler day we could survive this threat of corruption without serious damage. We could count on wearing out the brief spell of violence and corruption, or on circumscribing its effects. But now that we are a world power and our conduct affects the fate of every nation on the globe, we can no longer afford this piece of self-indulgence. Now we must square our conduct with principles of law and of morality that will withstand the scrutiny of public opinion everywhere and the tests of history as well.

James Baldwin

James Baldwin was born in Harlem in 1924, the oldest of nine children, and graduated from DeWitt Clinton High School, where he was editor of the literary magazine. After the death of his father in 1943 he lived in Greenwich Village, working by day as handyman, office boy, or factory worker, and writing at night. A Rosenwald Fellowship received in 1948 enabled him to go to Paris, where he wrote his first two novels, Go Tell It on the Mountain *(1953) and* Giovanni's Room *(1956), and the essays published as* Notes of a Native Son *(1955). In 1957 he returned to America and since then has continued his literary career with novels, plays, and essays. Baldwin has won many awards, among them a Guggenheim Fellowship (1954), a* Partisan Review *Fellowship (1956), and The National Institute for Arts and Letters Award (1956).* Nobody Knows My Name, *a collection of essays, was selected as one of the outstanding books of 1961 by The American Library Association.* The Fire Next Time *(1963) consists of two searing articles, or letters, on the relationship between black and white Americans. It secures Baldwin's lasting reputation both as essayist and as commentator on American*

culture. The second article originally appeared in The New
Yorker *under the title "Letter from a Region of My Mind." We
present below its concluding section.*

FROM **THE FIRE NEXT TIME**

No one seems to know where the Nation of Islam gets its money. A
vast amount, of course, is contributed by Negroes, but there are rumors
to the effect that people like Birchites and certain Texas oil million-
aires look with favor on the movement. I have no way of knowing
whether there is any truth to the rumors, though since these people
make such a point of keeping the races separate, I wouldn't be surprised if for this smoke there was some fire. In any case, during a
recent Muslim rally, George Lincoln Rockwell, the chief of the American Nazi party, made a point of contributing about twenty dollars to
the cause, and he and Malcolm X decided that, racially speaking,
anyway, they were in complete agreement. The glorification of one
race and the consequent debasement of another—or others—always has
been and always will be a recipe for murder. There is no way around
this. If one is permitted to treat any group of people with special
disfavor because of their race or the color of their skin, there is no
limit to what one will force them to endure, and, since the entire
race has been mysteriously indicted, no reason not to attempt to destroy it root and branch. This is precisely what the Nazis attempted.
Their only originality lay in the means they used. It is scarcely worthwhile to attempt remembering how many times the sun has looked
down on the slaughter of the innocents. I am very much concerned
that American Negroes achieve their freedom here in the United
States. But I am also concerned for their dignity, for the health of
their souls, and must oppose any attempt that Negroes may make to
do to others what has been done to them. I think I know—we see
it around us every day—the spiritual wasteland to which that road
leads. It is so simple a fact and one that is so hard, apparently, to
grasp: *Whoever debases others is debasing himself.* That is not a mystical
statement but a most realistic one, which is proved by the eyes of
any Alabama sheriff—and I would not like to see Negroes ever arrive
at so wretched a condition.

Now, it is extremely unlikely that Negroes will ever rise to power
in the United States, because they are only approximately a ninth of
this nation. They are not in the position of the Africans, who are

attempting to reclaim their land and break the colonial yoke and recover from the colonial experience. The Negro situation is dangerous
in a different way, both for the Negro qua Negro and for the country
of which he forms so troubled and troubling a part. The American
Negro is a unique creation; he has no counterpart anywhere, and no
predecessors. The Muslims react to this fact by referring to the
Negro as "the so-called American Negro" and substituting for the
names inherited from slavery the letter "X." It is a fact that every
American Negro bears a name that originally belonged to the white
man whose chattel he was. I am called Baldwin because I was either
sold by my African tribe or kidnapped out of it into the hands of a
white Christian named Baldwin, who forced me to kneel at the foot
of the cross. I am, then, both visibly and legally the descendant of
slaves in a white, Protestant country, and this is what it means to
be an American Negro, this is who he is—a kidnapped pagan, who
was sold like an animal and treated like one, who was once defined
by the American Constitution as "three-fifths" of a man, and who,
according to the Dred Scott decision, had no rights that a white man
was bound to respect. And today, a hundred years after his technical emancipation, he remains—with the possible exception of the
American Indian—the most despised creature in his country. Now,
there is simply no possibility of a real change in the Negro's situation
without the most radical and far-reaching changes in the American
political and social structure. And it is clear that white Americans
are not simply unwilling to effect these changes; they are, in the main,
so slothful have they become, unable even to envision them. It must
be added that the Negro himself no longer believes in the good faith
of white Americans—if, indeed, he ever could have. What the Negro
has discovered, and on an international level, is that power to intimi-
date which he has always had privately but hitherto could manipulate only privately—for private ends often, for limited ends always.
And therefore when the country speaks of a "new" Negro, which it
has been doing every hour on the hour for decades, it is not really
referring to a change in the Negro, which, in any case, it is quite
incapable of assessing, but only to a new difficulty in keeping him in
his place, to the fact that it encounters him (again! again!) barring yet
another door to its spiritual and social ease. This is probably, hard
and odd as it may sound, the most important thing that one human
being can do for another—it is certainly *one* of the most important
things; hence the torment and necessity of love—and this is the enormous contribution that the Negro has made to this otherwise shapeless
and undiscovered country. Consequently, white Americans are in
nothing more deluded than in supposing that Negroes could ever have
imagined that white people would "give" them anything. It is rare

indeed that people give. Most people guard and keep; they suppose that it is they themselves and what they identify with themselves that they are guarding and keeping, whereas what they are actually guarding and keeping is their system of reality and what they assume themselves to be. One can give nothing whatever without giving oneself—that is to say, risking oneself. If one cannot risk oneself, then one is simply incapable of giving. And, after all, one can give freedom only by setting someone free. This, in the case of the Negro, the American republic has never become sufficiently mature to do. White Americans have contented themselves with gestures that are now described as "tokenism." For hard example, white Americans congratulate themselves on the 1954 Supreme Court decision outlawing segregation in the schools; they suppose, in spite of the mountain of evidence that has since accumulated to the contrary, that this was proof of a change of heart—or, as they like to say, progress. Perhaps. It all depends on how one reads the word "progress." Most of the Negroes I know do not believe that this immense concession would ever have been made if it had not been for the competition of the Cold War, and the fact that Africa was clearly liberating herself and therefore had, for political reasons, to be wooed by the descendants of her former masters. Had it been a matter of love or justice, the 1954 decision would surely have occurred sooner; were it not for the realities of power in this difficult era, it might very well not have occurred yet. This seems an extremely harsh way of stating the case—ungrateful, as it were—but the evidence that supports this way of stating it is not easily refuted. I myself do not think that it can be refuted at all. In any event, the sloppy and fatuous nature of American good will can never be relied upon to deal with hard problems. These have been dealt with, when they have been dealt with at all, out of necessity—and in political terms, anyway, necessity means concessions made in order to stay on top. I think this is a fact, which it serves no purpose to deny, *but, whether it is a fact or not, this is what the black population of the world, including black Americans, really believe.* The word "independence" in Africa and the word "integration" here are almost equally meaningless; that is, Europe has not yet left Africa, and black men here are not yet free. And both of these last statements are undeniable facts, related facts, containing the gravest implications for us all. The Negroes of this country may never be able to rise to power, but they are very well placed indeed to precipitate chaos and ring down the curtain on the American dream.

This has everything to do, of course, with the nature of that dream and with the fact that we Americans, of whatever color, do not dare examine it and are far from having made it a reality. There are too many things we do not wish to know about ourselves. People are

202

not, for example, terribly anxious to be equal (equal, after all, to what and to whom?) but they love the idea of being superior. And this human truth has an especially grinding force here, where identity is almost impossible to achieve and people are perpetually attempting to find their feet on the shifting sands of status. (Consider the history of labor in a country in which, spiritually speaking, there are no workers, only candidates for the hand of the boss's daughter.) Furthermore, I have met only a very few people—and most of these were not Americans—who had any real desire to be free. Freedom is hard to bear. It can be objected that I am speaking of political freedom in spiritual terms, but the political institutions of any nation are always menaced and are ultimately controlled by the spiritual state of that nation. We are controlled here by our confusion, far more than we know, and the American dream has therefore become something much more closely resembling a nightmare, on the private, domestic, and international levels. Privately, we cannot stand our lives and dare not examine them; domestically, we take no responsibility for (and no pride in) what goes on in our country; and, internationally, for many millions of people, we are an unmitigated disaster. Whoever doubts this last statement has only to open his ears, his heart, his mind, to the testimony of—for example—any Cuban peasant or any Spanish poet, and ask himself what *he* would feel about us if *he* were the victim of our performance in pre-Castro Cuba or in Spain. We defend our curious role in Spain by referring to the Russian menace and the necessity of protecting the free world. It has not occurred to us that we have simply been mesmerized by Russia, and that the only real advantage Russia has in what we think of as a struggle between the East and the West is the moral history of the Western world. Russia's secret weapon is the bewilderment and despair and hunger of millions of people of whose existence we are scarcely aware. The Russian Communists are not in the least concerned about these people. But our ignorance and indecision have had the effect, if not of delivering them into Russian hands, of plunging them very deeply in the Russian shadow, for which effect—and it is hard to blame them—the most articulate among them, and the most oppressed as well, distrust us all the more. Our power and our fear of change help bind these people to their misery and bewilderment, and insofar as they find this state intolerable we are intolerably menaced. For if they find their state intolerable, but are too heavily oppressed to change it, they are simply pawns in the hands of larger powers, which, in such a context, are always unscrupulous, and when, eventually, they do change their situation—as in Cuba—we are menaced more than ever, by the vacuum that succeeds all violent upheavals. We should certainly know by now that it is one thing to overthrow a dictator or

203

repel an invader and quite another thing really to achieve a revolution. Time and time and time again, the people discover that they have merely betrayed themselves into the hands of yet another Pharaoh, who, since he was necessary to put the broken country together, will not let them go. Perhaps, people being the conundrums that they are, and having so little desire to shoulder the burden of their lives, this is what will always happen. But at the bottom of my heart I do not believe this. I think that people can be better than that, and I know that people can be better than they are. We are capable of bearing a great burden, once we discover that the burden is reality and arrive where reality is. Anyway, the point here is that we are living in an age of revolution, whether we will or no, and that America is the only Western nation with both the power and, as I hope to suggest, the experience that may help to make these revolutions real and minimize the human damage. Any attempt we make to oppose these outbursts of energy is tantamount to signing our death warrant.

Behind what we think of as the Russian menace lies what we do not wish to face, and what white Americans do not face when they regard a Negro: reality—the fact that life is tragic. Life is tragic simply because the earth turns and the sun inexorably rises and sets, and one day, for each of us, the sun will go down for the last, last time. Perhaps the whole root of our trouble, the human trouble, is that we will sacrifice all the beauty of our lives, will imprison ourselves in totems, taboos, crosses, blood sacrifices, steeples, mosques, races, armies, flags, nations, in order to deny the fact of death, which is the only fact we have. It seems to me that one ought to rejoice in the *fact* of death—ought to decide, indeed, to *earn* one's death by confronting with passion the conundrum of life. One is responsible to life: It is the small beacon in that terrifying darkness from which we come and to which we shall return. One must negotiate this passage as nobly as possible, for the sake of those who are coming after us. But white Americans do not believe in death, and this is why the darkness of my skin so intimidates them. And this is also why the presence of the Negro in this country can bring about its destruction. It is the responsibility of free men to trust and to celebrate what is constant—birth, struggle, and death are constant, and so is love, though we may not always think so—and to apprehend the nature of change, to be able and willing to change. I speak of change not on the surface but in the depths—change in the sense of renewal. But renewal becomes impossible if one supposes things to be constant that are not—safety, for example, or money, or power. One clings then to chimeras, by which one can only be betrayed, and the entire hope—the entire possibility—of freedom disappears. And by destruction I mean precisely the abdication by Americans of any effort really to be free.

The Negro can precipitate this abdication because white Americans have never, in all their long history, been able to look on him as a man like themselves. This point need not be labored; it is proved over and over again by the Negro's continuing position here, and his indescribable struggle to defeat the stratagems that white Americans have used, and use, to deny him his humanity. America could have used in other ways the energy that both groups have expended in this conflict. America, of all the Western nations, has been best placed to prove the uselessness and the obsolescence of the concept of color. But it has not dared to accept this opportunity, or even to conceive of it as an opportunity. White Americans have thought of it as their shame, and have envied those more civilized and elegant European nations that were untroubled by the presence of black men on their shores. This is because white Americans have supposed "Europe" and "civilization" to be synonyms—which they are not—and have been distrustful of other standards and other sources of vitality, especially those produced in America itself, and have attempted to behave in all matters as though what was east for Europe was also east for them. What it comes to is that if we, who can scarcely be considered a white nation, persist in thinking of ourselves as one, we condemn ourselves, with the truly white nations, to sterility and decay, whereas if we could accept ourselves *as we are*, we might bring new life to the Western achievements, and transform them. The price of this transformation is the unconditional freedom of the Negro; it is not too much to say that he, who has been so long rejected, must now be embraced, and at no matter what psychic or social risk. He is *the* key figure in his country, and the American future is precisely as bright or as dark as his. And the Negro recognizes this, in a negative way. Hence the question: Do I really *want* to be integrated into a burning house?

White Americans find it as difficult as white people elsewhere do to divest themselves of the notion that they are in possession of some intrinsic value that black people need, or want. And this assumption —which, for example, makes the solution to the Negro problem depend on the speed with which Negroes accept and adopt white standards— is revealed in all kinds of striking ways, from Bobby Kennedy's assurance that a Negro can become President in forty years to the unfortunate tone of warm congratulation with which so many liberals address their Negro equals. It is the Negro, of course, who is presumed to have become equal—an achievement that not only proves the comforting fact that perseverance has no color but also overwhelmingly corroborates the white man's sense of his own value. Alas, this value can scarcely be corroborated in any other way; there is certainly little enough in the white man's public or private life that one should desire to imitate. White men, at the bottom of their hearts, know this.

Therefore, a vast amount of the energy that goes into what we call the Negro problem is produced by the white man's profound desire not to be judged by those who are not white, not to be seen as he is, and at the same time a vast amount of the white anguish is rooted in the white man's equally profound need to be seen as he is, to be released from the tyranny of his mirror. All of us know, whether or not we are able to admit it, that mirrors can only lie, that death by drowning is all that awaits one there. It is for this reason that love is so desperately sought and so cunningly avoided. Love takes off the masks that we fear we cannot live without and know we cannot live within. I use the word "love" here not merely in the personal sense but as a state of being, or a state of grace—not in the infantile American sense of being made happy but in the tough and universal sense of quest and daring and growth. And I submit, then, that the racial tensions that menace Americans today have little to do with real antipathy—on the contrary, indeed—and are involved only symbolically with color. These tensions are rooted in the very same depths as those from which love springs, or murder. The white man's unadmitted— and apparently, to him, unspeakable—private fears and longings are projected onto the Negro. The only way he can be released from the Negro's tyrannical power over him is to consent, in effect, to become black himself, to become a part of that suffering and dancing country that he now watches wistfully from the heights of his lonely power and, armed with spiritual traveller's checks, visits surreptitiously after dark. How can one respect, let alone adopt, the values of a people who do not, on any level whatever, live the way they say they do, or the way they say they should? I cannot accept the proposition that the four-hundred-year travail of the American Negro should result merely in his attainment of the present level of the American civilization. I am far from convinced that being released from the African witch doctor was worthwhile if I am now—in order to support the moral contra-dictions and the spiritual aridity of my life—expected to become dependent on the American psychiatrist. It is a bargain I refuse. The only thing white people have that black people need, or should want, is power—and no one holds power forever. White people can-not, in the generality, be taken as models of how to live. Rather, the white man is himself in sore need of new standards, which will release him from his confusion and place him once again in fruitful communion with the depths of his own being. And I repeat: The price of the liberation of the white people is the liberation of the blacks—the total liberation, in the cities, in the towns, before the law, and in the mind. Why, for example—especially knowing the family as I do—I should *want* to marry your sister is a great mystery to me. But your sister and I have every right to marry if we wish to, and no

206

one has the right to stop us. If she cannot raise me to her level, perhaps I can raise her to mine.

In short, we, the black and the white, deeply need each other here if we are really to become a nation—if we are really, that is, to achieve our identity, our maturity, as men and women. To create one nation has proved to be a hideously difficult task; there is certainly no need now to create two, one black and one white. But white men with far more political power than that possessed by the Nation of Islam movement have been advocating exactly this, in effect, for generations. If this sentiment is honored when it falls from the lips of Senator Byrd, then there is no reason it should not be honored when it falls from the lips of Malcolm X. And any Congressional committee wishing to investigate the latter must also be willing to investigate the former. They are expressing exactly the same sentiments and represent exactly the same danger. There is absolutely no reason to suppose that white people are better equipped to frame the laws by which I am to be governed than I am. It is entirely unacceptable that I should have no voice in the political affairs of my own country, for I am not a ward of America; I am one of the first Americans to arrive on these shores.

This past, the Negro's past, of rope, fire, torture, castration, infanticide, rape; death and humiliation; fear by day and night, fear as deep as the marrow of the bone; doubt that he was worthy of life, since everyone around him denied it; sorrow for his women, for his kinfolk, for his children, who needed his protection, and whom he could not protect; rage, hatred, and murder, hatred for white men so deep that it often turned against him and his own, and made all love, all trust, all joy impossible—this past, this endless struggle to achieve and reveal and confirm a human identity, human authority, yet contains, for all its horror, something very beautiful. I do not mean to be sentimental about suffering—enough is certainly as good as a feast—but people who cannot suffer can never grow up, can never discover who they are. That man who is forced each day to snatch his manhood, his identity, out of the fire of human cruelty that rages to destroy it knows, if he survives his effort, and even if he does not survive it, something about himself and human life that no school on earth—and, indeed, no church—can teach. He achieves his own authority, and that is unshakable. This is because, in order to save his life, he is forced to look beneath appearances, to take nothing for granted, to hear the meaning behind the words. If one is continually surviving the worst that life can bring, one eventually ceases to be controlled by a fear of what life can bring; whatever it brings must be borne. And at this level of experience one's bitterness begins to be palatable, and hatred becomes too heavy a sack to carry. The apprehension of life here so briefly and inadequately sketched has been the experience of

generations of Negroes, and it helps to explain how they have endured
and how they have been able to produce children of kindergarten age
who can walk through mobs to get to school. It demands great force
and great cunning continually to assault the mighty and indifferent
fortress of white supremacy, as Negroes in this country have done so
long. It demands great spiritual resilience not to hate the hater whose
foot is on your neck, and an even greater miracle of perception and
charity not to teach your child to hate. The Negro boys and girls
who are facing mobs today come out of a long line of improbable
aristocrats—the only genuine aristocrats this country has produced.
I say "this country" because their frame of reference was totally
American. They were hewing out of the mountain of white supremacy
the stone of their individuality. I have great respect for that unsung
army of black men and women who trudged down back lanes and
entered back doors, saying "Yes, sir" and "No, Ma'am" in order to
acquire a new roof for the schoolhouse, new books, a new chemistry
lab, more beds for the dormitories, more dormitories. They did not
like saying "Yes, sir" and "No Ma'am," but the country was in no
hurry to educate Negroes, these black men and women knew that the
job had to be done, and they put their pride in their pockets in order
to do it. It is very hard to believe that they were in any way inferior
to the white men and women who opened those back doors. It is
very hard to believe that those men and women, raising their children,
eating their greens, crying their curses, weeping their tears, singing
their songs, making their love, as the sun rose, as the sun set, were in
any way inferior to the white men and women who crept over to share
these splendors after the sun went down. But we must avoid the
European error; we must not suppose that, because the situation, the
ways, the perceptions of black people so radically differed from those
of whites, they were racially superior. I am proud of these people
not because of their color but because of their intelligence and their
spiritual force and their beauty. The country should be proud of them,
too, but, alas, not many people in this country even know of their
existence. And the reason for this ignorance is that a knowledge of
the role these people played—and play—in American life would reveal
more about America to Americans than Americans wish to know.

The American Negro has the great advantage of having never
believed that collection of myths to which white Americans cling:
that their ancestors were all freedom-loving heroes, that they were
born in the greatest country the world has ever seen, or that Americans
are invincible in battle and wise in peace, that Americans have always
dealt honorably with Mexicans and Indians and all other neighbors or
inferiors, that American men are the world's most direct and virile,
that American women are pure. Negroes know far more about white

Americans than that; it can almost be said, in fact, that they know about white Americans what parents—or, anyway, mothers—know about their children, and that they very often regard white Americans that way. And perhaps this attitude, held in spite of what they know and have endured, helps to explain why Negroes, on the whole, and until lately, have allowed themselves to feel so little hatred. The tendency has really been, insofar as this was possible, to dismiss white people as the slightly mad victims of their own brainwashing. One watched the lives they led. One could not be fooled about that; one watched the things they did and the excuses that they gave themselves, and if a white man was really in trouble, deep trouble, it was to the Negro's door that he came. And one felt that if one had had that white man's worldly advantages, one would never have become as bewildered and as joyless and as thoughtlessly cruel as he. The Negro came to the white man for a roof or for five dollars or for a letter to the judge; the white man came to the Negro for love. But he was not often able to give what he came seeking. The price was too high; he had too much to lose. And the Negro knew this, too. When one knows this about a man, it is impossible for one to hate him, but unless he becomes a man—becomes equal—it is also impossible for one to love him. Ultimately, one tends to avoid him, for the universal characteristic of children is to assume that they have a monopoly on trouble, and therefore a monopoly on *you*. (Ask any Negro what he knows about the white people with whom he works. And then ask the white people with whom he works what they know about *him*.)

How can the American Negro past be used? It is entirely possible that this dishonored past will rise up soon to smite all of us. There are some wars, for example (if anyone on the globe is still mad enough to go to war) that the American Negro will not support, however many of his people may be coerced—and there is a limit to the number of people any government can put in prison, and a rigid limit indeed to the practicality of such a course. A bill is coming in that I fear America is not prepared to pay. "The problem of the twentieth century," wrote W. E. B. Du Bois around sixty years ago, "is the problem of the color line." A fearful and delicate problem, which compromises, when it does not corrupt, all the American efforts to build a better world—here, there, or anywhere. It is for this reason that everything white Americans think they believe in must now be reëxamined. What one would not like to see again is the consolidation of peoples on the basis of their color. But as long as we in the West place on color the value that we do, we make it impossible for the great unwashed to consolidate themselves according to any other principle. Color is not a human or a personal reality; it is a political reality. But this is a distinction so extremely hard to make that the

West has not been able to make it yet. And at the center of this dreadful storm, this vast confusion, stand the black people of this nation, who must now share the fate of a nation that has never accepted them, to which they were brought in chains. Well, if this is so, one has no choice but to do all in one's power to change that fate, and at no matter what risk—eviction, imprisonment, torture, death. For the sake of one's children, in order to minimize the bill that *they* must pay, one must be careful not to take refuge in any delusion—and the value placed on the color of the skin is always and everywhere and forever a delusion. I know that what I am asking is impossible. But in our time, as in every time, the impossible is the least that one can demand—and one is, after all, emboldened by the spectacle of human history in general, and American Negro history in particular, for it testifies to nothing less than the perpetual achievement of the impossible.

When I was very young, and was dealing with my buddies in those wine- and urine-stained hallways, something in me wondered, *What will happen to all that beauty?* For black people, though I am aware that some of us, black and white, do not know it yet, are very beautiful. And when I sat at Elijah's table and watched the baby, the women, and the men, and we talked about God's—or Allah's—vengeance, I wondered, when that vengeance was achieved, *What will happen to all that beauty then?* I could also see that the intransigence and ignorance of the white world might make that vengeance inevitable—a vengeance that does not really depend on, and cannot really be executed by, any person or organization, and that cannot be prevented by any police force or army: historical vengeance, a cosmic vengeance, based on the law that we recognize when we say, "Whatever goes up must come down." And here we are, at the center of the arc, trapped in the gaudiest, most valuable, and most improbable water wheel the world has ever seen. Everything now, we must assume, is in our hands; we have no right to assume otherwise. If we—and now I mean the relatively conscious whites and the relatively conscious blacks, who must, like lovers, insist on, or create, the consciousness of the others—do not falter in our duty now, we may be able, handful that we are, to end the racial nightmare, and achieve our country, and change the history of the world. If we do not now dare everything, the fulfillment of that prophecy, re-created from the Bible in song by a slave, is upon us: *God gave Noah the rainbow sign, No more water, the fire next time!*

RACE AND RACISM

The opening pages of Ruth Benedict's *Race: Science and Politics* (1940) serve as a better introduction to this section than any we could devise. The two Orwell essays that follow, characterized by his disarming honesty, deal primarily with the colonial experience. The first narrates his experience as a police officer in Burma which led to the recognition that "when the white man turns tyrant, it is his own freedom that he destroys"; the second describes a North African city as seen through the eyes of a white European and sounds a note of warning to all for whom the brown skin has been invisible.

The next four selections, together with the closing essay by James Baldwin in the preceding section, present, from varying points of view and in varying styles and tone, many of the implications of the black and white predicament in America. The closing piece by Frantz Fanon, African psychiatrist and revolutionary, brings to the problem of race and racism a broader and more universal perspective. Looking for a future, asking all to refuse being "sealed away in the materialized Tower of the Past" or "to accept the present as definitive," he concludes: "I recognize that I have one right alone: That of demanding human behavior from the other. One duty alone: That of not renouncing my freedom through my choices."

Ruth Benedict

Ruth Benedict was born in New York City in 1887. After receiving a B.A. degree from Vassar, she taught English in a girls' school and wrote and published some poetry under the name Anne Singleton. In 1914 she married Stanley R. Benedict, a biochemist. Five years later, at the age of thirty-two, Mrs. Benedict enrolled at Columbia, apparently because she wanted "busy work." Thus, almost by accident, she began the study of anthropology under Franz Boas, whom she later described as "the greatest of living anthropologists." She completed her doctorate in 1923 and immediately joined the faculty of Columbia, where she remained until her death in 1948. Mrs. Benedict's research, conducted on periodic field trips, made her a leading authority on the Indians of the American West. She has also been considered a pathfinder in her awareness of the relationship between anthropology and such other social sciences as psychology and sociology. This breadth of attention is evident in her Patterns of Culture *(1934). Other books by Mrs. Benedict are* The Concept of Guardian Spirit in North America *(1923),* Zuni Mythology *(1935), and* The Chrysanthemum and the Sword *(1946). As an introduction to this section, we reprint here the opening pages of the first chapter of* Race: Science and Politics *(1940).*

RACISM: THE ISM OF THE MODERN WORLD

As early as the late 1880's a French pro-Aryan, Vacher de Lapouge, wrote: "I am convinced that in the next century millions will cut each other's throats because of 1 or 2 degrees more or less of cephalic index." On the surface it appears a fantastic reason for world wars, and it was certainly a reason new under the sun. Was he right? What could it mean? The cephalic index is the quotient of the greatest breadth of the head divided by its length, and some tribes and peoples over the world run to high indices and some to low. Narrow heads are found among uncivilized primitives and among powerful and cultivated Western Europeans; broad heads are too. Neither the narrow heads of the whole world nor the broad heads stack up to show any obvious monopoly of glorious destiny or any corner on ability or virtue. Even in any one European nation or in America men of achievement have been some of them narrow-headed and some broad-

213

headed. What could it mean that "millions will cut each other's throats" because of the shape of the top of their skulls?

In the long history of the world men have given many reasons for killing each other in war: envy of another people's good bottom land or of their herds, ambition of chiefs and kings, different religious beliefs, high spirits, revenge. But in all these wars the skulls of the victims on both sides were generally too similar to be distinguished. Nor had the war leaders incited their followers against their enemies by referring to the shapes of their heads. They might call them the heathen, the barbarians, the heretics, the slayers of women and children, but never our enemy Cephalic Index 82.

It was left for high European civilization to advance such a reason for war and persecution and to invoke it in practice. In other words, racism is a creation of our own time. It is a new way of separating the sheep from the goats. The old parable in the New Testament separated mankind as individuals: on the one hand those who had done good, and on the other those who had done evil. The new way divides them by hereditary bodily characteristics—shape of the head, skin colour, nose form, hair texture, colour of the eyes—and those who have certain hallmarks are known by these signs to be weaklings and incapable of civilization, and those with the opposite are the hope of the world. Racism is the new Calvinism which asserts that one group has the stigmata of superiority and the other has those of inferiority. According to racism we know our enemies, not by their aggressions against us, not by their creed or language, not even by their possessing wealth we want to take, but by noting their hereditary anatomy. For the leopard cannot change his spots and by these you know he is a leopard.

For the individual, therefore, racism means that damnation or salvation in this world is determined at conception; an individual's good life cannot tip the balance in his favour and he cannot live a bad life if his physical type is the right sort. By virtue of birth alone each member of the "race" is high caste and rightly claims his place in the sun at the expense of men of other "races." He need not base his pride upon personal achievement nor upon virtue; he was born high caste.

From this postulate racism makes also an assertion about race: that the "good" anatomical hallmarks are the monopoly of a pure race which has always throughout history manifested its glorious destiny. The racialists have rewritten history to provide the scion of such a race with a long and glamorous group ancestry as gratifying as an individual coat of arms, and they assure him that the strength and vigour of his race are immutable and guaranteed by the laws of Nature. He must, however, guard this pure blood from contamination by that

214

of lesser breeds, lest degeneration follow and his race lose its supremacy. All over the world for the last generation this doctrine has been invoked in every possible kind of conflict: sometimes national, between peoples as racially similar as the French and Germans; sometimes across the colour line, as in Western fears of the Yellow Peril; sometimes in class conflicts, as in France; sometimes in conflicts between immigrants who arrived a little earlier and those who came a little later, as in America. It has become a bedlam.

Where all people claim to be tallest, not all can be right. In this matter of races, can the sciences to which they all appeal judge among the babel of contradictory claims and award the decision? Or is it a matter of false premises and bastard science? It is essential, if we are to live in this modern world, that we should understand Racism and be able to judge its arguments. We must know the facts first of Race, and then of this doctrine that has made use of them. For Racism is an *ism* to which everyone in the world today is exposed; for or against, we must take sides. And the history of the future will differ according to the decision which we make.

George Orwell

"Shooting an Elephant," based on Orwell's experiences in the Imperial Police in Burma, was written in the early 1930s and is the title essay in the collection Shooting an Elephant and Other Essays *(1950). "Marrakech," written in 1939, is included in the collection entitled* Such, Such Were the Joys *(1953). Both essays reflect Orwell's fear of the vague and abstract, his conviction that ideas derive from experience, and that experience is best conveyed in concrete and specific terms. For further information about the author, see page 79.*

SHOOTING AN ELEPHANT

In Moulmein, in Lower Burma, I was hated by large numbers of people—the only time in my life that I have been important enough for this to happen to me. I was sub-divisional police officer of the

215

town, and in an aimless, petty kind of way anti-European feeling was very bitter. No one had the guts to raise a riot, but if a European woman went through the bazaars alone somebody would probably spit betel juice over her dress. As a police officer I was an obvious target and was baited whenever it seemed safe to do so. When a nimble Burman tripped me up on the football field and the referee (another Burman) looked the other way, the crowd yelled with hideous laughter. This happened more than once. In the end the sneering yellow faces of young men that met me everywhere, the insults hooted after me when I was at a safe distance, got badly on my nerves. The young Buddhist priests were the worst of all. There were several thousands of them in the town and none of them seemed to have anything to do except stand on street corners and jeer at Europeans.

All this was perplexing and upsetting. For at that time I had already made up my mind that imperialism was an evil thing and the sooner I chucked up my job and got out of it the better. Theoretically —and secretly, of course—I was all for the Burmese and all against their oppressors, the British. As for the job I was doing, I hated it more bitterly than I can perhaps make clear. In a job like that you see the dirty work of Empire at close quarters. The wretched prisoners huddling in the stinking cages of the lock-ups, the grey, cowed faces of the long-term convicts, the scarred buttocks of the men who had been flogged with bamboos—all these oppressed me with an intolerable sense of guilt. But I could get nothing into perspective. I was young and ill-educated and I had had to think out my problems in the utter silence that is imposed on every Englishman in the East. I did not even know that the British Empire is dying, still less did I know that it is a great deal better than the younger empires that are going to supplant it. All I knew was that I was stuck between my hatred of the empire I served and my rage against the evil-spirited little beasts who tried to make my job impossible. With one part of my mind I thought of the British Raj as an unbreakable tyranny, as something clamped down, in *saecula saeculorum*, upon the will of prostrate peoples; with another part I thought that the greatest joy in the world would be to drive a bayonet into a Buddhist priest's guts. Feelings like these are the normal by-products of imperialism; ask any Anglo-Indian official, if you can catch him off duty.

One day something happened which in a roundabout way was enlightening. It was a tiny incident in itself, but it gave me a better glimpse than I had had before of the real nature of imperialism—the real motives for which despotic governments act. Early one morning the sub-inspector at a police station the other end of the town rang me up on the 'phone and said that an elephant was ravaging the bazaar. Would I please come and do something about it? I did not know what I could do, but I wanted to see what was happening and I got on to a pony and started out. I took my rifle, an old .44 Winchester and much too small to kill an elephant, but I thought the noise might be useful *in terrorem*. Various Burmans stopped me on the way and told me about the elephant's doings. It was not, of course, a wild elephant, but a tame one which had gone "must." It had been chained up, as tame elephants always are when their attack of "must" is due, but on the previous night it had broken its chain and escaped. Its mahout, the only person who could manage it when it was in that state, had set out in pursuit, but had taken the wrong direction and was now twelve hours' journey away, and in the morning the elephant had suddenly reappeared in the town. The Burmese population had no weapons and were quite helpless against it. It had already destroyed somebody's bamboo hut, killed a cow and raided some fruit-stalls and devoured the stock; also it had met the municipal rubbish van and, when the driver jumped out and took to his heels, had turned the van over and inflicted violences upon it.

The Burmese sub-inspector and some Indian constables were waiting for me in the quarter where the elephant had been seen. It was a very poor quarter, a labyrinth of squalid bamboo huts, thatched with palm-leaf, winding all over a steep hillside. I remember that it was a cloudy, stuffy morning at the beginning of the rains. We began questioning the people as to where the elephant had gone and, as usual, failed to get any definite information. That is invariably the case in the East; a story always sounds clear enough at a distance, but the nearer you get to the scene of events the vaguer it becomes. Some of the people said that the elephant had gone in one direction, some said that he had gone in another, some professed not even to have heard of any elephant. I had almost made up my mind that the whole story was a pack of lies, when we heard yells a little distance away. There was a loud, scandalized cry of "Go away, child! Go away this instant!" and an old woman with a switch in her hand came round the corner of a hut, violently shooing away a crowd of naked children. Some more women followed, clicking their tongues and exclaiming; evidently there was something that the children ought not to have seen. I rounded the hut and saw a man's dead body sprawling in the mud. He was an Indian, a black Dravidian coolie, almost naked, and he could not have been dead many minutes. The people said that the elephant had come suddenly upon him round the corner of the hut, caught him with its trunk, put its foot on his back and ground him into the earth. This was the rainy season and the ground was soft, and his face had scored a trench a foot deep and a couple of yards long. He was lying on his belly with arms crucified and head sharply twisted to one side. His face was coated with mud, the eyes wide open, the teeth bared and grinning with an expression of unendurable agony. (Never tell me, by the way, that the dead look peaceful. Most of the corpses I have seen looked devilish.) The friction of the great beast's foot had stripped the skin from his back as neatly as one skins a rabbit. As soon as I saw the dead man I sent an orderly to a friend's house nearby to borrow an elephant rifle. I had already sent back the pony, not wanting it to go mad with fright and throw me if it smelt the elephant.

The orderly came back in a few minutes with a rifle and five cartridges, and meanwhile some Burmans had arrived and told us that the elephant was in the paddy fields below, only a few hundred yards away. As I started forward practically the whole population of the quarter flocked out of the houses and followed me. They had seen the rifle and were all shouting excitedly that I was going to shoot the elephant. They had not shown much interest in the elephant when he was merely ravaging their homes, but it was different now that he was going to be shot. It was a bit of fun to them, as it would be to an English crowd; besides they wanted the meat. It made me vaguely uneasy. I had no intention of shooting the elephant—I had merely sent for the rifle to defend myself if necessary—and it is always unnerving to have a crowd following you. I marched down the hill, looking and feeling a fool, with the rifle over my shoulder and an ever-growing army of people jostling at my heels. At the bottom, when you got away from the huts, there was a metalled road and beyond that a miry waste of paddy fields a thousand yards across, not yet ploughed but soggy from the first rains and dotted with coarse grass. The elephant was standing eight yards from the road, his left side towards us. He took not the slightest notice of the crowd's approach. He was tearing up bunches of grass, beating them against his knees to clean them and stuffing them into his mouth.

I had halted on the road. As soon as I saw the elephant I knew with perfect certainty that I ought not to shoot him. It is a serious matter to shoot a working elephant—it is comparable to destroying a huge and costly piece of machinery—and obviously one ought not to do it if it can possibly be avoided. And at that distance, peacefully eating, the elephant looked no more dangerous than a cow. I thought then and I think now that his attack of "must" was already passing off; in which case he would merely wander harmlessly about until the mahout came back and caught him. Moreover, I did not in the least want to shoot him. I decided that I would watch him for a little while to make sure that he did not turn savage again, and then go home.

But at that moment I glanced round at the crowd that had followed me. It was an immense crowd, two thousand at the least and growing

218

every minute. It blocked the road for a long distance on either side. I looked at the sea of yellow faces above the garish clothes—faces all happy and excited over this bit of fun, all certain that the elephant was going to be shot. They were watching me as they would watch a conjurer about to perform a trick. They did not like me, but with the magical rifle in my hands I was momentarily worth watching. And suddenly I realized that I should have to shoot the elephant after all. The people expected it of me and I had got to do it; I could feel their two thousand wills pressing me forward, irresistibly. And it was at this moment, as I stood there with the rifle in my hands, that I first grasped the hollowness, the futility of the white man's dominion in the East. Here was I, the white man with his gun, standing in front of the unarmed native crowd—seemingly the leading actor of the piece; but in reality I was only an absurd puppet pushed to and fro by the will of those yellow faces behind. I perceived in this moment that when the white man turns tyrant it is his own freedom that he destroys. He becomes a sort of hollow, posing dummy, the conventionalized figure of a sahib. For it is the condition of his rule that he shall spend his life in trying to impress the "natives," and so in every crisis he has got to do what the "natives" expect of him. He wears a mask, and his face grows to fit it. I had got to shoot the elephant. I had committed myself to doing it when I sent for the rifle. A sahib has got to act like a sahib; he has got to appear resolute, to know his own mind and do definite things. To come all that way, rifle in hand, with two thousand people marching at my heels, and then to trail feebly away, having done nothing—no, that was impossible. The crowd would laugh at me. And my whole life, every white man's life in the East, was one long struggle not to be laughed at.

But I did not want to shoot the elephant. I watched him beating his bunch of grass against his knees, with that preoccupied grandmotherly air that elephants have. It seemed to me that it would be murder to shoot him. At that age I was not squeamish about killing animals, but I had never shot an elephant and never wanted to. (Somehow it always seems worse to kill a *large* animal.) Besides, there was the beast's owner to be considered. Alive, the elephant was worth at least a hundred pounds; dead, he would only be worth the value of his tusks, five pounds, possibly. But I had got to act quickly. I turned to some experienced-looking Burmans who had been there when we arrived, and asked them how the elephant had been behaving. They all said the same thing: he took no notice of you if you left him alone, but he might charge if you went too close to him.

It was perfectly clear to me what I ought to do. I ought to walk up to within, say, twenty-five yards of the elephant and test his behavior. If he charged, I could shoot; if he took no notice of me, it would be safe to leave him until the mahout came back. But also I knew that I was going to do no such thing. I was a poor shot with a rifle and the ground was soft mud into which one would sink at every step. If the elephant charged and I missed him, I should have about as much chance as a toad under a steam-roller. But even then I was not thinking particularly of my own skin, only of the watchful yellow faces behind. For at that moment, with the crowd watching me, I was not afraid in the ordinary sense, as I would have been if I had been alone. A white man mustn't be frightened in front of "natives"; and so, in general, he isn't frightened. The sole thought in my mind was that if anything went wrong those two thousand Burmans would see me pursued, caught, trampled on and reduced to a grinning corpse like that Indian up the hill. And if that happened it was quite probable that some of them would laugh. That would never do. There was only one alternative. I shoved the cartridges into the magazine and lay down on the road to get a better aim.

The crowd grew very still, and a deep, low, happy sigh, as of people who see the theatre curtain go up at last, breathed from innumerable throats. They were going to have their bit of fun after all. The rifle was a beautiful German thing with cross-hair sights. I did not then know that in shooting an elephant one would shoot to cut an imaginary bar running from ear-hole to ear-hole. I ought, therefore, as the elephant was sideways on, to have aimed straight at his ear-hole; actually I aimed several inches in front of this, thinking the brain would be further forward.

When I pulled the trigger I did not hear the bang or feel the kick—one never does when a shot goes home—but I heard the devilish roar of glee that went up from the crowd. In that instant, in too short a time, one would have thought, even for the bullet to get there, a mysterious, terrible change had come over the elephant. He neither stirred nor fell, but every line of his body had altered. He looked suddenly stricken, shrunken, immensely old, as though the frightful impact of the bullet had paralysed him without knocking him down. At last, after what seemed a long time—it might have been five seconds, I dare say—he sagged flabbily to his knees. His mouth slobbered. An enormous senility seemed to have settled upon him. One could have imagined him thousands of years old. I fired again into the same spot. At the second shot he did not collapse but climbed with desperate slowness to his feet and stood weakly upright, with legs sagging and head drooping. I fired a third time. That was the shot that did for him. You could see the agony of it jolt his whole body and knock the last remnant of strength from his legs. But in falling he seemed for a moment to rise, for as his hind legs collapsed beneath him he seemed to tower upward like a huge rock toppling, his trunk reaching skywards like a tree. He trumpeted, for the first and only time. And then down he came, his belly towards me, with a crash that seemed to shake the ground even where I lay.

I got up. The Burmans were already racing past me across the mud. It was obvious that the elephant would never rise again, but he was not dead. He was breathing very rhythmically with long rattling gasps, his great mound of a side painfully rising and falling. His mouth was wide open—I could see far down into caverns of pale pink throat. I waited a long time for him to die, but his breathing did not weaken. Finally I fired my two remaining shots into the spot where I thought his heart must be. The thick blood welled out of him like red velvet, but still he did not die. His body did not even jerk when the shots hit him, the tortured breathing continued without a pause. He was dying, very slowly and in great agony, but in some world remote from me where not even a bullet could damage him further. I felt that I had got to put an end to that dreadful noise. It seemed dreadful to see the great beast lying there, powerless to move and yet powerless to die, and not even to be able to finish him. I sent back for my small rifle and poured shot after shot into his heart and down his throat. They seemed to make no impression. The tortured gasps continued as steadily as the ticking of a clock.

In the end I could not stand it any longer and went away. I heard later that it took him half an hour to die. Burmans were bringing dahs and baskets even before I left, and I was told they had stripped his body almost to the bones by the afternoon.

Afterwards, of course, there were endless discussions about the shooting of the elephant. The owner was furious, but he was only an Indian and could do nothing. Besides, legally I had done the right thing, for a mad elephant has to be killed, like a mad dog, if its owner fails to control it. Among the Europeans opinion was divided. The older men said I was right, the younger men said it was a damn shame to shoot an elephant for killing a coolie, because an elephant was worth more than any damn Coringhee coolie. And afterwards I was very glad that the coolie had been killed; it put me legally in the right and it gave me a sufficient pretext for shooting the elephant. I often wondered whether any of the others grasped that I had done it solely to avoid looking a fool.

MARRAKECH

As the corpse went past the flies left the restaurant table in a cloud and rushed after it, but they came back a few minutes later.

The little crowd of mourners—all men and boys, no women—threaded their way across the market-place between the piles of pomegranates and the taxis and the camels, wailing a short chant over and over again. What really appeals to the flies is that the corpses here are never put into coffins, they are merely wrapped in a piece of rag and carried on a rough wooden bier on the shoulders of four friends. When the friends get to the burying-ground they hack an oblong hole a foot or two deep, dump the body in it and fling over it a little of the dried-up, lumpy earth, which is like broken brick. No grave-stone, no name, no identifying mark of any kind. The burying-ground is merely a huge waste of hummocky earth, like a derelict building-lot. After a month or two no one can even be certain where his own relatives are buried.

When you walk through a town like this—two hundred thousand inhabitants, of whom at least twenty thousand own literally nothing except the rags they stand up in—when you see how the people live, and still more how easily they die, it is always difficult to believe that you are walking among human beings. All colonial empires are in reality founded upon that fact. The people have brown faces—besides, there are so many of them! Are they really the same flesh as yourself? Do they even have names? Or are they merely a kind of undifferentiated brown stuff, about as individual as bees or coral insects? They rise out of the earth, they sweat and starve for a few years, and then they sink back into the nameless mounds of the grave-yard and nobody notices that they are gone. And even the graves themselves soon fade back into the soil. Sometimes, out for a walk, as you break your way through the prickly pear, you notice that it is rather bumpy underfoot, and only a certain regularity in the bumps tells you that you are walking over skeletons.

I was feeding one of the gazelles in the public gardens.

Gazelles are almost the only animals that look good to eat when they are still alive, in fact, one can hardly look at their hindquarters without thinking of mint sauce. The gazelle I was feeding seemed to know that this thought was in my mind, for though it took the piece of bread I was holding out it obviously did not like me. It nibbled rapidly at the bread, then lowered its head and tried to butt me, then took another nibble and then butted again. Probably its idea was that if it could drive me away the bread would somehow remain hanging in mid-air.

An Arab navvy working on the path nearby lowered his heavy hoe and sidled slowly towards us. He looked from the gazelle to the bread and from the bread to the gazelle, with a sort of quiet amazement, as though he had never seen anything quite like this before. Finally he said shyly in French:

"I could eat some of that bread."

I tore off a piece and he stowed it gratefully in some secret place under his rags. This man is an employee of the Municipality.

When you go through the Jewish quarters you gather some idea of what the medieval ghettoes were probably like. Under their Moorish rulers the Jews were only allowed to own land in certain restricted areas, and after centuries of this kind of treatment they have ceased to bother about overcrowding. Many of the streets are a good deal less than six feet wide, the houses are completely windowless, and sore-eyed children cluster everywhere in unbelievable numbers, like clouds of flies. Down the centre of the street there is generally running a little river of urine.

In the bazaar huge families of Jews, all dressed in the long black robe and little black skull-cap, are working in dark fly-infested booths that look like caves. A carpenter sits cross-legged at a prehistoric lathe, turning chair-legs at lightning speed. He works the lathe with a bow in his right hand and guides the chisel with his left foot, and thanks to a lifetime of sitting in this position his left leg is warped out of shape. At his side his grandson, aged six, is already starting on the simpler parts of the job.

I was just passing the coppersmiths' booths when somebody noticed that I was lighting a cigarette. Instantly, from the dark holes all round, there was a frenzied rush of Jews, many of them old grandfathers with flowing grey beards, all clamouring for a cigarette. Even a blind man somewhere at the back of one of the booths heard a rumour of cigarettes and came crawling out, groping in the air with his hand. In about a minute I had used up the whole packet. None of these people, I suppose, works less than twelve hours a day, and every one of them looks on a cigarette as a more or less impossible luxury.

As the Jews live in self-contained communities they follow the same trades as the Arabs, except for agriculture. Fruit-sellers, potters, silversmiths, blacksmiths, butchers, leatherworkers, tailors, water-carriers, beggars, porters—whichever way you look you see nothing but Jews. As a matter of fact there are thirteen thousand of them, all living in the space of a few acres. A good job Hitler wasn't here. Perhaps he was on his way, however. You hear the usual dark rumours about the Jews, not only from the Arabs but from the poorer Europeans.

"Yes, mon vieux, they took my job away from me and gave it to a Jew. The Jews! They're the real rulers of this country, you know.

GEORGE ORWELL

They've got all the money. They control the banks, finance—everything."

"But," I said, "isn't it a fact that the average Jew is a labourer working for about a penny an hour?"

"Ah, that's only for show! They're all moneylenders really. They're cunning, the Jews."

In just the same way, a couple of hundred years ago, poor old women used to be burned for witchcraft when they could not even work enough magic to get themselves a square meal.

All people who work with their hands are partly invisible, and the more important the work they do, the less visible they are. Still, a white skin is always fairly conspicuous. In northern Europe, when you see a labourer ploughing a field, you probably give him a second glance. In a hot country, anywhere south of Gibraltar or east of Suez, the chances are that you don't even see him. I have noticed this again and again. In a tropical landscape one's eye takes in everything except the human beings. It takes in the dried-up soil, the prickly pear, the palm tree and the distant mountain, but it always misses the peasant hoeing at his patch. He is the same colour as the earth, and a great deal less interesting to look at.

It is only because of this that the starved countries of Asia and Africa are accepted as tourist resorts. No one would think of running cheap trips to the Distressed Areas. But where the human beings have brown skins their poverty is simply not noticed. What does Morocco mean to a Frenchman? An orange-grove or a job in Government service. Or to an Englishman? Camels, castles, palm trees, Foreign Legionnaires, brass trays, and bandits. One could probably live there for years without noticing that for nine-tenths of the people the reality of life is an endless, backbreaking struggle to wring a little food out of an eroded soil.

Most of Morocco is so desolate that no wild animal bigger than a hare can live on it. Huge areas which were once covered with forest have turned into a treeless waste where the soil is exactly like broken-up brick. Nevertheless a good deal of it is cultivated, with frightful labour. Everything is done by hand. Long lines of women, bent double like inverted capital L's, work their way slowly across the fields, tearing up the prickly weeds with their hands, and the peasant gathering lucerne for fodder pulls it up stalk by stalk instead of reaping it, thus saving an inch or two on each stalk. The plough is a wretched wooden thing, so frail that one can easily carry it on one's shoulder, and fitted underneath with a rough iron spike which stirs the soil to a depth of about four inches. This is as much as the strength of the animals is

224

equal to. It is usual to plough with a cow and a donkey yoked together. Two donkeys would not be quite strong enough, but on the
other hand two cows would cost a little more to feed. The peasants
possess no harrows, they merely plough the soil several times over in
different directions, finally leaving it in rough furrows, after which the
whole field has to be shaped with hoes into small oblong patches to
conserve water. Except for a day or two after the rare rainstorms
there is never enough water. Along the edges of the fields channels
are hacked out to a depth of thirty or forty feet to get at the tiny
trickles which run through the subsoil.

Every afternoon a file of very old women passes down the road outside my house, each carrying a load of firewood. All of them are
mummified with age and the sun, and all of them are tiny. It seems
to be generally the case in primitive communities that the women,
when they get beyond a certain age, shrink to the size of children.
One day a poor old creature who could not have been more than four
feet tall crept past me under a vast load of wood. I stopped her and
put a five-sou piece (a little more than a farthing) into her hand. She
answered with a shrill wail, almost a scream, which was partly gratitude
but mainly surprise. I suppose that from her point of view, by taking
any notice of her, I seemed almost to be violating a law of nature.
She accepted her status as an old woman, that is to say as a beast
of burden. When a family is travelling it is quite usual to see a father
and a grown-up son riding ahead on donkeys, and an old woman following on foot, carrying the baggage.

But what is strange about these people is their invisibility. For
several weeks, always at about the same time of day, the file of old
women had hobbled past the house with their firewood, and though
they had registered themselves on my eyeballs I cannot truly say that
I had seen them. Firewood was passing—that was how I saw it. It
was only that one day I happened to be walking behind them, and the
curious up-and-down motion of a load of wood drew my attention to
the human being beneath it. Then for the first time I noticed the poor
old earth-coloured bodies, bodies reduced to bones and leathery skin,
bent double under the crushing weight. Yet I suppose I had not been
five minutes on Moroccan soil before I noticed the overloading of the
donkeys and was infuriated by it. There is no question that the donkeys are damnably treated. The Moroccan donkey is hardly bigger
than a St. Bernard dog, it carries a load which in the British Army
would be considered too much for a fifteen-hands mule, and very
often its pack-saddle is not taken off its back for weeks together.
But what is peculiarly pitiful is that it is the most willing creature on
earth, it follows its master like a dog and does not need either bridle

or halter. After a dozen years of devoted work it suddenly drops dead, whereupon its master tips it into the ditch and the village dogs have torn its guts out before it is cold.

This kind of thing makes one's blood boil, whereas—on the whole—the plight of the human beings does not. I am not commenting, merely pointing to a fact. People with brown skins are next door to invisible. Anyone can be sorry for the donkey with its galled back, but it is generally owing to some kind of accident if one even notices the old woman under her load of sticks.

As the storks flew northward the Negroes were marching southward —a long, dusty column, infantry, screw-gun batteries, and then more infantry, four or five thousand men in all, winding up the road with a clumping of boots and a clatter of iron wheels.

They were Senegalese, the blackest Negroes in Africa, so black that sometimes it is difficult to see whereabouts on their necks the hair begins. Their splendid bodies were hidden in reach-me-down khaki uniforms, their feet squashed into boots that looked like blocks of wood, and every tin hat seemed to be a couple of sizes too small. It was very hot and the men had marched a long way. They slumped under the weight of their packs and the curiously sensitive black faces were glistening with sweat.

As they went past a tall, very young Negro turned and caught my eye. But the look he gave me was not in the least the kind of look you might expect. Not hostile, not contemptuous, not sullen, not even inquisitive. It was the shy, wide-eyed Negro look, which actually is a look of profound respect. I saw how it was. This wretched boy, who is a French citizen and has therefore been dragged from the forest to scrub floors and catch syphilis in garrison towns, actually has feelings of reverence before a white skin. He has been taught that the white race are his masters, and he still believes it.

But there is one thought which every white man (and in this connection it doesn't matter twopence if he calls himself a socialist) thinks when he sees a black army marching past. "How much longer can we go on kidding these people? How long before they turn their guns in the other direction?"

It was curious, really. Every white man there had this thought stowed somewhere or other in his mind. I had it, so had the other onlookers, so had the officers on their sweating chargers and the white N.C.O.'s marching in the ranks. It was a kind of secret which we all knew and were too clever to tell; only the Negroes didn't know it. And really it was like watching a flock of cattle to see the long column, a mile or two miles of armed men, flowing peacefully up the road, while the great white birds drifted over them in the opposite direction, glittering like scraps of paper.

[1939]

Robert Coles

Robert Coles (born 1929) is a psychiatrist and student of the problems of poverty and racial discrimination. He was born in New England, attended Harvard, received his M.D. at Columbia, and then trained in child psychiatry, following the direction pointed by Anna Freud and Erik Erikson. After completing his residency he became head of an air force neuropsychiatric hospital in Biloxi, Mississippi. In 1961–1963 he returned to the South to study the psychiatric aspects of school desegregation. His work with both children and adults is vividly described in Children of Crisis: A Study of Courage and Fear *(1967), from which we take the present essay. He has since undertaken work with migrant and tenant farm children, as well as with northern city and ghetto children, and is now research psychiatrist and lecturer in education at Harvard. A recipient of many honors, including the Hofheimer research prize of the American Psychiatric Association, he is a prolific writer of magazine articles and books. Among the latter are* Wages of Neglect *(with Maria Piers, 1969),* Still Hungry in America *(1969), and* Teachers and the Children of Poverty *(1970).*

THE LAST DITCH

On August 5, 1964, a press service story quoted an FBI agent who was working in the area of Neshoba County, Mississippi, where the remains of three civil rights workers were found: "I wish I could have a psychiatrist examine whoever did this right now and see what they'd be thinking now that we've got the bodies."

I had heard a similar remark several weeks earlier from an agent in

McComb, Mississippi. A house occupied by several "integrationists" had just been badly damaged by dynamite, and while I was looking into some of the medical problems—two students were injured—the officer was trying to find out who was responsible for the explosion. Standing near the debris with soda pop in our hands we talked about the details of the incident. The officer assured me that it was a serious attempt at murder rather than a mere effort to warn and frighten, and then he turned his attention to explanations. Why would people want to do this? He asked it, then I asked it, both of us less curious than appalled. Yet, slowly the curiosity rose in him, and well after we had finished our talk he came back to the question. Why would anyone have nothing better to do in the middle of the night than plant dynamite? He was clearly suggesting that only an unhappy, a disturbed person would be awake so late, preparing that kind of deed. Perhaps, he suggested, I had some thoughts on that matter.

We each returned to our work, though I found myself ruminating about how indeed I might have explained to him exactly what my thoughts were. As I tried to lay that challenge to rest I kept on coming back to the chief capability we have in psychiatry, the case history. Perhaps if we had had the time I would have been able to show him what I felt to be the answer to his question by telling him about a particular segregationist's life, including of course the life of his mind.

This man did not murder the three civil rights workers, or plant dynamite in that home in the terror-stricken McComb area of Mississippi; but he has committed appallingly similar acts, in company with many others. He has been in mobs and will not deny having seen Negroes assaulted and killed as a result. I am sure he would satisfy those agents and all of us as a prototype of the bigot who is a potential killer. I thought of him immediately that morning in McComb, and again when I read the report of the government agent's dismayed call for psychiatric help in Philadelphia.

I first met John, as I shall call him, while he was protesting the archbishop's decision to admit some children who were Negro but also Catholic to the parochial schools of New Orleans. It was a warm, faintly humid early spring day, a Saturday too, and the next year's school opening hardly seemed a timely worry. Up and down he walked, picketing, tall, husky from the rear, an incipient paunch in front. He wore a brown suit, slightly frayed at the cuffs, and on its right shoulder rested his sign, wrought and lettered by himself: "Fight Integration. Communists Want Negroes With Whites." His shirt was starched and he wore a tie. He had brown eyes. He was bald but for the most meager line of black hair on his neck—baldness must have happened early and fast. His face was fleshy and largely unlined, and I thought, "Forty or forty-five."

Several of those in the picket line seemed unaware of the gazes they attracted. John, however, was the most engaging and communicative. Looking at people directly, he would talk with them if they showed the tiniest interest. He moved faster than the others, and seemed to be in charge, now signaling a new direction for walking, later approving or suggesting luncheon shifts.

We moved along the pavement side by side, he and I. Would I want a sign—he had several in reserve? I would rather talk with him; I was very much interested in his opinions. I felt it important that he, that they, not be misunderstood, and I would do my best to record fairly what he thought and wanted. I am a physician, I told him, a research physician specializing in problems of human adjustment under stress. A little amplification of this, and he laughed—it *was* a strain, the police and the scoffing people, and those reporters with the sly, obviously unfriendly questions. He would talk with reporters, any of them, so long as they were not niggers, not Communists, because he wanted to be heard. It was important to be heard or nothing could be accomplished. He wanted to do something, not merely have his say, and so he would surely talk with me if I were a teacher, if I wanted to report the truth to the educated. They needed the truth. I agreed. He was visibly impressed with certain credentials which, in my nervousness, I had offered: cards, pieces of paper which I now know were unnecessary for his cooperation. We began that day, later in the afternoon, signs put aside, over coffee. I arranged to meet him regularly, weekly, for several months at his home, or over coffee in a diner. He gradually told me about himself and his life, about what he believed and how he came to see things as he does.

He is a passionate segregationist ("you can put down the strongest, the strongest it's possible to be"). He has plans. He would like to exile most Negroes to Africa, perhaps sterilize a few quiet ones who would work at certain jobs fitting their animal nature, itself the work of God, he would emphasize. He would strip Jews of their fearful power, sending them off also, but to Russia, where they came from and yearn to return. There are other suspicious groups, Greeks, Lebanese—New Orleans is a port city, and he has worried about them leaving their boats. Do they try to *stay* on land? Unlike the niggers and Jews, whose clear danger to his city he had formulated for some time, he had not determined his exact position on such people, or his solution for them.

He was born in central Louisiana, say for example a town like Acme in Concordia Parish. The state is split into its southern, Catholic and French area and a northern section, basically Protestant and Anglo-

Saxon. Typically, his father was the former and his mother Scotch-Irish, a wayward Baptist who embraced the Roman Church (the only term used for the Catholic Church in certain areas of the so-called Bible Belt) a few weeks before her marriage. Born their second child in the month America entered the First World War, he was sickly and fatherless his first year of life. While his father fought in Europe the boy was taken with what we now call "allergies," a timid stomach which mostly rejected milk, a cranky skin which periodically exploded red, raw, itchy, and was often infected by his responsive scratches. His sister was five years older, and she remembered all this. She and her mother, still alive, have told him about his fretful infancy, and he knew it well enough to be able to pass on their memories. *His* first memory was a whipping from his father's strap. With his father home from war, a second son and last child was born. John was three. He had pinched the infant, done enough wrong to the child's skin to cause a cry and attract his father's punishing attention. That was to happen many times, though he held a special place in his mind for this earliest occasion: "My brother and I started off on the wrong track, and we've never got along with one another."

His brother is tall and thin, ruddy-faced and blue-eyed like his mother, wears a white shirt to a bank teller's job near their hometown. John, dark and short like his father, has several "blue-shirt" skills which at various times he has used. "I can build a house myself" was his way of summarizing them: carpentry, electric work, plumbing, even bricklaying.

The childhood development of the boys forked: one neat, precise, his mother's favorite as well as her physical reflection; the other, by his own description, naughty, often idle or busy being scrappy. John in short was an overlooked and troubled middle child. He resembled his father, yet had hated him for as long as he can remember. Oddly, though, his manner, his temperament sound like the father's as he describes the man and shows pictures of him, now ten years dead, a large blustery fellow, open, opinionated, rumpled, a mechanic pre-occupied with automobiles—under them daily, reading magazines about them by night. He had storms within him, and they fell upon his middle child, alone and arbitrarily, the boy felt.

Once John and I had talked long and hard—it seemed like a whole day. I noticed it had actually been three hours. The length of time measured a certain trust, a certain understanding that was developing between us. I found myself knowing him, recognizing some of the hardships he had endured, not just psychological ones, but the hunger and jobless panic which must have entered so many homes in a decade when I was scarcely born and he yet a child. I felt guilty for a moment, torn between him and the simple but of course complicated

230

facts and experiences of his life, and him as he now is, a shabby fanatic. He was feeling his own opening toward me, and with considerable emotion in his voice, lifting his right hand in a gesture which might well have been his father's, he interrupted our talk of Huey Long's racial attitudes and how they compared with those of his family: "Daddy [Southern fathers can be "daddy" to their children forever without embarrassment] had a bad temper, and I took it all myself. We had never had much money and bills would set him going, but he wouldn't touch my mother, or my brother or sister either. Yes" (I had asked), "my sister and brother both favored Ma, and Daddy, he'd feel no good because he couldn't get a week's pay, so he had to hit someone. Oh, he was for Huey boy all the way, except Huey was soft on niggers, but I think Daddy was, too. He used to say they were children, and we should protect them. But if they're like kids, they're like bad ones, and just like animals, so they've got to be watched over. You wouldn't let a wild animal go free in your home or in school with your kids, would you? It's right crazy how we forget that sometimes. Look at Harlem, and what happens when they let them go. They rape and kill our women and dirty the whole city up. I've been there and seen it. No" (prodded again), "I don't blame Daddy, because, you see, in those days we had them firm under our grip, so it was different and you didn't have to worry about them. But look at now." We did talk about current events for a few minutes, but each of us tired suddenly, and hardened.

Of course, from those old times to the present had been an eventful period for him as well as for the Negro race. He almost died twice. At seven he had a serious bout of pneumonia which—with no help from antibiotics—almost killed him. He recalled gratefully a Negro maid who cared for him through this, one of those (few now) who knew and willingly lived in her "place." She died shortly after he recovered. Abruptly and looking still young ("I think she was around forty, but you can't tell with niggers"), she collapsed before his very eyes while preparing supper for him. It was by his description probably a stroke that took her, and she proved irreplaceable. They had paid her a pittance, but she had stayed with them for lack of better. About that time several Negro families started moving North, while others trekked south to New Orleans. Though his father had not really been able to pay Willi-Jean her established wages for many months, only death ended her loyalty and their comfort. "I got pneumonia again when I was twelve, and so did my brother. It nearly killed Ma taking care of us. She used to try to keep everything in its place, I think that's why it was so hard without Willi-Jean. With us sick on top of it, she almost didn't get through it all, she got so nervous."

In telling him of my interest in his medical history, I asked him several times to describe in further detail his fits of illness, and the care given him during those times. It seemed clear that he had, in fact, suffered badly at his mother's hands, neglected by her for his sister or brother, blamed by her for getting sick. The Negro woman's sudden death was actually a severe and deeply resented blow to him. His affections for her were hastily buried with her. He had to keep on his guard against his mother's personality, now no longer buffered by Willi-Jean. During one of our last talks he said, "You know, Doc, I think I *did* have a bad time with sickness when I was a kid. When I was twelve I almost died of pneumonia, and then I broke my leg a few weeks after that and lost that year of school." He had tried to run away from home before he contracted pneumonia, and after his recovery, too, until his lame leg made such attempts impossible for a while.

If his mother was nervous, oppressively ritualistic, and hardly his advocate, his father was a heavy drinker, temper-ridden, and fearfully unpredictable. When drunk he was moody. He also became brutal, and his middle son was his customary target. Declaring a truth whose painful implications he could not look at too closely, John once reflected, "I never figured why Daddy picked on me. We got along fine when he was sober, but when he got liquored up, I got it first and hardest. I looked like him and helped him most in fixing things around the house, but he never remembered things like that when he was drunk." Not that his parents weren't "the nicest parents anyone could ever want." Any vision into their shortcomings, any criticism of them, had to be followed eventually by the atonement of heavy sentiment. He had long ago learned how dangerous it was to speak his mind. Perhaps his life, as we now see it, has been a quest for that very possibility. "I used to be afraid to say anything for fear it would get someone upset at home, so I just kept quiet and ran my trains." Trains were his chief hobby for a little longer than is usual, well into the early teens. He warmed while telling me about his empire of them, and he became wistful afterward. I wanted to hear of his childhood interests, and in speaking of them, he said ambiguously, "I knew trains better than anyone in town."

By the last two years of high school he had found an easier time. His mother reached menopause, surrendered in her war against dust and for order, and became cheerless and distant. His father now drank less, but had to struggle hard with another form of depression, an economic one which he shared with his country. Amid all this John strangely enough prospered. His sister married poorly, a marginal farmer soon dispossessed of his land. Slothful and malignant, he beat her regularly, fathered two children by her, and left shortly thereafter. She never remarried and has had to work hard to keep her two children fed and clothed. John's brother had trouble with learning. He left high school after one year, and for a time, nearly penniless, he drew food and small coin from government relief programs. Recently he has managed a job in a bank, but his wife is a heavy drinker, maybe worse, and they have five children. John says they "live like pigs," and apparently this state of decay set in very rapidly after their marriage. His brother's cleanest, most organized moments are at his job.

John, however, graduated from high school, the first in his family to do so, and went beyond that by securing a coveted job in the local hardware store. He had come to know its owner and his daughter, too. Always interested in fixing things—bicycles, injured cars, faltering plumbing, stray wires—he began in the hardware store as a willing and unpaid helper. The radio, new and mysterious, was his love, and he tinkered endlessly with the various models. The store had many other gadgets, and it also had his girl friend, the owner's daughter. He determined at about fifteen to marry her and did so at twenty. At the time of his marriage he was a relatively prosperous man, now wearing a white collar, regularly paid in dollars increasingly powerful out of their scarcity. ("My folks said I married real well, especially for those days.")

To hear him talk, the twelve months before and the twelve months after his wedding day were his best time. He remembers the pleasure and hope; but his nostalgia is brief, and is always tinctured with the bitterness which soon followed. His father-in-law's business collapsed, to be foreclosed by the handful of creditors who seemed to be gathering the entire countryside into their control. These provincial financiers, with their small banks all over the state, were controlled by Big Power and Big Money, both in New Orleans. Governor Huey had said so, and they killed him. John, with a wife and a boy of three months, had no choice but to try Huey's gambit—follow the Power, follow the Money. "We just up and moved. An uncle of my wife's thought he could get me work repairing radios. They were like TV today. No matter how poor you were, you needed some relaxation." John got a job and held it. He started by going into homes to repair wires or replace tubes. Soon he was selling radios themselves, all shapes and sizes on all kinds of payment plans. He was an exceptional salesman, seeing the radio as a box of easily summoned distraction for weary, uncertain people. He aimed at first not to sell but to explain, tracing with the future customer the webs and tangles of copper, informing his listener of their connections and rationale, pressing hard only at the end their whetted appetite, their need. ("Mostly they were people without cash.")

233

However, by the time a second world war was underway most Americans had radios, and his work slackened. In early 1942 he was the father of a four-year-old son, a two-year-old daughter. He owned a comfortable home in a distinctly middle-class area of white frame houses, each bulky, yet each a bit different. Most, though, had green shutters, high ceilings, thick walls, large, long windows, but no garage, all expressions of a warm, wet climate. More likely than not every residence had a single car so that the streets, palmy, well-paved, were lined on both sides just as from a plane's view the roofs asserted rows of radio antennae.

He still lives there, though many of his former neighbors have moved. For some the neighborhood was out of keeping with what they had recently become. They left for one-storied new houses in sprawling developments outside the city. The emigrants were replaced by others for whom the same neighborhood's value was defined by what they had just left. There are, however, a few who still prize those old houses, see their faintly shabby gentility and cherish their age and the memories they inspire. For John it is this way: "Those ranch houses are too expensive. Funny thing with a lot of the nigger lovers, they move out into the suburbs and then tell us how we should open our streets to them. I won't leave and I'd shoot to kill if they ever tried to buy a house nearby." (He cannot afford to leave. "They" are 2.4 miles away at their nearest.)

The war came as a relief. The economy was stagnant, floundering with too many unemployed. Poor people had bought their radios, and he was beginning to feel the pinch. ("Even the niggers had them. Some of them even had two.") Actually, he had sold many to Negroes in his years of salesmanship. He had collected money from them and taken showers after he came from their houses. Outweighing such services for Negroes was his participation in lynchings. He's been in two. His words: "We'd go home to see our folks, and you know in the country things are more direct, and there's no busybody reporters around. Once I heard one being organized, so I dropped by to see it." The other time was a rather spontaneous and informal affair. He noted that they "did it real quick like, the way you should. When you draw them out it makes it hard because you might get bad publicity. There are still lynchings around in farm country, I don't care what they tell you in the papers. We know how to take care of them when they get wise. We don't use rope, it's true, and get the crowds up we used to get. We may not always kill them, but we scare the Jesus out of them. You know the buckshot shootings you read about every now and then, it's the same thing as rope or fire. They know what'll happen if they get smart." Did he object at all to this? "Hell, no."

The Negroes were working for the Communists, any he would want to kill; I must know that. Had there been Communists in his town when he was a boy, during the twenties and thirties when lynchings were more public and common, some of them seen by him as a youth? Of course. The Communists took over in 1917, he knew the autumn month, but some of them had been working in this country even before that. He wasn't sure how far back, but he thought maybe twenty or thirty years, and they wanted to take this country, its free economy, for their prize. John was capable of broad, apocalyptic strokes: "This is a war between God and His Commandments and the Devil, and we may lose." I broached the subject of loss. How could God lose? "To punish us." Why would he want to do that? "We disobeyed him." Just an example or two—I was interested in them. "Nigger-loving."

In any case, he was glad to go to war in 1942, for he was accumulating unpaid bills. He yearned for the East—he wanted to go fight the Japs. He wasn't so sure about why we were fighting the Germans, who were combating the Reds, and might be our allies if we would have them. Hitler's enemies were his enemies: the Jews, moneyed, slyly alien and the main support of the Negroes, inferior lackeys who did their bidding for small reward. This was all communism, personified in those hundreds of thousands of hook-nosed or black-skinned natives who lived in New York, in Hollywood. They were the capitalists, too; they controlled publishing houses, banks and the stock exchanges. Their voices commanded a crippled, traitorous President's ear, bought the votes of errant, susceptible congressmen. "I was never against the Germans. I was proven right. Look at us now. They're our best protection against the Commies." Still, he added, the Germans would be of small help if the UN and integration took over America.

He never fought, though he helped others fight. He did his service at an army camp in New Jersey, a very small distance from Manhattan's subversion, perversion—and fascination. He went to New York all the time, to look, to see his enemy. He would always tell his friends how well he knew his New York enemies, and his friends, from what I could see, always seemed interested and stimulated by the details he supplied.

From all those furloughs to Union Square, Harlem and Greenwich Village he managed to return home alive, heavier by fifteen pounds, his balding completed. He worried about work after his discharge, with good reason. He came home to children grown older, a wife with moderate rheumatoid arthritis ("her joints are stiff all the time"). He was now irascible and sullen. His wife usually wanted to stay away from him—out of pain, out of lack of response. She was withdrawing into her narrowing world of routine care of the home and the symptoms of a chronic, slowly crippling disease. To help her she had a young Negro, a high school girl, not very experienced, but not very expensive. (The price of Negroes was rising, along with other postwar costs.) A mulatto, as thin and lissome—I gathered from pictures I saw of her with his children—as her mistress was fattening and severe, she stayed with them for three years, five part-time days a week, until her marriage bore unexpectedly heavy demands of her own in twin sons.

During those years right after the war John found life confusing and hard; and he became bitter. He tried television-repair work, but couldn't "connect with it" as with radio. He drew unemployment relief for a while, short rations in the face of consuming inflation. Finally, nearly drowning in doctor's bills, in debt even for essentials like food and the most urgently needed clothing, his home heavily mortgaged, he found rescue in the state government, a clerk's job in a motor vehicle registration office. Now barely secure, in his mid-thirties, he was free to settle into concentrated, serious suspicion and hate. It was, after all, the decade of the fifties, when many of our countrymen would seek far and wide for subversives—and when the Supreme Court would declare segregated schools unconstitutional.

I met him, of course, well ripened in such zeal and involved in actions based upon it. From our first meeting it was clear that he relished talking, and talked well. He had found comfort for his views from his employer, a Louisiana state government whose legislature, in its very chambers, had carried on a mock funeral of a federal judge, a native son who had ordered four Negro girls into two elementary schools in New Orleans.[1] The governor was a man whose chief merit seemed to be as a banjo player and singer whose theme song (composed by himself) was "You Are My Sunshine."

---

[1] Under the title of "Parents Stage Demonstration" the *New Orleans Times Picayune* of November 24, 1960, carried the following dispatch:

"Parents and children from integrated New Orleans schools bore a miniature black coffin, containing a blackened effigy of U.S. Judge J. Skelly Wright, into the Louisiana Capitol.

"Rep. Daniel Kelly, New Orleans, called House attention to the white parents and their children squeezing into aisles in the House open to spectators. Photographers had a field day.

"The House stood up and with a long roll of applause, saluted the parents. The legislature last week by resolution urged white parents to boycott the two integrated New Orleans schools.

"As the demonstrators moved into the legislative chambers, one woman in the group shouted, 'the judge is dead, we have slaughtered him.'

"Some of the group feigned weeping and mourning, others laughed.

"The blackened doll inside the yard-long coffin wore a black suit. In its pockets was a small gavel.

John dips constantly into the literature of segregation for support. It ranges all the way from the remarks of a scattering of biologists about a purported inferiority of the Negro on the basis of a supposedly lighter, smoother brain (fewer lines on the all-important frontal lobes) to the pathetic gibberish of the insane. He reads in such allied fields as the frantic anticommunism which holds the President and Supreme Court contaminated victims, even agents. There are always such diversions from the mainstream as the menacing ability fluorides have to erode America's freedom.

One of the first questions he had hurled at me, in our early tentative moments, was about his son. The young man was contemplating marriage and, a loyal Catholic, was about to attend a pre-marriage instruction course offered by their local church. The church was hellbent on integration, however, and John feared the worst for and of his son. Did I believe "in integrated marriage courses"? I wanted to know more about this. Well, he would kill his son if a Negro came into such a class and he, John Junior, remained. His customary composure cracked (one of the few times I was ever to see this, even when I knew him much better) and he shouted at me. I began to doubt whether he was "reasonable enough" for me ever to get to know "reasonably well." Yes, he'd kill his own son, he shouted. Would I? I thought not. Still, I told him I wanted to hear more about integrated marriage classes. Well, if I wanted to hear more, he would oblige.

The real truth was that he and his son hadn't been able to get along for many years, and for that matter he and his wife weren't now "together" as they used to be. Menopause along with arthritis had

---

"A small wreath of white flowers rested atop the coffin. Three pallbearers were on each side. Men, women and children were in the demonstration.

"Large and small black flags and some Confederate ensigns were carried by the demonstrators. Some women wore black veils.

"A little girl carried a black cross.

"Placards said, 'Thank God for the state legislature' and 'Davis our children's protector, thank God.'

"Chief villain in the eyes of the legislators Wednesday continued to be federal Judge Skelly Wright who issued an order for integration of four Negro first graders into New Orleans schools.

"Legislators still seethed over Wright's action in enjoining the Legislature from assuming control of the Orleans parish public school system.

"In the Senate, Sen. B. B. Rayburn of Bogalusa introduced a resolution calling for removal of Judge Wright. It called upon the congressional delegation to launch the action.

"Both the House and the Senate convened at about 10 A.M. Wednesday. There was little action in the Senate, which prepared to move over to the House for the joint session.

"Another resolution, approved by both Houses, called upon Judge Wright to recuse himself, 'because of his bias and prejudice against Louisiana.'"

come to his wife, heightening with its flashing signals her sense of decline, pulling her from her husband into a separate bed. (He still remembered his mother's menopausal depression, and he mentioned it when talking about his wife's health.) Once scornful of even an aspirin, she now juggled and swallowed seven separate encapsulated remedies. Their daughter, *his* daughter, his great delight for years, had rewarded him with excellent school work and high achievement in pre-college tests. Yet her success in the form of a full scholarship had eventually transported her away from home. Now it was their son, an office worker by day and part-time college student by night, who was about to leave. His family was dissolving, his marriage disintegrating. He was lonely.

"My boy is a fool, and he always has been." He became angry at first, but later appeared to regret his own remark. His son, it seems, cared little about Negroes and their threatening postures. He and his son had fought about ways of dressing, table manners and hobbies; had fought all along as the boy tried his own ways and John resisted, tried to pinion the lad, fashion him in his father's image. Murderous thoughts by a father at the shameful possibility of his son's "church marriage class" becoming desegregated were but a final expression of long-standing turmoil.

It was against a background of such family problems that John ardently pursued a world as white and shadowless as possible. His work for most of the fifteen-odd years since the war had been uncertain or dull. He tired of temporary jobs selling in stores, then became bored with the security but confinement and meager pay of his state position. About a year before I met him he had run for a significant political office, claiming he would ferret out Communists in his district, export Negroes North or across the Atlantic, deprive Jews of any local if hidden sovereignty, and keep a careful, alert eye upon Washington and New York. He lost, but polled a good vote. In the course of the campaign he met a man who shared his ideals. The man owned gas stations, more of them than he could operate by himself. ("He liked to watch the help, just like me. You can't trust a nigger out of the reach of your eye.") John, priding himself on his sharp vision, purchased one of the stations, mortgaging his house further. His wife was enraged; her arthritis worsened, a coincidence he noticed and wanted me to know about. Selling fuel was a tough but slimly profitable venture; a fortunate arrangement in some ways, however, because he was able to inform a fellow gasoline vendor, fast and angrily, about a Negro employee working for him whose child was one of the handful to initiate school desegregation. John helped organize the mobs around the city's desegregated schools. He was noisily attentive to those buildings, those nearly deserted and embattled buildings where a few

Negro and white children stubbornly persisted in getting educated together. To enable the Negro attendant to lose his job was actually as heartening an experience as John had enjoyed in a long time, and he referred back to this accomplishment frequently. He liked disorder in the streets, but he was not one to pass up private spite or intrigue either.

In time, we began to understand the design of his life, how old threads appear in apparently new patterns. Remember John while very young: a dark and sulky boy whose black-haired, ill-humored father preferred his fair wife, daughter and younger son. John understood all too well arbitrary discrimination, the kind that appearances (height, build, complexion) stimulate. He was born in a state split among many lines—northern, Anglo-Saxon, light-skinned, Protestant country farmers on the one hand; southern, Catholic, Mediterranean types on the other, many of the thousands who lived in a wicked, international port city. His parents brought these different traditions together in an uneasy marriage, and the boy grew up a victim of this delicate arrangement. How accidental is it to find him years later moodily resenting dark people?

A psychiatric evaluation finds him oriented and alert, in no trouble about who or where he is—his name, the date and place of our talks. His mind works in understandable fashion. He does not hallucinate, and though we may consider his beliefs delusional, they are held in common with thousands of others, and do not seem insistently private or as incomprehensible as those in schizophrenic delusional systems. His thinking is not psychotic; it flows in orderly and logical steps, given certain assumptions that are shared by many others and thus have social rather than idiosyncratic sources.

He is intelligent, beyond question so. He grasps issues, relates them to others, takes stock of problems and tries to solve them. He has read widely and deeply, if with self-imposed restrictions. Much of what he reads gives him real encouragement. Full of references to God and country, encouraging virulent racism, recommending violence as possibly necessary in some future Armageddon of white versus black, Gentile versus Jew, biblical patriotism versus atheistic internationalism, this "literature" seeks an America which we hope will never exist, but it also collects its readers into a fellowship. One can call *all* these people crazy, but it is a shared insanity not an individual one. John works; he has a family and friends. He is fitful, alternately cheerless and buoyant. He is not shy or withdrawn; and he is in definite contact with many people, and responds to their feelings. Can we call him "sick"?

In one of those compact appraisals of an individual person we might say that John is not insane, not psychotic in any operational sense of the word; neither retarded nor delinquent. He has no police record, has committed no crimes as his society defines them, is even careful to obey laws on picketing or demonstrations where they exist or are enforced. (*His* kind of demonstration has often been encouraged by some officials of his state.) Absurdly xenophobic, an anti-Semitic, anti-Negro "paranoiac"? Yes, along with many, many thousands in his region. A frustrated, defeated man, a sometime political candidate, a feckless sidewalk crank, occasionally irritable and only rarely dangerous? Yes, but far from alone.

Born in a region long poor and defeated, into a family itself humble and moneyless, often at the mercy of capricious economic, social or political forces, the boy at home faced those first insecurities, those early rivalries, hates and struggles which often set the pattern for later ones. White man against black embodied all those childhood hatreds, all those desperate, anxious attempts children make to locate themselves and their identities amid the strivings of siblings, amid the conscious and unconscious smiles and grudges, animosities and predilections of their parents. He was an active child, a fighter who managed to survive perilous disease and hard times. When grown he had some initial modest success at home and at work, only to return from war into a sliding, middle-aged depression, a personal one, but one that plagued his family, and some of his friends, too. (The papers talked of a "dislocated, postwar economy.") Individual psychopathology, social conflict and economic instability, each has its separate causes. On the other hand the mind can connect them together, and for many people they are keenly felt as three aspects of one unhappy, unpredictable life.

I looked first to "psychopathology" for the answer to the riddle of John, and those like him; for an explanation of their frightful actions. Rather than seek after political, social or economic ills, I chose medical or psychiatric ones, the kind that seemed "real" to me. John's life shows that it can be understood best by looking at it in several ways, and *one* of them is certainly psychiatric. Yet I have to keep on reminding myself that I have seen mobs such as he joined collect in one city while in another they were nowhere to be found. While the incidence of individual psychopathology probably is relatively constant in all Southern cities, the quality of police forces and politicians has varied, and so have their ideas about what constituted law and order. I have seen avowed segregationists—some of them unstable individuals in addition—submit quietly to the most radical kinds of integrated society because they worked on a federal air base. American laws and jobs seemed curiously more influential than "deep-rooted" attitudes.

The FBI agent who spoke to me in McComb was standing in front of a dynamited house in the very heart of the most oppressive area in the South. James Silver's "closed society,"[2] the state of Mississippi, has a long history to fall back upon, one enforced by social, economic and political power; no corner of the state had been more loyal to its past. Certainly I and others with me were frightened, though perhaps the FBI agent was not, by the hateful, suspicious attitude we were meeting at the hands of many of the townspeople. The Negroes were scared, and many of the whites had a kind of murder in their eyes. In the face of all that, the agent posed a question only in terms of illness, of individual eccentricity.

In McComb, in Mississippi, at that time, a dynamited house and even three murdered youths were not unique. There were klans, councils and societies there whose daily words or deeds encouraged the burning of churches, the dynamiting of houses, the beating, ambushing and killing of men. A few weeks after the "incident" in McComb I examined a minister brutally beaten in a doctor's office in Leake County, Mississippi.[3] The doctor—no redneck, not "ignorant"—had literally pushed the minister and a young student with him into the hands of a gang *in his own office.* Every bit of evidence suggests a plot arranged by that doctor—he knew in advance the two men were coming because they had telephoned to ask for medical help. Shall we suggest psychiatric examinations for him and for all the others in the state—businessmen, newspaper editors, lawyers—who ignore, condone, encourage or fail to conceal their pleasure at such episodes?

I wonder about the eager emphasis given private, aberrant motives by some in our society. Many ignore crying, horrible, concrete social and political realities whose effects—as a matter of fact—might lead us to understand how John and others like him continue to plague us. It is easier, I suppose, to look for the madman's impulse and make explaining it the doctor's task.

The bestiality I have seen in the South cannot be attributed only to its psychotic and ignorant people. Once and for all, in the face of what we have seen this century, we must all know that the animal in us can be elaborately rationalized in a society until an act of murder is seen as self-defense and dynamited houses become evidence of moral courage. Nor is the confused, damaged South the only region of this country in need of that particular knowledge.

---

[2] James W. Silver, *Mississippi: The Closed Society* (New York, Harcourt, Brace & World, 1964).

[3] Under the title of "Cleric and Student Tell of Attack in a Mississippi Doctor's Office" the *New York Times* of August 2, 1964, carried the following dispatch:

"Two civil rights workers, one a minister, were beaten in a physician's office where they were seeking medical care, it was disclosed today.

"The Rev. Edward K. Heininger, of Des Moines, Iowa, 45 years old, was said to have been injured severely by a gang of whites who attacked him in the presence of Dr. A. L. Thaggard Sr., who operates a private clinic in the Madden community near here."

Perry Morgan

Perry Morgan is Managing Editor of the Charlotte (N.C.) News. *Educated at the University of Georgia, he has also studied as a Nieman Fellow at Harvard. He has worked on newspapers in Georgia, Michigan, Virginia, and North Carolina and has won several prizes for editorial and news writing. The article we reprint below first appeared in the January 1962 issue of* Esquire.

THE CASE FOR THE WHITE SOUTHERNER

When the good citizens of New Rochelle, New York, were accused last year of admitting Jim Crow to their schools, they denied it. When they were taken to court, they resisted. When the judge looked and saw old Jim sitting there plain as day and ordered his remcval, a solid citizen of New Rochelle cried: "Nobody understands ou. situation."

New Rochelle is located in the Piety Belt that denounces racial discrimination and has it, too. The law is against it, but the majority of people are for it. Beginning in 1930, Judge Irving R. Kaufman found, the New Rochelle school board had confined Negro pupils exclusively to one school. This was the Lincoln School (presumably after Abraham Lincoln who signed the Emancipation Proclamation) from which transfers were denied even though all-white schools had twice as many vacant seats as children registered at Lincoln. Even after Judge Kaufman ordered Jim Crow expelled, a school board majority concocted a desegregation plan designed to sneak old Jim back into school by the side door. The judge, however, was adamant.

The Piety Belt is a varied land populated by people of good conscience. Their forefathers, according to much-loved myth, fought a war to free the slaves. And for the century since, by preachment and earnest exhortation, they have urged the white Southerner to conquer the evil in his heart and treat the Negro as a free and equal American. They have looked away to Dixie Land with fury and scorn and earnestly have hoped the downtrodden Negro would never doubt the constancy of their faith.

Abundance of precept, however, has been accompanied by a stringent shortage of example in the Piety Belt. Negroes migrating into the North early noted that, although the law was on their side, the people lacked some of the warmth and fellowship to which they were accustomed. "Up North," the saying sprang up, "they don't care how high you get just so you don't get too close; down South, they don't care how close you get, just so you don't get too high." The point has not lost its sharpness.

The South has been given far too much credit for ingenuity in shaping the law to its own purposes. The Southern lawyer seeking to circumvent the Supreme Court decision really had to look no farther than Philadelphia to find the model for what in the South the Northern press sniffily defines as "token integration." According to a Public Affairs Committee study by Will Maslow and Richard Cohen, "more Negro children attend what are in fact segregated schools in the major cities of the North than attend officially segregated schools in urban areas of the South." Note the authors: "When Lieutenant Nellie Forbush, the Navy nurse in *South Pacific*, tells the world she hails from Little Rock, she is greeted from Maine to Madagascar with hoots, catcalls and other indigenous expressions of disapproval . . . yet Little Rock . . . has fewer Negroes than the South Side of Chicago. More significant, school segregation is as prevalent in that corner of Chicago as it is in the Arkansas capital." So much for the soul of John Brown —in bivouac.

The non-Southerner naturally has ready excuses for this paradox. It is difficult to admit guilt. Having hidden his complicity in the crime of slavery for a century he cannot bring himself to face the fact now that the victim has caught up with him. His schools stagger from crisis to crisis under the weight of a vast influx of Negro children who lack the capacity to keep up with their white classmates. Achievement levels are dropping. The more affluent whites are fleeing. One school superintendent told *Look* Magazine's George B. Leonard, Jr. that a third of the children in his elementary schools may end up not only unemployed, but unemployable. But, as Leonard wrote, this is a shrouded crisis. Though Dr. James B. Conant has deplored the lack of statistics, school officials cannot publicly face the "delicate and complex matter of racial prejudice." Instead, "they cling to the vain old hope that racial prejudice will disappear if you pretend race does not exist."

So earnest is the innocent resident of the Piety Belt in his explanations that he forgets the white Southerner has heard them all before. In fact, he holds the patents on them. The Negro came to *him* on Yankee slave ships from the jungle. Yet in trying to shake the Northerner from his silly pretensions, *Look* indulged its own in a headline saying *"America's large cities are paying the grim price of a century of rural and Southern educational neglect."*

Southern neglect? God in heaven! By his standards of the time the Northerner perhaps had excuse for visiting unmerciful vengeance upon the whites of the defeated Confederacy. But what of the freed man in whose name, and out of strategic necessity, the Civil War was given a sacred cause through Lincoln's Emancipation Proclamation? Leaving the freed man and the white man together in a pit of poverty, pain and ignorance, the victorious Northerner turned to a feast of prosperity whose cynicism sickened and dismayed Henry Adams and other sensitive souls.

On reflection, though, it is not quite accurate to say the North merely wrought ruin and departed. More precisely, with a host of exploiting devices, it leeched out of a destroyed region many of the pitiful resources left for its meager sustenance. Long before Franklin D. Roosevelt rediscovered America's own viciously exploited colony to the South, the Piety Belt was grieving for the downtrodden in faraway corners of the world.

The white Southerner and the Negro climbed out of the pit together, and unassisted. It was a long, grim and demeaning journey, and if it scarred the Negro it also scarred the white. For its part in the crime of slavery, as Gerald Johnson has written, the South has paid and paid and paid. It owes neither the North nor the world apologies for its stewardship of the human dilemma deposited on American shores three centuries ago. What qualifications the Negro now brings in support of his demand for full participation in the world's most difficult citizenship, he has from the white Southerner. If he goes North with an inferior education, he was given that by a white man who has never been able to afford adequate schools for his own children.

The Southerner has believed a lot of comforting bushwa about his own region—moonlight, magnolias and all the rest. But having some little experience with the Negro problem, he is altogether disinclined to believe the North's nonsense too. He has observed that wherever the two races exist together in significant numbers—in London, Capetown or New Rochelle—walls are thrown up, and that when laws oppose, the walls somehow curve around the laws.

The case for the white Southerner is that he is a human being with a normal complement of virtues and vices. If he himself has been too much concerned with defending and vaunting his virtues, the North has been overly fascinated with condemning his vices. A Union officer made that point a century ago, as W. D. Workman has recalled, and so did Harriet Beecher Stowe when she got around to looking for herself.

Let the misunderstood citizen of affluent New Rochelle mark well this unique fact: twice in a hundred years the South has been forced to recast the laws, the mood and the mind of its people. In both cases, though it had no model for judgment, the nation decided to substitute revolutionary for evolutionary processes. The latter, to be sure, were still working injustices when the Supreme Court interrupted in 1954, but they had wrought profound changes too. The South at that point had begun rapidly to repair the spiritual and material ravages of a grim host of decades of poverty, ignorance, pain, disease and economic exploitation. A growing middle class was bringing a new stability to political processes flawed and half-paralyzed by the racial factor. The region had begun to surmount the bleak, crippling pessimism that was the natural inheritance of the past and to take new and promising initiatives even in the field of race relations. Great strides had been taken in education, medicine and agriculture. The fabled Southern female was slaving in field and factory, and sometimes both, to send sons and daughters to college and break once and for all the harsh grip of hoe and row. The winds of hope and progress, in sum, were quickening.

Then came May 17, 1954, and an historic decision concerned as much with conjectural foreign-policy needs for a purer national image as with the needs of the American Negro. Never before, not even in the Dred Scott case which wrecked the court's power and prestige on the reefs of Northern outrage, had there issued a writ touching so profoundly and personally the lives of so many millions of individuals. Yet out of his profound innocence, the Northerner fully expected the South—by taking thought—to swiftly swallow its sociological medicine, cleanse the national conscience and miraculously reorder its ancient social rhythms.

Be it noted that the court itself had no such expectations. Far less momentous writs of the court had failed before to run beyond the narrow bounds of the District of Columbia. Less than two decades had passed since the court had prevented its dismemberment by reversing —lock, stock, and barrel—its whole philosophy toward the New Deal.

The court, nonetheless, had set out to make a social laboratory out of a vast region whose history had led, in Robert Penn Warren's phrase, to a massive "fear of abstraction—the instinctive fear that the massiveness of experience, the concreteness of life, will be violated." Now, suddenly, so far as the rank-and-file Southerner knew, the most fearful of all abstractions had been struck into the law of the land. Once again, the vast engine of the Federal Government that had ground his fathers down was to undertake a transformation of his and his children's lives. Once again, the national press would smoke with moral rebuke and condemnation. Already, the NAACP was promising to wrap up the whole revolution in a year or two and, as at least one NAACP official gave as his personal opinion, intermarriage certainly *was* one goal of the revolution.

If this travail would make the world love America more, the Southerner asked himself, what would it do to his children? The very essence of the Supreme Court decision was admission that in the mass the Negro was culturally inferior. And the white schools themselves, despite tax support proportionally greater than the national average, sorely needed strengthening. Thus it was that the most liberal Southerner—and the South has a strain of liberalism unsurpassed for courage and toughness—was forced to ponder earnestly when the learned and gentle William Polk asked: "If the Negro is entitled to lift himself by enforced association with the white man, why should not the white man be entitled to prevent himself from being pulled down by enforced association with the Negro?"

And there were other questions for the heart: What would happen to the virtues of that paternalism which had bound black and white together in a relationship that, however unprogressive, was often warmly human in its sharing? If the Southerner *knew* he did not understand the lesser figure in this bond, was it not frightening to be forced to comprehend that this friendly, agreeable and sympathetic soul that jollied him and nursed his children was in reality a total stranger who changed vocabularies at quitting time?

Walter Lippmann once remarked that "all deliberate speed" in, say, Alabama might mean admission of Negro students to graduate schools of white universities by the tenth anniversary of the court's ruling. Lippmann offered a piercing insight into the fantastic complexity of rejiggering human attitudes plus calm acceptance that wherever such engineering is attempted social turbulence, fear and instability clog and distort the normal channels of social and political leadership. This, really, was not so strange a point—having been written down indelibly in blood and anguish throughout human history. But unhappily, American understanding that is capable of leaping an ocean often sinks midstream in the Potomac River.

As applied to Algeria, for example, the faithful reader of The New York *Times* and auditor of national television understands the difficulty very well. He sees clearly, for it has been movingly and expertly explained, why proud French generals, exquisitely mannered and magnificently educated, yielded to righteousness, insolence and finally to armed rebellion against the great de Gaulle himself at a moment when the very existence of France seemed at stake. Nor can the literate Northerner have failed to understand why in the teeth of the furies and the face of inevitable defeat the French *colon* incessantly riots to retain a way of life that must—and will—go with the wind. The parallels, of course, cannot be drawn too closely, but it says something meaningful about the universal frailties of the human condition.

But, in fairness, the Southerner who would be understood must not overly complain about the myopia of the Northern eye as it skims swiftly over the iron segregation of its Negro ghettos to focus intently upon the South. For if the Supreme Court decisions created opportunities and even felt necessities for false prophecy and senseless doctrine in the South, the market also turned bullish in the North.

Hearken to that admirable and sincerely self-righteous Senator from Illinois, Paul Douglas, regularly informing the South that it simply must throw off the palpable sins of segregation, get right with God and be born again in the image of the Americans for Democratic Action. Yes, verily, and let us not fret so much with the deliberateness of our speed. Keating of New York pats his foot. Ditto Javits and so also Clark of Pennsylvania and other evangelists of instant racial equality.

Let us not impute a lack of charity to these gentlemen. Indeed, they have the faith of their fathers. To befriend a recalcitrant South, they are ready at the drop of a hat to enact a force bill or to employ with Federal monies sociological shepherds to lead the region to redemption. And though all this piety falls sweetly upon the ears of Harlem and South Chicago, with their balances of power and their largely separate and patently unequal schools, it would be idle to charge these gentlemen with insincerity. Moreover, it would be immaterial. The Ku Klux Klan has been full of thugs who wielded the whip with absolute—and terrible—sincerity. John Brown, sainted by the sages of Concord for exploits including the insane murder and mutilation of five non-slaveholders in one night, was the acme of sincerity.

In the light of this heritage, then, which later unconstitutionally forced the fateful Fourteenth Amendment upon the South, does not Paul Douglas' impatience begin to seem entirely reasonable? And, in fact, isn't it understandable if just a bit insane that the last Democratic National Convention would declare an intention to abolish *all* literacy tests for voting in order finally and fully to extend the franchise to the Negro in the South . . . even in those many places where, as stubborn fact has it, he outnumbers the white? The answer is yes, of course, if one is prepared to admit that in the light of the Southerner's entirely different heritage the nation in 1954 would have foreseen that Faubus' rabble would for a time drown out the never-stilled voices of hope, faith and charity in the South. The answer is yes, if one is prepared, as the editors of The New York *Times* are not, to comprehend the resentment of Southerners when with merciless stupidity and frightening innocence "freedom riders" depart the ghettos and, with headlines and television cameras going on before, venture forth to tempt the violent boob from his lair.

Let us not turn so quickly away from this violent man, however. He, too, has a history. Perhaps he is kin to the tenant, Gudger, from whose barren, wasted life James Agee fashioned, in the 1930's, poignant prose for his *Let Us Now Praise Famous Men:*

"Gudger has no home, no land, no mule: none of the more important farming implements. He must get all of these of his landlord (who), for his share of the corn and cotton, also advances him rations money during four months of the year, March through June, and his fertilizer. Gudger pays him back with his labor and with the labor of his family. At the end of the season he pays him back further; with half his corn, with half his cottonseed. Out of his own half of these crops he also pays him back the rations money, plus interest, and his share of the fertilizer, plus interest, and such other debts, plus interest, as he may have incurred. What is left, once doctor bills and other debts have been deducted, is his year's earnings. . . . " Or perhaps this man screaming in the street was related to Ricketts who, with hope of good times, "went $400 into debt on a fine young pair of mules. One of the mules died before it had made its first crop; and the other died the year after; against his fear, amounting to full horror, of sinking to the half-crop level where nothing is owned, Ricketts went into debt for other, inferior mules; his cows went one by one into debts and desperate exchanges and by sickness; he got congestive chills; his wife got pellagra; a number of his children died; he got appendicitis and lay for days on end under the icecap; his wife's pellagra got into her brain; for ten consecutive years now, though they have lived on so little rations money and have turned nearly all their cottonseed money toward their debts, they have not cleared or had any hope of clearing a cent at the end of the year."

In all his variety from a Klansman plotting an atrocity to a school-board member secretly urging Negroes to apply for admission to the upper-class schools to the wan little interracial groups meeting in the church parlor, the white Southerner is a creature of a heritage that he can no more reject than a mother can reject her children. Splotched with evil, to be sure, that heritage also is compounded of triumphs of endurance, of courage, of selflessness that moved a world. Simply because it is gone does not mean it is forgotten or, indeed, could be forgotten. For if the "good Southerner" could break the bonds with the "bad Southerner" to whom he is bound irrevocably by ties, of blood, religion, race, memory, myth and love of land, where would he seek a new code of conduct? Not in the North, surely, for the Southerner knows in his bones what the historians know in fact: that the North has no moral credentials to preach in this matter, that whatever virtues that region may accidentally have earned by "freeing the slaves" was corrupted by a conscienceless "Reconstruction" of a freed man without freedom and a white man without hope or even youth. For the Negro there was no jubilee-jubilo. For neither white nor black was there a Marshall Plan.

The Southerner's senses told him rightly he had no corner on the corrupting of the American dream. He knew that the zeal of the abolitionist was not the reflection of a higher Northern morality—that to the North there was also greed, cynicism and calculation. He knew there was a reason that when the Supreme Court first came to the Fourteenth Amendment that charter of human freedom was converted to one of corporate privilege.

All this is remembered by the defeated as naturally as it is forgotten by the victorious. All this is the stubborn stuff of the barrier reef in the Potomac that keeps the white Northerner and Southerner forever strangers and prolongs the sterile ritual of finger-pointing that has woven both Paul Douglas and Orval Faubus into the sardonic and not-so-secret mirth of Negro intellectuals. Connoisseurs of that humor must await with relish the answer to the riddle: "What's the difference between a group of distressed Negroes being driven into a church by a white mob in Montgomery and another group being driven out of a church by a white mob in Chicago?" Only a dense literalist would torture that riddle with legalisms.

The legalisms remain, of course, and the white Southerner will make his peace with them. And though some of his number take secret pride in having been able with courage and statecraft to hew a path to compliance through a dense thicket of difficulties, he does not forget that the New Order requires most of the "poor white" Southerner who has been given least. He wonders, watching the flight to the suburbs and the proliferation of private pools, clubs and schools, if the grand design of 1954 does not trend North and South toward integration of the impoverished. Knowing something of the Negro's own intense concern for shadings of color that can reject as "too dark" a baby offered for adoption, he ponders earnestly whether the sociologists in their toneless tracts have not assumed too much in their vaunted knowledge of human nature. He understands the Negro professional man's remark to Harry Ashmore that he can always get a contribution for the cause but never an apartment in a New York Jewish neighborhood. He admires the frankness of another successful Negro who, having come up from squalor by dint of great determination, found himself "too busy to practice sociology." He can simultaneously admire the courage of a young Negro sit-in demonstrator, detest the white louts profaning the Confederate flag and wonder all the while whether the sit-ins will sabotage better job opportunities for Negroes. He is bound to wonder, too, if the Negro ever will turn from the faults of the white man's society to grapple with those grievous failings of his own that crowd the dockets of crime, disease and illegitimacy. For as the North ceaselessly has reminded the white Southerner, there is a limit to the number of excuses to be found in deprivation.

Writing that, I see in my mind's eye a white woman with a fifth-grade education, who, driven finally from the tyranny of the field, took a town job that paid $26 a month for sixteen hours a day in labor and transit, and who from this meager sum bought schoolbooks for three children; who, after washing their single sets of clothes at midnight, rose for work at 4 a.m. to leave biscuit dough in the oven and a stern note not to be late for school; who in all her life never bought unless she could pay and carries within her still a fierce independence that denies her pleasure from any gift, but who finds pleasure in giving. She is a Baptist who voted for Kennedy, but, may Myrdal forgive her, she is "prejudiced" against the Negro.

Not for the white Southerner is the sweet and innocent assurance of the slogan. No man better than he knows from mourning a dozen "New Souths" that died a-borning how swiftly the high rhetoric of progress can collapse into a wail and turn him back to the bleak rewards of the beloved and immemorial land.

He moves hesitantly, uncertainly into the New Order. Some of him dares to hope that this time a truly expanding economy will bathe both races in prosperity's magical sprays of tolerance. But he would also hope that some of the virtues of the old might be retained and perhaps even recognized beyond his borders: that in the new patterns the old civility and generosity and, yes, even the romanticism might find a cranny.

For if his fathers' dreams of a noble breed of learned men carried within itself a fatal flaw, was it otherwise so wild a dream? Was it one that a man—glimpsing it, as it were, in a smashed antique mirror —could quite relinquish in an age when men moved as ants beneath the edifice of the Great Machine?

The white Southerner will not fail his nation, nor himself. Out of the aged anguish and conflict of the human heart, the strongest of him will accommodate the pressures of the New Order into something comprehensible to the kin of Gudger and Ricketts and to the Negro who in the company of the white Southerner has at least learned to read the Declaration of Independence.

It may be true that the white Southerner could have done better in the past and that today he could move more swiftly to accommodate the New Order in the tangled skein of the old. Many of his own courageous prophets tell him so, and millions of his number are not averse to taking new paths laid out with care and reason.

It may be, as this loyal son believes, that the grinding mills of the New Order will in time refine the South's great virtues into a new statecraft that will not suffer by comparison with the wisdom and vision of the old.

Certain it is that few beyond are equipped to judge the Southerner's stewardship of the human dilemma the North so long ignored, but soon must face.

The white Southerner fears not history's judgment so much as the misjudgments of the non-Southerner who, armored in innocence and shielded by mass anonymity, sometimes forgets that allegiance to high principle purchases neither wisdom nor political responsibility.

James Baldwin

This essay is taken from a collection of the same name (1955). For information about the author, see page 199.

NOTES OF A NATIVE SON

On the 29th of July, in 1943, my father died. On the same day, a few hours later, his last child was born. Over a month before this, while all our energies were concentrated in waiting for these events, there had been, in Detroit, one of the bloodiest race riots of the century. A few hours after my father's funeral, while he lay in state in the undertaker's chapel, a race riot broke out in Harlem. On the morning of the 3rd of August, we drove my father to the graveyard through a wilderness of smashed plate glass.

The day of my father's funeral had also been my nineteenth birthday. As we drove him to the graveyard, the spoils of injustice, anarchy, discontent, and hatred were all around us. It seemed to me that God himself had devised, to mark my father's end, the most sustained and brutally dissonant of codas. And it seemed to me, too, that the violence which rose all about us as my father left the world had been devised as a corrective for the pride of his eldest son. I had declined to believe in that apocalypse which had been central to my father's vision; very well, life seemed to be saying, here is something that will certainly pass for an apocalypse until the real thing comes along. I had inclined to be contemptuous of my father for the conditions of his life, for the conditions of our lives. When his life had ended I began to wonder about that life and also, in a new way, to be apprehensive about my own.

I had not known my father very well. We had got on badly, partly because we shared, in our different fashions, the vice of stubborn pride. When he was dead I realized that I had hardly ever spoken to him. When he had been dead a long time I began to wish I had. It seems to be typical of life in America, where opportunities, real and fancied, are thicker than anywhere else on the globe, that the second generation has no time to talk to the first. No one, including my father, seems to have known exactly how old he was, but his mother had been born during slavery. He was of the first generation of free men. He, along with thousands of other Negroes, came North after 1919 and I was part of that generation which had never seen the landscape of what Negroes sometimes call the Old Country.

He had been born in New Orleans and had been a quite young man there during the time that Louis Armstrong, a boy, was running errands for the dives and honky-tonks of what was always presented to me as one of the most wicked of cities—to this day, whenever I think of New Orleans, I also helplessly think of Sodom and Gomorrah. My father never mentioned Louis Armstrong, except to forbid us to play his records; but there was a picture of him on our wall for a long time. One of my father's strong-willed female relatives had placed it there and forbade my father to take it down. He never did, but he eventually maneuvered her out of the house and when, some years later, she was in trouble and near death, he refused to do anything to help her.

He was, I think, very handsome. I gather this from photographs and from my own memories of him, dressed in his Sunday best and on his way to preach a sermon somewhere, when I was little. Handsome, proud, and ingrown, "like a toe-nail," somebody said. But he looked to me, as I grew older, like pictures I had seen of African tribal chieftains: he really should have been naked, with war-paint on and barbaric mementos, standing among spears. He could be chilling in the pulpit and indescribably cruel in his personal life and he was certainly the most bitter man I have ever met; yet it must be said that there was something else in him, buried in him, which lent him his tremendous power and, even, a rather crushing charm. It had something to do with his blackness, I think—he was very black—with his blackness and his beauty, and with the fact that he knew that he was black but did not know that he was beautiful. He claimed to be proud of his blackness but it had also been the cause of much humiliation and it had fixed bleak boundaries to his life. He was not a young man when we were growing up and he had already suffered many

252

kinds of ruin; in his outrageously demanding and protective way he loved his children, who were black like him and menaced, like him; and all these things sometimes showed in his face when he tried, never to my knowledge with any success, to establish contact with any of us. When he took one of his children on his knee to play, the child always became fretful and began to cry; when he tried to help one of us with our homework the absolutely unabating tension which emanated from him caused our minds and our tongues to become paralyzed, so that he, scarcely knowing why, flew into a rage and the child, not knowing why, was punished. If it ever entered his head to bring a surprise home for his children, it was, almost unfailingly, the wrong surprise and even the big watermelons he often brought home on his back in the summertime led to the most appalling scenes. I do not remember, in all those years, that one of his children was ever glad to see him come home. From what I was able to gather of his early life, it seemed that this inability to establish contact with other people had always marked him and had been one of the things which had driven him out of New Orleans. There was something in him, therefore, groping and tentative, which was never expressed and which was buried with him. One saw it most clearly when he was facing new people and hoping to impress them. But he never did, not for long. We went from church to smaller and more improbable church, he found himself in less and less demand as a minister, and by the time he died none of his friends had come to see him for a long time. He had lived and died in an intolerable bitterness of spirit and it frightened me, as we drove him to the graveyard through those unquiet, ruined streets, to see how powerful and overflowing this bitterness could be and to realize that this bitterness now was mine.

When he died I had been away from home for a little over a year. In that year I had had time to become aware of the meaning of all my father's bitter warnings, had discovered the secret of his proudly pursed lips and rigid carriage: I had discovered the weight of white people in the world. I saw that this had been for my ancestors and now would be for me an awful thing to live with and that the bitterness which had helped to kill my father could also kill me.

He had been ill a long time—in the mind, as we now realized, reliving instances of his fantastic intransigence in the new light of his affliction and endeavoring to feel a sorrow for him which never, quite, came true. We had not known that he was being eaten up by paranoia, and the discovery that his cruelty, to our bodies and our minds, had been one of the symptoms of his illness was not, then, enough to enable us to forgive him. The younger children felt, quite simply, relief that he would not be coming home anymore. My mother's observation that it was he, after all, who had kept them alive all these years meant nothing because the problems of keeping children alive are not real for children. The older children felt, with my father gone, that they could invite their friends to the house without fear that their friends would be insulted or, as had sometimes happened with me, being told that their friends were in league with the devil and intended to rob our family of everything we owned. (I didn't fail to wonder, and it made me hate him, what on earth we owned that anybody else would want.)

His illness was beyond all hope of healing before anyone realized that he was ill. He had always been so strange and had lived, like a prophet, in such unimaginably close communion with the Lord that his long silences which were punctuated by moans and hallelujahs and snatches of old songs while he sat at the living-room window never seemed odd to us. It was not until he refused to eat because, he said, his family was trying to poison him that my mother was forced to accept as a fact what had, until then, been only an unwilling suspicion. When he was committed, it was discovered that he had tuberculosis and, as it turned out, the disease of his mind allowed the disease of his body to destroy him. For the doctors could not force him to eat, either, and, though he was fed intravenously, it was clear from the beginning that there was no hope for him.

In my mind's eye I could see him, sitting at the window, locked up in his terrors; hating and fearing every living soul including his children who had betrayed him, too, by reaching towards the world which had despised him. There were nine of us. I began to wonder what it could have felt like for such a man to have had nine children whom he could barely feed. He used to make little jokes about our poverty, which never, of course, seemed very funny to us; they could not have seemed very funny to him, either, or else our all too feeble response to them would never have caused such rages. He spent great energy and achieved, to our chagrin, no small amount of success in keeping us away from the people who surrounded us, people who had all-night rent parties to which we listened when we should have been sleeping, people who cursed and drank and flashed razor blades on Lenox Avenue. He could not understand why, if they had so much energy to spare, they could not use it to make their lives better. He treated almost everybody on our block with a most uncharitable asperity and neither they, nor, of course, their children were slow to reciprocate.

The only white people who came to our house were welfare workers and bill collectors. It was almost always my mother who dealt with them, for my father's temper, which was at the mercy of his pride, was never to be trusted. It was clear that he felt their very presence in his home to be a violation: this was conveyed by his carriage, almost ludicrously stiff, and by his voice, harsh and vindictively polite. When I was around nine or ten I wrote a play which was directed by a young, white schoolteacher, a woman, who then took an interest in me, and gave me books to read and, in order to corroborate my theatrical bent, decided to take me to see what she somewhat tactlessly referred to as "real" plays. Theater-going was forbidden in our house, but, with the really cruel intuitiveness of a child, I suspected that the color of this woman's skin would carry the day for me. When, at school, she suggested taking me to the theater, I did not, as I might have done if she had been a Negro, find a way of discouraging her, but agreed that she should pick me up at my house one evening. I then, very cleverly, left all the rest to my mother, who suggested to my father, as I knew she would, that it would not be very nice to let such a kind woman make the trip for nothing. Also, since it was a schoolteacher, I imagine that my mother countered the idea of sin with the idea of "education," which word, even with my father, carried a kind of bitter weight.

Before the teacher came my father took me aside to ask *why* she was coming, what *interest* she could possibly have in our house, in a boy like me. I said I didn't know but I, too, suggested that it had something to do with education. And I understood that my father was waiting for me to say something—I didn't quite know what; perhaps that I wanted his protection against this teacher and her "education." I said none of these things and the teacher came and we went out. It was clear, during the brief interview in our living room, that my father was agreeing very much against his will and that he would have refused permission if he had dared. The fact that he did not dare caused me to despise him: I had no way of knowing that he was facing in that living room a wholly unprecedented and frightening situation.

Later, when my father had been laid off from his job, this woman became very important to us. She was really a very sweet and generous woman and went to a great deal of trouble to be of help to us, particularly during one awful winter. My mother called her by the highest name she knew: she said she was a "christian." My father could scarcely disagree but during the four or five years of our relatively close association he never trusted her and was always trying to surprise in her open, Midwestern face the genuine, cunningly hidden, and hideous motivation. In later years, particularly when it began to be clear that this "education" of mine was going to lead me to perdition, he became more explicit and warned me that my white friends in high school were not really my friends and that I would see, when I was older, how white people would do anything to keep a Negro down. Some of them could be nice, he admitted, but none of them were to be trusted and most of them were not even nice. The best thing was

255

to have as little to do with them as possible. I did not feel this way and I was certain, in my innocence, that I never would.

But the year which preceded my father's death had made a great change in my life. I had been living in New Jersey, working in defense plants, working and living among southerners, white and black. I knew about the south, of course, and about how southerners treated Negroes and how they expected them to behave, but it had never entered my mind that anyone would look at me and expect *me* to behave that way. I learned in New Jersey that to be a Negro meant, precisely, that one was never looked at but was simply at the mercy of the reflexes the color of one's skin caused in other people. I acted in New Jersey as I had always acted, that is as though I thought a great deal of myself—I had to *act* that way—with results that were, simply, unbelievable. I had scarcely arrived before I had earned the enmity, which was extraordinarily ingenious, of all my superiors and nearly all my co-workers. In the beginning, to make matters worse, I simply did not know what was happening. I did not know what I had done, and I shortly began to wonder what *anyone* could possibly do, to bring about such unanimous, active, and unbearably vocal hostility. I knew about jim-crow but I had never experienced it. I went to the same self-service restaurant three times and stood with all the Princeton boys before the counter, waiting for a hamburger and coffee; it was always an extraordinarily long time before anything was set before me; but it was not until the fourth visit that I learned that, in fact, nothing had ever been set before me: I had simply picked something up. Negroes were not served there, I was told, and they had been waiting for me to realize that I was always the only Negro present. Once I was told this, I determined to go there all the time. But now they were ready for me and, though some dreadful scenes were subsequently enacted in that restaurant, I never ate there again.

It was the same story all over New Jersey, in bars, bowling alleys, diners, places to live. I was always being forced to leave, silently, or with mutual imprecations. I very shortly became notorious and children giggled behind me when I passed and their elders whispered or shouted—they really believed that I was mad. And it did begin to work on my mind, of course; I began to be afraid to go anywhere and to compensate for this I went places to which I really should not have gone and where, God knows, I had no desire to be. My reputation in town naturally enhanced my reputation at work and my working day became one long series of acrobatics designed to keep me out of trouble. I cannot say that these acrobatics succeeded. It began to seem that the machinery of the organization I worked for was turning over, day and night, with but one aim: to eject me. I was fired once, and contrived, with the aid of a friend from New York, to get back on the payroll; was fired again, and bounced back again. It took a while to fire me for the third time, but the third time took. There were no loopholes anywhere. There was not even any way of getting back inside the gates.

That year in New Jersey lives in my mind as though it were the year during which, having an unsuspected predilection for it, I first contracted some dread, chronic disease, the unfailing symptom of which is a kind of blind fever, a pounding in the skull and fire in the bowels. Once this disease is contracted, one can never be really carefree again, for the fever, without an instant's warning, can recur at any moment. It can wreck more important things than race relations. There is not a Negro alive who does not have this rage in his blood—one has the choice, merely, of living with it consciously or surrendering to it. As for me, this fever has recurred in me, and does, and will until the day I die.

My last night in New Jersey, a white friend from New York took me to the nearest big town, Trenton, to go to the movies and have a few drinks. As it turned out, he also saved me from, at the very least, a violent whipping. Almost every detail of that night stands out very clearly in my memory. I even remember the name of the movie we saw because its title impressed me as being so patly ironical. It was a movie about the German occupation of France, starring Maureen O'Hara and Charles Laughton and called *This Land Is Mine.* I remember the name of the diner we walked into when the movie ended: it was the "American Diner." When we walked in the counterman asked what we wanted and I remember answering with the casual sharpness which had become my habit: "We want a hamburger and a cup of coffee, what do you think we want?" I do not know why, after a year of such rebuffs, I so completely failed to anticipate his answer, which was, of course, "We don't serve Negroes here." This reply failed to discompose me, at least for the moment. I made some sardonic comment about the name of the diner and we walked out into the streets.

This was the time of what was called the "brown-out," when the lights in all American cities were very dim. When we re-entered the streets something happened to me which had the force of an optical illusion, or a nightmare. The streets were very crowded and I was facing north. People were moving in every direction but it seemed to me, in that instant, that all of the people I could see, and many more than that, were moving toward me, against me, and that everyone was white. I remember how their faces gleamed. And I felt, like a physical sensation, a *click* at the nape of my neck as though some interior string connecting my head to my body had been cut. I began to walk. I heard my friend call after me, but I ignored him. Heaven only knows what was going on in his mind, but he had the good sense not to touch me—I don't know what would have happened if he had—and to keep me in sight. I don't know what was going on in my mind, either; I certainly had no conscious plan. I wanted to do something to crush these white faces, which were crushing me. I walked for perhaps a block or two until I came to an enormous, glittering, and fashionable restaurant in which I knew not even the intercession of the Virgin would cause me to be served. I pushed through the doors and took the first vacant seat I saw, at a table for two, and waited.

I do not know how long I waited and I rather wonder, until today, what I could possibly have looked like. Whatever I looked like, I frightened the waitress who shortly appeared, and the moment she appeared all of my fury flowed towards her. I hated her for her white face, and for her great, astounded, frightened eyes. I felt that if she found a black man so frightening I would make her fright worth-while.

She did not ask me what I wanted, but repeated, as though she had learned it somewhere, "We don't serve Negroes here." She did not say it with the blunt, derisive hostility to which I had grown so accustomed, but, rather, with a note of apology in her voice, and fear. This made me colder and more murderous than ever. I felt I had to do something with my hands. I wanted her to come close enough for me to get her neck between my hands.

So I pretended not to have understood her, hoping to draw her closer. And she did step a very short step closer, with her pencil poised incongruously over her pad, and repeated the formula: ". . . don't serve Negroes here."

Somehow, with the repetition of that phrase, which was already ringing in my head like a thousand bells of a nightmare, I realized that she would never come any closer and that I would have to strike from a distance. There was nothing on the table but an ordinary water-mug half full of water, and I picked this up and hurled it with all my strength at her. She ducked and it missed her and shattered against the mirror behind the bar. And, with that sound, my frozen blood abruptly thawed, I returned from wherever I had been, I *saw*, for the first time, the restaurant, the people with their mouths open, already, as it seemed to me, rising as one man, and I realized what I had done, and where I was, and I was frightened. I rose and began running for the door. A round, potbellied man grabbed me by the nape of the neck just as I reached the doors and began to beat me about the face. I kicked him and got loose and ran into the streets. My friend whispered, *"Run!"* and I ran.

My friend stayed outside the restaurant long enough to misdirect my pursuers and the police, who arrived, he told me, at once. I do not know what I said to him when he came to my room that night. I could not have said much. I felt, in the oddest, most awful way,

258

that I had somehow betrayed him. I lived it over and over and over again, the way one relives an automobile accident after it has happened and one finds oneself alone and safe. I could not get over two facts, both equally difficult for the imagination to grasp, and one was that I could have been murdered. But the other was that I had been ready to commit murder. I saw nothing very clearly but I did see this: that my life, my *real* life, was in danger, and not from anything other people might do but from the hatred I carried in my own heart.

[II]

I had returned home around the second week in June—in great haste because it seemed that my father's death and my mother's confinement were both but a matter of hours. In the case of my mother, it soon became clear that she had simply made a miscalculation. This had always been her tendency and I don't believe that a single one of us arrived in the world, or has since arrived anywhere else, on time. But none of us dawdled so intolerably about the business of being born as did my baby sister. We sometimes amused ourselves, during those endless, stifling weeks, by picturing the baby sitting within in the safe, warm dark, bitterly regretting the necessity of becoming a part of our chaos and stubbornly putting it off as long as possible. I understood her perfectly and congratulated her on showing such good sense so soon. Death, however, sat as purposefully at my father's bedside as life stirred within my mother's womb and it was harder to understand why he so lingered in that long shadow. It seemed that he had bent, and for a long time, too, all of his energies towards dying. Now death was ready for him but my father held back.

All of Harlem, indeed, seemed to be infected by waiting. I had never before known it to be so violently still. Racial tensions throughout this country were exacerbated during the early years of the war, partly because the labor market brought together hundreds of thousands of ill-prepared people and partly because Negro soldiers, regardless of where they were born, received their military training in the south. What happened in defense plants and army camps had repercussions, naturally, in every Negro ghetto. The situation in Harlem had grown bad enough for clergymen, policemen, educators, politicians, and social workers to assert in one breath that there was no "crime wave" and to offer, in the very next breath, suggestions as how to combat it. These suggestions always seemed to involve playgrounds, despite the fact that racial skirmishes were occurring in the playgrounds, too. Playground or not, crime wave or not, the Harlem police force had been augmented in March, and the unrest grew—perhaps, in fact, partly as a result of the ghetto's instinctive hatred of policemen. Perhaps

259

the most revealing news item, out of the steady parade of reports of muggings, stabbings, shootings, assaults, gang wars, and accusations of police brutality, is the item concerning six Negro girls who set upon a white girl in the subway because, as they all too accurately put it, she was stepping on their toes. Indeed she was, all over the nation.

I had never before been so aware of policemen, on foot, on horseback, on corners, everywhere, always two by two. Nor had I ever been so aware of small knots of people. They were on stoops and on corners and in doorways, and what was striking about them, I think, was that they did not seem to be talking. Never, when I passed these groups, did the usual sound of a curse or a laugh ring out and neither did there seem to be any hum of gossip. There was certainly, on the other hand, occurring between them communication extraordinarily intense. Another thing that was striking was the unexpected diversity of the people who made up these groups. Usually, for example, one would see a group of sharpies standing on the street corner, jiving the passing chicks; or a group of older men, usually, for some reason, in the vicinity of a barber shop, discussing baseball scores, or the numbers, or making rather chilling observations about women they had known. Women, in a general way, tended to be seen less often together—unless they were church women, or very young girls, or prostitutes met together for an unprofessional instant. But that summer I saw the strangest combinations: large, respectable, churchly matrons standing on the stoops or the corners with their hair tied up, together with a girl in sleazy satin whose face bore the marks of gin and the razor, or heavy-set, abrupt, no-nonsense older men, in company with the most disreputable and fanatical "race" men, or these same "race" men with the sharpies, or these sharpies with the churchly women. Seventh Day Adventists and Methodists and Spiritualists seemed to be hobnobbing with Holyrollers and they were all, alike, entangled with the most flagrant disbelievers; something heavy in their stance seemed to indicate that they had all, incredibly, seen a common vision, and on each face there seemed to be the same strange, bitter shadow.

The churchly women and the matter-of-fact, no-nonsense men had children in the Army. The sleazy girls they talked to had lovers there, the sharpies and the "race" men had friends and brothers there. It would have demanded an unquestioning patriotism, happily as uncommon in this country as it is undesirable, for these people not to have been disturbed by the bitter letters they received, by the newspaper stories they read, not to have been enraged by the posters, then to be found all over New York, which described the Japanese as "yellow-bellied Japs." It was only the "race" men, to be sure, who spoke ceaselessly of being revenged—how this vengeance was to be exacted was not clear—for the indignities and dangers suffered by Negro boys in uniform; but everybody felt a directionless, hopeless bitterness, as well as that panic which can scarcely be suppressed when one knows that a human being one loves is beyond one's reach, and in danger. This helplessness and this gnawing uneasiness does something, at length, to even the toughest mind. Perhaps the best way to sum all this up is to say that the people I knew felt, mainly, a peculiar kind of relief when they knew that their boys were being shipped out of the south, to do battle overseas. It was, perhaps, like feeling that the most dangerous part of a dangerous journey had been passed and that now, even if death should come, it would come with honor and without the complicity of their countrymen. Such a death would be, in short, a fact with which one could hope to live.

It was on the 28th of July, which I believe was a Wednesday, that I visited my father for the first time during his illness and for the last time in his life. The moment I saw him I knew why I had put off this visit so long. I had told my mother that I did not want to see him because I hated him. But this was not true. It was only that I *had* hated him and I wanted to hold on to this hatred. I did not want to look on him as a ruin: it was not a ruin I had hated. I imagine that one of the reasons people cling to their hates so stubbornly is because they sense, once hate is gone, that they will be forced to deal with pain.

We traveled out to him, his older sister and myself, to what seemed to be the very end of a very Long Island. It was hot and dusty and we wrangled, my aunt and I, all the way out, over the fact that I had recently begun to smoke and, as she said, to give myself airs. But I knew that she wrangled with me because she could not bear to face the fact of her brother's dying. Neither could I endure the reality of her despair, her unstated bafflement as to what had happened to her brother's life, and her own. So we wrangled and I smoked and from time to time she fell into a heavy reverie. Covertly, I watched her face, which was the face of an old woman; it had fallen in, the eyes were sunken and lightless; soon she would be dying, too.

In my childhood—it had not been so long ago—I had thought her beautiful. She had been quick-witted and quick-moving and very generous with all the children and each of her visits had been an event. At one time one of my brothers and myself had thought of running away to live with her. Now she could no longer produce out of her handbag some unexpected and yet familiar delight. She made me feel pity and revulsion and fear. It was awful to realize that she no longer caused me to feel affection. The closer we came to the hospital the more querulous she became and at the same time, naturally, grew more dependent on me. Between pity and guilt and fear

261

I began to feel that there was another me trapped in my skull like a jack-in-the-box who might escape my control at any moment and fill the air with screaming.

She began to cry the moment we entered the room and she saw him lying there, all shriveled and still, like a little black monkey. The great, gleaming apparatus which fed him and would have compelled him to be still even if he had been able to move brought to mind, not beneficence, but torture; the tubes entering his arm made me think of pictures I had seen when a child, of Gulliver, tied down by the pygmies on that island. My aunt wept and wept, there was a whistling sound in my father's throat; nothing was said; he could not speak. I wanted to take his hand, to say something. But I do not know what I could have said, even if he could have heard me. He was not really in that room with us, he had at last really embarked on his journey; and though my aunt told me that he said he was going to meet Jesus, I did not hear anything except that whistling in his throat. The doctor came back and we left, into that unbearable train again, and home. In the morning came the telegram saying that he was dead. Then the house was suddenly full of relatives, friends, hysteria, and confusion and I quickly left my mother and the children to the care of those impressive women, who, in Negro communities at least, automatically appear at times of bereavement armed with lotions, proverbs, and patience, and an ability to cook. I went downtown. By the time I returned, later the same day, my mother had been carried to the hospital and the baby had been born.

[III]

For my father's funeral I had nothing black to wear and this posed a nagging problem all day long. It was one of those problems, simple, or impossible of solution, to which the mind insanely clings in order to avoid the mind's real trouble. I spent most of that day at the downtown apartment of a girl I knew, celebrating my birthday with whiskey and wondering what to wear that night. When planning a birthday celebration one naturally does not expect that it will be up against competition from a funeral and this girl had anticipated taking me out that night, for a big dinner and a night club afterwards. Sometime during the course of that long day we decided that we would go out anyway, when my father's funeral service was over. I imagine *I* decided it, since, as the funeral hour approached, it became clearer and clearer to me that I would not know what to do with myself when it was over. The girl, stifling her very lively concern as to the possible effects of the whiskey on one of my father's chief mourners, concentrated on being conciliatory and practically helpful. She found a black shirt for me somewhere and ironed it and, dressed in the darkest pants and jacket I owned, and slightly drunk, I made my way to my father's funeral.

The chapel was full, but not packed, and very quiet. There were, mainly, my father's relatives, and his children, and here and there I saw faces I had not seen since childhood, the faces of my father's one-time friends. They were very dark and solemn now, seeming somehow to suggest that they had known all along that something like this would happen. Chief among the mourners was my aunt, who had quarreled with my father all his life; by which I do not mean to suggest that her mourning was insincere or that she had not loved him. I suppose that she was one of the few people in the world who had, and their incessant quarreling proved precisely the strength of the tie that bound them. The only other person in the world, as far as I knew, whose relationship to my father rivaled my aunt's in depth was my mother, who was not there.

It seemed to me, of course, that it was a very long funeral. But it was, if anything, a rather shorter funeral than most, nor, since there were no overwhelming, uncontrollable expressions of grief, could it be called—if I dare to use the word—successful. The minister who preached my father's funeral sermon was one of the few my father had still been seeing as he neared his end. He presented to us in his sermon a man whom none of us had ever seen—a man thoughtful, patient, and forbearing, a Christian inspiration to all who knew him, and a model for his children. And no doubt the children, in their disturbed and guilty state, were almost ready to believe this; he had been remote enough to be anything and, anyway, the shock of the incontrovertible, that it was really our father lying up there in that casket, prepared the mind for anything. His sister moaned and this grief-stricken moaning was taken as corroboration. The other faces held a dark, non-committal thoughtfulness. This was not the man they had known, but they had scarcely expected to be confronted with *him*; this was, in a sense deeper than questions of fact, the man they had not known, and the man they had not known may have been the real one. The real man, whoever he had been, had suffered and now he was dead: this was all that was sure and all that mattered now. Every man in the chapel hoped that when his hour came he, too, would be eulogized, which is to say forgiven, and that all of his lapses, greeds, errors, and strayings from the truth would be invested with coherence and looked upon with charity. This was perhaps the last thing human beings could give each other and it was what they demanded, after all, of the Lord. Only the Lord saw the midnight tears, only He was present when one of His children, moaning and wringing hands, paced up and down the room. When one slapped one's child in anger the recoil in the heart reverberated through heaven and became part of the pain of the universe. And when the children were hungry and sullen and distrustful and one watched them, daily, growing wilder, and further away, and running headlong into danger, it was the Lord who knew what the charged heart endured as the strap was laid to the backside; the Lord alone who knew what one *would* have said if one had had, like the Lord, the gift of the living word. It was the Lord who knew of the impossibility every parent in that room faced: how to prepare the child for the day when the child would be despised and how to *create* in the child—by what means?—a stronger antidote to this poison than one had found for oneself. The avenues, side streets, bars, billiard halls, hospitals, police stations, and even the playgrounds of Harlem—not to mention the houses of correction, the jails, and the morgue—testified to the potency of the poison while remaining silent as to the efficacy of whatever antidote, irresistibly raising the question of whether or not such an antidote existed; raising, which was worse, the question of whether or not an antidote was desirable; perhaps poison should be fought with poison. With these several schisms in the mind and with more terrors in the heart than could be named, it was better not to judge the man who had gone down under an impossible burden. It was better to remember: *Thou knowest this man's fall; but thou knowest not his wrassling.*

While the preacher talked and I watched the children—years of changing their diapers, scrubbing them, slapping them, taking them to school, and scolding them had had the perhaps inevitable result of making me love them, though I am not sure I knew this then—my mind was busily breaking out with a rash of disconnected impressions. Snatches of popular songs, indecent jokes, bits of books I had read, movie sequences, faces, voices, political issues—I thought I was going mad; all these impressions suspended, as it were, in the solution of the faint nausea produced in me by the heat and liquor. For a moment I had the impression that my alcoholic breath, inefficiently disguised with chewing gum, filled the entire chapel. Then someone began singing one of my father's favorite songs and, abruptly, I was with him, sitting on his knee, in the hot, enormous, crowded church which was the first church we attended. It was the Abyssinia Baptist Church on 138th Street. We had not gone there long. With this image, a host of others came. I had forgotten, in the rage of my growing up, how proud my father had been of me when I was little. Apparently, I had had a voice and my father had liked to show me off before the members of the church. I had forgotten what he had looked like when he was pleased but now I remembered that he had always been grinning with pleasure when my solos ended. I even remembered certain expressions on his face when he teased my mother

—had he loved her? I would never know. And when had it all begun to change? For now it seemed that he had not always been cruel. I remembered being taken for a haircut and scraping my knee on the footrest of the barber's chair and I remembered my father's face as he soothed my crying and applied the stinging iodine. Then I remembered our fights, fights which had been of the worst possible kind because my technique had been silence.

I remembered the one time in all our life together when we had really spoken to each other.

It was on a Sunday and it must have been shortly before I left home. We were walking, just the two of us, in our usual silence, to or from church. I was in high school and had been doing a lot of writing and I was, at about this time, the editor of the high school magazine. But I had also been a Young Minister and had been preaching from the pulpit. Lately, I had been taking fewer engagements and preached as rarely as possible. It was said in the church, quite truthfully, that I was "cooling off."

My father asked me abruptly, "You'd rather write than preach, wouldn't you?"

I was astonished at his question—because it was a real question. I answered, "Yes."

That was all we said. It was awful to remember that that was all we had *ever* said.

The casket now was opened and the mourners were being led up the aisle to look for the last time on the deceased. The assumption was that the family was too overcome with grief to be allowed to make this journey alone and I watched while my aunt was led to the casket and, muffled in black, and shaking, led back to her seat. I disapproved of forcing the children to look on their dead father, considering that the shock of his death, or, more truthfully, the shock of death as a reality, was already a little more than a child could bear, but my judgment in this matter had been overruled and there they were, bewildered and frightened and very small, being led, one by one, to the casket. But there is also something very gallant about children at such moments. It has something to do with their silence and gravity and with the fact that one cannot help them. Their legs, somehow, seem *exposed*, so that it is at once incredible and terribly clear that their legs are all they have to hold them up.

I had not wanted to go to the casket myself and I certainly had not wished to be led there, but there was no way of avoiding either of these forms. One of the deacons led me up and I looked on my father's face. I cannot say that it looked like him at all. His blackness had been equivocated by powder and there was no suggestion in that casket of what his power had or could have been. He was simply an old man dead, and it was hard to believe that he had ever given anyone either joy or pain. Yet, his life filled that room. Further up the avenue his wife was holding his newborn child. Life and death so close together, and love and hatred, and right and wrong, said something to me which I did not want to hear concerning man, concerning the life of man.

After the funeral, while I was downtown desperately celebrating my birthday, a Negro soldier, in the lobby of the Hotel Braddock, got into a fight with a white policeman over a Negro girl. Negro girls, white policemen, in or out of uniform, and Negro males—in or out of uniform—were part of the furniture of the lobby of the Hotel Braddock and this was certainly not the first time such an incident had occurred. It was destined, however, to receive an unprecedented publicity, for the fight between the policeman and the soldier ended with the shooting of the soldier. Rumor, flowing immediately to the streets outside, stated the soldier had been shot in the back, an instantaneous and revealing invention, and that the soldier had died protecting a Negro woman. The facts were somewhat different—for example, the soldier had not been shot in the back, and was not dead, and the girl seems to have been as dubious a symbol of womanhood as her white counterpart in Georgia usually is, but no one was interested in the facts. They preferred the invention because this invention expressed and corroborated their hates and fears so perfectly. It is just as well to remember that people are always doing this. Perhaps many of those legends, including Christianity, to which the world clings began their conquest of the world with just some such concerted surrender to distortion. The effect, in Harlem, of this particular legend was like the effect of a lit match in a tin of gasoline. The mob gathered before the doors of the Hotel Braddock simply began to swell and to spread in every direction, and Harlem exploded.

The mob did not cross the ghetto lines. It would have been easy, for example, to have gone over Morningside Park on the west side or to have crossed the Grand Central railroad tracks at 125th Street on the east side, to wreak havoc in white neighborhoods. The mob seems to have been mainly interested in something more potent and real than the white face, that is, in white power, and the principal damage done during the riot of the summer of 1943 was to white business establishments in Harlem. It might have been a far bloodier story, of course, if, at the hour the riot began, these establishments had still been open. From the Hotel Braddock the mob fanned out, east and west along 125th Street, and for the entire length of Lenox, Seventh, and Eighth avenues. Along each of these avenues, and along each major side street—116th, 125th, 135th, and so on—bars, stores, pawnshops, restaurants, even little luncheonettes had been smashed open and entered and looted—looted, it might be added, with more haste than efficiency. The shelves really looked as though a bomb had struck them. Cans of beans and soup and dog food, along with toilet paper, corn flakes, sardines and milk tumbled every which way, and abandoned cash registers and cases of beer leaned crazily out of the splintered windows and were strewn along the avenues. Sheets, blankets, and clothing of every description formed a kind of path, as though people had dropped them while running. I truly had not realized that Harlem *had* so many stores until I saw them all smashed open; the first time the word *wealth* ever entered my mind in relation to Harlem was when I saw it scattered in the streets. But one's first, incongruous impression of plenty was countered immediately by an impression of waste. None of this was doing anybody any good. It would have been better to have left the plate glass as it had been and the goods lying in the stores.

It would have been better, but it would also have been intolerable, for Harlem had needed something to smash. To smash something is the ghetto's chronic need. Most of the time it is the members of the ghetto who smash each other, and themselves. But as long as the ghetto walls are standing there will always come a moment when these outlets do not work. That summer, for example, it was not enough to get into a fight on Lenox Avenue, or curse out one's cronies in the barber shops. If ever, indeed, the violence which fills Harlem's churches, pool halls, and bars erupts outward in a more direct fashion, Harlem and its citizens are likely to vanish in an apocalyptic flood. That this is not likely to happen is due to a great many reasons, most hidden and powerful among them the Negro's real relation to the white American. This relation prohibits, simply, anything as uncomplicated and satisfactory as pure hatred. In order really to hate white people, one has to blot so much out of the mind—and the heart—that this hatred itself becomes an exhausting and self-destructive pose. But this does not mean, on the other hand, that love comes easily: the white world is too powerful, too complacent, too ready with gratuitous humiliation, and, above all, too ignorant and too innocent for that. One is absolutely forced to make perpetual qualifications and one's own reactions are always canceling each other out. It is this, really, which has driven so many people mad, both white and black. One is always in the position of having to decide between amputation and gangrene. Amputation is swift but time may prove that the amputation was not necessary—or one may delay the amputation too long. Gangrene is slow, but it is impossible to be sure that one is reading one's symptoms right. The idea of going through life as a cripple is more than one can bear, and equally unbearable is the risk of swelling up slowly, in agony, with poison. And the trouble, finally, is that the risks are real even if the choices do not exist.

"But as for me and my house," my father had said, "we will serve the Lord." I wondered, as we drove him to his resting place, what this line had meant for him. I had heard him preach it many times. I had preached it once myself, proudly giving it an interpretation different from my father's. Now the whole thing came back to me, as though my father and I were on our way to Sunday school and I were memorizing the golden text: *And if it seem evil unto you to serve the Lord, choose you this day whom you will serve; whether the gods which your fathers served that were on the other side of the flood, or the gods of the Amorites, in whose land ye dwell: but as for me and my house, we will serve the Lord.* I suspected in these familiar lines a meaning which had never been there for me before. All of my father's texts and songs, which I had decided were meaningless, were arranged before me at his death like empty bottles, waiting to hold the meaning which life would give them for me. This was his legacy: nothing is ever escaped. That bleakly memorable morning I hated the unbelievable streets and the Negroes and whites who had, equally, made them that way. But I knew that it was folly, as my father would have said, this bitterness was folly. It was necessary to hold on to the things that mattered. The dead man mattered, the new life mattered; blackness and whiteness did not matter; to believe that they did was to acquiesce in one's own destruction. Hatred, which could destroy so much, never failed to destroy the man who hated and this was an immutable law.

It began to seem that one would have to hold in the mind forever two ideas which seemed to be in opposition. The first idea was acceptance, the acceptance, totally without rancor, of life as it is, and men as they are: in the light of this idea, it goes without saying that injustice is a commonplace. But this did not mean that one could be complacent, for the second idea was of equal power: that one must never, in one's own life, accept these injustices as commonplace but must fight them with all one's strength. This fight begins, however, in the heart and it now had been laid to my charge to keep my own heart free of hatred and despair. This intimation made my heart heavy and, now that my father was irrecoverable, I wished that he had been beside me so that I could have searched his face for the answers which only the future would give me now.

Norman Podhoretz

Norman Podhoretz was born in New York City and educated at
Columbia College and Cambridge University, England, where he
was a Fulbright Scholar and a Kellet Fellow. A precociously
talented writer and critic, he was appointed editor of Commentary
in 1960, at the age of thirty. He has been a frequent contributor
to magazines, has published a ten-year collection of his articles,
entitled Doings and Undoings: The Fifties and After in
American Writing *(1964), and* Making It *(1968), a remark-*
ably candid account of his rise in the world of the New York
literary intelligentsia. The article we print below first appeared
in Commentary, *February 1963.*

MY NEGRO PROBLEM—AND OURS

If we—and . . . I mean the relatively conscious whites and the relatively conscious
blacks, who must, like lovers, insist on, or create, the consciousness of the others—
do not falter in our duty now, we may be able, handful that we are, to end the
racial nightmare, and achieve our country, and change the history of the world.
                                                                —JAMES BALDWIN

Two ideas puzzled me deeply as a child growing up in Brooklyn during
the 1930's in what today would be called an integrated neighborhood.
One of them was that all Jews were rich; the other was that all Negroes
were persecuted. These ideas had appeared in print; therefore they
must be true. My own experience and the evidence of my senses told
me they were not true, but that only confirmed what a day-dreaming
boy in the provinces—for the lower-class neighborhoods of New York
belong as surely to the provinces as any rural town in North Dakota
—discovers very early: *his* experience is unreal and the evidence of his
senses is not to be trusted. Yet even a boy with a head full of fantasies
incongruously synthesized out of Hollywood movies and English novels
cannot altogether deny the reality of his own experience—especially
when there is so much deprivation in that experience. Nor can he
altogether gainsay the evidence of his own senses—especially such
evidence of the senses as comes from being repeatedly beaten up,
robbed, and in general hated, terrorized, and humiliated.

And so for a long time I was puzzled to think that Jews were supposed to be rich when the only Jews I knew were poor, and that Negroes were supposed to be persecuted when it was the Negroes who were doing the only persecuting I knew about—and doing it, moreover, to *me*. During the early years of the war, when my older sister joined a left-wing youth organization, I remember my astonishment at hearing her passionately denounce my father for thinking that Jews were worse off than Negroes. To me, at the age of twelve, it seemed very clear that Negroes were better off than Jews—indeed, than *all* whites. A city boy's world is contained within three or four square blocks, and in my world it was the whites, the Italians and Jews, who feared the Negroes, not the other way around. The Negroes were tougher than we were, more ruthless, and on the whole they were better athletes. What could it mean, then, to say that they were badly off and that we were more fortunate? Yet my sister's opinions, like print, were sacred, and when she told me about exploitation and economic forces I believed her. I believed her, but I was still afraid of Negroes. And I still hated them with all my heart.

It had not always been so—that much I can recall from early childhood. When did it start, this fear and this hatred? There was a kindergarten in the local public school, and given the character of the neighborhood, at least half of the children in my class must have been Negroes. Yet I have no memory of being aware of color differences at that age, and I know from observing my own children that they attribute no significance to such differences even when they begin noticing them. I think there was a day—first grade? second grade?—when my best friend Carl hit me on the way home from school and announced that he wouldn't play with me any more because I had killed Jesus. When I ran home to my mother crying for an explanation, she told me not to pay any attention to such foolishness, and then in Yiddish she cursed the *goyim* and the *schwartzes*, the *schwartzes* and the *goyim*. Carl, it turned out, was a *schwartze*, and so was added a third to the categories into which people were mysteriously divided.

Sometimes I wonder whether this is a true memory at all. It is blazingly vivid, but perhaps it never happened: can anyone really remember back to the age of six? There is no uncertainty in my mind, however, about the years that followed. Carl and I hardly ever spoke, though we met in school every day up through the eighth or ninth grade. There would be embarrassed moments of catching his eye or of his catching mine—for whatever it was that had attracted us to one another as very small children remained alive in spite of the fantastic barrier of hostility that had grown up between us, suddenly and out of nowhere. Nevertheless, friendship would have been impossible, and even if it had been possible, it would have been unthinkable.

About that, there was nothing anyone could do by the time we were eight years old.

Item: The orphanage across the street is torn down, a city housing project begins to rise in its place, and on the marvelous vacant lot next to the old orphanage they are building a playground. Much excitement and anticipation as Opening Day draws near. Mayor LaGuardia himself comes to dedicate this great gesture of public benevolence. He speaks of neighborliness and borrowing cups of sugar, and of the playground he says that children of all races, colors, and creeds will learn to live together in harmony. A week later, some of us are swatting flies on the playground's inadequate little ball field. A gang of Negro kids, pretty much our own age, enter from the other side and order us out of the park. We refuse, proudly and indignantly, with superb masculine fervor. There is a fight, they win, and we retreat, half whimpering, half with bravado. My first nauseating experience of cowardice. And my first appalled realization that there are people in the world who do not seem to be afraid of anything, who act as though they have nothing to lose. Thereafter the playground becomes a battleground, sometimes quiet, sometimes the scene of athletic competition between Them and Us. But rocks are thrown as often as baseballs. Gradually we abandon the place and use the streets instead. The streets are safer, though we do not admit this to ourselves. We are not, after all, sissies—that most dreaded epithet of an American boyhood.

Item: I am standing alone in front of the building in which I live. It is late afternoon and getting dark. That day in school the teacher had asked a surly Negro boy named Quentin a question he was unable to answer. As usual I had waved my arm eagerly ("Be a good boy, get good marks, be smart, go to college, become a doctor") and, the right answer bursting from my lips, I was held up lovingly by the teacher as an example to the class. I had seen Quentin's face—a very dark, very cruel, very Oriental-looking face—harden, and there had been enough threat in his eyes to make me run all the way home for fear that he might catch me outside.

Now, standing idly in front of my own house, I see him approaching from the project accompanied by his little brother who is carrying a baseball bat and wearing a grin of malicious anticipation. As in a nightmare, I am trapped. The surroundings are secure and familiar, but terror is suddenly present and there is no one around to help. I am locked to the spot. I will not cry out or run away like a sissy, and I stand there, my heart wild, my throat clogged. He walks up, hurls the familiar epithet ("Hey, mo'f——r"), and to my surprise only pushes me. It is a violent push, but not a punch. A push is not as serious as a punch. Maybe I can still back out without entirely losing my dignity. Maybe I can still say, "Hey, c'mon Quentin, whaddya wanna do *that* for. I dint do nothin' to *you*," and walk away, not too rapidly. Instead, before I can stop myself, I push him back—a token gesture— and I say, "Cut that out, I don't wanna fight, I ain't got nothin' to fight about." As I turn to walk back into the building, the corner of my eye catches the motion of the bat his little brother has handed him. I try to duck, but the bat crashes colored lights into my head.

The next thing I know, my mother and sister are standing over me, both of them hysterical. My sister—she who was later to join the "progressive" youth organization—is shouting for the police and scream- ing imprecations at those dirty little black bastards. They take me upstairs, the doctor comes, the police come. I tell them that the boy who did it was a stranger, that he had been trying to get money from me. They do not believe me, but I am too scared to give them Quentin's name. When I return to school a few days later, Quentin avoids my eyes. He knows that I have not squealed, and he is ashamed. I try to feel proud, but in my heart I know that it was fear of what his friends might do to me that had kept me silent, and not the code of the street.

Item: There is an athletic meet in which the whole of our junior high school is participating. I am in one of the seventh-grade rapid- advance classes, and "segregation" has now set in with a vengeance. In the last three or four years of the elementary school from which we have just graduated, each grade had been divided into three classes, according to "intelligence." (In the earlier grades the divisions had either been arbitrary or else unrecognized by us as having anything to do with brains.) These divisions by IQ, or however it was arranged, had resulted in a preponderance of Jews in the "1" classes and a corresponding preponderance of Negroes in the "3's," with the Italians split unevenly along the spectrum. At least a few Negroes had always made the "1's," just as there had always been a few Jewish kids among the "3's" and more among the "2's" (where Italians dominated). But the junior high's rapid-advance class of which I am now a member is overwhelmingly Jewish and entirely white—except for a shy lonely Negro girl with light skin and reddish hair.

The athletic meet takes place in a city-owned stadium far from the school. It is an important event to which a whole day is given over. The winners are to get those precious little medallions stamped with the New York City emblem that can be screwed into a belt and that prove the wearer to be a distinguished personage. I am a fast runner, and so I am assigned the position of anchor man on my class's team in the relay race. There are three other seventh-grade teams in the race, two of them all Negro, as ours is all white. One of the all-Negro teams is very tall—their anchor man waiting silently next to me on the line looks years older than I am, and I do not recognize him. He is the first to get the baton and crosses the finishing line in a walk. Our team comes in second, but a few minutes later we are declared the winners, for it has been discovered that the anchor man on the first-place team is not a member of the class. We are awarded the medallions, and the following day our home-room teacher makes a speech about how proud she is of us for being superior athletes as well as superior students. We want to believe that we deserve the praise, but we know that we could not have won even if the other class had not cheated.

That afternoon, walking home, I am waylaid and surrounded by five Negroes, among whom is the anchor man of the disqualified team. "Gimme my medal, mo'f——r," he grunts. I do not have it with me and I tell him so. "Anyway, it ain't yours," I say foolishly. He calls me a liar on both counts and pushes me up against the wall on which we sometimes play handball. "Gimme my mo'f——n' medal," he says again. I repeat that I have left it home. "Le's search the li'l mo'f——r," one of them suggests, "he prolly got it *hid* in his mo'f——n' *pants*." My panic is now unmanageable. (How many times had I been surrounded like this and asked in soft tones, "Len' me a nickle, boy." How many times had I been called a liar for pleading poverty and pushed around, or searched, or beaten up, unless there happened to be someone in the marauding gang like Carl who liked me across that enormous divide of hatred and who would therefore say, "Aaah, c'mon, le's git someone else, *this* boy ain't got no money on 'im.") I scream at them through tears of rage and self-contempt, "Keep your f——n' filthy lousy black hands offa me! I swear I'll get the cops." This is all they need to hear, and the five of them set upon me. They bang me around, mostly in the stomach and on the arms and shoulders, and when several adults loitering near the candy store down the block notice what is going on and begin to shout, they run off and away.

I do not tell my parents about the incident. My team-mates, who have also been waylaid, each by a gang led by his opposite number from the disqualified team, have had their medallions taken from them, and they never squeal either. For days, I walk home in terror, expecting to be caught again, but nothing happens. The medallion is put away into a drawer, never to be worn by anyone.

Obviously experiences like these have always been a common feature of childhood life in working-class and immigrant neighborhoods, and Negroes do not necessarily figure in them. Wherever, and in whatever combination, they have lived together in the cities, kids of different groups have been at war, beating up and being beaten up: micks against kikes against wops against spicks against polacks. And even relatively homogeneous areas have not been spared the warring of the young: one block against another, one gang (called in my day, in a pathetic effort at gentility, an "S.A.C.," or social-athletic club) against another. But the Negro-white conflict had—and no doubt still has—a special intensity and was conducted with a ferocity unmatched by intramural white battling.

In my own neighborhood, a good deal of animosity existed between the Italian kids (most of whose parents were immigrants from Sicily) and the Jewish kids (who came largely from East European immigrant families). Yet everyone had friends, sometimes close friends, in the other "camp," and we often visited one another's strange-smelling houses, if not for meals, then for glasses of milk, and occasionally for some special event like a wedding or a wake. If it happened that we divided into warring factions and did battle, it would invariably be half-hearted and soon patched up. Our parents, to be sure, had nothing to do with one another and were mutually suspicious and hostile. But we, the kids, who all spoke Yiddish or Italian at home, were Americans, or New Yorkers, or Brooklyn boys: we shared a culture, the culture of the street, and at least for a while this culture proved to be more powerful than the opposing cultures of the home.

Why, *why* should it have been so different as between the Negroes and us? How was it borne in upon us so early, white and black alike, that we were enemies beyond any possibility of reconciliation? Why did we hate one another so?

I suppose if I tried, I could answer those questions more or less adequately from the perspective of what I have since learned. I could draw upon James Baldwin—what better witness is there?—to describe the sense of entrapment that poisons the soul of the Negro with hatred for the white man whom he knows to be his jailer. On the other side, if I wanted to understand how the white man comes to hate the Negro, I could call upon the psychologists who have spoken of the guilt that white Americans feel toward Negroes and that turns into hatred for lack of acknowledging itself as guilt. These are plausible answers and certainly there is truth in them. Yet when I think back upon my own experience of the Negro and his of me, I find myself troubled and puzzled, much as I was as a child when I heard that all Jews were rich and all Negroes persecuted. How could the Negroes in my neighborhood have regarded the whites across the street and around the corner as jailers? On the whole, the whites were not so poor as the Negroes, but they were quite poor enough, and the years were years of Depression. As for white hatred of the Negro, how could guilt have had anything to do with it? What share had these Italian and Jewish immigrants in the enslavement of the Negro? What share had they—downtrodden people themselves breaking their own necks to eke out a living—in the exploitation of the Negro?

274

No, I cannot believe that we hated each other back there in Brooklyn because they thought of us as jailers and we felt guilty toward them. But does it matter, given the fact that we all went through an unrepresentative confrontation? I think it matters profoundly, for if we managed the job of hating each other so well without benefit of the aids to hatred that are supposedly at the root of this madness everywhere else, it must mean that the madness is not yet properly understood. I am far from pretending that I understand it, but I would insist that no view of the problem will begin to approach the truth unless it can account for a case like the one I have been trying to describe. Are the elements of any such view available to us?

At least two, I would say, are. One of them is a point we frequently come upon in the work of James Baldwin, and the other is a related point always stressed by psychologists who have studied the mechanisms of prejudice. Baldwin tells us that one of the reasons Negroes hate the white man is that the white man refuses to *look* at him: the Negro knows that in white eyes all Negroes are alike; they are faceless and therefore not altogether human. The psychologists, in their turn, tell us that the white man hates the Negro because he tends to project those wild impulses that he fears in himself onto an alien group which he then punishes with his contempt. What Baldwin does *not* tell us, however, is that the principle of facelessness is a two-way street and can operate in both directions with no difficulty at all. Thus, in my neighborhood in Brooklyn, *I* was as faceless to the Negroes as they were to me, and if they hated me because I never looked at them, I must also have hated them for never looking at *me*. To the Negroes, my white skin was enough to define me as the enemy, and in a war it is only the uniform that counts and not the person.

So with the mechanism of projection that the psychologists talk about: it too works in both directions at once. There is no question that the psychologists are right about what the Negro represents symbolically to the white man. For me as a child the life lived on the other side of the playground and down the block on Ralph Avenue seemed the very embodiment of the values of the street—free, independent, reckless, brave, masculine, erotic. I put the word "erotic" last, though it is usually stressed above all others, because in fact it came last, in consciousness as in importance. What mainly counted for me about Negro kids of my own age was that they were "bad boys." There were plenty of bad boys among the whites—this was, after all, a neighborhood with a long tradition of crime as a career open to aspiring talents—but the Negroes were *really* bad, bad in a way that beckoned to one, and made one feel inadequate. *We* all went home every day for a lunch of spinach-and-potatoes; *they* roamed around during lunch hour, munching on candy bars. In winter *we* had to wear itchy woolen hats and mittens and cumbersome galoshes; *they* were bare-headed and loose as they pleased. *We* rarely played hookey, or got into serious trouble in school, for all our street-corner bravado; *they* were defiant, forever staying out (to do what delicious things?), forever making disturbances in class and in the halls, forever being sent to the principal and returning uncowed. But most important of all, they were *tough;* beautifully, enviably tough, not giving a damn for anyone or anything. To hell with the teacher, the truant officer, the cop; to hell with the whole of the adult world that held *us* in its grip and that we never had the courage to rebel against except sporadically and in petty ways.

This is what I saw and envied and feared in the Negro: this is what finally made him faceless to me, though some of it, of course, was actually there. (The psychologists also tell us that the alien group which becomes the object of a projection will tend to respond by trying to live up to what is expected of them.) But what, on his side, did the Negro see in me that made me faceless to *him?* Did he envy me my lunches of spinach-and-potatoes and my itchy woolen caps and my prudent behavior in the face of authority, as I envied him his noon-time candy bars and his bare head in winter and his magnificent rebelliousness? Did those lunches and caps spell for him the prospect of power and riches in the future? Did they mean that there were possibilities open to me that were denied to him? Very likely they did. But if so, one also supposes that he feared the impulses within himself toward submission to authority no less powerfully than I feared the impulses in myself toward defiance. If I represented the jailer to him, it was not because I was oppressing him or keeping him down: it was because I symbolized for him the dangerous and probably pointless temptation toward greater repression, just as he symbolized for me the equally perilous tug toward greater freedom. I personally was to be rewarded for this repression with a new and better life in the future, but how many of my friends paid an even higher price and were given only gall in return.

We have it on the authority of James Baldwin that all Negroes hate whites. I am trying to suggest that on their side all whites—all American whites, that is—are sick in their feelings about Negroes. There are Negroes, no doubt, who would say that Baldwin is wrong, but I suspect them of being less honest than he is, just as I suspect whites of self-deception who tell me they have no special feeling toward Negroes. Special feelings about color are a contagion to which white Americans seem susceptible even when there is nothing in their background to account for the susceptibility. Thus everywhere we look today in the North, we find the curious phenomenon of white middle-class liberals with no previous personal experience of Negroes

—people to whom Negroes have always been faceless in virtue rather than faceless in vice—discovering that their abstract commitment to the cause of Negro rights will not stand the test of a direct confrontation. We find such people fleeing in droves to the suburbs as the Negro population in the inner city grows; and when they stay in the city we find them sending their children to private school rather than to the "integrated" public school in the neighborhood. We find them resisting the demand that gerrymandered school districts be re-zoned for the purpose of overcoming de facto segregation; we find them judiciously considering whether the Negroes (for their own good, of course) are not perhaps pushing too hard; we find them clucking their tongues over Negro militancy; we find them speculating on the question of whether there may not, after all, be something in the theory that the races are biologically different; we find them saying that it will take a very long time for Negroes to achieve full equality, no matter what anyone does; we find them deploring the rise of black nationalism and expressing the solemn hope that the leaders of the Negro community will discover ways of containing the impatience and incipient violence within the Negro ghettos.[1]

But that is by no means the whole story; there is also the phenomenon of what Kenneth Rexroth once called "crow-jimism." There are the broken-down white boys like Vivaldo Moore in Baldwin's *Another Country* who go to Harlem in search of sex or simply to brush up against something that looks like primitive vitality, and who are so often punished by the Negroes they meet for crimes that they would have been the last ever to commit and of which they themselves have been as sorry victims as any of the Negroes who take it out on them. There are the writers and intellectuals and artists who romanticize Negroes and pander to them, assuming a guilt that is not properly theirs. And there are all the white liberals who permit Negroes to blackmail them into adopting a double standard of moral judgment, and who lend themselves—again assuming the responsibility for crimes they never committed—to cunning and contemptuous exploitation by Negroes they employ or try to befriend.

And what about me? What kind of feelings do I have about Negroes today? What happened to me, from Brooklyn, who grew up fearing and envying and hating Negroes? Now that Brooklyn is behind me, do I fear them and envy them and hate them still? The answer is yes, but not in the same proportions and certainly not in the same way. I now live on the upper west side of Manhattan, where there are many Negroes and many Puerto Ricans, and there are nights when I experi-

---

[1] For an account of developments like these, see "The White Liberal's Retreat" by Murray Friedman in the January 1963 *Atlantic Monthly*.

ence the old apprehensiveness again, and there are streets that I avoid when I am walking in the dark, as there were streets that I avoided when I was a child. I find that I am not afraid of Puerto Ricans, but I cannot restrain my nervousness whenever I pass a group of Negroes standing in front of a bar or sauntering down the street. I know now, as I did not know when I was a child, that power is on my side, that the police are working for me and not for them. And knowing this I feel ashamed and guilty, like the good liberal I have grown up to be. Yet the twinges of fear and the resentment they bring and the self-contempt they arouse are not to be gainsaid.

But envy? Why envy? And hatred? Why hatred? Here again the intensities have lessened and everything has been complicated and qualified by the guilts and the resulting over-compensations that are the heritage of the enlightened middle-class world of which I am now a member. Yet just as in childhood I envied Negroes for what seemed to me their superior masculinity, so I envy them today for what seems to me their superior physical grace and beauty. I have come to value physical grace very highly, and I am now capable of aching with all my being when I watch a Negro couple on the dance floor, or a Negro playing baseball or basketball. They are on the kind of terms with their own bodies that I should like to be on with mine, and for that precious quality they seem blessed to me.

The hatred I still feel for Negroes is the hardest of all the old feelings to face or admit, and it is the most hidden and the most over-larded by the conscious attitudes into which I have succeeded in willing myself. It no longer has, as for me it once did, any cause or justification (except, perhaps, that I am constantly being denied my right to an honest expression of the things I earned the right as a child to feel). How, then, do I know that this hatred has never entirely disappeared? I know it from the insane rage that can stir in me at the thought of Negro anti-Semitism; I know it from the disgusting prurience that can stir in me at the sight of a mixed couple; and I know it from the violence that can stir in me whenever I encounter that special brand of paranoid touchiness to which many Negroes are prone.

This, then, is where I am; it is not exactly where I think all other white liberals are, but it cannot be so very far away either. And it is because I am convinced that we white Americans are—for whatever reason, it no longer matters—so twisted and sick in our feelings about Negroes that I despair of the present push toward integration. If the pace of progress were not a factor here, there would perhaps be no cause for despair: time and the law and even the international political situation are on the side of the Negroes, and ultimately, therefore, victory—of a sort, anyway—must come. But from everything we have learned from observers who ought to know, pace has become as important to the Negroes as substance. They want equality and they want it *now*, and the white world is yielding to their demand only as much and as fast as it is absolutely being compelled to do. The Negroes know this in the most concrete terms imaginable, and it is thus becoming increasingly difficult to buy them off with rhetoric and promises and pious assurances of support. And so within the Negro community we find more and more people declaring—as Harold R. Isaacs recently put it in these pages[2]—that they want *out:* people who say that integration will never come, or that it will take a hundred or a thousand years to come, or that it will come at too high a price in suffering and struggle for the pallid and sodden life of the American middle class that at the very best it may bring.

The most numerous, influential, and dangerous movement that has grown out of Negro despair with the goal of integration is, of course, the Black Muslims. This movement, whatever else we may say about it, must be credited with one enduring achievement: it inspired James Baldwin to write an essay[3] which deserves to be placed among the classics of our language. Everything Baldwin has ever been trying to tell us is distilled here into a statement of overwhelming persuasiveness and prophetic magnificence. Baldwin's message is and always has been simple. It is this: "Color is not a human or personal reality; it is a political reality." And Baldwin's demand is correspondingly simple: color must be forgotten, lest we all be smited with a vengeance "that does not really depend on, and cannot really be executed by, any person or organization, and that cannot be prevented by any police force or army: historical vengeance, a cosmic vengeance based on the law that we recognize when we say, 'Whatever goes up must come down.' " The Black Muslims Baldwin portrays as a sign and a warning to the intransigent white world. They come to proclaim how deep is the Negro's disaffection with the white world and all its works, and Baldwin implies that no American Negro can fail to respond somewhere in his being to their message: that the white man is the devil, that Allah has doomed him to destruction, and that the black man is about to inherit the earth. Baldwin of course knows that this nightmare inversion of the racism from which the black man has suffered can neither win nor even point to the neighborhood in which victory might be located. For in his view the neighborhood of victory lies in exactly the opposite direction: the transcendence of color through love.

---

[2] "Integration and the Negro Mood," December 1962.

[3] Originally published last November in the *New Yorker* under the title "Letter From a Region in My Mind," it has just been reprinted (along with a new introduction) by Dial Press under the title *The Fire Next Time.*

Yet the tragic fact is that love is not the answer to hate—not in the world of politics, at any rate. Color is indeed a political rather than a human or a personal reality and if politics (which is to say power) has made it into a human and a personal reality, then only politics (which is to say power) can unmake it once again. But the way of politics is slow and bitter, and as impatience on the one side is matched by a setting of the jaw on the other, we move closer and closer to an explosion and blood may yet run in the streets.

Will this madness in which we are all caught never find a resting-place? Is there never to be an end to it? In thinking about the Jews I have often wondered whether their survival as a distinct group was worth one hair on the head of a single infant. Did the Jews have to survive so that six million innocent people should one day be burned in the ovens of Auschwitz? It is a terrible question and no one, not God himself, could ever answer it to my satisfaction. And when I think about the Negroes in America and about the image of integration as a state in which the Negroes would take their rightful place as another of the protected minorities in a pluralistic society, I wonder whether they really believe in their hearts that such a state can actually be attained, and if so *why* they should wish to survive as a distinct group. I think I know why the Jews once wished to survive (though I am less certain as to why we still do): they not only believed that God had given them no choice, but they were tied to a memory of past glory and a dream of imminent redemption. What does the American Negro have that might correspond to this? His past is a stigma, his color is a stigma, and his vision of the future is the hope of erasing the stigma by making color irrelevant, by making it disappear as a fact of consciousness.

I share this hope, but I cannot see how it will ever be realized unless color does *in fact* disappear: and that means not integration, it means assimilation, it means—let the brutal word come out—miscegenation. The Black Muslims, like their racist counterparts in the white world, accuse the "so-called Negro leaders" of secretly pursuing miscegenation as a goal. The racists are wrong, but I wish they were right, for I believe that the wholesale merging of the two races is the most desirable alternative for everyone concerned. I am not claiming that this alternative can be pursued programmatically or that it is immediately feasible as a solution; obviously there are even greater barriers to its achievement than to the achievement of integration. What I am saying, however, is that in my opinion the Negro problem can be solved in this country in no other way.

I have told the story of my own twisted feelings about Negroes here, and of how they conflict with the moral convictions I have since developed, in order to assert that such feelings must be acknowledged as honestly as possible so that they can be controlled and ultimately disregarded in favor of the convictions. It is *wrong* for a man to suffer because of the color of his skin. Beside that clichéd proposition of liberal thought, what argument can stand and be respected? If the arguments are the arguments of feeling, they must be made to yield; and one's own soul is not the worst place to begin working a huge social transformation. Not so long ago, it used to be asked of white liberals, "Would you like your sister to marry one?" When I was a boy and my sister was still unmarried, I would certainly have said no to that question. But now I am a man, my sister is already married, and I have daughters. If I were to be asked today whether I would like a daughter of mine "to marry one," I would have to answer: "No, I wouldn't *like* it at all. I would rail and rave and rant and tear my hair. And then I hope I would have the courage to curse myself for raving and ranting, and to give her my blessing. How dare I withhold it at the behest of the child I once was and against the man I now have a duty to be?"

Frantz Fanon

Frantz Fanon was born in Martinique in 1925. He studied medicine and psychiatry in France and was a French civil servant in charge of an Algerian psychiatric hospital, when the Algerian War broke out. He resigned his post, joined the rebels, became one of their leaders, and continued to work for them until his death from leukemia in 1961. A black West-Indian, yet a Frenchman; an intellectual in the white European tradition, yet an anti-European, anticolonial revolutionary, Fanon spent his whole adult life in an attempt to comprehend and to overcome the dilemma of racism. His passionate struggle is recorded in three books: Peau noire, masques blancs *(1952);* L'An cinq de la révolution Algérienne *(1959); and* Les Damnés de la terre *(1961). These have been translated as* Black Skin, White Masks *(1967), from which we print here the last chapter;* A Dying Colonialism *(1965); and* The Wretched of the Earth *(1967).*

Fanon's thought is mobile and complex, and cannot be summarized easily. Some readers, on the basis of passages in The Wretched of the Earth, *have made of him a romantic revolutionary, a simple-minded glorifier of violence. The historian*

J. E. Seigel suggests (American Scholar, vol. 38) *that this view does not do Fanon justice, that Fanon never wholly gave up the universalism evident in the conclusion of* Black Skin, White Masks; *beneath all of his work there remains the attempt "to find the means by which blackness could be made irrelevant by merging it in the larger fact of humanity."*

BY WAY OF CONCLUSION

The social revolution . . . cannot draw its poetry from the past, but only from the future. It cannot begin with itself before it has stripped itself of all its superstitions concerning the past. Earlier revolutions relied on memories out of world history in order to drug themselves against their own content. In order to find their own content, the revolutions of the nineteenth century have to let the dead bury the dead. Before, the expression exceeded the content; now, the content exceeds the expression.

—KARL MARX, *THE EIGHTEENTH BRUMAIRE*

I can already see the faces of all those who will ask me to be precise on this or that point, to denounce this or that mode of conduct.

It is obvious—and I will never weary of repeating this—that the quest for disalienation by a doctor of medicine born in Guadeloupe can be understood only by recognizing motivations basically different from those of the Negro laborer building the port facilities in Abidjan. In the first case, the alienation is of an almost intellectual character. Insofar as he conceives of European culture as a means of stripping himself of his race, he becomes alienated. In the second case, it is a question of a victim of a system based on the exploitation of a given race by another, on the contempt in which a given branch of humanity is held by a form of civilization that pretends to superiority.

I do not carry innocence to the point of believing that appeals to reason or to respect for human dignity can alter reality. For the Negro who works on a sugar plantation in Le Robert, there is only one solution: to fight. He will embark on this struggle, and he will pursue it, not as the result of a Marxist or idealistic analysis but quite simply because he cannot conceive of life otherwise than in the form of a battle against exploitation, misery, and hunger.

It would never occur to me to ask these Negroes to change their conception of history. I am convinced, however, that without even knowing it they share my views, accustomed as they are to speaking and thinking in terms of the present. The few working-class people whom I had the chance to know in Paris never took it on themselves to pose the problem of the discovery of a Negro past. They knew they were black, but, they told me, that made no difference in anything. In which they were absolutely right.

In this connection, I should like to say something that I have found in many other writers: Intellectual alienation is a creation of middle-class society. What I call middle-class society is any society that becomes rigidified in predetermined forms, forbidding all evolution, all gains, all progress, all discovery. I call middle-class a closed society in which life has no taste, in which the air is tainted, in which ideas and men are corrupt. And I think that a man who takes a stand against this death is in a sense a revolutionary.

The discovery of the existence of a Negro civilization in the fifteenth century confers no patent of humanity on me. Like it or not, the past can in no way guide me in the present moment.

The situation that I have examined, it is clear by now, is not a classic one. Scientific objectivity was barred to me, for the alienated, the neurotic, was my brother, my sister, my father. I have ceaselessly striven to show the Negro that in a sense he makes himself abnormal; to show the white man that he is at once the perpetrator and the victim of a delusion.

There are times when the black man is locked into his body. Now, "for a being who has acquired consciousness of himself and of his body, who has attained to the dialectic of subject and object, the body is no longer a cause of the structure of consciousness, it has become an object of consciousness."[1]

The Negro, however sincere, is the slave of the past. None the less I am a man, and in this sense the Peloponnesian War is as much mine as the invention of the compass. Face to face with the white man, the Negro has a past to legitimate, a vengeance to exact; face to face with the Negro, the contemporary white man feels the need to recall the times of cannibalism. A few years ago, the Lyon branch of the Union of Students From Overseas France asked me to reply to an article that made jazz music literally an irruption of cannibalism into the modern world. Knowing exactly what I was doing, I rejected the premises on which the request was based, and I suggested to the defender of European purity that he cure himself of a spasm that had nothing cultural in it. Some men want to fill the world with their presence. A German philosopher described this mechanism as *the pathology of freedom*. In the circumstances, I did not have to take up

---

[1] Maurice Merleau-Ponty, *La Phénoménologie de la perception* (Paris, Gallimard, 1945), p. 277.

a position on behalf of Negro music against white music, but rather to help my brother to rid himself of an attitude in which there was nothing healthful.

The problem considered here is one of time. Those Negroes and white men will be disalienated who refuse to let themselves be sealed away in the materialized Tower of the Past. For many other Negroes, in other ways, disalienation will come into being through their refusal to accept the present as definitive.

I am a man, and what I have to recapture is the whole past of the world. I am not responsible solely for the revolt in Santo Domingo.

Every time a man has contributed to the victory of the dignity of the spirit, every time a man has said no to an attempt to subjugate his fellows, I have felt solidarity with his act.

In no way should I derive my basic purpose from the past of the peoples of color.

In no way should I dedicate myself to the revival of an unjustly unrecognized Negro civilization. I will not make myself the man of any past. I do not want to exalt the past at the expense of my present and of my future.

It is not because the Indo-Chinese has discovered a culture of his own that he is in revolt. It is because "quite simply" it was, in more than one way, becoming impossible for him to breathe. When one remembers the stories with which, in 1938, old regular sergeants described the land of piastres and rickshaws, of cut-rate boys and women, one understands only too well the rage with which the men of the Viet-Minh go into battle.

An acquaintance with whom I served during the Second World War recently returned from Indo-China. He has enlightened me on many things. For instance, the serenity with which young Vietnamese of sixteen or seventeen faced firing squads. "On one occasion," he told me, "we had to shoot from a kneeling position: The soldiers' hands were shaking in the presence of those young 'fanatics.'" Summing up, he added: "The war that you and I were in was only a game compared to what is going on out there."

Seen from Europe, these things are beyond understanding. There are those who talk of a so-called Asiatic attitude toward death. But these basement philosophers cannot convince anyone. This Asiatic serenity, not so long ago, was a quality to be seen in the "bandits" of Vercors and the "terrorists" of the Resistance.

The Vietnamese who die before the firing squads are not hoping that their sacrifice will bring about the reappearance of a past. It is for the sake of the present and of the future that they are willing to die.

If the question of practical solidarity with a given past ever arose for me, it did so only to the extent to which I was committed to myself and to my neighbor to fight for all my life and with all my strength so that never again would a people on the earth be subjugated. It was not the black world that laid down my course of conduct. My black skin is not the wrapping of specific values. It is a long time since the starry sky that took away Kant's breath revealed the last of its secrets to us. And the moral law is not certain of itself.

As a man, I undertake to face the possibility of annihilation in order that two or three truths may cast their eternal brilliance over the world.

Sartre has shown that, in the line of an unauthentic position, the past "takes" in quantity, and, when solidly constructed, *informs* the individual. He is the past in a changed value. But, too, I can recapture my past, validate it, or condemn it through my successive choices.

The black man wants to be like the white man. For the black man there is only one destiny. And it is white. Long ago the black man admitted the unarguable superiority of the white man, and all his efforts are aimed at achieving a white existence.

Have I no other purpose on earth, then, but to avenge the Negro of the seventeenth century?

In this world, which is already trying to disappear, do I have to pose the problem of black truth?

Do I have to be limited to the justification of a facial conformation?

I as a man of color do not have the right to seek to know in what respect my race is superior or inferior to another race.

I as a man of color do not have the right to hope that in the white man there will be a crystallization of guilt toward the past of my race.

I as a man of color do not have the right to seek ways of stamping down the pride of my former master.

I have neither the right nor the duty to claim reparation for the domestication of my ancestors.

There is no Negro mission; there is no white burden.

I find myself suddenly in a world in which things do evil; a world in which I am summoned into battle; a world in which it is always a question of annihilation or triumph.

I find myself—I, a man—in a world where words wrap themselves in silence; in a world where the other endlessly hardens himself.

No, I do not have the right to go and cry out my hatred at the white man. I do not have the duty to murmur my gratitude to the white man.

My life is caught in the lasso of existence. My freedom turns me back on myself. No, I do not have the right to be a Negro.

I do not have the duty to be this or that. . . .

If the white man challenges my humanity, I will impose my whole weight as a man on his life and show him that I am not that "sho' good eatin'" that he persists in imagining.

I find myself suddenly in the world and I recognize that I have one right alone: That of demanding human behavior from the other.

One duty alone: That of not renouncing my freedom through my choices.

I have no wish to be the victim of the *Fraud* of a black world.

My life should not be devoted to drawing up the balance sheet of Negro values.

There is no white world, there is no white ethic, any more than there is a white intelligence.

There are in every part of the world men who search.

I am not a prisoner of history. I should not seek there for the meaning of my destiny.

I should constantly remind myself that the real *leap* consists in introducing invention into existence.

In the world through which I travel, I am endlessly creating myself.

I am a part of Being to the degree that I go beyond it.

And, through a private problem, we see the outline of the problem of Action. Placed in this world, in a situation, "embarked," as Pascal would have it, am I going to gather weapons?

Am I going to ask the contemporary white man to answer for the slave-ships of the seventeenth century?

Am I going to try by every possible means to cause Guilt to be born in minds?

Moral anguish in the face of the massiveness of the Past? I am a Negro, and tons of chains, storms of blows, rivers of expectoration flow down my shoulders.

But I do not have the right to allow myself to bog down. I do not have the right to allow the slightest fragment to remain in my existence. I do not have the right to allow myself to be mired in what the past has determined.

I am not the slave of the Slavery that dehumanized my ancestors.

To many colored intellectuals European culture has a quality of exteriority. What is more, in human relationships, the Negro may feel himself a stranger to the Western world. Not wanting to live the part of a poor relative, of an adopted son, of a bastard child, shall he feverishly seek to discover a Negro civilization?

Let us be clearly understood. I am convinced that it would be of the greatest interest to be able to have contact with a Negro literature or architecture of the third century before Christ. I should be very happy to know that a correspondence had flourished between some Negro philosopher and Plato. But I can absolutely not see how this fact would change anything in the lives of the eight-year-old children who labor in the cane fields of Martinique or Guadeloupe.

No attempt must be made to encase man, for it is his destiny to be set free.

The body of history does not determine a single one of my actions. I am my own foundation.

And it is by going beyond the historical, instrumental hypothesis that I will initiate the cycle of my freedom.

The disaster of the man of color lies in the fact that he was enslaved.

The disaster and the inhumanity of the white man lie in the fact that somewhere he has killed man.

And even today they subsist, to organize this dehumanization rationally. But I as a man of color, to the extent that it becomes possible for me to exist absolutely, do not have the right to lock myself into a world of retroactive reparations.

I, the man of color, want only this:

That the tool never possess the man. That the enslavement of man by man cease forever. That is, of one by another. That it be possible for me to discover and to love man, wherever he may be.

The Negro is not. Any more than the white man.

Both must turn their backs on the inhuman voices which were those of their respective ancestors in order that authentic communication be possible. Before it can adopt a positive voice, freedom requires an effort at disalienation. At the beginning of his life a man is always clotted, he is drowned in contingency. The tragedy of the man is that he was once a child.

It is through the effort to recapture the self and to scrutinize the self, it is through the lasting tension of their freedom that men will be able to create the ideal conditions of existence for a human world.

Superiority? Inferiority?

Why not the quite simple attempt to touch the other, to feel the other, to explain the other to myself?

Was my freedom not given to me then in order to build the world of the *You*?

At the conclusion of this study, I want the world to recognize, with me, the open door of every consciousness.

My final prayer:
O my body, make of me always a man who questions!

DISSENT AND CIVIL DIS- OBEDIENCE

B ehind every discussion on the nature and role of dissent and civil disobedience lie two questions: what is the relationship between the individual and society? between conscience and law? These are knotty questions, particularly today when authority is being challenged, when injustices are made visible, and when there is wide suspicion that rhetoric and temporizing are displacing ideas and action.

We begin the section with the Declaration of Independence, which establishes in our political tradition that the rights of men and the consent of the governed take precedence over the will of the State, and the Bill of Rights, which spells out and thus protects the rights of the individual. The article by Walter Lippmann which follows brings fresh dimension to the First Amendment by suggesting that in a democracy freedom of speech is important not so much for the speaker as for the listener: we must be free to hear what our critics have to say.

The next four pieces deal directly with civil disobedience. Thoreau, a dedicated individualist, and Martin Luther King, Jr., an eloquent spokesman for civil and human rights, both argue for the sovereignty of individual conscience. But many people say that civil disobedience within a civilized state is by definition immoral. This argument is felt to be especially cogent in a democracy, where law is adjustable. We voluntarily relinquish some of our freedom and accept the necessity and authority of the law in order to protect the community and guard it against anarchy. Defiance, then, strikes not only at specific laws but also at the concept of law and order and thus at the system itself. This is the argument which Plato presents so forcefully in *The Crito*, part of which is printed below. In reading the above arguments, the reader may wish to consider a paradox pointed out by George Orwell in his essay on Gandhi: that modern civil disobedience can only be effective in a democratic community. "It is difficult to see," says Orwell, "how Gandhi's methods [passive resistance] could be applied in a country where opponents to the regime disappear in the middle of the night and are never heard of again. Without a free press and the right of assembly, it is impossible not merely to appeal to out-side opinion, but to bring a mass movement into being, or even to make your intentions known to your adversary."

The above, then, deal essentially with social protest in the form of nonviolent dissent and disobedience. But what if the system is felt to be unresponsive to just demands? Malcolm X's speech, delivered in April 1964 and anticipating the 1964 national elections, clearly suggests the next step: if dissent cannot be satisfied with the ballot, the alternative is the bullet. Today, violence is encroaching upon nonviolence, and at times not only specific laws but the whole principle of civil order is being challenged. This is the concern of Erwin Griswold, whose sober and thoughtful speech closes the section. Fearful lest indiscriminate disobedience lead to the "legitimation of violence" and ultimately to the rejection of all civil order, he seeks to define the responsibilities that accompany our acknowledged right of dissent.

Thomas Jefferson

On June 11, 1776, the Continental Congress appointed a committee of five—Thomas Jefferson, Benjamin Franklin, John Adams, Robert Livingston, and Roger Sherman—to prepare a declaration of independence. It was decided that Jefferson should first write a draft. He did so, drawing heavily on the natural rights political philosophy of the time, but as he says, he turned to "neither book nor pamphlet" in its preparation. A few changes were made by Adams and Franklin, and it was then presented to Congress on June 28. On July 2 and 3 Congress debated the form and content of the Declaration, made a few further changes, and on July 4 approved it without dissent. Although we here credit Jefferson with authorship, we print the amended and official version, taken from the United States Government Senate Manual.

DECLARATION OF INDEPENDENCE (IN CONGRESS JULY 4, 1776)

THE UNANIMOUS DECLARATION OF THE THIRTEEN UNITED STATES OF AMERICA

When in the Course of human events, it becomes necessary for one people to dissolve the political bands which have connected them with another, and to assume among the powers of the earth, the separate and equal station to which the Laws of Nature and of Nature's God entitle them, a decent respect to the opinions of mankind requires that they should declare the causes which impel them to the separation.

We hold these truths to be self-evident, that all men are created equal, that they are endowed by their Creator with certain unalienable Rights, that among these are Life, Liberty and the pursuit of Happiness. That to secure these rights, Governments are instituted among Men, deriving their just powers from the consent of the governed, That whenever any Form of Government becomes destructive of these ends, it is the Right of the People to alter or to abolish it, and to institute new Government, laying its foundation on such principles and organizing its powers in such form, as to them shall seem most likely to effect their Safety and Happiness. Prudence, indeed, will dictate that Governments long established should not be changed for light and transient causes; and accordingly all experience hath shewn that mankind are more disposed to suffer, while evils are sufferable, than to right themselves by abolishing the forms to which they are accustomed. But when a long train of abuses and usurpations, pursuing invariably the same Object evinces a design to reduce them under absolute Despotism, it is their right, it is their duty, to throw off such Government, and to provide new Guards for their future security. Such has been the patient sufferance of these Colonies; and such is now the necessity which constrains them to alter their former Systems of Government. The history of the present King of Great Britain is a history of repeated injuries and usurpations, all having in direct object the establishment of an absolute Tyranny over these States. To prove this, let Facts be submitted to a candid world.

He has refused his Assent to Laws, the most wholesome and necessary for the public good.

He has forbidden his Governors to pass Laws of immediate and pressing importance, unless suspended in their operation till his Assent should be obtained; and when so suspended, he has utterly neglected to attend to them.

He has refused to pass other Laws for the accommodation of large districts of people, unless those people would relinquish the right of Representation in the Legislature, a right inestimable to them and formidable to tyrants only.

He has called together legislative bodies at places unusual, uncomfortable, and distant from the depository of their public Records, for the sole purpose of fatiguing them into compliance with his measures.

He has dissolved Representative Houses repeatedly, for opposing with manly firmness his invasions on the rights of the people.

He has refused for a long time, after such dissolutions, to cause others to be elected; whereby the Legislative powers, incapable of

Annihilation, have returned to the People at large for their exercise; the State remaining in the mean time exposed to all the dangers of invasion from without, and convulsions within.

He has endeavoured to prevent the population of these States; for that purpose obstructing the Laws for Naturalization of Foreigners; refusing to pass others to encourage their migrations hither, and raising the conditions of new Appropriations of Lands.

He has obstructed the Administration of Justice, by refusing his Assent to Laws for establishing Judiciary powers.

He has made Judges dependent on his Will alone, for the tenure of their offices, and the amount and payment of their salaries.

He has erected a multitude of New Offices, and sent hither swarms of Officers to harass our people, and eat out their substance.

He has kept among us, in times of peace, Standing Armies without the Consent of our legislatures.

He has affected to render the Military independent of and superior to the Civil power.

He has combined with others to subject us to a jurisdiction foreign to our constitution, and unacknowledged by our laws; giving his Assent to their Acts of pretended Legislation:

For quartering large bodies of armed troops among us:

For protecting them, by a mock Trial, from punishment for any Murders which they should commit on the Inhabitants of these States:

For cutting off our Trade with all parts of the world:

For imposing Taxes on us without our Consent:

For depriving us in many cases, of the benefits of Trial by Jury:

For transporting us beyond Seas to be tried for pretended offences:

For abolishing the free System of English Laws in a neighbouring Province, establishing therein an Arbitrary government, and enlarging its Boundaries so as to render it at once an example and fit instrument for introducing the same absolute rule into these Colonies:

For taking away our Charters, abolishing our most valuable Laws, and altering fundamentally the Forms of our Governments:

For suspending our own Legislatures, and declaring themselves invested with power to legislate for us in all cases whatsoever.

He has abdicated Government here, by declaring us out of his Protection and waging War against us.

He has plundered our seas, ravaged our Coasts, burnt our towns, and destroyed the lives of our people.

He is at this time transporting large Armies of foreign Mercenaries to compleat the works of death, desolation and tyranny, already begun with circumstances of Cruelty & perfidy scarcely paralleled in the most barbarous ages, and totally unworthy the Head of a civilized nation.

He has constrained our fellow Citizens taken Captive on the high

Seas to bear Arms against their Country, to become the executioners of their friends and Brethren, or to fall themselves by their Hands.

He has excited domestic insurrections amongst us, and has endeavoured to bring on the inhabitants of our frontiers, the merciless Indian Savages, whose known rule of warfare is an undistinguished destruction of all ages, sexes and conditions.

In every stage of these Oppressions We have Petitioned for Redress in the most humble terms: Our repeated Petitions have been answered only by repeated injury. A Prince, whose character is thus marked by every act which may define a Tyrant, is unfit to be the ruler of a free people.

Nor have We been wanting in attentions to our British Brethren. We have warned them from time to time of attempts by their legislature to extend an unwarrantable jurisdiction over us. We have reminded them of the circumstances of our emigration and settlement here. We have appealed to their native justice and magnanimity, and we have conjured them by the ties of our common kindred to disavow these usurpations, which would inevitably interrupt our connections and correspondence. They too have been deaf to the voice of justice and of consanguinity. We must, therefore, acquiesce in the necessity, which denounces our Separation, and hold them, as we hold the rest of mankind. Enemies in War, in Peace Friends.

WE, THEREFORE, the REPRESENTATIVES OF THE UNITED STATES OF AMERICA, IN GENERAL CONGRESS, Assembled, appealing to the Supreme Judge of the world for the rectitude of our intentions, do, in the Name, and by authority of the good People of these Colonies, solemnly PUBLISH and DECLARE, That these United Colonies are, and of Right ought to be FREE AND INDEPENDENT STATES; that they are Absolved from all Allegiance to the British Crown, and that all political connection between them and the State of Great Britain, is and ought to be totally dissolved; and that as FREE AND INDEPENDENT STATES, they have full Power to levy War, conclude Peace, contract Alliances, establish Commerce, and to do all other Acts and Things which INDEPENDENT STATES may of right do. And for the support of this Declaration, with a firm reliance on the protection of divine Providence, we mutually pledge to each other our Lives, our Fortunes and our sacred Honor.

The First Congress of the United States

*"The Bill of Rights" is the name given to the first ten amendments
to the United States Constitution. When the Constitution was
originally adopted in 1788, many of its framers had felt that a
spelling-out of rights already presumed to exist was unnecessary
and might even suggest an undue extension of governmental powers.
Some of the states, however, having explicit declarations of rights
in their own constitutions, recommended on ratifying the federal
Constitution that it too be so furnished. The Bill of Rights was
prepared by the first Congress under the leadership of James Madison
and was ratified by the states in 1791. It has turned out to be an
invaluable guide to the courts in decisions affecting civil rights
and is in fact the main protection American citizens have against
the diminution of their liberties by their government or by each
other.*

THE BILL OF RIGHTS

ARTICLES IN ADDITION TO, AND AMENDMENT OF, THE CONSTITUTION OF THE
UNITED STATES OF AMERICA, PROPOSED BY CONGRESS, AND RATIFIED BY THE
LEGISLATURES OF THE SEVERAL STATES, PURSUANT TO THE FIFTH ARTICLE OF
THE ORIGINAL CONSTITUTION.

ARTICLE I

Congress shall make no law respecting an establishment of religion,
or prohibiting the free exercise thereof; or abridging the freedom of
speech, or of the press; or the right of the people peaceably to assemble, and to petition the Government for a redress of grievances.

ARTICLE II

A well regulated Militia, being necessary to the security of a free
State, the right of the people to keep and bear Arms, shall not be
infringed.

ARTICLE III

No Soldier shall, in time of peace be quartered in any house, without the consent of the Owner, nor in time of war, but in a manner to be prescribed by law.

ARTICLE IV

The right of the people to be secure in their persons, houses, papers, and effects, against unreasonable searches and seizures, shall not be violated, and no Warrants shall issue, but upon probable cause, supported by Oath or affirmation, and particularly describing the place to be searched, and the persons or things to be seized.

ARTICLE V

No person shall be held to answer for a capital, or otherwise infamous crime, unless on a presentment or indictment of a Grand Jury, except in cases arising in the land or naval forces, or in the Militia, when in actual service in time of War or public danger; nor shall any person be subject for the same offence to be twice put in jeopardy of life or limb; nor shall be compelled in any criminal case to be a witness against himself; nor be deprived of life, liberty, or property, without due process of law; nor shall private property be taken for public use, without just compensation.

ARTICLE VI

In all criminal prosecutions, the accused shall enjoy the right to a speedy and public trial, by an impartial jury of the State and district wherein the crime shall have been committed, which district shall have been previously ascertained by law, and to be informed of the nature and cause of the accusation; to be confronted with the witnesses against him; to have compulsory process for obtaining witnesses in his favor, and to have the Assistance of Counsel for his defence.

ARTICLE VII

In Suits at common law, where the value in controversy shall exceed twenty dollars, the right of trial by jury shall be preserved, and no fact tried by a jury, shall be otherwise reexamined in any Court of the United States, than according to the rules of the common law.

ARTICLE VIII

Excessive bail shall not be required, nor excessive fines imposed, nor cruel and unusual punishments inflicted.

ARTICLE IX

The enumeration in the Constitution, of certain rights, shall not be construed to deny or disparage others retained by the people.

ARTICLE X

The powers not delegated to the United States by the Constitution, nor prohibited by it to the States, are reserved to the States respectively, or to the people.

Walter Lippmann

Walter Lippmann is one of the most honored of American newspapermen. Born in 1889, he was educated at Harvard and then taught philosophy there as an assistant to George Santayana. He joined the staff of The New Republic *at its founding in 1914, interrupted his journalistic career to serve as assistant to the Secretary of War—doing special work on peace negotiating—and then moved to an editorial position on the* New York World. *His writings have been syndicated in newspapers throughout the country and his column "Today and Tomorrow" won him Pulitzer Prizes in 1958 and 1962. The 1958 award cited the "wisdom, perception, and high sense of responsibility with which he has commented for many years on national and international affairs." He has received many honorary degrees, and such decorations as the Medal of Freedom, the Legion of Honor from France, and the Order of Leopold from Belgium. His books include* Liberty and the News *(1920),* Public Opinion *(1922),* The Good Society *(1937),* The Public Philosophy *(1955),* The Coming Tests with Russia *(1961),* Western Unity and the Common

Market *(1962), and* The Essential Lippmann: A Political Philosophy for Liberal Democracy *(1963). The essay we present below is taken from* The Atlantic Monthly *for August 1939.*

THE INDISPENSABLE OPPOSITION

[I]

Were they pressed hard enough, most men would probably confess that political freedom—that is to say, the right to speak freely and to act in opposition—is a noble ideal rather than a practical necessity. As the case for freedom is generally put to-day, the argument lends itself to this feeling. It is made to appear that, whereas each man claims his freedom as a matter of right, the freedom he accords to other men is a matter of toleration. Thus, the defense of freedom of opinion tends to rest not on its substantial, beneficial, and indispensable consequences, but on a somewhat eccentric, a rather vaguely benevolent, attachment to an abstraction.

It is all very well to say with Voltaire, 'I wholly disapprove of what you say, but will defend to the death your right to say it,' but as a matter of fact most men will not defend to the death the rights of other men: if they disapprove sufficiently what other men say, they will somehow suppress those men if they can.

So, if this is the best that can be said for liberty of opinion, that a man must tolerate his opponents because everyone has a 'right' to say what he pleases, then we shall find that liberty of opinion is a luxury, safe only in pleasant times when men can be tolerant because they are not deeply and vitally concerned.

Yet actually, as a matter of historic fact, there is a much stronger foundation for the great constitutional right of freedom of speech, and as a matter of practical human experience there is a much more compelling reason for cultivating the habits of free men. We take, it seems to me, a naïvely self-righteous view when we argue as if the right of our opponents to speak were something that we protect because we are magnanimous, noble, and unselfish. The compelling reason why, if liberty of opinion did not exist, we should have to invent it, why it will eventually have to be restored in all civilized countries where it is now suppressed, is that we must protect the right

298

of our opponents to speak because we must hear what they have to say.

We miss the whole point when we imagine that we tolerate the freedom of our political opponents as we tolerate a howling baby next door, as we put up with the blasts from our neighbor's radio because we are too peaceable to heave a brick through the window. If this were all there is to freedom of opinion, that we are too good-natured or too timid to do anything about our opponents and our critics except to let them talk, it would be difficult to say whether we are tolerant because we are magnanimous or because we are lazy, because we have strong principles or because we lack serious convictions, whether we have the hospitality of an inquiring mind or the indifference of an empty mind. And so, if we truly wish to understand why freedom is necessary in a civilized society, we must begin by realizing that, because freedom of discussion improves our own opinions, the liberties of other men are our own vital necessity.

We are much closer to the essence of the matter, not when we quote Voltaire, but when we go to the doctor and pay him to ask us the most embarrassing questions and to prescribe the most disagreeable diet. When we pay the doctor to exercise complete freedom of speech about the cause and cure of our stomachache, we do not look upon ourselves as tolerant and magnanimous, and worthy to be admired by ourselves. We have enough common sense to know that if we threaten to put the doctor in jail because we do not like the diagnosis and the prescription it will be unpleasant for the doctor, to be sure, but equally unpleasant for our own stomachache. That is why even the most ferocious dictator would rather be treated by a doctor who was free to think and speak the truth than by his own Minister of Propaganda. For there is a point, the point at which things really matter, where the freedom of others is no longer a question of their right but of our need.

The point at which we recognize this need is much higher in some men than in others. The totalitarian rulers think they do not need the freedom of an opposition: they exile, imprison, or shoot their opponents. We have concluded on the basis of practical experience, which goes back to Magna Carta and beyond, that we need the opposition. We pay the opposition salaries out of the public treasury.

In so far as the usual apology for freedom of speech ignores this experience, it becomes abstract and eccentric rather than concrete and human. The emphasis is generally put on the right to speak, as if all that mattered were that the doctor should be free to go out into the park and explain to the vacant air why I have a stomachache. Surely that is a miserable caricature of the great civic right which men have bled and died for. What really matters is that the doctor should tell *me* what ails me, that I should listen to him; that if I do not like what he says I should be free to call in another doctor; and that then the first doctor should have to listen to the second doctor; and that out of all the speaking and listening, the give-and-take of opinions, the truth should be arrived at.

This is the creative principle of freedom of speech, not that it is a system for the tolerating of error, but that it is a system for finding the truth. It may not produce the truth, or the whole truth all the time, or often, or in some cases ever. But if the truth can be found, there is no other system which will normally and habitually find so much truth. Until we have thoroughly understood this principle, we shall not know why we must value our liberty, or how we can protect and develop it.

[II]

Let us apply this principle to the system of public speech in a totalitarian state. We may, without any serious falsification, picture a condition of affairs in which the mass of the people are being addressed through one broadcasting system by one man and his chosen subordinates. The orators speak. The audience listens but cannot and dare not speak back. It is a system of one-way communication; the opinions of the rulers are broadcast outwardly to the mass of the people. But nothing comes back to the rulers from the people except the cheers; nothing returns in the way of knowledge of forgotten facts, hidden feelings, neglected truths, and practical suggestions.

But even a dictator cannot govern by his own one-way inspiration alone. In practice, therefore, the totalitarian rulers get back the reports of the secret police and of their party henchmen down among the crowd. If these reports are competent, the rulers may manage to remain in touch with public sentiment. Yet that is not enough to know what the audience feels. The rulers have also to make great decisions that have enormous consequences, and here their system provides virtually no help from the give-and-take of opinion in the nation. So they must either rely on their own intuition, which cannot be permanently and continually inspired, or, if they are intelligent despots, encourage their trusted advisers and their technicians to speak and debate freely in their presence.

On the walls of the houses of Italian peasants one may see inscribed in large letters the legend, 'Mussolini is always right.' But if that legend is taken seriously by Italian ambassadors, by the Italian General Staff, and by the Ministry of Finance, then all one can say is heaven help Mussolini, heaven help Italy, and the new Emperor of Ethiopia.

For at some point, even in a totalitarian state, it is indispensable that there should exist the freedom of opinion which causes opposing opinions to be debated. As time goes on, that is less and less easy under a despotism; critical discussion disappears as the internal opposition is liquidated in favor of men who think and feel alike. That is why the early successes of despots, of Napoleon I and of Napoleon III, have usually been followed by an irreparable mistake. For in listening only to his yes men—the others being in exile or in concentration camps, or terrified—the despot shuts himself off from the truth that no man can dispense with.

We know all this well enough when we contemplate the dictatorships. But when we try to picture our own system, by way of contrast, what picture do we have in our minds? It is, is it not, that anyone may stand up on his own soapbox and say anything he pleases, like the individuals in Kipling's poem who sit each in his separate star and draw the Thing as they see it for the God of Things as they are. Kipling, perhaps, could do this, since he was a poet. But the ordinary mortal isolated on his separate star will have an hallucination, and a citizenry declaiming from separate soapboxes will poison the air with hot and nonsensical confusion.

If the democratic alternative to the totalitarian one-way broadcasts is a row of separate soapboxes, then I submit that the alternative is unworkable, is unreasonable, and is humanly unattractive. It is above all a false alternative. It is not true that liberty has developed among civilized men when anyone is free to set up a soapbox, is free to hire a hall where he may expound his opinions to those who are willing to listen. On the contrary, freedom of speech is established to achieve its essential purpose only when different opinions are expounded in the same hall to the same audience.

For, while the right to talk may be the beginning of freedom, the necessity of listening is what makes the right important. Even in Russia and Germany a man may still stand in an open field and speak his mind. What matters is not the utterance of opinions. What matters is the confrontation of opinions in debate. No man can care profoundly that every fool should say what he likes. Nothing has been accomplished if the wisest man proclaims his wisdom in the middle of the Sahara Desert. This is the shadow. We have the substance of liberty when the fool is compelled to listen to the wise man and learn; when the wise man is compelled to take account of the fool, and to instruct him; when the wise man can increase his wisdom by hearing the judgment of his peers.

That is why civilized men must cherish liberty—as a means of promoting the discovery of truth. So we must not fix our whole attention on the right of anyone to hire his own hall, to rent his own broadcasting station, to distribute his own pamphlets. These rights are incidental; and though they must be preserved, they can be preserved only by regarding them as incidental, as auxiliary to the substance of liberty that must be cherished and cultivated.

Freedom of speech is best conceived, therefore, by having in mind the picture of a place like the American Congress, an assembly where opposing views are represented, where ideas are not merely uttered but debated, or the British Parliament, where men who are free to speak are also compelled to answer. We may picture the true condition of freedom as existing in a place like a court of law, where witnesses testify and are cross-examined, where the lawyer argues against the opposing lawyer before the same judge and in the presence of one jury. We may picture freedom as existing in a forum where the speaker must respond to questions; in a gathering of scientists where the data, the hypothesis, and the conclusion are submitted to men competent to judge them; in a reputable newspaper which not only will publish the opinions of those who disagree but will reëxamine its own opinion in the light of what they say.

Thus the essence of freedom of opinion is not in mere toleration as such, but in the debate which toleration provides: it is not in the venting of opinion, but in the confrontation of opinion. That this is the practical substance can readily be understood when we remember how differently we feel and act about the censorship and regulation of opinion purveyed by different media of communication. We find then that, in so far as the medium makes difficult the confrontation of opinion in debate, we are driven towards censorship and regulation.

There is, for example, the whispering campaign, the circulation of anonymous rumors by men who cannot be compelled to prove what they say. They put the utmost strain on our tolerance, and there are few who do not rejoice when the anonymous slanderer is caught, exposed, and punished. At a higher level there is the moving picture, a most powerful medium for conveying ideas, but a medium which does not permit debate. A moving picture cannot be answered effectively by another moving picture; in all free countries there is some censorship of the movies, and there would be more if the producers did not recognize their limitations by avoiding political controversy. There is then the radio. Here debate is difficult: it is not easy to make sure that the speaker is being answered in the presence of the same audience. Inevitably, there is some regulation of the radio.

When we reach the newspaper press, the opportunity for debate is so considerable that discontent cannot grow to the point where under normal conditions there is any disposition to regulate the press. But when newspapers abuse their power by injuring people who have no means of replying, a disposition to regulate the press appears. When we arrive at Congress we find that, because the membership of the

House is so large, full debate is impracticable. So there are restrictive rules. On the other hand, in the Senate, where the conditions of full debate exist, there is almost absolute freedom of speech.

This shows us that the preservation and development of freedom of opinion are not only a matter of adhering to abstract legal rights, but also, and very urgently, a matter of organizing and arranging sufficient debate. Once we have a firm hold on the central principle, there are many practical conclusions to be drawn. We then realize that the defense of freedom of opinion consists primarily in perfecting the opportunity for an adequate give-and-take of opinion; it consists also in regulating the freedom of those revolutionists who cannot or will not permit or maintain debate when it does not suit their purposes.

We must insist that free oratory is only the beginning of free speech; it is not the end, but a means to an end. The end is to find the truth. The practical justification of civil liberty is not that self-expression is one of the rights of man. It is that the examination of opinion is one of the necessities of man. For experience tells us that it is only when freedom of opinion becomes the compulsion to debate that the seed which our fathers planted has produced its fruit. When that is understood, freedom will be cherished not because it is a vent for our opinions but because it is the surest method of correcting them.

The unexamined life, said Socrates, is unfit to be lived by man. This is the virtue of liberty, and the ground on which we may best justify our belief in it, that it tolerates error in order to serve the truth. When men are brought face to face with their opponents, forced to listen and learn and mend their ideas, they cease to be children and savages and begin to live like civilized men. Then only is freedom a reality, when men may voice their opinions because they must examine their opinions.

[III]

The only reason for dwelling on all this is that if we are to preserve democracy we must understand its principles. And the principle which distinguishes it from all other forms of government is that in a democracy the opposition not only is tolerated as constitutional but must be maintained because it is in fact indispensable.

The democratic system cannot be operated without effective opposition. For, in making the great experiment of governing people by consent rather than by coercion, it is not sufficient that the party in power should have a majority. It is just as necessary that the party in power should never outrage the minority. That means that it must listen to the minority and be moved by the criticisms of the minority. That means that its measures must take account of the minority's objections, and that in administering measures it must remember that the minority may become the majority.

The opposition is indispensable. A good statesman, like any other sensible human being, always learns more from his opponents than from his fervent supporters. For his supporters will push him to disaster unless his opponents show him where the dangers are. So if he is wise he will often pray to be delivered from his friends, because they will ruin him. But, though it hurts, he ought also to pray never to be left without opponents; for they keep him on the path of reason and good sense.

The national unity of a free people depends upon a sufficiently even balance of political power to make it impracticable for the administration to be arbitrary and for the opposition to be revolutionary and irreconcilable. Where that balance no longer exists, democracy perishes. For unless all the citizens of a state are forced by circumstances to compromise, unless they feel that they can affect policy but that no one can wholly dominate it, unless by habit and necessity they have to give and take, freedom cannot be maintained.

Plato

Plato, one of the greatest philosophers of the Western world, was born in Athens. Originally named Aristocles, he was surnamed Plato because of his broad shoulders, or—as some would have it—his broad forehead. Early in his life he became a student of Socrates, and his subsequent writings are evidence of the profound influence his teacher had on him. After Socrates' trial, conviction, and death in 399 B.C., Plato spent thirteen years away from Athens, in Italy, Egypt, and parts of Greece. He returned in 386 B.C. and founded the Academy in which he taught until his death in 347 B.C. Aristotle was his student. Plato's extant works are in the form of conversations, or dialogues, in which the leading speaker is usually Socrates. Perhaps the best known of the dialogues is The Republic, *in which Socrates explores the nature of the ideal state. Plato records the last days of Socrates in three early dialogues,* The Apology, The Crito, *and* The Phaedo. The Apology *presents Socrates' defense at his trial on charges of corrupting youth and believing in gods other than the State's divinities.* The Phaedo *records Socrates' last conversation before death.* In The Crito, *Crito visits Socrates in prison and tries to persuade him to escape.* We print below, from the Jowett *translation, third edition, Socrates' argument for submitting to the death penalty that the law had imposed on him.*

FROM **THE CRITO**

Socrates . . . Ought a man to do what he admits to be right, or ought he to betray the right?

Crito. He ought to do what he thinks right.

Soc. But if this is true, what is the application? In leaving the prison against the will of the Athenians, do I wrong any? or rather do I not wrong those whom I ought least to wrong? Do I not desert the principles which were acknowledged by us to be just—what do you say?

Cr. I cannot tell, Socrates; for I do not know.

Soc. Then consider the matter in this way:—Imagine that I am about to play truant (you may call the proceeding by any name which you like), and the laws and the government come and interrogate me: 'Tell us, Socrates,' they say; 'what are you about? are you not going by an act of yours to overturn us—the laws, and the whole state, as far as in you lies? Do you imagine that a state can subsist and not be overthrown, in which the decisions of law have no power, but are set aside and trampled upon by individuals?' What will be our answer, Crito, to these and the like words? Any one, and especially a rhetorician, will have a good deal to say on behalf of the law which requires a sentence to be carried out. He will argue that this law should not be set aside; and shall we reply, 'Yes; but the state has injured us and given an unjust sentence.' Suppose I say that?

Cr. Very good, Socrates.

Soc. 'And was that our agreement with you?' the law would answer; 'or were you to abide by the sentence of the state?' And if I were to express my astonishment at their words, the law would probably add: 'Answer, Socrates, instead of opening your eyes—you are in the habit of asking and answering questions. Tell us,—What complaint have you to make against us which justifies you in attempting to destroy us and the state? In the first place did we not bring you into existence? Your father married your mother by our aid and begat you. Say whether you have any objection to urge against those of us who regulate marriage?' None, I should reply. 'Or against those of us who after birth regulate the nurture and education of children, in which you also were trained? Were not the laws, which have the charge of education, right in commanding your father to train you in music and gymnastic?' Right, I should reply. 'Well then, since you were brought into the world and nurtured and educated by us, can you deny in the first place that you are our child and slave, as your fathers were before you? And if this is true you are not on equal terms with us; nor can you think that you have a right to do to us what we are doing to you. Would you have any right to strike or revile or do any other evil to your father or your master, if you had one, because you have been struck or reviled by him, or received some other evil at his hands?—you would not say this? And because we think right to destroy you, do you think that you have any right to destroy us in return, and your country as far as in you lies? Will you, O professor of true virtue, pretend that you are justified in this? Has a philosopher like you failed to discover that our country is more to be valued and higher and holier far than mother or father or any ancestor, and more to be regarded in the eyes of the gods and of men of understanding? also to be soothed, and gently and reverently entreated when angry, even more than a father, and either to be persuaded, or if not persuaded, to be obeyed? And when we are punished by her, whether with imprisonment or stripes, the punishment is to be endured in silence; and if she leads us to wounds or death in battle, thither we follow as is right; neither may any one yield or retreat or leave his rank, but whether in battle or in a court of law, or in any other place, he must do what his city and his country order him; or he must change their view of what is just: and if he may do no violence to his father or mother, much less may he do violence to his country.' What answer shall we make to this, Crito? Do the laws speak truly, or do they not?

Cr. I think that they do.

Soc. Then the laws will say, 'Consider, Socrates, if we are speaking truly that in your present attempt you are going to do us an injury. For, having brought you into the world, and nurtured and educated you, and given you and every other citizen a share in every good which we had to give, we further proclaim to any Athenian by the liberty which we allow him, that if he does not like us when he has become of age and has seen the ways of the city, and made our acquaintance, he may go where he pleases and take his goods with him. None of us laws will forbid him or interfere with him. Any one who does not like us and the city, and who wants to emigrate to a colony or to any other city, may go where he likes, retaining his property. But he who has experience of the manner in which we order justice and administer the state, and still remains, has entered into an implied contract that he will do as we command him. And he who disobeys us is, as we maintain, thrice wrong; first, because in disobeying us he is disobeying his parents; secondly, because we are the authors of his education; thirdly, because he has made an agreement with us that he will duly obey our commands; and he neither obeys them nor convinces us that our commands are unjust; and we do not rudely impose them, but give him the alternative of obeying or convincing us;—that is what we offer, and he does neither.

'These are the sort of accusations to which, as we were saying, you, Socrates, will be exposed if you accomplish your intentions; you, above all other Athenians.' Suppose now I ask, why I rather than anybody else? they will justly retort upon me that I above all other men have acknowledged the agreement. 'There is clear proof,' they will say, 'Socrates, that we and the city were not displeasing to you. Of all Athenians you have been the most constant resident in the city, which, as you never leave, you may be supposed to love. For you never went out of the city either to see the games, except once when you went to the Isthmus, or to any other place unless when you were on military service; nor did you travel as other men do. Nor had you any curiosity to know other states or their laws: your affections did not go beyond us and our state; we were your special favourites, and you acquiesced in our government of you; and here in this city you begat your children, which is a proof of your satisfaction. Moreover, you might in the course of the trial, if you had liked, have fixed the penalty at banishment; the state which refuses to let you go now would have let you go then. But you pretended that you preferred death to exile, and that you were not unwilling to die. And now you have forgotten these fine sentiments, and pay no respect to us the laws, of whom you are the destroyer; and are doing what only a miserable slave would do, running away and turning your back upon the compacts and agreements which you made as a citizen. And first of all answer this very question: Are we right in saying that you agreed to be governed according to us in deed, and not in word only? Is that true or not?' How shall we answer, Crito? Must we not assent?

Cr. We cannot help it, Socrates.

Soc. Then will they not say: 'You, Socrates, are breaking the covenants and agreements which you made with us at your leisure, not in any haste or under any compulsion or deception, but after you have had seventy years to think of them, during which time you were at liberty to leave the city, if we were not to your mind, or if our covenants appeared to you to be unfair. You had your choice, and might have gone either to Lacedaemon or Crete, both which states are often praised by you for their good government, or to some other Hellenic or foreign state. Whereas you, above all other Athenians, seemed to be so fond of the state, or, in other words, of us her laws (and who would care about a state which has no laws?), that you never stirred out of her; the halt, the blind, the maimed were not more stationary in her than you were. And now you run away and forsake your agreements. Not so, Socrates, if you will take our advice; do not make yourself ridiculous by escaping out of the city.

'For just consider, if you transgress and err in this sort of way, what good will you do either to yourself or to your friends? That your friends will be driven into exile and deprived of citizenship, or will lose their property, is tolerably certain; and you yourself, if you fly to one of the neighbouring cities, as, for example, Thebes or Megara, both of which are well governed, will come to them as an enemy, Socrates, and their government will be against you, and all patriotic citizens will cast an evil eye upon you as a subverter of the laws, and you will confirm in the minds of the judges the justice of their own condemnation of you. For he who is a corrupter of the laws is more than likely to be a corrupter of the young and foolish portion of mankind. Will you then flee from well-ordered cities and virtuous men? and is existence worth having on these terms? Or will you go to them without shame, and talk to them, Socrates? And what will you say to them? What you say here about virtue and justice and institutions and laws being the best things among men? Would that be decent of you? Surely not. But if you go away from well-governed states to Crito's friends in Thessaly, where there is great disorder and licence, they will be charmed to hear the tale of your escape from prison, set off with ludicrous particulars of the manner in which you were wrapped in a goatskin or some other disguise, and metamorphosed as the manner is of runaways; but will there be no one to remind you that in your old age you were not ashamed to violate the most sacred laws from a miserable desire of a little more life? Perhaps not, if you keep them in a good temper; but if they are out of temper you will hear many degrading things; you will live, but how?—as the flatterer of all men, and the servant of all men; and doing what?—eating and drinking in Thessaly, having gone abroad in order that you may get a dinner. And where will be your fine sentiments about justice and virtue? Say that you wish to live for the sake of your children—you want to bring them up and educate them—will you take them into Thessaly and deprive them of Athenian citizenship? Is this the benefit which you will confer upon them? Or are you under the impression that they will be better cared for and educated here if you are still alive, although absent from them; for your friends will take care of them? Do you fancy that if you are an inhabitant of Thessaly they will take care of them, and if you are an inhabitant of the other world that they will not take care of them? Nay; but if they who call themselves friends are good for anything, they will—to be sure they will.

'Listen, then, Socrates, to us who have brought you up. Think not of life and children first, and of justice afterwards, but of justice first, that you may be justified before the princes of the world below. For neither will you nor any that belong to you be happier or holier or juster in this life, or happier in another, if you do as Crito bids. Now you depart in innocence, a sufferer and not a doer of evil; a victim, not of the laws but of men. But if you go forth, returning evil for evil, and injury for injury, breaking the covenants and agreements which you have made with us, and wronging those whom you ought least of all to wrong, that is to say, yourself, your friends, your country, and us, we shall be angry with you while you live, and our brethren, the laws in the world below, will receive you as an enemy; for they will know that you have done your best to destroy us. Listen, then, to us and not to Crito.'

This, dear Crito, is the voice which I seem to hear murmuring in my ears, like the sound of the flute in the ears of the mystic; that voice, I say, is humming in my ears, and prevents me from hearing any other. And I know that anything more which you may say will be vain. Yet speak, if you have anything to say.

Cr. I have nothing to say, Socrates.

Soc. Leave me then, Crito, to fulfil the will of God, and to follow whither he leads.

Henry David Thoreau

A social rebel with high principles, a man who loved nature and
solitude, Thoreau is considered by some a memorable individualist,
by others a perennial adolescent, and by still others as both.
E. B. White has called him a "regular hairshirt of a man." Born
in Concord in 1817, he was educated at Harvard and after
graduation returned to Concord where he first taught school and
on later occasions supported himself by making pencils. He became
a friend of Emerson, who was at the time leader of Concord's
intellectual and spiritual life; he joined the Transcendental Club
and contributed frequently to its journal, The Dial. *Some have*
said that Thoreau was the answer to Emerson's plea for an
American Scholar (see page 42). From July 4, 1845, to September
6, 1847, Thoreau lived in a hut at nearby Walden Pond, an

experience which he recorded in his most famous work, Walden.
*His stay there was interrupted for one day in the summer of 1846
when he was arrested for not paying the Massachusetts poll tax.
He explained his refusal as an act of protest against a government which sanctioned the Mexican War, a war he considered
in the interests of Southern slave holders; he later wrote an eloquent
defense of civil disobedience which was first published in 1849.
This essay, which has become an American classic, is reprinted
in full below; the text is that of the Riverside edition of Thoreau's
works.*

CIVIL DISOBEDIENCE

I heartily accept the motto,—"That government is best which governs
least;" and I should like to see it acted up to more rapidly and systematically.   Carried out, it finally amounts to this, which also I
believe,—"That government is best which governs not at all;" and
when men are prepared for it, that will be the kind of government
which they will have.   Government is at best but an expedient; but
most governments are usually, and all governments are sometimes,
inexpedient.   The objections which have been brought against a standing army, and they are many and weighty, and deserve to prevail,
may also at last be brought against a standing government.   The
standing army is only an arm of the standing government.   The government itself, which is only the mode which the people have chosen
to execute their will, is equally liable to be abused and perverted before
the people can act through it.   Witness the present Mexican war, the
work of comparatively a few individuals using the standing government as their tool; for, in the outset, the people would not have consented to this measure.

This American government,—what is it but a tradition, though a
recent one, endeavoring to transmit itself unimpaired to posterity, but
each instant losing some of its integrity?   It has not the vitality and
force of a single living man; for a single man can bend it to his will.
It is a sort of wooden gun to the people themselves.   But it is not the
less necessary for this; for the people must have some complicated
machinery or other, and hear its din, to satisfy that idea of government which they have.   Governments show thus how successfully
men can be imposed on, even impose on themselves, for their own

advantage. It is excellent, we must all allow. Yet this government never of itself furthered any enterprise, but by the alacrity with which it got out of its way. *It* does not keep the country free. *It* does not settle the West. *It* does not educate. The character inherent in the American people has done all that has been accomplished; and it would have done somewhat more, if the government had not sometimes got in its way. For government is an expedient by which men would fain succeed in letting one another alone; and, as has been said, when it is most expedient, the governed are most let alone by it. Trade and commerce, if they were not made of India-rubber, would never manage to bounce over the obstacles which legislators are continually putting in their way; and, if one were to judge these men wholly by the effects of their actions and not partly by their intentions, they would deserve to be classed and punished with those mischievous persons who put obstructions on the railroads.

But, to speak practically and as a citizen, unlike those who call themselves no-government men, I ask for, not at once no government, but *at once* a better government. Let every man make known what kind of government would command his respect, and that will be one step toward obtaining it.

After all, the practical reason why, when the power is once in the hands of the people, a majority are permitted, and for a long period continue, to rule is not because they are most likely to be in the right, nor because this seems fairest to the minority, but because they are physically the strongest. But a government in which the majority rule in all cases cannot be based on justice, even as far as men understand it. Can there not be a government in which majorities do not virtually decide right and wrong, but conscience?—in which majorities decide only those questions to which the rule of expediency is applicable? Must the citizen ever for a moment, or in the least degree, resign his conscience to the legislator? Why has every man a conscience, then? I think that we should be men first, and subjects afterward. It is not desirable to cultivate a respect for the law, so much as for the right. The only obligation which I have a right to assume is to do at any time what I think right. It is truly enough said, that a corporation has no conscience; but a corporation of conscientious men is a corporation *with* a conscience. Law never made men a whit more just; and, by means of their respect for it, even the well-disposed are daily made the agents of injustice. A common and natural result of an undue respect for law is, that you may see a file of soldiers, colonel, captain, corporal, privates, powder-monkeys, and all, marching in admirable order over hill and dale to the wars, against their wills, ay, against their common sense and consciences, which makes it very steep marching indeed, and produces a palpitation of the heart. They have no doubt that it is a damnable business in which they are concerned; they are all peaceably inclined. Now, what are they? Men at all? or small movable forts and magazines, at the service of some unscrupulous man in power? Visit the Navy-Yard, and behold a marine, such a man as an American government can make, or such as it can make a man with its black arts,—a mere shadow and reminiscence of humanity, a man laid out alive and standing, and already, as one may say, buried under arms with funeral accompaniments, though it may be,—

"Not a drum was heard, not a funeral note,
　As his corse to the rampart we hurried;
Not a soldier discharged his farewell shot
　O'er the grave where our hero we buried."

The mass of men serve the state thus, not as men mainly, but as machines, with their bodies. They are the standing army, and the militia, jailers, constables, posse comitatus, etc. In most cases there is no free exercise whatever of the judgment or of the moral sense; but they put themselves on a level with wood and earth and stones; and wooden men can perhaps be manufactured that will serve the purpose as well. Such command no more respect than men of straw or a lump of dirt. They have the same sort of worth only as horses and dogs. Yet such as these even are commonly esteemed good citizens. Others—as most legislators, politicians, lawyers, ministers, and office-holders—serve the state chiefly with their heads; and, as they rarely make any moral distinctions, they are as likely to serve the Devil, without *intending* it, as God. A very few, as heroes, patriots, martyrs, reformers in the great sense, and *men*, serve the state with their consciences also, and so necessarily resist it for the most part; and they are commonly treated as enemies by it. A wise man will only be useful as a man, and will not submit to be "clay," and "stop a hole to keep the wind away," but leave that office to his dust at least:—

"I am too high-born to be propertied,
To be a secondary at control,
Or useful serving-man and instrument
To any sovereign state throughout the world."

He who gives himself entirely to his fellow-men appears to them useless and selfish; but he who gives himself partially to them is pronounced a benefactor and philanthropist.

How does it become a man to behave toward this American government to-day? I answer, that he cannot without disgrace be associated with it. I cannot for an instant recognize that political organization as *my* government which is the *slave's* government also.

All men recognize the right of revolution; that is, the right to refuse allegiance to, and to resist, the government, when its tyranny or its inefficiency are great and unendurable. But almost all say that such is not the case now. But such was the case, they think, in the Revolution of '75. If one were to tell me that this was a bad government because it taxed certain foreign commodities brought to its ports, it is most probable that I should not make an ado about it, for I can do without them. All machines have their friction; and possibly this does enough good to counterbalance the evil. At any rate, it is a great evil to make a stir about it. But when the friction comes to have its machine, and oppression and robbery are organized, I say, let us not have such a machine any longer. In other words, when a sixth of the population of a nation which has undertaken to be the refuge of liberty are slaves, and a whole country is unjustly overrun and conquered by a foreign army, and subjected to military law, I think that it is not too soon for honest men to rebel and revolutionize. What makes this duty the more urgent is the fact that the country so overrun is not our own, but ours is the invading army.

Paley, a common authority with many on moral questions, in his chapter on the "Duty of Submission to Civil Government," resolves all civil obligation into expediency; and he proceeds to say, "that so long as the interest of the whole society requires it, that is, so long as the established government cannot be resisted or changed without public inconveniency, it is the will of God that the established government be obeyed, and no longer. . . . This principle being admitted, the justice of every particular case of resistance is reduced to a computation of the quantity of the danger and grievance on the one side, and of the probability and expense of redressing it on the other." Of this, he says, every man shall judge for himself. But Paley appears never to have contemplated those cases to which the rule of expediency does not apply, in which a people, as well as an individual, must do justice, cost what it may. If I have unjustly wrested a plank from a drowning man, I must restore it to him though I drown myself. This, according to Paley, would be inconvenient. But he that would save his life, in such a case, shall lose it. This people must cease to hold slaves, and to make war on Mexico, though it cost them their existence as a people.

In their practice, nations agree with Paley; but does any one think that Massachusetts does exactly what is right at the present crisis?

"A drab of state, a cloth-o'-silver slut,
To have her train borne up, and her soul trail in the dirt."

Practically speaking, the opponents to a reform in Massachusetts are not a hundred thousand politicians at the South, but a hundred thousand merchants and farmers here, who are more interested in commerce and agriculture than they are in humanity, and are not prepared to do justice to the slave and to Mexico, *cost what it may.* I quarrel not with far-off foes, but with those who, near at home, coöperate with, and do the bidding of, those far away, and without whom the latter would be harmless. We are accustomed to say, that the mass of men are unprepared; but improvement is slow, because the few are not materially wiser or better than the many. It is not so important that many should be as good as you, as that there be some absolute goodness somewhere; for that will leaven the whole lump. There are thousands who are *in opinion* opposed to slavery and to the war, who yet in effect do nothing to put an end to them; who, esteeming themselves children of Washington and Franklin, sit down with their hands in their pockets, and say that they know not what to do, and do nothing; who even postpone the question of freedom to the question of free-trade, and quietly read the prices-current along with the latest advices from Mexico, after dinner, and, it may be, fall asleep over them both. What is the price-current of an honest man and patriot to-day? They hesitate, and they regret, and sometimes they petition; but they do nothing in earnest and with effect. They will wait, well disposed, for others to remedy the evil, that they may no longer have it to regret. At most, they give only a cheap vote, and a feeble countenance and Godspeed, to the right, as it goes by them. There are nine hundred and ninety-nine patrons of virtue to one virtuous man. But it is easier to deal with the real possessor of a thing than with the temporary guardian of it.

All voting is a sort of gaming, like checkers or backgammon, with a slight moral tinge to it, a playing with right and wrong, with moral questions; and betting naturally accompanies it. The character of the voters is not staked. I cast my vote, perchance, as I think right; but I am not vitally concerned that that right should prevail. I am willing to leave it to the majority. Its obligation, therefore, never exceeds that of expediency. Even voting *for the right* is *doing* nothing for it. It is only expressing to men feebly your desire that it should prevail. A wise man will not leave the right to the mercy of chance, nor wish it to prevail through the power of the majority. There is but little virtue in the action of masses of men. When the majority shall at length vote for the abolition of slavery, it will be because they are indifferent to slavery, or because there is but little slavery left to be abolished by their vote. *They* will then be the only slaves. Only *his* vote can hasten the abolition of slavery who asserts his own freedom by his vote.

I hear of a convention to be held at Baltimore, or elsewhere, for the selection of a candidate for the Presidency, made up chiefly of editors, and men who are politicians by profession; but I think, what is it to any independent, intelligent, and respectable man what decision they may come to? Shall we not have the advantage of his wisdom and honesty, nevertheless? Can we not count upon some independent votes? Are there not many individuals in the country who do not attend conventions? But no: I find that the respectable man, so called, has immediately drifted from his position, and despairs of his country, when his country has more reason to despair of him. He forthwith adopts one of the candidates thus selected as the only *available* one, thus proving that he is himself *available* for any purposes of the demagogue. His vote is of no more worth than that of any unprincipled foreigner or hireling native, who may have been bought. O for a man who is a *man*, and, as my neighbor says, has a bone in his back which you cannot pass your hand through! Our statistics are at fault: the population has been returned too large. How many *men* are there to a square thousand miles in this country? Hardly one. Does not America offer any inducement for men to settle here? The American has dwindled into an Odd Fellow,—one who may be known by the development of his organ of gregariousness, and a manifest lack of intellect and cheerful self-reliance; whose first and chief concern, on coming into the world, is to see that the Almshouses are in good repair; and, before yet he has lawfully donned the virile garb, to collect a fund for the support of the widows and orphans that may be; who, in short, ventures to live only by the aid of the Mutual Insurance company, which has promised to bury him decently.

It is not a man's duty, as a matter of course, to devote himself to the eradication of any, even the most enormous wrong; he may still properly have other concerns to engage him; but it is his duty, at least, to wash his hands of it, and, if he gives it no thought longer, not to give it practically his support. If I devote myself to other pursuits and contemplations, I must first see, at least, that I do not pursue them sitting upon another man's shoulders. I must get off him first, that he may pursue his contemplations too. See what gross inconsistency is tolerated. I have heard some of my townsmen say, "I should like to have them order me out to help put down an insurrection of the slaves, or to march to Mexico;—see if I would go;" and yet these very men have each, directly by their allegiance, and so indirectly, at least, by their money, furnished a substitute. The soldier is applauded who refuses to serve in an unjust war by those who do not refuse to sustain the unjust government which makes the war; is applauded by those whose own act and authority he disregards and sets at naught; as if the state were penitent to that degree that it hired one to scourge it while it sinned, but not to that degree that it left off sinning for a moment. Thus, under the name of Order and Civil Government, we

315

are all made at last to pay homage to and support our own meanness. After the first blush of sin comes its indifference; and from immoral it becomes, as it were, *un*moral, and not quite unnecessary to that life which we have made.

The broadest and most prevalent error requires the most disinterested virtue to sustain it. The slight reproach to which the virtue of patriotism is commonly liable, the noble are most likely to incur. Those who, while they disapprove of the character and measures of a government, yield to it their allegiance and support are undoubtedly its most conscientious supporters, and so frequently the most serious obstacles to reform. Some are petitioning the state to dissolve the Union, to disregard the requisitions of the President. Why do they not dissolve it themselves,—the union between themselves and the state,—and refuse to pay their quota into its treasury? Do not they stand in the same relation to the state that the state does to the Union? And have not the same reasons prevented the state from resisting the Union which have prevented them from resisting the state?

How can a man be satisfied to entertain an opinion merely, and enjoy *it?* Is there any enjoyment in it, if his opinion is that he is aggrieved? If you are cheated out of a single dollar by your neighbor, you do not rest satisfied with knowing that you are cheated, or with saying that you are cheated, or even with petitioning him to pay you your due; but you take effectual steps at once to obtain the full amount, and see that you are never cheated again. Action from principle, the perception and the performance of right, changes things and relations; it is essentially revolutionary, and does not consist wholly with anything which was. It not only divides states and churches, it divides families; ay, it divides the *individual,* separating the diabolical in him from the divine.

Unjust laws exist: shall we be content to obey them, or shall we endeavor to amend them, and obey them until we have succeeded, or shall we transgress them at once? Men generally, under such a government as this, think that they ought to wait until they have persuaded the majority to alter them. They think that, if they should resist, the remedy would be worse than the evil. But it is the fault of the government itself that the remedy *is* worse than the evil. *It* makes it worse. Why is it not more apt to anticipate and provide for reform? Why does it not cherish its wise minority? Why does it cry and resist before it is hurt? Why does it not encourage its citizens to be on the alert to point out its faults, and *do* better than it would have them? Why does it always crucify Christ, and excommunicate Copernicus and Luther, and pronounce Washington and Franklin rebels?

One would think, that a deliberate and practical denial of its authority was the only offense never contemplated by government; else, why has it not assigned its definite, its suitable and proportionate penalty? If a man who has no property refuses but once to earn nine shillings for the state, he is put in prison for a period unlimited by any law that I know, and determined only by the discretion of those who placed him there; but if he should steal ninety times nine shillings from the state, he is soon permitted to go at large again.

If the injustice is part of the necessary friction of the machine of government, let it go, let it go: perchance it will wear smooth,—certainly the machine will wear out. If the injustice has a spring, or a pulley, or a rope, or a crank, exclusively for itself, then perhaps you may consider whether the remedy will not be worse than the evil; but if it is of such a nature that it requires you to be the agent of injustice to another, then, I say, break the law. Let your life be a counter friction to stop the machine. What I have to do is to see, at any rate, that I do not lend myself to the wrong which I condemn.

As for adopting the ways which the state has provided for remedying the evil, I know not of such ways. They take too much time, and a man's life will be gone. I have other affairs to attend to. I came into this world, not chiefly to make this a good place to live in, but to live in it, be it good or bad. A man has not everything to do, but something; and because he cannot do *everything*, it is not necessary that he should do *something* wrong. It is not my business to be petitioning the Governor or the Legislature any more than it is theirs to petition me; and if they should not hear my petition, what should I do then? But in this case the state has provided no way: its very Constitution is the evil. This may seem to be harsh and stubborn and unconciliatory; but it is to treat with the utmost kindness and consideration the only spirit that can appreciate or deserves it. So is all change for the better, like birth and death, which convulse the body.

I do not hesitate to say, that those who call themselves Abolitionists should at once effectually withdraw their support, both in person and property, from the government of Massachusetts, and not wait till they constitute a majority of one, before they suffer the right to prevail through them. I think that it is enough if they have God on their side, without waiting for that other one. Moreover, any man more right than his neighbors constitutes a majority of one already.

I meet this American government, or its representative, the state government, directly, and face to face, once a year—no more—in the person of its tax-gatherer; this is the only mode in which a man situated as I am necessarily meets it; and it then says distinctly, Recognize me; and the simplest, the most effectual, and, in the present posture of affairs, the indispensablest mode of treating with it on this head, of expressing your little satisfaction with and love for it, is to deny it then. My civil neighbor, the tax-gatherer, is the very man I have to deal with,—for it is, after all, with men and not with parchment that I quarrel,—and he has voluntarily chosen to be an agent of the government. How shall he ever know well what he is and does as an officer of the government, or as a man, until he is obliged to consider whether he shall treat me, his neighbor, for whom he has respect, as a neighbor and well-disposed man, or as a maniac and disturber of the peace, and see if he can get over this obstruction to his neighborliness without a ruder and more impetuous thought or speech corresponding with his action. I know this well, that if one thousand, if one hundred, if ten men whom I could name,—if ten *honest* men only,—ay, if *one* HONEST man, in this State of Massachusetts, *ceasing to hold slaves,* were actually to withdraw from this copartnership, and be locked up in the county jail therefor, it would be the abolition of slavery in America. For it matters not how small the beginning may seem to be: what is once well done is done forever. But we love better to talk about it: that we say is our mission. Reform keeps many scores of newspapers in its service, but not one man. If my esteemed neighbor, the State's ambassador, who will devote his days to the settlement of the question of human rights in the Council Chamber, instead of being threatened with the prisons of Carolina, were to sit down the prisoner of Massachusetts, that State which is so anxious to foist the sin of slavery upon her sister,—though at present she can discover only an act of inhospitality to be the ground of a quarrel with her,—the Legislature would not wholly waive the subject the following winter.

Under a government which imprisons any unjustly, the true place for a just man is also a prison. The proper place to-day, the only place which Massachusetts has provided for her freer and less desponding spirits, is in her prisons, to be put out and locked out of the State by her own act, as they have already put themselves out by their principles. It is there that the fugitive slave, and the Mexican prisoner on parole, and the Indian come to plead the wrongs of his race should find them; on that separate, but more free and honorable ground, where the State places those who are not *with* her, but *against* her,—the only house in a slave State in which a free man can abide with honor. If any think that their influence would be lost there, and their voices no longer afflict the ear of the State, that they would not be as an enemy within its walls, they do not know by how much truth is stronger than error, nor how much more eloquently and effectively he can combat injustice who has experienced a little in his own person. Cast your whole vote, not a strip of paper merely, but your whole influence. A minority is powerless while it conforms to the majority; it is not even a minority then; but it is irresistible when it clogs by its whole weight. If the alternative is to keep all just men in prison, or give up war and slavery, the State will not hesitate which to choose. If a thousand men were not to pay their tax-bills this year, that would not be a violent and bloody measure, as it would be to pay them, and enable the State to commit violence and shed innocent blood. This is, in fact, the definition of a peaceable revolution, if any such is possible. If the tax-gatherer, or any other public officer, asks me, as one has done, "But what shall I do?" my answer is, "If you really wish to do anything, resign your office." When the subject has refused allegiance, and the officer has resigned his office, then the revolution is accomplished. But even suppose blood should flow. Is there not a sort of blood shed when the conscience is wounded? Through this wound a man's real manhood and immortality flow out, and he bleeds to an everlasting death. I see this blood flowing now.

I have contemplated the imprisonment of the offender, rather than the seizure of his goods,—though both will serve the same purpose,—because they who assert the purest right, and consequently are most dangerous to a corrupt State, commonly have not spent much time in accumulating property. To such the State renders comparatively small service, and a slight tax is wont to appear exorbitant, particularly if they are obliged to earn it by special labor with their hands. If there were one who lived wholly without the use of money, the State itself would hesitate to demand it of him. But the rich man—not to make any invidious comparison—is always sold to the institution which makes him rich. Absolutely speaking, the more money, the less virtue; for money comes between a man and his objects, and obtains them for him; and it was certainly no great virtue to obtain it. It puts to rest many questions which he would otherwise be taxed to answer; while the only new question which it puts is the hard but superfluous one, how to spend it. Thus his moral ground is taken from under his feet. The opportunities of living are diminished in proportion as what are called the "means" are increased. The best thing a man can do for his culture when he is rich is to endeavor to carry out those schemes which he entertained when he was poor. Christ answered the Herodians according to their condition. "Show me the tribute-money," said he;—and one took a penny out of his pocket;—if you use money which has the image of Cæsar on it, which he has made current and valuable, that is, *if you are men of the State,* and gladly enjoy the advantages of Cæsar's government, then pay him back some of his own when he demands it. "Render therefore to Cæsar that which is Cæsar's, and to God those things which are God's,"—leaving them no wiser than before as to which was which; for they did not wish to know.

When I converse with the freest of my neighbors, I perceive that, whatever they may say about the magnitude and seriousness of the question, and their regard for the public tranquillity, the long and the short of the matter is, that they cannot spare the protection of the existing government, and they dread the consequences to their property and families of disobedience to it. For my own part, I should not like to think that I ever rely on the protection of the State. But, if I deny the authority of the State when it presents its tax-bill, it will soon take and waste all my property, and so harass me and my children without end. This is hard. This makes it impossible for a man to live honestly, and at the same time comfortably, in outward respects. It will not be worth the while to accumulate property; that would be sure to go again. You must hire or squat somewhere, and raise but a small crop, and eat that soon. You must live within yourself, and depend upon yourself always tucked up and ready for a start, and not have many affairs. A man may grow rich in Turkey even, if he will be in all respects a good subject of the Turkish government. Confucius said: "If a state is governed by the principles of reason, poverty and misery are subjects of shame; if a state is not governed by the principles of reason, riches and honors are the subjects of shame." No: until I want the protection of Massachusetts to be extended to me in some distant Southern port, where my liberty is endangered, or until I am bent solely on building up an estate at home by peaceful enterprise, I can afford to refuse allegiance to Massachusetts, and her right to my property and life. It costs me less in every sense to incur the penalty of disobedience to the State than it would to obey. I should feel as if I were worth less in that case.

Some years ago, the State met me in behalf of the Church, and commanded me to pay a certain sum toward the support of a clergyman whose preaching my father attended, but never I myself. "Pay," it said, "or be locked up in the jail." I declined to pay. But, unfortunately, another man saw fit to pay it. I did not see why the schoolmaster should be taxed to support the priest, and not the priest the schoolmaster; for I was not the State's schoolmaster, but I supported myself by voluntary subscription. I did not see why the lyceum should not present its tax-bill, and have the State to back its demand, as well as the Church. However, at the request of the selectmen, I condescended to make some such statement as this in writing:—"Know all men by these presents, that I, Henry Thoreau, do not wish to be regarded as a member of any incorporated society which I have not joined." This I gave to the town clerk; and he has it. The State, having thus learned that I did not wish to be regarded as a member of that church, has never made a like demand on me since; though it said that it must adhere to its original presumption that time. If I had known how to name them, I should then have signed off in detail from all the societies which I never signed on to; but I did not know where to find a complete list.

I have paid no poll-tax for six years. I was put into a jail once on this account, for one night; and, as I stood considering the walls of solid stone, two or three feet thick, the door of wood and iron, a foot thick, and the iron grating which strained the light, I could not help being struck with the foolishness of that institution which treated me as if I were mere flesh and blood and bones, to be locked up. I wondered that it should have concluded at length that this was the best use it could put me to, and had never thought to avail itself of my services in some way. I saw that, if there was a wall of stone between me and my townsmen, there was a still more difficult one to climb or break through before they could get to be as free as I was. I did not for a moment feel confined, and the walls seemed a great waste of stone and mortar. I felt as if I alone of all my townsmen had paid my tax. They plainly did not know how to treat me, but behaved like persons who are underbred. In every threat and in every compliment there was a blunder; for they thought that my chief desire was to stand the other side of that stone wall. I could not but smile to see how industriously they locked the door on my meditations, which followed them out again without let or hindrance, and *they* were really all that was dangerous. As they could not reach me, they had resolved to punish my body; just as boys, if they cannot come at some person against whom they have a spite, will abuse his dog. I saw that the State was half-witted, that it was timid as a lone woman with her silver spoons, and that it did not know its friends from its foes, and I lost all my remaining respect for it, and pitied it.

Thus the State never intentionally confronts a man's sense, intellectual or moral, but only his body, his senses. It is not armed with superior wit or honesty, but with superior physical strength. I was not born to be forced. I will breathe after my own fashion. Let us see who is the strongest. What force has a multitude? They only can force me who obey a higher law than I. They force me to become like themselves. I do not hear of *men* being *forced* to live this way or that by masses of men. What sort of life were that to live? When I meet a government which says to me, "Your money or your life," why should I be in haste to give it my money? It may be in a great strait, and not know what to do: I cannot help that. It must help itself; do as I do. It is not worth the while to snivel about it. I am not responsible for the successful working of the machinery of society. I am not the son of the engineer. I perceive that, when an acorn and a chestnut fall side by side, the one does not remain inert to make way for the other, but both obey their own laws, and spring and grow and flourish as best they can, till one, perchance, overshadows and destroys the other. If a plant cannot live according to its nature, it dies; and so a man.

The night in prison was novel and interesting enough. The prisoners in their shirt-sleeves were enjoying a chat and the evening air in the doorway, when I entered. But the jailer said, "Come, boys, it is time to lock up;" and so they dispersed, and I heard the sound of their steps returning into the hollow apartments. My room-mate was introduced to me by the jailer as "a first-rate fellow and a clever man." When the door was locked, he showed me where to hang my hat, and how he managed matters there. The rooms were whitewashed once a month; and this one, at least, was the whitest, most simply furnished, and probably the neatest apartment in the town. He naturally wanted to know where I came from, and what brought me there; and, when I had told him, I asked him in my turn how he came there, presuming him to be an honest man, of course; and, as the world goes, I believe he was. "Why," said he, "they accuse me of burning a barn; but I never did it." As near as I could discover, he had probably gone to bed in a barn when drunk, and smoked his pipe there; and so a barn was burnt. He had the reputation of being a clever man, had been there some three months waiting for his trial to come on, and would have to wait as much longer; but he was quite domesticated and contented, since he got his board for nothing, and thought that he was well treated.

He occupied one window, and I the other; and I saw that if one stayed there long, his principal business would be to look out the window. I had soon read all the tracts that were left there, and examined where former prisoners had broken out, and where a grate had been sawed off, and heard the history of the various occupants of that room; for I found that even here there was a history and a gossip which never circulated beyond the walls of the jail. Probably this is the only house in the town where verses are composed, which are afterward printed in a circular form, but not published. I was shown quite a long list of verses which were composed by some young men who had been detected in an attempt to escape, who avenged themselves by singing them.

I pumped my fellow-prisoner as dry as I could, for fear I should never see him again; but at length he showed me which was my bed, and left me to blow out the lamp.

It was like traveling into a far country, such as I had never expected to behold, to lie there for one night. It seemed to me that I never had heard the town-clock strike before, nor the evening sounds of the village; for we slept with the windows open, which were inside the grating. It was to see my native village in the light of the Middle

Ages, and our Concord was turned into a Rhine stream, and visions of knights and castles passed before me. They were the voices of old burghers that I heard in the streets. I was an involuntary spectator and auditor of whatever was done and said in the kitchen of the adjacent village-inn,—a wholly new and rare experience to me. It was a closer view of my native town. I was fairly inside of it. I never had seen its institutions before. This is one of its peculiar institutions; for it is a shire town. I began to comprehend what its inhabitants were about.

In the morning, our breakfasts were put through the hole in the door, in small oblong-square tin pans, made to fit, and holding a pint of chocolate, with brown bread, and an iron spoon. When they called for the vessels again, I was green enough to return what bread I had left; but my comrade seized it, and said that I should lay that up for lunch or dinner. Soon after he was let out to work at haying in a neighboring field, whither he went every day, and would not be back till noon; so he bade me good-day, saying that he doubted if he should see me again.

When I came out of prison,—for some one interfered, and paid that tax,—I did not perceive that great changes had taken place on the common, such as he observed who went in a youth and emerged a tottering and gray-headed man; and yet a change had to my eyes come over the scene,—the town, and State, and country,—greater than any that mere time could effect. I saw yet more distinctly the State in which I lived. I saw to what extent the people among whom I lived could be trusted as good neighbors and friends; that their friendship was for summer weather only; that they did not greatly propose to do right; that they were a distinct race from me by their prejudices and superstitions, as the Chinamen and Malays are; that in their sacrifices to humanity they ran no risks, not even to their property; that after all they were not so noble but they treated the thief as he had treated them, and hoped, by a certain outward observance and a few prayers, and by walking in a particular straight though useless path from time to time, to save their souls. This may be to judge my neighbors harshly; for I believe that many of them are not aware that they have such an institution as the jail in their village.

It was formerly the custom in our village, when a poor debtor came out of jail, for his acquaintances to salute him, looking through their fingers, which were crossed to represent the grating of a jail window, "How do ye do?" My neighbors did not thus salute me, but first looked at me, and then at one another, as if I had returned from a long journey. I was put into jail as I was going to the shoemaker's to get a shoe which was mended. When I was let out the next morning, I proceeded to finish my errand, and, having put on my mended shoe, joined a huckleberry party, who were impatient to put themselves under my conduct; and in half an hour,—for the horse was soon tackled,—was in the midst of a huckleberry field, on one of our highest hills, two miles off, and then the State was nowhere to be seen.

This is the whole history of "My Prisons."

I have never declined paying the highway tax, because I am as desirous of being a good neighbor as I am of being a bad subject; and as for supporting schools, I am doing my part to educate my fellow-countrymen now. It is for no particular item in the tax-bill that I refuse to pay it. I simply wish to refuse allegiance to the State, to withdraw and stand aloof from it effectually. I do not care to trace the course of my dollar, if I could, till it buys a man or a musket to shoot one with,—the dollar is innocent,—but I am concerned to trace the effects of my allegiance. In fact, I quietly declare war with the State, after my fashion, though I will still make what use and get what advantage of her I can, as is usual in such cases.

If others pay the tax which is demanded of me, from a sympathy with the State, they do but what they have already done in their own case, or rather they abet injustice to a greater extent than the State requires. If they pay the tax from a mistaken interest in the individual taxed, to save his property, or prevent his going to jail, it is because they have not considered wisely how far they let their private feelings interfere with the public good.

This, then, is my position at present. But one cannot be too much on his guard in such a case, lest his action be biased by obstinacy or an undue regard for the opinions of men. Let him see that he does only what belongs to himself and to the hour.

I think sometimes, Why, this people mean well, they are only ignorant; they would do better if they knew how: why give your neighbors this pain to treat you as they are not inclined to? But I think again, This is no reason why I should do as they do, or permit others to suffer much greater pain of a different kind. Again, I sometimes say to myself, When many millions of men, without heat, without ill will, without personal feeling of any kind, demand of you a few shillings only, without the possibility, such is their constitution, of retracting or altering their present demand, and without the possibility, on your side, of appeal to any other millions, why expose yourself to this overwhelming brute force? You do not resist cold and hunger, the winds and the waves, thus obstinately; you quietly submit to a thousand similar necessities. You do not put your head into the fire. But just in proportion as I regard this as not wholly a brute force, but partly a human force, and consider that I have relations to those millions as to so many millions of men, and not of mere brute or inanimate things, I see that appeal is possible, first and instantaneously, from them to the Maker of them, and, secondly, from them to themselves. But if I put my head deliberately into the fire, there is no appeal to fire or to the Maker of fire, and I have only myself to blame. If I could convince myself that I have any right to be satisfied with men as they are, and to treat them accordingly, and not according, in some respects, to my requisitions and expectations of what they and I ought to be, then, like a good Mussulman and fatalist, I should endeavor to be satisfied with things as they are, and say it is the will of God. And, above all, there is this difference between resisting this and a purely brute or natural force, that I can resist this with some effect; but I cannot expect, like Orpheus, to change the nature of the rocks and trees and beasts.

I do not wish to quarrel with any man or nation. I do not wish to split hairs, to make fine distinctions, or set myself up as better than my neighbors. I seek rather, I may say, even an excuse for conforming to the laws of the land. I am but too ready to conform to them. Indeed, I have reason to suspect myself on this head; and each year, as the tax-gatherer comes round, I find myself disposed to review the acts and position of the general and State governments, and the spirit of the people, to discover a pretext for conformity.

"We must affect our country as our parents,
And if at any time we alienate
Our love or industry from doing it honor,
We must respect effects and teach the soul
Matter of conscience and religion,
And not desire of rule or benefit."

I believe that the State will soon be able to take all my work of this sort out of my hands, and then I shall be no better a patriot than my fellow-countrymen. Seen from a lower point of view, the Constitution, with all its faults, is very good; the law and the courts are very respectable; even this State and this American government are, in many respects, very admirable, and rare things, to be thankful for, such as a great many have described them; but seen from a point of view a little higher, they are what I have described them; seen from a higher still, and the highest, who shall say what they are, or that they are worth looking at or thinking of at all?

However, the government does not concern me much, and I shall bestow the fewest possible thoughts on it. It is not many moments that I live under a government, even in this world. If a man is thought-free, fancy-free, imagination-free, that which *is not* never for a long time appearing *to be* to him, unwise rulers or reformers cannot fatally interrupt him.

I know that most men think differently from myself; but those whose lives are by profession devoted to the study of these or kindred subjects content me as little as any. Statesmen and legislators, standing so completely within the institution, never distinctly and nakedly behold it. They speak of moving society, but have no resting-place without it. They may be men of a certain experience and discrimination, and have no doubt invented ingenious and even useful systems, for which we sincerely thank them; but all their wit and usefulness lie within certain not very wide limits. They are wont to forget that the world is not governed by policy and expediency. Webster never goes behind government, and so cannot speak with authority about it. His words are wisdom to those legislators who contemplate no essential reform in the existing government; but for thinkers, and those who legislate for all time, he never once glances at the subject. I know of those whose serene and wise speculations on this theme would soon reveal the limits of his mind's range and hospitality. Yet, compared with the cheap professions of most reformers, and the still cheaper wisdom and eloquence of politicians in general, his are almost the only sensible and valuable words, and we thank Heaven for him. Comparatively, he is always strong, original, and, above all, practical. Still, his quality is not wisdom, but prudence. The lawyer's truth is not Truth, but consistency or a consistent expediency. Truth is always in harmony with herself, and is not concerned chiefly to reveal the justice that may consist with wrong-doing. He well deserves to be called, as he has been called, the Defender of the Constitution. There are really no blows to be given by him but defensive ones. He is not a leader, but a follower. His leaders are the men of '87. "I have never made an effort," he says, "and never propose to make an effort; I have never countenanced an effort, and never mean to countenance an effort, to disturb the arrangement as originally made, by which the various States came into the Union." Still thinking of the sanction which the Constitution gives to slavery, he says, "Because it was a part of the original compact,—let it stand." Notwithstanding his special acuteness and ability, he is unable to take a fact out of its merely political relations, and behold it as it lies absolutely to be disposed of by the intellect,—what, for instance, it behooves a man to do here in America to-day with regard to slavery,—but ventures, or is driven, to make some such desperate answer as the following, while professing to speak absolutely, and as a private man,—from which what new and singular code of social duties might be inferred? "The manner," says he, "in which the governments of those States where slavery exists are to regulate it is for their own consideration, under their responsibility to their constituents, to the general laws of propriety, humanity, and justice, and to God. Associations formed elsewhere, springing from a feeling of humanity, or any other cause, have nothing whatever to do with it. They have never received any encouragement from me, and they never will."

They who know of no purer sources of truth, who have traced up its stream no higher, stand, and wisely stand, by the Bible and the Constitution, and drink at it there with reverence and humility; but they who behold where it comes trickling into this lake or that pool, gird up their loins once more, and continue their pilgrimage toward its fountain-head.

No man with a genius for legislation has appeared in America. They are rare in the history of the world. There are orators, politicians, and eloquent men, by the thousand; but the speaker has not yet opened his mouth to speak who is capable of settling the much-vexed questions of the day. We love eloquence for its own sake, and not for any truth which it may utter, or any heroism it may inspire. Our legislators have not yet learned the comparative value of free-trade and of freedom, of union, and of rectitude, to a nation. They have no genius or talent for comparatively humble questions of taxation and finance, commerce and manufactures and agriculture. If we were left solely to the wordy wit of legislators in Congress for our guidance, uncorrected by the seasonable experience and the effectual complaints of the people, America would not long retain her rank among the nations. For eighteen hundred years, though perchance I have no right to say it, the New Testament has been written; yet where is the legislator who has wisdom and practical talent enough to avail himself of the light which it sheds on the science of legislation?

The authority of government, even such as I am willing to submit to,—for I will cheerfully obey those who know and can do better than I, and in many things even those who neither know nor can do so well,—is still an impure one: to be strictly just, it must have the sanction and consent of the governed. It can have no pure right over my person and property but what I concede to it. The progress from an absolute to a limited monarchy, from a limited monarchy to a democracy, is a progress toward a true respect for the individual. Even the Chinese philosopher was wise enough to regard the individual as the basis of the empire. Is a democracy, such as we know it, the last improvement possible in government? Is it not possible to take a further step towards recognizing and organizing the rights of man? There will never be a really free and enlightened State until the State comes to recognize the individual as a higher and independent power, from which all its own power and authority are derived, and treats him accordingly. I please myself with imagining a State at last which

can afford to be just to all men, and to treat the individual with respect as a neighbor; which even would not think it inconsistent with
its own repose if a few were to live aloof from it, not meddling with
it, nor embraced by it, who fulfilled all the duties of neighbors and
fellow-men. A State which bore this kind of fruit, and suffered it to
drop off as fast as it ripened, would prepare the way for a still more
perfect and glorious State, which also I have imagined, but not yet
anywhere seen.

Martin Luther King, Jr.

*Martin Luther King, Jr., was one of the most forceful advocates of
nonviolent disobedience in the struggle for civil and human rights.
Born in Georgia in 1929 and educated at Morehouse College,
Crozer Theological Seminary, and Boston University, he became
a Baptist minister in Montgomery, Alabama, in 1954. The next
year he launched the now famous Montgomery bus boycott.
Founder and President of the Southern Christian Leadership
Conference, he was a leader of the 1963 "March on Washington"
and of the 1965 voter registration drive in Selma, Alabama.
In 1964 he received the Nobel Peace Prize. He was assassinated
in Memphis, Tennessee, on April 4, 1968, while supporting a
strike of city garbage collectors.*

His writings include Stride Toward Freedom *(1958),* Strength
to Love *(1963),* Where Do We Go from Here: Chaos or
Community *(1967),* Conscience for Change *(1967),* The
Measure of Man *(1968), and* The Trumpet of Conscience
(1968). Why We Can't Wait, *published in 1964, includes a
revised version of the letter printed below, and an author's note
in which he says that "This response to a published statement by
eight fellow clergymen from Alabama . . . was composed under
somewhat constricting circumstances. Begun on the margins of
the newspaper in which the statement appeared while I was in jail,
the letter was continued on scraps of writing paper supplied by
a friendly Negro trusty, and concluded on a pad my attorneys
were eventually permitted to leave me. Although the text remains*

in substance unaltered, I have indulged in the author's prerogative
of polishing it for publication." For its greater immediacy, we
present here the unrevised version of the letter, together with the
public statement which occasioned it.

PUBLIC STATEMENT BY EIGHT ALABAMA CLERGYMEN

April 12, 1963

We the undersigned clergymen are among those who, in January, issued "An Appeal for Law and Order and Common Sense," in dealing with racial problems in Alabama. We expressed understanding that honest convictions in racial matters could properly be pursued in the courts, but urged that decisions of those courts should in the meantime be peacefully obeyed.

Since that time there had been some evidence of increased forbearance and a willingness to face facts. Responsible citizens have undertaken to work on various problems which cause racial friction and unrest. In Birmingham, recent public events have given indication that we all have opportunity for a new constructive and realistic approach to racial problems.

However, we are now confronted by a series of demonstrations by some of our Negro citizens, directed and led in part by outsiders. We recognize the natural impatience of people who feel that their hopes are slow in being realized. But we are convinced that these demonstrations are unwise and untimely.

We agree rather with certain local Negro leadership which has called for honest and open negotiation of racial issues in our area. And we believe this kind of facing of issues can best be accomplished by citizens of our own metropolitan area, white and Negro, meeting with their knowledge and experience of the local situation. All of us need to face that responsibility and find proper channels for its accomplishment.

Just as we formerly pointed out that "hatred and violence have no sanction in our religious and political traditions," we also point out that such actions as incite to hatred and violence, however technically peaceful those actions may be, have not contributed to the resolution of our local problems. We do not believe that these days of new hope are days when extreme measures are justified in Birmingham.

We commend the community as a whole, and the local news media and law enforcement officials in particular, on the calm manner in which these demonstrations have been handled. We urge the public to continue to show restraint should the demonstrations continue, and the law enforcement officials to remain calm and continue to protect our city from violence.

We further strongly urge our own Negro community to withdraw support from these demonstrations, and to unite locally in working peacefully for a better Birmingham. When rights are consistently denied, a cause should be pressed in the courts and in negotiations among local leaders, and not in the streets. We appeal to both our white and Negro citizenry to observe the principles of law and order and common sense.

Signed by:

C. C. J. CARPENTER, D.D., LL.D., *Bishop of Alabama*

JOSEPH A. DURICK, D.D., *Auxiliary Bishop, Diocese of Mobile-Birmingham*

Rabbi MILTON L. GRAFMAN, *Temple Emanu-El, Birmingham, Alabama*

Bishop PAUL HARDIN, *Bishop of the Alabama-West Florida Conference of the Methodist Church*

Bishop NOLAN B. HARMON, *Bishop of the North Alabama Conference of the Methodist Church*

GEORGE M. MURRAY, D.D., LL.D., *Bishop Coadjutor, Episcopal Diocese of Alabama*

EDWARD V. RAMAGE, *Moderator, Synod of the Alabama Presbyterian Church in the United States*

EARL STALLINGS, *Pastor, First Baptist Church, Birmingham, Alabama*

LETTER FROM BIRMINGHAM JAIL

MARTIN LUTHER KING, JR.
Birmingham City Jail
April 16, 1963

Bishop C. C. J. CARPENTER
Bishop JOSEPH A. DURICK
Rabbi MILTON L. GRAFMAN
Bishop PAUL HARDIN
Bishop NOLAN B. HARMON
The Rev. GEORGE M. MURRAY
The Rev. EDWARD V. RAMAGE
The Rev. EARL STALLINGS

My dear Fellow Clergymen,

While confined here in the Birmingham City Jail, I came across your recent statement calling our present activities "unwise and untimely." Seldom, if ever, do I pause to answer criticism of my work and ideas. If I sought to answer all of the criticisms that cross my desk, my secretaries would be engaged in little else in the course of the day and I would have no time for constructive work. But since I feel that you are men of genuine good will and your criticisms are sincerely set forth, I would like to answer your statement in what I hope will be patient and reasonable terms.

I think I should give the reason for my being in Birmingham, since you have been influenced by the argument of "outsiders coming in." I have the honor of serving as president of the Southern Christian Leadership Conference, an organization operating in every Southern state with headquarters in Atlanta, Georgia. We have some eighty-five affiliate organizations all across the South—one being the Alabama Christian Movement for Human Rights. Whenever necessary and possible we share staff, educational, and financial resources with our affiliates. Several months ago our local affiliate here in Birmingham invited us to be on call to engage in a nonviolent direct action program if such were deemed necessary. We readily consented and when the hour came we lived up to our promises. So I am here, along with several members of my staff, because we were invited here. I am here because I have basic organizational ties here. Beyond this, I am in Birmingham because injustice is here. Just as the eighth century prophets left their little villages and carried their "thus saith the Lord" far beyond the boundaries of their home town, and just as the Apostle Paul left his little village of Tarsus and carried the gospel of Jesus Christ to practically every hamlet and city of the Graeco-Roman world,

331

I too am compelled to carry the gospel of freedom beyond my particular home town. Like Paul, I must constantly respond to the Macedonian call for aid.

Moreover, I am cognizant of the interrelatedness of all communities and states. I cannot sit idly by in Atlanta and not be concerned about what happens in Birmingham. Injustice anywhere is a threat to justice everywhere. We are caught in an inescapable network of mutuality tied in a single garment of destiny. Whatever affects one directly affects all indirectly. Never again can we afford to live with the narrow, provincial "outside agitator" idea. Anyone who lives inside the United States can never be considered an outsider anywhere in this country.

You deplore the demonstrations that are presently taking place in Birmingham. But I am sorry that your statement did not express a similar concern for the conditions that brought the demonstrations into being. I am sure that each of you would want to go beyond the superficial social analyst who looks merely at effects, and does not grapple with underlying causes. I would not hesitate to say that it is unfortunate that so-called demonstrations are taking place in Birmingham at this time, but I would say in more emphatic terms that it is even more unfortunate that the white power structure of this city left the Negro community with no other alternative.

In any nonviolent campaign there are four basic steps: (1) collection of the facts to determine whether injustices are alive; (2) negotiation; (3) self-purification; and (4) direct action. We have gone through all of these steps in Birmingham. There can be no gainsaying of the fact that racial injustice engulfs this community. Birmingham is probably the most thoroughly segregated city in the United States. Its ugly record of police brutality is known in every section of this country. Its unjust treatment of Negroes in the courts is a notorious reality. There have been more unsolved bombings of Negro homes and churches in Birmingham than any city in this nation. These are the hard, brutal, and unbelievable facts. On the basis of these conditions Negro leaders sought to negotiate with the city fathers. But the political leaders consistently refused to engage in good faith negotiation.

Then came the opportunity last September to talk with some of the leaders of the economic community. In these negotiating sessions certain promises were made by the merchants—such as the promise to remove the humiliating racial signs from the stores. On the basis of these promises Rev. Shuttlesworth and the leaders of the Alabama Christian Movement for Human Rights agreed to call a moratorium on any type of demonstrations. As the weeks and months unfolded we realized that we were the victims of a broken promise. The signs remained. As in so many experiences of the past we were confronted with blasted hopes, and the dark shadow of a deep disappointment settled upon us. So we had no alternative except that of preparing for direct action, whereby we would present our very bodies as a means of laying our case before the conscience of the local and national community. We were not unmindful of the difficulties involved. So we decided to go through a process of self-purification. We started having workshops on nonviolence and repeatedly asked ourselves the questions, "Are you able to accept blows without retaliating?" "Are you able to endure the ordeals of jail?"

We decided to set our direct action program around the Easter season, realizing that with the exception of Christmas, this was the largest shopping period of the year. Knowing that a strong economic withdrawal program would be the by-product of direct action, we felt that this was the best time to bring pressure on the merchants for the needed changes. Then it occurred to us that the March election was ahead, and so we speedily decided to postpone action until after election day. When we discovered that Mr. Connor was in the run-off, we decided again to postpone action so that the demonstrations could not be used to cloud the issues. At this time we agreed to begin our nonviolent witness the day after the run-off.

This reveals that we did not move irresponsibly into direct action. We too wanted to see Mr. Connor defeated; so we went through postponement after postponement to aid in this community need. After this we felt that direct action could be delayed no longer.

You may well ask, "Why direct action? Why sit-ins, marches, etc.? Isn't negotiation a better path?" You are exactly right in your call for negotiation. Indeed, this is the purpose of direct action. Nonviolent direct action seeks to create such a crisis and establish such creative tension that a community that has constantly refused to negotiate is forced to confront the issue. It seeks so to dramatize the issue that it can no longer be ignored. I just referred to the creation of tension as a part of the work of the nonviolent resister. This may sound rather shocking. But I must confess that I am not afraid of the word tension. I have earnestly worked and preached against violent tension, but there is a type of constructive nonviolent tension that is necessary for growth. Just as Socrates felt that it was necessary to create a tension in the mind so that individuals could rise from the bondage of myths and half-truths to the unfettered realm of creative analysis and objective appraisal, we must see the need of having nonviolent gadflies to create the kind of tension in society that will help men rise from the dark depths of prejudice and racism to the majestic heights of understanding and brotherhood. So the purpose of the direct action is to create a situation so crisis-packed that it will inevitably open the door to negotiation. We, therefore, concur with you in your call for negotiation. Too long has our beloved Southland been bogged down in the tragic attempt to live in monologue rather than dialogue.

One of the basic points in your statement is that our acts are untimely. Some have asked, "Why didn't you give the new administration time to act?" The only answer that I can give to this inquiry is that the new administration must be prodded about as much as the outgoing one before it acts. We will be sadly mistaken if we feel that the election of Mr. Boutwell will bring the millennium to Birmingham. While Mr. Boutwell is much more articulate and gentle than Mr. Connor, they are both segregationists dedicated to the task of maintaining the status quo. The hope I see in Mr. Boutwell is that he will be reasonable enough to see the futility of massive resistance to desegregation. But he will not see this without pressure from the devotees of civil rights. My friends, I must say to you that we have not made a single gain in civil rights without determined legal and nonviolent pressure. History is the long and tragic story of the fact that privileged groups seldom give up their privileges voluntarily. Individuals may see the moral light and voluntarily give up their unjust posture; but as Reinhold Niebuhr has reminded us, groups are more immoral than individuals.

We know through painful experience that freedom is never voluntarily given by the oppressor; it must be demanded by the oppressed. Frankly I have never yet engaged in a direct action movement that was "well timed," according to the timetable of those who have not suffered unduly from the disease of segregation. For years now I have heard the word "Wait!" It rings in the ear of every Negro with a piercing familiarity. This "wait" has almost always meant "never." It has been a tranquilizing thalidomide, relieving the emotional stress for a moment, only to give birth to an ill-formed infant of frustration. We must come to see with the distinguished jurist of yesterday that "justice too long delayed is justice denied." We have waited for more than three hundred and forty years for our constitutional and God-given rights. The nations of Asia and Africa are moving with jet-like speed toward the goal of political independence, and we still creep at horse and buggy pace toward the gaining of a cup of coffee at a lunch counter.

I guess it is easy for those who have never felt the stinging darts of segregation to say wait. But when you have seen vicious mobs lynch your mothers and fathers at will and drown your sisters and brothers at whim; when you have seen hate filled policemen curse, kick, brutalize, and even kill your black brothers and sisters with impunity; when you see the vast majority of your twenty million Negro brothers smothering in an air-tight cage of poverty in the midst of an affluent society; when you suddenly find your tongue twisted and your speech stammering as you seek to explain to your six-year-old daughter why she can't go to the public amusement park that has just been advertised on television, and see tears welling up in her little eyes when she is told that Funtown is closed to colored children, and see the depressing clouds of inferiority begin to form in her little mental sky, and see her begin to distort her little personality by unconsciously developing a bitterness toward white people; when you have to concoct an answer for a five-year-old son asking in agonizing pathos: "Daddy, why do white people treat colored people so mean?"; when you take a cross country drive and find it necessary to sleep night after night in the uncomfortable corners of your automobile because no motel will accept you; when you are humiliated day in and day out by nagging signs reading "white" men and "colored"; when your first name becomes "nigger" and your middle name becomes "boy" (however old you are) and your last name becomes "John," and when your wife and mother are never given the respected title "Mrs."; when you are harried by day and haunted by night by the fact that you are a Negro, living constantly at tip-toe stance never quite knowing what to expect next, and plagued with inner fears and outer resentments; when you are forever fighting a degenerating sense of "nobodiness"; —then you will understand why we find it difficult to wait. There comes a time when the cup of endurance runs over, and men are no longer willing to be plunged into an abyss of injustice where they experience the bleakness of corroding despair. I hope, sirs, you can understand our legitimate and unavoidable impatience.

You express a great deal of anxiety over our willingness to break laws. This is certainly a legitimate concern. Since we so diligently urge people to obey the Supreme Court's decision of 1954 outlawing segregation in the public schools, it is rather strange and paradoxical to find us consciously breaking laws. One may well ask, "How can you advocate breaking some laws and obeying others?" The answer is found in the fact that there are two types of laws. There are *just* laws and there are *unjust* laws. I would be the first to advocate obeying just laws. One has not only a legal but moral responsibility to obey just laws. Conversely, one has a moral responsibility to disobey unjust laws. I would agree with Saint Augustine that "An unjust law is no law at all."

Now what is the difference between the two? How does one determine when a law is just or unjust? A just law is a man-made code that squares with the moral law or the law of God. An unjust law is a code that is out of harmony with the moral law. To put it in the terms of Saint Thomas Aquinas, an unjust law is a human law that is not rooted in eternal and natural law. Any law that uplifts human personality is just. Any law that degrades human personality

335

is unjust. All segregation statutes are unjust because segregation distorts the soul and damages the personality. It gives the segregator a false sense of superiority and the segregated a false sense of inferiority. To use the words of Martin Buber, the great Jewish philosopher, segregation substitutes an "I-it" relationship for the "I-thou" relationship, and ends up relegating persons to the status of things. So segregation is not only politically, economically, and sociologically unsound, but it is morally wrong and sinful. Paul Tillich has said that sin is separation. Isn't segregation an existential expression of man's tragic separation, an expression of his awful estrangement, his terrible sinfulness? So I can urge men to obey the 1954 decision of the Supreme Court because it is morally right, and I can urge them to disobey segregation ordinances because they are morally wrong.

Let us turn to a more concrete example of just and unjust laws. An unjust law is a code that a majority inflicts on a minority that is not binding on itself. This is *difference* made legal. On the other hand a just law is a code that a majority compels a minority to follow that it is willing to follow itself. This is *sameness* made legal.

Let me give another explanation. An unjust law is a code inflicted upon a minority which that minority had no part in enacting or creating because they did not have the unhampered right to vote. Who can say the legislature of Alabama which set up the segregation laws was democratically elected? Throughout the state of Alabama all types of conniving methods are used to prevent Negroes from becoming registered voters and there are some counties without a single Negro registered to vote despite the fact that the Negro constitutes a majority of the population. Can any law set up in such a state be considered democratically structured?

These are just a few examples of unjust and just laws. There are some instances when a law is just on its face but unjust in its application. For instance, I was arrested Friday on a charge of parading without a permit. Now there is nothing wrong with an ordinance which requires a permit for a parade, but when the ordinance is used to preserve segregation and to deny citizens the First Amendment privilege of peaceful assembly and peaceful protest, then it becomes unjust.

I hope you can see the distinction I am trying to point out. In no sense do I advocate evading or defying the law as the rabid segregationist would do. This would lead to anarchy. One who breaks an unjust law must do it *openly, lovingly* (not hatefully as the white mothers did in New Orleans when they were seen on television screaming "nigger, nigger, nigger") and with a willingness to accept the penalty. I submit that an individual who breaks a law that conscience tells him is unjust, and willingly accepts the penalty by staying in jail to arouse the conscience of the community over its injustice, is in reality expressing the very highest respect for law.

Of course there is nothing new about this kind of civil disobedience. It was seen sublimely in the refusal of Shadrach, Meshach, and Abednego to obey the laws of Nebuchadnezzar because a higher moral law was involved. It was practiced superbly by the early Christians who were willing to face hungry lions and the excruciating pain of chopping blocks, before submitting to certain unjust laws of the Roman Empire. To a degree academic freedom is a reality today because Socrates practiced civil disobedience.

We can never forget that everything Hitler did in Germany was "legal" and everything the Hungarian freedom fighters did in Hungary was "illegal." It was "illegal" to aid and comfort a Jew in Hitler's Germany. But I am sure that, if I had lived in Germany during that time, I would have aided and comforted my Jewish brothers even though it was illegal. If I lived in a communist country today where certain principles dear to the Christian faith are suppressed, I believe I would openly advocate disobeying these antireligious laws.

I must make two honest confessions to you, my Christian and Jewish brothers. First I must confess that over the last few years I have been gravely disappointed with the white moderate. I have almost reached the regrettable conclusion that the Negroes' great stumbling block in the stride toward freedom is not the White Citizens' "Counciler" or the Ku Klux Klanner, but the white moderate who is more devoted to "order" than to justice; who prefers a negative peace which is the absence of tension to a positive peace which is the presence of justice; who constantly says "I agree with you in the goal you seek, but I can't agree with your methods of direct action"; who paternalistically feels that he can set the time-table for another man's freedom; who lives by the myth of time and who constantly advises the Negro to wait until a "more convenient season." Shallow understanding from people of good will is more frustrating than absolute misunderstanding from people of ill will. Lukewarm acceptance is much more bewildering than outright rejection.

I had hoped that the white moderate would understand that law and order exist for the purpose of establishing justice, and that when they fail to do this they become the dangerously structured dams that block the flow of social progress. I had hoped that the white moderate would understand that the present tension in the South is merely a necessary phase of the transition from an obnoxious negative peace, where the Negro passively accepted his unjust plight, to a substance-filled positive peace, where all men will respect the dignity and worth of human personality. Actually, we who engage in nonviolent direct action are not the creators of tension. We merely bring to the surface

337

the hidden tension that is already alive. We bring it out in the open where it can be seen and dealt with. Like a boil that can never be cured as long as it is covered up but must be opened with all its pus-flowing ugliness to the natural medicines of air and light, injustice must likewise be exposed, with all of the tension its exposing creates, to the light of human conscience and the air of national opinion before it can be cured.

In your statement you asserted that our actions, even though peaceful, must be condemned because they precipitate violence. But can this assertion be logically made? Isn't this like condemning the robbed man because his possession of money precipitated the evil act of robbery? Isn't this like condemning Socrates because his unswerving commitment to truth and his philosophical delvings precipitated the misguided popular mind to make him drink the hemlock? Isn't this like condemning Jesus because His unique God consciousness and never-ceasing devotion to His will precipitated the evil act of crucifixion? We must come to see, as federal courts have consistently affirmed, that it is immoral to urge an individual to withdraw his efforts to gain his basic constitutional rights because the quest precipitates violence. Society must protect the robbed and punish the robber.

I had also hoped that the white moderate would reject the myth of time. I received a letter this morning from a white brother in Texas which said: "All Christians know that the colored people will receive equal rights eventually, but is it possible that you are in too great of a religious hurry? It has taken Christianity almost 2000 years to accomplish what it has. The teachings of Christ take time to come to earth." All that is said here grows out of a tragic misconception of time. It is the strangely irrational notion that there is something in the very flow of time that will inevitably cure all ills. Actually time is neutral. It can be used either destructively or constructively. I am coming to feel that the people of ill will have used time much more effectively than the people of good will. We will have to repent in this generation not merely for the vitriolic words and actions of the bad people, but for the appalling silence of the good people. We must come to see that human progress never rolls in on wheels of inevitability. It comes through the tireless efforts and persistent work of men willing to be co-workers with God, and without this hard work time itself becomes an ally of the forces of social stagnation.

We must use time creatively, and forever realize that the time is always ripe to do right. Now is the time to make real the promise of democracy, and transform our pending national elegy into a creative psalm of brotherhood. Now is the time to lift our national policy from the quicksand of racial injustice to the solid rock of human dignity.

You spoke of our activity in Birmingham as extreme. At first I was rather disappointed that fellow clergymen would see my nonviolent efforts as those of the extremist. I started thinking about the fact that I stand in the middle of two opposing forces in the Negro community. One is a force of complacency made up of Negroes who, as a result of long years of oppression, have been so completely drained of self-respect and a sense of "somebodiness" that they have adjusted to segregation, and of a few Negroes in the middle class who, because of a degree of academic and economic security, and because at points they profit by segregation, have unconsciously become insensitive to the problems of the masses. The other force is one of bitterness and hatred and comes perilously close to advocating violence. It is expressed in the various black nationalist groups that are springing up over the nation, the largest and best known being Elijah Muhammad's Muslim movement. This movement is nourished by the contemporary frustration over the continued existence of racial discrimination. It is made up of people who have lost faith in America, who have absolutely repudiated Christianity, and who have concluded that the white man is an incurable "devil." I have tried to stand between these two forces saying that we need not follow the "do-nothingism" of the complacent or the hatred and despair of the black nationalist. There is the more excellent way of love and nonviolent protest. I'm grateful to God that, through the Negro church, the dimension of nonviolence entered our struggle. If this philosophy had not emerged I am convinced that by now many streets of the South would be flowing with floods of blood. And I am further convinced that if our white brothers dismiss us as "rabble rousers" and "outside agitators"—those of us who are working through the channels of nonviolent direct action—and refuse to support our nonviolent efforts, millions of Negroes, out of frustration and despair, will seek solace and security in black nationalist ideologies, a development that will lead inevitably to a frightening racial nightmare.

Oppressed people cannot remain oppressed forever. The urge for freedom will eventually come. This is what has happened to the American Negro. Something within has reminded him of his birth-right of freedom; something without has reminded him that he can gain it. Consciously and unconsciously, he has been swept in by what the Germans call the *Zeitgeist*, and with his black brothers of Africa, and his brown and yellow brothers of Asia, South America, and the Caribbean, he is moving with a sense of cosmic urgency toward the promised land of racial justice. Recognizing this vital urge that has engulfed the Negro community, one should readily understand public demonstrations. The Negro has many pent-up resentments and latent frustrations. He has to get them out. So let him march sometime; let him have his prayer pilgrimages to the city hall; understand why he must have sit-ins and freedom rides. If his repressed emotions do not come out in these nonviolent ways, they will come out in ominous expressions of violence. This is not a threat; it is a fact of history. So I have not said to my people, "Get rid of your discontent." But I have tried to say that this normal and healthy discontent can be channeled through the creative outlet of nonviolent direct action. Now this approach is being dismissed as extremist. I must admit that I was initially disappointed in being so categorized.

But as I continued to think about the matter I gradually gained a bit of satisfaction from being considered an extremist. Was not Jesus an extremist in love? "Love your enemies, bless them that curse you, pray for them that despitefully use you." Was not Amos an extremist for justice —"Let justice roll down like waters and righteousness like a mighty stream." Was not Paul an extremist for the gospel of Jesus Christ— "I bear in my body the marks of the Lord Jesus." Was not Martin Luther an extremist—"Here I stand; I can do none other so help me God." Was not John Bunyan an extremist—"I will stay in jail to the end of my days before I make a butchery of my conscience." Was not Abraham Lincoln an extremist—"This nation cannot survive half slave and half free." Was not Thomas Jefferson an extremist—"We hold these truths to be self evident that all men are created equal." So the question is not whether we will be extremist but what kind of extremist will we be. Will we be extremists for hate or will we be extremists for love? Will we be extremists for the preservation of injustice—or will we be extremists for the cause of justice? In that dramatic scene on Calvary's hill three men were crucified. We must never forget that all three were crucified for the same crime—the crime of extremism. Two were extremists for immorality, and thus fell below their environment. The other, Jesus Christ, was an extremist for love, truth, and goodness, and thereby rose above His environment. So, after all, maybe the South, the nation, and the world are in dire need of creative extremists.

I had hoped that the white moderate would see this. Maybe I was too optimistic. Maybe I expected too much. I guess I should have realized that few members of a race that has oppressed another race can understand or appreciate the deep groans and passionate yearnings of those that have been oppressed, and still fewer have the vision to see that injustice must be rooted out by strong, persistent, and determined action. I am thankful, however, that some of our white brothers have grasped the meaning of this social revolution and committed themselves to it. They are still all too small in quantity, but they are big in quality. Some like Ralph McGill, Lillian Smith, Harry Golden, and James Dabbs have written about our struggle in eloquent, prophetic, and understanding terms. Others have marched with us down nameless streets of the South. They have languished in filthy, roach-infested jails, suffering the abuse and brutality of angry police-men who see them as "dirty nigger lovers." They, unlike so many of their moderate brothers and sisters, have recognized the urgency of the moment and sensed the need for powerful "action" antidotes to combat the disease of segregation.

Let me rush on to mention my other disappointment. I have been so greatly disappointed with the white Church and its leadership. Of course there are some notable exceptions. I am not unmindful of the fact that each of you has taken some significant stands on this issue. I commend you, Rev. Stallings, for your Christian stand on this past Sunday, in welcoming Negroes to your worship service on a non-segregated basis. I commend the Catholic leaders of this state for integrating Springhill College several years ago.

But despite these notable exceptions I must honestly reiterate that I have been disappointed with the Church. I do not say that as one of those negative critics who can always find something wrong with the Church. I say it as a minister of the gospel, who loves the Church; who was nurtured in its bosom; who has been sustained by its spiritual blessings and who will remain true to it as long as the cord of life shall lengthen.

I had the strange feeling when I was suddenly catapulted into the leadership of the bus protest in Montgomery several years ago that we would have the support of the white Church. I felt that the white ministers, priests, and rabbis of the South would be some of our strongest allies. Instead, some have been outright opponents, refusing to understand the freedom movement and misrepresenting its leaders; all too many others have been more cautious than courageous and have remained silent behind the anesthetizing security of stained glass windows.

In spite of my shattered dreams of the past, I came to Birmingham with the hope that the white religious leadership of the community would see the justice of our cause and, with deep moral concern, serve as the channel through which our just grievances could get to the power structure. I had hoped that each of you would understand. But again I have been disappointed.

I have heard numerous religious leaders of the South call upon their worshippers to comply with a desegregation decision because it is the law, but I have longed to hear white ministers say follow this decree because integration is morally right and the Negro is your brother. In the midst of blatant injustices inflicted upon the Negro, I have watched white churches stand on the sideline and merely mouth pious irrelevancies and sanctimonious trivialities. In the midst of a mighty struggle to rid our nation of racial and economic injustice, I have heard so many ministers say, "Those are social issues with which the

Gospel has no real concern," and I have watched so many churches commit themselves to a completely other-worldly religion which made a strange distinction between body and soul, the sacred and the secular.

So here we are moving toward the exit of the twentieth century with a religious community largely adjusted to the status quo, standing as a tail light behind other community agencies rather than a headlight leading men to higher levels of justice.

I have travelled the length and breadth of Alabama, Mississippi, and all the other Southern states. On sweltering summer days and crisp autumn mornings I have looked at her beautiful churches with their spires pointing heavenward. I have beheld the impressive outlay of her massive religious education buildings. Over and over again I have found myself asking: "Who worships here? Who is their God? Where were their voices when the lips of Governor Barnett dripped with words of interposition and nullification? Where were they when Governor Wallace gave the clarion call for defiance and hatred? Where were their voices of support when tired, bruised, and weary Negro men and women decided to rise from the dark dungeons of complacency to the bright hills of creative protest?"

Yes, these questions are still in my mind. In deep disappointment, I have wept over the laxity of the Church. But be assured that my tears have been tears of love. There can be no deep disappointment where there is not deep love. Yes, I love the Church; I love her sacred walls. How could I do otherwise? I am in the rather unique position of being the son, the grandson, and the great grandson of preachers. Yes, I see the Church as the body of Christ. But, oh! How we have blemished and scarred that body through social neglect and fear of being nonconformist.

There was a time when the Church was very powerful. It was during that period when the early Christians rejoiced when they were deemed worthy to suffer for what they believed. In those days the Church was not merely a thermometer that recorded the ideas and principles of popular opinion; it was a thermostat that transformed the mores of society. Wherever the early Christians entered a town the power structure got disturbed and immediately sought to convict them for being "disturbers of the peace" and "outside agitators." But they went on with the conviction that they were a "colony of heaven" and had to obey God rather than man. They were small in number but big in commitment. They were too God-intoxicated to be "astronomically intimidated." They brought an end to such ancient evils as infanticide and gladiatorial contest.

Things are different now. The contemporary Church is so often a weak, ineffectual voice with an uncertain sound. It is so often the arch-supporter of the status quo. Far from being disturbed by the presence of the Church, the power structure of the average community is consoled by the Church's silent and often vocal sanction of things as they are.

But the judgment of God is upon the Church as never before. If the Church of today does not recapture the sacrificial spirit of the early Church, it will lose its authentic ring, forfeit the loyalty of millions, and be dismissed as an irrelevant social club with no meaning for the twentieth century. I am meeting young people every day whose disappointment with the Church has risen to outright disgust.

Maybe again I have been too optimistic. Is organized religion too inextricably bound to the status quo to save our nation and the world? Maybe I must turn my faith to the inner spiritual Church, the church within the Church, as the true *ecclesia* and the hope of the world. But again I am thankful to God that some noble souls from the ranks of organized religion have broken loose from the paralyzing chains of conformity and joined us as active partners in the struggle for freedom. They have left their secure congregations and walked the streets of Albany, Georgia, with us. They have gone through the highways of the South on torturous rides for freedom. Yes, they have gone to jail with us. Some have been kicked out of their churches and lost the support of their bishops and fellow ministers. But they have gone with the faith that right defeated is stronger than evil triumphant. These men have been the leaven in the lump of the race. Their witness has been the spiritual salt that has preserved the true meaning of the Gospel in these troubled times. They have carved a tunnel of hope through the dark mountain of disappointment.

I hope the Church as a whole will meet the challenge of this decisive hour. But even if the Church does not come to the aid of justice, I have no despair about the future. I have no fear about the outcome of our struggle in Birmingham, even if our motives are presently misunderstood. We will reach the goal of freedom in Birmingham and all over the nation, because the goal of America is freedom. Abused and scorned though we may be, our destiny is tied up with the destiny of America. Before the pilgrims landed at Plymouth, we were here. Before the pen of Jefferson etched across the pages of history the majestic words of the Declaration of Independence, we were here. For more than two centuries our foreparents labored in this country without wages; they made cotton "king"; and they built the homes of their masters in the midst of brutal injustice and shameful humiliation —and yet out of a bottomless vitality they continued to thrive and develop. If the inexpressible cruelties of slavery could not stop us, the opposition we now face will surely fail. We will win our freedom because the sacred heritage of our nation and the eternal will of God are embodied in our echoing demands.

I must close now. But before closing I am impelled to mention one other point in your statement that troubled me profoundly. You warmly commended the Birmingham police force for keeping "order" and "preventing violence." I don't believe you would have so warmly commended the police force if you had seen its angry violent dogs literally biting six unarmed, nonviolent Negroes. I don't believe you would so quickly commend the policemen if you would observe their ugly and inhuman treatment of Negroes here in the city jail; if you would watch them push and curse old Negro women and young Negro girls; if you would see them slap and kick old Negro men and young Negro boys; if you will observe them, as they did on two occasions, refuse to give us food because we wanted to sing our grace together. I'm sorry that I can't join you in your praise for the police department.

It is true that they have been rather disciplined in their public handling of the demonstrators. In this sense they have been rather publicly "nonviolent." But for what purpose? To preserve the evil system of segregation. Over the last few years I have consistently preached that nonviolence demands that the means we use must be as pure as the ends we seek. So I have tried to make it clear that it is wrong to use immoral means to attain moral ends. But now I must affirm that it is just as wrong, or even more so, to use moral means to preserve immoral ends. Maybe Mr. Connor and his policemen have been rather publicly nonviolent, as Chief Prichett was in Albany, Georgia, but they have used the moral means of nonviolence to maintain the immoral end of flagrant racial injustice. T. S. Eliot has said that there is no greater treason than to do the right deed for the wrong reason.

I wish you had commended the Negro sit-inners and demonstrators of Birmingham for their sublime courage, their willingness to suffer, and their amazing discipline in the midst of the most inhuman provocation. One day the South will recognize its real heroes. They will be the James Merediths, courageously and with a majestic sense of purpose, facing jeering and hostile mobs and the agonizing loneliness that characterizes the life of the pioneer. They will be old, oppressed, battered Negro women, symbolized in a seventy-two year old woman of Montgomery, Alabama, who rose up with a sense of dignity and with her people decided not to ride the segregated buses, and responded to one who inquired about her tiredness with ungrammatical profundity: "My feets is tired, but my soul is rested." They will be young high school and college students, young ministers of the gospel and a host of the elders, courageously and nonviolently sitting in at lunch counters and willingly going to jail for conscience sake. One day the South will know that when these disinherited children of God sat down at lunch counters they were in reality standing up for the best in the American dream and the most sacred values in our Judeo-Christian heritage, and thus carrying our whole nation back to great wells of democracy which were dug deep by the founding fathers in the formulation of the Constitution and the Declaration of Independence.

Never before have I written a letter this long (or should I say a book?). I'm afraid that it is much too long to take your precious time. I can assure you that it would have been much shorter if I had been writing from a comfortable desk, but what else is there to do when you are alone for days in the dull monotony of a narrow jail cell other than write long letters, think strange thoughts, and pray long prayers?

If I have said anything in this letter that is an overstatement of the truth and is indicative of an unreasonable impatience, I beg you to forgive me. If I have said anything in this letter that is an understatement of the truth and is indicative of my having a patience that makes me patient with anything less than brotherhood, I beg God to forgive me.

I hope this letter finds you strong in the faith. I also hope that circumstances will soon make it possible for me to meet each of you, not as an integrationist or a civil rights leader, but as a fellow clergyman and a Christian brother. Let us all hope that the dark clouds of racial prejudice will soon pass away and the deep fog of misunderstanding will be lifted from our fear-drenched communities and in some not too distant tomorrow the radiant stars of love and brotherhood will shine over our great nation with all of their scintillating beauty.

Yours for the cause of
Peace and Brotherhood

MARTIN LUTHER KING, JR.

Malcolm X

Malcolm X was born Malcolm Little in Omaha, Nebraska, in 1925. He left school after the eighth grade, made his way to New York, and entered the Harlem underworld. He became a dope peddler and addict and in 1946 was sentenced to ten years in prison for burglary. His life was transformed in prison by the discovery of the religion of Islam and a library full of books. "My homemade education gave me," he records, "with every additional book that I read, a little bit more sensitivity to the deafness, dumbness, and blindness that was afflicting the black race in America." Paroled in 1952, he became nationally known as an outspoken defender of the Black Muslim doctrines of Elijah Muhammad. Expelled by the Muslims in 1963, he formed his own Black Nationalist group, the Organization of Afro-American Unity. He was gunned down in the Audubon Ballroom, New York City, February 21, 1965, while preparing to give one of the speeches for which he had become famous. Malcolm X's sometimes terrifying personality and eloquence have already made him a legendary figure in the history of black liberation. His Autobiography, written with Alex Haley, appeared posthumously in 1965. The speech we present here was given in Cleveland on April 3, 1964, and printed (from a tape recording) in the collection Malcolm X Speaks, *edited by George Breitman (1965). Mr. Breitman remarks that he counted in the tape almost 150 interruptions of applause and laughter from the audience. Other Malcolm X speeches may be found in* The Speeches of Malcolm X at Harvard *(ed. Archie Epps, 1969), and in* Malcolm X *(ed. John Henrik Clarke, 1969).*

THE BALLOT OR THE BULLET

Mr. Moderator, Brother Lomax, brothers and sisters, friends and enemies: I just can't believe everyone in here is a friend and I don't want to leave anybody out. The question tonight, as I understand it, is "The Negro Revolt, and Where Do We Go From Here?" or "What Next?" In my little humble way of understanding it, it points toward either the ballot or the bullet.

Before we try and explain what is meant by the ballot or the bullet, I would like to clarify something concerning myself. I'm still a Muslim, my religion is still Islam. That's my personal belief. Just as Adam Clayton Powell is a Christian minister who heads the Abyssinian Baptist Church in New York, but at the same time takes part in the political struggles to try and bring about rights to the black people in this country; and Dr. Martin Luther King is a Christian minister down in Atlanta, Georgia, who heads another organization fighting for the civil rights of black people in this country; and Rev. Galamison, I guess you've heard of him, is another Christian minister in New York who has been deeply involved in the school boycotts to eliminate segregated education; well, I myself am a minister, not a Christian minister, but a Muslim minister; and I believe in action on all fronts by whatever means necessary.

Although I'm still a Muslim, I'm not here tonight to discuss my religion. I'm not here to try and change your religion. I'm not here to argue or discuss anything that we differ about, because it's time for us to submerge our differences and realize that it is best for us to first see that we have the same problem, a common problem—a problem that will make you catch hell whether you're a Baptist, or a Methodist, or a Muslim, or a nationalist. Whether you're educated or illiterate, whether you live on the boulevard or in the alley, you're going to catch hell just like I am. We're all in the same boat and we all are going to catch the same hell from the same man. He just happens to be a white man. All of us have suffered here, in this country, political oppression at the hands of the white man, economic exploitation at the hands of the white man, and social degradation at the hands of the white man.

Now in speaking like this, it doesn't mean that we're anti-white, but it does mean we're anti-exploitation, we're anti-degradation, we're anti-oppression. And if the white man doesn't want us to be anti-him, let him stop oppressing and exploiting and degrading us. Whether we are Christians or Muslims or nationalists or agnostics or atheists, we must first learn to forget our differences. If we have differences, let us differ in the closet; when we come out in front, let us not have anything to argue about until we get finished arguing with the man. If the late President Kennedy could get together with Khrushchev and exchange some wheat, we certainly have more in common with each other than Kennedy and Khrushchev had with each other.

If we don't do something real soon, I think you'll have to agree that we're going to be forced either to use the ballot or the bullet. It's one or the other in 1964. It isn't that time is running out—time has run out! 1964 threatens to be the most explosive year America has ever witnessed. The most explosive year. Why? It's also a political year. It's the year when all of the white politicians will be back in the so-called Negro community jiving you and me for some votes. The year when all of the white political crooks will be right back in your and my community with their false promises, building up our hopes for a letdown, with their trickery and their treachery, with their false promises which they don't intend to keep. As they nourish these dissatisfactions, it can only lead to one thing, an explosion; and now we have the type of black man on the scene in America today—I'm sorry, Brother Lomax—who just doesn't intend to turn the other cheek any longer.

Don't let anybody tell you anything about the odds are against you. If they draft you, they send you to Korea and make you face 800 million Chinese. If you can be brave over there, you can be brave right here. These odds aren't as great as those odds. And if you fight here, you will at least know what you're fighting for.

I'm not a politician, not even a student of politics; in fact, I'm not a student of much of anything. I'm not a Democrat, I'm not a Republican, and I don't even consider myself an American. If you and I were Americans, there'd be no problem. Those Hunkies that just got off the boat, they're already Americans; Polacks are already Americans; the Italian refugees are already Americans. Everything that came out of Europe, every blue-eyed thing, is already an American. And as long as you and I have been over here, we aren't Americans yet.

Well, I am one who doesn't believe in deluding myself. I'm not going to sit at your table and watch you eat, with nothing on my plate, and call myself a diner. Sitting at the table doesn't make you a diner, unless you eat some of what's on that plate. Being here in America doesn't make you an American. Being born here in America doesn't make you an American. Why, if birth made you American, you wouldn't need any legislation, you wouldn't need any amendments to the Constitution, you wouldn't be faced with civil-rights filibustering in Washington, D.C., right now. They don't have to pass civil-rights legislation to make a Polack an American.

No, I'm not an American. I'm one of the 22 million black people who are the victims of Americanism. One of the 22 million black people who are the victims of democracy, nothing but disguised hypocrisy. So, I'm not standing here speaking to you as an American, or a patriot, or a flag-saluter, or a flag-waver—no, not I. I'm speaking as a victim of this American system. And I see America through the eyes of the victim. I don't see any American dream; I see an American nightmare.

These 22 million victims are waking up. Their eyes are coming open. They're beginning to see what they used to only look at. They're becoming politically mature. They are realizing that there are new political trends from coast to coast. As they see these new political trends, it's possible for them to see that every time there's an election the races are so close that they have to have a recount. They had to recount in Massachusetts to see who was going to be governor, it was so close. It was the same way in Rhode Island, in Minnesota, and in many other parts of the country. And the same with Kennedy and Nixon when they ran for president. It was so close they had to count all over again. Well, what does this mean? It means that when white people are evenly divided, and black people have a bloc of votes of their own, it is left up to them to determine who's going to sit in the White House and who's going to be in the dog house.

It was the black man's vote that put the present administration in Washington, D.C. Your vote, your dumb vote, your ignorant vote, your wasted vote put in an administration in Washington, D.C., that has seen fit to pass every kind of legislation imaginable, saving you until last, then filibustering on top of that. And your and my leaders have the audacity to run around clapping their hands and talk about how much progress we're making. And what a good president we have. If he wasn't good in Texas, he sure can't be good in Washington, D.C. Because Texas is a lynch state. It is in the same breath as Mississippi, no different; only they lynch you in Texas with a Texas accent and lynch you in Mississippi with a Mississippi accent. And these Negro leaders have the audacity to go and have some coffee in the White House with a Texan, a Southern cracker—that's all he is—and then come out and tell you and me that he's going to be better for us because, since he's from the South, he knows how to deal with the Southerners. What kind of logic is that? Let Eastland be president, he's from the South too. He should be better able to deal with them than Johnson.

In this present administration they have in the House of Representatives 257 Democrats to only 177 Republicans. They control two-thirds of the House vote. Why can't they pass something that will help you and me? In the Senate, there are 67 senators who are of the Democratic Party. Only 33 of them are Republicans. Why, the Democrats have got the government sewed up, and you're the one who sewed it up for them. And what have they given you for it? Four years in office, and just now getting around to some civil-rights legislation. Just now, after everything else is gone, out of the way, they're going to sit down now and play with you all summer long—the same old giant con game that they call filibuster. All those are in cahoots together. Don't you ever think they're not in cahoots together, for the man that is heading the civil-rights filibuster is a man from Georgia named Richard Russell. When Johnson became president, the first man he asked for when he got back to Washington, D.C., was "Dicky" —that's how tight they are. That's his boy, that's his pal, that's his buddy. But they're playing that old con game. One of them makes believe he's for you, and he's got it fixed where the other one is so tight against you, he never has to keep his promise.

So it's time in 1964 to wake up. And when you see them coming up with that kind of conspiracy, let them know your eyes are open. And let them know you got something else that's wide open too. It's got to be the ballot or the bullet. The ballot or the bullet. If you're afraid to use an expression like that, you should get on out of the country, you should get back in the cotton patch, you should get back in the alley. They get all the Negro vote, and after they get it, the Negro gets nothing in return. All they did when they got to Washington was give a few big Negroes big jobs. Those big Negroes didn't need big jobs, they already had jobs. That's camouflage, that's trickery, that's treachery, window-dressing. I'm not trying to knock out the Democrats for the Republicans, we'll get to them in a minute. But it is true—you put the Democrats first and the Democrats put you last.

Look at it the way it is. What alibis do they use, since they control Congress and the Senate? What alibi do they use when you and I ask, "Well, when are you going to keep your promise?" They blame the Dixiecrats. What is a Dixiecrat? A Democrat. A Dixiecrat is nothing but a Democrat in disguise. The titular head of the Democrats is also the head of the Dixiecrats, because the Dixiecrats are a part of the Democratic Party. The Democrats have never kicked the Dixiecrats out of the party. The Dixiecrats bolted themselves once, but the Democrats didn't put them out. Imagine, these lowdown Southern segregationists put the Northern Democrats down. But the Northern Democrats have never put the Dixiecrats down. No, look at that thing the way it is. They have got a con game going on, a political con game, and you and I are in the middle. It's time for you and me to wake up and start looking at it like it is, and trying to understand it like it is; and then we can deal with it like it is.

The Dixiecrats in Washington, D.C., control the key committees that run the government. The only reason the Dixiecrats control these committees is because they have seniority. The only reason they have seniority is because they come from states where Negroes can't vote. This is not even a government that's based on democracy. It is not a government that is made up of representatives of the people. Half of the people in the South can't even vote. Eastland is not even supposed to be in Washington. Half of the senators and congressmen who occupy these key positions in Washington, D.C., are there illegally, are there unconstitutionally.

I was in Washington, D.C., a week ago Thursday, when they were debating whether or not they should let the bill come onto the floor. And in the back of the room where the Senate meets, there's a huge map of the United States, and on that map it shows the location of Negroes throughout the country. And it shows that the Southern section of the country, the states that are most heavily concentrated with Negroes, are the ones that have senators and congressmen standing up filibustering and doing all other kinds of trickery to keep the Negro from being able to vote. This is pitiful. But it's not pitiful for us any longer; it's actually pitiful for the white man, because soon now, as the Negro awakens a little more and sees the vise that he's in, sees the bag that he's in, sees the real game that he's in, then the Negro's going to develop a new tactic.

These senators and congressmen actually violate the constitutional amendments that guarantee the people of that particular state or county the right to vote. And the Constitution itself has within it the machinery to expel any representative from a state where the voting rights of the people are violated. You don't even need new legislation. Any person in Congress right now, who is there from a state or a district where the voting rights of the people are violated, that particular person should be expelled from Congress. And when you expel him, you've removed one of the obstacles in the path of any real meaningful legislation in this country. In fact, when you expel them, you don't need new legislation, because they will be replaced by black representatives from counties and districts where the black man is in the majority, not in the minority.

If the black man in these Southern states had his full voting rights, the key Dixiecrats in Washington, D.C., which means the key Democrats in Washington, D.C., would lose their seats. The Democratic Party itself would lose its power. It would cease to be powerful as a party. When you see the amount of power that would be lost by the Democratic Party if it were to lose the Dixiecrat wing, or branch, or element, you can see where it's against the interests of the Democrats to give voting rights to Negroes in states where the Democrats have been in complete power and authority ever since the Civil War. You just can't belong to that party without analyzing it.

I say again, I'm not anti-Democrat, I'm not anti-Republican, I'm not anti-anything. I'm just questioning their sincerity, and some of the strategy that they've been using on our people by promising them promises that they don't intend to keep. When you keep the Democrats in power, you're keeping the Dixiecrats in power. I doubt that my good Brother Lomax will deny that. A vote for a Democrat is a vote for a Dixiecrat. That's why, in 1964, it's time now for you and me to become more politically mature and realize what the ballot is for; what we're supposed to get when we cast a ballot; and that if we don't cast a ballot, it's going to end up in a situation where we're going to have to cast a bullet. It's either a ballot or a bullet.

In the North, they do it a different way. They have a system that's known as gerrymandering, whatever that means. It means when Negroes become too heavily concentrated in a certain area, and begin to gain too much political power, the white man comes along and changes the district lines. You may say, "Why do you keep saying white man?" Because it's the white man who does it. I haven't ever seen any Negro changing any lines. They don't let him get near the line. It's the white man who does this. And usually, it's the white man who grins at you the most, and pats you on the back, and is supposed to be your friend. He may be friendly, but he's not your friend.

So, what I'm trying to impress upon you, in essence, is this: You and I in America are faced not with a segregationist conspiracy, we're faced with a government conspiracy. Everyone who's filibustering is a senator—that's the government. Everyone who's finagling in Washington, D.C., is a congressman—that's the government. You don't have anybody putting blocks in your path but people who are a part of the government. The same government that you go abroad to fight for and die for is the government that is in a conspiracy to deprive you of your voting rights, deprive you of your economic opportunities, deprive you of decent housing, deprive you of decent education. You don't need to go to the employer alone, it is the government itself, the government of America, that is responsible for the oppression and exploitation and degradation of black people in this country. And you should drop it in their lap. This government has failed the Negro. This so-called democracy has failed the Negro. And all these white liberals have definitely failed the Negro.

So, where do we go from here? First, we need some friends. We need some new allies. The entire civil-rights struggle needs a new interpretation, a broader interpretation. We need to look at this civil-rights thing from another angle—from the inside as well as from the outside. To those of us whose philosophy is black nationalism, the only way you can get involved in the civil-rights struggle is give it a new interpretation. That old interpretation excluded us. It kept us out. So, we're giving a new interpretation to the civil-rights struggle, an interpretation that will enable us to come into it, take part in it. And these handkerchief-heads who have been dillydallying and pussy-footing and compromising—we don't intend to let them pussyfoot and dillydally and compromise any longer.

How can you thank a man for giving you what's already yours? How then can you thank him for giving you only part of what's already yours? You haven't even made progress, if what's being given to you, you should have had already. That's not progress. And I love my Brother Lomax, the way he pointed out we're right back where we were in 1954. We're not even as far up as we were in 1954. We're behind where we were in 1954. There's more segregation now than there was in 1954. There's more racial animosity, more racial hatred, more racial violence today in 1964, than there was in 1954. Where is the progress?

And now you're facing a situation where the young Negro's coming up. They don't want to hear that "turn-the-other-cheek" stuff, no. In Jacksonville, those were teen-agers, they were throwing Molotov cocktails. Negroes have never done that before. But it shows you there's a new deal coming in. There's new thinking coming in. There's new strategy coming in. It'll be Molotov cocktails this month, hand grenades next month, and something else next month. It'll be ballots, or it'll be bullets. It'll be liberty, or it will be death. The only difference about this kind of death—it'll be reciprocal. You know what is meant by "reciprocal"? That's one of Brother Lomax's words, I stole it from him. I don't usually deal with those big words because I don't usually deal with big people. I deal with small people. I find you can get a whole lot of small people and whip hell out of a whole lot of big people. They haven't got anything to lose, and they've got everything to gain. And they'll let you know in a minute: "It takes two to tango; when I go, you go."

The black nationalists, those whose philosophy is black nationalism, in bringing about this new interpretation of the entire meaning of civil rights, look upon it as meaning, as Brother Lomax has pointed out, equality of opportunity. Well, we're justified in seeking civil rights, if it means equality of opportunity, because all we're doing there is trying to collect for our investment. Our mothers and fathers invested sweat and blood. Three hundred and ten years we worked in this country without a dime in return—I mean without a *dime* in return. You let the white man walk around here talking about how rich this country is, but you never stop to think how it got rich so quick. It got rich because you made it rich.

You take the people who are in this audience right now. They're poor, we're all poor as individuals. Our weekly salary individually amounts to hardly anything. But if you take the salary of everyone in here collectively it'll fill up a whole lot of baskets. It's a lot of wealth. If you can collect the wages of just these people right here for a year, you'll be rich—richer than rich. When you look at it like that, think how rich Uncle Sam had to become, not with this handful, but millions of black people. Your and my mother and father, who didn't work an eight-hour shift, but worked from "can't see" in the morning until "can't see" at night, and worked for nothing, making the white man rich, making Uncle Sam rich.

This is our investment. This is our contribution—our blood. Not only did we give of our free labor, we gave of our blood. Every time he had a call to arms, we were the first ones in uniform. We died on every battlefield the white man had. We have made a greater sacrifice than anybody who's standing up in America today. We have made a greater contribution and have collected less. Civil rights, for those of us whose philosophy is black nationalism, means: "Give it to us now. Don't wait for next year. Give it to us yesterday, and that's not fast enough."

I might stop right here to point out one thing. Whenever you're going after something that belongs to you, anyone who's depriving you of the right to have it is a criminal. Understand that. Whenever you are going after something that is yours, you are within your legal rights to lay claim to it. And anyone who puts forth any effort to deprive you of that which is yours, is breaking the law, is a criminal. And this was pointed out by the Supreme Court decision. It outlawed segregation. Which means segregation is against the law. Which means a segregationist is breaking the law. A segregationist is a criminal. You can't label him as anything other than that. And when you demonstrate against segregation, the law is on your side. The Supreme Court is on your side.

Now, who is it that opposes you in carrying out the law? The police department itself. With police dogs and clubs. Whenever you demonstrate against segregation, whether it is segregated education, segregated housing, or anything else, the law is on your side, and anyone who stands in the way is not the law any longer. They are breaking the law, they are not representatives of the law. Any time you demonstrate against segregation and a man has the audacity to put a police dog on you, kill that dog, kill him, I'm telling you, kill that dog. I say it, if they put me in jail tomorrow, kill—that—dog. Then you'll put a stop to it. Now, if these white people in here don't want to see that kind of action, get down and tell the mayor to tell the police department to pull the dogs in. That's all you have to do. If you don't do it, someone else will.

If you don't take this kind of stand, your little children will grow up and look at you and think "shame." If you don't take an uncompromising stand—I don't mean go out and get violent; but at the same time you should never be nonviolent unless you run into some nonviolence. I'm nonviolent with those who are nonviolent with me. But when you drop that violence on me, then you've made me go insane, and I'm not responsible for what I do. And that's the way every Negro should get. Any time you know you're within the law, within your legal rights, within your moral rights, in accord with justice, then die for what you believe in. But don't die alone. Let your dying be reciprocal. This is what is meant by equality. What's good for the goose is good for the gander.

When we begin to get in this area, we need new friends, we need new allies. We need to expand the civil-rights struggle to a higher level—to the level of human rights. Whenever you are in a civil-rights struggle, whether you know it or not, you are confining yourself to the jurisdiction of Uncle Sam. No one from the outside world can speak out in your behalf as long as your struggle is a civil-rights struggle. Civil rights comes within the domestic affairs of this country.

All of our African brothers and our Asian brothers and our Latin-American brothers cannot open their mouths and interfere in the domestic affairs of the United States. And as long as it's civil rights, this comes under the jurisdiction of Uncle Sam.

But the United Nations has what's known as the charter of human rights, it has a committee that deals in human rights. You may wonder why all of the atrocities that have been committed in Africa and in Hungary and in Asia and in Latin America are brought before the UN, and the Negro problem is never brought before the UN. This is part of the conspiracy. This old, tricky, blue-eyed liberal who is supposed to be your and my friend, supposed to be in our corner, supposed to be subsidizing our struggle, and supposed to be acting in the capacity of an adviser, never tells you anything about human rights. They keep you wrapped up in civil rights. And you spend so much time barking up the civil-rights tree, you don't even know there's a human-rights tree on the same floor.

When you expand the civil-rights struggle to the level of human rights, you can then take the case of the black man in this country before the nations in the UN. You can take it before the General Assembly. You can take Uncle Sam before a world court. But the only level you can do it on is the level of human rights. Civil rights keeps you under his restrictions, under his jurisdiction. Civil rights keeps you in his pocket. Civil rights means you're asking Uncle Sam to treat you right. Human rights are something you were born with. Human rights are your God-given rights. Human rights are the rights that are recognized by all nations of this earth. And any time any one violates your human rights, you can take them to the world court. Uncle Sam's hands are dripping with blood, dripping with the blood of the black man in this country. He's the earth's number-one hypocrite. He has the audacity—yes, he has—imagine him posing as the leader of the free world. The free world!—and you over here singing "We Shall Overcome." Expand the civil-rights struggle to the level of human rights, take it into the United Nations, where our African brothers can throw their weight on our side, where our Asian brothers can throw their weight on our side, where our Latin-American brothers can throw their weight on our side, and where 800 million Chinamen are sitting there waiting to throw their weight on our side.

Let the world know how bloody his hands are. Let the world know the hypocrisy that's practiced over here. Let it be the ballot or the bullet. Let him know that it must be the ballot or the bullet.

When you take your case to Washington, D.C., you're taking it to the criminal who's responsible; it's like running from the wolf to the fox. They're all in cahoots together. They all work political chicanery and make you look like a chump before the eyes of the world. Here you are walking around in America, getting ready to be drafted and sent abroad, like a tin soldier, and when you get over there, people ask you what are you fighting for, and you have to stick your tongue in your cheek. No, take Uncle Sam to court, take him before the world.

By ballot I only mean freedom. Don't you know—I disagree with Lomax on this issue—that the ballot is more important than the dollar? Can I prove it? Yes. Look in the UN. There are poor nations in the UN; yet those poor nations can get together with their voting power and keep the rich nations from making a move. They have one nation —one vote, everyone has an equal vote. And when those brothers from Asia, and Africa and the darker parts of this earth get together, their voting power is sufficient to hold Sam in check. Or Russia in check. Or some other section of the earth in check. So, the ballot is most important.

Right now, in this country, if you and I, 22 million African-Americans—that's what we are—Africans who are in America. You're nothing but Africans. Nothing but Africans. In fact, you'd get farther calling yourself African instead of Negro. Africans don't catch hell. You're the only one catching hell. They don't have to pass civil-rights bills for Africans. An African can go anywhere he wants right now. All you've got to do is tie your head up. That's right, go anywhere you want. Just stop being a Negro. Change your name to Hoogaga-gooba. That'll show you how silly the white man is. You're dealing with a silly man. A friend of mine who's very dark put a turban on his head and went into a restaurant in Atlanta before they called themselves desegregated. He went into a white restaurant, he sat down, they served him, and he said, "What would happen if a Negro came in here?" And there he's sitting, black as night, but because he had his head wrapped up the waitress looked back at him and says, "Why, there wouldn't no nigger dare come in here."

So, you're dealing with a man whose bias and prejudice are making him lose his mind, his intelligence, every day. He's frightened. He looks around and sees what's taking place on this earth, and he sees that the pendulum of time is swinging in your direction. The dark people are waking up. They're losing their fear of the white man. No place where he's fighting right now is he winning. Everywhere he's fighting, he's fighting someone your and my complexion. And they're beating him. He can't win any more. He's won his last battle. He failed to win the Korean War. He couldn't win it. He had to sign a truce. That's a loss. Any time Uncle Sam, with all his machinery for warfare, is held to a draw by some rice-eaters, he's lost the battle. He had to sign a truce. America's not supposed to sign a truce. She's supposed to be bad. But she's not bad any more. She's bad as long as she can use her hydrogen bomb, but she can't use hers for fear Russia might use hers. Russia can't use hers, for fear that Sam might use his. So, both of them are weaponless. They can't use the weapon because each's weapon nullifies the other's. So the only place where action can take place is on the ground. And the white man can't win another war fighting on the ground. Those days are over. The black man knows it, the brown man knows it, the red man knows it, and the yellow man knows it. So they engage him in guerrilla warfare. That's not his style. You've got to have heart to be a guerrilla warrior, and he hasn't got any heart. I'm telling you now.

I just want to give you a little briefing on guerrilla warfare because, before you know it, before you know it—It takes heart to be a guerrilla warrior because you're on your own. In conventional warfare you have tanks and a whole lot of other people with you to back you up, planes over your head and all that kind of stuff. But a guerrilla is on his own. All you have is a rifle, some sneakers and a bowl of rice, and that's all you need—and a lot of heart. The Japanese on some of those islands in the Pacific, when the American soldiers landed, one Japanese sometimes could hold the whole army off. He'd just wait until the sun went down, and when the sun went down they were all equal. He would take his little blade and slip from bush to bush, and from American to American. The white soldiers couldn't cope with that. Whenever you see a white soldier that fought in the Pacific, he has the shakes, he has a nervous condition, because they scared him to death.

The same thing happened to the French up in French Indochina. People who just a few years previously were rice farmers got together and ran the heavily-mechanized French army out of Indochina. You don't need it—modern warfare today won't work. This is the day of the guerrilla. They did the same thing in Algeria. Algerians, who were nothing but Bedouins, took a rifle and sneaked off to the hills, and de Gaulle and all of his highfalutin' war machinery couldn't defeat those guerrillas. Nowhere on this earth does the white man win in a guerrilla warfare. It's not his speed. Just as guerrilla warfare is prevailing in Asia and in parts of Africa and in parts of Latin America, you've got to be mighty naive, or you've got to play the black man cheap, if you don't think some day he's going to wake up and find that it's got to be the ballot or the bullet.

I would like to say, in closing, a few things concerning the Muslim Mosque, Inc., which we established recently in New York City. It's true we're Muslims and our religion is Islam, but we don't mix our religion with our politics and our economics and our social and civil activities—not any more. We keep our religion in our mosque. After our religious services are over, then as Muslims we become involved in political action, economic action, and social and civic action. We become involved with anybody, anywhere, any time and in any manner that's designed to eliminate the evils, the political, economic and social evils that are afflicting the people of our community.

The political philosophy of black nationalism means that the black man should control the politics and the politicians in his own community; no more. The black man in the black community has to be re-educated into the science of politics so he will know what politics is supposed to bring him in return. Don't be throwing out any ballots. A ballot is like a bullet. You don't throw your ballots until you see a target, and if that target is not within your reach, keep your ballot in your pocket. The political philosophy of black nationalism is being taught in the Christian church. It's being taught in the NAACP. It's being taught in CORE meetings. It's being taught in SNCC [Student Nonviolent Coordinating Committee] meetings. It's being taught in Muslim meetings. It's being taught where nothing but atheists and agnostics come together. It's being taught everywhere. Black people are fed up with the dillydallying, pussyfooting, compromising approach that we've been using toward getting our freedom. We want freedom *now*, but we're not going to get it saying "We Shall Overcome." We've got to fight until we overcome.

The economic philosophy of black nationalism is pure and simple. It only means that we should control the economy of our community. Why should white people be running all the stores in our community? Why should white people be running the banks of our community? Why should the economy of our community be in the hands of the white man? Why? If a black man can't move his store into a white community, you tell me why a white man should move his store into a black community. The philosophy of black nationalism involves a re-education program in the black community in regards to economics. Our people have to be made to see that any time you take your dollar out of your community and spend it in a community where you don't live, the community where you live will get poorer and poorer, and the community where you spend your money will get richer and richer. Then you wonder why where you live is always a ghetto or a slum area. And where you and I are concerned, not only do we lose it when we spend it out of the community, but the white man has got all our stores in the community tied up; so that though we spend it in the community, at sundown the man who runs the store takes it over across town somewhere. He's got us in a vise.

So the economic philosophy of black nationalism means in every church, in every civic organization, in every fraternal order, it's time now for our people to become conscious of the importance of controlling the economy of our community. If we own the stores, if we operate the businesses, if we try and establish some industry in our own community, then we're developing to the position where we are creating employment for our own kind. Once you gain control of the economy of your own community, then you don't have to picket and boycott and beg some cracker downtown for a job in his business.

The social philosophy of black nationalism only means that we have to get together and remove the evils, the vices, alcoholism, drug addiction, and other evils that are destroying the moral fiber of our community. We ourselves have to lift the level of our community, the standard of our community to a higher level, make our own society beautiful so that we will be satisfied in our own social circles and won't be running around here trying to knock our way into a social circle where we're not wanted.

So I say, in spreading a gospel such as black nationalism, it is not designed to make the black man re-evaluate the white man—you know him already—but to make the black man re-evaluate himself. Don't change the white man's mind—you can't change his mind, and that whole thing about appealing to the moral conscience of America—America's conscience is bankrupt. She lost all conscience a long time ago. Uncle Sam has no conscience. They don't know what morals are. They don't try and eliminate an evil because it's evil, or because it's illegal, or because it's immoral; they eliminate it only when it threatens their existence. So you're wasting your time appealing to the moral conscience of a bankrupt man like Uncle Sam. If he had a conscience, he'd straighten this thing out with no more pressure being put upon him. So it is not necessary to change the white man's mind. We have to change our own mind. You can't change his mind about us. We've got to change our own minds about each other. We have to see each other with new eyes. We have to see each other as brothers and sisters. We have to come together with warmth so we can develop unity and harmony that's necessary to get this problem solved ourselves. How can we do this? How can we avoid jealousy? How can we avoid the suspicion and the divisions that exist in the community? I'll tell you how.

I have watched how Billy Graham comes into a city, spreading what he calls the gospel of Christ, which is only white nationalism. That's what he is. Billy Graham is a white nationalist; I'm a black nationalist. But since it's the natural tendency for leaders to be jealous and look upon a powerful figure like Graham with suspicion and envy, how is it possible for him to come into a city and get all the cooperation of the church leaders? Don't think because they're church leaders that they don't have weaknesses that make them envious and jealous —no, everybody's got it. It's not an accident that when they want to choose a cardinal [as Pope] over there in Rome, they get in a closet so you can't hear them cussing and fighting and carrying on.

Billy Graham comes in preaching the gospel of Christ, he evangelizes the gospel, he stirs everybody up, but he never tries to start a church. If he came in trying to start a church, all the churches would be against him. So, he just comes in talking about Christ and tells everybody who gets Christ to go to any church where Christ is; and in this way the church cooperates with him. So we're going to take a page from his book.

Our gospel is black nationalism. We're not trying to threaten the existence of any organization, but we're spreading the gospel of black nationalism. Anywhere there's a church that is also preaching and practicing the gospel of black nationalism, join that church. If the NAACP is preaching and practicing the gospel of black nationalism, join the NAACP. If CORE is spreading and practicing the gospel of black nationalism, join CORE. Join any organization that has a gospel that's for the uplift of the black man. And when you get into it and see them pussyfooting or compromising, pull out of it because that's not black nationalism. We'll find another one.

And in this manner, the organizations will increase in number and in quantity and in quality, and by August, it is then our intention to have a black nationalist convention which will consist of delegates from all over the country who are interested in the political, economic and social philosophy of black nationalism. After these delegates convene, we will hold a seminar, we will hold discussions, we will listen to everyone. We want to hear new ideas and new solutions and new answers. And at that time, if we see fit then to form a black nationalist party, we'll form a black nationalist party. If it's necessary to form a black nationalist army, we'll form a black nationalist army. It'll be the ballot or the bullet. It'll be liberty or it'll be death.

It's time for you and me to stop sitting in this country, letting some cracker senators, Northern crackers and Southern crackers, sit there in Washington, D.C., and come to a conclusion in their mind that you and I are supposed to have civil rights. There's no white man going to tell me anything about *my* rights. Brothers and sisters, always remember, if it doesn't take senators and congressmen and presidential proclamations to give freedom to the white man, it is not necessary for legislation or proclamation or Supreme Court decisions to give freedom to the black man. You let that white man know, if this is a country of freedom, let it be a country of freedom; and if it's not a country of freedom, change it.

We will work with anybody, anywhere, at any time, who is genuinely interested in tackling the problem head-on, nonviolently as long as the enemy is nonviolent, but violent when the enemy gets violent.

We'll work with you on the voter-registration drive, we'll work with you on rent strikes, we'll work with you on school boycotts—I don't believe in any kind of integration; I'm not even worried about it because I know you're not going to get it anyway; you're not going to get it because you're afraid to die; you've got to be ready to die if you try and force yourself on the white man, because he'll get just as violent as those crackers in Mississippi, right here in Cleveland. But we will still work with you on the school boycotts because we're against a segregated school system. A segregated school system produces children who, when they graduate, graduate with crippled minds. But this does not mean that a school is segregated because it's all black. A segregated school means a school that is controlled by people who have no real interest in it whatsoever.

Let me explain what I mean. A segregated district or community is a community in which people live, but outsiders control the politics and the economy of that community. They never refer to the white section as a segregated community. It's the all-Negro section that's a segregated community. Why? The white man controls his own school, his own bank, his own economy, his own politics, his own everything, his own community—but he also controls yours. When you're under someone else's control, you're segregated. They'll always give you the lowest or the worst that there is to offer, but it doesn't mean you're segregated just because you have your own. You've got to *control* your own. Just like the white man has control of his, you need to control yours.

You know the best way to get rid of segregation? The white man is more afraid of separation than he is of integration. Segregation means that he puts you away from him, but not far enough for you to be out of his jurisdiction; separation means you're gone. And the white man will integrate faster than he'll let you separate. So we will work with you against the segregated school system because it's criminal, because it is absolutely destructive, in every way imaginable, to the minds of the children who have to be exposed to that type of crippling education.

Last but not least, I must say this concerning the great controversy over rifles and shotguns. The only thing that I've ever said is that in areas where the government has proven itself either unwilling or unable to defend the lives and the property of Negroes, it's time for Negroes to defend themselves. Article number two of the constitutional amendments provides you and me the right to own a rifle or a shotgun. It is constitutionally legal to own a shotgun or a rifle. This doesn't mean you're going to get a rifle and form battalions and go out looking for white folks, although you'd be within your rights— I mean, you'd be justified; but that would be illegal and we don't do anything illegal. If the white man doesn't want the black man buying rifles and shotguns, then let the government do its job. That's all. And don't let the white man come to you and ask you what you think about what Malcolm says—why, you old Uncle Tom. He would never ask you if he thought you were going to say, "Amen!" No, he is making a Tom out of you.

So, this doesn't mean forming rifle clubs and going out looking for people, but it is time, in 1964, if you are a man, to let that man know. If he's not going to do his job in running the government and providing you and me with the protection that our taxes are supposed to be for, since he spends all those billions for his defense budget, he certainly can't begrudge you and me spending $12 or $15 for a single-shot, or double-action. I hope you understand. Don't go out shooting people, but any time, brothers and sisters, and especially the men in this audience—some of you wearing Congressional Medals of Honor, with shoulders this wide, chests this big, muscles that big—any time you and I sit around and read where they bomb a church and murder in cold blood, not some grownups, but four little girls while they were praying to the same god the white man taught them to pray to, and you and I see the government go down and can't find who did it.

Why, this man—he can find Eichmann hiding down in Argentina somewhere. Let two or three American soldiers, who are minding somebody else's business way over in South Vietnam, get killed, and he'll send battleships, sticking his nose in their business. He wanted to send troops down to Cuba and make them have what he calls free elections—this old cracker who doesn't have free elections in his own country. No, if you never see me another time in your life, if I die in the morning, I'll die saying one thing: the ballot or the bullet, the ballot or the bullet.

If a Negro in 1964 has to sit around and wait for some cracker senator to filibuster when it comes to the rights of black people, why, you and I should hang our heads in shame. You talk about a march on Washington in 1963, you haven't seen anything. There's some more going down in '64. And this time they're not going like they went last year. They're not going singing "We Shall Overcome." They're not going with white friends. They're not going with placards already painted for them. They're not going with round-trip tickets. They're going with one-way tickets.

And if they don't want that non-nonviolent army going down there, tell them to bring the filibuster to a halt. The black nationalists aren't going to wait. Lyndon B. Johnson is the head of the Democratic Party. If he's for civil rights, let him go into the Senate next week and declare himself. Let him go in there right now and declare himself. Let him go in there and denounce the Southern branch of his party.

Let him go in there right now and take a moral stand—right now, not later. Tell him, don't wait until election time. If he waits too long, brothers and sisters, he will be responsible for letting a condition develop in this country which will create a climate that will bring seeds up out of the ground with vegetation on the end of them looking like something these people never dreamed of. In 1964, it's the ballot or the bullet. Thank you.

Erwin N. Griswold

Erwin Griswold (born 1904) was educated at Oberlin College and Harvard University Law School. After his admission to the bar in 1929 he became an attorney in the office of the U. S. Solicitor General and special assistant to the Attorney General. In 1934 he joined the Harvard University law faculty. He served as dean from 1946 to 1967, when he became Solicitor General of the United States. He has received many honors both in the United States and abroad and is the author of several books, including The Fifth Amendment Today *(1955) and* Law and Lawyers in the U.S. *(1964). The speech we print here was given at the Tulane University School of Law on April 16, 1968, less than two weeks after the assassination of Martin Luther King, Jr.*

DISSENT—1968 STYLE

"Preserving civil peace is the first responsibility of government."[1]

"Unfortunately, since the populace has been sluggish and complacent, occasional violence seems to be advantageous to wake people up. . . ."[2]

When I first accepted the invitation to deliver this year's Dreyfous Lecture, it was my intention to discuss, in a rather abstract way, some of the changes that have taken place in the modes of dissent over the

---

[1] *Report of the National Advisory Commission on Civil Disorders* 171 (March 1, 1968).

[2] Goodman, "The Resisters Support U.S. Traditions and Interests," in *On Civil Disobedience, 1967*, N.Y. Times Magazine, November 26, 1967, p. 124.

years. The sad events of the past ten days, however, have led me to revise my emphasis somewhat. Rather than recite the changes of the past, I wish to speak to you tonight about some fundamental postulates of our democratic society, principles which I believe must be kept in vivid focus and which must be meaningfully communicated to the community as a whole if true freedom—not frenetic license—is to endure.

Let me begin by confessing that I am aware that between the polar extremes which I shall discuss there are confusing overlays of principle and policy and there will remain very substantial areas where the conscientious judgment of the informed individual is the only operative standard. But for the individual to make a rational choice, he must be aware of the values and consequences at stake when he forms his conscience and determines to follow it, and it is in the hope that it will encourage reflective appreciation of what is truly involved in "civil disobedience"—which has become the most pervasive contemporary aspect of civil liberties—that I submit these remarks for your attention.

[I]

Ambassador Sol M. Linowitz touched on the core of the problem in his address last month before a conference organized by the American Assembly and the American Bar Association when he suggested that in recent years there has been a material change in the public attitude toward law. He observed that law is now too often viewed "not as the living model for a free society, but rather as a mode of callous repression, or—no less disturbingly—as a collection of precatory suggestions which can be flouted or ignored."[3]

The focus of these remarks, just as with the Ambassador's observation, is not professional crime engaged in by those who are indifferent to legal obstacles to their own enrichment. What is of more concern is that our society has become increasingly tolerant of the mischievous attempts to excuse deliberate violations of the law committed in furtherance of what the actor personally regards as a lofty cause. I shall advert later on to justifiable examples of civil disobedience, but what I suggest is that intellectual and practical consequence of indiscriminate civil disobedience is the "Legitimation of violence" of which we have seen too much in America. I borrow this phrase from the recent Presidential Riot Commission, which listed this sorry fact of American society as one of the basic causes of riots. The Commission's conclusion under this heading is as follows:[4]

---

[3] "Some Reflections on the Challenges to Lawyers and the Law," March 16, 1968.
[4] *Report of the National Advisory Commission on Civil Disorders* 92 (March 1, 1968).

A climate that tends toward the approval and encouragement of violence as a form of protest has been created by white terrorism directed against nonviolent protest, including instances of abuse and even murder of some civil rights workers in the South, by the open defiance of law and Federal authority by state and local officials resisting desegregation, and by some protest groups engaging in civil disobedience who turn their backs on non-violence, go beyond constitutionally protected rights of petition and free assembly and resort to violence to attempt to compel alteration of laws and policies with which they disagree. This condition has been reenforced by a general erosion of respect for authority in American society and the re-duced effectiveness of social standards and community restraints on violence and crime.

The ink is not yet dry on the latest confirmation of this conclusion. The almost inevitable retaliation that the Commission spoke of was not long in coming, and over a hundred cities have been wracked by the manifestation of grim, mindless destruction. To argue that massive retaliation against society at large is both unjustifiable and self-defeating[5]—while unquestionably correct—misses the point that our national temperament has become too much acclimated to violence as a method of social protest.

Perhaps you may interject that no one who champions the right of protest in general, or the privilege of civil disobedience in particular, would seek to justify either political assassinations or riots. Of course I would not dispute this caveat, but the troubling circumstances I have sketched have both a logical and a practical relevance to issues of protest and dissent. They are logically related to our focus because they represent the ultimate mode of dissent—rejection not merely of the position of the majority but of the very foundation of civilized society itself: Civil Order. They have a practical impact on our topic too, for these extreme acts I have adverted to are in a sense the prod-uct of the same undiscriminating and uncritical attitude toward indi-vidual choice about the binding nature of law that underlies less dramatic but similarly irresponsible forms of protest.

[II]

We Americans have always taken a considerable measure of pride in our personal independence and right to non-conformity. But in my view, effective self-government is nevertheless the greatest achieve-ment of mankind. I trust that most Americans share the conclusion that Government is not merely inevitable but highly desirable. And from this axiom, certain corollaries flow.

---

[5] *E.g.*, Leibman, *Civil Disobedience: A Threat to Our Law Society*, 51 A.B.A.J. 645, 646 (1965).

The *first* of these is, I think, that civil disobedience differs quite radically in important respects from ordinary modes of protest and dissent. The crucial attribute of civil disobedience is that it is expressed through deliberate violation of the law.[6] Read in the context of its origin, the First Amendment not only creates a right to dissent but in a very real sense encourages the exercise of this prerogative. That is why we are concerned about "chilling" First Amendment freedoms. But our law and custom have long been clear that the right to differ with society and to reject its code of behavior has limits, and the First Amendment will not do service to sanction every sort of activity that is sought to be justified as an expression of non-conformity.

Second, equally important and sometimes profoundly troubling, our political tradition has long recognized that a man's abiding duty to his conscience transcends his obligation to the State. Chief Justice Hughes once put it this way:[7]

Much has been said of the paramount duty to the State, a duty to be recognized, it is urged, even though it conflicts with convictions of duty to God. Undoubtedly that duty to the State exists within the domain of power, for government may enforce obedience to laws regardless of scruples. When one's belief collides with the power of the State, the latter is Supreme within its sphere and submission or punishment follows. But, in the forum of conscience, duty to a moral power higher than the State has always been maintained.

Third, in a democracy such as ours, each individual shares both a political and a moral duty "actively to participate—to some degree, at least—in the processes of government and law-making." I am quoting the words of my friend, Professor J. N. D. Anderson of the University of London.[8] He continues: "In a democracy, indeed, every citizen bears a measure of personal responsibility for misgovernment, bad laws, or wrong policies, unless he has played his full part in trying to get a better government into power, better laws on the statute book, and better policies adopted."

As my *fourth* corollary, and here perhaps I will meet with slightly less universal agreement, I suggest that what we have been classically concerned about protecting is the dissemination of ideas—protecting the individual's access to the intellectual market-place where he may offer his conception of the ills and remedies for social or political problems. Thus, historically, our motivation and our objective have

---

[6] One of the more thoughtful analyses of this topic is that given by Dean Francis Allen in *Civil Disobedience and the Legal Order*, 36 U. Cin. L. Rev. 1, 175 (1967).

[7] *United States v. Macintosh*, 283 U.S. 605, 633 (Hughes, C.J., and Holmes, Brandeis, and Stone, JJ., dissenting).

[8] Anderson, *Into the World—the Need and Limits of Christian Involvement* 41 (London 1968).

been the attempt to encourage the search for truth or wisdom, or both. To quote Chief Justice Hughes again:[9]

The maintenance of the opportunity for free political discussion to the end that government may be responsive to the will of the people and that changes may be obtained by lawful means, an opportunity essential to the security of the Republic, is a fundamental principle of our constitutional system.

Given these principles, which I regard as not merely orthodox but sound, let me turn to the forms of dissent and protest which are currently the vogue so that we may proceed to consider some of the problems of dissent and in particular of civil disobedience.

[III]

Toward the end of the last century, Justice Holmes observed that on the basis of his experience, "Behind every scheme to make the world over, lies the question, What kind of world do you want?"[10] It may well have been true in those times that dissent and protest and agitation—for women's suffrage, or prohibition, or socialism, or anarchism, or whatever—had a more or less conscious and systematic design for the objective which was sought to be achieved. But today, much protest seems reflexive rather than cerebral, motivated more by the desire to reject established positions and policies than by deliberate preference for some alternatives. Perhaps I am not perceptive enough to discern the latent wisdom and goals of movements that seek the elevation of dirty words on campus, or that exalt the virtues of "flower power," or that conduct a "strip in" in a public park. The message, if there is one, escapes me.

We have in this country, of course, recognized that the display of symbols as an expression of some dissenting position is entitled to constitutional protection. That was settled as long ago at least as the "red flag" case.[11] But all this presupposes that there is some intelligible and definable nexus between the form of the protest and what is being protested. Thus, when a prominent New York couple several years ago decided to express their indignation at increased municipal taxes by stringing clotheslines draped with rags and tattered uniforms in their front yard, the state courts found this "bizarre" manner of symbolic dissent unprotected, with Judge Stanley Fuld writing that it was clear that the "value of their 'protest' lay not in its message but

---

[9] *Stromberg* v. *California,* 283 U.S. 359, 369.

[10] *The Occasional Speeches of Justice Oliver Wendell Holmes* 75 (Howe ed. 1962).

[11] *Stromberg* v. *California,* 283 U.S. 359. Compare *West Virginia State Board of Education* v. *Barnette,* 319 U.S. 624.

in its offensiveness."[12]   And the Supreme Court summarily ruled that their claims of "free speech" were in the circumstances clearly frivolous.

I have similar difficulty with other popular forms of modern "dissent."   Have we reached the point in this country where anything is contributed to our shared desire for progress and achievement by "writing dirty words on a fence about the President of the country? Or calling members of his Administration names?"[13]   No less prominent a spokesman for dissent than Bayard Rustin has expressed his "puzzlement" at the tactics employed by some young people in proclaiming their disenchantment with present conditions.   He remarks rather pointedly that he is "concerned about their believing that you can educate people on the basis of simplistic slogans . . . rather than on the basis of a concrete program of concrete recommendations."[14] While satire and sharp rapier-thrusts have long been among the accepted, and effective, modes of social and political criticism, I doubt that personal ridicule or broad-gauge contumely has ever produced light rather than heat, or constructively contributed to the resolution of major questions.

I do not question the constitutional right to be irrelevant or intemperate or even unfair.   Our jurisprudence has made it clear that it is a prerogative of American citizenship "to criticize public men and measures—and that means not only informed and responsible criticism but the freedom to speak foolishly and without moderation."[15]   In part this is the consequence of the assumption of our democratic system that the people can be trusted to test competing ideas and proposals, after free discussion, and "to withstand ideas that are wrong."[16] And in part it reflects our policy that even damaging and false assertions, and those unrelated to alternative programs, must be suffered lest the submission of important and constructive suggestions be deterred.[17]

[IV]

There is a contemporary aspect of the problem to which, I think, too little attention has been given.

---

[12]   *People* v. *Stover*, 12 N.Y. 2d 462, 470, 240 N.Y.S. 2d 734, 191 N.E. 2d 272 (1963), appeal dismissed, 375 U.S. 42.

[13]   Farrell, "Today's Disobedience Is Uncivil," in *On Civil Disobedience, 1967*, N.Y. Times Magazine, November 26, 1967, p. 29.

[14]   Rustin, in *Civil Disobedience* 10 (Center for the Study of Democratic Institutions 1966).

[15]   *Baumgartner* v. *United States*, 322 U.S. 665, 673–674.   See also *Bridges* v. *California*, 314 U.S. 252.

[16]   *Barenblatt* v. *United States*, 360 U.S. 109, 146 (Black, J. dissenting).

[17]   See generally *New York Times Co.* v. *Sullivan*, 376 U.S. 254.

When our basic notions of freedom of speech, and of the right to dissent, were developed—largely in the eighteenth century—communication was very different from what it is now. There were fewer people—only three million in the United States. Most of them were close to the soil, and many were not unduly literate. The market place for political ideas was more limited than it is now.

Perhaps of even greater importance, though, was the fact that the speed of communication of ideas was very slow. Freedom of speech and press meant freedom for Thomas Paine to publish "Common Sense," or for John Adams to write an article for a newspaper and for the newspaper to publish it. When these and other things were printed, they were read in the privacy of the home, with few other persons around. Ideas had an opportunity to percolate, to be examined and considered, and to be refined and reformed in the thoughts of the people.

Of course, there was speech making, too. But one person's voice could reach perhaps a thousand people, perhaps somewhat more under very special circumstances. The speech, could, of course, be printed, but it would be the next day before it was read in the same community, and days or weeks before it was read elsewhere. Almost always, there was time for thoughtful consideration. Moreover, the volume of material which was communicated, in print or by speech, was very limited. There was adequate opportunity for thoughtful people to comprehend, to absorb, and digest. In the modern world, though, this has been changed completely. The change has been developing over the years, with the telegraph and telephone, and the speed of transportation. With the coming of the radio, it was possible for President Roosevelt to address fifty or one hundred million people at once, with an impact that had never been known before.

In recent years, the facilities of communication have continued to develop until our situation is utterly different from what it was even a generation ago. In older days, a person who had an idea to express —whether of dissent, or otherwise, had some difficulty in bringing this about. To publish it in a book or pamphlet might be beyond his means. There were few newspapers, and these did not have much space. Unless the idea was extremely good, or well expressed, it was not likely that a newspaper could be found to publish it.

Today, however, the news media are avid for news. Television stations are putting out news through all the hours of the day, and they are always seeking something new or different, something that will attract viewers to their station. Almost anyone who wants to do something bizarre on a public street can find his way on television, and be seen by millions or tens of millions of people all over the country, and, indeed, through much of the world.

369

Because the newspapers are in competition with the television stations, they have to present the same news. Thus, there has been an enormous increase in the opportunity to express dissent, and, perhaps even more important, an even greater increase in the immediacy of dissent and the impact which it can make. There may be real room to question whether we have psychologically caught up with the developments in communications' speed and distribution, whether we are capable of absorbing and evaluating all of the materials which are now communicated daily to hundreds of millions of people.

I do not mean to suggest that the communications agencies have acted irresponsibly. They, too, have had to learn their power while the public was beginning to become aware of it. There are clear signs that television and newspapers are aware of their responsibilities in these areas, and are accepting them. There is a hard line for them to follow. For they must serve the ideals of a free press. Yet, all of the problems are enormously magnified, and the essential nature of responsibility in the exercise of a free press stands out more clearly as the magnification increases. The power of communication, through press, radio and television, has become an awesome power. Its use is essential to the preservation of a free society. Only time will tell, I suppose, whether our system can adequately adjust itself to the impact of modern communications methods. I am only trying to point out here the importance of the exercise of responsibility in the expression of dissent in the modern world.

[V]

We must draw two fundamental distinctions when we speak of dissent; the first involves primarily legal and moral variables and divides permissible from unpermissible dissent; the second presupposes that the dissent is tolerable but involves the social and political considerations of whether, or when or how the protest *should* be made. The latter is not a question of right, but of judgment and morals, even of taste, and a proper sense of restraint and responsibility, qualities which are or should be inherent in the very concept of civil liberties.

We must begin any analysis of these questions with the undoubted fact that we live in a society, an imperfect and struggling one no doubt, but one where Government and order are not only a necessity but are the preference of an overwhelming majority of the citizenry. The rules that society has developed to organize and order itself are found in a body of law which has not been imposed from outside, but has been slowly built up from experience expressed through the consent of the governed, and now pervades all aspects of human activity.

Inevitably there are occasions when individuals or groups will chafe under a particular legal bond, or will bridle in opposition to a particular governmental policy, and the question presents itself, what can be done?

Vocal objection, of course—even slanderous or inane—is permissible. But the fact that one is a dissenter with a right to express his opposition entitles him to no special license. Thus, in expressing views that are themselves wholly immune to official strictures he gains no roving commission to ignore the rules and underlying assumption of society that relate in a neutral way to activity rather than to the maintenance or expression of ideas. Thus, I submit that one cannot rightly engage in conduct which is otherwise unlawful merely because he intends that either that conduct or the idea he wishes to express in the course of the conduct is intended to manifest his dissent from some governmental policy. I cannot distinguish in principle the legal quality of the determination to halt a troop train to protest the Vietnam war or to block workmen from entering a segregated job site to protest employment discrimination, from the determination to fire shots into a civil rights leader's home to protest integration. The right to disagree—and to manifest disagreement—which the Constitution allows to the individuals in those situations—does not authorize them to carry on their campaign of education and persuasion at the expense of someone else's liberty, or in violation of some laws whose independent validity is unquestionable.

This distinction runs deep in our history, but has too frequently been ignored in this decade. But the line is a clear one, and we should reestablish it in the thinking and understanding of our people. While I share Professor Harry Kalven's assessment that the "generosity and empathy with which [public streets and parks] are made available [as a 'public forum']" is an index of freedom,[18] I regard as unassailable the limitation that the mere fact that a person wishes to make a public point does not sanction any method he chooses to use to make it. Yet there seems to be currently a considerable tendency to ignore if not to reject this limitation. Certainly many of the modern forms of dissent, including those I have just mentioned, proceed on the basis of the contrary proposition. Only last Term the Supreme Court was asked to sustain the right of demonstrators active in a cause that most of us here and the Court itself no doubt regarded as laudable, to lodge their demand for an end to segregation on the grounds of a city jail where, it seemed, biased treatment was being accorded prisoners. The argument was made that a demonstration at that site was "particularly

---

[18] Kalvern, *The Concept of the Public Forum: Cox v. Louisiana,* 1965 Supreme Court Review 12.

appropriate," irrespective of the consequences. Speaking for the Court, Justice Black rejected this rationale, explaining that[19]

> Such an argument has as its major unarticulated premise the assumption that people who want to propagandize protests or views have a constitutional right to do so whenever and however and wherever they please.

That notion the Court expressly "vigorously and forthrightly rejected."

Another form of protest that can never, in my view, be excused or tolerated, is that which assumes the posture of a violent and forcible assault on public order, whatever the motivation. The interests at stake in such a situation must transcend the validity of the particular cause and the permissibility of adhering to it. Violent opposition to law—any law—or forcible disregard of another's freedom to disagree falls beyond the pale of legitimate dissent or even of civil disobedience, properly understood; it is nothing short of rebellion.

The utter indefensibility of violent opposition to law is that it proceeds on the foolhardy and immoral principle that might makes right. Centuries ago Rousseau rejected this approach as a viable political alternative:[20]

> For, if force creates right, the effect changes with the cause: every force that is greater than the first succeeds to its right. As soon as it is possible to disobey with impunity, disobedience is legitimate; and, the strongest being always in the right, the only thing that matters is to act so as to become the strongest. But what kind of right is that which perishes when force fails?

To permit factions that resort to force when they feel—however correctly—that a particular law or policy is wrong would be to renounce our own experience and that of the Founders. In support of this view, I offer two sentences written by Justice Frankfurter: "Law alone saves a society from being rent by internecine strife or ruled by mere brute power however disguised."[21] And, "Violent resistance to law cannot be made a legal reason for its suspension without loosening the fabric of our society."[22]

What is at stake is not mere order but also the lessons of history. True freedom and substantial justice come not from violent altercations or incendiary dissent. "No mob has ever protected any liberty, even its own."[23] While the First Amendment embodies a distrust of the collective conscience of the majority in areas of fundamental liberty, it no more intended to leave the limits of freedom to the judgment of

---

[19] *Adderley v. Florida*, 385 U.S. 39, 47–48.
[20] *The Social Contract*, Bk. I, Ch. 3.
[21] *United States v. United Mine Workers*, 330 U.S. 258, 308.
[22] *Cooper v. Aaron*, 358 U.S. 1, 22.
[23] *Terminiello v. Chicago*, 337 U.S. 1, 32 (Jackson, J., dissenting).

coercive dissenters. "Civil government cannot let any group ride rough-shod over others simply because their 'consciences' tell them to do so."[24]

[VI]

These reflections have dealt with the question when law and govern-ment may tolerate dissent, or dissent manifested in certain ways, and I have suggested that it is illicit to violate otherwise valid laws either as a symbol of protest or in the course of protest, and secondly that I regard it as indefensible to attempt to promote a viewpoint either by flagrant violence or by organized coercion. Now I will turn finally to the second distinction to which I referred earlier in this lecture. That is, assuming a legal or moral right to protest, what considerations of prudence and responsibility should infuse the determination to exercise these rights.

First, you will note that I imply that a line may be drawn between legal and moral rights to dissent. I am not now referring to what I accept as the genuine possibility that one may exercise his constitu-tional right to dissent in a way that, because of recklessness or unfair-ness, makes his conduct ethically improper. I mention this distinction, however, because I believe awareness and evaluation of it should always be taken into account in considering an exercise of the right to dissent. But for the present, I mean to concentrate on the converse of this dis-tinction, that there may be a moral right to dissent without a corre-sponding legal privilege to do so. It is in this context that "civil disobedience" must be viewed.

Earlier, I observed that our system contemplates that there may be a moral right to "civil disobedience" (properly understood) that exists notwithstanding a "legal" duty to obey. I also referred to the source of this moral right: the ultimate sanctity of a man's own conscience, as the intellectual and volitional composite that governs his conception of his relation to Eternal Truth. I wish now to emphasize the con-siderations which, in my view, condition the existence and exercise of this moral right, because I believe the current rhetoric—which some-times seems to consecrate "civil disobedience" as the noblest response in the pantheon of virtues—has obscured the nature and consequence of this activity. To define my term—I mean by "civil disobedience" the deliberate violation of a rule ordained by constituted government because of a conscientious conviction that the law is so unjust that it cannot morally be observed by the individual.

The most important point to be stressed is that this decision is one that should be made only after the most painful and introspective re-

---

[24] *Douglas* v. *City of Jeanette*, 319 U.S. 157, 179 (opinion of Jackson, J.).

flection, and only when the firm conclusion is reached that obedience offends the most fundamental personal values. It is self-evident that routine or random non-compliance with the law for transient or superficial reasons would negate the first principles of civilized behavior. Unless society can safely assume that *almost* without exception individuals will accept the will of the majority even when to do so is grudging and distasteful, the foundation of secure liberty will rather rapidly erode. John Locke, who in his profound *Letter Concerning Toleration* analyzed and defended the right of obedience to conscience over civil law in case of severe conflict, thereafter cautioned in his essay *Concerning Civil Government*:[25]

May [the sovereign] be resisted, as often as any one shall find himself aggrieved, and but imagine he has not right done him? This will unhinge and overturn all polities, and instead of government and order, leave nothing but anarchy and confusion.

Last year, in delivering this Lecture, Arthur Goodhart observed, "Thus, it has been correctly said that obedience to the law is a major part of patriotism."[26] He meant this not as a castigation of dissent or as an outburst of flag-waving chauvinism, but rather as a formulation of a central political truth: That if human society is to enjoy freedom, it cannot tolerate license. Henry David Thoreau is generally regarded as the most notable American exponent of civil disobedience, and all of us share admiration for his determination. But we must not ignore the vital aspect of Thoreau's non-conformity—his passionate attempt to dissociate himself from society. He was, as Harry Kalven has put it, "a man who does not see himself as belonging very intensely to the community in which he was raised,"[27] and who sought constantly but futilely to reject the society to which he had not voluntarily adhered.

Thoreau's poignant attitude was charming enough in mid-nineteenth century America. But it was, essentially, an effort to withdraw from the realities of life and it was, I suggest, myopic even then, for it was painfully inconsistent with the fact that man is a part of society by nature, by geography, and by citizenship. Unlike a member of a purely artificial group, like a bar association or country club, a citizen cannot resign from the "social compact" because he protests policies of the regime. Now in the last third of the Twentieth Century, we must be even more cognizant that there is nothing noble or salutary about foredoomed attempts to abdicate membership in society. Complex problems demand rational attention that can come only from personal focus

---

[25] Ch. XVIII, para. 203.

[26] *Recognition of the Binding Nature of Law*, 41 Tul. L. Rev. 769, 773 (1967).

[27] "On Thoreau" in *Civil Disobedience* 25, 28 (Center for the Study of Democratic Institutions 1966).

on solutions and never from stubbornly turning one's back on harsh and unpleasant realities.

This is precisely what non-conformity as a way of life is. It is the essential irrationality of the "hippie movement"—a mass endeavor to drop out of life. It is a protest of sorts, of course, but one that can bear no fruit, because it takes issue with what is not only inevitable, but more importantly, indispensible—social regulation of individual behavior.

Stretched to its logical extreme, this also is civil disobedience, and for this reason I urge that before any man embarks upon a unilateral nullification of any law he must appreciate that his judgment has not merely a personal significance but also portends grave consequences for his fellows.

In determining whether and when to exercise the moral right to disobey the dictates of the law, it must also be recognized that society not only does not but cannot recognize this determination as entitled to legal privilege. It is part of the Gandhian tradition of civil disobedience that the sincerity of the individual's conscience presupposes that the law will punish this assertion of personal principle. In the very formation of our country, in the Federalist Papers, Hamilton explained the reason why government cannot compromise its authority by offering a dispensation for individual conscience:[28]

Government implies the power of making laws. It is essential to the idea of a law, that it be attended with a sanction; or, in other words, a penalty or punishment for disobedience. If there be no penalty annexed to disobedience, the resolutions or commands which pretend to be laws will, in fact, amount to nothing more than advice or recommendation.

Thus, it is of the essence of law that it is equally applied to all, that it binds all alike, irrespective of personal motive. For this reason, one who contemplates civil disobedience out of moral conviction should not be surprised and must not be bitter if a criminal conviction ensues. And he must accept the fact that organized society cannot endure on any other basis. His hope is that he may aid in getting the law changed. But if he does not succeed in that, he cannot complain if the law is applied to him.

[VII]

Though I speak with seriousness about civil disobedience, I hope that my remarks are not misunderstood. I endeavored to make it plain in my opening analysis that a proper recognition of the rights

---

[28] *The Federalist, Number 15.*

of conscience is one of the basic assumptions of our society. The problem, of course, is to determine what is "proper." Like all questions worth discussing, it is inevitably one of degree.

In considering this question, it is well to examine not only *whether* civil disobedience is appropriate in a particular situation, but also *how* it is to be carried out. We have a vivid illustration of this in the experience of this generation. We are all aware of the fact that for many long years the legal structure was often used to perpetuate deprivations which were at odds with the most basic constitutional and moral values. During this time, conditions of political, social, and economic inequality made ineffective meaningful attempts to change these regulations and policies by petition within the customary channels of reform. In this situation, the only realistic recourse was deliberate refusal to abide by the restrictions any longer. Lunch-counter sit-ins and freedom rides are among the most dramatic examples of the techniques that were used to expose the injustices that were perpetrated under the banner of law. In many of these cases, these actions were not, indeed, illegal, since the restrictive laws were plainly invalid if one had the time, energy, and money to take them up to higher courts. In other cases, though, the line was not clear, and sometimes the actions taken were undoubtedly illegal. We cannot fail to recognize the fact that it was these tactics which succeeded in putting the basic issues squarely before the courts and the public. And it was in this way that the law was clarified in the courts and that legislative changes were brought about.

There are great lessons to be learned from this experience. Perhaps the greatest of these is that what mattered was not merely the moral fervor of the demonstrators, or the justice of their cause, but also the way in which they conducted themselves. They and their leaders were aware of the moral dimensions of their cause, and they knew that this required an equal adherence to morality in the means by which they sought to vindicate their cause. Because of this, rigid adherence to the philosophy of non-violence was sought and widely achieved. In retrospect, I am sure that our Nation will point with pride not only to the courage of those who risked punishment in order to challenge injustice, but also to the morality of their actions in scrupulously avoiding violence, even in reaction to the force which was exerted on them. The affirmation of the close relation between morality and non-violence will be one of the many monuments of the Rev. Martin Luther King, Jr.

As this experience shows, the ultimate legal success as well as the intrinsic moral quality of civil disobedience turns on the restraint with which it is exercised. This is an extremely hard line to draw, but it is one which must be earnestly sought out. Unfortunately, some of those who claim this mantle today do not appreciate the moral quality of thought and action which made their predecessors worthy to wear it.

Of course, it has not been my intention to disparage the objectives of any individual or group, or to discourage the honest and forthright and candid prophylaxis and therapy that are the legacy of reflective and constructive criticism. My only concern has been that some contemporary forms and philosophies of protest may in fact unwittingly retard the improvements in society which we all seek. I hope the ideas I have sought to present here may contribute to the thoughtful consideration of critical issues with which we must all deal in the creative evolution of our cherished land.

THE
STUDENT
AND THE
UNIVERSITY

"Youth movements have come and gone," writes Walter Laqueur in one of the essays in this section, "but never before has one been taken so seriously." The question is: does the current generation merit the attention it is getting? We think so. At any rate, since the university is one of the principal places in which the youth movement has been working out its career, the question is an inevitable one for university discussion. Students have been making a frontal examination, if not attack, on the basic assumptions about the university, and the way in which the university responds in the next few years will very likely determine the nature of the institution and of its governance for a long time.

The section begins with a piece of student writing, James Simon Kunen's description of the 1968 uprising at Columbia. Kunen's understated, somewhat ingenuous tone does more to catch the attractiveness and force of the student point of view than a more strident and assertive piece might have done. The essays that follow are by older hands. Nicola Chiaromonte comments on the international character of the student movement, and while he rejects the idea "that the young must be right simply because they are young," he identifies a state of affairs in modern culture that explains the revolt of youth. John Holt describes the progressive deepening of his sympathy with student activism on one campus; he tries to show some of the defects in the character of university administration that seem to require activism, and he ends with a bold proposal on university admissions.

Professors Bettelheim and Laqueur try to put the student movement in larger perspective: the former by discussing the psychological and social character of the leaders of the student left; the latter by discussing the history of student movements back to the Middle Ages. Both offer some unsettling modern parallels to the youth movement that accompanied Hitler's rise in Germany.

Robert Brustein confronts student demands for equality in campus governance with the argument that "it is absurd to identify electoral with educational institutions." Richard Hofstadter and George W. Wetherill end the section with pieces on the proper role of the university. Both agree that the university's unique function is uninhibited critical examination. From this position, Hofstadter offers principles of personal conduct toward the university, while Wetherill defines the limits of appropriate university research and public service.

James Simon Kunen

James Simon Kunen was born in Massachusetts in 1948, attended Andover, and entered Columbia in 1966. When the 1968 student uprising broke out he was a member of the sophomore class, going out for crew, and already keeping a sort of journal "on napkins and cigarette packs and hitchhiking signs." An early installment of the journal was published in New York magazine in May; and by July 8 Kunen refers to it as "this ego-blast book I'm writing." The journal ends on August 6, was published as The Strawberry Statement: Notes of a College Revolutionary *(1969), and made into a film in 1970. Two principal symbols of student concern at the time were Columbia's affiliation in the I.D.A. (Institute for Defense Analysis), a group of universities doing research for the Department of Defense; and "The Gym," which Columbia had arranged to build in Morningside Park, public land on the edge of Harlem, in exchange for allowing limited public use of the building at certain times. The uprising was led by Mark Rudd, a junior, president of the Columbia Chapter of S.D.S., Students for a Democratic Society.*

FROM **THE STRAWBERRY STATEMENT**

I wrote the Book.

I should like to point out immediately that just because I happened to be born in 1948, it doesn't mean that what I have to say as a nineteen-year-old is worth any more than what nineteen-year-olds had to say in, to pick a year at random, 1920. To say that youth is what's happening is absurd. It's always been happening. Everyone is nineteen, only at different times. This youth-cult scene is a disservice to everyone. I'm anticipating a severe psychological set-back when I turn twenty, and I don't know what I'm going to do when my youth-fare card runs out. As for this "don't-trust-anyone-over-30" shit, I agree in principle, but I think they ought to drop the zero.

What sort of man gets busted at Columbia? I don't know. I got busted at Columbia and I, for one, strongly support trees (and, in the larger sense, forests), flowers, mountains and hills, also valleys, the ocean, wiliness (when used for good), good, little children, people, tremendous record-setting snowstorms, hurricanes, swimming underwater, nice policemen, unicorns, extra-inning ball games up to twelve innings, pneumatic jackhammers (when they're not too close), the dunes in North Truro on Cape Cod, liberalized abortion laws, and Raggedy Ann dolls, among other things.

I do not like Texas, people who go to the zoo to be arty, the Defense Department, the name "Defense Department," the fly buzzing around me as I write this, protective tariffs, little snowstorms that turn to slush, the short days of winter, extra-inning ball games over twelve innings, calling people consumers, pneumatic jackhammers immediately next to the window, and G.I. Joe dolls. Also racism, poverty and war. The latter three I'm trying to do something about.

But I am not a nihilist. I do like some things.

I should add that I have never been able to stand at a high place without thinking about jumping off.

• • •

Thursday, April 4, 1968: I was going to work for Martin Luther King's poor people's march, but now he's dead. I suppose there'll be one anyway. Anyway is the way things always end up going these days.

Then Rudd did the thing at the King Memorial Service. I wasn't there because we had double crew practice to take advantage of the suspension of classes. But there was a memorial service on campus, and President Kirk attended, and pious phrases were uttered honoring the memory of what the powerful choose to remember of Dr. King. And Rudd got up, in the middle of the service, and called the memorial service an obscenity, which it was, because, as he explained, while President Kirk was in there "honoring" Dr. King, his university was paying black maids less than they could collect on welfare, and insistently refusing collective bargaining and obstructing unionization of its kitchen workers, not to mention continuing the expansion policies which had in ten years almost completely expunged non-whites from Morningside Heights. Also, President Kirk's university was helping to form imperialist policy and prosecute the imperialist war that Dr. King opposed. President Kirk's little religious service was obscenely hypocritical, it was filthy. Rudd walked out. He was followed by many people. Soon he would be followed by many more.

• • •

Monday, April 22: A mimeograph has appeared around the campus charging SDS with using coercion to gain its political ends. SDS is for free speech for itself only, it is charged. SDS physically threatens the administration. SDS breaks rules with impunity while we (undefined) are subject to dismissal for tossing a paper airplane out a dorm window. Aren't you TIRED, TIRED, TIRED of this? Will Mark Rudd be our next dean? Do something about it. Come to the SDS rally tomorrow and *be prepared.* At first anonymous, the leaflet reappears in a second edition signed Students for a Free Campus. The jocks have done it again. As with the demonstrations against Marine campus recruiting in the spring of '67, threats of violence from the right will bring hundreds of the usually moderate to the SDS ranks just to align themselves against jock violence. I personally plan to be there, but I'm not up tight about it. At the boat house, a guy says he's for the jock position. Don't get me wrong, I say, I'm not against beating up on a few pukes, I just don't think you should stoop to their level by mimeographing stuff. We both go out and kill ourselves trying to row a boat faster than eight students from MIT will be able to.

Tuesday, April 23: Noon. At the sundial are 500 people ready to follow Mark Rudd (whom they don't particularly like because he always refers to President Kirk as "that shithead") into the Low Library administration building to demand severance from IDA, an end to gym construction, and to defy Kirk's recent edict prohibiting indoor demonstrations. There are around 100 counterdemonstrators. They are what Trustee Arthur Ochs Sulzberger's newspapers refers to as "burly white youths" or "students of considerable athletic attainment"—jocks. Various deans and other father surrogates separate the two factions. Low Library is locked. For lack of a better place to go we head for the site of the gym in Morningside Park, chanting "Gym Crow must go." I do not chant because I don't like chanting.

I have been noncommittal to vaguely against the gym, but now I see the site for the first time. There is excavation cutting across the whole park. It's really ugly. And there's a chain link fence all around the hole. I don't like fences anyway so I am one of the first to jump on it and tear it down. Enter the New York Police Department. One of them grabs the fence gate and tries to shut it. Some demonstrators grab him. I yell "Let that cop go," partly because I feel sorry for the cop and partly because I know that the night sticks will start to flagellate on our heads, which they proceed to do. One of my friends goes down and I pull him out. He's on adrenaline now and tries to get back at the cops but I hold him, because I hit a cop at Whitehall and I wished I hadn't very shortly thereafter.* After the usual hassle, order is restored and the cops let Rudd mount a dirt pile to address

---

* In October of 1967, there was a series of "Stop the Draft Week" demonstrations at Whitehall, the Army Induction Center for Manhattan. At about 6 A.M. on a Thursday morning a blue cossack rode his lumbering steed at me on the sidewalk. It was just too early in the morning to get run over by a horse. I slugged him (the cop) in the thigh, which was as high as I could reach, and was immediately brought to bay and apprehended by a detective, who smashed me in the knee with a movie camera, and later let me go when he deduced from my name that I was Irish, which I'm not.

us. As soon as he starts to talk he is drowned out by jackhammers but, at the request of the police, they are turned off. Rudd suggests we go back to the sundial and join with 300 demonstrators there, but we know that he couldn't possibly know whether there are 300 demonstrators there and we don't want to leave. He persists and we defer.

Back at the sundial there is a large crowd. It's clear we've got something going. An offer comes from Vice-President Truman to talk with us in McMillin Theatre but Rudd, after some indecision, refuses. It seems we have the initiative and Truman just wants to get us in some room and bullshit till we all go back to sleep. Someone suggests we go sit down for awhile in Hamilton, the main college classroom building, and we go there. Sitting down turns to sitting-in, although we do not block classes. Rudd asks, "Is this a demonstration?" "Yes!" we answer, all together. "Is it indoors?" "Yes!"

An immediate demand is the release of the one student arrested at the park, Mike Smith, who might as well be named John Everyman, because nobody knows him. To reciprocate for Mike's detention, Dean Coleman is detained.

At four o'clock, like Pavlov's dog, I go to crew, assuring a long-hair at the door that I'll be back. At practice it is pointed out to me that the crew does not have as many WASPS as it should have according to the population percentage of WASPS in the nation, so don't I think that crew should be shut down? I answer no, I don't think crew should be shut down. . . .

Wednesday, April 24, 5:30 A.M. Someone just won't stop yelling that we've got to get up, that we're leaving, that the blacks occupying Hamilton with us have asked us to leave. I get up and leave. The column of evicted whites shuffles over to Low Library. A guy in front rams a wooden sign through the security office side doors and about 200 of us rush in. Another 150 hang around outside because the breaking glass was such a bad sound. They become the first "sundial people." Inside we rush up to Kirk's office and someone breaks the lock. I am not at all enthusiastic about this and suggest that perhaps we ought to break up all the Ming Dynasty art that's on display while we're at it. A kid turns on me and says in a really ugly way that the exit is right over there. I reply that I am staying, but that I am not a sheep and he is.

Rudd calls us all together. He looks very strained. He elicits promises from the *Spectator* reporters in the crowd not to report what he is about to say. Then he says that the blacks told us to leave Hamilton because they do not feel that we are willing to make the sacrifices they are willing to make. He says that they have carbines and grenades and that they're not leaving. I think that's really quite amazing.

We all go into Kirk's office and divide into three groups, one in each room. We expect the cops to come any moment. After an hour's discussion my room votes 29–16 to refuse to leave, to make the cops carry us out. The losing alternative is to escape through the windows and then go organize a strike. The feeling is that if we get busted, *then* there will be something to organize a strike about. The man chairing the discussion is standing on a small wooden table and I am very concerned lest he break it. We collect water in wastebaskets in case of tear gas. Some of it gets spilled and I spend my time trying to wipe it up. I don't want to leave somebody else's office all messy.

We check to see what other rooms have decided. One room is embroiled in a political discussion, and in the other everyone is busy playing with the office machines.

At about 8:30 A.M. we hear that the cops are coming. One hundred seventy-three people jump out the window. (I don't jump because I've been reading *Lord Jim*.) That leaves twenty-seven of us sitting on the floor, waiting to be arrested. In stroll an inspector and two cops. We link arms and grit our teeth. After about five minutes of gritting our teeth it dawns on us that the cops aren't doing anything. We relax a little and they tell us they have neither the desire nor the orders to arrest us. In answer to a question they say they haven't got MACE either.

In through the window like Batman climbs Professor Orest Ranum, liberal, his academic robes billowing in the wind. We laugh at his appearance. He tells us that our action will precipitate a massive right-wing reaction in the faculty. He confides that the faculty had been nudging Kirk toward resignation, but now we've blown everything; the faculty will flock to support the President. We'll all be arrested, he says, and we'll all be expelled. He urges us to leave. We say no. One of us points out that Sorel said only violent action changes things. Ranum says that Sorel is dead. He gets on the phone to Truman and offers us trial by a tripartite committee if we'll leave. We discuss it and vote no. Enter Mark Rudd, through the window. He says that twenty-seven people can't exert any pressure, and the best thing we could do would be to leave and join a big sit-in in front of Hamilton. We say no, we're not leaving until our demands on the gym, IDA and amnesty for demonstrators are met. Rudd goes out and comes back and asks us to leave again, and we say no again. He leaves to get reinforcements. Ranum leaves. Someone comes in to take pictures. We all cover our faces with different photographs of Grayson Kirk.

It's raining out, and the people who are climbing back in are marked by their wetness. Offered a towel by one of the new people, a girl pointedly says "No, thank you, I haven't been out." Rationally, we twenty-seven are glad that there are now 150 people in the office, but emotionally we resent them. As people dry out, the old and new become less easily differentiable, and I am trying for a field promotion in the movement so that I will not fade into the masses who jumped and might jump again.

The phone continues to ring and we inform the callers that we are sorry, but Dr. Kirk will not be in today because Columbia is under new management. After noon, all the phones are cut off by the administration.

At 3:45 I smoke my first cigarette in four months and wonder if Lenin smoked. I don't go to crew. I grab a typewriter and, though preoccupied by its electricness, manage to write:

The time has come to pass the time.

I am not having good times here. I do not know many people who are here, and I have doubts about why they are here. Worse, I have doubts about why I am here. (Note the frequency of the word *here*. The place I am is the salient characteristic of my situation.) It's possible that I'm here to be cool or to meet people or to meet girls (as distinct from people) or to get out of crew or to be arrested. Of course the possibility exists that I am here to precipitate some change at the University. I am willing to accept the latter as true or, rather, I am willing, even anxious, not to think about it any more. If you think too much on the second tier (think about why you are thinking what you think) you can be paralyzed.

I really made the conflicting-imperative scene today. I have never let down the crew before, I think. Let down seven guys. I am one-eighth of the crew. I am one-fiftieth of this demonstration. And I am not even sure that this demonstration is right. But I multiplied these figures by an absolute importance constant. I hate to hamper the hobby of my friends (and maybe screw, *probably* screw, my own future in it), I am sorry about that, but death is being done by this University and I would rather fight it than row a boat.

But then I may, they say, be causing a right-wing reaction and hurting the cause. Certainly it isn't conscionable to hold Dean Coleman captive. But attention is being gotten. Steps will be taken in one direction or another. The polls will fluctuate and the market quiver. Our being here is the cause of an effect. We're trying to make it good; I don't know what else to say or do. That is, I have no further statement to make at this time, gentlemen.

The news comes in that Avery Hall, the architecture school, has been liberated. We mark it as such on Grayson's map. At about 8 P.M. we break back into Kirk's inner office, which had been relocked by security when we gathered into one room when the cops came in the morning. The $450,000 Rembrandt and the TV have gone with the cops.

We explore. The temptation to loot is tremendous, middle-class morality notwithstanding, but there is no looting. I am particularly attracted by a framed diploma from American Airlines declaring Grayson Kirk a V.I.P., but I restrict myself to a few Grayson Kirk introduction cards. Someone finds a book on masochism behind a book on government. Someone else finds what he claims is Grayson's draft card and preparations are made to mail it back to the Selective Service. On his desk is an American Airlines jigsaw puzzle which has apparently been much played with.

We have a meeting to discuss politics and defense, but I sit at the door as a guard. A campus guard appears and, before I can do anything, surprises me by saying, "As long as you think you're right, fuck 'em." He hopes something good for him might come out of the whole thing. He makes eighty-six dollars a week after twenty years at the job.

I go down to the basement of Low, where the New York City Police have set up shop. There are approximately forty of them; there is precisely one of me. I ask one for the score of the Red Sox game. He seems stunned that a hippie faggot could be interested in such things, but he looks it up for me. Rained out.

I use the pay-phone to call a girl at Sarah Lawrence. I tell her how isolated I feel and how lonely I am and hungry and tired and she says oh. I explain that I'll be busted any minute and she says she knows that.

I return upstairs. One of these people who knows how to do things has reconnected a phone, but he needs someone to hold the two wires together while he talks. I do it. I'll do anything to feel like I'm doing something.

Thursday, April 25: I get up and shave with Grayson Kirk's razor, use his toothpaste, splash on his after-shave, grooving on it all. I need something morale-building like this, because my revolutionary fervor takes about half an hour longer than the rest of me to wake up.

Someone asks if anyone knows how to fix a Xerox 3000, and I say yes, lying through my teeth. Another man and I proceed to take it apart and put it back together. To test it I draw a pierced heart with "Mother" in the middle and feed it to the machine. The machine gives back three of the same. Much rejoicing. Now we can get to work on Kirk's files. My favorite documents are a gym letter which ends with the sentence "Bring on the bull-dozers!" and a note to a Columbia representative to the land negotiations telling him to be careful *not* to mention to Parks Commissioner Hoving that the date for digging has been moved up. ("We don't want him to know that we decided on this over a year ago," the note explains.)

Since a bust does not seem imminent, I climb out the window and go to crew at four. I talk to the coach and we agree that I will sleep in Low but will show up for the bus to Cambridge the next morning if I'm not in jail.

When I get back from crew I have to run a police cordon and leap for the second-story ledge. A cop, much to my surprise, bothers to grab me and tries to pull me down, but some people inside grab me and pull me up.

A meeting is going on discussing defense. J.J. wants to pile art treasures on the windows so the cops will have to break them to get in. I'm for that. But he also wants to take poles and push cops off the ledge. When this is criticized he tries to make it clear that it will be done in a nonviolent way. A friend whispers to me that J.J. is SDS's answer to the jock. A guy in a red crash helmet begins to say that maybe we won't fight because we're not as manly as the blacks, but it is well known that he is loony as hell and he is shouted down in a rare violation of the democratic process. After two hours' debate it is decided to man the barricades until they start to fall, then gather in groups with locked arms and resist passively. A motion to take off all our clothes when the police arrive is passed, with most girls abstaining.

I get back to the Xerox and copy seventy-three documents, including clippings from *The New York Times*. I hear over the radio that Charles 37X Kenyatta and the Mau Maus are on campus. This does not surprise me.

J.J. is recruiting volunteers to liberate another building. He had thirty, male and female, and at 2 A.M. he's ready to move. I go out on the ledge to check for cops. There are only three, so we climb down and sprint to Mathematics Hall. There we are joined by twenty radicals who could no longer stand the Establishment-liberal atmosphere of the previously liberated Fayerweather Hall. We get inside and immediately pile up about 2000 pounds of furniture at the front door. Only then do we discover two housekeepers still in the building. They are quite scared but only say "Why didn't you tell us you were coming?" and laugh. We help them out a window and along a ledge with the aid of the just-arrived-press movie lights.

We hold the standard two-hour meeting to decide how to deal with the cops, whom we understand to be on their way. The meeting is chaired by Tom Hayden, who is an Outside Agitator. Reverend Starr, the Protestant counselor, tells us the best positions for firehoses and so on. Dean Alexander B. Platt is allowed in through the window.

He looks completely dead. We consider capturing him, but no one has the energy, so we let him go after thanking him for coming. Professor Allen Westin, liberal, comes and offers us a tripartite committee which he has no authority to constitute and which we don't want. He is thanked and escorted to the window.

At 6 A.M. I go to sleep.

Friday, April 26: I wake up at 8:55 and run to the crew bus and leave for MIT. From Cambridge I call my home in Marlboro. My mother asks me, "Are you on the side of the law-breakers in this thing?" For ten minutes we exchange mother talk and revolutionary rhetoric. She points out that neither Gandhi nor Thoreau would have asked for amnesty. I admit I haven't read them. But Gandhi had no Gandhi to read and Thoreau hadn't read Thoreau. They had to reach their own conclusions and so will I.

Saturday, April 27: I row a boat race and split. That wraps up the crew season—for me. On the MTA to Logan Airport a middle-aged man starts winking and smiling and gesticulating at my right lapel. Looking down, I see that I am wearing a broken rifle pin, symbol of the War Resisters' League. I tell him that it so happens I am on my way back to Columbia right now to carry on a Revolution. He thinks that's fine.

I get back to Math around 4:30 and sit down on the public-relations ledge over Broadway. People from a peace demonstration downtown are depositing money and food in a bucket at the bottom of a rope. Each time we haul it up and re-lower it we include I.D.'s for people who want to get into the campus. A remarkable number of cars toot their support, and when a bus driver pulls over to wave us a victory sign, ten people nearly fall off the ledge.

In the evening I discover that the electricity to the kitchen is cut off. I run downstairs and almost call for "someone important" but somehow I am unwilling to accept that kind of status relation. I tell several of my peers and one of them finds the fuse box and sets things right.

I volunteer for shopping. We buy twenty dollars of food for eighteen dollars (the merchants earlier had contributed food outright) and on the way back meet a gentleman who seems to belong to Drunken Faculty to Forget the Whole Mess. Someone whom I think of as a friend threatens to punch me because I am carrying food.

As the evening wears on I feel less useful and more alienated, so I assign myself the task of keeping the mayonnaise covered. After covering it twelve times I give up and decide to write home. I wonder whether the Paris Commune was this boring.

In the letter I try to justify rebelling on my father's money. I point out that one of the dangers of going to college is that you learn things, and that my present actions are much influenced by my Contemporary Civilization (C1001y) readings. After sealing the letter I realize that my conception of the philosophy of law comes not so much from Rousseau as from Fess Parker as Davy Crockett. I remember his saying that you should decide what you think is right and then go ahead and do it. Walt Disney really bagged that one; the old fascist inadvertently created a whole generation of radicals.

I discover a phone which has not been cut off and call my brother. As I am talking someone puts a piece of paper beside me and writes "This . . . phone . . . is . . . tapped." I address myself briefly to the third party and go on talking. It feels good to talk to someone on the outside, although it is disappointing to find out that the outside world is going on as usual.

· · ·

Tuesday, May 21: As a result of the proliferation of my diary in *New York* magazine, I am now a qualified spokesman for the Columbia strikers, the international peace movement, and everyone in the world younger than thirty. Nonetheless, I agree to go on a Mutual Radio Network interview with some misgivings concerning my expertise on its subject, "The Generation Gap." It turns out, however, that the interviewer lives but three doors from Mark Rudd back in New Jersey, and this, coupled with my absolute inability to conceive of anyone listening to such a program, allays my nervousness to the point where I can go ahead and incriminate myself on seven counts of everything. When it's all over I am too embarrassed to ask about money and therefore get none, not even cab fare. This is The Big City.

I take the subway back and arrive at campus at about 5 P.M., just in time for the meeting with our lawyers. But there is no one there. Enquiring as to what is going on here, I find that everybody is over at Hamilton where a sit-in is now in progress. The facts, as they are related to me, are that Dean Platt has sent letters to Rudd and others demanding their appearance before him; that they have exercised their right (Constitutional) not to appear while their case is in court; that they have consequently been suspended; and that everyone else in the world has shown up to protest. That's good enough for me. We're nearing the bottom of the barrel in unarrested radical manpower, so there are only about 150 sitting-in in the building, but I join the let's say 1500 standing outside in non-trespassing support. Every so often I get hit with eggs, which a small group of jocks are having good clean fun throwing. Since they have no arguments and no support for their arguments (of which they have none), they have no recourse but to assault us like this and sing fight songs—that's right,

390

fight songs. They are standing there—I beg you to believe this—throwing eggs and singing "Roar, Lion, Roar" all the while. They sing "Who Owns New York?" (C-O-L-U-M-B-I-A) which I think is particularly amusing, because it is precisely our point that Columbia is such a huge real-estate enterprise (owning four percent of New York, to be exact). They top it all off by launching into "America." We join them in this one.

I leave Hamilton to aid in the construction of barricades at either end of College Walk. This is one of the more purely symbolic acts I have ever indulged in, since there are at least seven other gates and countless tunnels through which the cops can get in. At the Amsterdam Avenue end we are having trouble barricading one of the gates. The cops, who are awaiting orders just outside, offer us all sorts of advice, interspersed with statements impugning the value of a college education if we can't figure out how to wedge a gate shut. Finally one of them digs into his pocket and offers me a padlock, which I accept with some thanks and considerable amazement. Unfortunately, it doesn't fit, so I give it back.

At 2:30 A.M. the cops are inside Hamilton, having emerged from the tunnels within. The arrestees are removed through the tunnels, but there is a large confrontation between demonstrators and police at the doors. The police are keeping the demonstrators from getting into the building but the demonstrators, on the other hand, are keeping the police from getting out on the campus.

Near Schermerhorn Hall, a crowd gathers to attempt to hold up the paddy wagons. People are incredibly mad. These navy-blue masses may be the Law, but to us they are the same bunch of animals who, totally unprovoked, beat up 150 people at the first bust, and they're back, they're back on our campus, and we want to get them the hell out. I see bricks, signs, and a potted tree hurled onto police cars parked seventy feet below us. The cars are empty. I don't think anyone wants to hurt policemen, but at least we can make their visit cost them something in technology.

Elsewhere a group of thirty cops has come through a gate which leads, via the hallways of two dormitories, onto campus. As they begin to emerge from the dorm a group of about two hundred students confronts them screaming "Cops must go!" and meaning it. I see one of my more moderate friends at the front of the group and just go up to him and shake his hand. Then we all start moving toward the cops. They back up a little and we move forward a little, and we move forward a lot and they back up a lot until we've marched them backwards right off the campus. We slam the gate between us.

The Fire Department makes the scene, since smoke seems to be pouring out of one of the classroom buildings, and I sit around and

watch them for a while. So do a lot of other kids. Those extension
ladders are amazing. Someone yells "Hooray for the Fire Department!
They don't beat people up."

There is a big crowd at the sundial, so I go there to see what's up.
Dean Platt is up. He has a bullhorn, and says it's his sad duty to announce that the campus will be cleared by the police. Everyone is
to leave or return to his dormitory. Some kid rushes up and grabs
the bullhorn from him. A strike leader apologizes profusely for this,
which I think is sort of funny, in a way.

One minute, at the most, after his announcement there are shouts
that the TPF are coming through the barricade. I figure that I didn't
really have time to leave the campus, did I; in fact, I might not even
have heard the announcement. I rush to the falling barricade at
Amsterdam Avenue.

A huge column of TPF are trudging in. Their front ranks are already right on top of us. I keep yelling walk, don't run, to everybody.
We can back up slowly; we mustn't panic and trample each other.
Suddenly the TPF are unleashed. They charge us, swinging their
clubs. I have to turn and run and after about six steps I trip over
someone who has tripped over someone else. I curl up into a rolling
ball and watch a lot of blue legs run past me. When I get up, I'm
right in the middle of the police. Two of them single me out and
start chasing me with clubs raised. I run like a thief for the other
side of the campus, for Broadway, for *away*, that's all, far away. A
cop in front of me turns and waits for me. I notice that he has his
weight on the balls of his feet, his club parallel to the ground, ready
for me to go either way. I'm thinking what a goddamn shame it is
that I'm wearing my goddamn loafers because I can't run very well in
them. I veer off to the right and he gets a good backhand stroke into
my left calf, but I don't fall down. I see a first-aid circle and jump
into it like goals in tag. Twenty feet away a kid has tripped and two
cops are on him, one kicking, one clubbing. I run down to help him
(which consists of yelling "Hey, leave him alone"), but the cops are
through with him. A stretcher is brought but he says "That's all
right, I'm fine." There is blood streaming down his face. I think
that he obviously doesn't know what he is talking about. He is put
on the stretcher. Someone, I think he's the head of the Columbia
cheerleaders, is standing nearby saying "Oh my God, Oh my
God," not addressing God really, but just sort of saying it over
and over. I resolve that nothing is going to get me off this campus
tonight.

The cops are regrouping, so I have a chance to join a concentration
of students on South Field. They rush us again, but I manage to get
into the lobby of Ferris Booth Hall. The TPF are right on the patio,

separated from us only by glass doors. We see them putting tape over their badge numbers.

We withdraw to the auditorium to hold a meeting about whether to leave, or stay on campus and get arrested and suspended. Nothing is decided. It's up to the individual. When we come out, the cops have withdrawn to the center of the campus, so I go outside. It is getting light.

I'm standing with some friends when I notice two husky grey-suited gentlemen, walking up to a long-haired kid standing alone on the edge of the lawn with a camera. Suddenly they run up to him and knock him to the ground and start punching him and dragging him away. He screams "Leave me alone, please, I was just standing there!" They're plainclothesmen. I yell "Come on, there's just two of them. Let's get him back." Five of us start to run towards them. I am terribly frightened and I don't know what I'm going to do when I get there. Someone behind us throws an empty Seven-up can which bounces off one of the plainclothesmen's heads. Right off his grey crew cut. He yells "Get back or somebody's going to get killed," and reaches to his side, pulls out a gun and waves it at us. I yell "He's got a gun" and bolt away, not knowing whether or not I am going to hear a bang.

I stop alongside a friend who was in on this episode. We light cigarettes. I'm thinking it's lucky my cigarettes are Marlboros, with the crush-proof box, or they would have been ruined by now. He tells me that our mutual acquaintance Larry was clubbed inside his dorm, on the mezzanine floor, as he stood with his key in his door. We laugh about what an amazing loser Larry is, how that was bound to happen to him. I'm thinking it's great that we're able to stand and joke with each other right after we almost got killed.

A bunch of plainclothesmen rush our group and we run into Carmen Hall. As soon as they leave, we come out again, and they rush us again, and we come out again. It reminds me of a game of red-light.

One time we pile up at the door and one of us doesn't quite make it in. Three cops grab him in the doorway and try to drag him away, but we grab him too and try to pull him in. It's a stalemate; he's bent over, not going either way. One of the cops takes the opportunity to punch him again and again in the back of the head. I cup my hands over the back of his head. The puncher grabs my arm and bends it around the door frame and yells "Let's drag this guy out," which they start to do. I extend my free arm in and say as clearly as I can, "Take my hand, they're dragging me out." Someone does and everyone gets in. The kid who was pounded is standing there saying "Whew," that's all. I can't figure out how he can continue to exist, how he can breath in and breath out and beat his heart and

393

just continue as a person. I don't see how anyone can be in such danger without ending his self. For my part, I put my face in my hands and think, "I am putting my face in my hands."

At 8 A.M. I go to bed.

Nicola Chiaromonte

Nicola Chiaromonte was born in southern Italy in 1905. Before World War II he wrote for the important literary magazine Solaria *and for the underground anti-Fascist journal* Giustizia e Libertà. *On account of his opposition to Fascism, he lived from 1934 to 1946 in France and the United States. He has been for a long while the theater critic of* Il Mondo, *the liberal weekly published in Rome, and with Ignazio Silone was editor, from its inception, of the monthly cultural review* Tempo Presente. *He has also been a steady contributor of literary and political pieces to* Partisan Review *in New York and* Encounter *in London. His books are* Il Tempo della malafede *(1953), on Communist intellectuals, and* La Situazione drammatica *(1960), a collection of his dramatic criticism. Many of Chiaromonte's writings in English have been in the form of "letters" or reports from the Continent. The present one appeared in* Encounter, *July 1968.*

LETTER FROM ROME

Some three years ago, in an article in *Tempo Presente* called "Rebellious Youth," I came to the conclusion that only one thing seems to have shaken the political inertia that characterises our age and aroused political passions and a real sense of participation: and that is the idea of freedom. The Hungarian rising, directed by intellectuals and fought by the young and the very young in the name of unadorned freedom, was the main and most memorable example of this. Before that there was Poznan and the "Polish October," where in the main intellectuals and young people were demanding their freedom. In

Italy, there was July 1960; more significantly, there was the upsurge of action and opinion in France against the Algerian war. Then, in July '63, there was the miners' strike in Asturias in which the demand for freedom of association and of speech was raised before the question of wages, and was much the more important demand. And I also dealt at length in that article with the revolt of American students against racialism and the war in Viet Nam.

It was perfectly clear that freedom was again the leaven in the political struggle, and that the young find themselves quite naturally in the vanguard of the movement, without waiting for the politicians to finish their calculations, organise their tactics, and put out their slogans.

But I felt that it was not enough to rejoice that a wave of rebellion (or rebelliousness), rather than some "realistic" conformity, seemed to have engulfed young people immediately after the war: "We must also consider each manifestation of rebellion case by case. . . ."

All right, then: let us consider what is happening in this rebellion of the young—and not only of students. Since 1965 it has spread across Europe, indeed across the world, from North and South America to China; in China, with the approval of its intellectual hot-heads and hangers-on, the remarkable event known as the "Cultural Revolution" has increasingly appeared to be an astute operation intended to unleash the rebelliousness of the young against the party machine, to the greater glory and support of Chairman Mao, and with the army to prevent things getting too much out of hand. In Europe, the young are in revolt in nearly all the countries of both East and West, including Scandinavia and Britain on the one hand, and the Soviet Union and Poland on the other.

But we must distinguish between these various forms of rebellion and consider their differences.

First, the Russian students and intellectuals protesting against the régime's repressive refusal to listen and the open revolt of students, teachers and intellectuals in Warsaw to the cry of "freedom," are not at all the same as the uprisings of students in Turin, Milan, Florence and Rome against their respective vice-chancellors, teachers and ministers, even though the Italian students may challenge the whole of society in their slogans and manifestos, may talk about a "total rejection," refuse what they call "concessions," and declare their wish to change everything from top to bottom, independently, with their own methods and according to their own standards. The freedom the Polish students are demanding is a clear, specific challenge to a clearly and specifically oppressive régime; whereas the "global confrontation" the Italian and German students are talking about is a formula as vague as it is violent. If we are speaking of the universities, then a challenge to their academic power means at most asking for the students' direct participation in discussions and decisions that affect their studies. Whereas if we are speaking of society as a whole —"the famous consumer goods society"—then "total rejection" means rebellion against everything and against nothing.

In fact, apart from their extremely significant refusal to accept guidance from the political parties, what the rebellious Italian students seem to be protesting against is mainly the war in Viet Nam, and what they approve of are men and events wholly alien to the situation, both educational and political, in Italy—men like Guevara and Castro, or exotic figures like Mao Tse-tung. Freedom, in fact, is the last thing they consider or even care about.

On the other hand, apart from violent clashes with the police (sometimes deliberately sought), and painfully confused stands taken by members of the academic establishment—who are either warily submissive or toughly determined (and occasionally both, in quick succession)—the students have done as they pleased and continue to do so. One is still waiting to see what direction their revolt is going to take and what objects it really aims at, and not merely who is going to lead it and in what direction. But it is obvious that there is no question of seeking freedom—rather its opposite: anger at the lack of authority, and at the lack of any established order that commands respect.

We have yet to see what the Italian students are capable of doing, after this great wave of revolt, in which indignation against the scandalous conditions of the universities and of schooling in general in Italy, and against the brutality and madness of the American war in Viet Nam, went with a cult (not unlike that of film star fans) of Ché Guevara and an enthusiasm for Mao Tse-tung, a dictator and thinker whose authority stems more from his power of command than from any qualities of his thought. It is impossible not to see in this revolt, however, an urge towards violence fatally combined with the idea of obtaining, at once and through direct action, what it is impossible to obtain at once and through direct action—namely, the reform of education and the reform of society. Impossible, that is, without total guidance by the hand of a dictator—and where that leads we know all too well.

The Italian students may have been doing as they pleased, but they have used this freedom of theirs for serious ends—or at least they are meant to be serious. Their revolt was a result of their anger towards and contempt for a so-called ruling class that primarily rules the affairs of the political parties into which it is divided and subdivided; and in this it was fully justified. But until now theirs have been mass riots, in which the voice of reason was drowned; and anyone who wanted to know what the whole thing was about had to go and listen to individuals, one by one.

But why was the students' revolt so confused, both in its ideas (or rather in its slogans) and in its behaviour? It was justified by the facts, in particular by the Italian Parliament's shameful refusal to pass the reform which would have abolished the most scandalous privilege in present-day Italian universities—the right of Deputies, Senators, and Ministers to hold an academic chair purely for prestige. Was it because of their youth? We are told to understand and not discourage the muddled enthusiasm of the young (because if we discourage it this means we want everything to continue as it is: corrupt, inert, torpid). And so we should, on condition that we reject absolutely the idea that the young must be right simply because they are young. It was on this principle that Fascism advanced, and something equally evil might even grow out of it today, whether its label is socialist, anarchist, or simply humanitarian. We have already had the startling spectacle of teachers in their fifties rushing to join the rioting young, urging them on to the "total rejection" and even to violence, in the certainty that they are marching with History.

But the young are in revolt not merely to reform the universities. As they themselves admit, their protest goes further than that. Indeed, it seems likely that the wretched conditions of education in Italy today, the teaching cliques, the academic charlatanism, the physical impossibility of following courses and even of seeing the professor's face except at exams, are all secondary reasons, and almost excuses for rebellion, not its primary cause. That lies elsewhere, and it is, I think, very simple: it is the fact that the young—those born after 1940—find themselves living in a society that neither commands nor deserves respect, a society whose authority merely weighs on them and so seems to license every kind of lawlessness and rebellion, open and covert. This is so from the top of the social hierarchy (if there is still such a thing, apart from a hierarchy of power) down to the forms of political life and the circumstances of everyday Italian life. But the most irresponsible and corrupt group of all is, I would say unhesitatingly, today's intellectuals: they follow the crowd instead of setting an example, quibble instead of thinking, offer political factionalism instead of critical guidance, hold forth on undigested questions of ideology, and, in fact, instead of acting as the voice of a people of which they are part, themselves make up a special party, one which furthers their own particular aims and needs.

It is against this lack of moral guidance and an authority worth respecting that young people are rebelling today, all over the world;

397

and it is a serious matter, not to be answered by police attacks or tricky manoeuvres. This explains why, in the absence of anyone or anything to respect—and of an authority that can be either respected or hated, but which at least exists—the Italian young, like the young in France or Germany, create exotic myths out of Ché and Ho and Mao. These myths are by their very nature either empty or totalitarian: they lead either to nothing or else to mass demagogy and, sooner or later, to a technocratic authoritarianism cloaked in ideology. This authoritarianism—which is today's, *not* yesterday's or the day before yesterday's, which is generally called up as a bogey—does not even demand a charismatic leader: all it needs is the existing state of affairs, the endless complexity, the vast inertia, and the enormous, almost supernatural authority of industrial society; a society borne up not so much by the *capitalists,* as the current cliché maintains, as by the very ideas to which those in revolt have appealed. For has modern man, in his collective existence, laid claim to any god or ideal but the god of possession and enjoyment and the limitless satisfaction of material needs? Has he put forward any reason for working but the reward of pleasure and prosperity? Has he, in fact, evolved anything but this "consumer society" that is so easily and so falsely repudiated?

In these conditions it is suspiciously romantic to talk about "revolution." How will it be achieved except by a *coup d'état,* executed by a highly-placed few, and in secret? . . .

Are the young mistaken, then, in their revolt? No. But neither are they right. You can talk about right only when you talk reasonably, person to person. A rioting crowd never reasons, nor can it ever be right: it is an explosion, and nothing more, an event that may have its proper causes and reasons, and so logically cannot be either approved or disapproved except in detail, case by case, individual by individual. You do not approve of an earthquake, you try to clear things up after it. But as far as the earthquake of which the revolt of the young is only *one* symptom is concerned, the present Italian ruling classes (indeed, the present rulers of the world in general, for the whole business is universal) show no sign of clearing anything up, only of aggravating the difficulties.

If there is a remedy at all, it lies elsewhere, and is a very long-term one. In my view, it consists of a determined secession from a society (or rather from a state of affairs, since "society" implies a community and a purpose, which is exactly what collective life nowadays lacks) which is not actually evil by nature, indeed may well be improved; but is neither good nor bad, only indifferent, which is the worst thing of all and the most deadening. From this society—from this state of affairs—people must detach themselves, must become resolute "heretics." They must detach themselves quietly, without shouting or riots, indeed in silence and secrecy; not alone but in groups, in real "societies" that will create, as far as is possible, a life that is independent and wise, not utopian or phalansterian, in which each man learns to govern himself first of all and to behave rightly towards others, and works at his own job according to the standards of the craft itself, standards that in themselves are the simplest and strictest of moral principles and by their very nature cut out deception and prevarication, charlatanism and the love of power and possession. This would not mean detaching oneself from either the life of like-minded others, or politics in the real sense of the word. It would be, all the same, a non-rhetorical form of "total rejection." The French student revolt by sharply attacking the principle of centralised authority and demanding a reorganisation of collective life from the ground up has raised precisely this question.

John Holt

The essay we print below first appeared in the Yale Alumni Magazine, *November 1969. For further information about the author, see page 111.*

LETTER FROM BERKELEY

I spent last winter at the University of California at Berkeley. I'd been invited by their English Department to teach some writing courses during the winter quarter to a group of students almost all of whom were working for teachers' credentials. I lived in the faculty club on campus and was therefore very close to, though not very actively involved in, the student strike and the uprisings and riots that followed it. Very soon after the strike—it was really a boycott, but since students everywhere call this kind of operation a strike I will use that word—my students and I decided to move our classes off campus, not so much because we strongly or actively supported the strike as because we did not want to appear to be opposing it or flaunting it.

Also, some of my students were very strongly in support of the strike and to continue to meet on campus would have made it impossible for them to go on attending the class, which they very much wanted to do.

When the strike began, I was more irritated than sympathetic. One day the black students announced a set of "final demands"; a day or two later they announced the beginning of the strike. I was walking toward Wheeler Hall, where the department office was, and first saw pickets—not many of them—in front of some of the doors. Instantly I felt myself put in a difficult position and resented it. I have long since lost any feeling I might have had about the sanctity of picket lines. Still, it seemed to me that I was being asked either to join the picket lines or consider myself an ally of the university, Governor Reagan, and all they stood for. I found myself thinking angrily that, ordinarily, before a union calls a strike it gives its membership a chance to hear, discuss, and vote on the issues. I had been given no such chance; indeed, I found out after a while that the strike leaders had deliberately decided not to present a referendum on their demands to the university community, sure that it would have been decisively outvoted. At that time, this made me angry. It does not any more.

Immediately my students, themselves holding many different views, asked me what I thought about the strike, and in our discussion of these matters I got a good deal of education myself. I began by saying that there was much in the demands of the Third World students that I sympathized with; that I thought some of their demands had consequences which they had not really considered; that I resented being told that I must actively support a strike when I had nothing to say either about calling it or about the terms under which it was called. I also felt that, by the way in which they called the strike and by the violence—not very extensive, but real enough—which the strikers used against people and property in the early days of the strike, they were hurting their cause. It had seemed to me that the strikers were using or trying to use me and other members of the university community as hostages, perhaps as some kind of collective battering ram against the university administration, and I resented this. I found myself thinking wryly that it was easy from a distance to feel sympathetic to the rebels at Columbia who had seized buildings. But when I was compelled—against my will and at a time when I felt that I had other things to think about—to make hard decisions about whose side I was on, I did not like it much, and felt it an imposition and injustice.

This was my position in late January when the strike began. By the middle of March, when my classes came to an end, and everyone agreed to cool the strike until the end of exams and the beginning of the spring term, my opinions on all of these matters had changed. I found myself agreeing very strongly with virtually everything that the Third World group was demanding, and, what is more important, feeling not only that their tactics had been wise and effective, but that virtually no other options had been open to them. It seemed unarguably clear that only by taking action as they did could they have persuaded not only the university administration but the faculty and the student body at large to take their problems seriously and put them in the center of their consciousness—where indeed they rightly belong. It seemed to me clear, from the way in which the university spoke and acted during the crisis, that it had not dealt in the past and would not in the future deal seriously or honestly with the Third World students, unless compelled to by the kind of action they took. In short, it seems to me that when universities say to students, "It is wrong and foolish of you to try to get us to discuss these issues and make what you think are necessary changes by making trouble; the thing to do is sit down and discuss this quietly and rationally," they are either deceiving themselves or lying outright.

I may be wrong about this, but I don't think I am. I don't mean to argue the point here. What seems to me significant is that the events themselves that took place on the campus during the seven or eight weeks in question changed my mind, and the minds of a considerable number of other faculty members and a large part of the student body. In short, it is the way in which the university dealt with the strike, far more than anything that the strikers said or did, that convinced large numbers of people who had initially been unsympathetic that the strikers were right or, perhaps, that the university was wrong.

Tactically, the university made serious mistakes. It brought police on the campus before it needed to. It brought in police over whose actions it had no control, when it might have hired private agents or perhaps even deputized order-keepers from among its own people. It brought in too many police and kept them around when there was no longer any need for them. It allowed police to use the campus and, far worse, the administration building itself, as a base of operations. It repeated these errors over and over again. Instead of at any moment calling for enough police to deal with whatever situation might be at hand, and then sending them home when the particular situation had been taken care of, it acted as if it felt that the presence of many police on campus would prevent incidents from occurring. Of course, it did quite the opposite. Moreover, it soon created a situation in which the police and their politically ambitious leaders realized

401

that the campus was a kind of battlefield where they could wage, for private or political reasons, the kind of war against young people which they were glad to wage on any pretense.

The university talked as stupidly as it acted. I think that Hayakawa of San Francisco State is a bad, ambitious, and dangerous man, but there was at least something refreshing in the honest and sometimes hysterical anger with which he faced and shouted down his opponents. They must at least have had the feeling that they were talking to a live human being, bad as he might be. The University of California's pronouncements on the strike were always written or spoken in a kind of bureaucratese which made one feel that what they were saying must be lies, because if they were telling the truth they wouldn't need or want to talk that way.

I think in fact that the university administration was probably more sympathetic to the Third World demands than many of their own faculty or than the regents, the governor, or the people of California. But even when they were telling the truth, they *sounded* as if they were lying, and as time went on they grew less and less truthful. It is not just as an English teacher, a writer, or a lover of the English language that I say that if you want to talk seriously to people who are angry and distrustful, you must speak in the plainest and most direct English possible. Academics are so accustomed to use language as a kind of display, like the tail feathers on a peacock or the stripes on a naval officer's sleeve, that it will be hard for them to learn this lesson.

Something on the order of 90 or 95 per cent of the violence that took place on campus was initiated by the police. We have learned by now, as a result of uncountable experiences in the past few years, that when police stand for long in the presence of people whom they dislike and fear, they cannot be trusted to remain orderly. Indeed, it is only rarely, and with the greatest difficulty, that they can be compelled to do so. One of the things a policeman learns very quickly is whom he may safely hit on the head with his stick and whom he may not. Police now recognize that within every part of the country young people, students, hippies, and radicals are the safest targets they have—safer even than blacks. Any university president who calls police onto his campus knows that they will use far more violence against students than the situation demands, that they will indeed use the situation as a pretext for expressing their own rage, and that their superiors, far from trying to control them in such instances, will encourage them as a way of gaining further political support and power within the community.

The way in which these large gatherings became violent was usually the same. There would be large numbers of students gathered in the plaza in front of Sproul Hall, the administration building. Facing them would be squads of police with blue motorcycle helmets and plastic visors. At some point the police would begin to make what is usually called "a sweep," that is, they would move toward and into a large group of people and, at first prodding and pushing with their clubs, try to clear a path. The path might not be needed, they might not in fact be opening the way *to* anything; the point was that they were simply getting people out of the way. As long as the crowd was not too thick and there was plenty of room to move in front of them, the crowd would often disperse and reform behind the police. But the police know that large numbers of people do not move very quickly, so eventually they were sure of finding some people who could not get out of their way fast enough. When this happened, they had the excuse they needed to begin clubbing. Nobody who saw them on the campus doubted that their intent was to provoke violence. A rumor, probably well founded and certainly widely believed, was that the number of police on campus grew larger and larger because policemen were volunteering for this duty.

On many occasions the police did not even need a pretext to start clubbing people. My office was on the fourth floor of Wheeler Hall and overlooked Sproul Plaza. One day a fellow faculty member and friend was looking down at the scene when he saw, in many parts of the large crowd gathered below, plainclothes policemen suddenly take out blackjacks and begin striking, *from behind,* people standing in front of them.

One day, one of my students, a very pretty girl from a rich California suburb, said, obviously in a good deal of agitation, that she wanted to speak to me. I said something about office hours on Wednesday and Friday, but she was in a greater hurry than that, so we arranged to meet at lunch. The following day she appeared, still agitated, trembling uncontrollably, scarcely coherent. She told me in bits and pieces the following story.

The papers had for a day or two been full of reports of the brutal beating by the police of a Los Angeles reporter named Vaughn. While standing, equipped with the proper press credentials, in front of the administration building, he had been suddenly set upon by four policemen, who clubbed him to the ground and beat him with their clubs as he lay there. Many people—hundreds—saw this. A student was standing not far away. Unable to tolerate any longer what he was seeing he rushed at the police and tried to push or drag them away from the fallen Vaughn. Suddenly four policemen—I'm not sure whether they were the same or different ones—knocked him to the ground and began beating him. One knocked all his front teeth out with a club. After a while they dragged him—blood pouring from his mouth, screaming in mingled pain and terror, into the administration building itself.

What I learned from my student was that the student who had been beaten, a friend of hers, was himself not political, and was not involved in the strike, and was not even a supporter of it. I'm not sure why he was there; in any case, he had a right to be. When he was being beaten, she herself was not very far away. She was quite naturally too terrified to try to help him—how could she have helped? —and she watched, helpless, as her good friend was dragged away and out of sight into the building.

She was shaking as she told me all this. She kept saying, and in the context the words sounded ludicrously inadequate, that she felt so frustrated, so frustrated. We are so accustomed to hearing the word used in trivial contexts that it is easy to forget how accurately it describes how she must have felt. This was clearly a situation in which something had to be done, yet there was nothing to do. Her friend was down on the ground, being beaten, with every possibility of being very seriously injured, and to whom could she call for help? Where was law and order? Where, in this emergency, were all the people whom she had grown up believing she could depend on?

She told me that night, still in terrible agitation, still looking for help and support and sympathy, she had called up her family. Her father's response to her tale was that if her friend had been minding his own business, nothing would have happened to him. I found myself thinking of Kitty Genovese, murdered—over a period of about a half an hour—outside her apartment in Long Island, while 30 or 40 neighbors, seeing and hearing everything, did nothing. What torrents of moral indignation have since then been poured over that scene.

In one of my classes another girl, the daughter of a rich family in a big West Coast city, told me of what might be called her Unsentimental Education. She had gone, a few years before, to watch a big demonstration at the induction center in Oakland. She did not go as a participant or active supporter. She was by no means then convinced of the rightness of the demonstrators' cause or the wisdom of their actions. Why did she go? The question is important. Many of her friends were there; some were quite closely involved; she wanted to see what happened to them; more important, since such demonstrations are a vital part of today's history, she wanted, like any curious and intelligent person, to be present while this particular episode in the drama of history was being written. Who, given the opportunity to travel back in time and watch it, would pass up the Boston Tea Party?

She was standing in the crowd, not carrying a placard, not obstructing the door, not doing anything. There was confused and violent action, police rushed from all directions, and as she put it, the next thing she knew, she was being dragged by her feet, just like Christopher Robin's bear, bump bump bump, down the steps into the basement of the police station. Today, only a couple of years later, and still in her very early twenties, she is a radical—tough-minded, unsentimental, untrusting, unforgiving, utterly determined to shake to the foundations the existing order of things.

The universities seem genuinely surprised and puzzled that bringing police on the campus should, as it always does, enormously increase the size and touchiness of student demonstrations, instead of doing away with them. They ask, like the perplexed father of my student in his comfortable suburb, "Why, when these students know that there are police standing around there just waiting to hit them on the head, do they persist in going where the police are? Why don't they go about their own business quietly, go to classes, do the assignments, take the tests? When being bad brings such swift and hard punishment, why don't they be good?"

It is a real question, a serious one, an important one. When I first came to Berkeley I was not sure myself why the presence of police on campus attracted crowds of students like honey collecting flies. I came to understand only gradually.

Perhaps I've already suggested the reasons. The students gather where the police are, first, because their friends are there, because they feel a solidarity with them, because they want to see what happens to them and share in it. They have a sense that history is being written at such places, and every whole man wants to be a part of the history of his own times. Also, they go as witnesses. They know that the police can be counted on to lie—and, in general, authority supports their lies—about what happens at these occasions. Thus the University of California, after a very considerable amount of police violence, could issue a statement from the Chancellor's office—heaven only knows who writes these statements—that the reports of police violence had not been supported by its own observers, two or three of them, and would in any case be taken up and dealt with in the usual way by competent authorities. In other words, if a policeman hits you on the head with his club, report him to police headquarters and they will conduct an official and impartial investigation as a result of which the true facts will be made known. This is really what the university said, though not so simply or directly. So the students know that the only way to be sure about what happens on these occasions is to be there.

405

There is more to it than that. I avoided the center of the campus at times of the day when there was likely to be violence. My reason or excuse was that I had not really come to the university to take part in such things, that this was not my first interest, that I was not a permanent member of the university community, and therefore not committed or involved, and that my first responsibility at least during this quarter was to the students who had signed up for my classes. This excuse seemed good enough at the time. At any rate, I was able to skirt round the center of the campus when there was trouble, although as it overflowed into the adjoining Berkeley streets it grew harder to get away from it, and on a couple of occasions I had my first good whiff of the latest model tear gas, which is quite remarkable stuff.

But as time went on, as the violence mounted, I grew more and more uneasy about staying out of the center of things. It was fortunate for me that I was only there for a quarter and that, as the crisis reached its peak, final exams for the quarter came along and everyone agreed to cool things for a while. Had I been there for another month, and had the violence continued to mount, I would have felt more and more strongly that my staying out of it was simply an act of cowardice, that what primarily moved me was a desire to stay out of trouble, that I was abandoning and betraying the strikers with whom I was feeling deeper and deeper sympathy. I've often been moved by the old hymn, "Once to every man and nation/comes the moment to decide/in the strife twixt truth and falsehood/for the good or evil side." Feeling as I did about the crisis, I could find less and less excuse for staying from the action, and I really doubt whether my conscience would have allowed me to take the easy way out much longer. This would have been even more true as more and more of my students got directly involved.

To all this, the crackpot realists (as C. Wright Mills called them) will snort that it is always possible to raise the price of public opposition high enough so that people will stop opposing. If the government, like the government of Mexico, brings troops with machine guns onto campuses, and orders them to fire at crowds of students that do not disperse, there will be no crowds. It is just a question of raising the ante high enough to make your opponent drop out of the game.

The argument has a certain internal logic. I once read about a general—true, fictional?—who in an argument said angrily that it was a lot of nonsense that you couldn't kill an idea, all you had to do was to find everybody who believed in that idea and shoot them. It sounds workable, and it is hard to see the flaw in it.

It would seem that if you have very much more force at your disposal

406

than your opponent you can eventually raise the ante high enough to make him do your bidding. But this depends on a number of things being true. There's no use saying to someone, "Do what I tell you or I will kill you," if he would rather be dead than do what you tell him. Nor is there any use if he thinks that, having by the use of this threat made him yield once, you will simply use it again and again with no limit. He then feels that since he must resist and die sometime, better to do it sooner than later.

What our romantic lovers of violence—General LeMay, Hayakawa, the Pentagon, many university administrators, some students, and who knows how large a percentage of the American people—forget is that the aim of violence, even of war, is reconciliation, peace, accord. You fight your opponent in order to persuade him to stop fighting, to win him over to your way of looking at things, to persuade him that whatever state of affairs you have in mind for him is better than the state of affairs he will be in if he resists you. You must, therefore, hold out a tolerable alternative. But this is what our universities and our society, in their struggle with the young, quite simply cannot do. They cannot say, "Go along with us, do what we say, and we will give you a world to live in which—even if it is not perfect, even if it is not in accord with your hopes and dreams—is at least something." We cannot say that. We have no alternatives. We offer nothing at all. My sister once wisely said of one of her sons, "He may not know what he wants, but he knows what he can't stand." To our students and young, who cannot tolerate our society as it is, we only offer more and more of what they can't stand. Bigger, noisier, dirtier cities, more war, more exploitation, more corruption, more cruelty, more ugliness, more depersonalization, and at the end of it, the virtual certainty that if the world is not destroyed by war it will be made uninhabitable by the waste products of an ever larger gross industrial product.

By making the penalties ever higher, we may be able to prevent certain kinds of opposition and rebellion. But this is folly. What makes us think that we will like better what comes next? We scream in pain and indignation about the students breaking the rules. But really they are sticking quite closely to the rules. When they seize university buildings or march around campuses talking about demands, they are not really imposing ultimata, they are still accepting the idea of the university as a community in which problems can be discussed and worked out, with the important difference that they want to be in on the discussions and decisions. It's absolute nonsense to claim that the students are out to destroy the university. Indeed, they love the university—at least in a kind of ideal form which exists mostly in their imaginations and in its own propaganda—in a way that the university scarcely loves itself. I met this winter, during my stay in Berkeley, Mario Savio and Michael Rossman, two of the leaders of the Free Speech Movement at Berkeley several years ago. What astonished me more than anything else was the degree to which they are frustrated academics. There is nothing that these two young men would really rather be than professors in a university that they could trust and feel proud of. If we convince students, as we may if we send enough of them to jail for long enough, that the university cannot really be dealt with or reformed, that there is no chance of ever getting it to take students seriously, to say nothing of the problems of mankind, then they may seriously think about how to destroy it, and when they do its days are numbered.

The fatal flaw in the arguments of the crackpot realists is that our society is terribly vulnerable to internal attack and disruption. It is a dreadful mistake to take the angry rhetoric of our black power leaders and student radicals for reality. They really have *not* given up on society; they really *are* thinking of ways to make it human, decent, viable—none of which it is right now. Whatever they may *say*, they are not seriously thinking about how to bring it down in ruins. This would not be a hard thing to do. I have occasionally played the game of thinking myself into the mind of an angry guerrilla, and the things I can think of in only a short space of time scare me enough so that I don't want to tell anyone else about them. If a hundred thousand people—or perhaps even ten thousand, or a thousand—with determination, knowledge, and a certain macabre sense of humor were to give their serious attention to making our highly complicated and vulnerable society grind to a halt, they could probably do it quite easily. But they would have to be serious—that is to say, they would really have to have given up the hope of making it into a good society. The young people have not given up. If we want them to, all we have to do is raise the stakes high enough.

Not long after arriving at Berkeley I was invited by a new friend on the faculty to go with him to a noon performance in the university music theater of Purcell's *Dido and Aeneas*. This was produced, played, sung, and danced entirely by the students. It was a beautiful production, up to the highest professional standards, imaginatively, wittily, and convincingly done. I left the hall with my heart swelling and my feet scarcely touching the ground. I looked about the campus, which, particularly in that section, is very beautiful, with rolling grass and lovely trees, and I had a vision of what that university might be. Seeing the vision, like my friends from the Free Speech Movement, I fell in love with it, and at the same time realized how very far from its promise and potential the university had fallen. I looked about the buildings and the campus and thought what an extraordinary gathering there was here of human knowledge, skill, and talent. How much the university might be, how close it was even now to being a kind of distillation of everything we mean by civilization in its best sense, a collection of so much of the finest things that men have thought and done. I thought what a lovely thing it would be if we could have, here and in many places, such a gathering of man's finest works, and people who knew them and understood them and loved them and could use them, a pool of wealth for anyone and everyone to dip into as they needed or wanted. How lovely it was too to walk in broad spaces between buildings which if not always handsome were at least not covered by neon signs and constant appeals to people's greed, envy, and fear. I thought of the streets of downtown Berkeley itself, of the people who lived there—and I often thought of this when the police were on campus—and reflected how seldom if ever in their lives they must have had the opportunity even of walking in so spacious and so gracious a place. Why shouldn't the university be like a park, but a park of the mind and hands and spirit as well as a park in space? Why not a place to stretch and refresh the soul as well as the legs?

And with this thought I became painfully aware, then and for the rest of my stay, of the signs sprinkled all over the campus—THIS IS THE PROPERTY OF THE REGENTS AND THE STATE OF CALIFORNIA—something full of talk about trespassers being prosecuted and so forth. I thought to myself, why should an institution supported by the public funds not be open to the public? By what right is it run like a private club?

And I was very painfully reminded, then and later, of the mean-spirited and bureaucratic way in which the university deals with its own students. Just to read the notices circulated by the university and pinned on its bulletin boards is enough to make the heart sink. Not a speck of grace, wit, or courtesy. Nothing really different from what one would expect to find in a large corporation or even the army itself. I thought of the classes, the assignments, the tests, the threats, the grading, the invidious comparisons, the setting of student against student, the treating of knowledge and skill like some saleable commodity, and for the rest of my visit I was horrified and saddened by the distance between the promise of what that university and all universities might be and what they had become and were.

Even the minority of adults—and I fear it is a fairly small one—that does not deeply hate and fear the young, that feels at least somewhat sympathetic and benevolent, finds it hard to understand what they are so angry about. Or, why they are so angry about what they are angry about. Their anger seems disproportionate. Not long ago I thought it was myself.

It is impossible any longer to say to young people that this is a benevolent or trustworthy or even in any reasonable degree sane society. We talk, at least to the students, as if this society had nothing much wrong with it, and as if its institutions, used in the prescribed ways, were perfectly capable of correcting what is wrong. But the students do not find out from SDS alone in what desperate shape our society and civilization find themselves, and how little idea anyone in the older generation has of how they may be saved. They find this out in our TV, newspapers, and mass media. Nobody seriously believes that we are likely to solve, or are even moving towards a solution, of any of the most urgent problems of our times—war, the proliferation of atomic, chemical, and bacteriological weapons, overpopulation, poverty, the destruction of the earth's natural resources, the degradation of man's physical and biological environment, the fossilization and depersonalization of his political and economic institutions, his increasing alienation, boredom, anger. We do not think any more that we can really make the world a fit and happy and beautiful place for people to live; we scarcely think that we can keep it a place where people can live at all. Only when we talk to students do we talk as if these problems were not real or serious or urgent. Only to the young do we keep saying that daddy knows best. But it is no good; they hear us talking to each other.

Nothing worth saving, or worth having, in the university is seriously threatened by the demands of even the most radical students. Indeed, in their efforts to get agreement from the university, the Third World people at Berkeley very quickly watered down their original demands to the point where I, for one, felt they were nowhere near radical enough.

One of the student demands that most terrified the university, and at first most puzzled and startled me, was the demand for open admissions.

During the strike I thought about this a great deal, and it is worth saying again that it was the fact of the strike, and only that, that made me think about it. Indeed, I felt the strike as a kind of pressure on my mind, often an unwanted pressure. I often wished angrily that they would get the thing settled and over with so I could again think about what I wanted to think about. It was not really until the strike ended, and even after I left Berkeley altogether that I began to realize that what the strikers wanted me to think about were indeed the things that I ought to be thinking about. There is no more crucial question

410

in our society than this question of relationships between the old and the young, between educational institutions and their students, between the people who hold effective power in our society in and out of universities and the young people who increasingly demand to be given more and more of it. The revolt of the young, or the battle between young and old (look at it how you will) is the most important question of our time, and on the way we resolve it or fail to resolve it will probably depend, more than on any other one thing, our society's prospects for survival.

But I was puzzled by the proposal for open admissions. I found myself thinking, if anybody could get into the university, why wouldn't ten thousand, twenty thousand, a hundred thousand people come here, and if they did, what would the university do with them? And I began thinking freshly about a question that people have been asking me many times in my lecturing on education. Hundreds of teachers and parents have said to me, "If children are educated the way you want, if they can learn whatever they like in the way it seems best to them, how are the colleges going to solve their admissions problem?" My answer was usually that I did not consider the solving of the college admissions problem a high priority question, for me or even for the elementary or secondary schools of this country. I usually followed this by suggesting one or more ways in which colleges might, by my lights, improve their admissions procedures so as to make places available to students of a much wider variety of talents and backgrounds. But I accepted almost without realizing it the assumption on the part of my hearers that a college must make decisions about who *can* come in and who *cannot*. After all, their facilities are limited, aren't they? They can't take in everyone, can they?

Then one day I found myself thinking of the Boston Public Library, which I go to quite often, more to borrow classical records than books. Here is what must certainly be called an educational institution. Yet it does not make decisions and judgments about who can come in and who cannot, and—what is more important—who is good enough to come in and who is not. It simply says like libraries everywhere, "Here are some facilities—books, records, films, exhibits. If you want, come in and use them, as much as you want, as long as you want." I thought of many other educational institutions that serve society, none of which exclude anybody, and it suddenly occurred to me that the admissions problem of our universities is not a real problem but a manufactured one—that is, it exists because the universities want it to exist, not because it has to.

Why shouldn't a school, college, or university be like a museum, a library, a concert hall, a lecture hall, a sports facility? Why shouldn't it, like them, say to the public, "Here is what we have to offer you;

here are the possibilities. If they appeal to you, come in and use them, for as little or as long as you like." If more people want to get in than there is room for, let them handle this situation the way a concert hall or theater handles it. Why not hang out a sign saying "Sold Out—next performance tomorrow afternoon, next week, next month, next year." If a student wanted to take a course with Professor So-and-So and there were hundreds of other students wanting to take the same course, why not let him make the kind of choice that someone makes who wants to see a very popular play? Let him either, in effect, wait until there is an opportunity to get in the course, or, if that seems like too long a wait, think about getting the same sort of information or help somewhere else? If I want to see a doctor, and someone says that he has so many patients that I won't be able to see him for four months, the sensible thing to do is find some other doctor, maybe not quite as good but with fewer patients.

Let the student worry about overcrowding. The university can say, we can provide university housing for so many thousand students; after that, people will have to find their own. Large numbers of students at Berkeley and other state universities do in fact live off campus. This often makes housing both scarce and expensive, and this may in turn make a student decide that a particular university is or is not a good place to go. But let this be his worry, not the university's. If the housing, facilities, and courses at one university are terribly crowded so that desirable courses are hard or impossible to get into —as indeed they are now in many cases at places like Berkeley—the student can decide either to try to wait it out or go somewhere else.

Nor is there any necessary reason why universities should worry so about qualifications. This will seem startling at first. But after all, when I borrow a book or record from the Boston Public Library, nobody gives me a quiz to be sure I will understand it. It's up to me to decide how I want to spend my time and to run the risk of wasting it. Similarly, if I go to the Boston Symphony to hear a piece of difficult modern music, nobody examines me in the hall to make sure I'm educated enough to appreciate it. I pay my money and I take my choice. If I go home later feeling angrily that it was a waste of an evening, all right, that's my tough luck. But why should anyone else make this decision for me?

It is perfectly true that universities of this kind would be in important ways different from the ones we know today. The universities as they exist have come to think of themselves as private clubs. They are in a race with each other for prestige, which is quickly translated into money and power—the professor from a prestigious university has more chance of getting a big foundation or government grant than a

412

professor from some less prestigious one. Therefore, they have an interest in convincing the world that their club is harder to get into than anybody else's. At the same time, they try to convince the on-coming generations of students that membership in this club will in the long run prove more valuable—again in terms of power and money—than membership in any other. That is what creates the admissions problem. I make a great many people think that my club is the one to be in, and then I stand at the door and tell large numbers of them that they aren't good enough to get in. On the other hand, since the Boston Public Library isn't trying to convince people that because it is harder to get in it is a "better" library than the New York Public Library, it doesn't have to urge large numbers of people to come to it because it is the best and then put somebody at the door turning most of these people away because they aren't good enough to get in.

The universities that consider themselves superior have an enormous investment, financial and psychological, in the notion of their own superiority, and I don't expect them to give it up quickly or lightly. Given its present concerns, which do not for the most part have much to do with education, I can understand why the University of California should feel threatened by the demand of the Third World students that they open their doors to any Third World people who want to come in, and I can understand their wanting to resist this demand as much as they can. As long as universities are interested in prestige and power, they will want to go on saying to the world that people are coming to them because they are so good, and that they are turning away most of their applicants or supplicants because they in turn are not good enough. But a university truly dedicated to education, to the spreading of knowledge, skill, and—most important—wisdom to all who wanted or needed it, would think in other terms.

People ask, what about the granting of degrees? If anybody who wants can come to a university and there study as much or as little as he wants, how will the university issue its credentials? I don't think the university ought to be in the credentials-granting business. Why should our universities be hiring halls for business and government? It does not seem to me to be a vital or necessary or even acceptable part of the process of education. In any case, people even now take courses in the extension divisions of universities and, depending on the length of the course, get a certain number of credits for work done. There's no reason at all why people could not over a number of years take courses in an assortment of universities, depending on where they lived and who they wanted to study with, and simply have some kind of certificate listing the total number of credits they had collected. In any case, there is plenty of evidence that educational institutions do not and cannot teach competence. Since they don't and can't, why go on any longer with the pretense that an academic degree is a certificate of competence? All it shows or can show is that such-and-such a person has taken so many courses and played the school game for a certain length of time; it says nothing about what he will or will not be able to do in his later working life. The prestige universities have worked hard, for reasons already given, to convince employers and the public at large that their degrees are indeed certificates of exceptional competence and worth. They have to do this to create among the students a demand for these degrees and among employers a demand for holders of them. But it is a con, and there is really nothing in it. If the universities grew interested in education they could give up this fiction along with others.

To the dissatisfied, the universities like to say, in one way or another, "If you don't like our rules, you don't have to play our game." This seems the height of reasonableness. It is nothing of the kind. The universities, which in other circumstances like to think of themselves sometimes as exclusive clubs, sometimes as temples of the higher truth and learning, are comparing themselves here to any kind of store. You go to the supermarket, pay some money, walk out the door with a little food. If you don't like their food or their prices, you don't go to that supermarket; you go to some other. In the same way, the universities say, we offer certain kinds of learning, skill, and money-attracting credentials, in return for a good deal of the students' money and time.

The trouble with this—and it should be obvious to anyone who takes half a minute to think about it—is that the stores we trade at do not exercise the kind of influence and pressure on our lives that the universities, singly and collectively, exercise on the lives of their students. The supermarkets do not post people at the door deciding whether or not I am good enough to get in. Nor do they stamp on my forehead in indelible ink for the world to see whether or not I *was* good enough. They do not grade me like the meat they sell. The universities, on the other hand, do exactly this. They have arrived at a situation, and to a considerable extent contrived it, in which their opinion of a young person determines to a very large degree what that person can or cannot do, will or will not become during the rest of his life. There is probably no other single institution in society, even the armed forces, which has as much to say about our lives. (The armed forces, it is true, can put a man in a position where he may be killed or injured, but once he gets out of their hands, so to speak, they don't cast much of a shadow over his future.)

Our young people start living under the shadow of universities almost as soon as they're born. What the universities want, what they think is good, bad, valuable, valueless, certainly determines and creates the kinds of pressures that our young people live under beginning as early as age three or four. Our young people spend a very large part of their time, even before they go on to college, doing what the schools think the universities want; they go on doing what they want while they're at the universities, which may be anything from four to heaven-knows-how-many years; and, as I said before, they carry on them for the rest of their lives whatever sort of brand the university has chosen to put on them. Their demand—that since universities exercise this enormous control over the lives of their students, students should have something to say about them and the way they are run—seems to me to be altogether right and just. If universities want to say to our young people in effect, "We are just a gathering of scholars doing our thing; please stop bothering us and interfering with us, and let us do our own thing the way we want," then they have got to get their feet off the collective necks of the young and give up the extraordinary and unjustifiable power that they have acquired over their lives.

Bruno Bettelheim

Bruno Bettelheim is a psychoanalyst and teacher who was born and educated in Vienna. He received his Ph.D. from the University of Vienna in 1938, the year Hitler marched into Austria; he was then imprisoned in concentration camps at both Dachau and Buchenwald, an experience described in The Informed Heart *(1960). In 1939 he managed to come to the United States and he became a citizen in 1944. He has been teaching at the University of Chicago since 1944, where he is now the Rowley Distinguished Service Professor of Education. He is perhaps best known for his pioneering work with autistic children as head of the University of Chicago's Sonia Shankman Orthogenic School. The application of psychoanalysis to social problems, particularly to the rearing of children, has been a steady concern that forms the basis for many of his books. These include* Love Is Not Enough—The Treatment of Emotionally Disturbed Children *(1950),* Truants from Life *(1955),* Dialogues with Mothers *(1962),* The Empty Fortress *(1967), and* The Children of the Dream *(1969), a study of child-rearing practices in the kibbutz. In recent years he*

has become an outspoken critic of some aspects of student protest.
We print below an article from Change in Higher Education
(May–June 1969), based on a statement submitted by the author
to the House Special Subcommittee on Education, March 20, 1969.

THE ANATOMY OF ACADEMIC DISCONTENT

While history does not repeat itself, and while the present situation
in the United States is radically different from that of pre-Hitler Germany, some similarities between the present student rebellion in this
country and what happened in the German universities to spearhead
Hitler's rise to power are nevertheless striking.   Politically, of course,
the German student rebels embraced the extreme right, while here
the dissenters embrace the extreme left, but what is parallel is the
determination to bring down the establishment.   In Germany the philosophy which gained the rebels a mass following was racist and
directed against a discriminated minority (the Jews), while here the
radical students intend to *help* a discriminated minority.   This is an
important difference, but it does not change the parallel that universities then and now were forced to make decisions with respect to
the race of students, rather than on the basis of disregard of racial
origin.   To use only one example, German universities began to cave
in when students coerced faculties to appoint professorships in *Rassen-
wissenschaft;* that is, professorships devoted to teaching the special aspects, merits and achievements of one race as opposed to others, rather
than teaching the contributions to knowledge, whatever the origins of
the contributors.

Professor Walter Z. Laqueur (*Young Germany,* Basic Books, 1962) says,
"National Socialism came to power as the party of youth."   Its cult
of youth was as pronounced as that of Italian fascism whose very
hymn was called "Youth" (Giovinezza).   Hitler insisted all along
that his movement was a revolt "of the coming generation against all
that was senile and rotten with decay in German democratic society."
Professor Peter Gay (*Weimar Culture: The Outsider as Insider,* Harper
and Row, 1968), stresses the prevalence in pre-Hitler days of an
ideology that pitted sons against fathers and insisted that the generations cannot understand each other, that they are deadly enemies;
in short, an ideology that said exactly the same thing in this respect
that our rebellious students, who insist that nobody over thirty is

416

trustworthy, say today. Then, as now, the student rebels were pictured as the new generation, disgusted with the complacency of their parents, fighting courageously for a better world. And what were then the mass media often depicted them as idealists, as young people concerned with the real issues of society. They were, in their time, the wave of the future. And leftist student activists in 1968 burned books they did not like in the same manner and at the same place—Berlin— as did Hitler's youthful followers in 1933.

Then, as now, these youthful followers of the extremists were anti-intellectual, resting their case on convictions based on their emotions. They were fascinated with violence. Their favorite technique was to disrupt meetings, not just because they were not to their liking, but more as a demonstration of their power; and they created disorder which then was claimed to demonstrate that the establishment was unable to function, and hence had to be replaced by one based on their creed.

Having stressed these parallels, one must also recognize the vast differences between the present American student rebelliousness and that of pre-Hitler Germany. It is these differences which should permit us to work toward an entirely different outcome. If I read the signs of the time correctly, I do not think that the rebellious students in and by themselves are a serious danger to this country, although they are a real danger to the universities. The danger, I fear, is rather an opposite one: that the disgusting behavior of a very small group of students —the overwhelming majority of our students are sound and wish nothing more than to take advantage of the opportunities higher education offers them—will arouse a severe counterreaction, so much so that their leftist radicalism may lead to a fascist type of backlash. This is the greatest danger inherent in their efforts to create chaos. To prevent chaos, and in desperation—and the rebels do succeed in creating desperation—repressive measures might be embraced which would be dangerous to our democratic institutions. Because of this danger, student rebellions must be dealt with in the best interest of all society, including that of the rebelling students themselves. But they can be dealt with intelligently and constructively only if the measures adopted are designed to eliminate the causes of the widespread discontent.

To understand this discontent, one has to realize first that many more young people go to college today than ever before, and hence many more are much less prepared for it. Taking advantage of college and being satisfied with the experience, rather than being defeated by it, requires a considerable amount of self-discipline and a high degree of satisfaction with developing one's intellect. Present-day education, both at home and in school, teaches very little self-discipline compared to even very recent times. The expectation now is that education can hand over knowledge and skills, and nearly instantly; and there is a widespread feeling that if students do not do well in school, then this is the failing of the educational system, not the result of a lack of personal application. With each year in school, this feeling becomes stronger in those who do not do well academically. And with it, the system becomes the enemy which deliberately withholds from them what they believe it could so easily give; hence their hatred of the system.

To understand why pressures erupt in adolescence on a growing scale nowadays, and why society's controls seem to grow weaker, we must recognize that adolescent revolt is not a stage of development that follows automatically from our natural makeup. What makes for adolescent revolt is the fact that our society keeps the younger generation too long dependent in terms of mature responsibility and a striving for independence. Years ago, when formal schooling ended for the vast majority at the age of fourteen or fifteen and thereafter one became self-supporting, married and had children, there was no need for adolescent revolt. Because while puberty is a biological given, adolescence as we know it with its identity crises is not. All children grow up and become pubertal; but by no means do they all become adolescents. To be adolescent means that one has reached, and even passed, the age of puberty, is at the height of physical development—healthier, stronger, even handsomer than one has been or will be for the rest of one's life; but to be adolescent also means that one must nevertheless postpone full adulthood long beyond what any other period in history has considered reasonable. And the educational experiences in home and school prepare well only a small minority of young people for such a prolonged waiting, for being able to control their angry impatience while waiting.

It is this waiting for the real life that creates a climate in which a sizeable segment of college students can at least temporarily be seduced into following the lead of small groups of militants. It seems to give them a chance to prove themselves as real men. Thus it is the empty wait for real life which makes for student rebellions. This can be seen from the fact that most of the rebellious students, here and abroad, are either undergraduates, are studying the social sciences and the humanities, or both. There are few militants among students of medicine, engineering, the natural sciences; they are busy doing things that are important to them: they are working in the laboratory and at their studies. It is those students who do not quite know what they are preparing themselves for and why, those students who sit around waiting for examinations rather than doing active work, who form the cadres of the student rebellion.

418

One example may stand for many. In a class I am presently teaching, a student who was close to the activists gave me, at first, a very hard time in class. Two months later he was one of my most interested, cooperative students. I asked him what happened. He answered: "A few weeks ago I got a job which interests me, and I also began to be interested in my classes; that did it."

There are today far too many students in college who essentially have no business there. Some are there to evade the draft; many others are there out of a vague idea that it will help them to find better paying jobs, although they do not know what jobs they want. And many go to college simply because they do not know what better to do and because it is expected of them. Their deep dissatisfaction with themselves and their inner confusion is projected first against the university, and second against all institutions of society, which are blamed for their own inner weakness.

To make matters worse, our institutions of higher learning have expanded much too rapidly; under public pressure for more education for everybody, they have increased enrollment beyond reason. The result is classes which are too large, and which are often taught in our large universities by teaching assistants, some of whom, out of their own inner dissatisfaction and insecurity, tend to side with the rebellion. All this leads to the anonymity, the impersonal nature of student-faculty contacts, about which many students rightly complain. And since many of them are essentially not interested in the intellectual adventure, the knowledge which the faculty can convey to them is not what they want. What they do want, essentially, is group therapeutic experiences to help them to mature, to be secure, to find themselves. But since colleges are not mass therapeutic institutions, they disappoint the students where their greatest need lies.

Because of the vast expansion in numbers, moreover, the old methods to lend coherence to the college experience, and to offer students a life geared to the needs of late adolescence, have disintegrated. This the fraternities and sororities used to do by offering group homes to ease the transition from family to society at large. But they no longer can contain the large proportion of students. The demand of some black students for separate black housing should therefore be understood, at least in part, as the consequence of their feeling lost in the anonymous mass of students. Indeed, most white students are similarly lost until they find themselves in their work and study experiences. The old rituals which enhanced student life and bound students both to each other and to their college—the football rallies, the homecomings—have lost most of their meaning and have been replaced by nothing equalling the excitement which the sit-ins and protests provide. The spirit of intimate comradeship—important as at no other time in life—that used to prevail in the fraternity house is now found by all too many students in their demonstrations, where they feel closely bound together, doing things which they deep down know they do also for the emotional satisfaction of simply being together, whatever high sounding issues they think are motivating their actions. Nor should the symbolic meaning of students invading the dean's or president's office, whether violently or non-violently, be overlooked; big in age and size, they inwardly feel like little boys, and hence they need to play big by sitting in papa's big chair. They want to have a say in how things are run, want to sit in the driver's seat, not because they feel competent to do so, but because they cannot bear to feel incompetent.

It is unnatural to keep large numbers of young people in dependency and attending school for some twenty years. This was the way of life for that small elite which always in the past went to universities, but never did they represent more than a small percentage of the youth population, the vast majority of which actively met life early and proved itself as men and women, as real and strong human beings. Now, however, the tremendous push to send everybody to college has brought into the university an incredibly large number of young people who do not find their self-realization through study, or through the intellectual adventure. Yet, still needing to find their early manhood, they try to change the university into something in which they can find it by engaging in an active, sometimes violent, battle against the existing order or all of society. Their victory would change the university into an institution no longer dedicated to the intellectual virtues, to the frontiers of knowledge, but dedicated, rather, to the belligerent reshaping of society; and this is exactly what the militants want—not to engage in study and research, but in political battles. The reason we didn't have student revolts of this kind and this scope before is partly because only those went to college who wanted to be educated, and partly because those students who had to put themselves through school proved their early manhood—at least to some degree—by the very fact that they could do so. I think many of the rebellious students today are essentially guilt-ridden individuals. They feel terribly guilty about all their advantages, including their exemption from the draft, which is a serious guilt. Unable to bear living with their inner guilt, they try to destroy society or certain of its institutions rather than deal with it.

Since all too many students who now go to college have little interest, ability and use for what constitutes a college education, they would be better off with a high-level vocational education closely linked to a work program to give scope to their needs for physical activity and visible, tangible achievement. The complaint of many of these students is that nobody needs them. They view themselves as parasites of society, and therefore come to hate the society which they think makes them feel this way. Here we should learn from the communist countries where studies are combined with work in factories and in the fields. This, I believe, would be a much better arrangement for those students who do not feel a deep commitment to the intellectual enterprise (that is, study and research), and those who are so committed will never constitute more than a relatively small segment of youth.

I would, in fact, urge the creation of a government program of a couple of years' duration—a civilian Peace Corps—in which young people would work on socially significant projects while earning pay for it, and simultaneously receive higher vocational training. After such service and training, only those who really wish to do so would enter the universities, while the rest would feel a much greater stake in a society they helped to rebuild; at the least, they would be well-prepared for permanent jobs. Such a program should be an alternative to the draft. Only those young men who volunteer should serve in the armed forces. And I am convinced that if every able-bodied person were required to serve two years in national service of some kind, there would be no scarcity of volunteers for the armed forces, particularly if military servicemen received advantages in pay or other special advantages at the end of their service. This would also eliminate the draft exemption of college students which, in connection with the war in Vietnam, is behind so much of the student unrest. *If I am exempt from service when others are not, I can live in peace with myself only if convinced this is a vile war.*

In calming the dissent that is so widespread on our campuses now, we should concentrate our efforts on separating the ready followers from the small group of rebellion leaders. Were it not for the widespread discontent, protest leaders would find a scant following, and if they should break the law without such followers, they could be readily dealt with. It is the mass following they can arouse because of the widespread malaise which alone makes them dangerous.

There has always been a small percentage of persons bent on destroying society and on fomenting revolution. In earlier generations there were the Wobblies; later there were the campus communists. But the present brand of campus revolutionaries, who are of anarchist and nihilist persuasion, are much more dangerous because they can point to success after success with their disrupting tactics. And nothing succeeds like success. Two hundred years ago Immanuel Kant warned that we shall never be able to control violence if it is rewarded. "It

421

is far more convenient," he wrote, "to commit an act of violence, and afterwards excuse it, than laboriously to consider convincing arguments and lose time in listening to objections. This very boldness itself indicates a sort of conviction of the legitimacy of the action, and the God of success is afterwards the best advocate."

The greatest danger presently, then, is the readiness with which violence is excused, and the seemingly convincing arguments which are brought forth to justify it before and after the act. Worst and most dangerous of all, there seems to be a tendency in our society to legitimize the results of violence so that, as Kant put it, the God of success afterwards serves as advocate for the violent action that preceded it, and suggests its future use. On our campuses, those committed to violence (to quote Kant again) "lose no time on considering arguments, or on listening to objections." They refuse to be rational about their grievances and, by violent means, insist on having their way, no matter what. And if they get it, as Kant knew, their success then legitimizes their disruptive actions.

The rebels gain their success by arousing a sizeable number of students through the tactic of confrontation, and by the universities' fear of confrontation. Confrontation has one important aim—to use the reaction of the provoked to generate a new unity among the demonstrators. In its most direct form, militants have stood in front of policemen and denounced them as pigs until the men in uniform hit out. The art of demonstrating then lies in ensuring that the blows are directed against the less-committed demonstrators and, if possible, against completely uninvolved persons. This provides the mass following required for success.

Of the small group of leaders of the radical left, it has been observed that most come from well-educated, very liberal families. Of those whom I know, I would say, too, that they have had their intellectual abilities developed very highly at much too early an age, at the expense of their emotional development. Although often very bright, emotionally some of them remained fixated at the age of the temper tantrum. It is this discrepancy between great intellectual maturity and utter emotional immaturity which is so baffling, often even to the universities, where some members of the faculty fail to see behind the obvious intelligence the inability to act rationally, and most of all, the inability to act responsibly. It is one of the weaknesses of university professors that, as persons committed to value intellectual ability most highly, they are captivated by the intelligence of these students to the degree that they are ready to excuse or brush aside the students' disruptiveness and intellectual arrogance.

As for the discontented students themselves, psychologically I always found them hating themselves as intensely as they hate the establishment, a self-hatred they try to escape by fighting *any* establishment. They need help in overcoming their emotional difficulties, and punishment is hardly the answer. If we bring them to the universities, we should provide facilities for helping them. It is their emotional immaturity that explains both their call for immediate action, and the retreat of the dropout and the hippy into utter non-action; each masks the inability of very intelligent young people to take time to think things out. The militants must want to destroy the universities because they do not want to be students, for to be a student means to prepare oneself to do something more worthwhile in the future. The militant student's cry is for action now, not preparation for action later. In this sense, he is no longer a student at all, since he clearly rejects knowledge as a precondition of meaningful activity. Truth, moreover, is no longer sought but "revealed"; the contempt for free speech and free thought is demonstrated as much by his actions as by his words. Were he ever to capture the university, it would cease to be a university.

In their inability to delay action for thought, both right and left extremists, the militants of all colors, are brothers under the skin. This is among the reasons why historically it has happened before that the young followers of the extreme right have become those of the extreme left, or the other way around. The mainspring of the rebels' action is more their wish to prove themselves strong—and less any particular political conviction—superimposed on self-doubt and hatred of a society which they feel has left them out in the cold. In Germany the National Socialists and the Communists voted together and worked together to bring down the democratic Weimar government, and in the same context, it is not so surprising that former Nazis easily involved themselves in the communistic government of East Germany.

But there are also good reasons why it is mainly the children of leftist parents who become hippies or student revolutionaries in our society, just as in other places and other times the children of conservative parents, under similar emotional conditions, spearheaded rightwing radicalism. It was the children of conservative German parents, for example, who first embraced the Emperor's War and enthusiastically went to their death because they felt a need to lay their bodies on the line for ideas their parents had only luke-warmly held; for thus they proved themselves strong, while at the same time proving their parents weak, wishy-washy and unworthy of true respect. They felt, too, that this was a means of rebirth, a way to revitalize an ossified society, to create a new society; with little patience for the

423

voice of reason, they asked for authenticity and confrontation. All these were the main tenets of Hitler's academic youth, as they are now those of our own student left.

Thus, while the emotional constellations which make for very different student revolts are strangely similar, the specific political content of a student revolt depends to a large degree on the beliefs of the students' parents. For in many ways rebellion represents a desperate wish by youth to do better than their parents in exactly those beliefs in which parents seem weakest. In this sense, rebellion also represents a desperate desire for parental approval, but even more it represents a desperate wish that parents had been stronger in their convictions. So many of our radicals embrace Maoism and chant "Ho, Ho, Ho Chi Minh" much as another generation chanted at football rallies. These are strong father-figures with strong convictions who powerfully coerce their "children" to follow their commands. While consciously the students demand freedom and participation, unconsciously their commitment to Mao and other dictatorships suggests their desperate need for controls from the outside, since without them they are unable to bring order into their inner chaos. Such controls, however, must not be imposed punitively, nor for the benefit of others. They must be controls that clearly and definitely benefit the individual, so that he will eventually make them his own.

The inability of militant students to wait and work hard for long-range goals marks them as emotionally disturbed; so does their hatred for their parents who failed to give them direction and set them against the world by exposing their immature minds to criticism of all that could have given meaning to their lives. Indeed, it is their hatred of society that makes it so easy for the militant student leaders to make common cause with another small group that provides temporary leadership for some of the rebellions: outright paranoid individuals. The proportion of paranoids among students is no greater than in any comparable group of the population. But they are more dangerous because of their high intelligence, which permits them to conceal more successfully the degree of their disturbance. And student revolt permits them to act out their paranoia to a degree that no other position in society permits. How understandable, then, that all paranoids who can, do flock into the ranks of the militants. Unfortunately, most non-experts do not know how persuasive paranoids can be, at least until they are recognized. The persuasiveness of a Hitler or a Stalin is now regarded as the consequence of his own paranoia and his unconscious appeal to the vague paranoid tendencies among the immature and disgruntled. I have no doubt that the ranks of today's militants contain some would-be Hitlers and Stalins.

Paranoids make a persuasive appeal to any group in the population which rightly or wrongly feels persecuted, and they seek out such groups because they are most likely to view their own paranoia as true understanding of a persecuted group's particular predicament. Which brings me to the special problems of some of our black students who, fortunately, seem to recognize more and more that SDS is using them rather than helping them. (They are not quite as successfully seeing through the motives of some of the paranoid student leaders.)

The overwhelming majority of black students desires exactly the same as does the overwhelming majority of white students: a rightful place in society. Only a very small minority of black and white students wishes to destroy it. Thus if the blacks could be convinced that there is a good place for them in society, their attitude would change and they would part ways with SDS, as many of them have already done. But the difficulty is that many black students, because of the nature of the commitment of the university, do not feel that being a student is necessarily the best way for them to find their rightful place in society. It is here that our wish and theirs, that they should become part of the elite, runs afoul of what for many of them is their reality. Many black students in our colleges are often ill-prepared academically and lacking in the skills required for academic success. At the same time, they have been imbued with the notion that it is the fault of the establishment that they are disadvantaged. While this is true to some degree, awareness of such truth offers an easy way out if one does not succeed. All students find the transition from home to college difficult. In past times the student placed the blame for this on himself, and most students therefore tried to do something about themselves and sooner or later succeeded. Today both white and black students tend to blame the faculty for the difficulties they encounter in adjusting to a different way of life and study. The demand for black-study programs originated, not only in the justified feeling that one must be familiar and proud of one's own background, but to a large degree in the feeling that such studies would be easier, and that the faculty would have greater understanding.

The fact is that the preparation of some black students who are induced to go to college is inferior to that of the white majority of the college population. While the faculty is ready to make allowances for this, compensation runs counter to the self-respect of the black student, who rightly does not wish to be treated as a second-class citizen. But if he cannot compete successfully with his fellow students who have had so many educational and social advantages, he is in a terrible conflict. Brought to college to do as well as the others, when he fails his background does not permit him to accept the fact of failure because of his lack of preparation; to do so would make him feel second-class, a position he is seeking to escape by obtaining a college education. Although intellectually able, he has difficulty in adjusting, and he comes to feel that the very place which promised to make him equal fails to do so. Disappointed, he rages against the institution which once more makes him feel inferior, and special programs of assistance only make his feelings of inferiority even deeper. The many black students who are well able to hold their own with the best feel they must not desert their fellow black comrades, and in times of protest, they make their comrades' burden their own.

If we want to bring a large number of black students into our universities, as we should, we must start much earlier than college. From high school on, it will be necessary to educate a larger number of blacks, together with white youngsters from culturally deprived backgrounds, in true prep schools to permit them to enter college as well prepared academically and socially as the more advantaged students.

There is today a fascination in society with sex and violence, with drugs and insanity, which both influences the student militants and provides them with a noteworthiness which they exploit to the full. If students protest in an orderly and rational fashion, they receive little public attention. But if they shed their clothes and walk around naked, this makes news all over the nation, whatever case they may or may not have had; it is part of a dangerous fascination with youth and its extreme positions. What passes for modern literature which these youngsters read in junior high school intoxicates their minds with the appeal of drug-induced madness, with sexual acting out and with violence.

The universities, because of their intellectual prestige, give the student activists a platform for their revolutionary claims which they otherwise would never have. For example, for days not more than some twenty to thirty students recently occupied the administration building of the University of Chicago. They got headlines every day and were prominently featured on radio and television. Had thirty people demonstrated in any other place, they would have received no attention whatever. This SDS knows, and this is why it aims at the universities. The contrast between an institution devoted to the highest achievements of reason, and the obscenity and violence perpetrated there, makes it all the more fascinating, a fascination on which SDS tries to build its revolutionary success.

An idea in itself may amount to next to nothing, but it becomes news by interfering with something else which is considered to be of public importance. In themselves, a couple of hundred demonstrators somewhere in New York or Chicago would amount to very little; but when fifty students march into a lecture hall, seize control of the podium and broadcast their claims and philosophy to people who came to hear something quite different—then they have made news. If someone advocates urinating on graves (as the Fugs did), or if a few girls dress up as witches and put curses on professors (as they did in Chicago), if they did so without reference to politics, people would rightly wonder about their sanity. But when they do so as a condemnation of the Vietnam war or in the name of some progressive cause, they win the support of many older liberals and enlightened radicals who invariably consider it all very socially significant. When a teen-ager wrestles with the police for the sake of the moral superiority of a future social order, he cannot fail to obtain the sympathetic attention of radio and television editors, if not psychiatrists. The ritualistic invocation of ideology is thus both an alibi and a defense.

Perhaps it all has made too many headlines, perhaps it has been talked about too much for people to accept the fact, but the truth of the matter is that these rebellions can and do paralyze our universities. Not only are classes interrupted and buildings occupied, but faculty members must devote their energies to calming things down. Even more importantly, the time and energy which should be devoted to more lasting achievements are drained away on plans to forestall new confrontations. A last comparison with pre-Hitler days: In Germany at that time, as Professor George L. Mosse (*The Crisis of German Ideology*, Grosset and Dunlap, 1964) puts it, "professors tended to be either scholars who withdrew into their own specialty, taking scant notice of the world around them, or men who attempted to play the role of prophets. The first kind of academic wanted only to be left in peace. . . . The professor as prophet, with very few exceptions indeed, was to be found on the side of the revolting students." Of the students of that time he says, "They had found a basis for action that opposed existing authority yet remained independent of any political movement directed by their elders." And the faculties, he says, "failed to provide any opposition, failed to use administrative powers and failed to organize effective alternative groups of students. At best they displayed a detached passivity . . . at worst they joined in the harassment."

In our universities today we have faculty members who are trying to remain aloof from it all, and others who are trying to anticipate even the most radical student demands so as to avoid confrontations. Worse, though, there are few efforts being made to organize effective alternative groups of students. Worst of all, many professors are so intimidated that they cave in even before the students exercise pressure.

It is the continuous worry about what the militant students may do next, the anxious efforts to give them no offense, which saps the universities of their strength to the point of paralysis. And this anxious avoidance of taking a firm stand gives not only these militants, but also many non-committed students, the feeling that they have the faculty on the run.

If the colleges and universities would take a determined stand against coercion and intimidation—though always open to, indeed inviting, reasonable and non-coercive discussion about much-needed reform— then student rebellions could be reduced to the point where they would no longer threaten either the universities or society. The university must strengthen its will to resist disruption and coercion. If it succeeds, it will have little need to take recourse to punitive measures, beyond setting into practice the principle that those who do not wish to have any part of our universities should have their will: they should not be permitted to be, live or work in a place they hate, not as a punishment, but because to remain in a place they hate and despise serves no good purpose and is detrimental to their emotional well-being.

Walter Laqueur

Walter Laqueur is Professor of the History of Ideas at Brandeis University and director of the Institute of Contemporary History, London. He was born in Germany in 1921. At seventeen he left for Palestine; he dropped out of Hebrew University after a year, joined a kibbutz, and worked as a bricklayer's mate, tractor driver, book seller, and auxiliary policeman. From 1945 to 1955 he was a newspaper correspondent and free-lance writer, doing the traveling, reading, and observing that prepared him for his present career. Professor Laqueur is a specialist in international studies, with a particular interest in the Soviet Union and the Middle East. He is coeditor of The Journal of Contemporary History. *His many publications include* Young Germany: A History of the German Youth Movement *(1962),* The Road to Jerusalem: The Origins of the Israeli-Arab Conflict *(1969), and* The Struggle for the Middle East: The Soviet Union

in the Mediterranean 1958–1968 *(1969). He is a regular
contributor of articles to* Commentary; *the following appeared
in the June 1969 issue.*

REFLECTIONS ON YOUTH MOVEMENTS

I can well imagine that on Saturday nights across this country, at
hundreds of faculty parties where a year and a half ago the main
subject of discussion was the war in Vietnam, thousands of professors
and their wives now passionately debate the pros and cons of the
student movement, the tactics of the SDS, and the significance of the
generational conflict. I myself have attended several such gatherings,
and have been struck not so much by the intensity with which the
actions of the students are either approved of or condemned by their
elders, as by the baffled consensus among those elders that the movement is both unprecedented and totally inexplicable in terms of what
the university has historically represented. When I am asked, as I
invariably am, for the European view on these matters, I rarely manage
more than a few words, to the effect that the American situation is
unique and that anyway history never repeats itself—which, needless
to say, is of no great help to anyone. And yet, I believe there *is*
something to be learned from the European experience, even if the
lesson is an ambiguous one. Not the least thing to be learned is that
the Western university has by no means always represented that
tranquil meeting-ground, so fondly misremembered now by American
professors, of those who would gladly learn with those who would
gladly teach.

Quite the contrary. Organized youth revolt has for a long time
been an integral part of European history. That, on the one hand.
On the other, the idea of the university as a quiet place, devoted to
the pursuit of learning and unaffected by the turbulence of the outside
world, is of comparatively recent date. The medieval university certainly was no such place. As Nathan Schachner has pointed out, it
was a place characterized more by bloody affrays, pitched battles,
mayhem, rape, and homicide: "Indeed by the frequency of riots one
may trace the rise of the University to power and privilege." In his
monumental study, *Universities of Europe in the Middle Ages*, Hastings
Rashdall relates the violence of the medieval university to the violence

of medieval times in general, when the slitting of a throat was not regarded even by the Church as the worst of mortal sins. Thus, a Master of Arts at the University of Prague who had cut the throat of a Friar Bishop was merely expelled, while in the case of other offenders punishment consisted in the confiscation of scholastic effects and garments. The police were openly ridiculed by students, and the universities did nothing to exact discipline from their own scholars. In dealing with the subject of students' morals, Rashdall is constrained to write in Latin. According to Charles Thurot's history of Paris University in the Middle Ages, masters frolicked with their pupils and even took part in their disorders. The university was a great concourse of men and boys freed from all parental restrictions; morality, as Schachner notes, was a private affair, as were the comings and goings of the students. Nor was the trouble localized; the same complaints were to be heard from Oxford to Vienna and Salamanca.

As for the professor, his position in the medieval university was not what it became in later days. He was, first of all, paid by the students. A professor at Bologna needed his students' permission if he wanted to leave town even for a single day; he had to pay a fine if he arrived late in class or if he ended his lecture before the chiming of the church bells; should his lectures not meet with favor, there was a good chance that he would be interrupted, hissed, or even stoned. Supported by King and Church, medieval students enjoyed almost unlimited freedom. It was an unwritten rule, for instance, that they were always in the right in their clashes with townspeople. Of course, from time to time the citizenry would get even by killing a few students; the Oxford town-and-gown riots of 1354 were one such response, if a major one, to student provocation—provocation that took the form, in the words of a contemporary chronicler, of "atrociously wounding and slaying many, carrying off women, ravishing virgins, committing robberies and many other enormities hateful to God." To be sure, the real troublemakers were a minority, some of them not even students but young vagabonds enjoying the immunities of the scholar, drifting from master to master and from university to university. For every scholar involved in felonious offenses there were dozens whose story is unknown. "They studied conscientiously, attended lectures and disputations, worked hard, ate frugally, drank their modest stoup of wine, and had no time for the delights of tavern and brothel. The annals of the virtuous, like the annals of a happy people, are short and barren" (Schachner). Nevertheless, it is a fact that only in later ages did the university begin to impose stricter discipline on its students.

If student violence in the Middle Ages can be ascribed mainly to the high spirits of youth, by the 18th century a new figure had appeared on the scene: the student as freedom fighter. *Die Raeuber* ("The

Robbers"), the play that made Schiller famous, tells the story of a group of students who, disgusted by society and its inequities, take to the mountains to lead partisan warfare against the oppressors. (In the 1920's when Piscator staged the play in Berlin, he had Spiegelberg, one of the leaders of the gang and incidentally a Jew, appear in the mask of Trotsky.) *Sturm und Drang*, the first real literary movement of youth revolt, combined opposition to social conventions with a style of life that is familiar enough today: wild language, long hair, and strange attire. Within a few decades after its inception, the romantics had made this movement fashionable, if not respectable, all over Europe. Suddenly there was Young England and Young Germany, Young Italy, Young Hungary, and Young Russia—all up in arms against the tyranny of convention, tradition, and outworn beliefs. One of the very few places untouched by the cult of youth at that time was America, itself a young country, unencumbered by the dead weight of tradition: *America,* Goethe apostrophized, *du hast es besser. . . .*

Some youth groups in the modern period have done much good, while others have caused a great deal of harm. It has been the custom in writing about them to divide them into the progressive and the reactionary, the wholesome and the decadent, so that, for example, the revolutionary Russian student movement of the 19th century, the Italian Risorgimento, and the Chinese May 1919 movement fall in one camp, and the fascist youth movements fall in the other. But this scheme is at best an oversimplification, since almost all movements of youthful revolt have contained in themselves both elements at once. The historical role a movement finally played depended in each case on political conditions in the society at large, the gravity of the problems the movement faced, the degree of its cultural development, and the quality of the guidance it received from its mentors.

The dual character of youth movements is illustrated with particular clarity by the example of the early German student circles, the *Burschenschaften.* In his recent book [*The Conflict of Generations*], Lewis Feuer characterizes the members of these circles as "historicists, terrorists, totalitarians and anti-Semites"—all of which is perfectly true. But they were also genuine patriots who dreamed of German unity and set out to combat the tyranny and oppression of the Holy Alliance. Most of them, in addition, were democrats of sorts and their movement was regarded by the liberals of the day as one of great promise. Their story is briefly told. The leader of the group was Karl Follen, a lecturer at Jena, of whom a contemporary wrote that "no one could be compared with him for purity and chastity of manners and morals. He seemed to concentrate all his energies upon one great aim—the revolution." In 1818, a certain Karl Sand, an idealistic and highly unstable student of theology who had come under Follen's influence, assassinated a minor playwright by the name of August Kotzebue who was suspected of being a Russian agent. Sand genuinely expected that this action, undertaken in the service of a holy cause, would trigger a revolution. But the choice of victim was haphazard, and the consequences regrettable: the government seized the opportunity to suppress the *Burschenschaft* as well as the whole democratic movement. Follen escaped to America, where he became professor of German literature and preacher at Harvard (he later drowned at sea in a shipwreck). It took almost thirty years for the movement he had led to recover from the blow dealt it by the authorities.

The idealism, spirit of sacrifice, devotion to one's people, and revolutionary fervor that marked the *Burschenshaft* have been an inherent part of all youth movements over the last hundred years. It is a mistake to assume that the fascist youth movements were an exception to this rule, that their members were mainly sadistic, blindly destructive young thugs. To be sure, they preached a doctrine of violence, but as Mussolini said, "there is a violence that liberates, and there is a violence that enslaves; there is moral violence and stupid, immoral violence" (compare Marcuse: "In terms of historical function, there is a difference between revolutionary and reactionary violence, between violence practiced by the oppressed and by the oppressors"). The ideological forerunners of Italian fascism, men like Corradini and Federzoni, were second to none in their condemnation of capitalism and imperialism and in their defense of the rights of the "proletarian nations." Early fascist programs demanded a republic, the abolition of all titles, a unified education, the control and taxation of all private income, and the confiscation of unproductive capital. They also placed great stress on youth. Giovanni Gentile, the philosopher of fascism, considered the sole aim of the new movement to be the "spiritual liberation of the young Italians." The very anthem of the fascist regime was an appeal to the young generation: *Giovinezza, Giovinezza, primavera di bellezza.*

Similarly in Germany, where the student movement after the First World War was strongly nationalist; the Nazi student association emerged as the leading force in the German universities (and in Austria) in 1930, well before Hitler had become the leader of the strongest German party. With 4,000 registered members out of a total of 132,000 students, the Nazis easily took control of the chief organization of German students several years before the party's seizure of national power. The declared aim of the Nazi student association was to destroy liberalism and international capitalism; point two on its program was to "purge the university of the influence of private capital"; point nine called on students to join the ranks of the workers. The slogan of "student power" made its first appearance at the *Goettingen Studententag* in 1920. Later on it was linked to the demand that the university be made political, a real "people's university," and that all the academic cobwebs and so-called "objective sciences" be cleaned out. Even before Hitler came to power, leading German professors attacked the "idea of false tolerance" of the humanist university. Invoking Fichte, Hegel, and Schleiermacher, they held that liberal democracy was the main enemy of the true scientific spirit, and demanded that henceforth only one political philosophy be taught. The Nazis, needless to say, were still more radical: academic life, they said, had largely become an end in itself; located outside the sphere of real life, the university educated two types of students— the only-expert and the only-philosopher. These two types produced a great many books and much clever and refined table-talk, but neither they nor the universities which sustained them were in a position to give clear answers to the burning questions of the day.

Criticisms like these were common at the time all over Europe. An observer of the French scene wrote in 1931 that the main characteristic of the young generation was its total rejection of the existing order: "almost no one defends the present state of affairs." One of the most interesting French youth groups was *L'Ordre Nouveau,* whose manifesto, written by Dandieu and Robert Aron, had the title, *La Révolution Nécessaire. Ordre Nouveau* stood for the liberation of man from capitalist tyranny and materialistic slavery; Bolshevism, fascism, and National Socialism, it declared, had assumed the leadership of the young generation and for that reason would prevail everywhere. The young in France were deeply affected—to quote yet another contemporary witness —by a "tremendous wave of revolutionary enthusiasm, of holy frenzy and disgust." When several prominent young socialists seceded from the SFIO in opposition to the rule of the old gang and established a movement of their own, this too was welcomed as one more manifestation of the rebellion of the young generation. All these people were deeply troubled by the existing state of affairs and no doubt well meaning in their intentions; together with Jean Luchaire, the leader of *Ordre Nouveau,* many of them ended up as Nazi collaborators during World War II.

The tactics adopted by these youth groups vis-à-vis the universities were the tactics of agitation. Even before the First World War, members of the *Action Française* had made it a custom to disrupt systematically the lectures of professors at the Sorbonne who had provoked their ire for political reasons. Nazi students perfected the system, forcing universities to dismiss Jewish professors, and even one Christian pacifist, well before 1933. But the question must be asked again: was this rowdyism, or an action undertaken in the genuine conviction that one's

433

country was in grave danger and that the professors were enemies of the people who had to be removed? Among the fascist youth movements in the late 20's, one of the most sinister was the Rumanian terrorist band, the *Archangel Michael,* which later became the Iron Guard. Yet even the members of this group were not devoid of sincerity and idealism; Eugen Weber recently wrote of their leader: "From a mendacious people he demanded honesty, in a lazy country he demanded work, in an easy-going society he demanded self-discipline and persistence, from an exuberant and windy folk he demanded brevity and self-control." Whoever describes a youth movement as idealistic only states the obvious. Youth movements have never been out for personal gain; what motivates them is different from what motivates an association for the protection of the interests of small shopkeepers. The fascist experience has shown that the immense potential which inheres in every youth movement can be exploited in the most disastrous way; but the potential itself must be seen as neutral.

Almost everything that is great has been done by youth, wrote Benjamin Disraeli, himself at one time a fighter in the ranks of generational revolt. Professor Feuer would counter: many disasters in modern European politics have been caused by students and youth movements. The exploits of the *Burschenschaften,* he argues, set back the cause of German freedom thirty years. Russian student terrorism in the 1880's put an end to progress toward constitutionalism in that country. But for the terror and stress of the First World War (inaugurated by a bomb thrown by yet another student hero, Gavrilo Princip), Russia would have evolved in a liberal capitalist direction, and European civilization would not have been maimed by fascism and a second World War. According to Professor Feuer, the qualities needed to bring about peaceful social and political change are not those usually found in youth movements, and he accuses students of almost always acting irrationally in pursuing their objectives. Unfortunately, however, peaceful change is not always possible in history, nor are patience and prudence invariably the best counsel. Take the Munich students who revolted against Hitler in 1943 and the student rebels who were recently sentenced in the Soviet Union; had they acted entirely rationally, they might well have convinced themselves that as a consequence of long-term political and social processes, the dictatorship would disappear anyway or at least be mitigated in its ferocity. Why therefore endanger their lives? To their eternal credit, such rational considerations did not enter the students' minds. The impetuosity, the impatience, and sometimes the madness of youth movements has been a liberating force in the struggle against tyranny and dictatorship.

Tyranny cannot be overthrown unless at least some people are willing to sacrifice their lives, and those willing to do so usually do not come from the ranks of the senior citizens. It is only when youth movements have launched a total attack against democratic regimes and societies—in Germany, France, and Italy in the 20's and in other countries later on—that they have come to play by necessity a reactionary and destructive role.

Most of the basic beliefs and even the outward fashions of the present world youth movements can be traced back to the period in Europe just before and after the First World War. The German *Neue Schar* of 1919 were the original hippies: long-haired, sandaled, unwashed, they castigated urban civilization, read Hermann Hesse and Indian philosophy, practiced free love, and distributed in their meetings thousands of asters and chrysanthemums. They danced, sang to the music of the guitar, and attended lectures on the "Revolution of the Soul." The modern happening was born in 1910 in Trieste, Parma, Milan, and other Italian cities where the Futurists arranged public meetings to recite their poems, read their manifestoes, and exhibit their ultra-modern paintings. No one over thirty, they demanded, should in future be active in politics. The public participated actively at these gatherings, shouting, joking, and showering the performers with rotten eggs. In other places, things were not so harmless. "Motiveless terror" formed part of the program of a group of young Russian anarchists, the *Bezmotivniki*, in their general struggle against society. The *Bezmotivniki* threatened to burn down whole cities, and their news sheets featured diagrams for the production of home-made bombs. Drug-taking as a social phenomenon, touted as a way of gaining new experience and a heightened sensibility, can be traced back to 19th-century France and Britain. The idea of a specific youth culture was first developed in 1913–14 by the German educator Gustav Wyneken and a young man named Walter Benjamin who later attained literary fame. In 1915, Friedrich Bauermeister, an otherwise unknown member of the youth movement, developed the idea of the "class struggle of youth." Bauermeister regarded the working class and the socialist movement (including Marx and Engels) as "eudaimonistic"; the socialists, he admitted, stood for a just order and higher living standards, but he feared that once their goals were achieved they would part ways with the youth movement. Bauermeister questioned whether even the social revolution could create a better type of man, or release human beings from their "bourgeois and proletarian distortions."

The ideas of this circle were developed in a little magazine called *Der Anfang* in 1913–14. Youth, the argument ran (in anticipation of Professor Kenneth Keniston), was *milieulos*, not yet integrated into

435

society. Unencumbered by the ties of family or professional careers, young people were freer than other elements of society. As for their lack of experience, for which they were constantly criticized by their elders, this, far from being a drawback, was in fact a great advantage. Walter Benjamin called experience the "mask of the adult." For what did the adult wish above all to prove? That he, too, had once been young, had disbelieved his parents, and had harbored revolutionary thoughts. Life, however, had taught the adult that his parents had been right after all, and now he in turn smiled with condescending superiority and said to the younger generation: this will be your fate too.

For the historian of ideas, the back issues of the periodicals of the youth movement, turned yellow with age, make fascinating reading. The great favorites of 1918–19 were Hermann Hesse, Spengler's *Decline of the West*, Zen Buddhism and Siddharta, Tagore's gospel of spiritual unity *(Love not Power)*, and Lenin. It is indeed uncanny how despite all the historical differences, the German movement preempted so many of the issues agitating the American movement of today, as well as its literary fashions.

Some youth movements in the last hundred years have been unpolitical in character. Most, however, have had definite political aims. Of this latter group, some have belonged to the extreme Left, others have gravitated to the extreme Right; some have sought absolute freedom in anarchy, others have found fulfillment in subordinating themselves to a leader. To find a common denominator seems therefore very nearly hopeless. But the contradictions are often more apparent than real, not only because many of those who originally opted for the extreme Left later moved to the Right, or vice versa, or because the extremes sometimes found common ground as in the National Bolshevik movement which gained some prominence in various countries in the 1920's. Whether a certain movement became political or unpolitical, whether it opted for the Left or the Right, depended on the historical context: it hardly needs to be explained in detail why youth movements were preponderantly right-wing after the First World War, while more recently most have tended toward the Left. But beyond the particular political orientation there are underlying motives which have remained remarkably consistent throughout.

Youth movements have always been extreme, emotional, enthusiastic; they have never been moderate or rational (again, no major excursion into the psychology of youth is needed to explain this). Underlying their beliefs has always been a common anti-capitalist, anti-bourgeois denominator, a conviction that the established order is corrupt to the bones and beyond redemption by parliamentary means of reform. The ideologies of democracy and liberalism have always been seen as an irretrievable part of the whole rotten system; all politicians, of course, are crooks. Equally common to all youth groups is a profound pessimism about the future of present-day culture and an assumption that traditional enlightened concepts like tolerance are out of date. The older generation has landed the world in a mess, and a radical new beginning, a revolution, is needed. Youth movements have never been willing to accept the lessons of the past; each generation is always regarded as the first (and the last) in history. And the young have always found admiring adults to confirm them in their beliefs.

This leads us to the wider issue of *Kulturpessimismus.* The idea that the world is in decline—an idea that is about as old as the world itself—had an impact on modern youth movements through the mediating influence of neo-romanticism. The themes of decadence and impending doom can be traced like a bright threat through the 19th century from Alfred de Musset *("Je suis venu trop tard dans un monde trop vieux"),* to Carlyle, Ruskin, and Arnold with their strictures against the universal preoccupation with material gain. So widespread a fashion did *Kulturpessimismus* enjoy that one can scarcely find a single self-respecting 19th-century author who did not complain about the disjunction between mankind and the world, between idea and reality, or about the spiritual bankruptcy and moral consumption of his age. In Germany, as *mal du siècle* turned into *fin de siècle,* a whole phalanx of Cassandras raised their voices, denouncing mass culture, crass materialism, and the lack of a sense of purpose in modern life. *Kulturpessimismus* induced in some a sense of resignation and gave rise to decadent moods in literature and the arts; at the same time, however, it acted as a powerful stimulus to movements of regeneration. Whereas dissatisfaction led some to ennui and perversions (*La jeune France,* an all-out revolt against social conventions, was decadent and wholly unpolitical in character), elsewhere and in other periods boredom gave birth to activism. Thus, on the eve of the First World War, a whole generation of young Europeans, having pronounced themselves culturally suffocated, welcomed the outbreak of hostilities as heralding a great purge, a liberation that would somehow put things right. The close connection between *Kulturpessimismus* and boredom deserves more study than it has received so far, as does the connection between boredom and prosperity. Max Eyth, the German popular writer, astutely diagnosed the illness of his age in the autobiography he wrote during the Wilhelminian era: *"Es ist uns seit einer Reihe von Jahren zu gut gegangen"* (We had it too good for a number of years).

One of the main problems facing the decadents was that of combining their hatred of modern civilization with their love of the refinements that civilization had made possible. (This is still very much of a problem, although some of today's revolutionaries seem to have solved it on the personal if not on the ideological level.) The decadents also faced the dilemma of squaring their *langueur*—Verlaine: *Je suis l'Empire à la fin de la décadence*—with their fascination with violence and revolutionary action. The indiscriminate assassinations and bombings carried out by the French anarchists found many admirers among both the decadents and the right-wing futurists. "What matter the victims, provided the gesture is beautiful," Laurent Tailhade wrote. D'Annunzio's career as a writer progressed from descriptions of courtesans in modish clothes, luminous landscapes, and villas by the sea, to the most lavish praise of the freshness and joy of war. Having begun by calling on youth to "abolish all moral restrictions," he ended as the prophet of moral regeneration and the poet laureate of fascism. The list could be lengthened: Maurice Barrès made his way from the decadent movement to the *Action Française*; Johannes R. Becher, who in the early 20's was known in Germany as the mad expressionist poet who had killed his girl friend, was to become in later life minister of culture in Walter Ulbricht's East Germany.

If the youth movements of the early 20th century arose, then, in a milieu in which the sense of decadence was widespread, they represented at the same time an attempt to overcome it. Their leaders were moralists, forever complaining about the evils of corporate guilt. Like all moralists, they exaggerated those evils, speaking out of the anti-historical perspective which is a hallmark of the moralist. For the study of history teaches that other periods have, broadly speaking, not been much better than one's own. This is why the moralist and the revolutionary regard history as a reactionary discipline, the story of big failures and small successes. The study of history is a breeding-ground of skepticism; the less the moralist knows of it, the more effectively will he pursue his mission with an untroubled conscience. Thomas Mann, pleading in a famous speech to German students in the 1920's for "aristocratic skepticism in a world of frenetic fools," was sadly out of touch with the mood of an audience longing for firm belief and certain truths.

If in what I have said up till now my remarks have indicated a certain ambivalence of feeling toward youth movements in general, it is because I have been trying to distinguish between the various ideas which they have espoused—ideas which are certainly deserving of criticism—and, what I take to be of even greater significance, the depth of emotional experience which they have provided their members.[1] (I say this as one who shared that experience at one stage in his life.)   The politics and culture of youth movements have always been a reflection of the Zeitgeist, a hodgepodge, often, of mutually exclusive ideas.   A proto-Nazi wrote about the unending and fruitless discussions of German youth movements in 1920: "Look at those *Freideutsche* leaders and their intellectual leap-frogging from Dostoevsky to Chuang-tse, Count Keyserling, Spengler, Buddha, Jesus, Landauer, Lenin, and whichever literary Jew happens to be fashionable to the moment.   Of their own substance they have little or nothing." There was, let's face it, more than a grain of truth in this criticism; a list of the main formative intellectual influences on the American movement would look even more incongruous.   But what was essential about the German youth movement, at least in its first phase, was not its "intellectual leap-frogging" and confused politics but something else entirely.   The movement represented an *un*political form of opposition to a civilization that had little to offer the young generation, a protest against the lack of vitality, warmth, emotion, and ideals in German society.   (Hoelderlin: "I can conceive of no people more dismembered. . . .   You see workmen but no human beings, thinkers but no human beings, priests but no human beings, masters and servants, youth and staid people, but no human beings. . . .")   It wanted to develop qualities of sincerity, decency, open-mindedness, to free its members from petty egoism and careerism, to oppose artificial conventions, snobbery, and affectation.   Its basic character was formless and intangible, its authentic and deepest experience difficult to describe and perhaps impossible to analyze: the experience of marching together, of participating in common struggles, of forming lasting friendships. There was, of course, much romantic exaltation as well, but although it is easier to ridicule the extravagances of this state of mind than to do it justice, the temptation should be resisted: experiences of such depth are very serious matters indeed.

The non-political phase of the German youth movement ended roughly speaking with the First World War.   Summarizing that early phase, I wrote several years ago that "if lack of interest in politics could provide an alibi from history, the youth movement would then leave the court without a stain on its character."[2]   In retrospect, this judgment seems a trifle misplaced; the truth is that the movement was

---

[1] Although I originally intended this as a statement about youth movements of the past, I now read in Martin Duberman's review of Christopher Lasch's new book, *The Agony of the American Left*: "I think what is most impressive about the radical young people is not their politics or their social theories, but the cultural revolution they have inaugurated—the change in life style."

[2] *Young Germany: A History of the German Youth Movement.*

simply not equipped to deal with politics. Being romantic and opposed to "arid intellectualism," its thought was confused and its outlook illiberal. Oriented toward a mythic past and an equally mythic future, it was darkly suspicious of the values of the Enlightenment—an attitude that did not have much to commend it in a country where the Enlightenment had not met with conspicuous success anyway—and it was easily swayed in different directions by philosophical charlatans and political demagogues preaching all kinds of eccentric doctrines.

All this appeared very clearly in the second, political phase of the German youth movement after the First World War. By 1930, the youth movement was displaying an incontinent eagerness to rid Germany of democracy. Almost all its members shared the assumption that anything at all would be better than the detested old regime. Lacking experience and imagination, they clearly misjudged the major political forces of their time. One of their leaders wrote much later: "We had no real principles. We thought everything possible. The ideas of natural law, of the inalienable rights of man, were strange to us. As far as our ideas were concerned we were in mid-air, without a real basis for our artificial constructions." It was, in brief, not an intellectual movement, and any attempt to evaluate it on the cultural and political level alone will not do it justice; it moved on a different plane. The movement arose in response to a certain malaise; it attempted, without success, to solve the conflicts facing it; and it was, in retrospect, a splendid failure. With all its imperfections, it did succeed in inspiring loyalties and a deep sense of commitment among its members.

I am not sure whether today's youth movements can achieve even this much. "People who screw together, glue together," claims the Berkeley SDS, but if that were true, the Roman Empire would still be in existence. Some time ago, I happened to meet with members of a radical pacifist communal settlement in upstate New York. This settlement had had its origins in the early German youth movement; its members were believing Christians who took their cue from the New Testament: "Ye cannot serve God and Mammon," and "the love of money is the root of all evil." Setting out to realize the ideal of social justice in their own lives, they established two settlements in Germany, moved to England in 1934, then to Paraguay, and finally to New York State. Still convinced that their way of life is the best of all possible ways, the surviving members have recently been trying to find supporters and active followers. On their tours of college campuses they are invariably met with tremendous enthusiasm and a great show of willingness to join. Then, a few days after each appearance, they send a bus around to take prospective candidates for a tour of the settlement. No one shows up. One could argue that it is unfair to compare the depth of commitment and the ardor of present-day revolutionaries with that shown by those who challenged less permissive societies in bygone days. Where the 19th-century revolutionary risked the gallows or a lifetime in Siberia, the rebel of the 60's risks a warning from a disciplinary committee. In these adverse circumstances a breed of devoted revolutionaries is unlikely to arise. That may be finally all to the good, but I for one confess to a certain nostalgia for the breed.

It has been said of youth movements: blessed is the land that has no need of them. For a long time, America was such a land. In the 19th and early 20th centuries, it alone among the major Western countries did not experience a widespread movement of generational conflict. The reasons for this are not particularly obscure. For one thing, the burden of the past was not felt as heavily in America as it was in Europe. Less distance separated parents and children, teachers and students; adventurous young men went West, the country was forever expanding; society as a whole was far less rigid. Then in the 20th century, when these factors had ceased to be quite so important, America was spared a movement of youth revolt by a series of economic and foreign political crises. For it is a rule of youth movements that, like *Kulturpessimismus*, they prosper only against a background of rising affluence. Another rule appears to be that they cannot strike deep roots in a country whose general mood is basically optimistic.

America in the 60's is a prosperous society, but it is no longer optimistic: the American dream has been lost on the way to affluence. It was thus in a sense inevitable that when the worldwide wave of youth revolt broke earlier in this decade, American youth should assume a leading role. (I am not speaking here of the black student revolt, because this is not a generational conflict but part of a wider movement for full political and social emancipation, and the success or failure of this movement will depend ultimately on the blacks themselves.) But the American situation is a complicated one, not only because it is accompanied by such factors as a general breakdown of authority, a crisis in the universities, and a widespread sense of cultural malaise, but also because of the response it has elicited in the society at large. Youth movements have come and gone, but never before has one been taken so seriously. Never in the past has an older generation been so disconcerted by the onslaught of the young. Previous generations of adults, more certain of their traditions and values, less ridden by feelings of guilt, have shown little patience with their rebellious sons and daughters. The middle-aged, middle-class parents of today clearly do not feel themselves to be in any such position of certainty. The milieu in which the youth of America have grown up bears striking resemblance to the European 1890's as described by Max Nordau:

There is a sound of rending in every tradition and it is as though the morrow would not link itself with today. Things as they are totter and plunge, and they are suffered to reel and fall because man is weary, and there is no faith that it is worth an effort to uphold them. Views that have hitherto governed minds are dead or driven hence, meanwhile interregnum in all its terrors prevails and there is confusion among the powers that be . . . what shall inspire us? So rings the question from the thousand voices of the people, and where a market-vendor sets up his booth and claims to give an answer, where a fool or a knave begins suddenly to prophesy in verse or prose, in sound or color, or professes to practice his art otherwise than his predecessors and competitors, there gathers a great concourse around him to seek in what he has wrought, as in Oracles of the Pythia, some meaning to be divined and interpreted. . . . It is only a very small minority who honestly find pleasure in the new tendencies, and announce them with genuine conviction as that which is sound, a sure guide for the future, a pledge of pleasure and of moral benefit. But this minority has the gift of covering the whole visible surface of society, as a little oil extends over a large area of the surface of the sea. It consists chiefly of rich educated people, or of fanatics. The former give the *ton* to all the snobs, the fools, and the blockheads; the latter make an impression upon the weak and dependent, and it intimidates the nervous. . . .

Nordau's *Degeneration* is an exaggerated, polemical tract, but much of what he wrote about the malady of his age was pertinent; he realized correctly that ideas, books, and works of art exercise a powerful, suggestive influence far beyond the small circle of the avant-garde: "It is from these productions that an age derives its ideals of morality and beauty. If they are absurd and anti-social they exert a disturbing and corrupting influence on the views of a whole generation." The moral and aesthetic ideals of today's avant-garde theater and cinema have certainly had their effect—as have the works of Jean Genet and Frantz Fanon. The deliberate gibberish of recent movies and novels finds its reflection in the involuntary gibberish of certain strands of youth politics; the message of John Cage's "Silent Sonata 4.33" (in which a performer sits in front of a piano for precisely that amount of time, poised to play but never playing) has its parallel in certain aspects of the wider cultural revolution; the theater of the absurd is not unconnected with the politics of the absurd. Indeed, the crisis of rationality has had a powerful impact: affirmation replaces analysis and argumentation; *fin de siècle* revolutionaries arrange happenings and call it a revolution, or discuss *salon* Maoism before enthusiastic audiences and call it radical commitment. Afraid to appear unfashionable or out of step with the avant-garde, those who ought to know better seem willing to take every idiocy seriously, trying to "understand" if not to accept.

Corruptio optimi pessima. The American youth movement, with its immense idealistic potential, has gone badly, perhaps irrevocably, off the rails. For this, a great responsibility falls on the shoulders of the gurus who have provided the ideological justification for the movement in its present phase—those intellectuals, their own bright dream having faded, who now strain to recapture their ideological virginity. There is perhaps some tragedy to be glimpsed in this endeavor of the old to keep pace with the young, but at the moment one cannot permit himself the luxury of a tragic sense. The doctors of the American youth movement are in fact part of its disease. They have helped to generate a great deal of passion, but aside from the most banal populism they have failed to produce a single new idea. Most of them stress their attachment to Marx. But one need only read *The Eighteenth Brumaire* to find Marx's opinion on the value of bohemianism in the revolutionary struggle; and his polemics against Bakunin leave little doubt as to his feelings with regard to the idea, first propagated one hundred years ago, of a coalition between *lumpenproletariat* and *lumpenintelligentsia.* Students should not be criticized for ignoring the lessons of the past and the dangers of chiliastic movements. They always do; the historical memory of a generation does not usually extend back very far, and the lessons of historical experience cannot be bequeathed by will or testament. But their mentors do remember, and their betrayal of memory cannot be forgiven.

The American youth revolt was sparked off by Vietnam, by race conflict, and later on by the crisis of the university. At any point along the line rational alternatives could have been formulated and presented. Instead, the movement preferred a total, unthinking rejection, and so became politically irrelevant. Yet a revolution is in fact overdue in the universities. There is nothing more appalling than the sight of enormous aggregations of students religiously writing down pearls of wisdom that can be found more succinctly and profoundly put in dozens of books. There is nothing more pathetic than to behold the proliferation of social-science non-subjects in which the body of solid knowledge proffered stands usually in inverse ratio to the scientific pretensions upheld. Whole sections of the universities could be closed down for a year or two, and the result, far from being the disaster to civilization which some appear to anticipate, would probably be beneficial. Unfortunately, this is about the last thing that is likely to happen, for it is precisely the non-subjects, the fads, and the bogus sciences to which the "radicals" in their quest for social relevance are attracted as if by magnetic force. As for the consequences of all this, one thing can be predicted with certainty: those to be most directly affected by the new dispensation in the universities will emerge from the experience more confused and disappointed than ever, and more desperately in need of certain truths, firm beliefs.

An American youth movement was bound to occur sooner or later; youth revolt is a natural phenomenon, part of the human condition. But the particular direction the American movement would take was not at all foreordained, and it is therefore doubly sad that in its extreme form it has taken a destructive course, self-defeating in terms of its own aims. It seems fairly certain at this point that the American movement will result in a giant hangover, for the more utopian a movement's aims, the greater the disappointment which must inevitably ensue. The cultural and political idiocies perpetrated with impunity in this permissive age have clearly gone beyond the borders of what is acceptable for any society, however liberally it may be structured. No one knows whether the right-wing backlash, so long predicted, will in fact make its dreadful appearance; perhaps we shall be spared this reaction. It is more likely that there will be a backlash from within the extremist movement itself, as ideas and ideologies undergo change and come into conflict with underlying attitudes. Insofar as those attitudes are intolerant and irrational, they will not quickly mellow, and for that reason America is likely to experience a great deal more trouble with its *enragés*.

The American youth movement of the 60's, infected by the decadence of the age, missed the opportunity to become a powerful agent of regeneration and genuine social and political change. But decadence, contrary to popular belief, is not necessarily a fatal disease. It is a phase through which many generations pass at various stages of their development. The boredom that gives rise to decadence contains the seeds of its own destruction, for who, after a time, would not become bored with boredom? In 1890, the prevailing mood in France was expressed in the term *fin de siècle;* the most popular sport was national self-degradation; and everyone was convinced that the decay of the country had reached its ultimate stage. Charles Gide, the economist, compared France with a sugarloaf drowning in the sea. Fifteen years later the crisis was suddenly over. Almost overnight, pessimism was transformed into optimism, defeatism into aggressive nationalism, a preoccupation with eroticism into a new enthusiasm for athletics. No one knew exactly why this happened: French society and politics remained essentially the same, the demographic problem was still in full force, moral and religious uncertainties were as rampant as before. I do not mean to suggest that recovery is always so certain; indeed, the form the cure takes is sometimes almost as

444

bad as the disease. But generations seldom commit collective suicide. As they rush toward the abyss, a guardian angel seems to watch over them, gently deflecting them at the very last moment. Nevertheless, even the patience of angels must not be tried too severely.

Robert Brustein

Robert Brustein was born in New York in 1927, attended Amherst, Yale, and Nottingham and received a doctorate at Columbia in 1957. He has taught at Cornell, Vassar, and Columbia, and is now Dean of the Drama School at Yale. He has been drama critic for The New Republic *since 1959 and has received the George Jean Nathan Award (1962) and the George Polk Memorial Award (1965) for outstanding criticism. Many of his magazine pieces are collected in* Season of Discontent: Dramatic Opinions 1959–65 *(1967). A study,* The Theatre of Revolt: An Approach to Modern Drama, *appeared in 1964. The following article is from* The New Republic, *April 26, 1969.*

THE CASE FOR PROFESSIONALISM

> In such a state of society [a state of democratic anarchy], the master fears and flatters his scholars, and the scholars despise their masters and tutors; young and old are alike; and the young man is on a level with the old, and is ready to compete with him in word and deed; and old men condescend to the young and are full of pleasantry and gaiety; they are loth to be thought morose and authoritative, and therefore they adopt the manners of the young. . . .
>
> PLATO, *THE REPUBLIC,* BOOK VIII

Among the many valuable things on the verge of disintegration in contemporary America is the concept of professionalism—by which I mean to suggest a condition determined by training, experience, skill, and achievement (by remuneration, too, but this is secondary). In our intensely Romantic age, where so many activities are being politicized and objective judgments are continually colliding with subjective demands, the amateur is exalted as a kind of democratic culture hero, subject to no standards or restrictions. This development has been of concern to me because of its impact upon my immediate areas of interest—the theater and theater training—but its consequences can be seen everywhere, most conspicuously in the field of liberal education. If the amateur is coequal—and some would say, superior—to the professional, then the student is coequal or superior to the professor, and "the young man," as Plato puts it in his discourse on the conditions that lead to tyranny, "is on a level with the old, and is ready to compete with him in word and deed."

As recently as five years ago, this proposition would have seemed remote; today, it has virtually become established dogma, and its implementation is absorbing much of the energy of the young. Although student unrest was originally stimulated, and rightly so, by such external issues as the war in Vietnam and the social grievances of the blacks and the poor, it is now more often aroused over internal issues of power and influence in the university itself. Making an analogy between democratic political systems and the university structure, students begin by demanding a representative voice in the "decisions that affect our lives," including questions of faculty tenure, curriculum changes, grading, and academic discipline. As universities begin to grant some of these demands, thus tacitly accepting the analogy, the demands escalate to the point where students are now insisting on a voice in electing the university president, a role in choosing the faculty, and even a place on the board of trustees.

I do not wish to comment here on the validity of individual student demands—certainly, a student role in university affairs is both practical and desirable, as long as that role remains advisory. Nor will I take the time to repeat the familiar litany of admiration for the current student generation—it has, to my mind, already been sufficiently praised, even overpraised, since for all its intrinsic passion, intelligence, and commitment, the proportion of serious, gifted, hardworking students remains about what it always was (if not actually dwindling for reasons I hope soon to develop). I do want, however, to examine the analogy which is now helping to politicize the university, and scholarship itself, because it seems to me full of falsehood.

Clearly, it is absurd to identify electoral with educational institutions. To compare the state with the academy is to assume that the primary function of the university is to govern and to rule. While the relationship between the administration and the faculty does have certain political overtones, the faculty and administration can no more be considered the elected representatives of the student body than the students—who were admitted after voluntary application on a selective and competitive basis—can be considered freeborn citizens of a democratic state: the relationship between teacher and student is strictly tutorial. Thus, the faculty member functions not to represent the student's interests in relation to the administration, but rather to communicate knowledge from one who knows to one who doesn't. That the reasoning behind this analogy has not been more frequently questioned indicates the extent to which some teachers are refusing to exercise their roles as professionals. During a time when all authority is being radically questioned, faculty members are becoming more reluctant to accept the responsibility of their wisdom and experience and are, therefore, often willing to abandon their authoritative position in order to placate the young.

The issue of authority is a crucial one here, and once again we can see how the concept of professionalism is being vitiated by false analogies. Because *some* authority is cruel, callow, or indifferent (notably the government in its treatment of certain urgent issues of the day), the Platonic *idea* of authority comes under attack. Because some faculty members are remote and pedantic, the credentials of distinguished scholars, artists, and intellectuals are ignored or rejected, and anyone taking charge of a classroom or a seminar is open to charges of "authoritarianism." This explains the hostility of many students towards the lecture course—where an "authority" communicates the fruits of his research, elaborating on unclear points when prodded by student questioning (still a valuable pedagogical technique, especially for beginning students, along with seminars and tutorials). Preferred to this, and therefore replacing it in some departments, is the discussion group or "bull session," where the student's opinion about the material receives more attention than the material itself, if indeed the material is still being treated. The idea—so central to scholarship— that there is an inherited body of knowledge to be transmitted from one generation to another—loses favor because it puts the student in an unacceptably subordinate position, with the result that the learning process gives way to a general free-for-all in which one man's opinion is as good as another's.

The problem is exacerbated in the humanities and social sciences with their more subjective criteria of judgment; one hardly senses the same difficulties in the clinical sciences. It is unlikely (though anything is possible these days) that medical students will insist on making a diagnosis through majority vote, or that students entering surgery will refuse anaesthesia because they want to participate in the decisions that affect their lives and, therefore, demand to choose the surgeon's instruments or tell him where to cut. Obviously, some forms of authority are still respected, and some professionals remain untouched by the incursions of the amateur. In liberal education, however, where the development of the individual assumes such weight and importance, the subordination of mind to material is often looked on as some kind of repression. One begins to understand the current loss of interest in the past, which offers a literature and history verified to some extent by time, and the passionate concern with the immediate present, whose works still remain to be objectively evaluated. When one's educational concerns are contemporary, the material can be subordinated to one's own interests, whether political or aesthetic, as the contemporary literary journalist is often more occupied with his own ideas than with the book he reviews.

Allied to this problem, and compounding it, is the problem of the black students, who are sometimes inclined to reject the customary university curriculum as "irrelevant" to their interests, largely because of its orientation towards "white" culture and history. In its place, they demand courses dealing with the history and achievements of the black man, both in Africa and America. Wherever history or anthropology departments have failed to provide appropriate courses, this is a serious omission and should be rectified: such an omission is an insult not only to black culture but to scholarship itself. But when black students begin clamoring for courses in black law, black business, black medicine, or black theater, then the university is in danger of becoming the instrument of community hopes and aspirations rather than the repository of an already achieved culture. It is only one more step before the university is asked to serve propaganda purposes, usually of an activist nature: a recent course, demanded by black law students at Yale, was to be called something like "white capitalist exploitation of the black ghetto poor."

On the one hand, the demand for "relevance" is an effort to make the university undertake the reparations that society should be paying. On the other, it is a form of solipsism, among both black students and white. And such solipsism is a serious threat to that "disinterestedness" that Matthew Arnold claimed to be the legitimate function of the scholar and the critic. The proper study of mankind becomes contemporary or future man; and the student focuses not on the outside world, past or present, so much as on a parochial corner of his own immediate needs. But this is childish, in addition to being Romantic, reflecting as it does the student's unwillingness to examine or conceive a world beyond the self. And here, the university seems to be paying a debt not of its own making—a debt incurred in the permissive home and the progressive school, where knowledge was usually of considerably less importance than self-expression.

In the schools, particularly, techniques of education always seemed to take precedence over the material to be communicated; lessons in democracy were frequently substituted for training in subjects; and

448

everyone learned to be concerned citizens, often at the sacrifice of a solid education. I remember applying for a position many years ago in such a school. I was prepared to teach English literature, but was told no such subject was being offered. Instead, the students had a course called *Core*, which was meant to provide the essence of literature, history, civics, and the like. The students sat together at a round table to dramatize their essential equality with their instructor; the instructor—or rather, the coordinator, as he was called—remained completely unobtrusive; and instead of determining answers by investigation or the teacher's authority, they were decided upon by majority vote. I took my leave in haste, convinced that I was witnessing democracy totally misunderstood. That misunderstanding has invaded our institutions of higher learning.

For the scholastic habits of childhood and adolescence are now being extended into adulthood. The graduates of the *Core* course, and courses like it, are concentrating on the development of their "life styles," chafing against restrictions of all kinds (words like "coercion" and "co-option" are the current jargon), and demanding that all courses be geared to their personal requirements and individual interests. But this is not at all the function of the university. As Paul Goodman has observed, in *The Community of Scholars*, when you teach the child, you teach the person; when you teach the adolescent, you teach the subject through the person; *but when you teach the adult, you teach the subject.* Behind Goodman's observation lies the assumption that the university student is, or should already be, a developed personality, that he comes to the academy not to investigate his "life style" but to absorb what knowledge he can, and that he is, therefore, preparing himself, through study, research, and contemplation, to enter the community of professional scholars. In resisting this notion, some students reveal their desire to maintain the conditions of childhood, to preserve the liberty they enjoyed in their homes and secondary schools, to extend the privileges of a child- and youth-oriented culture into their mature years. They wish to remain amateurs.

One can see why Goodman has concluded that many of the university young do not deserve the name of students: they are creating conditions in which it is becoming virtually impossible to do intellectual work. In turning their political wrath from the social world, which is in serious need of reform (partly because of a breakdown in professionalism), to the academic world, which still has considerable value as a learning institution, they have determined, on the one hand, that society will remain as venal, as corrupt, as retrogressive as ever, and, on the other hand, that the university will no longer be able to proceed with the work of free inquiry for which it was founded. As an added irony, students, despite their professed distaste for the bureaucratic administration of the university, are now helping to construct—through the insane proliferation of student-faculty committees—a far vaster network of bureaucracy than ever before existed. This, added to their continual meetings, confrontations, and demonstrations —not to mention occupations and sit-ins—is leaving precious little time or energy either for their intellectual development, or for that of the faculty. As a result, attendance at classes has dropped drastically; exams are frequently skipped; and papers and reports are either late, under-researched, or permanently postponed. That the university needs improvement goes without saying. And students have been very helpful in breaking down its excesses of impersonality and attempting to sever its ties with the military-industrial complex. But students need improvement too, which they are hardly receiving through all this self-righteous bustle over power. That students should pay so much attention to this activity creates an even more serious problem: the specter of an ignorant, uninformed group of graduates or dropouts who (when they finally leave the academic sanctuary) are incompetent to deal with society's real evils or to function properly in professions they have chosen to enter.

It is often observed that the word *amateur* comes from the Latin verb, to love—presumably because the amateur is motivated by passion rather than money. Today's amateur, however, seems to love not his subject but himself. And his assault on authority—on the application of professional standards in judgment of his intellectual development —is a strategy to keep this self-love unalloyed. The permanent dream of this nation, a dream still to be realized, has been a dream of equal opportunity—the right of each man to discover wherein he might excel. But this is quite different from that sentimental egalitarianism which assumes that each man excels in everything. There is no blinking the fact that some people are brighter than others, some more beautiful, some more gifted. Any other conclusion is a degradation of the democratic dogma and promises a bleak future if universally insisted on— a future of monochromatic amateurism in which everybody has opinions, few have facts, nobody has an idea.

Richard Hofstadter

Richard Hofstadter (1916–1970) was educated at the University of Buffalo and at Columbia, where he received the Ph.D. in 1942 and later became De Witt Clinton Professor of American History. He

450

was the author of a long series of studies marked by rich historical learning and a precise control of ideas. Among the best known are Social Darwinism in American Thought 1860–1915 *(1944),* The American Political Tradition *(1948),* The Development of Academic Freedom in the U.S. *(with Walter P. Metzger, 1952),* The Age of Reform *(1955), for which he received the 1956 Pulitzer Prize in History, and* Anti-Intellectualism in American Life *(1963). Professor Hofstadter gave the Commencement Address at Columbia on June 4, 1968, under trying circumstances, in the wake of the disturbances partly chronicled in James Simon Kunen's journal (see pages 381–394). The text of the address is from the Autumn 1968* American Scholar.

COMMENCEMENT ADDRESS

For a long time, Columbia University has been part of my life. I came here as a graduate student in 1937, returned as a member of the faculty in 1946, and have since remained. In these years, I have had at this University many admired and cherished colleagues, and many able students. In this respect, I am but one of a large company of faculty members who, differing as they do on many matters, are alike in their sense of the greatness of this institution and in their affection for it. In this hour of its most terrible trial, it could surely have found a great many of us willing to speak. Quite frankly I have never been very much interested in Commencements, although I recognize their important symbolic function. But it seems to me entirely appropriate, and also symbolic, that on this unusual occasion a member of the faculty should have been asked to speak. Trustees, administrators and students tend to agree that in ultimate reality the members of the faculty *are* the university, and we of the faculty have not been disposed to deny it.

Yet while I hope I am speaking in the interest of my university, it would be wrong to suggest that I am precisely speaking for it. It is in fact of the very essence of the conception of the modern university that I wish to put before you that no one is authorized to speak for it. A university is firmly committed to certain basic values of freedom, rationality, inquiry, discussion, and to its own internal order; but it does not have corporate views of public questions. Administrators and trustees are, of course, compelled by practical neces-

451

sity to take actions that involve some assumptions about the course and meaning of public affairs; but they know that in so doing they are not expressing a corporate university judgment or committing other minds. Members of the faculties often express themselves vigorously on public issues, but they acknowledge the obligation to make it clear that they are not speaking in the name of their university. This fact of our all speaking separately is in itself a thing of great consequence, because in this age of rather overwhelming organizations and collectivities, the university is singular in being a collectivity that serves as a citadel of intellectual individualism.

Although I mean to say a few things about our prospects at Columbia, let me first suggest to you how I think the modern university as such ought to be regarded.

A university is a community, but it is a community of a special kind—a community devoted to inquiry. It exists so that its members may inquire into truths of all sorts. Its presence marks our commitment to the idea that somewhere in society there must be an organization in which anything can be studied or questioned—not merely safe and established things but difficult and inflammatory things, the most troublesome questions of politics and war, of sex and morals, of property and national loyalty. It is governed by the ideal of academic freedom, applicable both to faculty and students. The ideal of academic freedom does indeed put extraordinary demands upon human restraint and upon our capacity for disinterested thought. Yet these demands are really of the same general order as those we regard as essential to any advanced civilization. The very possibility of civilized human discourse rests upon the willingness of people to consider that they may be mistaken. The possibility of modern democracy rests upon the willingness of governments to accept the existence of a loyal opposition, organized to reverse some of their policies and to replace them in office. Similarly, the possibility of the modern free university rests upon the willingness of society to support and sustain institutions part of whose business it is to examine, critically and without stint, the assumptions that prevail in that society. Professors are hired to teach and students are sent to learn with the quite explicit understanding that they are not required to agree with those who hire or send them.

Underlying these remarkable commitments is the belief that in the long run the university will best minister to society's needs not alone through its mundane services but through the far more important office of becoming an intellectual and spiritual balance wheel. This is a very demanding idea, an idea of tremendous sophistication, and it is hardly surprising that we have some trouble in getting it fully accepted by society or in living up to it ourselves. But just because it is demanding we should never grow tired of explaining or trying to realize it. Nor should we too quickly become impatient with those who do not immediately grasp it.

We are very much impressed now not simply by the special character of the free university but also by its fragility. The delicate thing about freedom is that while it requires restraints, it also requires that these restraints normally be self-imposed, and not forced from outside. The delicate thing about the university is that it has a mixed character, that it is suspended between its position in the external world, with all its corruption and evils and cruelties, and the splendid world of our imagination. The university does in fact perform certain mundane services of instruction and information to society—and there are those who think it should aspire to nothing more. It does in fact constitute a kind of free forum—and there are those who want to convert it primarily into a center of political action. But above these aspects of its existence stands its essential character as a center of free inquiry and criticism—a thing not to be sacrificed for anything else. A university is not a service station. Neither is it a political society, nor a meeting place for political societies. With all its limitations and failures, and they are invariably many, it is the best and most benign side of our society insofar as that society aims to cherish the human mind. To realize its essential character, the university has to be dependent upon something less precarious than the momentary balance of forces in society. It has to pin its faith on something that is not hard-boiled or self-regarding. It has to call not merely upon critical intelligence but upon self-criticism and self-restraint. There is no group of professors or administrators, of alumni or students, there is no class or interest in our society that should consider itself exempt from exercising the self-restraint or displaying the generosity that is necessary for the university's support.

Some people argue that because the modern university, whether public or private, is supported by and is part of the larger society, it therefore shares in all the evils of society, and must be quite ruthlessly revolutionized as a necessary step in social reform, or even in social revolution. That universities do share in, and may even at some times and in some respects propagate, certain ills of our society seems to me undeniable. But to imagine that the best way to change a social order is to start by assaulting its most accessible centers of thought and study and criticism is not only to show a complete disregard for the intrinsic character of the university but also to develop a curiously self-destructive strategy for social change. If an attempt is made to politicize completely our primary centers of free argument and inquiry, they will only in the end be forced to lose their character and be reduced to centers of vocational training, nothing more. Total and pure neutrality for the university is in fact impossible, but neutrality should continue to define our aim, and we should resist the demand that the university espouse the political commitments of any of its members. This means, too, that the university should be extraordinarily chary of relationships that even suggest such a political commitment.

The university is the only great organization in modern society that considers itself obliged not just to tolerate but even to give facilities and protection to the very persons who are challenging its own rules, procedures and policies. To subvert such a fragile structure is all too easy, as we now know. That is why it requires, far more than does our political society, a scrupulous and continued dedication to the conditions of orderly and peaceable discussion. The technique of the forceable occupation and closure of a university's buildings with the intention of bringing its activities to a halt is no ordinary bargaining device—it is a thrust at the vitals of university life. It is a powerful device for control by a determined minority, and its continued use would be fatal to any university. In the next few years the universities of this country will have to find the effective strategy to cope with it, and to distinguish it sharply and permanently from the many devices of legitimate student petition, demonstration and protest.

This brings me to our own problem. Our history and situation, our own mistakes, have done a great deal to create this problem; but it must not be regarded as an isolated incident, since it is only the most severe, among American universities, of a number of such incidents. We are at a crisis point in the history of American education and probably in that of the Western world. Not only in New York and Berkeley, but in Madrid and Paris, in Belgrade and Oxford, in Rome, Berlin and London, and on many college and university campuses throughout this country, students are disaffected, restive and rebellious.

I cannot pretend to offer a theory that will pull together all these events in a single coherent pattern. Nothing could be more dissimilar, for example, than the intramural situation of students at Columbia and students at the Sorbonne—nor, for that matter, than the response of the community to their actions—and yet the common bond of dissatisfaction is obvious. It is easier to account for the general rise in activism on American campuses, for all our students are troubled today by two facts of the most fundamental consequence for all of us— the persistence at home of poverty and racial injustice, and abroad of the war in Vietnam. It is the first of these that we will have to live with the longer and address ourselves to much more fully, imaginatively and generously than we have so far done. But in the short run the escalation of this cruel and misconceived venture in Vietnam has done more than any other thing to inflame our students, to undermine their belief in the legitimacy of our normal political processes, and to

454

convince them that violence is the order of the day. I share their horror at this war, and I consider that the deep alienation it has inflicted on young Americans who would otherwise be well disposed toward their country is one of the staggering uncountable costs of the Vietnam undertaking. This war has already toppled a President; but its full effects on our national life have not yet been reckoned.

Here at Columbia, we have suffered a disaster whose precise dimensions it is impossible to state, because the story is not yet finished, and the measure of our loss still depends upon what we do. For every crisis, for every disaster, there has to be some constructive response. At Columbia the constructive response has been a call for university reform. I have spoken to no one who does not believe in its desirability, and I believe that the idea of reform commands an extraordinarily wide positive response in all bodies from trustees to students, although when we come to discussing particulars, we will surely differ sharply about them. Our foundation dates from the eighteenth century, and although we have made elaborate and ingenious improvisations upon it through the generations, we have never had a decisive, concerted moment of thorough and imaginative reconsideration of our procedures. Powers need to be redistributed. Some new organs of decision and communication need to be created. A greater participation of students in university decisions seems to me to be bound to come here and elsewhere. Some students call for student power— others shrink from the term because they have some sense of the arduous work, the sheer tedium, the high responsibilities that are always a part of administrative power. I would suggest that, except for certain areas in which student decision has proved workable, what students need and should have is influence, not power; but they also need formal channels to assure them that their influence is in fact effective.

About university reform certain guiding principles ought to be observed. Columbia has been a distinguished university these many decades because it has been doing *some* things right. Plans for the future should be based upon an evolution from existing structures and arrangements, not upon a utopian scheme for a perfect university. The business of reforming a university takes time, requires a certain willingness to experiment and to retreat from experiment when it does not work, and indeed a willingness not to undertake too many interlocking experiments all at once. As reform demands time, it demands peace of mind, the ability to exchange views and proposals in a calm and deliberative spirit. It cannot be carried out, although it can be begun, in a moment of crisis. It cannot be carried out under duress.

What we need then is stability, peace, mutual confidence. The time will soon come when the first halting gestures toward conciliation can be multiplied and strengthened, when we can move more rapidly toward the reconstruction of the frame of trust.

Friends outside the university who know how serious is the damage we have suffered have asked me: How can Columbia go on after this terrible wound? I can only answer: How can it not go on? The question is not whether it will continue but in what form. Will it fall into a decline and become a third- or fourth-rate institution, will it be as distinguished as it has been for generations past, or will it somehow be made even more distinguished? Columbia is a great and —in the way Americans must reckon time—an ancient university. In this immense, rich country, we have only a limited number of institutions of comparable quality. We are living through a period in which the need for teaching and research—for the services a university performs and the things it stands for—is greater than it ever was before. What kind of a people would we be if we allowed this center of our culture and our hope to languish and fail? That is the question I must leave with you.

George W. Wetherill

George W. Wetherill was born in 1925 and served during World War II as a radar technician and instructor for the Army and Navy. He then entered the University of Chicago, received bachelor's degrees in both philosophy and science, and a Ph.D. in physics (1953) with a dissertation on fission of radioactive elements. After working at the Carnegie Institute of Washington on terrestrial magnetism, he became Professor of Geology and Geophysics at U.C.L.A. and is at present chairman of the Department of Planetary and Space Science. His most recent research has been on meteorites, comets, and the geology of the moon.

In 1969 Professor Wetherill was appointed to a seven-member Special Committee of University of California faculty members charged "to consider the appropriateness of the present relationship between the University and the research laboratories at Livermore and Los Alamos." The laboratories are operated by the University under contract to the Atomic Energy Commission. They are enormous establishments, between them having 11,000 employees, a plant valued at $700 million, and "the total national responsi-

bility for developing new nuclear and thermonuclear explosives."
In their Report, *published by the Assembly of the Academic*
Senate, May 11, 1970, six committee members recommended that
the University's relationship with the laboratories could be con-
tinued, though "only with substantial modifications." Professor
Wetherill's dissenting "Personal Addendum" follows.

UNIVERSITY RESEARCH AT LIVERMORE AND LOS ALAMOS

I. INTRODUCTION

In writing about the work of the Livermore and Los Alamos laboratories, I find it difficult at first to see beyond the horror that may one day, sooner or later, result from the weapons which have been invented there. Without minimizing the terrible consequences of warfare using more conventional weapons, I feel these devices carry the insanity of warfare to its senseless conclusion; their effects go beyond genocide in eliminating not only entire populations, but destroy the physical basis of their culture as well; even the land itself may become unfit for life.

However, one should pause a bit before going on to a more objective discussion of why I believe the development of nuclear weapons is an unfit business for the University of California to engage in, and wonder why there has been so little outcry against these weapons in our University community. In some way the danger of thermonuclear annihilation has failed to motivate us to serious protest. A curious insensitivity exists, illustrated by such actions as that of a land investment company which ran a full page advertisement in the *Los Angeles Times* on February 14, 1970, consisting of a photograph of an explosion of a nuclear weapon, beneath which was printed: "Even if they drop a bomb on it, you still own the hole." How much of the horror is unconsciously ameliorated by the fact that a great university, presumably dedicated to humanistic values, is the sole contractor for the design, development, and testing of all U. S. nuclear weapons?

By writing of this, I certainly don't wish to create the impression that my co-workers on this committee are less sensitive to these matters than myself. I am also aware that in making recommendations of this kind it is necessary to go beyond one's immediate, sometimes emotional response and to deal with the truly complex issues involved. This was done by the majority in writing their report, and I am also obligated to do so.

In order to do this, it is necessary to propose criteria for deciding whether or not an activity is an appropriate one for the University to engage in, and then to decide whether or not the operation of these laboratories meets these criteria.

Particularly since the end of World War II, most major American universities, including the University of California, have engaged in various activities which appear to be of rather direct benefit to the military power of the country. Until recently, this practice has not been widely criticized, and it is not hard to recall the traditional reasons given in support of these practices. These generally stress the need for military power in an armed world, the obligation of the University to use its resources for public service, and the right of an individual to pursue research of his choice without intimidation from others.

In the last few years there has arisen among many people a strong feeling that traditional arguments of this kind require reexamination. This widespread questioning of traditional values and assumptions is a direct consequence of the shocking impact of recent events and developments upon our lives. These include the profound dismay of viewing in Viet Nam the consequences of our shallow belief in our innate moral superiority and historical role as the global champion of freedom, fear and misgivings concerning the monstrous weapons arrayed against us and with which we are threatening others, the assassination of our most popular leaders, the extreme and often self-destructive alienation of many in the new generation, a realization of man's abuse of the finite capacity of our planet to support life, and the recognition of the racism infecting the core of this society which had seemed well on the road to perfection.

II. THE PROPER SERVICE OF THE UNIVERSITY

In seeking how to adequately respond to these developments it is necessary to examine the fundamental assumptions of many areas of society and its institutions, to see wherein they have failed, and what can be done about it. Among these institutions is the university. The charge to this committee constitutes but one facet of the reexamination which is currently going on in many areas of university affairs, and must be viewed in this broader context. Simply changing the relationship between the University and the Livermore and Los Alamos laboratories would effect little change in the nature of the University. However, it is one step, among many, which can be taken to place the University more in harmony with the needs of society.

I express it this way, because I believe that the general purpose of the university is to serve society. This is true, if for no other reason, because otherwise it would be rather unreasonable for us to expect society to support us. By "serving society," I by no means wish to imply that the university should be an instrument of the state. To achieve the former without becoming (or remaining) the latter is part of the task before us.

This requirement that the university serve society has led to the demand that the university work directly on environmental pollution, the urban crisis, nuclear weapons, training of military officers, agricultural automation, the problems of farm laborers, and many other things. One of the major arguments given in support of the university's assuming these roles, is that the most able people are to be found in the university community, and that the problems are so pressing that enlistment of the most able people in their solution is mandatory. It is also asserted that only in the university are the necessary intellectual and technological skills combined with human values, and that this humanization of such things as weapons technology demands University participation. While there could be some truth in this flattering picture we have drawn of ourselves, I feel that our too ready acceptance of it has led to delusions of grandeur on our part, and will, in many areas, lead to disappointment in our actual performance on the part of others.

I think it necessary to go beyond the general requirement that the university must serve society, because this is the general function not only of the university, but all other institutions as well. It is the task of each of these institutions to define as clearly as possible the specific and unique service which they can perform. Such clear definition is essential if we are to expect the financial support and freedom from interference needed to properly perform our special service and to avoid disappointing those who have been led by our own self-image to expect more than we are able to achieve. It is not surprising that many persons outside the University, both in government and in private life, seem to have little appreciation of the needs and functions of a university, when the University has permitted itself to become an almost formless conglomerate.

I believe that the specific service of the university is to study, understand, and interpret all aspects of our physical and cultural universe, past and present, to synthesize this knowledge, give it new form, and transmit it to society by teaching, publication, and public expression. As a consequence, the university serves society as a source of enlightenment and critical commentary. Artificial barriers to the acquisition and dissemination of knowledge, such as security classification, are incompatible with this concept of the role of a university. Furthermore, these roles, roughly referred to as research and teaching, are not unrelated functions, but are in a synergistic relationship, and only when

459

they reinforce each other in this way should an institution be considered to be a university.

In addition, there is another way in which the university may be distinguished from other similar institutions, which is a corollary of the foregoing, and follows from the role of the university in teaching. This is the time scale in which it operates. Most institutions of our society are forced to focus their attention on the immediate present, and must deal with the complex day-to-day details of our world. The university, on the other hand, has the obligation of preparing its students for their lifetime and of helping them acquire the basic understanding and skills they will need to live creatively well into the twenty-first century. The curricula and courses offered must constantly be tested against this criterion rather than reflect the latest fashion.

An example of the pitfalls of being a follower of educational fashion may be seen by remembering that in the late 1950's, following the early Soviet successes in space, great emphasis was placed on the fact that the U.S.S.R. was graduating more engineers and scientists than our country. In order to survive as a nation it was thought necessary to correct this situation; high school courses in mathematics and sciences were overhauled and emphasized, and university programs in these areas were enlarged. Now it is ten years later; within the past two or three years we have graduated the first Ph.D.'s who were inspired to enter science and engineering as a result of the post-Sputnik changes in high school education. We have landed on the moon, and we have clearly gained world leadership in space science and technology. Now we learn that somehow this was a mistake. Whereas in 1959 our major national problem was affluence, now it is poverty. The Ph.D.'s in physics can't find jobs. Perhaps it is not reasonable to have expected Congress and the White House to have foreseen this result, but the universities don't appear to have been any more far-sighted.

In the area of research, this need to operate on a long time scale is represented by the importance to the university of basic, rather than applied research. It is not that applied research is impure and beneath our intellectual dignity, but it is that basic research is badly needed, it is the type of research most easy to associate with teaching, and it is that kind of research of most enduring significance.

There has arisen a somewhat frivolous image of the nature of basic research to which its supporters have contributed. It is that basic research is pursued at random and for fun. In fact, basic research is no more random than any other kind of research; there are definite criteria which are used in choosing between different research projects and in evaluating these choices. Such evaluation is made routinely in deciding which of our colleagues merit promotion and in reviewing research proposals. One of the principal criteria is that the research must involve a fundamental problem, the solution to which will provide some general understanding and reduce the need for trial and error experimentation. With regard to the "fun," this is simply a way of saying that we enjoy our work, although sometimes the enjoyment may resemble a form of masochism.

Amidst the clamor for immediate solution of our many problems, it should be remembered that many of these problems have been caused, or at least aggravated, by excessively rapid application of research. The internal combustion engine, pesticides, and psychological testing are a few examples. The only preventative for this is broad basic understanding which will permit us to see beyond the immediate benefits of technological innovations to their longer range and broader consequences.

In saying this, I don't mean to imply that applied research has no place at all in the university; actually there is no clear line between basic and applied research. However, the extremes of each are clearly distinguishable, and a research program which most nearly resembles the research and development division of an industrial manufacturer is clearly out of place in a university.

Another corollary of the special and unique function of a university, as defined, is that appropriate university projects will be generated from within the university and will be neither imposed nor controlled by outside forces.

I wish to make clear that I do not think the foregoing represents an ivory tower concept of a university, the faculty of which is hibernating in an academic cocoon, insensitive to the real world outside. In fact, it is difficult to take this possibility seriously. The clear and present danger to the University comes from the opposite direction; the threat comes from the trend toward such deep involvement in the detailed everyday problems of society that the ability of the University to perform its special role is endangered.

What then is the obligation of the University in performing "public service"? I suggest that the functions described above encompass the *entire* public service which the University can perform without jeopardizing its capacity to fulfill its special role.

It may be expected that a number of projects which originate in the University, and were at one time appropriate, will so grow in size and complexity that the work of these projects will cease to interact effectively with the teaching role of the University. Upon achieving a viability of their own, such enterprises should be severed from the University, and go on their own. This should not be considered a traumatic experience for either, but a normal development, analogous to one's children becoming of age and leaving home. The University can then turn anew to its fundamental innovative role.

While the university I am describing is not an ivory tower, neither is it unlimited. This more limited role of the university may be expected to result in the need for other institutions to perform functions relinquished by the university. It is therefore imperative that the means to perform these functions be provided to these institutions. To some extent, this has been done in various governmental laboratories. Many persons working in laboratories of such agencies as the U. S. Geological Survey, NASA, the National Center for Atmospheric Research, the Kitt Peak Observatory, etc. are permitted freedom in their work comparable to that found in a university. A number of outstanding investigators have been attracted to positions which permit them to devote full time to research. These people belong essentially to the same intellectual community as university people, and their interaction with those in universities is comparable to that between the faculties of different universities. Much further development of this kind is necessary, including the extension of this freedom to industrial laboratories. If a "university atmosphere" is essential to work of high quality, and high quality work is needed in government or industry, there is no fundamental reason why workers in civil service or industrial laboratories cannot obtain the privileges necessary to do their job properly. As the problems of society become more complex, it is clear that the already overburdened universities must be relieved of the responsibility of being the only institutions capable of excellence.

In summary, appropriate University research activities should interact constructively with its teaching function, should not introduce impediments to the free exchange of knowledge such as security classification, should emphasize basic, rather than applied research, even though a certain amount of the latter may be desirable. Furthermore, the initiative and control of University projects should be from within the University, rather than external to it.

III. THE LIVERMORE AND LOS ALAMOS LABORATORIES

We now turn to the question of whether or not the operation of these laboratories fulfills the foregoing criteria for an appropriate university activity. It appears to me that it does not.

First, the relationship of the work of these laboratories to the teaching program of the University is minimal and peripheral. The University possesses on its campuses facilities and faculty more than sufficient to absorb the small number of students associated with these laboratories.

Much of the work done at these laboratories is subject to security classification, a situation inimical to the free exchange of ideas and information characteristic of a university. For this reason, the University of California has moved to virtually eliminate such classified research from its campuses; almost all other major universities have done the same. Furthermore, the need for security classification imposes a political test upon University personnel, a practice disavowed on the campuses by all segments of the University community. It has been argued that at present this test is not a severe one. Even if this is true, there is no guarantee that it will remain so. The history of our country shows that the political climate changes, and from time to time we become obsessed with the threat of internal subversion. It is not reasonable to suppose that we have finally outgrown this custom.

Many of the research projects carried out in these laboratories could certainly qualify as the kind of basic and applied research appropriate to a university, except that in some cases the physical size of the project makes it difficult for students to contribute in an individually meaningful way. However, the basic function, the reason for existence of these laboratories, remains what it always has been—the design, development and testing of nuclear weapons. Even if one puts out of mind the uses of these devices, to a large extent the kind of work is more nearly that of the research division of a manufacturing corporation than that of a university. A considerable distortion of the term "research" is necessary in order to apply it to the redesign of a nuclear warhead to be compatible with a new type of missile.

Finally, the criterion that appropriate University activities be internally generated and controlled is not fulfilled. The development of weapons is ultimately under the direction of the military branches of government. Much of the non-classified work, such as the use of nuclear explosives for excavation and other non-military purposes, the development of nuclear-powered rocket engines, and the development of thermonuclear power are national programs of the Atomic Energy Commission and subject to their direction and control. Even that portion of the work which is generated internally by the staff of these laboratories is external to most of the University, since the laboratory staff is not part of the University community, either through physical proximity or through academic status and privileges.

I have avoided introducing arguments which may be considered to be based on the morality or immorality of the work done in these laboratories. I have followed this course because I would feel excessively self-righteous if I were to attempt to bind my colleagues' actions by my personal moral beliefs, and also because I don't think that morality is a prime characteristic of a university. There is a certain incompatibility between freedom and morality. There are many repressive people in our society who would constrain the University by their ideas of what is moral and immoral, and I am reluctant to join their numbers.

However, there is an aspect of the operation of these laboratories which I believe is immoral in a different sense. It is related to the matter of external, rather than University, control of the work done there. Everyone should agree that the work of these laboratories is at least relevant to moral consideration. The question of whether one should develop weapons, which might kill or disable hundreds of millions of people in a few minutes, is clearly a moral question, even if one feels the morally correct answer to be yes (for example, on the grounds that the development of these weapons makes this outcome less probable). By operating these laboratories the University and the individuals which comprise it are assuming a large measure of responsibility for the consequences, moral or immoral, of the work done there. For example, it is generally agreed that the use of the name of the University is an important factor in recruiting scientists and technicians of high ability to work in these laboratories. Because of the secrecy of the work, the University is in ignorance of what is actually being done in the laboratories. Should it turn out that the consequences of this work are generally held by ourselves and others to be clearly detrimental to mankind, we and others in the University are not in a position to say that we knew the risks and took the responsibility. Rather, we will have to say that we didn't really know what was being done there and that the University was only taking orders from the military forces. I cannot see how a university can believe this to be a morally justifiable position in which to find itself.

If the foregoing seems to some to represent a hypothetical problem unlikely to arise in the real world, they should be reminded that this has already happened at least once. During the early 1950's both of these laboratories were heavily engaged in developing weapons which combined thermonuclear reactions with fission, to produce a weapon a thousand times as powerful as those which destroyed Hiroshima and Nagasaki. Knowledge of the nature of these weapons, in particular the vastly increased radioactive fallout which would bring death to people far beyond the blast area, was kept from the public, including the University community, until an arsenal of these weapons was already deployed. The combination of these weapons with the intercontinental missile has brought about the present balance of terror.

It is therefore apparent that the operation of these laboratories fails to meet every one of the criteria set forth in defining an appropriate University activity. It is of interest to compare this conclusion with the conclusions reached by the majority of the membership of this committee. I find myself in essential agreement with the factual material presented in the first two parts of the majority report. It is

464

obvious that I disagree with much that is written in the remaining two parts of that report. However, it is noteworthy, that in spite of significant differences in our basic assumptions regarding the proper role of a modern university, both reports come to the conclusion that continuation of the existing relationship with the laboratories is not appropriate. I am sure there are many who will not accept all of my criteria defining an appropriate University activity, but it appears that the combination of the secret nature of much of the work of these laboratories, their minimization of the educational role, and their external control and direction violate almost anyone's concept of the proper nature of a university. Regardless of one's basic assumptions, most will admit that it is possible for a university activity to be inappropriate.

I propose that if anything is inappropriate it is the operation of these laboratories.

I must strongly differ with my colleagues on this committee in their belief that closer relationships between the University and the laboratories will change things sufficiently to transform the present inappropriate relationship to an appropriate one. The only reason the present relationship with the laboratories has been tolerable, in spite of the inconsistencies between their work and the proper tasks of a university, is that the laboratories interact very little with the campuses of the University. Integration of the laboratories into the University system, as proposed in the majority report, would only make manifest how inappropriate their activities are. The changes proposed would do little to alter the basic function of the laboratories—the development of nuclear weapons under the direction of control of the military forces. These agencies will still require that this military work remain secret, and investigations of the political beliefs of those working in the laboratories will continue. Much of the work of the laboratories will continue to have little interaction with the educational functions of the University.

The consequences of this integration will be a mixture of some proper University functions with activities fundamentally inappropriate. The incompatibility of these activities will be much more visible than before and will quite properly lead to a demand for the separation of the weapons work from University sponsorship. This will be much more difficult to accomplish after integration of the laboratories has intermingled this work with proper University functions. Our position would then more resemble that of M.I.T. where, in the Lincoln Laboratory, military research is combined with activities, particularly in the field of radio astronomy, which are a vital part of the work of M.I.T. faculty and students. Their dilemma is more acute, and I cannot recommend voluntarily moving into a similar situation.

Rather, I feel that we should recognize that at the present time operation of laboratories such as these is an anomaly that can be removed without significant dislocation of legitimate University activities, and that we should take the opportunity to do so, rather than move forward a situation where the anomaly will be more apparent, and in which removal could be accomplished only at the cost of considerable damage to the operation of the University.

IV. RECOMMENDATION

It is recommended that the University inform the Atomic Energy Commission that it does not plan to continue the operation of these laboratories beyond the expiration of the present contracts on September 30, 1972. Between now and that date, the University and the A.E.C. should take measures to terminate this operation in an orderly way so as to minimize sudden disruption of University activities carried out in conjunction with the laboratories, such as the Applied Science Department of the Davis campus.

Respectfully submitted,
GEORGE W. WETHERILL

TECH-
NOLOGY
AND HUMAN
VALUES

The successful application of science to our practical problems has been truly described as "one of the miracles of mankind." But unless it be in partisan defense of free enterprise or the democratic way of life, no serious writer today can discuss technological progress without misgivings. Most of us, at least, are aware of some of the terrifying losses that seem always to accompany the gains: the atomic balance of terror; the population explosion; the poisoning of our air, water, and soil; the electronic and psychological threat to privacy; the displacement of skilled workers by skilled machines; and the recent advances in brain chemistry and genetics which promise the means of even more terrifying damage to mankind.

The first three writers in the present section share the assumption, spoken or unspoken, that technology itself will not solve the problems it creates, and that in order to find a way out of the dilemma, we need to understand it in the broadest terms. Erich Fromm offers a wide-ranging general estimate of where we stand now with our technological society. He insists that some of the key concepts of it, such as "maximal efficiency and output," need to be reexamined, and that its dehumanizing effect on man needs to be reckoned in the balance sheet along with its progress. Lynn White, Jr., takes up technology in long historical perspective, tracing the idea of man's domination of nature back to Western Christianity itself and boldly proposing that "we find a new religion, or rethink our old one." More radically yet, Theodore Roszak asks us to reject a culture based on science and technology, on "the myth of objective consciousness" itself, preparatory to turning toward an entirely antithetic system of values. As a balancing agent, we print next F. M. Esfandiary's account of technological progress from the point of view of one who knows the unscientific passivity, and corresponding suffering, of the civilization of the Orient.

The section ends with two satires of technology: Jonathan Swift expresses his misgivings concerning applied science still in its infancy; E. B. White's comical science fiction of 1950 is already too true.

W. H. Auden (1907–)

MOON LANDING

It's natural the Boys should whoop it up for
so huge a phallic triumph, an adventure
    it would not have occurred to women
    to think worthwhile, made possible only

because we like huddling in gangs and knowing
the exact time: yes, our sex may with reason
    hurrah the deed, although the motives
    that primed it were somewhat less than *menschlich*.

A grand gesture. But what does it period?
What does it osse? We were always adroiter
    with objects than lives and more facile
    at courage than kindness: from the moment

the first flint was flaked, this landing was merely
a matter of time. But our selves, like Adam's,
    still don't fit us exactly, modern
    only in this—our lack of decorum.

Homer's heroes were no braver than Armstrong,
Aldrin, Collins, but more fortunate: Hector
    was excused the insult of having
    his valor covered by television.

Worth *going* to see? I can well believe it.
Worth *seeing?* Mneh! I once rode through a desert
    and was not charmed: give me a watered
    lively garden, remote from blatherers

about the New, the von Brauns and their ilk, where
on August mornings I can count the morning
    glories, where to die has a meaning,
    and no engine can shift my perspective.

Unsmudged, thank God, my Moon still queens the Heavens
as She ebbs and fulls, a Presence to glop at,
    Her Old Man, made of grit not protein,
    still visits my Austrian several

with His old detachment, and the old warnings
still have power to scare me: Hybris comes to
    a nasty finish, Irreverence
    is a greater oaf than Superstition.

Our apparatniks will continue making
the usual squalid mess called History:
    all we can pray for is that artists,
    chefs and saints may still appear to blithe it.

(1969)

Erich Fromm

Erich Fromm, born in Germany in 1900, studied sociology and
psychology at Heidelberg, Frankfort, and Munich and received
the Ph.D. from Heidelberg in 1922. He then trained in psycho-
analysis at Munich and at the Psychoanalytic Institute in Berlin.
In 1934 he settled in the United States and eventually became an
American citizen. He became Professor of Psychiatry at New
York University in 1962, has lectured at Columbia, was for a
long time on the faculty of Bennington College, and from 1951 to
1967 taught psychoanalysis at the National University of Mexico.
His particular interest is the application of psychoanalytic theory
to the problems of culture and society, and he has published a
number of widely read books in this area. Among them are
Escape from Freedom *(1941),* Man for Himself *(1947),*
The Sane Society *(1955),* Zen Buddhism and Psychoanalysis
(1960), The Heart of Man *(1964),* You Shall Be as Gods:

A Radical Interpretation of the Old Testament and Its
Tradition *(1966), and* The Revolution of Hope: Toward a
Humanized Technology *(1968), from which we print here a
major portion of Chapter 3.*

WHERE ARE WE NOW AND WHERE ARE WE HEADED?

1. WHERE ARE WE NOW?

It is difficult to locate our exact position on the historical trajectory
leading from eighteenth- and nineteenth-century industrialism to the
future. It is easier to say where we are *not*. We are not on the way
to free enterprise, but are moving rapidly away from it. We are not
on the way to greater individualism, but are becoming an increasingly
manipulated mass civilization. We are not on the way to the places
toward which our ideological maps tell us we are moving. We are
marching in an entirely different direction. Some see the direction
quite clearly; among them are those who favor it and those who fear
it. But most of us look at maps which are as different from reality
as was the map of the world in the year 500 B.C. It is not enough to
know that our maps are false. It is important to have correct maps if
we are to be able to go in the direction we want to go. The most
important feature of the new map is the indication that we have passed
the stage of the first Industrial Revolution and have begun the period
of the second Industrial Revolution.

The first Industrial Revolution was characterized by the fact that
man had learned to replace live energy (that of animals and men)
by mechanical energy (that of steam, oil, electricity, and the atom).
These new sources of energy were the basis for a fundamental change
in industrial production. Related to this new industrial potential was
a certain type of industrial organization, that of a great number of
what we would call today small- or medium-sized industrial enterprises, which were managed by their owners, which competed with
each other, and which exploited their workers and fought with them
about the share of the profits. The member of the middle and upper
class was the master of his enterprise, as he was the master of his
home, and he considered himself to be the master of his destiny.
Ruthless exploitation of nonwhite populations went together with
domestic reform, increasingly benevolent attitudes toward the poor,

and eventually, in the first half of this century, the rise of the working class from abysmal poverty to a relatively comfortable life.

The first Industrial Revolution is being followed by the second Industrial Revolution, the beginning of which we witness at the present time. It is characterized by the fact not only that *living energy* has been replaced by mechanical energy, but that *human thought* is being replaced by the thinking of machines. Cybernetics and automation ("cybernation") make it possible to build machines that function much more precisely and much more quickly than the human brain for the purpose of answering important technical and organizational questions. Cybernation is creating the possibility of a new kind of economic and social organization. A relatively small number of mammoth enterprises has become the center of the economic machine and will rule it completely in the not-too-distant future. The enterprise, although legally the property of hundreds of thousands of stockholders, is managed (and for all practical purposes managed independently of the legal owners) by a self-perpetuating bureaucracy. The alliance between private business and government is becoming so close that the two components of this alliance become ever less distinguishable. The majority of the population in America is well fed, well housed, and well amused, and the sector of "underdeveloped" Americans who still live under substandard conditions will probably join the majority in the foreseeable future. We continue to profess individualism, freedom, and faith in God, but our professions are wearing thin when compared with the reality of the organization man's obsessional conformity guided by the principle of hedonistic materialism.

If society could stand still—which it can do as little as an individual—things might not be as ominous as they are. But we are headed in the direction of a new kind of society and a new kind of human life, of which we now see only the beginning and which is rapidly accelerating.

2. THE VISION OF THE DEHUMANIZED SOCIETY OF A.D. 2000

What is the kind of society and the kind of man we might find in the year 2000, provided nuclear war has not destroyed the human race before then?

If people knew the likely course which American society will take, many if not most of them would be so horrified that they might take adequate measures to permit changing the course. If people are not aware of the direction in which they are going, they will awaken when it is too late and when their fate has been irrevocably sealed. Unfortunately, the vast majority are not aware of where they are going.

472

They are not aware that the new society toward which they are moving is as radically different from Greek and Roman, medieval and traditional industrial societies as the agricultural society was from that of the food gatherers and hunters. Most people still think in the concepts of the society of the first Industrial Revolution. They see that we have more and better machines than man had fifty years ago and mark this down as progress. They believe that lack of direct political oppression is a manifestation of the achievement of personal freedom. Their vision of the year 2000 is that it will be the full realization of the aspirations of man since the end of the Middle Ages, and they do not see that the year 2000 may be not the fulfillment and happy culmination of a period in which man struggled for freedom and happiness, but the beginning of a period in which man ceases to be human and becomes transformed into an unthinking and unfeeling machine.

It is interesting to note that the dangers of the new dehumanized society were already clearly recognized by intuitive minds in the nineteenth century, and it adds to the impressiveness of their vision that they were people of opposite political camps.[1]

A conservative like Disraeli and a socialist like Marx were practically of the same opinion concerning the danger to man that would arise from the uncontrolled growth of production and consumption. They both saw how man would become weakened by enslavement to the machine and his own ever-increasing cupidity. Disraeli thought the solution could be found by containing the power of the new bourgeoisie; Marx believed that a highly industrialized society could be transformed into a humane one, in which man and not material goods were the goal of all social efforts.[2] One of the most brilliant progressive thinkers of the last century, John Stuart Mill, saw the problem with all clarity:

I confess I am not charmed with the ideal of life held out by those who think that the normal state of human beings is that of struggling to get on; that the trampling, crushing, elbowing, and treading on each other's heels, which form the existing type of social life, are the most desirable lot of human kind, or anything but the disagreeable symptoms of one of the phases of industrial progress. . . . Most fitting, indeed, is it, that while riches are power, and to grow as rich as possible the universal object of ambition, the path to its attainment should be open to all, without favour or partiality. But the best state for human nature is that in which, while no one is poor, no one desires to be richer, nor has any reason to fear being thrust back by the efforts of others to push themselves forward.[3]

---

[1] Cf. the statements by Burckhardt, Proudhon, Baudelaire, Thoreau, Marx, Tolstoy quoted in *The Sane Society*, pp. 184 ff.

[2] Cf. Erich Fromm, *Marx's Concept of Man* (New York: Ungar, 1961).

[3] *Principles of Political Economy* (London: Longmans, 1929; 1st edition, 1848).

It seems that great minds a hundred years ago saw what would happen today or tomorrow, while we to whom it is happening blind ourselves in order not to be disturbed in our daily routine. It seems that liberals and conservatives are equally blind in this respect. There are only few writers of vision who have clearly seen the monster to which we are giving birth. It is not Hobbes' *Leviathan*, but a Moloch, the all-destructive idol, to which human life is to be sacrificed. This Moloch has been described most imaginatively by Orwell and Aldous Huxley, by a number of science-fiction writers who show more perspicacity than most professional sociologists and psychologists.

I have already quoted Brzezinski's description of the technetronic society, and only want to quote the following addition: "The largely humanist-oriented, occasionally ideologically-minded intellectual-dissenter . . . is rapidly being displaced either by experts and specialists . . . or by the generalists-integrators, who become in effect house-ideologues for those in power, providing overall intellectual integration for disparate actions."[4]

A profound and brilliant picture of the new society has been given recently by one of the most outstanding humanists of our age, Lewis Mumford.[5] Future historians, if there are any, will consider his work to be one of the prophetic warnings of our time. Mumford gives new depth and perspective to the future by analyzing its roots in the past. The central phenomenon which connects past and future, as he sees it, he calls the "megamachine."

The "megamachine" is the totally organized and homogenized social system in which society as such functions like a machine and men like its parts. This kind of organization by total coordination, by "the constant increase of order, power, predictability and above all control," achieved almost miraculous technical results in early megamachines like the Egyptian and Mesopotamian societies, and it will find its fullest expression, with the help of modern technology, in the future of the technological society.

Mumford's concept of the megamachine helps to make clear certain recent phenomena. The first time the megamachine was used on a large scale in modern times was, it seems to me, in the Stalinist system of industrialization, and after that, in the system used by Chinese Communism. While Lenin and Trotsky still hoped that the Revolution would eventually lead to the mastery of society by the individual, as Marx had visualized, Stalin betrayed whatever was left of these hopes and sealed the betrayal by the physical extinction of all those in whom the hope might not have completely disappeared. Stalin

---

[4] "The Technetronic Society," p. 19.
[5] Lewis Mumford, *The Myth of the Machine.*

could build his megamachine on the nucleus of a well-developed industrial sector, even though one far below those of countries like
England or the United States. The Communist leaders in China were
confronted with a different situation. They had no industrial nucleus
to speak of. Their only capital was the physical energy and the passions and thoughts of 700 million people. They decided that by means
of the complete coordination of this human material they could create
the equivalent of the original accumulation of capital necessary to
achieve a technical development which in a relatively short time would
reach the level of that of the West. This total coordination had to be
achieved by a mixture of force, personality cult, and indoctrination
which is in contrast to the freedom and individualism Marx had
foreseen as the essential elements of a socialist society. One must not
forget, however, that the ideals of the overcoming of private egotism
and of maximal consumption have remained elements in the Chinese
system, at least thus far, although blended with totalitarianism, nationalism, and thought control, thus vitiating the humanist vision of Marx.

The insight into this radical break between the first phase of industrialization and the second Industrial Revolution, in which society itself
becomes a vast machine, of which man is a living particle, is obscured
by certain important differences between the megamachine of Egypt
and that of the twentieth century. First of all, the labor of the live
parts of the Egyptian machine was forced labor. The naked threat of
death or starvation forced the Egyptian worker to carry out his task.
Today, in the twentieth century, the worker in the most developed
industrial countries, such as the United States, has a comfortable life
—one which would have seemed like a life of undreamed-of luxury to
his ancestor working a hundred years ago. He has, and in this point
lies one of the errors of Marx, participated in the economic progress
of capitalist society, profited from it, and, indeed, has a great deal more
to lose than his chains.

The bureaucracy which directs the work is very different from the
bureaucratic elite of the old megamachine. Its life is guided more or
less by the same middle-class virtues that are valid for the worker;
although its members are better paid than the worker, the difference
in consumption is one of quantity rather than quality. Employers and
workers smoke the same cigarettes and they ride in cars that look the
same even though the better cars run more smoothly than the cheaper
ones. They watch the same movies and the same television shows,
and their wives use the same refrigerators.[6]

The managerial elite are also different from those of old in another

---

[6] The fact that the underdeveloped sector of the population does not take part in this
new style of life has been mentioned above.

respect: they are just as much appendages of the machine as those whom they command. They are just as alienated, or perhaps more so, just as anxious, or perhaps more so, as the worker in one of their factories. They are bored, like everyone else, and use the same antidotes against boredom. They are not as the elites were of old—a culture-creating group. Although they spend a good deal of their money to further science and art, as a class they are as much consumers of this "cultural welfare" as its recipients. The culture-creating group lives on the fringes. They are creative scientists and artists, but it seems that, thus far, the most beautiful blossom of twentieth-century society grows on the tree of science, and not on the tree of art.

3. THE PRESENT TECHNOLOGICAL SOCIETY

a. Its Principles

The technetronic society may be the system of the future, but it is not yet here; it can develop from what is already here, and it probably will, unless a sufficient number of people see the danger and redirect our course. In order to do so, it is necessary to understand in greater detail the operation of the present technological system and the effect it has on man.

What are the guiding principles of this system as it is today?

It is programed by two principles that direct the efforts and thoughts of everyone working in it: The first principle is the maxim that something *ought* to be done because it is technically *possible* to do it. If it is possible to build nuclear weapons, they must be built even if they might destroy us all. If it is possible to travel to the moon or to the planets, it must be done, even if at the expense of many unfulfilled needs here on earth. This principle means the negation of all values which the humanist tradition has developed. This tradition said that something should be done because it is needed for man, for his growth, joy, and reason, because it is beautiful, good, or true. Once the principle is accepted that something ought to be done because it is technically possible to do it, all other values are dethroned, and technological development becomes the foundation of ethics.[7]

---

[7] While revising this manuscript I read a paper by Hasan Ozbekhan, "The Triumph of Technology: 'Can' Implies 'Ought.'" This paper, adapted from an invited presentation at MIT and published in mimeographed form by System Development Corporation, Santa Monica, California, was sent to me by the courtesy of Mr. George Weinwurm. As the title indicates, Ozbekhan expresses the same concept as the one I present in the text. His is a brilliant presentation of the problem from the standpoint of an outstanding specialist in the field of management science, and I find it a very encouraging fact that the same idea appears in the work of authors in fields as different as his and mine. I quote a sentence that shows the identity of his concept and the one presented

The second principle is that of *maximal efficiency and output*. The requirement of maximal efficiency leads as a consequence to the requirement of minimal individuality. The social machine works more efficiently, so it is believed, if individuals are cut down to purely quantifiable units whose personalities can be expressed on punched cards. These units can be administered more easily by bureaucratic rules because they do not make trouble or create friction. In order to reach this result, men must be de-individualized and taught to find their identity in the corporation rather than in themselves.

The question of economic efficiency requires careful thought. The issue of being economically efficient, that is to say, using the smallest possible amount of resources to obtain maximal effect, should be placed in a historical and evolutionary context. The question is obviously more important in a society where real material scarcity is the prime fact of life, and its importance diminishes as the productive powers of a society advance.

A second line of investigation should be a full consideration of the fact that efficiency is only a known element in already existing activities. Since we do not know much about the efficiency or inefficiency of untried approaches, one must be careful in pleading for things as they are on the grounds of efficiency. Furthermore, one must be very careful to think through and specify the area and time period being examined. What may appear efficient by a narrow definition can be highly inefficient if the time and scope of the discussion are broadened. In economics there is increasing awareness of what are called "neighborhood effects"; that is, effects that go beyond the immediate activity and are often neglected in considering benefits and costs. One example would be evaluating the efficiency of a particular industrial project only in terms of the immediate effects on this enterprise—forgetting, for instance, that waste materials deposited in nearby streams and the air represent a costly and a serious inefficiency with regard to the community. We need to clearly develop standards of efficiency that take account of time and society's interest as a whole. Eventually, the human element needs to be taken into account as a basic factor in the system whose efficiency we try to examine.

Dehumanization in the name of efficiency is an all-too-common occurrence; e.g., giant telephone systems employing Brave New World techniques of recording operators' contacts with customers and asking customers to evaluate workers' performance and attitudes, etc.—all aimed at instilling "proper" employee attitude, standardizing service,

---

in the text: "Thus, feasibility, which is a strategic concept, becomes elevated into a normative concept, with the result that whatever technological reality indicates we *can* do is taken as implying that we *must* do it" (p. 7).

and increasing efficiency. From the narrow perspective of immediate company purposes, this may yield docile, manageable workers, and thus enhance company efficiency. In terms of the employees, as human beings, the effect is to engender feelings of inadequacy, anxiety, and frustration, which may lead to either indifference or hostility. In broader terms, even efficiency may not be served, since the company and society at large doubtless pay a heavy price for these practices.

Another general practice in organizing work is to constantly remove elements of creativity (involving an element of risk or uncertainty) and group work by dividing and subdividing tasks to the point where no judgment or interpersonal contact remains or is required. Workers and technicians are by no means insensitive to this process. Their frustration is often perceptive and articulate, and comments such as "We are human" and "The work is not fit for human beings" are not uncommon. Again, efficiency in a narrow sense can be demoralizing and costly in individual and social terms.

If we are only concerned with input-output figures, a system may give the impression of efficiency. If we take into account what the given methods do to the human beings in the system, we may discover that they are bored, anxious, depressed, tense, etc. The result would be a twofold one: (1) Their imagination would be hobbled by their psychic pathology, they would be uncreative, their thinking would be routinized and bureaucratic, and hence they would not come up with new ideas and solutions which would contribute to a more productive development of the system; altogether, their energy would be considerably lowered. (2) They would suffer from many physical ills, which are the result of stress and tension; this loss in health is also a loss for the system. Furthermore, if one examines what this tension and anxiety do to them in their relationship to their wives and children, and in their functioning as responsible citizens, it may turn out that for the system as a whole the seemingly efficient method is most inefficient, not only in human terms but also as measured by merely economic criteria.

To sum up: efficiency is desirable in any kind of purposeful activity. But it should be examined in terms of the larger systems, .of which the system under study is only a part; it should take account of the human factor within the system. Eventually efficiency as such should not be a *dominant* norm in any kind of enterprise.

The other aspect of the same principle, that of *maximum output*, formulated very simply, maintains that the more we produce of whatever we produce, the better. The success of the economy of the country is measured by its rise of total production. So is the success of a company. Ford may lose several hundred million dollars by the failure of a costly new model, like the Edsel, but this is only a minor
478

mishap as long as the production curve rises. The growth of the economy is visualized in terms of ever-increasing production, and there is no vision of a limit yet where production may be stabilized. The comparison between countries rests upon the same principle. The Soviet Union hopes to surpass the United States by accomplishing a more rapid rise in economic growth.

Not only industrial production is ruled by the principle of continuous and limitless acceleration. The educational system has the same criterion: the more college graduates, the better. The same in sports: every new record is looked upon as progress. Even the attitude toward the weather seems to be determined by the same principle. It is emphasized that this is "the hottest day in the decade," or the coldest, as the case may be, and I suppose some people are comforted for the inconvenience by the proud feeling that they are witnesses to the record temperature. One could go on endlessly giving examples of the concept that constant increase of quantity constitutes the goal of our life; in fact, that it is what is meant by "progress."

Few people raise the question of *quality*, or what all this increase in quantity is good for. This omission is evident in a society which is not centered around man any more, in which one aspect, that of quantity, has choked all others. It is easy to see that the predominance of this principle of "the more the better" leads to an imbalance in the whole system. If all efforts are bent on doing *more*, the quality of living loses all importance, and activities that once were means become ends.[8]

If the overriding economic principle is that we produce more and more, the consumer must be prepared to want—that is, to consume—

---

[8] I find in C. West Churchman's *Challenge to Reason* (New York: McGraw-Hill, 1968) an excellent formulation of the problem:

"If we explore this idea of a larger and larger model of systems, we may be able to see in what sense completeness represents a challenge to reason. One model that seems to be a good candidate for completeness is called an *allocation* model; it views the world as a system of activities that use resources to "output" usable products.

"The process of reasoning in this model is very simple. One searches for a central quantitative measure of system performance, which has the characteristic: the more of this quantity the better. For example, the more profit a firm makes, the better. The more qualified students a university graduates, the better. The more food we produce, the better. It will turn out that the particular choice of the measure of system performance is not critical, so long as it is a measure of general concern.

"We take this desirable measure of performance and relate it to the feasible activities of the system. The activities may be the operations of various manufacturing plants, of schools and universities, of farms, and so on. Each significant activity contributes to the desirable quantity in some recognizable way. The contribution, in fact, can often be expressed in a mathematical function that maps the amount of activity onto the amount of the desirable quantity. The more sales of a certain product, the higher the profit of a firm. The more courses we teach, the more graduates we have. The more fertilizer we use, the more food [pp. 156–57]."

more and more. Industry does not rely on the consumer's spontaneous desires for more and more commodities. By building in obsolescence it often forces him to buy new things when the old ones could last much longer. By changes in styling of products, dresses, durable goods, and even food, it forces him psychologically to buy more than he might need or want. But industry, in its need for increased production, does not rely on the consumer's needs and wants but to a considerable extent on advertising, which is the most important offensive against the consumer's right to know what he wants. The spending of 16.5 billion dollars on direct advertising in 1966 (in newspapers, magazines, radio, TV) may sound like an irrational and wasteful use of human talents, of paper and print. But it is not irrational in a system that believes that increasing production and hence consumption is a vital feature of our economic system, without which it would collapse. If we add to the cost of advertising the considerable cost for restyling of durable goods, especially cars, and of packaging, which partly is another form of whetting the consumer's appetite, it is clear that industry is willing to pay a high price for the guarantee of the upward production and sales curve.

The anxiety of industry about what might happen to our economy if our style of life changed is expressed in this brief quote by a leading investment banker:

Clothing would be purchased for its utility; food would be bought on the basis of economy and nutritional value; automobiles would be stripped to essentials and held by the same owners for the full 10 or 15 years of their useful lives; homes would be built and maintained for their characteristics of shelter, without regard to style or neighborhood. And what would happen to a market dependent upon new models, new styles, new ideas?[9]

b. Its Effect on Man

What is the effect of this type of organization on man? It reduces man to an appendage of the machine, ruled by its very rhythm and demands. It transforms him into *Homo consumens*, the total consumer, whose only aim is to *have* more and to *use* more. This society produces many useless things, and to the same degree many useless people. Man, as a cog in the production machine, becomes a thing, and ceases to be human. He spends his time doing things in which he is not interested, with people in whom he is not interested, producing things in which he is not interested; and when he is not producing, he is consuming. He is the eternal suckling with the open mouth, "taking in," without effort and without inner activeness, whatever the boredom-

---

[9] Paul Mazur, *The Standards We Raise*, New York, 1953, p. 32.

preventing (and boredom-producing) industry forces on him—cigarettes, liquor, movies, television, sports, lectures—limited only by what he can afford. But the boredom-preventing industry, that is to say, the gadget-selling industry, the automobile industry, the movie industry, the television industry, and so on, can only succeed in preventing the boredom from becoming conscious. In fact, they increase the boredom, as a salty drink taken to quench the thirst increases it. However unconscious, boredom remains boredom nevertheless.

The passiveness of man in industrial society today is one of his most characteristic and pathological features. He takes in, he wants to be fed, but he does not move, initiate, he does not digest his food, as it were. He does not reacquire in a productive fashion what he inherited, but he amasses it or consumes it. He suffers from a severe systemic deficiency, not too dissimilar to that which one finds in more extreme forms in depressed people.

Man's passiveness is only one symptom among a total syndrome, which one may call the "syndrome of alienation." Being passive, he does not relate himself to the world actively and is forced to submit to his idols and their demands. Hence, he feels powerless, lonely, and anxious. He has little sense of integrity or self-identity. Conformity seems to be the only way to avoid intolerable anxiety—and even conformity does not always alleviate his anxiety.

No American writer has perceived this dynamism more clearly than Thorstein Veblen. He wrote:

In all the received formulations of economic theory, whether at the hands of the English economists or those of the continent, the human material with which the inquiry is concerned is conceived in hedonistic terms; that is to say, in terms of a passive and substantially inert and immutably given human nature. . . . The hedonistic conception of man is that of a lightning calculator of pleasures and pains, who oscillates like a homogeneous globule of desire of happiness under the impulse of stimuli that shift him about the area, but leave him intact. He has neither antecedent nor consequent. He is an isolated, definitive human datum, in stable equilibrium except for the buffets of the impinging forces that displace him in one direction or another. Self-imposed in elemental space, he spins symmetrically about his own spiritual axis until the parallelogram of forces bears down upon him, whereupon he follows the line of the resultant. When the force of the impact is spent, he comes to rest, a self contained globule of desire as before. Spiritually, the hedonistic man is not a prime mover. *He is not the seat of a process of living, except in the sense that he is subject to a series of permutations enforced upon him by circumstances external and alien to him.*[10]

---

[10] "Why Is Economics Not an Evolutionary Science?," in *The Place of Science in Modern Civilization and Other Essays* (New York: B. W. Huebsch, 1919), p. 73. (Emphasis added.)

Aside from the pathological traits that are rooted in passiveness, there are others which are important for the understanding of today's pathology of normalcy. I am referring to the growing split of cerebral-intellectual function from affective-emotional experience; the split of thought from feeling, mind from the heart, truth from passion.

Logical thought is not rational if it is merely logical[11] and not guided by the concern for life, and by the inquiry into the total process of living in all its concreteness and with all its contradictions. On the other hand, not only thinking but also emotions can be rational. *"Le coeur a ses raisons que la raison ne connaît point,"* as Pascal put it. (The heart has its reasons which reason knows nothing of.) Rationality in emotional life means that the emotions affirm and help the person's psychic structure to maintain a harmonious balance and at the same time to assist its growth. Thus, for instance, irrational love is love which enhances the person's dependency, hence anxiety and hostility. Rational love is a love which relates a person intimately to another, at the same time preserving his independence and integrity.

Reason flows from the blending of rational thought and feeling. If the two functions are torn apart, thinking deteriorates into schizoid intellectual activity, and feeling deteriorates into neurotic life-damaging passions.

The split between thought and affect leads to a sickness, to a low-grade chronic schizophrenia, from which the new man of the technetronic age begins to suffer. In the social sciences it has become fashionable to think about human problems with no reference to the feelings related to these problems. It is assumed that scientific objectivity demands that thoughts and theories concerning man be emptied of all emotional concern with man.

An example of this emotion-free thinking is Herman Kahn's book on thermonuclear warfare. The question is discussed: how many millions of dead Americans are "acceptable" if we use as a criterion the ability to rebuild the economic machine after nuclear war in a reasonably short time so that it is as good as or better than before. Figures for GNP and population increase or decrease are the basic categories in this kind of thinking, while the question of the human results of nuclear war in terms of suffering, pain, brutalization, etc., is left aside.

Kahn's *The Year 2000* is another example of the writing which we may expect in the completely alienated megamachine society. Kahn's concern is that of the figures for production, population increase, and various scenarios for war or peace, as the case may be. He impresses

---

[11] Paranoid thinking is characterized by the fact that it can be completely logical, yet lack any guidance by concern or concrete inquiry into reality; in other words, logic does not exclude madness.

many readers because they mistake the thousands of little data which he combines in ever-changing kaleidoscopic pictures for erudition or profundity. They do not notice the basic superficiality in his reasoning and the lack of the human dimension in his description of the future.

When I speak here of low-grade chronic schizophrenia, a brief explanation seems to be needed. Schizophrenia, like any other psychotic state, must be defined not only in psychiatric terms but also in social terms. Schizophrenic experience *beyond* a certain threshold would be considered a sickness in any society, since those suffering from it would be unable to function under any social circumstances (unless the schizophrenic is elevated into the status of a god, shaman, saint, priest, etc.). But there are low-grade chronic forms of psychoses which can be shared by millions of people and which—precisely because they do not go beyond a certain threshold—do not prevent these people from functioning socially. As long as they share their sickness with millions of others, they have the satisfactory feeling of not being alone; in other words, they avoid that sense of complete isolation which is so characteristic of full-fledged psychosis. On the contrary, they look at themselves as normal and at those who have not lost the link between heart and mind as being "crazy." In all low-grade forms of psychoses, the definition of sickness depends on the question as to whether the pathology is shared or not. Just as there is low-grade chronic schizophrenia, so there exist also low-grade chronic paranoia and depression. And there is plenty of evidence that among certain strata of the population, particularly on occasions where a war threatens, the paranoid elements increase but are not felt as pathological as long as they are common.[12]

The tendency to install technical progress as the highest value is linked up not only with our overemphasis on intellect but, most importantly, with a deep emotional attraction to the mechanical, to all that is not alive, to all that is man-made. This attraction to the non-alive, which is in its more extreme form an attraction to death and decay (necrophilia), leads even in its less drastic form to indifference toward life instead of "reverence for life." Those who are attracted

---

[12] The difference between that which is considered to be sickness and that which is considered to be normal becomes apparent in the following example. If a man declared that in order to free our cities from air pollution, factories, automobiles, airplanes, etc., would have to be destroyed, nobody would doubt that he was insane. But if there is a consensus that in order to protect our life, our freedom, our culture, or that of other nations which we feel obliged to protect, thermonuclear war might be required as a last resort, such opinion appears to be perfectly sane. The difference is not at all in the kind of thinking employed but merely in that the first idea is not shared and hence appears abnormal while the second is shared by millions of people and by powerful governments and hence appears to be normal.

to the non-alive are the people who prefer "law and order" to living structure, bureaucratic to spontaneous methods, gadgets to living beings, repetition to originality, neatness to exuberance, hoarding to spending. They want to control life because they are afraid of its uncontrollable spontaneity; they would rather kill it than to expose themselves to it and merge with the world around them. They often gamble with death because they are not rooted in life; their courage is the courage to die and the symbol of their ultimate courage is the Russian roulette.[13] The rate of our automobile accidents and the preparation for thermonuclear war are a testimony to this readiness to gamble with death. And who would not eventually prefer this exciting gamble to the boring unaliveness of the organization man?

One symptom of the attraction of the merely mechanical is the growing popularity, among some scientists and the public, of the idea that it will be possible to construct computers which are no different from man in thinking, feeling, or any other aspect of functioning.[14] The main problem, it seems to me, is not whether such a computer-man can be constructed; it is rather why the idea is becoming so popular in a historical period when nothing seems to be more important than to transform the existing man into a more rational, harmonious, and peace-loving being. One cannot help being suspicious that often the attraction of the computer-man idea is the expression of a flight from life and from humane experience into the mechanical and purely cerebral.

The possibility that we can build robots who are like men belongs, if anywhere, to the future. But the present already shows us men who act like robots. When the majority of men are like robots, then indeed there will be no problem in building robots who are like men. The idea of the manlike computer is a good example of the alternative between the human and the inhuman use of machines. The computer can serve the enhancement of life in many respects. But the idea that it replaces man and life is the manifestation of the pathology of today.

The fascination with the merely mechanical is supplemented by an increasing popularity of conceptions that stress the animal nature of man and the instinctive roots of his emotions or actions. Freud's was

---

[13] Michael Maccoby has demonstrated the incidence of the life-loving versus the death-loving syndrome in various populations by the application of an "interpretative" questionnaire. Cf. his "Polling Emotional Attitudes in Relation to Political Choices" (to be published).

[14] Dean E. Wooldridge, for instance, in *Mechanical Man* (New York: McGraw-Hill, 1968), writes that it will be possible to manufacture computers synthetically which are "completely undistinguishable from human beings produced in the usual manner" [!] (p. 172). Marvin L. Minsky, a great authority on computers, writes in his book *Computation* (Englewood Cliffs, N.J.: Prentice-Hall, 1967): "There is no reason to suppose machines have any limitations not shared by man" (p. vii).

such an instinctive psychology; but the importance of his concept of libido is secondary in comparison with his fundamental discovery of the unconscious process in waking life or in sleep. The most popular recent authors who stress instinctual animal heredity, like Konrad Lorenz (*On Aggression*) or Desmond Morris (*The Naked Ape*), have not offered any new or valuable insights into the specific human problem as Freud has done; they satisfy the wish of many to look at themselves as determined by instincts and thus to camouflage their true and bothersome human problems.[15] The dream of many people seems to be to combine the emotions of a primate with a computerlike brain. If this dream could be fulfilled, the problem of human freedom and of responsibility would seem to disappear. Man's feelings would be determined by his instincts, his reason by the computer; man would not have to give an answer to the questions his existence asks him. Whether one likes the dream or not, its realization is impossible; the naked ape with the computer brain would cease to be human, or rather "he" would not *be*.[16]

Among the technological society's pathogenic effects upon man, two more must be mentioned: the disappearance of *privacy* and of *personal human contact*.

"Privacy" is a complex concept. It was and is a privilege of the middle and upper classes, since its very basis, private space, is costly. This privilege, however, can become a common good with other economic privileges. Aside from this economic factor, it was also based on a hoarding tendency in which *my* private life was *mine* and nobody else's, as was *my* house and any other property. It was also a concomitant of *cant*, of the discrepancy between moral appearances and reality. Yet when all these qualifications are made, privacy still seems to be an important condition for a person's productive development.

---

[15] This criticism of Lorenz refers only to that part of his work in which he deals by analogy with the psychological problems of man, not with his work in the field of animal behavior and instinct theory.

[16] In revising this manuscript I became aware that Lewis Mumford had expressed the same idea in 1954 in *In the Name of Sanity* (New York: Harcourt, Brace & Co.):

"Modern man, therefore, now approaches the last act of this tragedy, and I could not, even if I would, conceal its finality or its horror. We have lived to witness the joining, in intimate partnership, of the automaton and the id, the id rising from the lower depths of the unconscious, and the automaton, the machine-like thinker and the manlike machine, wholly detached from other life-maintaining functions and human reactions, descending from the heights of conscious thought. The first force has proved more brutal, when released from the whole personality, than the most savage of beasts; the other force, so impervious to human emotions, human anxieties, human purposes, so committed to answering only the limited range of questions for which its apparatus was originally loaded, that it lacks the saving intelligence to turn off its own compulsive mechanism, even though it is pushing science as well as civilization to its own doom [p. 198]."

First of all, because privacy is necessary to collect oneself and to free oneself from the constant "noise" of people's chatter and intrusion, which interferes with one's own mental processes. If all private data are transformed into public data, experiences will tend to become more shallow and more alike. People will be afraid to feel the "wrong thing"; they will become more accessible to psychological manipulation which, through psychological testing, tries to establish norms for "desirable," "normal," "healthy" attitudes. Considering that these tests are applied in order to help the companies and government agencies to find the people with the "best" attitudes, the use of psychological tests, which is by now an almost general condition for getting a good job, constitutes a severe infringement on the citizen's freedom. Unfortunately, a large number of psychologists devote whatever knowledge of man they have to his manipulation in the interests of what the big organization considers efficiency. Thus, psychologists become an important part of the industrial and governmental system while claiming that their activities serve the optimal development of man. This claim is based on the rationalization that what is best for the corporation is best for man. It is important that the managers understand that much of what they get from psychological testing is based on the very limited picture of man which, in fact, management requirements have transmitted to the psychologists, who in turn give it back to management, allegedly as a result of an independent study of man. It hardly needs to be said that the intrusion of privacy may lead to a control of the individual which is more total and could be more devastating than what totalitarian states have demonstrated thus far. Orwell's 1984 will need much assistance from testing, conditioning, and smoothing-out psychologists in order to come true. It is of vital importance to distinguish between a psychology that understands and aims at the well-being of man and a psychology that studies man as an object, with the aim of making him more useful for the technological society.

Lynn White, Jr.

Lynn White, Jr., was born in San Francisco in 1907. He attended Stanford, Union Theological Seminary, and Harvard, where he received the Ph.D. in 1934. After teaching at Princeton and Stanford, he became President of Mills College in 1943.

*Fourteen years later he returned to full-time teaching and research
as Professor of History at U.C.L.A. and founder and director of
the Center for Medieval and Renaissance Studies. During an
energetic career as educator and historian, Professor White has
received three honorary degrees, the Pfizer prize of the History of
Science Society, and the Leonardo da Vinci Medal of the Society
for the History of Technology. Among his books are* Educating
Our Daughters: A Challenge to Colleges *(1950),* Medieval
Technology and Social Change *(1962), and* Machina ex Deo:
Essays in the Dynamism of Western Culture *(1968), from
which we take the present essay. It first appeared in* Science *for
March 10, 1967; subsequent issues of that journal record the very
diverse reactions to it.*

THE HISTORICAL ROOTS OF OUR ECOLOGIC CRISIS

A conversation with Aldous Huxley not infrequently put one at the
receiving end of an unforgettable monologue. About a year before
his lamented death he was discoursing on a favorite topic: man's
unnatural treatment of nature and its sad results. To illustrate his
point he told how, during the previous summer, he had returned to a
little valley in England where he had spent many happy months as a
child. Once it had been composed of delightful grassy glades; now it
was becoming overgrown with unsightly brush because the rabbits that
formerly kept such growth under control had largely succumbed to a
disease, myxomatosis, that was deliberately introduced by the local
farmers to reduce the rabbits' destruction of crops. Being something
of a Philistine, I could be silent no longer, even in the interests of
great rhetoric. I interrupted to point out that the rabbit itself had
been brought as a domestic animal to England in 1176, presumably to
improve the protein diet of the peasantry.

All forms of life modify their contexts. The most spectacular and
benign instance is doubtless the coral polyp. By serving its own ends,
it has created a vast undersea world favorable to thousands of other
kinds of animals and plants. Ever since man became a numerous
species he has affected his environment notably. The hypothesis that
his fire-drive method of hunting created the world's great grasslands
and helped to exterminate the monster mammals of the Pleistocene
from much of the globe is plausible, if not proved. For six millennia

at least, the banks of the lower Nile have been a human artifact rather than the swampy African jungle which nature, apart from man, would have made it. The Aswan Dam, flooding 5000 square miles, is only the latest stage in a long process. In many regions terracing or irrigation, over-grazing, the cutting of forests by Romans to build ships to fight Carthaginians or by Crusaders to solve the logistics problems of their expeditions have profoundly changed some ecologies. Observation that the French landscape falls into two basic types, the open fields of the north and the *bocage* of the south and west, inspired Marc Bloch to undertake his classic study of medieval agricultural methods. Quite unintentionally, changes in human ways often affect nonhuman nature. It has been noted, for example, that the advent of the automobile eliminated huge flocks of sparrows that once fed on the horse manure littering every street.

The history of ecologic change is still so rudimentary that we know little about what really happened, or what the results were. The extinction of the European aurochs as late as 1627 would seem to have been a simple case of overenthusiastic hunting. On more intricate matters it often is impossible to find solid information. For a thousand years or more the Frisians and Hollanders have been pushing back the North Sea, and the process is culminating in our own time in the reclamation of the Zuider Zee. What, if any, species of animals, birds, fish, shore life, or plants have died out in the process? In their epic combat with Neptune have the Netherlanders overlooked ecological values in such a way that the quality of human life in the Netherlands has suffered? I cannot discover that the questions have ever been asked, much less answered.

People, then, have often been a dynamic element in their own environment, but in the present state of historical scholarship we usually do not know exactly when, where, or with what effects man-induced changes came. As we enter the last third of the twentieth century, however, concern for the problem of ecologic backlash is mounting feverishly. Natural science, conceived as the effort to understand the nature of things, had flourished in several eras and among several peoples. Similarly, there had been an age-old accumulation of technological skills, sometimes growing rapidly, sometimes slowly. But it was not until about four generations ago that Western Europe and North America arranged a marriage between science and technology, a union of the theoretical and the empirical approaches to our natural environment. The emergence in widespread practice of the Baconian creed that scientific knowledge means technological power over nature can scarcely be dated before about 1850, save in the chemical industries, where it is anticipated in the eighteenth century. Its acceptance as a normal pattern of action may mark the greatest event in human history since the invention of agriculture, and perhaps in nonhuman terrestrial history as well.

Almost at once the new situation forced the crystallization of the novel concept of ecology; indeed, the word *ecology* first appeared in the English language in 1873. Today, less than a century later, the impact of our race upon the environment has so increased in force that it has changed in essence. When the first cannons were fired, in the early fourteenth century, they affected ecology by sending workers scrambling to the forests and mountains for more potash, sulfur, iron ore, and charcoal, with some resulting erosion and deforestation. Hydrogen bombs are of a different order: a war fought with them might alter the genetics of all life on this planet. By 1285 London had a smog problem arising from the burning of soft coal, but our present combustion of fossil fuels threatens to change the chemistry of the globe's atmosphere as a whole, with consequences which we are only beginning to guess. With the population explosion, the carcinoma of planless urbanism, the now geological deposits of sewage and garbage, surely no creature other than man has ever managed to foul its nest in such short order.

There are many calls to action, but specific proposals, however worthy as individual items, seem too partial, palliative, negative: ban the bomb, tear down the billboards, give the Hindus contraceptives and tell them to eat their sacred cows. The simplest solution to any suspect change is, of course, to stop it, or, better yet, to revert to a romanticized past: make those ugly gasoline stations look like Anne Hathaway's cottage or (in the Far West) like ghost-town saloons. The "wilderness area" mentality invariably advocates deep-freezing an ecology, whether San Gimignano or the High Sierra, as it was before the first Kleenex was dropped. But neither atavism nor prettification will cope with the ecologic crisis of our time.

What shall we do? No one yet knows. Unless we think about fundamentals, our specific measures may produce new backlashes more serious than those they are designed to remedy.

As a beginning we should try to clarify our thinking by looking, in some historical depth, at the presuppositions that underlie modern technology and science. Science was traditionally aristocratic, speculative, intellectual in intent; technology was lower-class, empirical, action-oriented. The quite sudden fusion of these two toward the middle of the nineteenth century is surely related to the slightly prior and contemporary democratic revolutions which, by reducing social barriers, tended to assert a functional unity of brain and hand. Our ecologic crisis is the product of an emerging, entirely novel, democratic culture. The issue is whether a democratized world can survive its own implications. Presumably we cannot unless we rethink our axioms.

One thing is so certain that it seems stupid to verbalize it: both modern technology and modern science are distinctively *Occidental*. Our technology has absorbed elements from all over the world, notably from China; yet everywhere today, whether in Japan or in Nigeria, successful technology is Western. Our science is the heir to all the sciences of the past, especially perhaps to the work of the great Islamic scientists of the Middle Ages, who so often outdid the ancient Greeks in skill and perspicacity: ibn-al-Haytham in optics, for example; or Omar Khayyám in mathematics. Indeed, not a few works of such geniuses seem to have vanished in the original Arabic and to survive only in medieval Latin translations that helped to lay the foundation for later Western developments. Today, around the globe, all significant science is Western in style and method, whatever the pigmentation or language of the scientists.

A second pair of facts is less well recognized because they result from quite recent historical scholarship. The leadership of the West, both in technology and in science, is far older than the so-called Scientific Revolution of the seventeenth century or the so-called Industrial Revolution of the eighteenth century. These terms are in fact outmoded and obscure the true nature of what they try to describe—significant stages in two long and separate developments. By 1000 A.D. at the latest—and perhaps, feebly, as much as two hundred years earlier—the West began to apply water power to industrial processes other than milling grain. This was followed in the late twelfth century by the harnessing of wind power. . . . From simple beginnings, but with remarkable consistency of style, the West rapidly expanded its skills in the development of power machinery, labor-saving devices, and automation. Not in craftsmanship but in basic technological capacity, the Latin West of the later Middle Ages far outstripped its elaborate, sophisticated, and aesthetically magnificent sister cultures, Byzantium and Islam. In 1444 a great Greek ecclesiastic, Bessarion, who had gone to Italy, wrote a letter to a prince in Greece. He is amazed by the superiority of Western ships, arms, textiles, glass. But above all he is astonished by the spectacle of water wheels sawing timbers and pumping the bellows of blast furnaces. Clearly, he had seen nothing of the sort in the Near East.

By the end of the fifteenth century the technological superiority of Europe was such that its small, mutually hostile nations could spill out over all the rest of the world, conquering, looting, and colonizing. The symbol of this technological superiority is the fact that Portugal, one of the weakest states of the Occident, was able to become, and to remain for a century, mistress of the East Indies. And we must remember that the technology of Vasco da Gama and Albuquerque was built by pure empiricism, drawing remarkably little support or inspiration from science.

In the present-day vernacular understanding, modern science is supposed to have begun in 1543, when both Copernicus and Vesalius published their great works. It is no derogation of their accomplishments, however, to point out that such structures as the *Fabrica* and the *De revolutionibus* do not appear overnight. The distinctive Western tradition of science, in fact, began in the late eleventh century with a massive movement of translation of Arabic and Greek scientific works into Latin. A few notable books—Theophrastus, for example—escaped the West's avid new appetite for science, but within less than two hundred years effectively the entire corpus of Greek and Muslim science was available in Latin, and was being eagerly read and criticized in the new European universities. Out of criticism arose new observation, speculation, and increasing distrust of ancient authorities. By the late thirteenth century Europe had seized global scientific leadership from the faltering hands of Islam. It would be as absurd to deny the profound originality of Newton, Galileo, or Copernicus as to deny that of the fourteenth-century scholastic scientists like Buridan or Oresme on whose work they built. Before the eleventh century, science scarcely existed in the Latin West, even in Roman times. From the eleventh century onward, the scientific sector of Occidental culture has increased in a steady crescendo.

Since both our technological and our scientific movements got their start, acquired their character, and achieved world dominance in the Middle Ages, it would seem that we cannot understand their nature or their present impact upon ecology without examining fundamental medieval assumptions and developments.

Until recently, agriculture has been the chief occupation even in "advanced" societies; hence, any change in methods of tillage has much importance. Early plows, drawn by two oxen, did not normally turn the sod but merely scratched it. Thus, cross-plowing was needed, and fields tended to be squarish. In the fairly light soils and semi-arid climates of the Near East and Mediterranean, this worked well. But such a plow was inappropriate to the wet climate and often sticky soils of Northern Europe. By the latter part of the seventh century after Christ, however, following obscure beginnings, certain Northern peasants were using an entirely new kind of plow, equipped with a vertical knife to cut the line of the furrow, a horizontal share to slice under the sod, and a moldboard to turn it over. The friction of this plow with the soil was so great that it normally required not two but eight oxen. It attacked the land with such violence that cross-plowing was not needed, and fields tended to be shaped in long strips.

In the days of the scratch plow, fields were distributed generally in units capable of supporting a single family. Subsistence farming was the presupposition. But no peasant owned eight oxen: to use the new and more efficient plow, peasants pooled their oxen to form large plow teams, originally receiving (it would appear) plowed strips in proportion to their contribution. Thus, distribution of land was based no longer on the needs of a family but, rather, on the capacity of a power machine to till the earth. Man's relation to the soil was profoundly changed. Formerly man had been part of nature; now he was the exploiter of nature. Nowhere else in the world did farmers develop any analogous agricultural implement. Is it coincidence that modern technology, with its ruthlessness toward nature, has so largely been produced by descendants of these peasants of Northern Europe?

This same exploitive attitude appears slightly before 830 A.D. in Western illustrated calendars. In older calendars the months were shown as passive personifications. The new Frankish calendars, which set the style for the Middle Ages, are very different: they show men coercing the world around them—plowing, harvesting, chopping trees, butchering pigs. Man and nature are two things, and man is master.

These novelties seem to be in harmony with larger intellectual patterns. What people do about their ecology depends on what they think about themselves in relation to things around them. Human ecology is deeply conditioned by beliefs about our nature and destiny —that is, by religion. To Western eyes this is very evident in, say, India or Ceylon. It is equally true of ourselves and of our medieval ancestors.

The victory of Christianity over paganism was the greatest psychic revolution in the history of our culture. It has become fashionable today to say that for better or worse we live in "the post-Christian age." Certainly the forms of our thinking and language have largely ceased to be Christian, but to my eye the substance often remains amazingly akin to that of the past. Our daily habits of action, for example, are dominated by an implicit faith in perpetual progress which was unknown either to Greco-Roman Antiquity or to the Orient. It is rooted in, and is indefensible apart from, Judeo-Christian teleology. The fact that Communists share it merely helps to show what can be demonstrated on many other grounds: that Marxism, like Islam, is a Judeo-Christian heresy. We continue today to live, as we have lived for about 1700 years, very largely in a context of Christian axioms.

What did Christianity tell people about their relations with the environment?

While many of the world's mythologies provide stories of creation, Greco-Roman mythology was singularly incoherent in this respect. Like Aristotle, the intellectuals of the ancient West denied that the visible world had had a beginning. Indeed, the idea of a beginning was impossible in the framework of their cyclical notion of time. In sharp contrast, Christianity inherited from Judaism not only a concept of time as nonrepetitive and linear but also a striking story of creation. By gradual stages a loving and all-powerful God had created light and darkness, the heavenly bodies, the earth and all its plants, animals, birds, and fishes. Finally, God had created Adam and, as an afterthought, Eve to keep man from being lonely. Man named all the animals, thus establishing his dominance over them. God planned all of this explicitly for man's benefit and rule: no item in the physical creation had any purpose save to serve man's purposes. And, although man's body is made of clay, he is not simply part of nature: he is made in God's image.

Especially in its Western form, Christianity is the most anthropocentric religion the world has seen. As early as the second century both Tertullian and St. Irenaeus of Lyons were insisting that when God shaped Adam he was foreshadowing the image of the incarnate Christ, the Second Adam. Man shares, in great measure, God's transcendence of nature. Christianity, in absolute contrast to ancient paganism and Asia's religions (except, perhaps, Zoroastrianism), not only established a dualism of man and nature but also insisted that it is God's will that man exploit nature for his proper ends.

At the level of the common people this worked out in an interesting way. In Antiquity every tree, every spring, every stream, every hill had its own *genius loci*, its guardian spirit. These spirits were accessible to men, but were very unlike men; centaurs, fauns, and mermaids show their ambivalence. Before one cut a tree, mined a mountain, or dammed a brook, it was important to placate the spirit in charge of that particular situation, and to keep it placated. By destroying pagan animism, Christianity made it possible to exploit nature in a mood of indifference to the feelings of natural objects.

It is often said that for animism the Church substituted the cult of saints. True; but the cult of saints is functionally quite different from animism. The saint is not *in* natural objects; he may have special shrines, but his citizenship is in heaven. Moreover, a saint is entirely a man; he can be approached in human terms. In addition to saints, Christianity of course also had angels and demons inherited from Judaism and perhaps, at one remove, from Zoroastrianism. But these were all as mobile as the saints themselves. The spirits *in* natural objects, which formerly had protected nature from man, evaporated. Man's effective monopoly on spirit in this world was confirmed, and the old inhibitions to the exploitation of nature crumbled.

When one speaks in such sweeping terms, a note of caution is in order. Christianity is a complex faith, and its consequences differ in differing contexts. What I have said may well apply to the medieval West, where in fact technology made spectacular advances. But the Greek East, a highly civilized realm of equal Christian devotion, seems to have produced no marked technological innovation after the late seventh century, when Greek fire was invented. The key to the contrast may perhaps be found in a difference in the tonality of piety and thought which students of comparative theology find between the Greek and the Latin Churches. The Greeks believed that sin was intellectual blindness, and that salvation was found in illumination, orthodoxy—that is, clear thinking. The Latins, on the other hand, felt that sin was moral evil, and that salvation was to be found in right conduct. Eastern theology has been intellectualist. Western theology has been voluntarist. The Greek saint contemplates; the Western saint acts. The implications of Christianity for the conquest of nature would emerge more easily in the Western atmosphere.

The Christian dogma of creation, which is found in the first clause of the Creeds, has another meaning for our comprehension of today's ecologic crisis. By revelation, God had given man the Bible, the Book of Scripture. But since God had made nature, nature also must reveal the divine mentality. The religious study of nature for the better understanding of God was known as natural theology. In the early Church, and always in the Greek East, nature was conceived primarily as a symbolic system through which God speaks to men: the ant is a sermon to sluggards; rising flames are the symbol of the soul's aspiration. This view of nature was essentially artistic rather than scientific. While Byzantium preserved and copied great numbers of ancient Greek scientific texts, science as we conceive it could scarcely flourish in such an ambience.

However, in the Latin West by the early thirteenth century natural theology was following a very different bent. It was ceasing to be the decoding of the physical symbols of God's communication with man and was becoming the effort to understand God's mind by discovering how his creation operates. The rainbow was no longer simply a symbol of hope first sent to Noah after the Deluge: Robert Grosseteste, Friar Roger Bacon, and Theodoric of Freiberg produced startlingly sophisticated work on the optics of the rainbow, but they did it as a venture in religious understanding. From the thirteenth century onward into the eighteenth, every major scientist, in effect, explained his motivations in religious terms. Indeed, if Galileo had not been so expert an amateur theologian he would have got into far less trouble: the professionals resented his intrusion. It was not until the late eighteenth century that the hypothesis of God became unnecessary to many scientists.

It is often hard for the historian to judge, when men explain why they are doing what they want to do, whether they are offering real reasons or merely culturally acceptable reasons. The consistency with which scientists during the long formative centuries of Western science said that the task and the reward of the scientist were "to think God's thoughts after him" leads one to believe that this was their real motivation. If so, then modern Western science was cast in a matrix of Christian theology. The dynamism of religious devotion, shaped by the Judeo-Christian dogma of creation, gave it impetus.

We would seem to be headed toward conclusions unpalatable to many Christians. Since both *science* and *technology* are blessed words in our contemporary vocabulary, some may be happy at the notions, first, that, viewed historically, modern science is an extrapolation of natural theology and, second, that modern technology is at least partly to be explained as an Occidental, voluntarist realization of the Christian dogma of man's transcendence of, and rightful mastery over, nature. But, as we now recognize, somewhat over a century ago science and technology, hitherto quite separate activities, joined to give mankind powers which, to judge by many of the ecologic effects, are out of control. If so, Christianity bears a huge burden of guilt.

I personally doubt that disastrous ecologic backlash can be avoided simply by applying to our problems more science and more technology. Our science and technology have grown out of Christian attitudes toward man's relation to nature which are almost universally held not only by Christians and neo-Christians but also by those who fondly regard themselves as post-Christians. Despite Copernicus, all the cosmos rotates around our little globe. Despite Darwin, we are *not*, in our hearts, part of the natural process. We are superior to nature, contemptuous of it, willing to use it for our slightest whim. A governor of California, like myself a churchman but less troubled than I, spoke for the Christian tradition when he said (as is alleged), "When you've seen one redwood tree, you've seen them all." To a Christian a tree can be no more than a physical fact. The whole concept of the sacred grove is alien to Christianity and to the ethos of the West. For nearly two millennia Christian missionaries have been chopping down sacred groves, which are idolatrous because they assume spirit in nature.

What we do about ecology depends on our ideas of the man-nature relationship. More science and more technology are not going to get us out of the present ecologic crisis until we find a new religion, or rethink our old one. The beatniks and hippies, who are the basic revolutionaries of our time, show a sound instinct in their affinity for Zen Buddhism and Hinduism, which conceive of the man-nature relationship as very nearly the mirror image of the Christian view. These faiths, however, are as deeply conditioned by Asian history as Christianity is by the experience of the West, and I am dubious of their viability among us.

Possibly we should ponder the greatest radical in Christian history since Christ: St. Francis of Assisi. The prime miracle of St. Francis is the fact that he did not end at the stake, as many of his left-wing followers did. He was so clearly heretical that a General of the Franciscan Order, St. Bonaventura, a great and perceptive Christian, tried to suppress the early accounts of Franciscanism. The key to an understanding of Francis is his belief in the virtue of humility, not merely for the individual but for man as a species. Francis tried to depose man from his monarchy over creation and set up a democracy of all God's creatures. With him the ant is no longer simply a homily for the lazy, flames a sign of the thrust of the soul toward union with God; now they are Brother Ant and Sister Fire, praising the Creator in their own ways as Brother Man does in his.

Later commentators have said that Francis preached to the birds as a rebuke to men who would not listen. The records do not read so; he urged the little birds to praise God, and in spiritual ecstasy they flapped their wings and chirped rejoicing. Legends of saints, especially the Irish saints, had long told of their dealings with animals but always, I believe, to show their human dominance over creatures. With Francis it is different. The land around Gubbio in the Apennines was being ravaged by a fierce wolf. St. Francis, says the legend, talked to the wolf and persuaded him of the error of his ways. The wolf repented, died in the odor of sanctity, and was buried in consecrated ground.

What Sir Steven Runciman calls "the Franciscan doctrine of the animal soul" was quickly stamped out. Quite possibly it was in part inspired, consciously or unconsciously, by the belief in reincarnation held by the Cathar heretics who at that time teemed in Italy and southern France, and who presumably had got it originally from India. It is significant that at just the same moment, about 1200, traces of metempsychosis are found also in Western Judaism, in the Provençal *Cabbala*. But Francis held neither to transmigration of souls nor to pantheism. His view of nature and of man rested on a unique sort of pan-psychism of all things animate and inanimate, designed for the glorification of their transcendent Creator, who, in the ultimate gesture of cosmic humility, assumed flesh, lay helpless in a manger, and hung dying on a scaffold.

I am not suggesting that many contemporary Americans who are concerned about our ecologic crisis will be either able or willing to counsel with wolves or exhort birds. However, the present increasing disruption of the global environment is the product of a dynamic technology and science which were originating in the Western medieval world and against which St. Francis was rebelling in so original a way. Their growth cannot be understood historically apart from distinctive attitudes toward nature which are deeply grounded in Christian dogma. The fact that most people do not think of these attitudes as Christian is irrelevant. No new set of basic values has been accepted in our society to displace those of Christianity. Hence we shall continue to have a worsening ecologic crisis until we reject the Christian axiom that nature has no reason for existence save to serve man.

The greatest spiritual revolutionary in Western history, St. Francis, proposed what he thought was an alternative Christian view of nature and man's relation to it: he tried to substitute the idea of the equality of all creatures, including man, for the idea of man's limitless rule of creation. He failed. Both our present science and our present technology are so tinctured with orthodox Christian arrogance toward nature that no solution for our ecologic crisis can be expected from them alone. Since the roots of our trouble are so largely religious, the remedy must also be essentially religious, whether we call it that or not. We must rethink and refeel our nature and destiny. The profoundly religious, but heretical, sense of the primitive Franciscans for the spiritual autonomy of all parts of nature may point a direction. I propose Francis as a patron saint for ecologists.

Theodore Roszak

Theodore Roszak (born 1933) attended U.C.L.A. and received his Ph.D. from Princeton in 1958. He is now Associate Professor of History at California State College at Hayward, where he heads the Western Culture program. Professor Roszak is a vigorous social philosopher and critic who has contributed much to such journals as The Nation, Liberation, *and* New Politics. *He was editor of and contributor to* The Dissenting Academy *(1968), and his* The Making of a Counter Culture: Reflections on the Technocratic Society and Its Youthful Opposition *(1969) was nominated for a National Book Award. The latter work analyzes some of the major influences on the modern youth culture, showing how that culture calls into question the conventional world view of science and technology; it ends with the author's recommendation of a new culture in which the magical, visionary world view would give a deeper meaning and purpose*

*to life. We print here the appendix to the book, "Objectivity
Unlimited," designed to illustrate in detail the psychology of
"objective consciousness," which the author discusses in Chapter 7.
A few of the opening pages of Chapter 7 introduce the subject.*

FROM THE MYTH OF OBJECTIVE CONSCIOUSNESS

If there is one especially striking feature of the new radicalism we
have been surveying, it is the cleavage that exists between it and the
radicalism of previous generations where the subjects of science and
technology are concerned. To the older collectivist ideologies, which
were as given to the value of industrial expansion as the capitalist class
enemy, the connection between totalitarian control and science was not
apparent. Science was almost invariably seen as an undisputed social
good, because it had become so intimately related in the popular mind
(though not often in ways clearly understood) to the technological progress that promised security and affluence. It was not foreseen even by
gifted social critics that the impersonal, large-scale social processes to
which technological progress gives rise—in economics, in politics, in
education, in every aspect of life—generate their own characteristic
problems. When the general public finds itself enmeshed in a gar-
gantuan industrial apparatus which it admires to the point of idolization
and yet cannot comprehend, it must of necessity defer to those who
are experts or to those who own the experts; only they appear to know
how the great cornucopia can be kept brimming over with the good
things of life.

Centralized bigness breeds the regime of expertise, whether the big
system is based on privatized or socialized economies. Even within
the democratic socialist tradition with its stubborn emphasis on
workers' control, it is far from apparent how the democratically governed units of an industrial economy will automatically produce a
general system which is not dominated by co-ordinating experts. It
is both ironic and ominous to hear the French Gaullists and the Wilson
Labourites in Great Britain—governments that are heavily committed
to an elitist managerialism—now talking seriously about increased
workers' "participation" in industry. It would surely be a mistake to
believe that the technocracy cannot find ways to placate and integrate
the shop floor without compromising the continuation of super-scale
social processes. "Participation" could easily become the god-word

of our official politics within the next decade; but its reference will be to the sort of "responsible" collaboration that keeps the technocracy growing. We do well to remember that one of the great secrets of successful concentration camp administration under the Nazis was to enlist the "participation" of the inmates.

It is for this reason that the counter culture, which draws upon a profoundly personalist sense of community rather than upon technical and industrial values, comes closer to being a radical critique of the technocracy than any of the traditional ideologies. If one starts with a sense of the person that ventures to psychoanalytical depths, one may rapidly arrive at a viewpoint that rejects many of the hitherto undisputed values of industrialism itself. One soon begins talking about "standards of living" that transcend high productivity, efficiency, full employment, and the work-and-consumption ethic. Quality and not quantity becomes the touchstone of social value.

The critique is pushed even further when the counter culture begins to explore the modes of non-intellective consciousness. Along this line, questions arise which strike more deeply at technocratic assumptions. For if the technocracy is dependent on public deference to the experts, it must stand or fall by the reality of expertise. But what *is* expertise? What are the criteria which certify someone as an expert?

If we are foolishly willing to agree that experts are those whose role is legitimized by the fact that the technocratic system needs them in order to avoid falling apart at the seams, then of course the technocratic status quo generates its own internal justification: the technocracy is legitimized because it enjoys the approval of experts; the experts are legitimized because there could be no technocracy without them. This is the sort of circular argument student rebels meet when they challenge the necessity of administrative supremacy in the universities. They are invariably faced with the rhetorical question: but who will allocate room space, supervise registration, validate course requirements, coordinate the academic departments, police the parking lots and dormitories, discipline students, etc., if not the administration? Will the multiversity not collapse in chaos if the administrators are sent packing? The students are learning the answer: yes, the multiversity will collapse; but *education* will go on. Why? Because the administrators have nothing to do with the reality of education; their expertise is related to the illusory busywork that arises from administrative complexity itself. The multiversity creates the administrators and they, in turn, expand the multiversity so that it needs to make place for more administrators. One gets out of this squirrel cage only by digging deep into the root meaning of education itself.

The same radicalizing logic unfolds if, in confronting the technocracy, we begin looking for a conception of expertise which amounts to something more than the intimidating truism that tells us experts are those in the absence of whom the technocracy would collapse.

An expert, we say, is one to whom we turn because he is in control of reliable knowledge about that which concerns us. In the case of the technocracy, the experts are those who govern us because they know (reliably) about all things relevant to our survival and happiness: human needs, social engineering, economic planning, international relations, invention, education, etc. Very well, but what is "reliable knowledge"? How do we know it when we see it? The answer is: reliable knowledge is knowledge that is scientifically sound, since science is that to which modern man refers for the definitive explication of reality. And what in turn is it that characterizes scientific knowledge? The answer is: objectivity. Scientific knowledge is not just feeling or speculation or subjective ruminating. It is a verifiable description of reality that exists independent of any purely personal considerations. It is true . . . real . . . dependable. . . . It works. And that at last is how we define an expert: he is one who *really* knows what is what, because he cultivates an objective consciousness.

Thus, if we probe the technocracy in search of the peculiar power it holds over us, we arrive at the myth of objective consciousness. There is but one way of gaining access to reality—so the myth holds— and this is to cultivate a state of consciousness cleansed of all sub- jective distortion, all personal involvement. What flows from this state of consciousness qualifies as knowledge, and nothing else does. This is the bedrock on which the natural sciences have built; and under their spell all fields of knowledge strive to become scientific. The study of man in his social, political, economic, psychological, historical aspects—all this, too, must become objective: rigorously, painstakingly objective. At every level of human experience, would-be scientists come forward to endorse the myth of objective consciousness, thus certifying themselves as experts. And because they know and we do not, we yield to their guidance.

•   •   •

OBJECTIVITY UNLIMITED

The items contained in this appendix are meant to give at least a mini- mal illustration of the psychology of objective consciousness as charac- terized in Chapter VII. The examples offered are few in number; but they could be multiplied many times over.

It is likely that some readers will protest that these items do not give a "balanced" picture of science and technology, but unfairly emphasize certain enormities and absurdities. Let me therefore make three points in explanation of why and how the examples of objectivity below were selected.

(1) Often, when one enters into a discussion of the less encouraging aspects of scientific research and technical innovation, the cases brought forward for consideration are either obviously extreme examples that are universally condemned (like that of the Nazi physicians who experimented on human specimens), or they are images conjured up from science fiction, which are easily waved aside precisely because they *are* fictitious. The items in this appendix are not drawn from either of these sources. Rather, they derive from what I believe can fairly be called mainstream science (I include the behavioral sciences in the term) and technology. I have tried to offer reports, examples, and statements from thoroughly reputable sources which can pass muster as possessing professional respectability. My object is to present items that have a routine, if not an almost casual, character and can therefore stand as the voice of normal, day-to-day science and technology as they are practiced in our society with a sense of complete innocence and orthodoxy—and often with the massive subsidization of public funds. Indeed, I suspect that many scientists and technicians would find nothing whatever to object to in the remarks and projects referred to here, but would view them as perfectly legitimate, if not extremely interesting, lines of research to which only a perversely anti-scientific mentality would object.

(2) Further, I would contend that the material presented here typifies what the technocracy is most eager to reward and support. These are the kinds of projects and the kinds of men we can expect to see becoming ever more prominent as the technocratic society consolidates its power. Whatever enlightening and beneficial "spin-off" the universal research explosion of our time produces, the major interest of those who lavishly finance that research will continue to be in weapons, in techniques of social control, in commercial gadgetry, in market manipulation, and in the subversion of democratic processes by way of information monopoly and engineered consensus. What the technocracy requires, therefore, is men of unquestioning objectivity who can apply themselves to any assignment and deliver the goods, with few qualms regarding the ultimate application of their work.

As time goes on, it may well be that gifted and sensitive talents will find it more and more difficult to serve the technocratic system. But such conscience-stricken types—the potential Norbert Wieners and Otto Hahns and Leo Szilards—will be easily replaced by acquiescent routineers who will do what is expected of them, who will play dumb

501

as they continue grinding out the research, and who will be able to convince themselves that the high status they receive is, in truth, the just and happy reward their idealistic quest for knowledge deserves. One would think that a man who had been hired by pyromaniacs to perfect better matches would begin to sense, at some point, how much of a culprit he was. But fame and cash can do wonders to bolster one's sense of innocence.

Not long before his death, the greatest scientific mind since Newton confessed to the world that, if he had to choose over again, he would rather have been a good shoemaker. I have often felt that, long before he learns a single thing about mesons or information theory or DNA, every aspiring young scientist and technician in our schools should be confronted with that heartbroken admission and forced to fathom its implications. But alas, I suspect there is in the great man's lament a pathos too deep any longer to be appreciated by the sorcerer's apprentices who crowd forward in disconcerting numbers to book passage on the technocratic gravy train. And where the scientists and technicians lead, the pseudo-scientists and social engineers are quick to follow. Given the dazzling temptations of a sky's-the-limit research circus, what time is there to dally over traditional wisdom or moral doubt? It distracts from the bright, hard, monomaniacal focus that pays off for the expert—especially if one bears in mind that in the technical fields these days apprentices make their mark early . . . or perhaps never. So the sweaty quest for quick, stunning success goes off in all directions. If only one can find a way to graft the head of a baboon on to a blue jay (after all, why not?) . . . if only one can synthesize a virus lethal enough to wipe out a whole nation (after all, why not?) . . . if only one can invent a Greek-tragedy writing machine (after all, why not?) . . . if only one can dope out a way to condition the public into believing that War is Peace and that the fallout shelter is our home away from home (after all, why not?) . . . if only one can devise a way to program dreams so that perhaps commercial announcements can be inserted (after all, why not?) . . . if only one can find out how to scramble DNA so that parents can order their progeny tailor-made as guaranteed-or-money-back Mozarts, Napoleons, or Jesus Christs (after all, why not?) . . . if only one can invent a method of shooting passengers like bullets from Chicago to Istanbul (after all, why not?) . . . if only one can develop a computer that will simulate the mind of God (after all, why not?) . . . one's name is made!

It is, once again, the key strategy of the technocracy. It monopolizes the cultural ground; it sponges up and anticipates all possibilities. Where science and technology are concerned, its concern is to keep its magician's hat filled with every conceivable form of research and development, the better to confound and stupefy the populace. Thus it must stand prepared to subvene every minor intellectual seizure that lays claim to being or pursuing some form of scientific knowledge. For after all, one never can tell what may come of pure research. Best buy it all up, so that one can be in the position to pick and choose what to exploit and develop.

(3) The notion of "balance," as applied to the evaluation of scientific and technical work, implies the existence of well-defined values which can be brought to bear to distinguish a desirable from an undesirable achievement. The supposition that such values exist in our culture is misleading in the extreme; but that supposition plays a critically important part in the politics of the technocracy and is, indeed, one of its stoutest bulwarks.

To begin with, we must understand that there exists no way whatever, on strictly scientific grounds, to invalidate *any* objective quest for knowledge, regardless of where it may lead or how it may proceed. The particular project may be unpalatable to the more squeamish among us—for "purely personal reasons"; but it does not thereby cease to be a legitimate exercise of objectivity. After all, knowledge is knowledge; and the more of it, the better. Just as Leigh-Mallory set out to climb Everest simply because it was *there,* so the scientific mind sets out to solve puzzles and unravel mysteries because it perceives them as being *there.* What further justification need there be?

Once an area of experience has been identified as an object of study or experimental interference, there is no rational way in which to deny the inquiring mind its right to know, without calling into question the entire scientific enterprise. In order to do so, one would have to invoke some notion of the "sacred" or the "sacrosanct" to designate an area of life that must be closed to inquiry and manipulation. But since the entire career of the objective consciousness has been one long running battle against such suspiciously nebulous ideas, these concepts survive in our society only as part of an atavistic vocabulary. They are withered roses we come upon, crushed in the diaries of a pre-scientific age.

We are sadly deceived by the old cliché which mournfully tells us that morality has failed to "keep up with" technical progress (as if indeed morality were a "field of knowledge" in the charge of unidentified, but presumably rather incompetent, experts). The expansion of objective consciousness must, of necessity, be undertaken at the expense of moral sensibility. Science deracinates the experience of sacredness wherever it abides, and does so unapologetically, if not with fanatic fervor. And lacking a warm and lively sense of the sacred, there can be no ethical commitment that is anything more than superficial humanist rhetoric. We are left with, at best, good intentions and well-meaning gestures that have no relationship to authoritative experience, and which therefore collapse into embarrassed confusion as soon as a more hard-headed, more objective inquirer comes along and asks, "But why not?" Having used the keen blade of scientific skepticism to clear our cultural ground of all irrational barriers to inquiry and manipulation, the objective consciousness is free to range in all directions. And so it does.

It is only when we recognize the essentially no-holds-barred character of the objective consciousness—its illimitable thrust toward knowledge and technical mastery of every kind—that the demand for a balanced appreciation of its achievements becomes irrelevant, as well as sleazy in the extreme. The defense of science and technology by reference to balance is, in fact, the worst vice of our culture, betraying an ethical superficiality that is truly appalling. For the balance that is called for is *not* something the scientific community itself provides, or in any sense employs as a control upon its activities. Rather, it is *we* the public who are expected to supply the balance by way of our private assessments of what the objective consciousness lays before us. The scientists and technicians enjoy the freedom—indeed they demand the freedom—to do *absolutely anything* to which curiosity or a research contract draws them. And while they undertake their completely indiscriminate activities, the technocracy which sponsors them provides the public with a scorecard. On this scorecard we can, on the basis of our personal predilections, chalk up the pluses and minuses in any way we see fit. It is all admirably pluralistic: the technocracy can afford to be pluralistic in the matter, because it knows that over the long run there will be achievements and discoveries a-plenty to meet everybody's tastes. After all, if one keeps reaching into a grab bag filled with an infinite number of things, sooner or later one is bound to pluck out enough nice things to offset the undesirable things one has acquired. But the balance involved is hardly guaranteed by those who fill the bag; it is based entirely on chance and personal evaluation.

So we arrive at the lowest conceivable level of moral discourse: ex post facto tabulation and averaging within a context of randomized human conduct. The balance that emerges from such a situation might just as well be gained if our society were to agree to subsidize every whim that arose within a community of certified lunatics, on the assumption that a certain amount of what such a procedure eventually produced would meet any standard of worthwhileness one cared to name. Where moral discrimination is concerned, the scientific and technical mandarins of the technocracy operate not very differently from the composer of chance music who offers us a chaos of sound: if we do not like what we hear, we need only wait a little longer. Eventually . . . eventually . . . there will come a concatenation of noises that charms our taste. At that point, presumably, the score as a whole is vindicated.

The demand for a balanced view of science and technology amounts, then, to something rather like a con game which the technocracy plays with the general public. Since balance is in no sense an ethical discipline the technocracy imposes upon itself by reference to a pre-established moral end, we have absolutely no guarantee that the future of scientific and technical work has anything to offer us but more of everything. All we can be sure of is that the objective consciousness will expand into more areas of life militantly and inexorably, entrenching its alienative dichotomy, invidious hierarchy, and mechanistic imperative ever more deeply in our experience. As that happens, the dreams of reason are bound to become more and more a nightmare of depersonalization. If one wonders how the world will then look to men, one need scarcely turn to the inventions of science fiction; we need only examine the activities and sentiments of those whose capacity for experience has already been raped by the ethos of objectivity. And that is what the items offered here are meant to illustrate.

(1) The first item dates back nearly a century; but it is cited without criticism in a recent survey of psychology as a significant example of pioneering neurological research. It concerns the work of Dr. Roberts Bartholow of the Medical College of Ohio. In 1874 Dr. Bartholow conducted a number of experiments on a "rather feeble-minded" woman of thirty named Mary Rafferty. The experiments involved passing an electric current into the young woman's brain through a portion of the skull that had eroded away. Here is a selection from the records of Dr. Bartholow, who introduces his findings by saying, "It has seemed to me most desirable to present the facts as I observed them, without comment."

Observation 3. Passed an insulated needle into the left posterior lobe. . . . Mary complained of a very strong and unpleasant feeling of tingling in both right extremities. In order to develop more decided reactions, the strength of the current was increased. . . . her countenance exhibited great distress, and she began to cry. . . . left hand was extended . . . the arms agitated with clonic spasms, her eyes became fixed, with pupils widely dilated, lips were blue and she frothed at the mouth. (Quoted in David Krech, "Cortical Localization of Function," in Leo Postman, ed., *Psychology in the Making* [New York: A. A. Knopf, 1962], pp. 62–63.)

Three days after this experiment, Mary Rafferty was dead. Those who think such experimentation on human specimens—especially on imprisoned persons like Mary Rafferty—is uncommon, should see M.

H. Pappworth's *Human Guinea Pigs: Experimentation on Man* (London: Routledge & Kegan Paul, 1967).

(2) To spare a sigh for the fate of animals undergoing laboratory experimentation is generally considered cranky in the extreme. The reasons for this no doubt include the layman's inability to gain a clear picture of what is happening to the animals through the technical terminology of such accounts as appear in the many journals of physiology, psychology, and medical research, as well as the prevailing assumption that such research is directly related to human benefit and is therefore necessary. The following is a fairly comprehensible report of research done for the British Ministry of Supply during World War II on the effects of poison gases. If the account detours into too many technicalities, the situation is simply this: the experimenter has forced a large dose of Lewisite gas into the eye of a rabbit and is recording over the next two weeks precisely how the animal's eye rots away. But note how the terminology and the reportorial style distance us from the reality of the matter. As in the case of Mary Rafferty above, it is impossible to focus on the fact that the event is happening before a human observer.

Very severe lesions ending in loss of the eye: . . . In two eyes of the 12 in the series of very severe lesions the destructive action of the Lewisite produced necrosis [decay] of the cornea before the blood vessels had extended into it. Both lesions were produced by a large droplet. In one case the rabbit was anaesthetized, in the other it was not anaesthetized and was allowed to close the eye at once, thus spreading the Lewisite all over the conjunctival sac [eyeball]. The sequence of events in this eye begins with instantaneous spasm of the lids followed by lacrimation in 20 seconds (at first clear tears and in one minute 20 seconds milky Harderian secretion). In six minutes the third lid is becoming oedematous [swollen] and in 10 minutes the lids themselves start to swell. The eye is kept closed with occasional blinks. In 20 minutes the oedema [swelling] is so great that the eye can hardly be kept closed as the lids are lifted off the globe. In three hours it is not possible to see the cornea and there are conjunctival petechiae [minute hemorrhages]. Lacrimation continues.

In 24 hours the oedema is beginning to subside and the eye is discharging muco-pus. There is a violent iritis [inflammation] and the cornea is oedematous all over in the superficial third. . . . On the third day there is much discharge and the lids are still swollen. On the fourth day the lids are stuck together with discharge. There is severe iritis. The corneae are not very swollen. . . . On the eighth day there is hypopyon [pus], the lids are brawny and contracting down on the globe so that the eye cannot be fully opened. . . . In 10 days the cornea is still avascular, very opaque and covered with pus. On the 14th day the center of the cornea appears to liquify and melt away, leaving a Descemetocoele [a membrane over the cornea], which remains intact till the 28th day, when it ruptures leaving only the remains of an eye in a mass of pus. (Ida Mann, A. Pirie, B. D. Pullinger, "An Experimental and Clinical Study of the Reaction of the Anterior Segment of the Eye to Chemical Injury, With Special Reference to Chemical Warfare Agents," *British Journal of Ophthalmology,* Monograph Supplement XIII, 1948, pp. 146–47.)

By way of explaining the methodological validity of such research, P. B. Medawar offers the following hard-headed observation:

For all its crudities, Behaviorism, conceived as a methodology rather than as a psychological system, taught psychology with brutal emphasis that "the dog is whining" and "the dog is sad" are statements of altogether different empirical standing, and heaven help psychology if it ever again overlooks the distinction. (P. B. Medawar, *The Art of the Soluble* [London: Methuen, 1967], p. 89.)

Professor Medawar does not make clear, however, on whom the "brutal emphasis" of this distinction has fallen: the experimenter or the experimental subject. Does it, for example, make any difference to the methodology if the subject is capable of saying, "I am sad," "I am hurt"?

For a wise discussion of the ethics and psychology of animal experimentation (as well as a few more ghastly examples of the practice), see Catherine Roberts, "Animals in Medical Research" in her *The Scientific Conscience* (New York: Braziller, 1967).

(3) The following comes from a study of the effects of wartime bombing on civilian society, with special reference to the probable results of thermonuclear bombardment. The research was done under grants from the U. S. Air Force and the Office of the Surgeon General at the Columbia University Bureau of Applied Social Research, and published with the aid of a Ford Foundation subsidy. It should be mentioned that the scholar's conclusions are generally optimistic about the possibilities of rapid recovery from a nuclear war. He even speculates that the widespread destruction of cultural artifacts in such a war might have the same long-term effect as the barbarian devastation of Greco-Roman art and architecture: namely, a liberation from the dead hand of the artistic past such as that which prepared the way for the Italian Renaissance.

We have deliberately avoided arousing emotions. In this area, which so strongly evokes horror, fear, or hope, a scientist is seriously tempted to relax his standards of objectivity and to give vent to his own subjective feelings. No one can fail to be deeply aroused and disturbed by the facts of nuclear weapons. These sentiments are certainly necessary to motivate actions, but they should not distort an investigation of the truth or factual predictions.

This book deals with the social consequences of actual bombing, starting with different types of destruction as given physical events, tracing step by step the effects upon urban populations—their size, composition, and activities—and finally investigating the repercussions upon national populations and whole countries. . . . While we are deeply concerned with the moral and humanitarian implications of bomb destruction, we excluded them from this book, not because we judged them to be of secondary importance, but because they are better dealt with separately and in a different context.

This "different context," however, has not to date been explored by the author. But he does turn to considering "the effect upon morale" of wholesale carnage. Note how the use of phrases like "apparently" and "it appears" and "it can be argued" and "there is evidence of" neatly denature the horror of the matters under discussion.

The impact of casualties upon morale stems mainly from actually seeing dead or injured persons and from the emotional shock resulting from the death of family and friends. . . . No other aspect of an air raid causes as severe an emotional disturbance as the actual witnessing of death and agony. Interviews with persons who have experienced an atomic explosion reveal that ⅓ of them were emotionally upset because of the casualties they saw, while only 5 percent or fewer experienced fear or some other form of emotional disturbance on account of the flash of the explosion, the noise, the blast, the devastation, and the fires.

An atomic bombing raid causes more emotional reactions than a conventional raid. Janis declares:
"Apparently it was not simply the large number of casualties but also the specific character of the injuries, particularly the grossly altered physical appearance of persons who suffered severe burns, that had a powerful effect upon those who witnessed them. Hence, it appears to be highly probable that, as a correlate of the exceptional casualty-inflicting properties of the atomic weapon, there was an unusually intense emotional impact among the uninjured evoked by the perception of those who were casualties."
The strong emotional disturbance that results from the sight of mangled bodies has also been reported from lesser peacetime disasters such as a plant explosion.

We are interested here in this emotional agitation only as it affects the overt behavior of city dwellers. Two contradictory reactions could be suggested as short-range effects. It can be argued that apathy and disorganization will prevail. On the other hand, it is conceivable that the emotional disturbance from casualties will intensify rescue or defense activities. While there is evidence of both forms of reactions after a disaster, the latter is encouraged by effective leadership which directs survivors toward useful activities. (Fred C. Iklé, *The Social Impact of Bomb Destruction* [Norman, Okla.: University of Oklahoma Press, 1958], pp. vii–viii; 27–29.)

(4) As the selection above suggests, the new social science of operations analysis has done an impressively ambitious job of opening up hitherto neglected avenues of research. Here, for example, are some suggested research subjects for which the RAND Corporation received government grants totaling several million dollars during 1958 as part of its civilian defense studies:

A study should be made of the survival of populations in environments similar to overcrowded shelters (concentration camps, Russian and German use of crowded freight cars, troopships, crowded prisons, crowded life-boats, submarines, etc.). Some useful guiding principles might be found and adapted to the shelter program.

The object of such research would be to "act as reassurance that the more unpleasant parts of the experience had been foreseen and judged to be bearable by a peacetime government." (Herman Kahn, "Some Specific Suggestions for Achieving Early Non-Military Defense Capabilities and Initiating Long-Range Programs," RAND Corporation Research Memorandum RM-2206-RC, 1959, pp. 47–48.)

And to give but one more example of the truly Faustian élan of our military-oriented research, we have this prognosis from a naval engineer:

Weather and climate are never neutral. They are either formidable enemies or mighty allies. Try to imagine the fantastic possibilities of one nation possessing the capability to arrange over large areas, or perhaps the entire globe, the distribution of heat and cold, rain and sunshine, flood and drought, to the advantage of itself and its allies and to the detriment of its enemies. We *must* think about it—*now*—for this is the direction in which technology is leading us. . . .

The question is no longer: "Will mankind be able to modify the weather on a large scale and control the climate?" Rather, the question is: "Which scientists will do it first, American or Russian?" . . . (Commander William J. Kotsch, USN, "Weather Control and National Strategy," *United States Naval Institute Proceedings*, July 1960, p. 76.)

(5) The classic justification for technological progress has been that it steadily frees men from the burdens of existence and provides them with the leisure in which to make "truly human uses" of their lives. The following selections would suggest, however, that by the time we arrive at this high plateau of creative leisure, we may very well find it already thickly inhabited by an even more beneficent species of inventions which will have objectified creativity itself. It is quite unclear what the justification for this form of progress is, other than the technocratic imperative: "What can be done must be done."

I would like to teach a machine how to write a limerick, and I suspect I can do it. I am quite sure that in the first batch it will be easy for any-

509

body to pick out from a random array those limericks created by an IBM machine. But perhaps in a little while the distinctions will not be so clear. The moment we can do that we will have carried out a psychological experiment in new terms which for the first time may give a sharp definition of what is meant by a joke. (Edward Teller, "Progress in the Nuclear Age," *Mayo Clinic Proceedings*, January 1965.)

Can a computer be used to compose a symphony? As one who has been engaged in programming a large digital computer to program original musical compositions, I can testify that the very idea excites incredulity and indignation in many quarters. Such response in part reflects the extreme view of the nineteenth-century romantic tradition that regards music as direct communication of emotion from composer to listener—"from heart to heart," as Wagner said. In deference to this view it must be conceded that we do not *yet* understand the subjective aspect of musical communication well enough to study it in precise terms. . . . On the other hand, music does have its objective side. The information encoded there relates to such quantitative entities as pitch and time, and is therefore accessible to rational and ultimately mathematical analysis. . . . it is possible, at least in theory, to construct tables of probabilities describing a musical style, such as Baroque, Classical or Romantic, and perhaps even the style of an individual composer. Given such tables, one could then reverse the process and compose music in a given style. (Lejaren A. Hiller, Jr., in *Scientific American*, December 1959. Italics added.)

The most ominous aspect of such statements is the ever-present "yet" that appears in them. To offer another example: "No technology as *yet* promises to duplicate human creativity, especially in the artistic sense, if only because we do not *yet* understand the conditions and functioning of creativity. (This is not to deny that computers can be useful aids to creative activity.)" (Emmanuel G. Mesthene, *How Technology Will Shape the Future*, Harvard University Program on Technology and Society, Reprint Number 5, pp. 14–15.) The presumption involved in such statements is almost comic. For the man who thinks that creativity might *yet* become a technology is the man who stands no chance of ever understanding what creativity is. But we can be sure the technicians will eventually find us a bad mechanized substitute and persuade themselves that it is the real thing.

(6) The literature of our society dealing with imprisonment and capital punishment is extensive, including contributions by Tolstoy, Camus, Dostoyevsky, Sartre, and Koestler. Since, however, these men offer us only imaginative fiction, their work is obviously of little scientific value. What follows is an attempt by two psychiatrists to gain, at long last, some hard data on the experience of awaiting execution. The sample population is nineteen people in the Sing Sing death house.

510

"One might expect them," the researchers state, "to show severe depression and devastating anxiety, yet neither symptom was conspicuous among these 19 doomed persons. By what mechanisms did they avoid these expected reactions to such overwhelming stress? Do their emotional patterns change during a year or two in a death cell? And do these defenses function to the moment of execution—or do they crumble towards the end?"

Here are the psychiatrists' thumbnail sketches of their specimens—all of whom, they observe, come from "deprived backgrounds," with extensive experience of institutional confinement, and none of whom had long premeditated the killings they were convicted of. Notice how effectively the terminology and the data provided screen out the observer so that we have no sense of the character of the human presence with which these pathetic prisoners were interacting—surely a key factor in the situation. Note, too, how the concluding table of findings turns the life-and-death matter into a statistical abstraction.

This inmate is the only woman in this series. She is of dull intelligence, acts in a playful and flirtatious manner. She was usually euphoric, but became transiently depressed when she thought her case was going badly. She frequently complained of insomnia and restlessness. These symptoms quickly disappeared when she was visited by a psychiatrist whom she enjoyed seeing and talking to in a self-justifying and self-pitying manner. Psychological tests showed pervasive feelings of insecurity, repressive defenses, and an inability to handle angry and aggressive feelings in an effectual manner.

This inmate is an illiterate, inadequate individual who was convicted as an accomplice to a robbery-murder. He had an overall IQ of 51. He showed primarily depression, withdrawal, and obsessive rumination over the details of his crime and conviction. He eventually evolved a poorly elaborated paranoid system whereby he supposedly was betrayed and framed by his girl friend and one of the codefendants. Despite the looseness of his persecutory thinking, it was accompanied by a clear-cut elevation in his mood and reduction of anxiety.

He is one of the two inmates in this series who uses religious preoccupation as his major defense mechanism. He repeatedly in an almost word for word way stated his situation as follows. "No one can understand how I feel unless it happened to you. Christ came to me and I know He died for my sins. It doesn't matter if I am electrocuted or not. I am going to another world after this and I am prepared for it." As his stay progresses he becomes increasingly more hostile and antagonistic, and his behavior progressively out of keeping with his professed religious ideas. In addition to obsessive rumination, projection and withdrawal are employed to ward off feelings of anxiety and depression.

511

The researchers summarize their findings as follows:

Psychological defense mechanisms used
(Totals more than 19; some used more than one)
Denial by isolation of affect 7
Denial by minimizing the predicament 4
Denial by delusion formation 1
Denial by living only in the present 4
Projection 7
Obsessive rumination in connection with appeals 3
Obsessive preoccupation with religion 2
Obsessive preoccupation with intellectual or philosophical
   matters 5

(Harvey Bluestone and Carl L. McGahee, "Reaction to Extreme Stress: Impending Death by Execution," *The American Journal of Psychiatry*, November 1962, pp. 393-96.)

(7) Reportedly, within the last decade, the most promising scientific brains have been drifting away from physics to biology and medical science, where the frontiers of research have begun to reveal more intriguing prospects. Some of them, like that which follows, vie with the ingenuity of H. G. Wells' Dr. Moreau.

Dr. Vladimir Demikhov, an eminent Soviet experimental surgeon whose grafting of additional or different heads and limbs on to dogs has drawn considerable attention, has come up with a new suggestion for the advancement of transplantation surgery.

According to "Soviet Weekly," Dr. Demikhov believes that it would be simple to store organs for spare-part surgery—not by developing techniques for banks of particular organs or tissues but by temporarily grafting the stored organ on to the exterior of human "vegetables."

A human "vegetable" is a human being who, through accident or disease, has lost all intelligent life, but is otherwise functioning normally. The surgeon's "bank" would consist of technically living bodies, each supporting externally a number of additional organs. (Anthony Tucker, science correspondent, *The Guardian* [London], January 20, 1968.)

For a popularized survey of recent work in the biological sciences, see Gordon Rattray Taylor, *The Biological Time-Bomb* (New York: World, 1968). Among other breathtaking possibilities the biologists have in store for us, there will be the capacity to produce carbon-copy human beings with interchangeable parts and faultless collective co-ordination. We shall then have, we are told, "exceptional human beings in unlimited numbers," as well as ideal basketball teams . . . and (no doubt) armies.

(8) The following are two examples of scientists doing their utmost

to defend the dignity of pure research against any moralizing encroachments.

In December 1967, Dr. Arthur Kornberg, a Nobel prize winning geneticist, announced the first successful synthesis of viral DNA, an important step toward the creation of test-tube life. After the announcement Dr. Kornberg was interviewed by the press.

At the end, the moral problem was posed. "Dr. Kornberg, do you see the time when your work will come into conflict with traditional morality?" Again he took off his glasses and looked down and meditated. Very gently, he replied: "We can never predict the benefits that will flow from advancements in our fundamental knowledge. There is no knowledge that cannot be abused, but I hope that our improved knowledge of genetic chemistry will make us better able to cope with hereditary disease. I see no possibility of conflict in a decent society which uses scientific knowledge for human improvement." . . . He left it to us to define, or redefine, a decent society. (Alistair Cooke, reporting in *The Guardian* [London], December 17, 1967.)

In the summer of 1968, a controversy blew up in Great Britain over the part played by academic scientists in the activities of the Ministry of Defence Microbiological Establishment at Porton, one of the world's most richly productive centers of chemical and biological warfare research. (Porton, for example, developed some of the gases most extensively used by American forces in Vietnam.) Professor E. B. Chain of Imperial College protested this "irresponsible scoop hunting" in a lengthy letter to *The Observer*, detailing the many worthwhile lines of research that had come out of the work done at Porton.

What is wrong with accepting research grants from the Ministry of Defence? As is well known, thousands of scientists have, for many years, accepted such grants from the US Navy, the US Air Force, NATO, and similar national and international organisations for fundamental research in many branches of the physical and biological sciences: this does not mean that such work involved them in research on military technology. One can only be grateful for the wisdom and foresight shown by those responsible for formulating and deciding the policies of these organisations in allowing their funds to be made available for sponsoring fundamental university research which bears no immediate, and usually not even a remote, relation to problems of warfare technology.

Of course, almost any kind of research, however academic, and almost any invention, however beneficial to mankind, from the knife to atomic energy, from anaesthetics to plant hormones, can be used for war and other destructive purposes, but it is, of course, not the scientist and inventor who carries the responsibility for how the results of his research or his inventions are used. (*The Observer* [London], June 1, 1968.)

It is actually a dubious proposition that any scientist worth his salt cannot make a pretty accurate prediction of how his findings might be used. But even if one were to grant the point, there is one kind of result which is completely predictable and which is bound never to be far from the awareness of the researcher. Productive research results in a handsomely rewarded career, in acclaim and wide recognition. Is it too cynical to suggest that this all-too-predictable result frequently makes it ever so much harder to foresee the probable abuses of one's research?

(9) C. Wright Mills once called the middle class citizenry of our polity a collection of "cheerful robots." Perhaps it is because the human original has fallen so far short of authenticity that our behavioral scientists can place such easy confidence in the simulated caricatures of humanity upon which their research ever more heavily comes to bear. One begins to wonder how much of what our society comes to accept as humanly normal, legitimate, and appropriate in years to come will be patterned upon the behavior of such electronic homunculi as those described below.

A pioneering demonstration of the feasibility of computer simulation appeared in 1957 when Newell, Shaw, and Simon published a description of their Logic Theorist program, which proved theorems in elementary symbolic logic—a feat previously accomplished only by humans. Among subsequent applications of information processing programs to classical problems of psychological theory are Feigenbaum's Elementary Perceiver and Memorizer, a computer model of verbal rote memorization; Feldman's simulation of the behavior of subjects in a binary-choice experiment, and Hovland and Hunt's model of human concept formulation. Lindsay explores another facet of cognitive activity in his computer processing of syntactic and semantic information to analyze communications in Basic English, and Bert Green and associates have programmed a machine to respond to questions phrased in ordinary English. Still another aspect of human decision-making appears in Clarkson's model of the trust investment process. At a more general level, Newell, Shaw, and Simon have programmed an information processing theory of human problem solving, a model whose output has been compared systematically with that of human problem solvers. Reitman has incorporated elements of this general problem-solving system in simulating the complex creative activity involved in musical composition.

While early applications of information processing models focus on relatively logical aspects of human behavior, recent simulation models incorporate emotional responses. Concerned by the singlemindedness of cognitive activity programmed in the Newell, Shaw, and Simon General Problem Solver, Reitman and associates recently have programmed a Hebbian-type model of human thinking that is not in complete control of what it remembers and forgets, being subject to interruptions and to conflict. Kenneth Colby, a psychiatrist, has developed a computer model for simulating therapeutic manipulation of emotions as well as a patient's responses. In HOMUNCULUS, our computer model of elementary social behavior, simulated subjects may at times emit anger or guilt reactions, or they may suppress aggression and later vent it against a less threatening figure than the one who violated norms regarding distributive justice.

. . . Among other computer applications involving considerations of emotional behavior are Coe's simulation of responses to frustration and conflict, Loehlin's simulation of socialization, and Abelson's design for computer simulation of "hot," affect-laden cognition. Imaginative computer simulations of voting behavior have been done by Robert Abelson, William McPhee, and their associates. Using the fluoridation controversies as a case in point, Abelson and Bernstein blend theories from several disciplines and from both field and experimental phenomena in constructing their model. Simulated individuals are assigned characteristics known to be relevant, and the programmed model specifies the processes by which they may change during the fluoridation campaign. . . .

In another study . . . Raymond Breton has simulated a restriction-of-output situation. According to this model, under most conditions pressures from fellow workmen result in a more homogeneous output, presumably in conformity with the norm. When motivation for monetary reward is intensified, however, some simulated workers develop negative sentiments toward those attempting to apply constraints, and variability of output increases.

(J. T. and J. E. Gullahorn, "Some Computer Applications in Social Science," *American Sociological Review*, vol. 30, June 1965, pp. 353–365.)

F. M. Esfandiary

F. M. Esfandiary was born in 1930 in Teheran, Iran, attended schools in the Middle East, Europe, and the United States, and currently lives in New York City. He was a member of the U.N. Conciliation Commission for Palestine, has done research on social problems in Iran, and has worked as a counselor for delinquent children in New York and California. He has received many foundation grants for his writing and has contributed articles to The Nation, Saturday Review, Texas Quarterly, *and other*

periodicals. *His three novels are* Day of Sacrifice *(1959),* The
Beggar *(1965), and* Identity Card *(1966). The present essay
appeared in* The New York Times Magazine, *February 5, 1967.*

THE MYSTICAL WEST PUZZLES THE PRACTICAL EAST

An American couple recently spent two weeks in the Middle East
crawling in and out of archeological sites, visiting the Pyramids, the
Sphinx, the ruins of Baalbek, the ruins of Jerash and Petra, and many
"holy" places. In Jordan they met a Middle Easterner who urged them
to visit a camp of squatters in Old Jerusalem. Sprawled within a
stone's throw of stately temples, churches and mosques, it is one of
the world's most horrifying shantytowns. Several thousand Arabs,
some of them refugees, fester in dark, damp hovels that are no more
than holes in the ground. Families of five, eight or 10 live huddled
together in cells with hardly room enough for three or four. The
stench of urine permeates the trapped air. There are sick and old
people down there who have not seen the light of day in months;
they lie rotting on damp floors, waiting for death to deliver them.
Children, naked and cadaverous, cower in dingy corners or rummage
in garbage heaps for food.

The Middle Easterner led the American couple to one of the open-
ings in the ground and asked them to follow him down. The Americans stared at the steep stairs and the darkness below and refused to
go. "These stairs look dangerous," the American woman said. "Besides, there is nothing to see down below."

"If you had been told that two or three thousand years ago people
lived down there, you would have crawled on your hands and knees
just to have a glimpse of the place, but because people live there now,
you refuse to see it."

"But what is there to see anyway?"

"You would have seen some of the poverty and misery of these
people."

"I'm not so sure these people are all that miserable," the American
interposed. "They look peaceful enough to me. They are probably
a lot happier than some Americans we know back home." He stopped,
looked about and with memorable inattention to logic, added: "In fact,
there is something spiritual, something Biblical, about the way these
people live."

Westerners have this dispiriting propensity for contorting reality, for weaving fantasies. They have a childlike need to idolize and romanticize. Self-proclaimed prophets, LSD zealots, Black Muslims, beat poets and artists, students, intellectuals and others have all turned to what they call the Wisdom of the East. Today Buddhism, Hinduism, Zen, Yoga, Islam, Baha'iism are attracting countless followers in America and Western Europe. A mass of literature glorifies the East and the past, but books which attempt to deal realistically with its underdeveloped countries are largely ignored. If reality threatens to obtrude, it is tampered with until it miraculously fits in with cherished fantasies.

This might seem harmless enough but for the fact that in refusing to see things as they are, in reviving stale philosophies and romanticizing the past, the West is helping to perpetuate Eastern backwardness. It encourages those in our own cultures who resist progress, and it is the peoples of the East who must finally endure the suffering and the destitution.

After they have uttered their empty praises, Westerners run back to New York and Beverly Hills and languish in their comfortable apartments while benefiting from all the social and economic amenities of the 20th century—the 20th century which so many of them claim to despise.

The East they glorify is a famished, ailing man sprawled on the side of the road who is struggling to arise while they stand around congratulating him and his ancestors on being spiritual, and living so close to the earth.

There are Americans and Europeans who know every rose petal that dropped from the mouth of a Buddha or a Confucius, who know every stone of the Pyramids or the Taj Mahal, yet who know nothing of the peoples living in Eastern lands today, nothing of their needs and sorrows, their struggles and hopes. Can this preoccupation with the romanticized past help us understand or in any way alter the sad fact that today, this very day, millions are hungry and homeless and suffering from agonizing maladies of body and mind?

This same unrealism is reflected in Western foreign policy, which refuses to acknowledge, much less support, the genuine revolutionary aspirations of disadvantaged peoples all over the world, which sometimes even refuses to acknowledge the existence of governments and peoples whose orientation is different from its own. The Washington officials who support reactionary regimes in backward countries are rendering the same disservice, perpetuating the same ills, as the beat poet who revives the archaic philosophies of a Lao-Tze or a Buddha.

The American and Western European Underground, which considers itself avant-garde, is in fact pathetically regressive. It does not look ahead; it looks back. It is romantic and mawkish. Bearded zealots, sitting cross-legged on the ground, wallowing in Haiku poetry, Bhagavad-Gitas and Zen in an atmosphere saturated with the exoticisms of incense, opiates and lanterns—the "scene," in short, smacks of a Dr. Fu Manchu melodrama. The dialogue of the Underground, like its poetry, is heavily spiced with pretentious allusions to Nirvana, Karma, Satori . . . Its idols are the swami, the guru, the mystic and other high priests of Eastern occultism who go about murmuring such profound revelations as, "Life is like a fountain."

In Greenwich Village, as in other bohemias of the Western world, one can often see displayed in cafes and shop windows posters of some swami or yogi. The large head, dark piercing eyes, benign smile and flowing gray beard bear a disquieting resemblance to the popular ideas of the Judeo-Christian God. Looking at these posters, I cannot help wondering if Western man, who has just come back from the highly publicized burial of his late God, is not now fervently looking for a new one.

In the big cities, there is a noticeable restlessness, a groping, a desperation to believe in something. In New York and Los Angeles, Chicago and San Francisco, innumerable cults, religions and spiritual groups flourish and win fanatic adherents. It is appalling to see bright, educated city-dwellers swallow the nonsense that these soothsayers, clairvoyants, spiritualists, prophets, dish out. There is something pathetic about this hunger for fairy tales.

Consciously or unconsciously, the West does not want the old societies to change. It would rather they remained languid and inert—what it calls spiritual. It would rather the Easterner remained cross-legged and contemplative. The West needs this vision to nourish and titillate its fantasies, while it goes on building better homes, richer economies, better societies for itself.

But young revolutionary Asians and Africans do not want to play the spiritual buffoon for the West. They are not amused by suffering and destitution. They are apprehensive of their backwardness and see in it no beauty, no dignity, no spirituality, nothing sacred or worth holding. They are struggling to disembarrass themselves of the very philosophies which a section of the West is striving to regenerate.

These ancient teachings, for the most part, encouraged passivity, withdrawal, involvement with self, submission. They instilled the belief that fate or reincarnation decided everything; that suffering and affliction were rewards or punishment or irreversible destiny and that all effort, all merit, all endeavor was therefore futile. Through the centuries these teachings have seeped into the fabric of Eastern cultures, infecting our economies, our politics, our social and familial institutions, our very self-image.

Twenty-five hundred years ago, Buddha, like other Eastern philosophers before and after him, said: "He who sits still, wins." Asia, then immobilized in primitive torpor, had no difficulty responding. It sat still. What it won for sitting still was the perpetuation of famines and terrorizing superstitions, oppression of children, subjugation of women, emasculation of men, fratricidal wars, persecutions, mass-killings. The history of Asia, like the history of all mankind, is a horrendous account of human suffering.

Thus when life was a relentless cycle of anguish, it was probably inevitable that some, in their desperation and helplessness, should reject reality and withdraw. Their resignation and submission were defenses against suffering. When Lao-Tze, Solomon—even Rousseau centuries later—exhorted their fellow men to go back to nature or spend their lives in contemplation, they were reacting to a world that was hostile and unmanageable, a world that generated anxiety and terror, a sense of nihilism and alienation.

But times have changed. Man is no longer helpless; his problems no longer insurmountable. Ancient exhortations to asceticism and self-renunciation are irrelevant in our modern world. Buddhism, Zen, Sufiism, Islam, Judaism—indeed, all the theologies and philosophies of the past—have nothing to teach modern man. Ahead of *their* time, they are far behind ours. Do not kill; do not hate; love your neighbor; love your fellow man—these were revolutionary concepts at one time. Today they are platitudes—though easier said than done.

The injunction against killing cows, noble in itself, did not deter people from killing one another. The religionist who spoke of the brotherhood of man had no difficulty persecuting members of other religions. But now that man is slowly reaching adulthood, he does not need to be reminded of the teachings of his childhood—he must find ways to implement them.

Americans and Western Europeans, in their sensitivity to lingering problems around them, tend to make science and progress their scapegoats. There is a belief that progress has precipitated widespread unhappiness, anxieties and other social and emotional problems. Science is viewed as a cold mechanical discipline having nothing to do with human warmth and the human spirit.

But to many of us from the nonscientific East, science does not have such repugnant associations. We are not afraid of it, nor are we disappointed by it. We know all too painfully that our social and emotional problems festered long before the age of technology. To us, science is warm and reassuring. It promises hope. It is helping us at long last gain some control over our persecutory environments, alleviating age-old problems—not only physical but also, and especially, problems of the spirit.

Shiraz, for example, a city in southern Iran, has long been renowned for its rose gardens and nightingales; its poets, Sadi and Hafiz, and its mystical, ascetic philosophy, Sufiism. Much poetry has been written in glorification of the spiritual attributes of this oasis city. And to be sure, Shiraz is a green, picturesque town, with a quaint bazaar and refreshing gardens. But in this "romantic" city thousands of emotionally disturbed and mentally retarded men, women and children were, until recently, kept in chains in stifling prison cells and lunatic asylums.

Every now and again, some were dragged, screaming and pleading, to a courtyard and flogged for not behaving "normally." But for the most part, they were made to sit against damp walls, their hands and feet locked in chains, and thus immobilized, without even a modicum of affection from their helpless families and friends, they sat for weeks and months and years—often all their lives. Pictures of these wretched men, women and children can still be seen in this "city of poetry," this "city with the spiritual way of life."

It was only recently that a wealthy young Shirazi who, against the admonitions of his family, had studied psychology at the University of Teheran and foreign universities, returned to Shiraz and after considerable struggle with city officials succeeded in opening a psychiatric clinic, the first in those regions. After still more struggle, he arranged to have the emotionally disturbed and the mentally retarded transferred from prison to their homes, to hospitals and to his clinic, where he and his staff now attend them.

They are fortunate. All over Asia and other backward areas, emotionally disturbed men and women are still incarcerated in these medieval dungeons called lunatic asylums. The cruel rejection and punishment are intended to teach them a lesson or help exorcise evil spirits.

The West, however, still bogged down in its ridiculous romanticism, would like to believe that emotional disturbances, dope addiction, delinquency are all modern problems brought on by technological progress, and that backward societies are too spiritual and beautiful to need the ministrations of science. But while the West can perhaps afford to think this way, the people of backward lands cannot.

Young Middle Eastern men and women are daily flouting the devitalizing repressions and fatalism of Islam. India is valiantly straining to extricate itself from the dead weight of social traditions whose corrosive nihilism and spiritualism the realist Nehru disdained. Japan's new industrialism and pragmatism are obvious renunciations of the debilitating influences of Zen. China's revolutionary leaders are prodding their people to reject the ancient traditions and philosophies which had helped perpetuate the country's backwardness and misery, making it prey to incessant foreign rapacities.

If at times these struggles have been erratic and violent, it is only because the obstacles are awesome, the inertia too entrenched, the people's suffering too anguished, their impatience too eruptive. Moreover, the total cultural reorganizations such as Asia and Africa are undergoing inevitably engender their own temporary dislocations and confusions. But the goals, the direction remain constant. We are on the move, however awkwardly at first, to a saner, better world.

It is precisely this new voice of Asia, this new spirit, that the West must heed and, where necessary, uphold. It is encouraging that in the Western world today, particularly in America, university professors, teachers, students, artists, writers, Negroes, housewives and others who traditionally were uninvolved in politics are now more and more asserting their rights, making their voices heard. The increasing numbers of people who travel each year are also helping all societies to outgrow their insularity, their provincialism, their social, economic and political traditions.

In spite of colossal obstacles, man has come a long way. Let him not be afraid to believe that he will go still farther; that he will remake the world—that, indeed, he *is* remaking the world.

If man has to believe in something, let him believe in his own infinite potential, his own future.

Jonathan Swift

*Swift (1667–1745), born of an English family in Dublin, became
an Anglican clergyman in a period of disappointment over his
hopes for a political career in England. He nevertheless pursued
politics and by 1710 had achieved a powerful position in the Tory
party. In 1713 he was rewarded for his service to the Tory
government—in the manner of those times—with the Deanship of*

*St. Patrick's, Dublin. However, he spent little time in Ireland
until the fall of the party forced his return to Dublin a few years
later, where he became for the rest of his life a champion of the
Irish people against English oppression. Meanwhile, he had
become an intimate of the best English writers of his day, a leading
political pamphleteer, and had begun the series of writings that
make him the greatest of English satirists. Especially notable are*
A Tale of a Tub *and* The Battle of the Books *published in
1704,* A Modest Proposal *(1720), and the incomparable* Gulliver's Travels *(1726). It is from the third part of this work,
"A Voyage to Laputa, Balnibarbi, Luggnagg, Glubbdubdrib, and
Japan," that the present account (Chapter 5) is taken. Some of
the specific details in the description would have been recognized by
Swift's contemporaries as comic versions of actual experiments
reported in the* Transactions *of the Royal Society, the leading
scientific group in England. The suggestion for the abolition of
words probably refers to Thomas Sprat's ideal of an economical
scientific prose that would express "so many 'Things,' almost in
an equal number of 'Words.' " Critics have sometimes been
inclined to apologize for the attitude toward scientific experiment
here expressed by Swift. They point out that no one at the time
(Sir Isaac Newton was still alive) could have predicted the
enormous achievements of science and technology, and Swift does
seem to have attacked "projectors" in part because of the impracticality of their schemes. But in the context of the other readings
in this section, the reader may find that Swift's satire still contains
some prophecy in it.*

THE GRAND ACADEMY OF LAGADO

This Academy is not an entire single Building, but a Continuation of
several Houses on both Sides of a Street; which growing waste, was
purchased and applyed to that Use.

I was received very kindly by the Warden, and went for many Days
to the Academy. Every Room hath in it one or more Projectors; and
I believe I could not be in fewer than five Hundred Rooms.

The first Man I saw was of a meagre Aspect, with sooty Hands and
Face, his Hair and Beard long, ragged and singed in several Places.

His Clothes, Shirt, and Skin were all of the same Colour. He had been Eight Years upon a Project for extracting Sun-Beams out of Cucumbers, which were to be put into Vials hermetically sealed, and let out to warm the Air in raw inclement Summers. He told me, he did not doubt in Eight Years more, that he should be able to supply the Governors Gardens with Sun-shine at a reasonable Rate; but he complained that his Stock was low, and intreated me to give him something as an Encouragement to Ingenuity, especially since this had been a very dear Season for Cucumbers. I made him a small Present, for my Lord had furnished me with Money on purpose, because he knew their Practice of begging from all who go to see them.

I went into another Chamber, but was ready to hasten back, being almost overcome with a horrible Stink. My Conductor pressed me forward, conjuring me in a Whisper to give no Offence, which would be highly resented; and therefore I durst not so much as stop my Nose. The Projector of this Cell was the most ancient Student of the Academy. His Face and Beard were of a pale Yellow; his Hands and Clothes dawbed over with Filth. When I was presented to him, he gave me a very close Embrace, (a Compliment I could well have excused.) His Employment from his first coming into the Academy, was an Operation to reduce human Excrement to its original Food, by separating the several Parts, removing the Tincture which it receives from the Gall, making the Odour exhale, and scumming off the Saliva. He had a weekly Allowance from the Society, of a Vessel filled with human Ordure, about the Bigness of a *Bristol* Barrel.

I saw another at work to calcine Ice into Gunpowder; who likewise shewed me a Treatise he had written concerning the Malleability of Fire, which he intended to publish.

There was a most ingenious Architect who had contrived a new Method for building Houses, by beginning at the Roof, and working downwards to the Foundation; which he justified to me by the like Practice of those two prudent Insects the Bee and the Spider.

There was a Man born blind, who had several Apprentices in his own Condition: Their Employment was to mix Colours for Painters, which their Master taught them to distinguish by feeling and smelling. It was indeed my Misfortune to find them at that Time not very perfect in their Lessons; and the Professor himself happened to be generally mistaken: This Artist is much encouraged and esteemed by the whole Fraternity.

In another Apartment I was highly pleased with a Projector, who had found a Device of plowing the Ground with Hogs, to save the Charges of Plows, Cattle, and Labour. The Method is this: In an Acre of Ground you bury at six Inches Distance, and eight deep, a

Quantity of Acorns, Dates, Chesnuts, and other Maste or Vegetables whereof these Animals are fondest; then you drive six Hundred or more of them into the Field, where in a few Days they will root up the whole Ground in search of their Food, and make it fit for sowing, at the same time manuring it with their Dung. It is true, upon Experiment they found the Charge and Trouble very great, and they had little or no Crop. However, it is not doubted that this Invention may be capable of great Improvement.

I went into another Room, where the Walls and Ceiling were all hung round with Cobwebs, except a narrow Passage for the Artist to go in and out. At my Entrance he called aloud to me not to disturb his Webs. He lamented the fatal Mistake the World had been so long in of using Silk-Worms, while we had such plenty of domestick Insects, who infinitely excelled the former, because they understood how to weave as well as spin. And he proposed farther, that by employing Spiders, the Charge of dying Silks would be wholly saved; whereof I was fully convinced when he shewed me a vast Number of Flies most beautifully coloured, wherewith he fed his Spiders; assuring us, that the Webs would take a Tincture from them; and as he had them of all Hues, he hoped to fit every Body's Fancy, as soon as he could find proper Food for the Flies, of certain Gums, Oyls, and other glutinous Matter, to give a Strength and Consistence to the Threads.

There was an Astronomer who had undertaken to place a Sun-Dial upon the great Weather-Cock on the Town-House, by adjusting the annual and diurnal Motions of the Earth and Sun, so as to answer and coincide with all accidental Turnings of the Wind.

I was complaining of a small Fit of the Cholick; upon which my Conductor led me into a Room, where a great Physician resided, who was famous for curing that Disease by contrary Operations from the same Instrument. He had a large Pair of Bellows, with a long slender Muzzle of Ivory. This he conveyed eight Inches up the Anus, and drawing in the Wind, he affirmed he could make the Guts as lank as a dried Bladder. But when the Disease was more stubborn and violent, he let in the Muzzle while the Bellows was full of Wind, which he discharged into the Body of the Patient; then withdrew the Instrument to replenish it, clapping his Thumb strongly against the Orifice of the Fundament; and this being repeated three or four Times, the adventitious Wind would rush out, bringing the noxious along with it (like Water put into a Pump) and the Patient recovers. I saw him try both Experiments upon a Dog, but could not discern any Effect from the former. After the latter, the Animal was ready to burst, and made so violent a Discharge, as was very offensive to me and my Companions. The Dog died on the Spot, and we left the Doctor endeavouring to recover him by the same Operation.

I visited many other Apartments, but shall not trouble my Reader with all the Curiosities I observed, being studious of Brevity.

I had hitherto seen only one Side of the Academy, the other being appropriated to the Advancers of speculative Learning; of whom I shall say something when I have mentioned one illustrious Person more, who is called among them *the universal Artist*. He told us, he had been Thirty Years employing his Thoughts for the Improvement of human Life. He had two large Rooms full of wonderful Curiosities, and Fifty Men at work. Some were condensing Air into a dry tangible Substance, by extracting the Nitre, and letting the aqueous or fluid Particles percolate: Others softening Marble for Pillows and Pin-cushions; others petrifying the Hoofs of a living Horse to preserve them from foundring. The Artist himself was at that Time busy upon two great Designs: The first, to sow Land with Chaff, wherein he affirmed the true seminal Virtue to be contained, as he demonstrated by several Experiments which I was not skilful enough to comprehend. The other was, by a certain Composition of Gums, Minerals, and Vegetables outwardly applied, to prevent the Growth of Wool upon two young Lambs; and he hoped in a reasonable Time to propagate the Breed of naked Sheep all over the Kingdom.

We crossed a Walk to the other Part of the Academy, where, as I have already said, the Projectors in speculative Learning resided.

The first Professor I saw was in a very large Room, with Forty Pupils about him. After Salutation, observing me to look earnestly upon a Frame, which took up the greatest Part of both the Length and Breadth of the Room; he said, perhaps I might wonder to see him employed in a Project for improving speculative Knowledge by practical and mechanical Operations. But the World would soon be sensible of its Usefulness; and he flattered himself, that a more noble exalted Thought never sprang in any other Man's Head. Every one knew how laborious the usual Method is of attaining to Arts and Sciences; whereas by his Contrivance, the most ignorant Person at a reasonable Charge, and with a little bodily Labour, may write Books in Philosophy, Poetry, Politicks, Law, Mathematicks and Theology, without the least Assistance from Genius or Study. He then led me to the Frame, about the Sides whereof all his Pupils stood in Ranks. It was Twenty Foot square, placed in the Middle of the Room. The Superficies was composed of several Bits of Wood, about the Bigness of a Dye, but some larger than others. They were all linked together by slender Wires. These Bits of Wood were covered on every Square with Paper pasted on them; and on these Papers were written all the Words of their Language in their several Moods, Tenses, and Declensions, but without any Order. The Professor then desired me to observe, for he was going to set his Engine at work. The Pupils at his Command took each of them hold

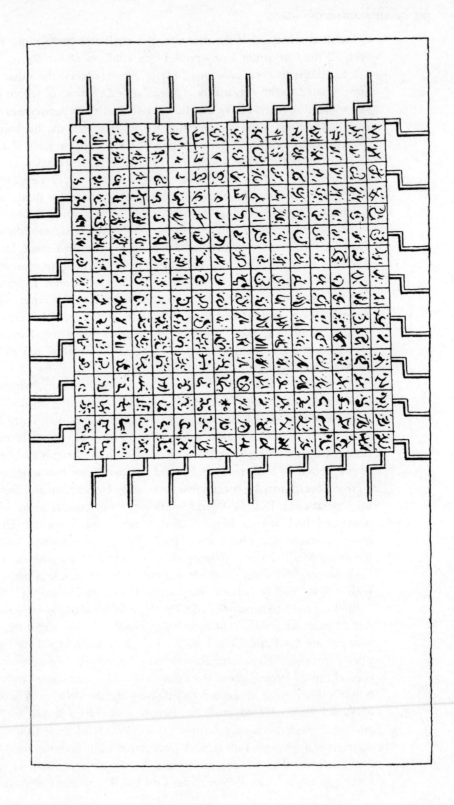

of an Iron Handle, whereof there were Forty fixed round the Edges of the Frame; and giving them a sudden Turn, the whole Disposition of the Words was entirely changed. He then commanded Six and Thirty of the Lads to read the several Lines softly as they appeared upon the Frame; and where they found three or four Words together that might make Part of a Sentence, they dictated to the four remaining Boys who were Scribes. This Work was repeated three or four Times, and at every Turn the Engine was so contrived that the Words shifted into new Places, as the square Bits of Wood moved upside down.

Six Hours a-Day the young Students were employed in this Labour; and the Professor shewed me several Volumes in large Folio already collected, of broken Sentences, which he intended to piece together; and out of those rich Materials to give the World a compleat Body of all Arts and Sciences; which however might be still improved, and much expedited, if the Publick would raise a Fund for making and employing five Hundred such Frames in *Lagado,* and oblige the Managers to contribute in common their several Collections.

He assured me, that this Invention had employed all his Thoughts from his Youth; that he had emptied the whole Vocabulary into his Frame, and made the strictest Computation of the general Proportion there is in Books between the Numbers of Particles, Nouns, and Verbs, and other Parts of Speech.

I made my humblest Acknowledgments to this illustrious Person for his great Communicativeness; and promised if ever I had the good Fortune to return to my native Country, that I would do him Justice, as the sole Inventer of this wonderful Machine; the Form and Contrivance of which I desired Leave to delineate upon Paper as in the Figure here annexed. I told him, although it were the Custom of our Learned in *Europe* to steal Inventions from each other, who had thereby at least this Advantage, that it became a Controversy which was the right Owner; yet I would take such Caution, that he should have the Honour entire without a Rival.

We next went to the School of Languages, where three Professors sat in Consultation upon improving that of their own Country.

The first Project was to shorten Discourse by cutting Polysyllables into one, and leaving out Verbs and Participles; because in Reality all things imaginable are but Nouns.

The other, was a Scheme for entirely abolishing all Words whatsoever: And this was urged as a great Advantage in Point of Health as well as Brevity. For, it is plain, that every Word we speak is in some Degree a Diminution of our Lungs by Corrosion; and consequently contributes to the shortning of our Lives. An Expedient was therefore offered, that since Words are only Names for *Things,* it would be more convenient for all Men to carry about them, such *Things* as were necessary to express the particular Business they are to discourse on. And this Invention would certainly have taken Place, to the great Ease as well as Health of the Subject, if the Women in Conjunction with the Vulgar and Illiterate had not threatened to raise a Rebellion, unless they might be allowed the Liberty to speak with their Tongues, after the Manner of their Forefathers: Such constant irreconcileable Enemies to Science are the common People. However, many of the most Learned and Wise adhere to the new Scheme of expressing themselves by *Things;* which hath only this Inconvenience attending it; that if a Man's Business be very great, and of various Kinds, he must be obliged in Proportion to carry a greater Bundle of *Things* upon his Back, unless he can afford one or two strong Servants to attend him. I have often beheld two of those Sages almost sinking under the Weight of their Packs, like Pedlars among us; who when they met in the Streets would lay down their Loads, open their Sacks, and hold Conversation for an Hour together; then put up their Implements, help each other to resume their Burthens, and take their Leave.

But, for short Conversations a Man may carry Implements in his Pockets and under his Arms, enough to supply him, and in his House he cannot be at a Loss; therefore the Room where Company meet who practice this Art, is full of all *Things* ready at Hand, requisite to furnish Matter for this Kind of artificial Converse.

Another great Advantage proposed by this Invention, was, that it would serve as an universal Language to be understood in all civilized Nations, whose Goods and Utensils are generally of the same Kind, or nearly resembling, so that their Uses might easily be comprehended. And thus, Embassadors would be qualified to treat with foreign Princes or Ministers of State, to whose Tongues they were utter Strangers.

I was at the Mathematical School, where the Master taught his Pupils after a Method scarce imaginable to us in *Europe.* The Proposition and Demonstration were fairly written on a thin Wafer, with Ink composed of a Cephalick Tincture. This the Student was to swallow upon a fasting Stomach, and for three Days following eat nothing but Bread and Water. As the Wafer digested, the Tincture mounted to his Brain, bearing the Proposition along with it. But the Success hath not hitherto been answerable, partly by some Error in the *Quantum* or Composition, and partly by the Perverseness of Lads; to whom this Bolus is so nauseous, that they generally steal aside, and discharge it upwards before it can operate; neither have they been yet persuaded to use so long an Abstinence as the Prescription requires.

E. B. White

Elwyn Brooks White, born in 1899, was graduated from Cornell in 1921 and joined the staff of The New Yorker *in 1926. He regularly wrote its "Notes and Comment" section until 1938 and contributed to the page in the 1940s and 1950s. His sensitive, humorous character and his witty yet natural and exact literary style, along with the congenial talents of James Thurber and of a few others, were in part responsible for the extraordinary reputation of* New Yorker *writing at that time. He contributed a monthly column, entitled "One Man's Meat," to* Harper's *from 1938 to 1943 and resumed writing for* The New Yorker *on a free-lance basis in 1945. Since 1937 he has taken periodic refuge in a Maine farm. He has been awarded honorary degrees from Dartmouth, Maine, Bowdoin, Hamilton, Colby, Yale, and Harvard, the National Institute of Arts and Letters gold medal in 1960 for his contribution to literature, and the Presidential Medal of Freedom in 1963. White has published two excellent children's books,* Stuart Little *(1945) and* Charlotte's Web *(1952), and received the 1970 Laura Ingalls Wilder Award for his "substantial and lasting contribution to literature for children." Among his best-known other books are* Is Sex Necessary?, *written with James Thurber (1929),* Every Day Is Saturday *(1934),* One Man's Meat *(1942),* The Wild Flag *(1946), and* The Elements of Style *(1959), a reverent reediting of the textbook of his former professor William Strunk, Jr. The story we present below, taken from* The Second Tree from the Corner *(1954), was first published in* The New Yorker *in February 1950.*

THE MORNING OF THE DAY THEY DID IT (February 25, 1950)

My purpose is to tell how it happened and to set down a few impressions of that morning while it is fresh in memory. I was in a plane that was in radio communication with the men on the platform. To put the matter briefly, what was intended as a military expedient turned suddenly into a holocaust. The explanation was plain enough to me, for, like millions of others, I was listening to the conversation between the two men and was instantly aware of the quick shift it took. That part is clear. What is not so clear is how I myself survived, but I am beginning to understand that, too. I shall not burden the reader with an explanation, however, as the facts are tedious and implausible. I am now in good health and fair spirits, among friendly people on an inferior planet, at a very great distance from the sun. Even the move from one planet to another has not relieved me of the nagging curse that besets writing men—the feeling that they must produce some sort of record of their times.

The thing happened shortly before twelve noon. I came out of my house on East Harding Boulevard at quarter of eight that morning, swinging my newspaper and feeling pretty good. The March day was mild and springlike, the warmth and the smells doubly welcome after the rotten weather we'd been having. A gentle wind met me on the Boulevard, frisked me, and went on. A man in a leather cap was loading bedsprings into a van in front of No. 220. I remember that as I walked along I worked my tongue around the roof of my mouth, trying to dislodge a prune skin. (These details have no significance; why write them down?)

A few blocks from home there was a Contakt plane station and I hurried in, caught the 8:10 plane, and was soon aloft. I always hated a jet-assist takeoff right after breakfast, but it was one of the discomforts that went with my job. At ten thousand feet our small plane made contact with the big one, we passengers were transferred, and the big ship went on up to fifty thousand, which was the height television planes flew at. I was a script writer for one of the programs. My tour of duty was supposed to be eight hours.

I should probably explain here that at the period of which I am writing, the last days of the planet earth, telecasting was done from planes circling the stratosphere. This eliminated the coaxial cable, a form of relay that had given endless trouble. Coaxials worked well enough for a while, but eventually they were abandoned, largely because of the extraordinary depredations of earwigs. These insects had developed an alarming resistance to bugspray and were out of control most of the time. Earwigs increased in size and in numbers, and the forceps at the end of their abdomen developed so that they could cut through a steel shell. They seemed to go unerringly for coaxials. Whether the signals carried by the cables had anything to do with it I don't know, but the bugs fed on these things and were enormously stimulated. Not only did they feast on the cables, causing the cables to disintegrate, but they laid eggs in them in unimaginable quantities, and as the eggs hatched the television images suffered greatly, there was more and more flickering on the screen, more and more eyestrain and nervous tension among audiences, and of course a further debasement of taste and intellectual life in general. Finally the coaxials were given up, and after much experimenting by Westinghouse and the Glenn Martin people a satisfactory substitute was found in the high-flying planes. A few of these planes, spotted around the country, handled the whole television load nicely. Known as Strato-video planes, they were equipped with studios; many programs originated in the air and were transmitted directly, others were beamed to the aircraft from ground stations and then relayed. The planes flew continuously, twenty-four hours a day, were refuelled in air, and dropped down to ten thousand feet every eight hours to meet the Contakt planes and take on new shifts of workers.

I remember that as I walked to my desk in the Stratoship that morning, the nine-o'clock news had just ended and a program called "Author, Please!" was going on, featuring Melonie Babson, a woman who had written a best-seller on the theme of euthanasia, called "Peace of Body." The program was sponsored by a dress-shield company.

I remember, too, that a young doctor had come aboard the plane with the rest of us. He was a newcomer, a fellow named Cathcart, slated to be the physician attached to the ship. He had introduced himself to me in the Contakt plane, had asked the date of my Tri-D shot, and had noted it down in his book. (I shall explain about these shots presently.) This doctor certainly had a brief life in our midst. He had hardly been introduced around and shown his office when our control room got a radio call asking if there was a doctor in the stratosphere above Earthpoint F-plus-6, and requesting medical assistance at the scene of an accident.

F-plus-6 was almost directly below us, so Dr. Cathcart felt he ought to respond, and our control man gave the word and asked for particulars and instructions. It seems there had been a low-altitude collision above F-plus-6 involving two small planes and killing three people. One plane was a Diaheliper, belonging to an aerial diaper service that flew diapers to rural homes by helicopter. The other was one of the familiar government-owned sprayplanes that worked at low altitudes over croplands, truck gardens, and commercial orchards, delivering a heavy mist of the deadly Tri-D solution, the pesticide that had revolutionized agriculture, eliminated the bee from nature, and given us fruits and vegetables of undreamed-of perfection but very high toxicity.

The two planes had tangled and fallen onto the observation tower of a whooping-crane sanctuary, scattering diapers over an area of half a mile and releasing a stream of Tri-D. Cathcart got his medical kit, put on his parachute, and paused a moment to adjust his pressurizer, preparatory to bailing out. Knowing that he wouldn't be back for a while, he asked if anybody around the shop was due for a Tri-D shot that morning, and it turned out that Bill Foley was. So the Doctor told Foley to come along, and explained that he would give him his injection on the way down. Bill threw me a quick look of mock anguish, and started climbing into his gear. This must have been six or seven minutes past nine.

It seems strange that I should feel obliged to explain Tri-D shots. They were a commonplace at this time—as much a part of a person's life as his toothbrush. The correct name for them was Anti-Tri-D, but people soon shortened the name. They were simply injections that everyone had to receive at regular twenty-one-day intervals, to counteract the lethal effect of food, and the notable thing about them was the great importance of the twenty-one-day period. To miss one's Tri-D shot by as much as a couple of hours might mean serious consequences, even death. Almost every day there were deaths reported in the papers from failure to get the injection at the proper time. The whole business was something like insulin control in diabetes. You can easily imagine the work it entailed for doctors in the United States, keeping the entire population protected against death by poisoning.

As Dr. Cathcart and Bill eased themselves out of the plane through the chute exit, I paused briefly and listened to Miss Babson, our author of the day.

"It is a grand privilege," she was saying, "to appear before the television audience this morning and face this distinguished battery of critics, including my old sparring partner, Ralph Armstrong, of the *Herald Tribune*. I suppose after Mr. Armstrong finishes with me I will be a pretty good candidate for euthanasia myself. Ha. But seriously, ladies and gentlemen, I feel that a good book is its own defense."

The authoress had achieved a state of exaltation already. I knew that her book, which she truly believed to be great, had been suggested to her by an agent over a luncheon table and had been written largely by somebody else, whom the publisher had had to bring in to salvage the thing. The final result was a run-of-the-can piece of rubbish easily outselling its nearest competitor.

Mis Babson continued, her exaltation stained with cuteness:

"I have heard my novel criticized on the ground that the theme of euthanasia is too daring, and even that it is anti-Catholic. Well, I can remember, way back in the dark ages, when a lot of things that are accepted as commonplace today were considered daring or absurd. My own father can recall the days when dairy cows were actually bred by natural methods. The farmers of those times felt that the artificial-breeding program developed by our marvellous experiment stations was highfalutin nonsense. Well, we all know what has happened to the dairy industry, with many of our best milch cows giving milk continuously right around the clock, in a steady stream. True, the cows do have to be propped up and held in position in special stanchions and fed intravenously, but I always say it isn't the hubbub that counts, it's the butterfat. And I doubt if even Mr. Armstrong here would want to return to the days when a cow just gave a bucket of milk and then stopped to rest."

Tiring of the literary life, I walked away and looked out a window. Below, near the layer of cumulus, the two chutes were visible. With the help of binoculars I could see Bill manfully trying to slip his chute over next to the Doc, and could see Cathcart fumbling for his needle. Our telecandid man was at another window, filming the thing for the next newscast, as it was a new wrinkle in the Tri-D world to have somebody getting his shot while parachuting.

I had a few chores to do before our program came on, at eleven-five. "Town Meeting of the Upper Air" was the name of it. "Town Meeting" was an unrehearsed show, but I was supposed to brief the guests, distribute copies of whatever prepared scripts there were, explain the cuing, and make everybody happy generally. The program we were readying that morning had had heavy advance billing, and there was tremendous interest in it everywhere, not so much because of the topic ("Will the fear of retaliation stop aggression?") or even the cast of characters, which included Major General Artemus T. Recoil, but because of an incidental stunt we were planning to pull off. We had arranged a radio hookup with the space platform, a gadget the Army had succeeded in establishing six hundred miles up, in the regions of the sky beyond the pull of gravity. The Army, after many years of experimenting with rockets, had not only got the platform established but had sent two fellows there in a Spaceship, and also a liberal supply of the New Weapon.

The whole civilized world had read about this achievement, which swung the balance of power so heavily in our favor, and everyone was aware that the damned platform was wandering around in its own orbit at a dizzy distance from the earth and not subject to gravitational pull. Every kid in America had become an astrophysicist overnight and talked knowingly of exhaust velocities, synergy curves, and Keplerian ellipses. Every subway rider knew that the two men on the platform were breathing oxygen thrown off from big squash vines that they had taken along. The *Reader's Digest* had added to the fun by translating and condensing several German treatises on rockets and space travel, including the great *Wege zur Raumschiffahrt*. But to date, because of security regulations and technical difficulties, there had been no radio-television hookup. Finally we got clearance from Washing-

ton, and General Recoil agreed to interview the officers on the platform as part of the "Town Meeting" program. This was big stuff—
to hear directly from the Space Platform for Checking Aggression,
known pretty generally as the SPCA.

I was keyed up about it myself, but I remember that all that morning in the plane I felt disaffected, and wished I were not a stratovideo
man. There were often days like that in the air. The plane, with its
queer cargo and its cheap goings on, would suddenly seem unaccountably remote from the world of things I admired. In a physical sense
we were never very remote: the plane circled steadily in a fixed circle
of about ten miles diameter, and I was never far from my own home
on East Harding Boulevard. I could talk to Ann and the children, if
I wished, by radiophone.

In many respects mine was a good job. It paid two hundred and
twenty-five dollars a week, of which two hundred and ten was with-
held. I should have felt well satisfied. Almost everything in the way
of social benefits was provided by the government—medical care,
hospitalization, education for the children, accident insurance, fire and
theft, old-age retirement, Tri-D shots, vacation expense, amusement and
recreation, welfare and well-being, Christmas and good will, rainy-day
resource, staples and supplies, beverages and special occasions, baby-
sitzfund—it had all been worked out. Any man who kept careful
account of his pin money could get along all right, and I guess I should
have been happy. Ann never complained much, except about one
thing. She found that no matter how we saved and planned, we never
could afford to buy flowers. One day, when she was a bit lathered up
over household problems, she screamed, "God damn it, I'd rather live
dangerously and have one dozen yellow freesias!" It seemed to prey
on her mind.

Anyway, this was one of those oppressive days in the air for me.
Something about the plane's undeviating course irritated me; the circle
we flew seemed a monstrous excursion to nowhere. The engine noise
(we flew at subsonic speed) was an unrelieved whine. Usually I didn't
notice the engines, but today the ship sounded in my ears every
minute, reminding me of a radiotherapy chamber, and there was
always the palpable impact of vulgar miracles—the very nature of
television—that made me itchy and fretful.

Appearing with General Recoil on "Town Meeting of the Upper
Air" were to be Mrs. Florence Gill, president of the Women's Auxiliary of the Sons of Original Matrons; Amory Buxton, head of the
Economics and Withholding Council of the United Nations; and a
young man named Tollip, representing one of the small, ineffectual
groups that advocated world federation. I rounded up this stable
of intellects in the reception room, went over the procedure with them,

534

gave the General a drink (which seemed to be what was on his mind), and then ducked out to catch the ten-o'clock news and to have a smoke.

I found Pete Everhardt in the control room. He looked bushed. "Quite a morning, Nuncle," he said. Pete not only had to keep his signal clean on the nine-o'clock show (Melonie Babson was a speaker who liked to range all over the place when she talked) but he had to keep kicking the ball around with the two Army officers on the space platform, for fear he would lose them just as they were due to go on. And on top of that he felt obliged to stay in touch with Dr. Cathcart down below, as a matter of courtesy, and also to pick up incidental stuff for subsequent newscasts.

I sat down and lit a cigarette. In a few moments the day's authoress wound up her remarks and the news started, with the big, tense face of Ed Peterson on the screen dishing it out. Ed was well equipped by nature for newscasting; he had the accents of destiny. When he spread the news, it penetrated in depth. Each event not only seemed fraught with meaning, it seemed fraught with Ed. When he said "I predict . . ." you felt the full flow of his pipeline to God.

To the best of my recollection the ten-o'clock newscast on this awful morning went as follows:

(Announcer) "Good morning. Tepky's Hormone-Enriched Dental Floss brings you Ed Peterson and the news."

(Ed) "Flash! Three persons were killed and two others seriously injured a few minutes ago at Earthpoint F-plus-6 when a government sprayline collided with a helicopter of the Diaheliper Company. Both pilots were thrown clear. They are at this moment being treated by a doctor released by parachute from Stratovideo Ship 3, from which I am now speaking. The sprayplane crashed into the observation tower of a whooping-crane sanctuary, releasing a deadly mist of Tri-D and instantly killing three wardens who were lounging there watching the love dance of the cranes. Diapers were scattered widely over the area, and these sterile garments proved invaluable to Dr. Herbert L. Cathcart in bandaging the wounds of the injured pilots, Roy T. Bliss and Homer Schenck. [Here followed a newsreel shot showing Cathcart winding a diaper around the head of one of the victims.] You are now at the scene of the disaster," droned Ed. "This is the first time in the history of television that an infant's napkin has appeared in the role of emergency bandage. Another first for American Tel. & Vid.!

"Washington! A Senate committee, with new facts at its disposal, will reopen the investigation to establish the blame for Pearl Harbor.

"Chicago! Two members of the Department of Sanitation were removed from the payroll today for refusal to take the loyalty oath.

Both are members of New Brooms, one of the four hundred thousand organizations on the Attorney General's subversive list.

"Hollywood! It's a boy at the Roscoe Pews. Stay tuned to this channel for a closeup of the Caesarean section during the eleven-o'clock roundup!

"New York! Flash! The Pulitzer Prize in editorial writing has been awarded to Frederick A. Mildly, of the New York *Times*, for his nostalgic editorial 'The Old Pumphandle.'

"Flash! Donations to the Atlantic Community Chest now stand at a little over seven hundred billion dollars. Thanks for a wonderful job of giving—I mean that from my heart.

"New York! The vexing question of whether Greek athletes will be allowed to take part in next year's Olympic Games still deadlocks the Security Council. In a stormy session yesterday the Russian delegate argued that the presence of Greek athletes at the games would be a threat to world peace. Most of the session was devoted to a discussion of whether the question was a procedural matter or a matter of substance.

"Flash! Radio contact with the two United States Army officers on the Space Platform for Checking Aggression, known to millions of listeners as the SPCA, has definitely been established, despite rumors to the contrary. The television audience will hear their voices in a little more than one hour from this very moment. You will *not* see their faces. Stay tuned! This is history, ladies and gentlemen—the first time a human voice freed from the pull of gravity has been heard on earth. The spacemen will be interviewed by Major General Artemus T. Recoil on the well-loved program 'Town Meeting of the Upper Air.'

"I predict: that because of SPCA and the Army's Operation Space, the whole course of human destiny will be abruptly changed, and that the age-old vision of peace is now on the way to becoming a reality."

Ed finished and went into his commercial, which consisted of digging a piece of beef gristle out of his teeth with dental floss.

I rubbed out my cigarette and walked back toward my cell. In the studio next ours, "The Bee" was on the air, and I paused for a while to watch. "The Bee" was a program sponsored by the Larry Cross Pollination Company, aimed principally at big orchardists and growers —or rather at their wives. It was an interminable mystery-thriller sort of thing, with a character called the Bee, who always wore a green hood with two long black feelers. Standing there in the aisle of the plane, looking into the glass-enclosed studio, I could see the Bee about to strangle a red-haired girl in slinky pajamas. This was America's pollination hour, an old standby, answer to the housewife's dream.

The Larry Cross outfit was immensely rich. I think they probably handled better than eighty per cent of all fertilization in the country. Bees, as I have said, had become extinct, thanks to the massive doses of chemicals, and of course this had at first posed a serious agricultural problem, as vast areas were without natural pollination. The answer came when the Larry Cross firm was organized, with the slogan "We Carry the Torch for Nature." The business mushroomed, and branch offices sprang up all over the nation. During blossom time, field crews of highly trained men fanned out and pollinized everything by hand—a huge job and an arduous one. The only honey in the United States was synthetic—a blend of mineral oil and papaya juice. Ann hated it with a morbid passion.

When I reached my studio I found everybody getting ready for the warmup. The Town Crier, in his fusty costume, stood holding his bell by the clapper, while the makeup man touched up his face for him. Mrs. Gill, the S.O.M. representative, sat gazing contemptuously at young Tollip. I had riffled through her script earlier, curious to find out what kind of punch she was going to throw. It was about what I expected. Her last paragraph contained the suggestion that all persons who advocated a revision of the Charter of the United Nations be automatically deprived of their citizenship. "If these well-meaning but misguided persons," ran the script, "with their utopian plans for selling this nation down the river are so anxious to acquire world citizenship, I say let's make it easy for them—let's take away the citizenship they've already got and see how they like it. As a lineal descendant of one of the Sons of Original Matrons, I am sick and tired of these cuckoo notions of one world, which come dangerously close to simple treachery. We've enough to do right here at home without . . ."

And so on. In my mind's ear I could already hear the moderator's salutary and impartial voice saying, "Thank you, Mrs. Florence Gill."

At five past eleven, the Crier rang his bell. "Hear ye! See ye! Town Meetin' today! Listen to both sides and make up your own minds!" Then George Cahill, the moderator, started the ball rolling.

I glanced at Tollip. He looked as though his stomach were filling up with gas. As the program got under way, my own stomach began to inflate, too, the way it often did a few hours after breakfast. I remember very little of the early minutes of that morning's Town Meeting. I recall that the U.N. man spoke first, then Mrs. Gill, then Tollip (who looked perfectly awful). Finally the moderator introduced General Recoil, whose stomach enjoyed the steadying effects of whiskey and who spoke in a loud, slow, confident voice, turning frequently to smile down on the three other guests.

"We in the Army," began the General, "don't pretend that we know all the answers to these brave and wonderful questions. It is not the

537

Army's business to know whether aggression is going to occur or not. Our business is to put on a good show if it *does* occur. The Army is content to leave to the United Nations and to idealists like Mr. Tollip the troublesome details of political progress. I certainly don't know, ladies and gentlemen, whether the fear of retaliation is going to prevent aggression, but I *do* know that there is no moss growing on we of Operation Space. As for myself, I guess I am what you might call a retaliatin' fool. [Laughter in the upper air.] Our enemy is well aware that we are now in a most unusual position to retaliate. That knowledge on the part of our enemy is, in my humble opinion, a deterrent to aggression. If I didn't believe that, I'd shed this uniform and get into a really well-paid line of work, like professional baseball."

Will this plane never quit circling? (I thought). Will the words never quit going round and round? Is there no end to this noisy carrousel of indigestible ideas? Will no one ever catch the brass ring?

"But essentially," continued the General, "our job is not to deal with the theoretical world of Mr. Tollip, who suggests that we merge in some vast superstate with every Tom, Dick, and Harry, no matter what their color or race or how underprivileged they are, thus pulling down our standard of living to the level of the lowest common denominator. Our job is not to deal with the diplomatic world of Mr. Buxton, who hopes to find a peaceful solution around a conference table. No, the Army must face the world as it is. We know the enemy is strong. In our dumb way, we think it is just horse sense for us to be stronger. And I'm proud, believe me, ladies and gentlemen, proud to be at one end of the interplanetary conversation that is about to take place on this very, *very* historic morning. The achievement of the United States Army in establishing the space platform—which is literally a man-made planet—is unparalleled in military history. We have led the way into space. We have given Old Lady Gravity the slip. We have got there, and we have got there fustest with the mostest. [Applause.]

"I can state without qualification that the New Weapon, in the capable hands of the men stationed on our platform, brings the *entire* globe under our dominion. We can pinpoint any spot, anywhere, and sprinkle it with our particular brand of thunder. Mr. Moderator, I'm ready for this interview if the boys out there in space are ready."

Everyone suspected that there might be a slipup in the proceedings at this point, that the mechanical difficulties might prove insuperable. I glanced at the studio clock. The red sweep hand was within a few jumps of eleven-thirty—the General had managed his timing all right. Cahill's face was tenser than I had ever seen it before. Because of the advance buildup, a collapse at this moment would put him in a nasty hole, even for an old experienced m.c. But at exactly eleven-thirty the interview started, smooth as silk. Cahill picked it up from the General.

"And now, watchers of television everywhere, you will hear a conversation between Major General Artemus T. Recoil, who pioneered Operation Space, and two United States Army officers on the platform —Major James Obblington, formerly of Brooklyn, New York, now of Space, and Lieutenant Noble Trett, formerly of Sioux City, Iowa, now of Space. Go ahead, General Recoil!"

"Come in, Space!" said the General, his tonsils struggling in whiskey's undertow, his eyes bearing down hard on the script. "Can you hear me, Major Obblington and Lieutenant Trett?"

"I hear you," said a voice. "This is Trett." The voice, as I remember it, astonished me because of a certain laconic quality that I had not expected. I believe it astonished everyone. Trett's voice was cool, and he sounded as though he were right in the studio.

"Lieutenant Trett," continued the General, "tell the listeners here on earth, tell us, in your position far out there in free space, do you feel the pull of gravity?"

"No, sir, I don't," answered Trett. In spite of the "sir," Trett sounded curiously listless, almost insubordinate.

"Yet you are perfectly comfortable, sitting there on the platform, with the whole of earth spread out before you like a vast target?"

"Sure I'm comfortable."

The General waited a second, as though expecting amplification, but it failed to come. "Well, ah, how's the weather up there?" he asked heartily.

"There isn't any," said Trett.

"No weather? No weather in space? That's very interesting."

"The hell it is," said Trett. "It's God-damn dull. This place is a dump. Worse than some of the islands in the Pacific."

"Well, I suppose it must get on your nerves a bit. That's all part of the game. Tell us, Lieutenant, what's it like to be actually a part of the solar system, with your own private orbit?"

"It's all right, except I'd a damn sight rather get drunk," said Trett.

I looked at Cahill. He was swallowing his spit. General Recoil took a new hold on his script.

"And you say you don't feel the pull of gravity, not even a little?"

"I just told you I didn't feel any pull," said Trett. His voice now had a surly quality.

"Well, ah," continued the General, who was beginning to tremble, "can you describe, briefly, for the television audience—" But it was at this point that Trett, on the platform, seemed to lose interest in talking with General Recoil and started chinning with Major Obblington, his sidekick in space. At first the three voices clashed and blurred, but the General, on a signal from the moderator, quit talking, and the conversation that ensued between Trett and Obblington was audible and clear. Millions of listeners must have heard the dialogue.

"Hey, Obie," said Trett, "you want to know something else I don't feel the pull of, besides gravity?"

"What?" asked his companion.

"Conscience," said Trett cheerfully. "I don't feel my conscience pulling me around."

"Neither do I," said Obblington. "I ought to feel some pulls but I don't."

"I also don't feel the pull of duty."

"Check," said Obblington.

"And what is even more fantastic, I don't feel the pull of dames."

Cahill made a sign to the General. Stunned and confused by the turn things had taken, Recoil tried to pick up the interview and get it back on the track. "Lieutenant Trett," he commanded, "you will limit your remarks to the—"

Cahill waved him quiet. The next voice was the Major's.

"Jesus, now that you mention it, I don't feel the pull of dames, either! Hey, Lieutenant—you suppose gravity has anything to do with sex?"

"God damn if I know," replied Trett. "I know I don't *weigh* anything, and when you don't weigh anything, you don't seem to *want* anything."

The studio by this time was paralyzed with attention. The General's face was swollen, his mouth was half open, and he struggled for speech that wouldn't come.

Then Trett's cool, even voice again: "See that continent down there, Obie? That's where old Fatso Recoil lives. You feel drawn toward that continent in any special way?"

"Naa," said Obblington.

"You feel like doing a little shooting, Obie?"

"You're rootin' tootin' I feel like shootin'."

"Then what are we waiting for?"

I am, of course, reconstructing this conversation from memory. I am trying to report it faithfully. When Trett said the words "Then what are we waiting for?" I quit listening and dashed for the phones in the corridor. As I was leaving the studio, I turned for a split second and looked back. The General had partially recovered his power of speech. He was mumbling something to Cahill. I caught the words "phone" and "Defense Department."

The corridor was already jammed. I had only one idea in my head —to speak to Ann. Pete Everhardt pushed past me. He said crisply,

540

"This is it." I nodded. Then I glanced out of a window. High in the east a crazy ribbon of light was spreading upward. Lower down, in a terrible parabola, another streak began burning through. The first blast was felt only slightly in the plane. It must have been at a great distance. It was followed immediately by two more. I saw a piece of wing break up, saw one of the starboard engines shake itself loose from its fastenings and fall. Near the phone booths, the Bee, still in costume, fumbled awkwardly for a parachute. In the crush one of his feelers brushed my face. I never managed to reach a phone. All sorts of things flashed through my mind. I saw Ann and the children, their heads in diapers. I saw again the man in the leather cap, loading bedsprings. I heard again Pete's words, "This is it," only I seemed to hear them in translation: "Until the whole wide world to nothingness do sink." (How durable the poets are!) As I say, I never managed the phone call. My last memory of the morning is of myriads of bright points of destruction where the Weapon was arriving, each pyre in the characteristic shape of an artichoke. Then a great gash, and the plane tumbling. Then I lost consciousness.

I cannot say how many minutes or hours after that the earth finally broke up. I do not know. There is, of course, a mild irony in the fact that it was the United States that was responsible. Insofar as it can be said of any country that it had human attributes, the United States was well-meaning. Of that I am convinced. Even I, at this date and at this distance, cannot forget my country's great heart and matchless ingenuity. I can't in honesty say that I believe we were wrong to send the men to the platform—it's just that in any matter involving love, or high explosives, one can never foresee all the factors. Certainly I can't say with any assurance that Tollip's theory was right; it seems hardly likely that anyone who suffered so from stomach gas could have been on the right track. I did feel sympathetic toward some of his ideas, perhaps because I suffered from flatulence myself. Anyway, it was inevitable that it should have been the United States that developed the space platform and the new weapon that made the H-bomb obsolete. It was inevitable that what happened, at last, was conceived in good will.

Those times—those last days of earth! I think about them a lot. A sort of creeping ineptitude had set in. Almost everything in life seemed wrong to me, somehow, as though we were all hustling down a blind alley. Many of my friends seemed mentally confused, emotionally unstable, and I have an idea I seemed the same to them. In the big cities, horns blew before the light changed, and it was clear that motorists no longer had the capacity to endure the restrictions they had placed on their own behavior. When the birds became extinct (all

541

but the whooping crane), I was reasonably sure that human beings were on the way out, too. The cranes survived only because of their dance—which showmen were quick to exploit. (Every sanctuary had its television transmitter, and the love dance became a more popular spectacle than heavyweight prizefighting.) Birds had always been the symbol of freedom. As soon as I realized that they were gone, I felt that the significance had gone from my own affairs. (I was a cranky man, though—I must remember that, too—and am not trying here to suggest anything beyond a rather strong personal sadness at all this.)

Those last days! There were so many religions in conflict, each ready to save the world with its own dogma, each perfectly intolerant of the other. Every day seemed a mere skirmish in the long holy war. It was a time of debauch and conversion. Every week the national picture magazines, as though atoning for past excesses, hid their cheesecake carefully away among four-color reproductions of the saints. Television was the universal peepshow—in homes, schools, churches, bars, stores, everywhere. Children early formed the habit of gaining all their images at second hand, by looking at a screen; they grew up believing that anything perceived directly was vaguely fraudulent. Only what had been touched with electronics was valid and real. I think the decline in the importance of direct images dated from the year television managed to catch an eclipse of the moon. After that, nobody ever looked at the sky, and it was as though the moon had joined the shabby company of buskers. There was really never a moment when a child, or even a man, felt free to look away from the television screen—for fear he might miss the one clue that would explain everything.

In many respects I like the planet I'm on. The people here have no urgencies, no capacity for sustained endeavor, but merely tackle things by fits and starts, leaving undone whatever fails to hold their interest, and so, by witlessness and improvidence, escape many of the errors of accomplishment. I like the apples here better than those on earth. They are often wormy, but with a most wonderful flavor. There is a saying here: "Even a very lazy man can eat around a worm."

But I would be lying if I said I didn't miss that other life, I loved it so.

THE FATE OF THE CITY

arl Sandburg's opening poem, "Chicago," voices an exuberant vitality rarely associated with cities today. Technology and the growth of populations have radically changed the boundaries and complexions of cities everywhere, and the tendency of large urban centers to grow out and coalesce suggests that some day, for instance, our East and West coasts will become urban sprawls extending for hundreds of miles from Boston to Washington and from San Francisco to the Mexican border. What kind of life will there be in these "cities" of the future?

Lewis Mumford feels that because city planners and architects have lost sight of the human function of the city, they have no "formative idea," no image of the city, and he deplores the resulting nondesign and formless urbanization, so vividly described by Dan Jacobson in the following essay. Jane Jacobs presents an approach to city planning which Mumford calls sentimental but which merits the wide attention it has nevertheless received. Her main concern here is the sterile and anonymous life style fostered by planned streets and planned communities. Harvey Cox, however, sees in our urban anonymity great possibilities of choice and, therefore, of freedom from "saddling traditions and burdensome expectations of town life."

Although the last three selections are specifically about New York City, their ideas are relevant elsewhere. Tom Wolfe's disturbing essay is based on a recent study of how much space is needed by animals for survival. He describes human overcrowding and its possible consequences: the disintegration of people under intolerable stress. Kenneth Clark's excerpts from interviews with Harlem residents highlight the complexities and intensities of ghetto life. Norman Mailer's concluding essay, with its humane perceptions of the myriad problems facing the city, proposes a return to the city-state and "power to the neighborhoods."

Carl Sandburg (1878–1967)

CHICAGO

Hog Butcher for the World,
Tool Maker, Stacker of Wheat,
Player with Railroads and the Nation's
    Freight Handler;
Stormy, husky, brawling,
City of the Big Shoulders:
They tell me you are wicked, and I believe
    them; for I have seen your painted
    women under the gas lamps luring the
    farm boys.
And they tell me you are crooked, and I
    answer: Yes, it is true I have seen the
    gunman kill and go free to kill again.
And they tell me you are brutal, and my
    reply is: On the faces of women and
    children I have seen the marks of wanton
    hunger.
And having answered so I turn once more
    to those who sneer at this my city, and I
    give them back the sneer and say to
    them:
Come and show me another city with lifted
    head singing so proud to be alive and
    coarse and strong and cunning.
Flinging magnetic curses amid the toil of
    piling job on job, here is a tall bold
    slugger set vivid against the little soft
    cities;
Fierce as a dog with tongue lapping for
    action, cunning as a savage pitted against
    the wilderness,
    Bareheaded,
    Shoveling,
    Wrecking,
    Planning,
    Building, breaking, rebuilding,

Under the smoke, dust all over his mouth,
  laughing with white teeth,
Under the terrible burden of destiny
  laughing as a young man laughs,
Laughing even as an ignorant fighter laughs
  who has never lost a battle,
Bragging and laughing that under his wrist
  is the pulse, and under his ribs the heart
  of the people,
              Laughing!
Laughing the stormy, husky, brawling
  laughter of youth; half-naked, sweating,
  proud to be Hog-butcher, Tool-maker,
  Stacker of Wheat, Player with Railroads,
  and Freight-handler to the Nation.

                        (1914)

Lewis Mumford

*Lewis Mumford (born 1895) has been called a "man of the
renaissance" for the breadth of his knowledge and influence in the
areas of literature, history, art, architecture, and city planning.
Although he holds no academic degrees, and is neither a professional
architect nor city planner, he has held many professorships,
lectureships, and awards in these fields. In 1961 he was the first
American to receive the Royal Gold Medal for architecture from
Queen Elizabeth II, and he received the Award of Merit of the
American Institute of Architects in 1962, the U. S. Medal of
Freedom in 1964, and the National Institute of Arts and Letters
Gold Medal Award for 1970. He was brought up an Episcopalian,
but he considers himself a "religious humanist" in the tradition
of Emerson and Whitman. A strong influence on his intellectual
development was Sir Patrick Geddes, a Scottish biologist and
sociologist who was a pioneer in civic and regional studies. One of
the major themes in Mumford's writings is that man's only
hope lies in a rediscovery of human feelings and values. "In
a mature society," he has said, "man himself, not his machines or
his organizations, is the chief work of art." He wrote in the*

*1920s and 1930s a number of books important to students of
American art and literature, and more recently a more general
series, including* The Condition of Man *(1944),* The Conduct
of Life *(1951),* The City in History *(1961), which won the
National Book Award in 1962,* The Highway and the City
(1963), The Myth of the Machine: Technics and Human
Development *(1967), and* The Urban Prospect *(1968). "The
Disappearing City" was the first (October 1962) in a series of
five articles entitled "The Future of the City" written for*
The Architectural Record.

THE DISAPPEARING CITY

Nobody can be satisfied with the form of the city today. Neither as
a working mechanism, as a social medium, nor as a work of art does
the city fulfill the high hopes that modern civilization has called forth
—or even meet our reasonable demands. Yet the mechanical processes of fabricating urban structures have never before been carried
to a higher point: the energies even a small city now commands would
have roused the envy of an Egyptian Pharaoh in the Pyramid Age.
And there are moments in approaching New York, Philadelphia or
San Francisco by car when, if the light is right and the distant masses
of the buildings are sufficiently far away, a new form of urban splendor, more dazzling than that of Venice or Florence, seems to have
been achieved.

Too soon one realizes that the city as a whole, when one approaches
it closer, does not have more than a residue of this promised form in
an occasional patch of good building. For the rest, the play of light
and shade, of haze and color, has provided for the mobile eye a
pleasure that will not bear closer architectural investigation. The illusion fades in the presence of the car-choked street, the blank glassy
buildings, the glare of competitive architectural advertisements, the
studied monotony of high-rise slabs in urban renewal projects: in short,
new buildings and new quarters that lack any esthetic identity and
any human appeal except that of superficial sanitary decency and bare
mechanical order.

In all the big cities of America, the process of urban rebuilding is
now proceeding at a rapid rate, as a result of putting both the financial
and legal powers of the state at the service of the private investor and

builder. But both architecturally and socially the resulting forms have been so devoid of character and individuality that the most sordid quarters, if they have been enriched over the years by human intercourse and human choice, suddenly seem precious even in their ugliness, even in their disorder.

Whatever people made of their cities in the past, they expressed a visible unity that bound together, in ever more complex form, the cumulative life of the community; the face and form of the city still recorded that which was desirable, memorable, admirable. Today a rigid mechanical order takes the place of social diversity, and endless assembly-line urban units automatically expand the physical structure of the city while destroying the contents and meaning of city life. The paradox of this period of rapid "urbanization" is that the city itself is being effaced. Minds still operating under an obsolete 19th century ideology of unremitting physical expansion oddly hail this outcome as "progress."

The time has come to reconsider the whole process of urban design. We must ask ourselves what changes are necessary if the city is again to become architecturally expressive, and economically workable, without our having to sacrifice its proper life to the mechanical means for keeping that life going. The architect's problem is again to make the city visually "imageable"—to use Kevin Lynch's term. Admittedly neither the architect nor the planner can produce, solely out of his professional skill, the conditions necessary for building and rebuilding adequate urban communities; but their own conscious reorientation on these matters is a necessary part of a wider transformation in which many other groups, professions and institutions must in the end participate.

The multiplication and expansion of cities which took place in the 19th century in all industrial countries occurred at a moment when the great city builders of the past—the kings and princes, the bishops and the guilds—were all stepping out of the picture; and the traditions that had guided them, instead of being modified and improved, were recklessly discarded by both municipal authorities and business enterprisers.

Genuine improvements took place indeed in the internal organization of cities during the 19th century: the first substantial improvements since the introduction of drains, piped drinking water, and water closets into the cities and palaces of Sumer, Crete and Rome. But the new organs of sanitation, hygiene and communication had little effect on the visible city, while the improvements of transportation by railroad, elevated railroad and trolley car brought in visual disorder and noise and, in the case of railroad cuts and marshalling yards, disrupted urban space as recklessly as expressways and parking lots do today. In both the underground and the above-ground city, these new gains in mechanical efficiency were mainly formless, apart from occasional by-products like a handsome railroad station or a bridge.

In consequence, the great mass of metropolitan buildings since the 19th century has been disorganized and formless, even when it has professed to be mechanically efficient. Almost until today, dreams of improvement were either cast into archaic, medieval, classic or renascence molds, unchanged except in scale, or into purely industrial terms of mechanical innovations, collective "Crystal Palaces," such as H. G. Wells pictured in his scientific romances, and even Ebenezer Howard first proposed for a garden city shopping mall. In America, despite the City Beautiful movement of the Nineties, urban progress is still identified with high buildings, wide avenues, long vistas: the higher, the wider, the longer, the better.

Current suggestions for further urban improvement still tend to fall automatically into a purely mechanical mold: gouging new expressways into the city, multiplying skyscrapers, providing moving sidewalks, building garages and underground shelters, projecting linear Road-towns, or covering the entire area with a metal and plastic dome to make possible total control of urban weather—on the glib theory that uniform conditions are "ideal" ones. So long as the main human functions and purposes of the city are ignored, these subsidiary processes tend to dominate the architect's imagination. All the more because the resulting fragments of urbanoid tissue can be produced anywhere, at a profit, in limitless quantities. We are now witnessing the climax of this process.

The great exception to the routine processes of 19th century urban expansion was the replanning of the center of Paris. Paris became in fact *the* model 19th century city. Here, in a consistent organic development that began under Colbert and was carried to a temporary climax under Baron Haussmann during the Second Empire, a new central structure was created—first in the handsome monumental masonry of the Seine embankment, and then in the great boulevards and new parks. By creating a new outlet for sociability and conversation in the tree-lined promenade and the sidewalk café, accessible even to older quarters that were still dismally congested and hygienically deplorable, the planners of Paris democratized and humanized the otherwise sterile Baroque plan. The beauty and order of this new frame, which at once preserved the complexities of the older neighborhoods and opened up new quarters threaded with broad public greens, attracted millions of visitors to Paris and—what was more important—helped increase the daily satisfaction of its inhabitants.

But while Paris improved its rich historic core, it lost out in form, as badly as London or Berlin, Philadelphia or Chicago, on its spreading periphery. The vitality and individuality that had been heightened by

549

the boulevards, parks and parkways of Paris were dependent upon historic institutions and many-sided activities that the new quarters lacked. Left to themselves, these residential quarters were deserts of pretentious monotony. Today central Paris, too, is being annihilated by the same forces that produce the vast areas of urban nonentity that surround the living core of our own big cities. These forces are choking Paris today as they have choked cities in the United States, as new as Fort Worth and as old as Boston.

Not the weakest of these destructive forces are those that operate under the guise of "up-to-date planning," in extravagant engineering projects, like the new motorway along the Left Bank of the Seine—a self-negating improvement just as futile as the motorways that have deprived Boston and Cambridge of access to their most convenient and potentially most delightful recreation area along the Charles. This new order of planning makes the city more attractive temporarily to motor cars, and infinitely less attractive permanently to human beings. On the suburban outskirts of our cities everywhere in both Europe and America, high-rise apartments impudently counterfeit the urbanity they have actually left behind. Present-day building replaces the complex structure of the city with loose masses of "urbanoid" tissue.

This formless urbanization, which is both dynamic and destructive, has become almost universal. Though it utilizes one kind of structure in metropolitan renewal projects and a slightly different kind in suburbia, the two types have basically the same defect. They have been built by people who lack historical or sociological insight into the nature of the city, considered as anything but the largest number of consumers that can be brought together in the most accessible manufacturing and marketing area.

If this theory were an adequate one, it would be hard to account for the general exodus that has been taking place from the center of big cities for the last generation or more; and even harder to account for the fact that suburbs continue to spread relentlessly around every big metropolis, forming ever-widening belts of population at low residential density per acre, ever further removed from the jobs and cultural opportunities that big cities are by their bigness supposed to make more accessible. In both cases, cities, villages and countryside, once distinct entities with individuality and identity, have become homogenized masses. Therewith one of the main functions of architecture, to symbolize and express the social idea, has disappeared.

During the last generation an immense amount of literature on cities has belatedly appeared, mostly economic and social analysis of a limited kind, dealing with the subsidiary and peripheral aspects of urban life. Most of these studies have been entirely lacking in concrete architectural understanding and historical perspective. Though they emphasize dynamic processes and technological change, they quaintly assume that the very processes of change now under observation are themselves unchanging; that is, that they may be neither retarded, halted nor redirected nor brought within a more complex pattern that would reflect more central human needs and would alter their seeming importance.

For the exponents of aimless dynamism, the only method of controlling the urban processes now visible is to hasten them and widen their province. Those who favor this automatic dynamism treat the resultant confusions and frustrations as the very essence of city life, and cheerfully write off the accompanying increase in nervous tensions, violence, crime and health-depleting sedatives, tranquillizers and atmospheric poisons.

The effect of this literature has been, no doubt, to clarify the economic and technical processes that are actually at work in Western urban society. But that clarification, though it may help the municipal administrator in performing his daily routines and making such plans as can be derived from five-year projections, has so far only served to reinforce and speed up the disruptive processes that are now in operation. From the standpoint of the architect and the city planning, such analysis would be useful only if it were attached to a formative idea of the city; and such an idea of the city is precisely what is lacking.

"Idea" comes from the original Greek term for "image." Current proposals for city improvement are so imageless that city planning schools in America, for the last half-generation, have been turning out mainly administrators, statisticians, economists, traffic experts. For lack of an image of the modern city, contemporary "experts" covertly fall back on already obsolete clichés, such as Le Corbusier's Voisin plan for Paris. Following the humanly functionless plans and the purposeless processes that are now producing total urban disintegration, they emerge, like the sociologist Jean Gottmann, with the abstract concept of "Megalopolis"—the last word in imageless urban amorphousness. And unfortunately, people who have no insight into the purposes of urban life have already begun to talk of this abstraction as the new "form" of the city.

The emptiness and sterility of so much that now goes under the rubric of modern city design is now being widely felt. Hence the interest that has been awakened by books like Jane Jacobs' *The Death and Life of Great American Cities,* with its keen appreciation of some of the more intimate aspects of urban life, and with its contrasting criticism, largely deserved, of radical human deficiencies in the standardized, high-rise, "urban renewal" projects.

But unfortunately Mrs. Jacobs, despite her healthy reaction against bad design, has, to match her phobia about open spaces, an almost pathological aversion to good urban design. In order to avoid officious municipal demolition and regulation, she would return to Victorian *laissez faire;* in order to overcome regimentation, she would invite chaos. Mrs. Jacobs has made a sentimental private utopia out of a very special case—a few streets in a little urban backwater—a special neighborhood of New York that happily retained its historical identity longer than any other area except Brooklyn Heights. In any large sense, she lacks an image of the modern city. Her new model is only the old muddle from which less whimsical planners are belatedly trying to escape.

The fact is that 20th century planning still lacks a fresh multidimensional image of the city, partly because we have not discussed and sorted out the true values, functions and purposes of modern culture from many pseudo-values and apparently automatic processes that promise power or profit to those who promote them.

What has passed for a fresh image of the city turns out to be two forms of anti-city. One of these is a multiplication of standard, de-individualized high-rise structures, almost identical in form, whether they enclose offices, factories, administrative headquarters or family apartments, set in the midst of a spaghetti tangle of traffic arteries, expressways, parking lots and garages. The other is the complementary but opposite image of urban scatter and romantic seclusion often called suburban, though it has in fact broken away from such order as the 19th century suburb had actually achieved, and even lacks such formal coherence as Frank Lloyd Wright proposed to give it in his plans for Broadacre City. As an agent of human interaction and cooperation, as a stage for the social drama, the city is rapidly sinking out of sight.

If either the architect or the planner is to do better in the future, he must understand the historical forces that produced the original miscarriage of the city, and the contemporary pressures that have brought about this retreat and revolt.

Dan Jacobson

Dan Jacobson is a poet, story writer, and essayist who was born and educated in South Africa and now lives in London. His first jobs were in teaching, journalism, and business. In 1956–1957 he held a Fellowship in Creative Writing at Stanford University,

and No Further West: California Visited *(1957) is a record
of the impression California made on him. We reprint below its
second chapter. Mr. Jacobson has written many stories and
reviews for* Commentary, The New Yorker, The Atlantic
Monthly, The New Statesman, *and other magazines in both
England and the United States. Some of his other writings are*
A Long Way from London *(1958),* Evidence of Love *(1960),*
Time of Arrival and Other Essays *(1962),* The Beginners
(1966), and Through the Wilderness and Other Stories
(1968).

THE SEVERED TENDON

Why hadn't anyone *told* me? That was the question I asked of myself
in awe, in fear, in anger, in despair. What I saw was all new, brand-
new, and of a size and a populousness and a busyness that I couldn't
begin to comprehend. Why hadn't anyone told me about it? Why
hadn't I been warned?

And I asked this question though what we saw of Palo Alto by day-
light on our first morning there confirmed my first impression that
the town was very similar to the small towns I had known in South
Africa. There was the same sense of space, newness, and sandi-
ness; there were the same wide tarred streets, empty in the sun; there
were the same lawns of grass shrivelling at the edges; the leaves of
familiar trees hung down spiritlessly in front of houses that were often
of a style I had known in South Africa; there was a main street, with
its shop windows and department stores stretching away from the
pavements, and few people about.

But the difficulty was that this main street wasn't main at all, and
the town wasn't a small one, if it existed at all; and of that I wasn't
sure. What I saw in the days following our arrival seemed to be a
single sprawl that stretched all the thirty miles between San Francisco
and Palo Alto and for another thirty miles beyond; and what it was
anywhere along the length was precisely what it was anywhere else
along its length. And what *that* was—I had no word for it. It was a
sprawl, a mess, a nightmare of repetition and disjunction and incoherence, all grown permanent and powerful.

There were shops, identical houses in tracts, drive-ins, motels, factories, shopping centres, supermarkets, giant billboards, filling-stations, used-car lots all along El Camino Real. There were identical houses in tracts, drive-ins, motels, shopping-centres, supermarkets, giant billboards all along the Bayshore Highway; there were whole towns of identical houses in tracts between the Bayshore Highway and El Camino Real; and further again, and further yet, there were used-car lots and giant billboards and shopping centres and supermarkets . . .

And all the buildings sprawled wide, drunkenly, sharing no style, no size, having no relation to one another but that imposed on them by the single thing they did share: a frontage of the road, a view of the traffic, a gaze across to the other side of the road where there were other motels, drive-ins, gas-stations and other names—The Crown, Crazy Jack's, Ole Olsen's, Top-T Service, and a supermarket spaciously spelling out its name with a single letter in each of its stucco arches. They were all spread away from one another, pushed apart physically. Every car of the thousands that rushed at all times and along all the length of the roads had to have a place for it when it swung off the road and stopped. So, sprawling enough in themselves, the places spread their grounds wider still, in hope that one car or a hundred would stop in this drive-in rather than the fifty others over the last few miles, this supermarket rather than the last. Perhaps the car would stop because in front of this supermarket someone had taken the trouble to advertise—in black letters six inches high against a white illuminated background—*Celery: 10 Cents a Stick.* How could anyone go to so much trouble to sell sticks of celery, one wondered; but one wondered about nothing very long on that road, because next there was a car mounted on a platform twenty feet high, and slowly the whole platform turned round, bearing the car on its palm. Below it, and stretching away from it was a used-car lot, and another, all decorated with streamers and bunting and strings of plastic whirligigs, as if royalty were soon to pass by, to inspect the acres upon acres of used cars, glittering in their lots on the sand. Then a service-station, or two, or three, a motel with all its Swiss-style gabled little chalets in a row along the road, a second-hand furniture mart, a liquor store, more used-car lots. It was impossible to tell which of all the cars in rows belonged to one lot and which to another, for there were no fences between them; but there were names on poles, names on billboards, names as high as the little wooden offices that bore them, and each name was different from the last—unless it was a name that had been seen before, fifty times before, in front of other lots, on other hoardings, further back along the road.

The used-car lots covered their spaces, they stretched down the road, and then beyond them there rose the grandeur of a new shopping centre. This one looked something like the Palais de Chaillot in Paris. It was white, it gleamed, it flung its arms open as if to embrace not a terraced garden but a plain of parked cars as wide as that first one we saw in front of the airport. These shopping centres were things that we had never seen before—places that under a single sprawling roof housed enough shops to supply the wants of a town. That one was like the Palais de Chaillot; the next was quaint, rural, timbered, with flagged walks, low buildings with overhanging eaves, at every corner a loudspeaker playing soft music. In this shopping centre there was a shop that sold only electronically-operated garage doors; but otherwise there was nothing in it that was not repeated shabbily or elegantly by some single shop belonging to the sprawl directly and not through the *imperium in imperio* of the shopping centre. They both contributed to the sprawl, and who could say which contribution was the greater—that of the shopping centre, with all its elegant arcades and galleries, or of this shabby drive-in shaped like a Mexican hat, with its brim over the place where cars were parked?

But what did shabby mean here, and what did elegant mean? Here was a shack of shingles and nails all smeared and disfigured with the great letters that give it its name—but within there was wall-to-wall carpeting, marble-topped desks, mobiles hanging from the ceilings, and sheer glass partitions; there was a neon sign blazing away so fiercely that it almost hid the little barn behind it where food was served. And the cars in the used-car lots, were they shabby or are they elegant? And that hospital for dogs, where on the roof a neon dog wagged its long neon tail?

But it was gone too, behind us, in a moment, for one always travelled by car down the roads, one never walked.

Those highways were able along their length to provide you with any material thing you might ever need. There were all the shops of various kinds; there were banks, travel-agencies, money-lenders, real-estate agents who would sell you a house, and furniture stores that would sell you the furniture to fill it with. There were bookstores and shops selling the latest selection of records, and little establishments that offered tropical fish in bowls, and imported Danish cutlery. There were the shops and the facilities for whole cities of prosperous people; but the curious, the frightening thing was that all the shops and facilities belonged only to the highways and to no city.

Nowhere along their length did the highways seem to contract, confine themselves, centre themselves for a community around them. There were no parks along the highways, no statues, no plaques commemorating notable events; there were no vistas, no views, no streets that radiated from this point or that; there was nowhere that one could turn and look back the way one had come. The highways ran with all their businesses and townships from San Francisco to Palo Alto and beyond, simply ploughing across the country; and it was as if some kind of vital tendon had been severed, so that they could grasp nothing to themselves, could enclose nothing in themselves, could make no order of themselves, but could only lie sprawling, incoherent, centreless, viewless, shapeless, faceless—offering all the products a community might need and yet making the establishment of a community impossible.

For it was by the roads and from the roads that the towns like ours seemed to live. Every morning half of the male inhabitants of the towns seemed to get into their cars and go thundering along the highways to San Francisco or elsewhere, and every evening they thundered back again. The women drove along the highways to do their shopping; the very air of the towns was filled night and day with the whisper of the traffic on the highways. As our town seemed to be, so seemed all the others—flat, indistinguishable appendages to the highways, equal parts of a brand-new nameless sprawl across a country.

Jane Jacobs

Jane Jacobs was born in 1916 in Scranton, Pennsylvania, and came to New York at the age of eighteen. She worked at a variety of jobs, sold some magazine articles, and explored the city. In 1947, three years after her marriage to an architect, she moved into a three-story slum building on Hudson Street in the western part of Greenwich Village and immediately began to rehabilitate it. She became chairman of the Committee to Save the West Village and led a battle which prevented New York City from redeveloping a fourteen-block portion of her neighborhood. From 1952 to 1962 she was an editor of Architectural Forum. *Her writings include* The Economy of the Cities *(1969) and her controversial earlier book,* The Death and Life of Great American Cities *(1961). We reprint two parts of that book which were adapted for magazine publication. The first is "Violence in the City Streets," from the September 1961* Harper's; *the second, "How City Planners Hurt Cities," from* The Saturday Evening Post, *October 14, 1961. "To approach a city," Mrs. Jacobs has written, "as if it were a larger architec-*

*tural problem, capable of being given order by converting it into
a disciplined work of art, is to make the mistake of substituting
art for life."*

VIOLENCE IN THE CITY STREETS

To build city districts that are custom-made for easy crime is idiotic.
Yet that is what we do. Today barbarism has taken over many city
streets—or people fear it has, which comes to much the same thing
in the end.

"I live in a lovely quiet residential area," says a friend of mine who
is hunting for another place to live. "The only disturbing sound at
night is the occasional scream of someone being mugged."

It does not take many incidents of violence to make people fear the
streets. And as they fear them, they use them less, which makes the
streets still more unsafe.

This problem is not limited to the older parts of cities. Sidewalk
and doorstep insecurity are as serious in cities that have made conscientious efforts to rebuild as they are in those cities that have lagged.
Nor is it illuminating to tag minority groups, or the poor, or the out-
casts, with responsibility for city danger. Some of the safest—as well
as some of the most dangerous—sidewalks in New York, for example,
are those along which poor people or minority groups live. And this
is true elsewhere.

Deep and complicated social ills underlie delinquency and crime—in
suburbs and towns as well as great cities. But if we are to maintain
a city society that can diagnose and keep abreast of these profoundly
difficult problems, the starting point must be to strengthen the workable forces that now exist for maintaining urban safety and civilization.
In fact we do precisely the opposite.

First, we must understand that the public peace—the sidewalk and
street peace—of cities is not kept primarily by the police, necessary
though they are. It is kept primarily by an intricate, almost unconscious, network of voluntary controls and standards among the
people themselves. In some city areas—notably older public-housing
projects and streets with very high population turnover—the keeping
of public sidewalk law and order is left almost entirely to the police
and special guards. Such places are jungles.

Nor can the problem be solved by spreading people out more thinly, trading the characteristics of cities for the characteristics of suburbs. If this were possible, then Los Angeles should be in good shape because superficially it is almost all suburban. It has virtually no districts compact enough to qualify as dense city. Yet Los Angeles' crime figures are flabbergasting. Among the seventeen standard metropolitan areas with populations over a million, Los Angeles stands pre-eminent in crime, especially the crimes associated with personal attack, which make people fear the streets. (Los Angeles, for example, has a forcible rape rate more than twice as high as either of the next two cities, which happen to be St. Louis and Philadelphia, three times as high as the rate for Chicago, and more than four times the rate for New York.)

The reasons for Los Angeles' high crime rates are complex, and at least in part obscure. But of this we can be sure: thinning out a city does not insure safety from crime and fear of crime. This is demonstrable too in cities where pseudosuburbs or superannuated suburbs are ideally suited to rape, muggings, beatings, holdups, and the like. The all-important question is: How much easy opportunity does any city street offer to crime? It may be that there is some absolute amount of crime in a given city, which will find an outlet somehow (I do not believe this). In any case, different kinds of city streets garner radically different shares of barbarism.

Some city streets afford no such opportunity. The streets of the North End of Boston are outstanding examples. City planners officially consider this area a "slum" but the streets are probably as safe as any place on earth. Although most of the North End's residents are Italian or of Italian descent, the district's streets are heavily and constantly used also by people of every race and background. Some of the strangers from outside work in or close to the district; some come to shop and stroll; many make a point of cashing their paychecks in North End stores and immediately making their big weekly purchases in streets where they know they will not be parted from their money between the getting and the spending.

Frank Havey, director of the North End Union, the local settlement house, says, "In twenty-eight years I have never heard of a single case of rape, mugging, molestation of a child, or other street crime of that sort in the district. And if there had been any, I would have heard of it even if it did not reach the papers." Half-a-dozen times or so in the past three decades, says Havey, would-be molesters have made a try toward luring a child or, late at night, attacking a woman. In every such case the try was thwarted by passers-by, by kibitzers from windows, or shopkeepers.

Meantime, in the Elm Hill Avenue section of Roxbury, a part of inner Boston that is suburban in superficial character, prudent people

558

stay off the streets at night because of the ever-present possibility of street assaults with no kibitzers to protect the victims. For this and other related reasons—dispiritedness and dullness—most of Roxbury has run down. It has become a place to leave.

Roxbury's disabilities, and especially its Great Blight of Dullness, are all too common in other cities too. But differences like these in public safety within the same city are worth noting. The once fine Elm Hill Avenue section's basic troubles are not due to a criminal or a discriminated-against or a poverty-stricken population. Its troubles are due to the fundamental fact that it is physically unsuited to function with vitality as a city district, and so cannot function safely.

Even within supposedly similar parts of supposedly similar places, drastic differences in public safety exist. For example, at Washington Houses, a public-housing project in New York, a tenants' group put up three Christmas trees in mid-December 1958. The biggest tree—a huge one—went into the project's inner "street," a landscaped central mall. Two smaller trees were placed at the outer corners of the project where it abuts a busy avenue and lively cross streets. The first night, the large tree and all its trimmings were stolen. The two smaller ones remained intact, lights, ornaments, and all, until they were taken down at New Year's. The inner mall is *theoretically* the most safe and sheltered place in the project. But, says a social worker who has been helping the tenants' group, "People are no safer in that mall than the Christmas tree. On the other hand, the place where the other trees were safe, where the project is just one corner out of four, happens to be safe for people."

Everyone knows that a well-used city street is apt to be safe. A deserted one is apt to be unsafe. But how does this work, really? And what makes a city street well used or shunned? Why is the inner sidewalk mall in Washington Houses—which is supposed to be an attraction—shunned when the sidewalks of the old city just to its west are not? What about streets that are busy part of the time and then empty abruptly? A city street equipped to make a safety asset out of the presence of strangers, as successful city neighborhoods always do, must have three main qualities:

First, there must be a clear demarcation between public and private spaces. They cannot ooze into each other as they do typically in housing projects where streets, walks, and play areas may seem at first glance to be open to the public but in effect are special preserves. (The fate of Washington Houses' large Christmas tree is a classic example of what happens when the distinction between public and private space is blurred, and the area which should be under public surveillance has no clear practicable limits.)

Second, there must be *eyes* upon the street, eyes belonging to what we might call its natural proprietors. To insure the safety of both residents and strangers, the buildings on a street must be oriented to it. They cannot turn their backs or blank sides on it and leave it blind.

And third, the sidewalk must have users on it fairly continuously, both to add more effective eyes and to induce plenty of people in buildings along the street to watch the sidewalks. Nobody enjoys sitting on a stoop or looking out a window at an empty street. But large numbers of people entertain themselves, off and on, by watching street activity.

In settlements smaller than cities, public behavior (if not crime) is controlled to some extent by a web of reputation, gossip, approval, disapproval, and sanctions. All of these are powerful if people know each other and word travels. But a city's streets must control not only the behavior of city people but also of visitors who want to have a big time away from the gossip and sanctions at home. It is a wonder cities have solved such a difficult problem at all. And yet in many streets they do it magnificently.

The issue of unsafe streets cannot be evaded by trying to make some other features of a locality safe instead—for example, interior courtyards, or sheltered play spaces. The streets of a city are where strangers come and go. The streets must not only defend the city against predatory strangers. They must also insure the safety of the many peaceable strangers who pass through. Moreover no normal person can spend his life in some artificial haven, and this includes children. Everyone must use the streets.

On the surface, we seem to have here some simple aims: To try for streets where the public space is unequivocally public and to see that these public street spaces have eyes on them as continually as possible.

But it is far from simple to accomplish these things. You can't make people use streets without reason. You can't make people watch streets if they do not want to. The safety of the street works best— and with least taint of hostility or suspicion—where people are using and enjoying the city streets voluntarily.

The basic requisite for such surveillance is a substantial quantity of stores and other public places sprinkled along the sidewalks; it is especially important that places frequented during the evening and night be among them. Stores, bars, and restaurants—the chief examples—abet sidewalk safety in different and complex ways.

First, they give people concrete reasons for using the sidewalks.

Second, they draw people along the sidewalks past places which have few attractions in themselves; this influence does not carry very far geographically, so there must be many—and different—enterprises in a city district if they are to give walkers reason for criss-crossing paths and populating barren stretches on the street.

Third, small businessmen and their employees are typically strong proponents of peace and order themselves; they hate broken windows, holdups, and nervous customers. If present in sufficient abundance, they are great street watchers and sidewalk guardians.

Fourth, the activity generated by people on errands, or people aiming for food or drink, in itself attracts more people to the street.

This last point seems incomprehensible to city planners and architectural designers. They operate on the premise that city people seek emptiness, obvious order, and quiet. Nothing could be less true. The love of people for watching activity and other people is evident in cities everywhere. This trait reaches an almost ludicrous extreme on upper Broadway in New York, where the street is divided by a narrow, central mall, right in the middle of traffic. Benches have been placed at the cross-street intersections of this long mall, and on any day when the weather is even barely tolerable they are filled with people watching the pedestrians, the traffic, and each other.

Eventually Broadway reaches Columbia University and Barnard College, one to the right, the other to the left. Here all is obvious order and quiet. No more stores and the activity they generate, almost no more pedestrians—and no more watchers on the benches. I have tried them and can see why. No place could be more boring. Even the students shun it. They do their outdoor loitering, homework, and street watching on the steps overlooking the busiest campus crossing.

It is just so elsewhere. A lively street always has both its users and watchers. Last year I was in the Lower East Side of Manhattan, waiting for a bus on a street full of errand-goers, children playing, and loiterers on the stoops. In a minute or so a woman opened a third floor tenement window, vigorously yoo-hooed at me, and shouted down that "The bus doesn't run here on Saturdays!" Then she directed me around the corner. This woman was one of thousands of New Yorkers who casually take care of the streets. They notice strangers. They observe everything going on. If they need to take action, whether to direct a stranger or to call the police, they do so. Such action usually requires, to be sure, a certain self-assurance about the actor's proprietorship of the street and the support he will get if necessary, and this raises special problems I will not deal with here. But the fundamental thing is the watching itself.

Not everyone in cities helps to take care of the streets, and many a resident or worker is unaware of why his neighborhood is safe. Consider, for example, a recent incident which occurred on the street where I live.

My block is a small one, but it contains a remarkable range of buildings, varying from several vintages of tenements to three- or four-story houses. Some of these have been converted into low-rent flats with stores on the ground floor; some, like ours, have been returned to single-family use. Across the street are some four-story brick tenements with stores below. Half of them were converted twelve years ago into small high-rent elevator apartments.

From my second-story window I happened to see a suppressed struggle going on between a man and a little girl. He seemed to be trying to get her to go with him, by turns cajoling her, and then acting nonchalant. The child was making herself rigid against the wall.

I wondered whether I should intervene, but then it became unnecessary. The wife of the butcher emerged from their ship with a determined look on her face. Joe Cornacchia came out of his delicatessen and stood solidly to the other side. Several heads poked out of the tenement windows above; one was withdrawn quickly, and its owner reappeared a moment later in the doorway behind the man. Two men from the bar next to the butcher shop came to the doorway and waited. On my side of the street, the locksmith, the fruit man, and the laundry proprietor came out of their shops, and other eyes peered from windows. That man did not know it, but he was surrounded. Nobody was going to allow a little girl to be dragged off, even if nobody knew who she was. I am sorry—for dramatic reasons—to have to report that the little girl turned out to be the man's daughter.

Throughout this little drama, perhaps five minutes in all, *no eyes appeared in the windows of the high-rent apartments.* It was the only building of which this was true. When we first moved to our block, I used to hope that soon all the old tenements would be rehabilitated in the same way. I know better now, and am filled with gloom by the recent news that such a transformation is scheduled for the rest of the block. The high-rent tenants, most of whom are so transient[1] we cannot even keep track of their faces, have not the remotest idea of who takes care of their street, or how. A city neighborhood can absorb and protect a substantial number of these birds of passage. But if and when they *become* the neighborhood, the streets will gradually grow less secure, and if things get bad enough they will drift away to another neighborhood which is mysteriously safer.

In some rich neighborhoods, where there is little do-it-yourself surveillance, street watchers are hired. The monotonous sidewalks of residential Park Avenue in New York, for example, are surprisingly

---

[1] Some, according to the storekeepers, live on beans and bread and spend their sojourn looking for a place to live where all their money will not go for rent.

little used; their logical users are populating instead the interesting sidewalks of Lexington and Madison Avenues to the east and west, filled with bars, stores, and restaurants. A network of doormen and superintendents, of delivery boys and nursemaids—a form of *hired* neighborhood—keeps residential Park Avenue supplied with eyes. At night, dog walkers safely venture forth and supplement the doormen. But this street is blank of built-in eyes, and devoid of concrete reasons for using or watching it. If its rents were to slip below the point where they could support a plentiful hired neighborhood of doormen and elevator men, it would become a woefully dangerous street.

Once a street has effective demarcation between private and public spaces and has a basic supply of activity and eyes, it is equipped to handle strangers, in fact the more the merrier.

Strangers can be a safety asset, particularly at night. The street on which I live is fortunate in having a locally supported bar, another around the corner, and a famous one—the White Horse—that draws continuous troops of strangers. (Dylan Thomas used to go there, and mentioned it in his writing.) This bar, indeed, works two distinct shifts. In the morning and early afternoon it is a social gathering place for Irish longshoremen and other craftsmen in the area, as it always was. But beginning in midafternoon it changes to kind of a college bull session combined with a literary cocktail party, and this continues until the early hours of the morning. On a cold winter's night, when the doors of the White Horse open, a solid wave of conversation surges out—very warming. The comings and goings from this bar do much to keep our street reasonably populated until three in the morning, make it safe to come home to. The only instance I know of a beating in our street occurred in the dead hours between the closing of the bar and dawn. (The beating was halted by one of our neighbors who saw it from his window.)

I know a street uptown where a church youth and community center, with many night dances and other activities, performs about the same service as the White Horse bar. Orthodox planning is much imbued with puritanical conceptions of how people should spend their free time. But there is room in cities for many differences in people's tastes, proclivities, and occupations. And these differences are in fact *needed.* Utopians and other compulsive managers of other people's leisure openly prefer one kind of legal enterprise over others—youth centers and restaurants are "better" than bars and poolrooms. This kind of thinking is worse than irrelevant for cities. It is harmful. The greater and more plentiful the range of all legitimate interests—in the strictly legal sense—that city streets and their enterprises can satisfy, the better for the streets and for the safety of the city.

Bars, and indeed all commerce, have a bad name in many city districts precisely because they do draw strangers and the strangers do not work out as an asset.

This is especially true in the dispirited gray belts of great cities and in once-fashionable (or at least once-solid) inner residential areas gone into decline. Because these neighborhoods are so dangerous, and the streets typically so dark, it is commonly believed that their troubles with strangers may result from insufficient street lighting. Good lighting is important, but darkness alone does not account for the gray areas' deep, functional sickness, the Great Blight of Dullness.

Bright lights do give some reassurance to people who need or want to go out. Thus lights induce these people to contribute their own eyes to the upkeep of the street. Moreover, as is obvious, good lighting makes the eyes count for more because their range is greater. Each additional pair of eyes, and every increase in their range, is that much to the good. But unless eyes are there, and unless in the brains behind those eyes is the almost unconscious reassurance of general street support in upholding civilization, lights can do no good. Horrifying public crimes can, and do, occur in well-lighted subway stations when no effective eyes are present (although a few people may be). They virtually never occur in darkened theatres where many people and eyes are present.

To explain the troubling effect of strangers on the streets of gray city areas, it is useful to examine the peculiarities of another and figurative kind of street—the corridors of high-rising, public-housing projects which have become standard all over America. The elevators and corridors of these projects are, in a sense, streets piled up in the sky to permit the ground to become deserted parks like the mall at Washington Houses where the tree was stolen.

These interior parts of the building are not only streets in the sense that they serve the comings and goings of residents—few of whom may know each other or recognize, necessarily, who is a resident and who is not. They are streets also in the sense of being accessible to the public. They have been designed in an imitation of upper-class standards for apartment living without upper-class cash for doormen and elevator men. Anyone can go into these buildings, unquestioned, and use the elevator and corridors. These blind-eyed streets, although completely accessible to public use, are closed to public view and thus lack the checks and inhibitions exerted by eye-policed city streets.

The New York Housing Authority some years back experimented with corridors open to public view in a Brooklyn project which I shall call Blenheim Houses although that is not its name. (I do not wish to add to its troubles by advertising it.)

Because the buildings of Blenheim Houses are sixteen stories high, the open corridors cannot really be watched from the ground or from other buildings. But their psychological openness has had some effect. More importantly, the corridors were well designed to induce surveillance from within the buildings themselves. They were equipped to serve as play space, and as narrow porches, as well as passageways. This all turned out to be so lively and interesting that the tenants added still another use: picnic grounds—this in spite of continual pleas and threats from the management which did not *plan* that the balcony corridors should serve as picnic grounds. (One of the main tenets of planners is that the Plan should anticipate everything and then permit no changes.) The tenants are devoted to the balcony-corridors which are, as a result, under intense surveillance. There has been no problem of crime in these corridors nor of vandalism either. Not even light bulbs are stolen or broken.

Nonetheless, Blenheim Houses has a fearsome problem of vandalism and scandalous behavior. The lighted balconies which are, as the manager puts it, "the brightest and most attractive scene in sight," draw strangers, especially teen-agers, from all over Brooklyn. But these strangers do not halt at the visible corridors. They go into other "streets" of the buildings, streets that lack surveillance—the elevators and, more important in this case, the fire stairs and their landings. The housing police run up and down after the malefactors—who behave barbarously and viciously in the blind-eyed, sixteen-story stairways—and the malefactors elude them. It is easy to run the elevators up to a high floor, jam the doors so the elevators cannot be brought down, and then play hell with a building and anyone you can catch. So serious is the problem and apparently so uncontrollable, that the advantage of the safe corridors is all but canceled out—at least in the harried manager's eyes.

What happens at Blenheim Houses is somewhat the same as in dull gray areas of cities. Their pitifully few and thinly spaced patches of life are like the visible corridors at Blenheim Houses. They do attract strangers. But the relatively deserted, blind streets leading from these places are like the fire stairs at Blenheim Houses. They lack the kind of street life which could equip them to handle strangers safely, and the presence of strangers in them is thus an automatic menace.

The temptation in such cases is to blame the balconies—or the commerce or bars that serve as a magnet. A typical train of thought is exemplified in the Hyde Park–Kenwood renewal project now under way in Chicago. This piece of gray area adjoining the University of Chicago contains many splendid houses and grounds, but for thirty years it has been plagued with a frightening street-crime problem, accompanied in recent years by considerable physical decay. The "cause" of Hyde Park–Kenwood's decline has been brilliantly identified, by the city planners, as the presence of "blight." By this they mean that too many of the college professors and other middle-class families steadily deserted this dull and dangerous area and their places were often, quite naturally, taken by those with little economic or social choice among living places.

What does the Hyde Park–Kenwood plan do? It designates and removes these chunks of blight and replaces them with housing projects designed, as usual, to minimize use of the streets. The plan also adds still more empty spaces here and there, blurs even further the district's already poor distinctions between private and public space, and amputates the existing commerce, which is no great shakes.

The early plans for this renewal included, for example, a relatively large imitation-suburban shopping center. But further thought gave the planners a faint glimmer of the realities. A large center—larger than that required for the standard shopping needs of the renewal district's residents—"might draw into the area extraneous people," as one of the architectural planners put it. A small shopping center was thereupon settled on. Large or small matters little.

It matters little because Hyde Park–Kenwood, like all city districts, is, in real life, surrounded by "extraneous" people—hundreds of thousands of them. The area is an embedded part of Chicago. It cannot wish away its location. It cannot bring back its one-time condition, long gone, of semi-suburbia. To plan as if it could, and to evade its deep, functional inadequacies, can have only one of two possible results so far as safety is concerned:

(1) Extraneous people will continue to come into the area as they please, including some who are not at all nice, and the opportunity for street crime will be a little easier, if anything, because of the added emptiness. (2) Or a determined effort can be made to keep extraneous people out of the area. Indeed, according to the *New York Times*, the adjoining University of Chicago—the institution that was the moving spirit in getting the plan under way—took the extraordinary measure of loosing police dogs every night to patrol its campus. The dogs are trained to hold at bay any human in this dangerous unurban inner keep. The barriers formed by new projects at the edges of Hyde Park–Kenwood, plus extraordinary policing, may be able to keep out strangers. If so, the price will be hostility from the surrounding city and an ever more beleaguered feeling within the fort. And who can be sure, either, that all those thousands rightfully within the fort are trustworthy in the dark?

I do not wish to single out one area, or in this case one plan, as uniquely opprobrious. Hyde Park–Kenwood is significant mainly because the diagnosis and the corrective measures of its plan typify in slightly more ambitious form plans conceived for cities all over the country. And in city after city, we are seeing the results of orthodox city planning of this kind: great cyclone fences are erected to "protect" sequestered projects and developments from their surroundings and special police are hired to chase intruding boys—while the crime rates rise, and people cling to their cars at night. Hyde Park–Kenwood, in short, is not a local aberration but an example of how we are deliberately building unsafe cities.

In this article I have pointed to some lively and well-used city streets and neighborhoods where lives are secure and civilized and public violence and barbarism are rare. I am not suggesting, however, that we should therefore try to imitate routinely and mechanically the districts that do display strength and success as fragments of city life. That would be impossible, and, moreover, even the best city streets and districts can stand improvement, especially in their amenity. But if life in our cities is to be safe and satisfying, we must first be aware of where it now succeeds and fails, and why. Then we shall at least have some idea both of the kind of city we want and the failure of most urban planning today to achieve anything resembling it. And this first step we have not yet begun to take.

HOW CITY PLANNERS HURT CITIES

City planners and rebuilders are killing our cities, not on purpose, but because they do not understand how cities work. Their well-meant but ignorant actions, supported by public money and political power, can be fearsomely destructive.

We are continually assured that planners are producing healthful city environments for us. But most planners and rebuilders do not recognize a healthful city environment when they see one, much less know how to create one. Consider, for example, a district called the North End, in Boston.

Twenty years ago, when I first saw the North End, its buildings were badly overcrowded. Rundown brick houses had been converted into flats. Four- or five-story walk-ups had been built to house immigrants first from Ireland, then Eastern Europe and finally from Sicily. You did not have to look far to see that the district was taking a severe physical beating and was desperately poor.

When I saw the North End again in 1959, I was amazed. Scores of buildings had been rehabilitated. Instead of mattresses against the windows, there were Venetian blinds and glimpses of fresh paint. Many of the small, converted houses were now occupied by one or two families instead of three or four. Some of the families in the tenements had uncrowded themselves by throwing two flats together, equipping them with new bathrooms and kitchens. Mingled among the buildings were splendid food stores. Small industries—upholstery making, metalworking, food processing, and the like—rimmed the neighborhood. The streets were alive with children playing, people shopping, strolling and talking.

I had seen a lot of Boston in the past few days, most of it dull, gloomy and decaying. This place struck me as the healthiest district in the city. To find out more about it, I went into a bar and phoned a Boston planner I know.

"Why in the world are you down in the North End?" he said. "Nothing's going on there. Eventually, yes, but not yet. That's a slum!"

"It doesn't seem like a slum to me," I said.

"Why that's the worst slum in the city. It has 275 dwelling units to the net acre! [Excluding streets, nonresidential land, etc.] I hate to admit we have anything like that in Boston, but it's a fact."

"Do you have any other figures on it?" I asked.

He did. Statistics showed that the neighborhood's delinquency, disease and infant-mortality rates are among the lowest in the city. The child population is just about average. The death rate is low, 8.8 per 1000, against the average city rate of 11.2.

"You should have more slums like this," I said. "Don't tell me there are plans to wipe this out. You ought to be down here learning as much as you can from it."

"I know how you feel," he said. "I often go down there myself just to walk around the streets and feel that wonderful, cheerful street life. You'd be crazy about it in summer. But we have to rebuild it eventually. We've got to get those people off the street."

My planner friend's instincts told him the North End was a healthful place. Statistics confirmed it. But his training as a city planner told him the North End *had* to be a "bad" place. It has little park land. Children play on the sidewalks. It has small blocks. In city-planning parlance, the district is "badly cut up by wasteful streets." It also has "mixed uses"—another sin. It is made up of the plans of hundreds of people—not planners. Such freedom represents, as one of the wise men of city planning put it, "a chaotic accident . . . the summation of the haphazard, antagonistic whims of many self-centered, ill-advised individuals."

Under the seeming chaos of a lively place like the North End is a marvelous and intricate order—a complicated array of urban activities.

These activities support and supplement each other, keeping the neighborhood interesting and vital. The planners would kill it.

The North End is not unique. In city after city, there are districts that refuse to decay, districts that hold people even when their incomes rise and their "status" improves, districts that spontaneously repair and renovate in spite of discouragement by government officials and mortgage lenders. These interesting and vital areas are the ones that have everything possible wrong with them—according to city-planning theory. Equally significant, in city after city the districts in decline and decay are frequently the ones that ought to be successful—according to planning theory.

The Morningside Heights area in New York City is such an example. According to theory, it should not be in trouble. It has a great abundance of park land, campus areas, playgrounds and other open spaces. It has plenty of grass. It occupies high and pleasant ground with magnificient river views. It is a famous educational center. It has good hospitals and fine churches. It has no industries. Its residential streets are zoned against "incompatible uses."

Yet by the early 1950's Morningside Heights was becoming the kind of slum in which people fear to walk the streets. Columbia University, other institutions and the planners from the city government got together. At great cost the most blighted part of the area was wiped out. In the torn-down area a middle-income project complete with shopping center was built. Nearby a fenced-off low-income project was erected. The projects were hailed as a great demonstration in city saving.

After that Morningside Heights went downhill even faster. It continues to pile up new mountains of crime and troubles to this day. The "remedy" didn't work. Dull, sorted-out "quiet residential areas" in cities fail because they are inconvenient, uninteresting and dangerous. The dark, empty grounds of housing projects breed crime. And it is much the same with dark, empty streets of "quiet residential areas" in big cities.

Our cities need help desperately. If places like Morningside Heights are to be helped, the help must be based not on imitations of genteel, "good" addresses, but on understanding the real needs of those who live in big cities. A little involvement with the life of city streets, a little recognition that empty grass festooned with used tissue paper is no treat for anyone, a little common sense—these are the first requirements.

The New York City neighborhood where I live is considered a mess by planners. They have plans to sort out its differing land uses from one another and isolate residences from working places with a buffer strip. Such a strip would be useful primarily to muggers. For months

569

residents and businessmen of the neighborhood have been combating the scheme to simplify and regiment the area with Federal funds. Simplification would be the avenue to its ruin.

One need only watch the sidewalks to see how the neighborhood is built upon a complicated set of activities. Each day Hudson Street, my street, is the scene of an endlessly varied parade of persons, some of them neighbors, many of them strangers. This scene is all composed of interesting movement and change.

I make my first entrance a little after eight A.M. when I put out the garbage can. Around me, droves of junior-high-school students and people coming to work in the district walk by the center of the stage. While I sweep the sidewalk, I watch the signs and rituals of morning. Mr. Halpert unlocking his laundry hand-cart from its mooring to a cellar door. Joe Cornacchia's son-in-law stacking out empty crates from the delicatessen. The barber bringing out his sidewalk folding chair. Mr. Goldstein arranging coils of wire that proclaim the hardware store is open. The primary children, heading for St. Luke's to the south. The children for St. Veronica's heading west. The children for P.S. 41 heading east. Well-dressed and even elegant women, and men with briefcases, emerge now from doorways and side streets. Simultaneously numbers of women in house dresses emerge and pause for quick conversations. Longshoremen who are not working gather at the White Horse Tavern or the International Bar for beer and conversation.

As noontime arrives, the executives and business lunchers from the industries in the neighborhood throng the Dorgene Restaurant and the Lion's Head coffee house down the street. If there were no workers to support these places at noon, we residents would not have them to use at night. Character dancers come onstage: a strange old man with strings of old shoes over his shoulders; motor-scooter riders with big black beards and girl friends who bounce on the back of their scooters. Mr. Koochagian, the tailor, waters the plants in his window, gives them a look from the outside and accepts a compliment on them from two passers-by. The baby carriages come out.

As the residents return home from work in other places, the ballet reaches its crescendo. This is the time of roller skates and stilts and tricycles and games with bottle tops and plastic cowboys. This is the time of bundles and packages and zigzagging from the drugstore to the fruit stand. This is the time when teenagers, all dressed up, are pausing to ask if their slips show or their collars look right. This is the time when anybody you know in the neighborhood will go by.

As darkness thickens and Mr. Halpert moors the laundry cart to the cellar door again, the ballet goes on under lights. It eddies back and forth, intensifying at the bright spotlight pools of Joe's sidewalk pizzeria, the bars and the drugstore. On Hudson Street we do not barricade ourselves indoors when darkness falls.

I know the deep night ballet from waking long after midnight to tend a baby. Sitting in the dark I have seen the shadows and heard the sounds of the sidewalk. Mostly it is snatches of party conversation. When the bars have closed, it is the sound of singing. Sometimes there is anger or sad weeping; sometimes a flurry of searching for a string of broken beads. One night a young man came along bellowing invectives at two girls who apparently were disappointing him. Doors opened, a wary semicircle of men and women formed around him; the police came. Out came the heads, too, along Hudson Street, offering opinion, "Drunk. . . . Crazy. . . . A wild kid from the suburbs." (It turned out he *was* a wild kid from the suburbs.)

I have not begun to describe the many differences that keep our sidewalks bustling. Among businesses and industries alone there are more than fifty different kinds within a few blocks. On Hudson Street, just as in the North End of Boston, we are the lucky possessors of a complex city order that is anything but the chaos that city planners proclaim it to be. Such neighborhoods as ours engender intense affection among those who live or work in them. As a result, they are stable places where people of many different incomes and tastes remain permanently—by choice.

The true problem of city planning and rebuilding in a free society is how to cultivate more city districts that are free, lively and fertile places for the differing plans of thousands of individuals—not planners. Nothing could be farther from the aims of planners today. They have been trained to think of people as interchangeable statistics to be pushed around, to think of city vitality and mixture as a mess. Planners are the enemies of cities because they offer us only the poisonous promise of making every place in a city more like dull and standardized Morningside Heights. They have failed to pursue the main point: to study the success and failure of the real life of the cities. With their eyes on simple-minded panaceas, they destroy success and health. Planners will become helpful only when they abandon what they have learned about what "ought" to be good for cities.

When they learn how fulfilling life in a city really can be, then they will finally stop working against the very goals they set out to achieve.

Harvey Cox

*Harvey Cox (born 1929) was educated at the University of
Pennsylvania, Yale, and Harvard (Ph.D., 1963). He has been
director of religious activities at Oberlin College and worked for a
year at an East Berlin mission. In 1965, after teaching for two
years at the Andover Newton Theological School, he joined the
faculty of Harvard, where he is now Professor of Divinity.*
He has contributed to such magazines as Christian Century,
Commonweal, Harper's, *and* Playboy *and is a member of the
editorial board of* Christianity and Crisis. *His books include*
God's Revolution and Man's Responsibility *(1965),* On Not
Leaving It to the Snake *(a collection of essays, 1967), and* The
Feast of Fools *(1969).*

*We print here a section from the second chapter of his best-known
work,* The Secular City *(1964). The book was originally
designed as a study resource for a series of student conferences
planned by the National Student Christian Federation and is thus
aimed at a young audience. In it Cox argues that the secularization
and urbanization of our society need not represent "sinister curses
to be escaped," but are instead "opportunities to be embraced."
The book has been astonishingly popular and is the subject of*
The Secular City Debate *(ed. Daniel Callahan, 1966), a collection of reviews and rejoinders.*

ANONYMITY

Every college sophomore knows that modern man is a faceless cipher.
The stock in trade of too many humanities courses and religious-
emphasis weeks is the featureless "mass man," reduced to a number
or a series of holes in an IBM card, wandering through T. S. Eliot's
"waste land" starved for a name. "Loss of identity" and "disappearance of selfhood" have come to play an ever larger role in the popular
pastime of flagellating urban culture. Where does this fear of anonymity originate?

Regardless of how cheapened and trite such criticisms have become
in our time, they do stem from an impressive intellectual ancestry.
Søren Kierkegaard fulminated brilliantly against certain elements of
mass society and urban life in *The Present Age* (1846). José Ortega y

Gasset, the Spanish philosopher, exemplifies the aristocratic repugnance for the erasing of class lines and the anonymous character of modern society in his *Revolt of the Masses* (1932). Rainer Maria Rilke's book *Notebooks of Malte Lauridi Brigge* (English translation, 1930) displays a metaphysical horror for the impersonality of life and for the loss of the mystery of things which he found in the city. Above all, the refusal of Franz Kafka to endow the main characters of two of his later novels with any name has sometimes been interpreted as a protest against urban and bureaucratic anonymity.

Must the modern writer be antiurban?

The truth is that, for a genuine literary artist, the city is the setting but not the real target of his onslaught. Many nineteenth- and early twentieth-century writers did not see that urban anonymity has its distinct benefits as well as its horrors. A writer who becomes *essentially* antiurban forfeits his claim to greatness, for what is often left unsaid by the morbid critics of anonymity is, first, that without it, life in a modern city could not be human, and second, that anonymity represents for many people a liberating even more than a threatening phenomenon. It serves for large numbers of people as the possibility of freedom in contrast to the bondage of the law and convention. The anonymity of city living helps preserve the privacy essential to human life. Furthermore, anonymity can be understood theologically as Gospel versus Law.

THE MAN AT THE GIANT SWITCHBOARD

Technopolitan man sits at a vast and immensely complicated switchboard. He is *homo symbolicus*, man the communicator, and the metropolis is a massive network of communications. A whole world of possibilities for communication lies within his reach. The contemporary urban region represents an ingenious device for vastly enlarging the range of human communication and widening the scope of individual choice. Urbanization thus contributes to the freedom of man. This is perfectly evident when we think, for example, of cinema theaters and restaurants. Residents of a city of ten thousand may be limited to one or two theaters, while people who live in a city of a million can choose among perhaps fifty films on a given night. The same principle holds for restaurants, schools, and even in some measure for job opportunities or prospective marriage partners. Urban man is free to choose from a wider range of alternatives. Thus his manhood as *homo symbolicus* is enhanced.

But freedom always demands discipline. The mere availability of such a wide spectrum of possibilities requires an adjustment of urban man's behavior. He must exercise choice more frequently, and choice

573

always means exclusion. He doesn't just "go to the movies" on a free evening, as his more rural counterpart might; he must choose one from among the fifty films now showing. This means a conscious decision *not* to see the other forty-nine.

In the area of personal relationships this selectivity becomes more demanding. Urban man has a wider variety of "contacts" than his rural counterpart; he can choose only a limited number for friends. He must have more or less impersonal relationships with most of the people with whom he comes in contact precisely in order to nourish and cultivate certain friendships. This selectivity can best be symbolized perhaps by the unplugged telephone or the unlisted number. A person does not request an unlisted number to cut down on the depth of his relationships. Quite the opposite; he does so to guard and deepen the worthwhile relationships he has against being dissolved in the deluge of messages that would come if one were open on principle and on an equal basis to anyone who tried to get through, including the increasing army of telephone salesmen who violate one's privacy so arrogantly. Those we want to know have our number; others do not. We are free to use the switchboard without being victimized by its infinite possibilities.

Urban man must distinguish carefully between his private life and his public relationships. Since he depends on such a complex net of services to maintain himself in existence in a modern city, the majority of his transactions will have to be public and will be what sociologists call functional or secondary. In most of his relationships he will be dealing with people he cannot afford to be interested in as individuals but must deal with in terms of the services they render to him and he to them. This is essential in urban life. Supermarket checkers or gas-meter readers who became enmeshed in the lives of the people they were serving would be a menace. They would soon cause a total breakdown in the essential systems of which they are integral parts. Urban life demands that we treat most of the people we meet as persons—not as things, but not as intimates either. This in turn produces the kind of "immunization" against personal encounters which Louis Wirth explains this way:

Characteristically, urbanites meet one another in highly segmental roles. They are, to be sure, dependent upon more people for the satisfactions of their life-needs than are rural people and thus are associated with a greater number of organized groups, but they are less dependent upon particular persons, and their dependence upon others is confined to a highly fractionalized aspect of the other's round of activity. This is essentially what is meant by saying that the city is characterized by secondary rather than primary contacts. The contacts of the city may indeed be face to face, but they are nevertheless impersonal, superficial, transitory, and segmental.

574

The reserve, the indifference, and the blasé outlook which urbanites manifest in their relationships may thus be regarded as devices for immunizing themselves against the personal claims and expectations of others.[1]

This immunization results in a way of life which often appears cold and even heartless to those unfamiliar with the dynamics of urban living. Here both writers and sociologists have missed the point. Cultural romantics such as Rilke and Ortega recoiled in distaste at what they took to be the cruelty of the city. In sociology a similar criticism was also voiced. Relationships in the city, it was complained, tended to be divested of their really human substance and made mechanical and lifeless.

One of the most influential sociological critics of the shape of urban life was the German scholar Ferdinand Tönnies (1855-1936), whose work has continued to exert a considerable influence on modern sociology and cultural analysis. In 1887 Tönnies published a book in which he contrasted the coherent, organic togetherness of *Gemeinschaft* (community) with the more rational, planned, and partial nexus of the *Gesellschaft* (society). Kaspar Naegele summarizes Tönnies' distinction:

Relations of the *Gemeinschaft* type are more inclusive; persons confront each other as ends, they cohere more durably. . . . In *Gesellschaft* their mutual regard is circumscribed by a sense of specific, if not formal obligations. . . . A transaction can occur without any other encounters, leaving both parties virtually anonymous.[2]

Tönnies is talking about what some sociologists describe as "primary" versus "secondary" relationships, or "organic" versus "functional" relationships. Having lived both as a villager and as an urbanite I know just what these terms mean. During my boyhood, my parents never referred to "the milkman," "the insurance agent," "the junk collector." These people were, respectively, Paul Weaver, Joe Villanova, and Roxy Barazano. All of our family's market transactions took place within a web of wider and more inclusive friendship and kinship ties with the same people. They were never anonymous. In fact, the occasional salesman or repairman whom we did not know was always viewed with dark suspicion until we could make sure where he came from, who his parents were, and whether his family was "any good." Trips to the grocery store, gasoline station, or post office were inevitably social visits, never merely functional contacts.

Now, as an urbanite, my transactions are of a very different sort. If I need to have the transmission on my car repaired, buy a television

---

[1] Louis Wirth, "Urbanism as a Way of Life" in Paul K. Hatt and Albert J. Reiss, Jr. (eds.), *Cities and Society* (New York: The Free Press, 1957), p. 54.

[2] Kaspar D. Naegele, "The Institutionalization of Action," in Talcott Parsons, *et al.* (eds.), *Theories of Society* (New York: The Free Press, 1961), p. 184.

antenna, or cash a check, I find myself in functional relationships with mechanics, salesmen, and bank clerks whom I never see in any other capacity. These "contacts" are in no sense "mean, nasty, or brutish," though they do tend to be short, at least not any longer than the time required to make the transaction and to exchange a brief pleasantry. Some of these human contacts occur with considerable frequency, so that I come to know the mannerisms and maybe even the names of some of the people. But the relationships are unifaceted and "segmental." I meet these people in no other context. To me they remain essentially just as anonymous as I do to them. Indeed, in the case of the transmission repairman, I hope I never see him again—not because he is in any way unpleasant, but because my only possible reason for seeing him again would be a new and costly breakdown in my car's gearbox. The important point here is that my relationships with bank clerks and garagemen are no less human or authentic merely because we both prefer to keep them anonymous. Here is where much theological analysis of urbanization has gone hopelessly astray.

Theologians have spent themselves in well-intentioned forays against the "depersonalization of urban life," often fed by a misunderstanding of Martin Buber's philosophy of "I and Thou" relationships. In contrast to those who utilize his categories in a different manner, Buber himself never claimed that *all* our relationships should be of the deep, interpersonal I-Thou variety. He knew this experience was a rich and rare one. But Buber did open the door for misunderstanding by neglecting to study with sufficient thoroughness the place of types of relationships which actually constitute most of our lives, a point to which we shall return shortly.

A recent survey by some Protestant ministers in a new urban highrise apartment area where they intended to establish house church groups illustrates the misplaced emphasis on I-Thou relationships that has marked modern Christian theology. In conducting their study, the pastors were shocked to discover that the recently arrived apartment dwellers, whom they expected to be lonely and desperate for relationships, did not want to meet their neighbors socially and had no interest whatever in church or community groups. At first the ministers deplored what they called a "social pathology" and a "hedgehog" psychology. Later, however, they found that what they had encountered was a sheer survival technique. Resistance against efforts to subject them to neighborliness and socialization is a skill apartment dwellers must develop if they are to maintain any human relationships at all. It is an essential element in the shape of the secular city.

In condemning urban anonymity, the ministers had made the mistake of confusing a preurban ethos with the Christian concept of *koinonia.* The two are not the same. The ministers had wanted to develop a kind of village togetherness among people, one of whose main reasons for moving to high-rise apartments is to escape the relationships enforced on them by the lack of anonymity of the village. Apartment dwellers, like most urbanites, live a life in which relationships are founded on free selection and common interest, usually devoid of spatial proximity. Studies have shown that even friendship patterns within a large apartment complex follow age, family size, and personal interest lines. They do not ordinarily spring from the mere proximity of apartments. Thus, to complain that apartment people often live for years just down the hall from another family but do not "really get to know them" overlooks the fact that many specifically choose *not* to "know" their spatial neighbors in any intimate sense. This allows them more time and energy to cultivate the friends they themselves select. This does not mean the apartment dweller cannot love his next-door neighbor. He can and often does so, certainly no less frequently than the small-town resident. But he does so by being a dependable fellow tenant, by bearing his share of the common responsibility they both have in that segment of their lives shaped by residence. This does not require their becoming cronies.

All this means that the urban secular man is summoned to a different *kind* of neighborliness than his town-dwelling predecessor practiced. Much like the Samaritan described by Jesus in the story he told in response to the question "Who is my neighbor?," his main responsibility is to do competently what needs to be done to assure his neighbor's health and well-being. The man who fell among thieves was not the next-door neighbor of the Samaritan, but he helped him in an efficient, unsentimental way. He did not form an I-Thou relationship with him but bandaged his wounds and made sure the innkeeper had enough cash to cover his expenses.

Urban anonymity need not be heartless. Village sociability can mask murderous hostility. Loneliness is undoubtedly a serious problem in the city, but it cannot be met by dragooning urban people into relationships which sabotage their privacy and reduce their capacity to live responsibly with increasing numbers of neighbors. The church investigators who shook their heads over the evasiveness of the apartment dwellers had forgotten this. They had come to the city with a village theology and had stumbled upon an essential protective device, the polite refusal to be chummy without which urban existence could not be human. They had overlooked the fact that technopolitan man *must* cultivate and guard his privacy. He must restrict the number of people who have his number or know his name.

The small-town dweller, on the other hand, lives within a restricted web of relationships and senses a larger world he may be missing. Since the people he knows also know one another, he gossips more and yearns to hear gossip. His private life is public and vice versa. While urban man is unplugging his telephone, town man (or his wife) may be listening in on the party line or its modern equivalent, gossiping at the kaffee-klatsch.

Urban man, in contrast, wants to maintain a clear distinction between private and public. Otherwise public life would overwhelm and dehumanize him. His life represents a point touched by dozens of systems and hundreds of people. His capacity to know some of them better necessitates his minimizing the depth of his relationships to many others. Listening to the postman gossip becomes for urban man an act of sheer graciousness, since he probably has no interest in the people the postman wants to talk about. Unlike my parents, who suspected all strangers, he tends to be wary not of the functionaries he doesn't know but of those he does.

ANONYMITY AS DELIVERANCE FROM THE LAW

How can urban anonymity be understood theologically? Here the traditional distinction between Law and Gospel comes to mind. In using these terms we refer not to religious rules or to fiery preaching, but to the tension between bondage to the past and freedom for the future. In this sense Law means anything that binds us uncritically to inherited conventions, and Gospel is that which frees us to decide for ourselves.

As the contemporary German theologian Rudolf Bultmann once wrote, Law means the "standards of this world."[3] It is what Riesman calls the power of "other-direction" driving us toward conformity to the expectations and customs of the culture, enforced in a thousand small, nearly unnoticeable ways by the people who make our choices for us. When Law rather than Gospel becomes the basis for our lives, it militates against choice and freedom. It decides for us, thus sapping our powers of responsibility. Similarly, Gospel in a broader sense means a summons to choice and answerability. It designates not merely the verbal message of the church, but also the call which comes to any man when he is confronted with the privilege and necessity of making a free and responsible decision, not determined by cultural background or social convention. Our use of the Law-Gospel dialectic here suggests that it has a broader relevance than is ordi-

---

[3] Bultmann's discussion of the Law can be found in his *Theology of the New Testament* (New York: Scribner, 1951; London: SCM Press), Section 27, pp. 259–269. The best discussion of the broader significance of the Law is found in Friedrich Gogarten's *Mensch zwischen Gott und Welt* (Stuttgart: Friedrich Vorwerk Verlag, 1956), especially Section I and the first part of Section II.

narily accorded it in theology. It suggests that in the historical process itself man meets the One who calls him into being as a free deciding self, and knows that neither his past history nor his environment determines what he does. In the anonymity of urban culture, far from the fishbowl of town life, modern man experiences both the terror and the delight of human freedom more acutely. The biblical God is present for man today in the world of social reality, and Law and Gospel provide us an angle of vision by which to understand secular events, including urbanization. The God of the Gospel is the One who wills freedom and responsibility, who points toward the future in hope. The Law, on the other hand, includes any cultural phenomenon which holds men in immaturity, in captivity to convention and tradition. The Law is enforced by the weight of human opinion; the Gospel is the activity of God creating new possibilities in history. Law signifies the fact that man does live in society; Gospel points to the equally important fact that he is more than the intersection of social forces. He feels himself summoned to choose, to actualize a potential selfhood which is more than the sum of genes plus glands plus class. Man cannot live without Law, but when Law becomes wholly determinative, he is no longer really man.

From this perspective, urbanization can be seen as a liberation from some of the cloying bondages of preurban society. It is the chance to be free. Urban man's deliverance from enforced conventions requires that he choose for himself. His being anonymous to most people permits him to have a face and a name for others.

This is not an easy thing to accomplish. The challenge of living responsibly within segmental relationships is formidable, especially for those who have been reared in small-town or traditional cultures. Often a nagging sense of guilt plagues the urban man with rural roots because he cannot possibly cultivate an I-Thou relationship with everyone. Unfortunately the church, largely bound to a preurban ethos, often exacerbates his difficulty by seeking to promote small-town intimacy among urban people and by preaching the necessity of I-Thou relationships as the only ones that are really human. But this represents a misreading of the Gospel and a disservice to urban man. Relationships among urbanites do not have to be lifeless or callous just because they are impersonal. Jane Jacobs in her *Death and Life of Great American Cities* has caught the flavor of urban neighborliness exceptionally well. It necessitates learning how to enjoy public relationships without allowing them to become private:

Nobody can keep open house in a great city. Nobody wants to. And yet if interesting, useful and significant contacts among the people of cities are confined to acquaintanceships suitable for private life, the city becomes stultified. Cities are full of people with whom, from your viewpoint, or mine, or any other individual's, a certain degree of contact is useful or enjoyable; but you do not want them in your hair. And they do not want you in theirs either.[4]

Theologians would do well to appreciate this characteristically urban "togetherness" so aptly described by Jane Jacobs and to see in its impersonal, even anonymous, interrelatedness an authentic form of corporate human existence in the urban epoch.

We need to develop a viable theology of anonymity. In doing so, it might be useful to add another type of human relationship to Buber's famous pair. Besides I-It relationships, in which the other person is reduced to the status of an object, and in addition to the profound, personally formative I-Thou encounter, why could we not evolve a theology of the I-*You* relationship? Buber's philosophy suffers from an unnecessary dichotomy. Perhaps between the poles of the two types of human relationship he has elaborated we could designate a third. It would include all those public relationships we so enjoy in the city but which we do not allow to develop into private ones. These contacts can be decidedly human even though they remain somewhat distant. We like and enjoy these people, but as Jane Jacobs says, we "don't want them in our hair, and they don't want us in theirs either."

The danger with an I-Thou typology is that all relationships which are not deeply personal and significant tend to be swept or shoved into the I-It category. But they need not be. The development of an I-*You* theology would greatly clarify the human possibilities of urban life, and would help stall attempts to lure urban people back into pre-urban conviviality under the color of saving their souls.

The development of such a theology would help expose the *real* dangers inherent in urban anonymity, as opposed to the pseudodangers. Technopolitan possibilities *can* harden into rigid new conventions. Freedom can always be used for antihuman purposes. The Gospel can ossify into a new legalism. But none of these hazards can be exposed if we continue to insist on judging urban life by preurban norms. Despite its pitfalls, the anonymous shape of urban life helps free man from the Law. For many people it is a glorious liberation, a deliverance from the saddling traditions and burdensome expectations of town life and an entry into the exciting new possibilities of choice which pervade the secular metropolis.

---

[4] Jane Jacobs, *The Death and Life of Great American Cities* (New York: Vintage, 1963; London: Cape), pp. 55–56.

Tom Wolfe

*Tom Wolfe, born in Virginia in 1931, attended Washington and
Lee University and took a Ph.D. in American Studies at Yale
in 1957. He turned at once from scholarship to journalism,
working as reporter for the Springfield (Mass.)* Union *and as
reporter and Latin American correspondent for the* Washington
Post. *In 1961 the Washington Newspaper Guild gave him a
Front Page award for humor and foreign news reporting. In 1962
he began an association with the* New York Herald Tribune
*as reporter and magazine writer, and he remains contributing editor
to that now-defunct newspaper's surviving section, the magazine*
New York. *Mr. Wolfe is a prolific contributor to other
magazines and is famous (or perhaps notorious) for his uninhibited
satire and his sometimes frantic style, well reflected even in the titles
of his books:* The Kandy-Kolored Tangerine-Flake Streamline
Baby *(1965),* The Electric Kool-Aid Acid Test *(1968), and*
The Pump House Gang *(1968), from which we take the present
article; it appeared first in* New York *in 1966 with the title
"O Rotten Gotham—Sliding Down into the Behavioral Sink."*

O ROTTEN GOTHAM

I just spent two days with Edward T. Hall, an anthropologist, watching
thousands of my fellow New Yorkers short-circuiting themselves into
hot little twitching death balls with jolts of their own adrenalin. Dr.
Hall says that it is overcrowding that does it. Overcrowding gets the
adrenalin going, and the adrenalin gets them hyped up. And here
they are, hyped up, turning bilious, nephritic, queer, autistic, sadistic,
barren, batty, sloppy, hot-in-the-pants, chancred-on-the-flankers, leer-
ing, puling, numb—the usual in New York, in other words, and God
knows what else. Dr. Hall has the theory that overcrowding has
already thrown New York into a state of behavioral sink. Behavioral
sink is a term from ethology, which is the study of how animals relate
to their environment. Among animals, the sink winds up with a
"population collapse" or "massive die-off." O rotten Gotham.

It got to be easy to look at New Yorkers as animals, especially looking down from some place like a balcony at Grand Central at the rush

hour Friday afternoon. The floor was filled with the poor white humans, running around, dodging, blinking their eyes, making a sound like a pen full of starlings or rats or something.

"Listen to them skid," says Dr. Hall.

He was right. The poor old etiolate animals were out there skidding on their rubber soles. You could hear it once he pointed it out. They stop short to keep from hitting somebody or because they are disoriented and they suddenly stop and look around, and they skid on their rubber-sole shoes, and a screech goes up. They pour out onto the floor down the escalators from the Pan-Am Building, from 42nd Street, from Lexington Avenue, up out of subways, down into subways, railroad trains, up into helicopters—

"You can also hear the helicopters all the way down here," says Dr. Hall. The sound of the helicopters using the roof of the Pan-Am Building nearly fifty stories up beats right through. "If it weren't for this ceiling"—he is referring to the very high ceiling in Grand Central— "this place would be unbearable with this kind of crowding. And yet they'll probably never 'waste' space like this again."

They screech! And the adrenal glands in all those poor white animals enlarge, micrometer by micrometer, to the size of cantaloupes. Dr. Hall pulls a Minox camera out of a holster he has on his belt and starts shooting away at the human scurry. The Sink!

Dr. Hall has the Minox up to his eye—he is a slender man, calm, 52 years old, young-looking, an anthropologist who has worked with Navajos, Hopis, Spanish-Americans, Negroes, Trukese. He was the most important anthropologist in the government during the crucial years of the foreign aid program, the 1950's. He directed both the Point Four training program and the Human Relations Area Files. He wrote The Silent Language and The Hidden Dimension, two books that are picking up the kind of "underground" following his friend Marshall McLuhan started picking up about five years ago. He teaches at the Illinois Institute of Technology, lives with his wife, Mildred, in a high-ceilinged town house on one of the last great residential streets in downtown Chicago, Astor Street; has a grown son and daughter, loves good food, good wine, the relaxed, civilized life—but comes to New York with a Minox at his eye to record—perfect!—The Sink.

We really got down in there by walking down into the Lexington Avenue line subway stop under Grand Central. We inhaled those nice big fluffy fumes of human sweat, urine, effluvia, and sebaceous secretions. One old female human was already stroked out on the upper level, on a stretcher, with two policemen standing by. The other humans barely looked at her. They rushed into line. They bellied each other, haunch to paunch, down the stairs. Human heads shone through the gratings. The species North European tried to

582

create bubbles of space around themselves, about a foot and a half in diameter—

"See, he's reacting against the line," says Dr. Hall.

—but the species Mediterranean presses on in. The hell with bubbles of space. The species North European resents that, this male human behind him presses forward toward the booth . . . *breathing* on him, he's disgusted, he pulls out of the line entirely, the species Mediterranean resents him for resenting it, and neither of them realizes what the hell they are getting irritable about exactly. And in all of them the old adrenals grow another micrometer.

Dr. Hall whips out the Minox. Too perfect! The bottom of The Sink.

It is the sheer overcrowding, such as occurs in the business sections of Manhattan five days a week and in Harlem, Bedford-Stuyvesant, southeast Bronx every day—sheer overcrowding is converting New Yorkers into animals in a sink pen. Dr. Hall's argument runs as follows: all animals, including birds, seem to have a built-in, inherited requirement to have a certain amount of territory, space, to lead their lives in. Even if they have all the food they need, and there are no predatory animals threatening them, they cannot tolerate crowding beyond a certain point. No more than two hundred wild Norway rats can survive on a quarter acre of ground, for example, even when they are given all the food they can eat. They just die off.

But why? To find out, ethologists have run experiments on all sorts of animals, from stickleback crabs to Sika deer. In one major experiment, an ethologist named John Calhoun put some domesticated white Norway rats in a pen with four sections to it, connected by ramps. Calhoun knew from previous experiments that the rats tend to split up into groups of ten to twelve and that the pen, therefore, would hold forty to forty-eight rats comfortably, assuming they formed four equal groups. He allowed them to reproduce until there were eighty rats, balanced between male and female, but did not let it get any more crowded. He kept them supplied with plenty of food, water, and nesting materials. In other words, all their more obvious needs were taken care of. A less obvious need—space—was not. To the human eye, the pen did not even look especially crowded. But to the rats, it was crowded beyond endurance.

The entire colony was soon plunged into a profound behavioral sink. "The sink," said Calhoun, "is the outcome of any behavioral process that collects animals together in unusually great numbers. The unhealthy connotations of the term are not accidental: a behavioral sink does act to aggravate all forms of pathology that can be found within a group."

For a start, long before the rat population reached eighty, a status hierarchy had developed in the pen. Two dominant male rats took over the two end sections, acquired harems of eight to ten females each, and forced the rest of the rats into the two middle pens. All the overcrowding took place in the middle pens. That was where the "sink" hit. The aristocrat rats at the ends grew bigger, sleeker, healthier, and more secure the whole time.

In The Sink, meanwhile, nest building, courting, sex behavior, reproduction, social organization, health—all of it went to pieces. Normally, Norway rats have a mating ritual in which the male chases the female, the female ducks down into a burrow and sticks her head up to watch the male. He performs a little dance outside the burrow, then she comes out, and he mounts her, usually for a few seconds. When The Sink set in, however, no more than three males—the dominant males in the middle sections—kept up the old customs. The rest tried everything from satyrism to homosexuality or else gave up on sex altogether. Some of the subordinate males spent all their time chasing females. Three or four might chase one female at the same time, and instead of stopping at the burrow entrance for the ritual, they would charge right in. Once mounted, they would hold on for minutes instead of the usual seconds.

Homosexuality rose sharply. So did bisexuality. Some males would mount anything—males, females, babies, senescent rats, anything. Still other males dropped sexual activity altogether, wouldn't fight and, in fact, would hardly move except when the other rats slept. Occasionally a female from the aristocrat rats' harems would come over the ramps and into the middle sections to sample life in The Sink. When she had had enough, she would run back up the ramp. Sink males would give chase up to the top of the ramp, which is to say, to the very edge of the aristocratic preserve. But one glance from one of the king rats would stop them cold and they would return to The Sink.

The slumming females from the harems had their adventures and then returned to a placid, healthy life. Females in The Sink, however, were ravaged, physically and psychologically. Pregnant rats had trouble continuing pregnancy. The rate of miscarriages increased significantly, and females started dying of tumors and other disorders of the mammary glands, sex organs, uterus, ovaries, and Fallopian tubes. Typically, their kidneys, livers, and adrenals were also enlarged or diseased or showed other signs associated with stress.

Child-rearing became totally disorganized. The females lost the interest or the stamina to build nests and did not keep them up if they did build them. In the general filth and confusion, they would not put themselves out to save offspring they were momentarily separated from. Frantic, even sadistic competition among the males was going on all around them and rendering their lives chaotic. The males

584

began unprovoked and senseless assaults upon one another, often in the form of tail-biting. Ordinarily, rats will suppress this kind of behavior when it crops up. In The Sink, male rats gave up all policing and just looked out for themselves. The "pecking order" among males in The Sink was never stable. Normally, male rats set up a three-class structure. Under the pressure of overcrowding, however, they broke up into all sorts of unstable subclasses, cliques, packs—and constantly pushed, probed, explored, tested one another's power. Anyone was fair game, except for the aristocrats in the end pens.

Calhoun kept the population down to eighty, so that the next stage, "population collapse" or "massive die-off," did not occur. But the autopsies showed that the pattern—as in the diseases among the female rats—was already there.

The classic study of die-off was John J. Christian's study of Sika deer on James Island in the Chesapeake Bay, west of Cambridge, Maryland. Four or five of the deer had been released on the island, which was 280 acres and uninhabited, in 1916. By 1955 they had bred freely into a herd of 280 to 300. The population density was only about one deer per acre at this point, but Christian knew that this was already too high for the Sikas' inborn space requirements, and something would give before long. For two years the number of deer remained 280 to 300. But suddenly, in 1958, over half the deer died; 161 carcasses were recovered. In 1959 more deer died and the population steadied at about 80.

In two years, two-thirds of the herd had died. Why? It was not starvation. In fact, all the deer collected were in excellent condition, with well-developed muscles, shining coats, and fat deposits between the muscles. In practically all the deer, however, the adrenal glands had enlarged by 50 percent. Christian concluded that the die-off was due to "shock following severe metabolic disturbance, probably as a result of prolonged adrenocortical hyperactivity. . . . There was no evidence of infection, starvation, or other obvious cause to explain the mass mortality." In other words, the constant stress of overpopulation, plus the normal stress of the cold of the winter, had kept the adrenalin flowing so constantly in the deer that their systems were depleted of blood sugar and they died of shock.

Well, the white humans are still skidding and darting across the floor of Grand Central. Dr. Hall listens a moment longer to the skidding and the darting noises, and then says, "You know, I've been on commuter trains here after everyone has been through one of these rushes, and I'll tell you, there is enough acid flowing in the stomachs in every car to dissolve the rails underneath."

Just a little invisible acid bath for the linings to round off the day. The ulcers the acids cause, of course, are the one disease people have already been taught to associate with the stress of city life. But over-crowding, as Dr. Hall sees it, raises a lot more hell with the body than just ulcers. In everyday life in New York—just the usual, getting to work, working in massively congested areas like 42nd Street between Fifth Avenue and Lexington, especially now that the Pan-Am Building is set in there, working in cubicles such as those in the editorial offices at Time-Life, Inc., which Dr. Hall cites as typical of New York's poor handling of space, working in cubicles with low ceilings and, often, no access to a window, while construction crews all over Manhattan drive everybody up the Masonite wall with air-pressure generators with noises up to the boil-a-brain decibel levels, then rushing to get home, piling into subways and trains, fighting for time and for space, the usual day in New York—the whole now-normal thing keeps shooting jolts of adrenalin into the body, breaking down the body's defenses and winding up with the work-a-daddy human animal stroked out at the breakfast table with his head apoplexed like a cauliflower out of his $6.95 semispread Pima-cotton shirt, and nosed over into a plate of No-Kloresto egg substitute, signing off with the black thrombosis, cancer, kidney, liver, or stomach failure, and the adrenals ooze to a halt, the size of eggplants in July.

One of the people whose work Dr. Hall is interested in on this score is Rene Dubos at the Rockefeller Institute. Dubos's work indicates that specific organisms, such as the tuberculosis bacillus or a pneumonia virus, can seldom be considered "the cause" of a disease. The germ or virus, apparently, has to work in combination with other things that have already broken the body down in some way—such as the old adrenal hyperactivity. Dr. Hall would like to see some autopsy studies made to record the size of adrenal glands in New York, especially of people crowded into slums and people who go through the full rush-hour-work-rush-hour cycle every day. He is afraid that until there is some clinical, statistical data on how overcrowding actually ravages the human body, no one will be willing to do anything about it. Even in so obvious a thing as air pollution, the pattern is familiar. Until people can actually see the smoke or smell the sulphur or feel the sting in their eyes, politicians will not get excited about it, even though it is well known that many of the lethal substances polluting the air are invisible and odorless. For one thing, most politicians are like the aristocrat rats. They are insulated from The Sink by practically sultanic buffers—limousines, chauffeurs, secretaries, aides-de-camp, doormen, shuttered houses, high-floor apartments. They almost never ride subways, fight rush hours, much less live in the slums or work in the Pan-Am Building.

We took a cab from Grand Central to go up to Harlem, and by 48th Street we were already socked into one of those great, total traffic jams on First Avenue on Friday afternoon. Dr. Hall motions for me to survey the scene, and there they all are, humans, male and female, behind the glass of their automobile windows, soundlessly going through the torture of their own adrenalin jolts. This male over here contracts his jaw muscles so hard that they bunch up into a great cheese Danish pattern. He twists his lips, he bleeds from the eyeballs, he shouts . . . soundlessly behind glass . . . the fat corrugates on the back of his neck, his whole body shakes as he pounds the heel of his hand into the steering wheel. The female human in the car ahead of him whips her head around, she bares her teeth, she screams . . . soundlessly behind glass . . . she throws her hands up in the air, Whaddya expect me— Yah, yuh stupid—and they all sit there, trapped in their own congestion, bleeding hate all over each other, shorting out the ganglia and —goddam it—

Dr. Hall sits back and watches it all. This is it! The Sink! And where is everybody's wandering boy?

Dr. Hall says, "We need a study in which drivers who go through these rush hours every day would wear GSR bands."

GSR?

"Galvanic skin response. It measures the electric potential of the skin, which is a function of sweating. If a person gets highly nervous, his palms begin to sweat. It is an index of tension. There are some other fairly simple devices that would record respiration and pulse. I think everybody who goes through this kind of experience all the time should take his own pulse—not literally—but just be aware of what's happening to him. You can usually tell when stress is beginning to get you physically."

In testing people crowded into New York's slums, Dr. Hall would like to take it one step further—gather information on the plasma hydrocortisone level in the blood or the corticosteroids in the urine. Both have been demonstrated to be reliable indicators of stress, and testing procedures are simple.

The slums—we finally made it up to East Harlem. We drove into 101st Street, and there was a new, avant-garde little church building, the Church of the Ephiphany, which Dr. Hall liked—and, next to it, a pile of rubble where a row of buildings had been torn down, and from the back windows of the tenements beyond several people were busy "airmailing," throwing garbage out the window, into the rubble, beer cans, red shreds, the No-Money-Down Eames roller stand for a TV set, all flying through the air onto the scaggy sump. We drove around some more in Harlem, and a sequence was repeated, trash, buildings falling down, buildings torn down, rubble, scaggy sumps or, suddenly, a cluster of high-rise apartment projects with fences around the grass.

587

"You know what this city looks like?" Dr. Hall said. "It looks bombed out. I used to live at Broadway and 124th Street back in 1946 when I was studying at Columbia. I can't tell you how much Harlem has changed in twenty years. It looks bombed out. It's broken down. People who live in New York get used to it and don't realize how filthy the city has become. The whole thing is typical of a behavioral sink. So is something like the Kitty Genovese case—a girl raped and murdered in the courtyard of an apartment complex and forty or fifty people look on from their apartments and nobody even calls the police. That kind of apathy and anomie is typical of the general psychological deterioration of The Sink."

He looked at the high-rise housing projects and found them mainly testimony to how little planners know about humans' basic animal requirements for space.

"Even on the simplest terms," he said, "it is pointless to build one of these blocks much over five stories high. Suppose a family lives on the fifteenth floor. The mother will be completely cut off from her children if they are playing down below, because the elevators are constantly broken in these projects, and it often takes half an hour, literally half an hour, to get the elevator if it is running. That's very common. A mother in that situation is just as much a victim of overcrowding as if she were back in the tenement block. Some Negro leaders have a bitter joke about how the white man is solving the slum problem by stacking Negroes up vertically, and there is a lot to that."

For one thing, says Dr. Hall, planners have no idea of the different space requirements of people from different cultures, such as Negroes and Puerto Ricans. They are all treated as if they were minute, compact middle-class whites. As with the Sika deer, who are overcrowded at one per acre, overcrowding is a relative thing for the human animal, as well. Each species has its own feeling for space. The feeling may be "subjective," but it is quite real.

Dr. Hall's theories on space and territory are based on the same information, gathered by biologists, ethologists, and anthropologists, chiefly, as Robert Ardrey's. Ardrey has written two well-publicized books, *African Genesis* and *The Territorial Imperative*. *Life* magazine ran big excerpts from *The Territorial Imperative*, all about how the drive to acquire territory and property and add to it and achieve status is built into all animals, including man, over thousands of centuries of genetic history, etc., and is a more powerful drive than sex. *Life*'s big display prompted Marshall McLuhan to crack, "They see this as a great historic justification for free enterprise and Republicanism. If the birds do it and the stickleback crabs do it, then it's right for man." To people like Hall and McLuhan, and Ardrey, for that matter, the right or wrong of it is irrelevant. The only thing they find inexcusable is the kind of thinking, by influential people, that isn't even aware of all this. Such as the thinking of most city planners.

"The planners always show you a bird's-eye view of what they are doing," he said. "You've seen those scale models. Everyone stands around the table and looks down and says that's great. It never occurs to anyone that they are taking a bird's-eye view. In the end, these projects do turn out fine, when viewed from an airplane."

As an anthropologist, Dr. Hall has to shake his head every time he hears planners talking about fully integrated housing projects for the year 1980 or 1990, as if by then all cultural groups will have the same feeling for space and will live placidly side by side, happy as the happy burghers who plan all the good clean bird's-eye views. According to his findings, the very fact that every cultural group does have its own peculiar, unspoken feeling for space is what is responsible for much of the uneasiness one group feels around the other.

It is like the North European and the Mediterranean in the subway line. The North European, without ever realizing it, tries to keep a bubble of space around himself, and the moment a stranger invades that sphere, he feels threatened. Mediterranean peoples tend to come from cultures where everyone is much more involved physically, publicly, with one another on a day-to-day basis and feels no uneasiness about mixing it up in public, but may have very different ideas about space inside the home. Even Negroes brought up in America have a different vocabulary of space and gesture from the North European Americans who, historically, have been their models, according to Dr. Hall. The failure of Negroes and whites to communicate well often often boils down to things like this: some white will be interviewing a Negro for a job; the Negro's culture has taught him to show somebody you are interested by looking right at him and listening intently to what he has to say. But the species North European requires something more. He expects his listener to nod from time to time, as if to say, "Yes, keep going." If he doesn't get this nodding, he feels anxious, for fear the listener doesn't agree with him or has switched off. The Negro may learn that the white expects this sort of thing, but he isn't used to the precise kind of nodding that is customary, and so he may start overresponding, nodding like mad, and at this point the North European is liable to think he has some kind of stupid Uncle Tom on his hands, and the guy still doesn't get the job.

The whole handling of space in New York is so chaotic, says Dr. Hall, that even middle-class housing now seems to be based on the bird's-eye models for slum project. He took a look at the big Park West Village development, set up originally to provide housing in Manhattan for families in the middle-income range, and found its handling of space very much like a slum project with slightly larger balconies. He felt the time has come to start subsidizing the middle class in New York on its own terms—namely, the kind of truly "human" spaces that still remain in brownstones.

"I think New York City should seriously consider a program of encouraging the middle-class development of an area like Chelsea, which is already starting to come up. People are beginning to renovate houses there on their own, and I think if the city would subsidize that sort of thing with tax reliefs and so forth, you would be amazed at what would result. What New York needs is a string of minor successes in the housing field, just to show everyone that it can be done, and I think the middle class can still do that for you. The alternative is to keep on doing what you're doing now, trying to lift a very large lower class up by main force almost and finding it a very slow and discouraging process."

"But before deciding how to redesign space in New York," he said, "people must first simply realize how severe the problem already is. And the handwriting is already on the wall."

"A study published in 1962," he said, "surveyed a representative sample of people living in New York slums and found only 18 percent of them free from emotional symptoms. Thirty-eight percent were in need of psychiatric help, and 23 percent were seriously disturbed or incapacitated. Now, this study was published in 1962, which means the work probably went on from 1955 to 1960. There is no telling how bad it is now. In a behavioral sink, crises can develop rapidly."

Dr. Hall would like to see a large-scale study similar to that undertaken by two sociopsychologists, Chombart de Lauwe and his wife, in a French working-class town. They found a direct relationship between crowding and general breakdown. In families where people were crowded into the apartment so that there was less than 86 to 108 square feet per person, social and physical disorders doubled. That would mean that for four people the smallest floor space they could tolerate would be an apartment, say, 12 by 30 feet.

What would one find in Harlem? "It is fairly obvious," Dr. Hall wrote in *The Hidden Dimension*, "that the American Negroes and people of Spanish culture who are flocking to our cities are being very seriously stressed. Not only are they in a setting that does not fit them, but they have passed the limits of their own tolerance of stress. The United States is faced with the fact that two of its creative and sensitive peoples are in the process of being destroyed and like Samson could bring down the structure that houses us all."

Dr. Hall goes out to the airport, to go back to Chicago, and I am coming back in a cab, along the East River Drive. It is four in the afternoon, but already the damned drive is clogging up. There is a

590

1959 Oldsmobile just to the right of me. There are about eight people in there, a lot of popeyed silhouettes against a leopard-skin dashboard, leopard-skin seats—and the driver is classic. He has a mustache, sideburns down to his jaw socket, and a tattoo on his forearm with a Rossetti painting of Jane Burden Morris with her hair long. All right; it is even touching, like a postcard photo of the main drag in San Pedro, California. But suddenly Sideburns guns it and cuts in front of my cab so that my driver has to hit the brakes, and then hardly 100 feet ahead Sideburns hits a wall of traffic himself and has to hit his brakes, and then it happens. A stuffed white Angora animal, a dog, no, it's a Pekingese cat, is mounted in his rear window—as soon as he hits the brakes its *eyes* light up, Nighttown pink. To keep from ramming him, my driver has to hit the brakes again, too, and so here I am, out in an insane, jammed-up expressway at four in the afternoon, shuddering to a stop while a stuffed Pekingese grows bigger and bigger and brighter in the eyeballs directly in front of me. Jolt! Nighttown pink! Hey—that's me the adrenalin is hitting, *I* am this white human sitting in a projectile heading amid a mass of clotted humans toward a white Angora stuffed goddam leopard-dash Pekingese freaking cat— kill that damned Angora—Jolt!—got me—another micrometer on the old adrenals—

Kenneth B. Clark

Kenneth B. Clark was born in Panama in 1914. He attended public schools in Harlem, then Howard University and Columbia, receiving his Ph.D. in Psychology in 1940. He did wartime work in the Office of War Information, then taught at Hampton Institute and at C.C.N.Y., where he has been Professor of Social Psychology since 1949. Professor Clark's main interests are child, social, and clinical psychology. He has been chief psychologist of the Northside Center for Child Development in New York, director of the Metropolitan Applied Research Center, and was one of the founders of Haryou, Harlem Youth Opportunities Unlimited. His book Dark Ghetto: Dilemmas of Social Power *(1965) arose out of his role as an "involved observer" in the research and planning stage of the Haryou program. The prologue to the book, presented here, consists of excerpts from taped interviews with Harlem residents. Professor*

Clark remarks that the presence of the microphone did not inhibit genuine responses. "Intensity of feeling, anguish, and concern were freely expressed. But even the most obvious hyperbole reflected a level of reality which can not be ignored if the complexities and the potential explosiveness of the American ghetto are to be understood." He is also author of Prejudice and Your Child *(1955) and editor of* The Negro Protest *(1963) and* The Negro American *(with Talcott Parsons, 1966).*

THE CRY OF THE GHETTO

A lot of times, when I'm working, I become as despondent as hell and I feel like crying. I'm not a man, none of us are men! I don't own anything. I'm not a man enough to own a store; none of us are.

—MAN, AGE ABOUT 30

You know the average young person out here don't have a job, man, they don't have anything to do. They don't have any alternative, you know, but to go out there and try to make a living for themselves. Like when you come down to the Tombs down there, they're down there for robbing and breaking in. They want to know why you did it and where you live, but you have to live. You go down to the employment agency and you can't get a job. They have you waiting all day, but you can't get a job. They don't have a job for you. Yet you have to live. I'm ready to do anything anyone else is ready to do—because I want to live—I want to live. No one wants to die. I want to live.

—DRUG ADDICT, MALE, AGE 30

If a man qualifies, it should be first come, first serve. You understand what I mean? Regardless of whether we're black or white, we all have families! It should be first come, first serve. But that's not how they do you! If you're black, you're automatically turned down on a lot of jobs. They'll take your application, but no sooner than you walk out of the office, or wherever it is, they take the application and put it in the wastebasket, and tell you they'll let you know in a couple of weeks.

—MAN, AGE ABOUT 24

No one with a mop can expect respect from a banker, or an attorney, or men who create jobs, and all you have is a mop. Are you crazy? Whoever heard of integration between a mop and a banker?

—MAN, AGE ABOUT 38

The way the Man has us, he has us wanting to kill one another. Dog eat dog, amongst us! He has us, like we're so hungry up here, he has us up so tight! Like his rent is due, my rent is due. It's Friday. The Man wants sixty-five dollars. If you are three days over, or don't have the money; like that, he wants to give you a dispossess! Take you to court! The courts won't go along with you, they say get the money or get out! Yet they don't tell you how to get the money, you understand? They say get the money and pay the Man, but they don't say how to get it. Now, if you use illegal means to obey his ruling to try to get it—which he's not going to let you do—if you use illegal means to pay your bills according to his ruling—he will put you in jail.

—MAN, AGE 31

They are raising the rents so high, like that, with a job, the menial jobs that we have or get, the money we will receive—we won't be able to pay the rent! So where we going to go? They are pushing us further, and further, and further—out of Harlem.

—MAN, AGE 31

If you could get onto the ninth floor of the Tombs, you would see for yourself. They are lying there like dogs, vomiting and what not, over one another. It is awful. It smells like a pigpen up there. If you look, you'll see nothing but Spanish. And the black man. You'll seldom see a white man. When you do, he is from a very poor group. They are 20 years old, looking like they were 40.

—DRUG ADDICT, MALE, AGE ABOUT 37

I want to go to the veins.
You want to do what?
I want to go to the veins.
You want to go to the veins; you mean you want to get high?
Yeah.
Why do you want to get high, man?
To make me think.
You can't think without getting high?
No.

Discrimination is even in the school I attend right now. I know my teacher is very prejudiced because I have certain questions that have

593

to be answered for my knowledge, but he will never answer. He would always call on a little white boy to give the answer. I told him one night, to his face, that if he didn't want to answer my questions just tell me and I would leave. There are always other teachers. He didn't say anything. He just looked at me and figured I was going to—so he said, "Well, maybe next time." There is no next time—this is the time and I'm not taking second best from any white man.

—BOY, AGE 17

Well, the gang, they look for trouble, and then if they can't find no trouble, find something they can do, find something they can play around. Go in the park, find a bum, hit him in the face, pee in his face, kick him down, then chase him, grab him and throw him over the fence.

—BOY, AGE 15

The conditions here are the way they are because of white domination of this community, and when that changes, as is being attempted here, by these [Black] Nationalists, or by any other nationalist groups, or by the Muslims; when they can unite and change these conditions, change the white domination for Black domination, the conditions will change.

—MAN, AGE 28

Why in the hell—now this is more or less a colored neighborhood— why do we have so many white cops? As if we got to have somebody white standing over us. Not that I am prejudiced or anything, but I can't understand why we have to have so many white cops! Now if I go to a white neighborhood, I'm not going to see a lot of colored cops in no white neighborhood, standing guard over the white people. I'm not going to see that; and I know it, and I get sick and tired of seeing so many white cops, standing around.

—WOMAN, AGE 38

My wife was even robbed coming back from the store. They tried to snatch her pocketbook, and she came upstairs crying to me. What could I do? Where was the police? Where is the protection?

—MAN, AGE ABOUT 50

The white cops, they have a damn sadistic nature. They are really a sadistic type of people and we, I mean me, myself, we don't need them here in Harlem. We don't need them! They don't do the neighborhood any good. They deteriorate the neighborhood. They start

594

more violence than any other people start. They start violence, that's right. A bunch of us could be playing some music, or dancing, which we have as an outlet for ourselves. We can't dance in the house, we don't have clubs or things like that. So we're out on the sidewalk, right on the sidewalk; we might feel like dancing, or one might want to play something on his horn. Right away here comes a cop. "You're disturbing the peace!" No one has said anything, you understand; no one has made a complaint. Everyone is enjoying themselves. But here comes one cop, and he'll want to chase everyone. And gets mad. I mean, he gets mad! We aren't mad. He comes into the neighborhood, aggravated and mad.

—MAN, AGE ABOUT 33

Last night, for instance, the officer stopped some fellows on 125th Street, Car No. ——, that was the number of the car, and because this fellow spoke so nicely for his protection and his rights, the officer said, "All right, everybody get off the street or inside!" Now, it's very hot. We don't have air-conditioned apartments in most of these houses up here, so where are we going if we get off the streets? We can't go back in the house because we almost suffocate. So we sit down on the curb, or stand on the sidewalk, or on the steps, things like that, till the wee hours of the morning, especially in the summer when it's too hot to go up. Now where were we going? But he came out with his nightstick and wants to beat people on the head, and wanted to—he arrested one fellow. The other fellow said, "Well, I'll move, but you don't have to talk to me like a dog." I think we should all get together—everybody—all get together and every time one draws back his stick to do something to us, or hits one of us on the head, take the stick and hit *him* on *his* head, so he'll know how it feels to be hit on the head, or kill him, if necessary. Yes, kill him, if necessary. That's how I feel. There is no other way to deal with this man. The only way you can deal with him is the way he has been dealing with us.

—MAN, ABOUT 35

Everything is a big laugh in this dump unless you kill a cop. Then they don't laugh. I had a cop walk up to me a couple of days ago. You know what he said? "Move over." They have the street blocked up and he's going to tell me you can go around them. I said, "Hell if I do." He said, "What did you say?" I said, "Hell if I do." He said, "I'll slap your black ass." I told him, "That's one day you'll know if you're living or dying." He just looked at me. I said, "Why don't you say it? You want to say nigger so bad."

—MAN, AGE 21
595

The flag here in America is for the white man. The blue is for justice; the fifty white stars you see in the blue are for the fifty white states; and the white you see in it is the White House. It represents white folks. The red in it is the white man's blood—he doesn't even respect your blood, that's why he will lynch you, hang you, barbecue you, and fry you.

—MAN, AGE ABOUT 35

A stereotyped Negro you see him in the movies or on TV, walking down the levee with a watermelon in his hand, his shiny teeth, and his straw hat on his head. That's the one you see on television, yassuh, yassuh, and the showboys come in Stepin Fetchit, because that's what every Negro is associated with. To me, the middle-class Negro and the upper-class Negro is one that's trying to get away from that stereotype. They're the ones trying to get away.

—MAN, AGE 18

I don't see why we've got to always look up to the white man's life. That's what we've been exposed to, you know. Be like the white man. I think we have to have criteria of our own. They had "Amos and Andy" on radio, they were done by white men. You hear the fellows saying, "Oh, I'm going to get me a white broad." We should form our own criteria. We should try and have some more people like Martin Luther King, like James Baldwin. We can send some draftsmen to school, some engineers; people can come back and build a city for Negroes to live in, or you know, not just for Negroes but for Negroes and anyone else who wants to live there. Why do we always have to get up—come up to the white man's level? We struggle like the devil to get up there, and we hardly ever do it. Why can't we form our own level?

—GIRL, AGE 15

I have been uncomfortable being a Negro. I came from the South—Kentucky, on the Ohio River line—and I have had white people spit on me in my Sunday suit.

—WOMAN

The main thing is to know just where he comes from, knowing about his race. The main thing. He will then disregard every time he turns on the television that he sees a white face. That won't mean anything to him; it will be just another program because he will know that the conditions of the way of this world are based on only the white man's psychology, that makes these things. It won't be because this man is better fitted than he is on the television; it is because he dominates, he capitalizes, he corrupts.

—MAN, AGE 35

First stop wearing the white man's clothes. Dress in your ancestral clothes. Learn your history and your heritage. This is part of my culture and I'm proud. Wear your clothes! Put on your *abdaba,* your *dashiki* and your *fella.* You can do it.

—WOMAN, AGE ABOUT 45

The Honorable Elijah Mohammed teaches, but the only thing is, some of our people still don't take that old blue-eyed, hook-nosed picture of Christ off their wall—take it down and step on it. These people have been exploiting us for years.

—MAN, AGE ABOUT 35

Hear me now, hear me. Thy kingdom come, thy will be done, on earth as it is in Heaven. The kingdom is ours, black man's kingdom. We want our own God, our own paradise, our own joys on this earth, and if we are not getting that, then something must be wrong somewhere, so with all of your Gospel and all your preaching, if you cannot benefit the children, it has no value.

—MAN, AGE ABOUT 50

Churches don't mean us no good. We've been having churches all our lives under the same conditions, and look at the condition we're still in. The church must not have meant anything. See, when you go to church you don't learn how to read and write, and count, at church. You learn that in school. See what I mean? So what good the churches doing us? They are not doing us any good! You could build some factories or something in Harlem and give our people some work near home. That would do us more good than a church.

—MAN, AGE ABOUT 45

The preacher is a hustler. He creates a system for people to believe in that makes faggots, homosexuals, and lesbians out of the population of the black people, and this is exactly what Whitey wants him to do. If you keep the damn preachers out of it, we'd solve our whole problem, just like the NAACP and the CORE over here in Brooklyn now; they don't want no part of the medicine, so that's it. But I'm a U-Pad member of the National Black Nationalists, and that's all I have to say. I don't go with this. His members that are here can believe him, they can fall behind or whatsoever. The only thing he wants—

you never see a rabbi ride in a Cadillac, you never see a Jew rabbi, a charity rabbi, ride in nothing. They walk—They're doing a big enough job in the church, we don't need any leaders out here. In fact, we need to get rid of preachers like this because they are the very first ones who are going to sell us down the creek like he has done, like ministers have been doing over and over again. And incidentally, there was a big crook over in Brooklyn who sold everybody out on the picket line.

—MAN, AGE 35

We don't want any bloodshed if we can help it, but if there has to be a little bloodletting, well and good. But this is only the beginning —what happened here today. Our next big step is the Harlem Police Department—we want black captains and we're going to have them. I've been fighting for dozens of years here in Harlem, where the so-called leaders play—Uncle Tom—play politics and let the people starve. You have district leaders here that draw a big fat salary. You can't hardly walk the street for trash. You have captains here—district captains and what not—all kinds of leaders here in Harlem. You never see them until election.

—WOMAN, AGE ABOUT 30

I think there's a great lack of offensive direction and most of the adults have, more or less, succumbed to the situation and have decided, what the hell can I do? This is the attitude; that we can do nothing, so leave it alone. People think you're always going to be under pressure from the white man and he owns and runs everything, and we are so dependent on him that there's nothing I can do. This is the general impression I've gotten from most of the adults in Harlem.

—GIRL, AGE 15

It's got to get better. It can't get worse—it's got to get better, and they'll open up. They have to open up because they will find themselves going down all over the world, not only here. It's not just us picketing that forced them to do this; all over the world people are talking about American imperialism, and it's forcing them to do all these things. Because whether I walk the line or not, whoever walks the line that has a black face is walking the line for me. Whether they are walking in Alabama, Arizona, Mississippi, or wherever they're walking. And there isn't anything for the Man to do but begin giving us an equal chance if he wants to save himself, because he's going down and we're the only ones that are holding him up.

—MAN, AGE ABOUT 45

All right, so you get into the school and you get your rights, but in the whole scope of the black man in America, how can you accomplish anything by doing this? Yes, all right, you are accepted into Woolworths; you fought and got your heads beat in. But what do your children think of you? Do you have any economic or political power? The people like you who're going into Greenwood, Mississippi, say, where the people are living—you are all dependent. It's unthinkable. The people have nothing. At this point they are living on things that are being sent to them from New York, Chicago, and other places in the United States. Do you know how much money we spend on foreign aid while here in the United States we people are starving?

—MAN, AGE 18, AND GIRL, AGE 15

When the time comes, it is going to be too late. Everything will explode because the people they live under tension now; they going to a point where they can't stand it no more. When they get to that point. . . . They want us to go to Africa, they say.

That would be the best thing they would want in the world because then they could get all of us together. All they would have to do is drop one bomb and we're dead.

—MEN, AGES 30 TO 35

I would like to see the day when my people have dignity and pride in themselves as black people. And when this comes about, when they realize that we are capable of all things, and can do anything under the sun that a man can do, then all these things will come about—equality, great people, presidents—everything.

—MAN, AGE 19

I would like to be the first Negro president.

—BOY, AGE ABOUT 17

Norman Mailer

Norman Mailer (born 1923) was a precocious success as a writer of fiction. While at Harvard in 1941 he won the annual college contest of Story Magazine; *his first published novel,* The Naked and the Dead *(1948), drawing on his wartime experience in the*

*Pacific, was a best seller. Other, less successful, novels have
followed, among them* The Deer Park *(1955),* An American
Dream *(1965), and* Why Are We in Vietnam? *(1967).
Mailer's reputation as a writer has nevertheless continued
to grow, partly because of the increasing role of nonfiction, mostly
autobiographical and political, in his work. He had published
two volumes of essays,* Advertisements for Myself *(1959) and*
The Presidential Papers *(1963), when* The Armies of the
Night *(1968), an account of the 1967 antiwar march on
Washington, won him a National Book Award and a Pulitzer
Prize. The 1968 nominating conventions occasioned his* Miami
and the Siege of Chicago *(1968), and in line with his deepening
personal involvement in politics, he ran in the 1969 Democratic
primary as candidate for Mayor of New York. Columnist Jimmy
Breslin ran with him for City Council President. In the election,
the Mailer-Breslin ticket was badly defeated. The major literature
of the campaign is collected in* Running Against the Machine
(ed. Peter Manso, 1969).

The following piece was written for the May 18 New York
Times Magazine, *just before the election. The occasion does not
evoke the full, novelistic range of expression that Mailer is capable
of in expository prose, but it has much of his directness and his
political idealism.*

WHY ARE WE IN NEW YORK?

How is one to speak of the illness of a city? A clear day can come,
a morning in early May like the pride of June. The streets are cool,
the buildings have come out of shadow, and silences are broken by
the voices of children. It is as if the neighborhood has slept in the
winding sheet of the past. Forty years go by—one can recollect the
milkman and the clop of a horse. It is a great day. Everyone speaks
of the delight of the day on the way to work. It is hard on such
mornings to believe that New York is the victim "etherized on a
table."

Yet by afternoon the city is incarcerated once more. Haze covers
the sky, a grim, formless glare blazes back from the horizon. The city
has become unbalanced again. By the time work is done, New Yorkers
push through the acrid lung-rotting air and work their way home,

avoiding each other's eyes in the subway. Later, near midnight, thinking of a walk to buy The Times, they hesitate—in the darkness a familiar sense of dread returns, the streets are not quite safe, the sense of waiting for some apocalyptic fire, some night of long knives hangs over the city. We recognize one more time that the city is ill, that our own New York, the Empire City, is not too far from death.

Recollect: When we were children, we were told air was invisible, and it was. Now we see it shift and thicken, move in gray depression over a stricken sky. Now we grow used to living with colds all year, and viruses suggestive of plague. Tempers shorten in our hideous air. The sick get sicker, the violent more violent. The frayed tissue of New York manners seems ready to splatter on every city street. It is the first problem of the city, our atrocious air. People do not die dramatically like the one-day victims of Donora, rather they dwindle imperceptibly, die five years before their time, 10 years before, cough or sneeze helplessly into the middle of someone else's good mood, stroll about with the hot iron of future asthma manacled to their lungs. The air pollution in New York is so bad, and gives so much promise of getting worse, that there is no solution to any other problem until the air is relieved of its poisonous ingestions. New York has conceivably the worst air of any city in the universe today—certainly it is the worst air in the most technologically developed nation in the world, which is to say it is the air of the future if the future is not shifted from its program. Once Los Angeles was famous for the liver-yellow of its smog; we have surpassed her.

That is our pervasive ill. It is fed by a host of tributary ills which flow into the air, fed first by our traffic, renowned through the world for its incapacity to move. Midtown Manhattan is next to impenetrable by vehicle from midday to evening—the average rate of advance is, in fact, 6 miles an hour, about the speed of a horse at a walk. Once free of the center, there is the threat of hourlong tie-ups at every bridge, tunnel and expressway if even a single car breaks down in a lane. In the course of a year, people lose weeks of working time through the sum of minutes and quarter-hours of waiting to crawl forward in traffic. Tempers blow with lost schedules, work suffers everywhere. All the while stalled cars gun their motors while waiting in place, pumping carbon monoxide into air already laden with caustic sulphur-oxide from fuel oil we burn to make electricity.

Given this daily burden, this air pollution, noise pollution, stagnant transport, all-but-crippled subways, routes of new transportation 20 years unbuilt—every New Yorker sallies forth into an environment which strips him before noon of his good cheer, his charity, his calm nerve, and his ability to discipline his anger.

Yet, beneath that mood of pestilential clangor, something worse is ticking away—our deeper sense of a concealed and continuing human horror. If there are eight million people in New York, one million live on welfare, no, the figure is higher now, it will be one million two hundred thousand by the end of the year. Not a tenth of these welfare cases will ever be available for work; they are women and children first, then too old, too sick, too addicted, too illiterate, too unskilled, too ignorant of English. Fatherless families and motherless families live at the end of an umbilical financial cord which perpetuates them in an embryonic economic state. Welfare is the single largest item in the city budget—two years ago it surpassed the figure we reserve for education, yet it comes down to payments of no more than $3,800 a year for a family of four. Each member of that family is able to spend a dollar a day for food, at most $1.25 a day.

Still, it is worse than that. If one of eight people in New York is on welfare, half as many again might just as well be on welfare because their minimum wage brings in no more than such a check. So the natural incentive is to cease working. Close to $1.5-billion is spent on welfare now. The figure will go up. Manpower Training, in contrast, spends about a twenty-fifth as much. Looking to skill the poor for work, it will train as many as 4,000 men a year, and place perhaps 10,000 men out of 100,000 applicants in bad jobs without foreseeable future, the only jobs indeed available for the untrained. Sometimes in the Job Corps it cost $13,000 to train a man for a job where he might be able to make $6,000 a year if he could find a job, but the skills he had learned were not related to the jobs he might return to at home. Poverty lies upon the city like a layer of smog.

Our housing offers its unhappy figures. If we have calculated that it is necessary to build 7,500 new low-income apartments a year, merely to keep on the same terms with the problem, we end in fact with 4,000 units constructed. Never mind how most of it looks—those grim, high-rise, new-slum prisons on every city horizon. Face rather the fact that we lose near to the same number of units a year as old buildings which could have been saved run down into a state requiring condemnation. Of the $100,000,000 the city spends each budget year for new housing, $20,000,000 goes into demolition. If four times as much were spent by present methods on low- and middle-income housing, 36,000 new and rehabilitated units could be provided a year, but housing needs would still be huge and unmet—the average family could wait 25 years to benefit from the program.

Our finances are intolerable. If New York States delivers $17-billion in income tax and $5-billion in corporate taxes to the Federal Government, it is conservative to assume that $14-billion of the total of $22-

billion has come from the people of New York City. But our city budget is about $7.5-billion: of that sum only $3-billion derives from the State and from Washington. New York must find another $4.5-billion in real estate and other local taxes. Consider then: We pay $14-billion in income tax to the Federal Government and to Albany: back comes $3-billion. We put out 5 dollars for every dollar which returns. So we live in vistas of ironbound civic poverty. Four of those lost 5 dollars are going to places like Vietnam and Malmstrom in North Dakota where the ABM will find a site, or dollars are going to Interstate highways which pass through regions we probably will never visit. In relation to the Federal Government, the city is like a sharecropper who lives forever in debt at the company store.

Yes, everything is wrong. The vocations of the past disintegrate. Jewish teachers who went into the education system 20 years ago to have security for themselves and to disseminate enlightenment among the children of the poor, now feel no security in their work, and are rejected in their liberal sociological style of teaching. The collective ego of their life style is shattered. They are forced to comprehend that there are black people who would rather be taught by other black people than by experts. The need for authenticity has become the real desire in education. "Who am I? What is the meaning of my skin, my passion, my dread, my fury, my dream of glories undreamed, my very need for bread?"—these questions are now become so powerful they bring the pumps of blood up to pressure and leave murder in the heart. What can education be in the womb of a dying city but a fury to discover for oneself whether one is victim or potential hero, stupid or too bright for old pedagogical ways? Rage at the frustration of the effort to find a style became the rage at the root of the uproar in the schools last year, and the rage will be there until the schools are free to discover a new way to learn. Let us not be arrogant toward the ignorant—their sensitivity is often too deep to dare the knowledge of numbers or the curlicue within a letter. Picasso, age of 11, could still not do arithmetic because the figure 7 looked like a nose upside down to him.

Among the poor, genius may stay buried behind the mask of the most implacable stupidity, for if genius can have no issue in a man's life, he must conceal it, and protect it, reserve it for his seed, or his blessing, or, all else gone, for his curse. No wonder we live with dread in our heart, and the nicest of the middle class still padlock their doors against the curse. We are like a Biblical city which has fallen from grace. Our parks deteriorate, and after duty our police go home to suburbs beyond the city—they come back to govern us from without. And municipal employes drift in the endless administrative bogs of

Wagnerian systems of apathy and attrition. Work gets done at the rate of work accomplished by a draft army in peacetime at a sullen out-of-the-way post. The Poverty Program staggers from the brilliance of its embezzlements. But, of course, if you were a bright young black man, might you not want to steal a million from the Feds?

Here, let us take ourselves to the problem. It goes beyond the Durham gang. Our first problem is that no one alive in New York can answer with honesty the question: Can New York be saved? None of us can know. It is possible people will emigrate from New York in greater and greater numbers, and administration will collapse under insufferable weights, order will be restored from without. Then, everyone who can afford it will redouble his efforts to go, and New York will end as the first asylum of the megacity of the technological future. We who leave will carry with us the infection of the cowardice and apathy, the sense of defeat of the terminal years. We will move into other cities similarly affected or into a countryside wary of us, for we are then packers and peddlers from an expiring social world. So our first problem is to find whether we can find a way to rally our morale.

Part of the tragedy, part of the unbelievable oncoming demise of New York is that none of us can simply believe it. We were always the best and the strongest of cities, and our people were vital to the teeth. Knock them down eight times and they would get up with that look in the eye which suggests the fight has barely begun. We were the city of optimists. It is probably why we settled so deep into our mistakes. We simply couldn't believe that we weren't inexhaustible as a race—an unspoken race of New Yorkers.

Now all our problems have the magnitude of junkie problems—they are so coexistent with our life that New Yorkers do not try to solve them but escape them. Our fix is to put the blame on the blacks and Puerto Ricans. But everybody knows that nobody can really know where the blame resides. Nobody but a candidate for Mayor. It is the only way he can have the optimism to run. So the prospective candidate writing these words has the heart to consider entering the Democratic primary on June 17 because he thinks he sees a way out of the swamp: better, he believes he glimpses a royal road.

The face of the solution may reside in the notion that the Left has been absolutely right on some critical problems of our time, and the Conservatives have been altogether correct about one enormous matter —which is that the Federal Government has no business whatever in local affairs. The style of New York life has shifted since the Second World War (along with the rest of the American cities) from a scene of local neighborhoods and personalities to a large dull impersonal style of life which deadens us with its architecture, its highways, its abstract welfare, and its bureaucratic reflex to look for government solutions which come into the city from without (and do not work). So the old confidence that the problems of our life were roughly equal to our abilities has been lost. Our authority has been handed over to the Federal power. We expect our economic solutions, our habitats, yes, even our entertainments, to derive from that remote abstract power, remote as the other end of a television tube. We are like wards in an orphan asylum. The shaping of the style of our lives is removed from us—we pay for huge military adventures and social experiments so separated from our direct control that we do not even know where to begin to look to criticize the lack of our power to criticize. We cannot—the words are now a cliché, the life has gone out of them—we cannot forge our destiny. So our condition is spiritless. We wait for abstract impersonal powers to save us, we despise the abstractness of those powers, we loathe ourselves for our own apathy. Orphans.

Who is to say that the religious heart is not right to think the need of every man and woman alive may be to die in a state of grace, a grace which for atheists and agnostics may reside in the basic act of having done one's best, of having found some part of a destiny to approach, and having worked for the view of it? New York will not begin to be saved until its men and women begin to believe that it must become the greatest city in the world, the most magnificent, most creative, most extraordinary, most just, dazzling, bewildering and balanced of cities. The demand upon us has come down to nothing less than that.

How can we begin? By the most brutal view, New York City is today a legislative pail of dismembered organs strewn from Washington to Albany. We are without a comprehensive function or a skin. We cannot begin until we find a function which will become our skin. It is simple: Our city must become a state. We must look to become a state of the United States separate from New York State: the Fifty-First, in fact, of the United States. New York City State, or The State of New York City. It is strange on the tongue, but not so strange.

Think on the problem of this separation. People across the state are oriented toward Buffalo or Albany or Rochester or Montreal or Toronto or Boston or Cleveland. They do not think in great numbers of coming to New York City to make their life. In fact the good farmers and small-town workers of New York State rather detest us. They hear of the evils of our city with quiet thin-lipped glee; in the State Legislature they rush to compound those evils. Every time the city needs a program which the state must approve, the city returns with a part of its package—the rest has been lost in deals, compromises and imposts.

605

The connection of New York City to New York State is a marriage of misery, incompatibility and abominable old quarrels.

While the separation could hardly be as advantageous to New York State as it would be for the city, it might nonetheless begin the development of what has been hitherto a culturally undernourished hinterland, a typically colorless national tract.

But we will not weep for New York State—look, rather, to the direct advantages to ourselves. We have, for example, received no money so far for improving our city transit lines, yet the highway program for America in 1968 was $5-billion. Of this, New York State received at least $350,000,000 for its roads. New York City received not a dollar from Washington or Albany for reconstruction of its 6,000 miles of streets and avenues.

As a city-state we could speak to the Federal Government in the unmistakable tones of a state. If so many hundreds of millions go to Pennsylvania and Oklahoma and Colorado and Maine for their highway programs, then we could claim that a comparable amount is required for our transportation problems which can better be solved by the construction of new rapid transit. Add the monies attainable by an increased ability as the Fifty-First State to press for more equitable return on our taxes. Repeat: we give to Washington and Albany almost 5 tax dollars for every dollar which returns; Mississippi, while declaiming the virtues and inviolability of states' rights, still gets four Federal dollars for every income-tax dollar she pays up.

As the center of the financial and communications industries, as the first victim of a nuclear war, the new State of the City of New York would not have the influence of one state in fifty-one, but rather would exist as one of the two or three states whose force and influence could be felt upon every change in the country's policy. With the power implicit in this grip, it may not be excessive to assume that divorce from Albany would produce an extra billion in real savings and natural efficiency, and still another billion (not to mention massive allocations for transit problems) could derive from our direct relation with the Federal Government: The first shift in our ability to solve our problems might have begun.

It would not, however, be nearly enough. The ills of New York cannot be solved by money. New York will be ill until it is magnificent. For New York must be ready to show the way to the rest of Western civilization. Until it does, it will be no more than the first victim of the technological revolution no matter how much money it receives in its budget. Money bears the same relation to social solutions that water does to blood.

Yet the beginning of a city-state and the tonic of a potential budget of $8- or $9- or $10-billion would offer a base on which to build. Where then could we take it? How would we build?

We could direct our effort first against the present thickets of the City Charter. The Charter is a formidable document. There are some who would say it is a hideous document. Taken in combination with the laws of New York State, it is a legal mat guaranteed to deaden the nerve of every living inquiry. The Charter in combination with the institutional and municipal baggage surrounding it is guaranteed to inhibit any honest man from erecting a building, beginning an enterprise, organizing a new union, searching for a sensible variety of living zone, or speaking up for local control in education. It would strangle any honest Mayor who approached the suffocations of air pollution or traffic, tried to build workable on-the-job training, faced the most immediate problems of law and order, attacked our shortage of housing or in general even tried to conceive of a new breath of civic effort. There is no way at present to circumvent the thicket without looking to power-brokers in the trade unions, the Mafia and real estate.

Only if the people of New York City were to deliver an overwhelming mandate for a city-state could anything be done about the thicket. Then the legal charter of the new state could rewrite the means by which men and women could work to make changes in the intimate details of their neighborhoods and their lives.

Such a new document would most happily be built upon one concept so fundamental that all others would depend upon it. This concept might state that power would return to the neighborhoods.

Power to the neighborhoods! In the new city-state, every opportunity would be offered to neighborhoods to vote to become townships, villages, hamlets, sub-boroughs, tracts or small cities, at which legal point they would be funded directly by the fifty-first state. Many of these neighborhoods would manage their own municipal services, their police, sanitation, fire protection, education, parks, or, like very small towns, they could, if they wished, combine services with other neighborhoods. Each neighborhood would thus begin to outline the style of its local government by the choice of its services.

It may be recognized that we are at this point not yet vastly different from a patch of suburbs and townships in Westchester or Jersey. The real significance of power to the neighborhoods is that people could come together and constitute themselves upon any principle. Neighborhoods which once existed as separate towns or districts, like Jamaica or New Utrecht or Gravesend, might wish to become towns again upon just such a historic base. Other neighborhoods with a sense of unity provided by their geography like Bay Ridge, Park Slope, Washington Heights, Yorkville, Fordham Road, Riverdale,

Jackson Heights, Canarsie or Corona might be able without undue discussion to draw their natural lines.

Poorer neighborhoods would obviously look to establish themselves upon their immediate problems, rather than upon historical or geographical tradition. So Harlem, Bedford-Stuyvesant and the Barrio in East Harlem might be the first to vote for power to their own neighborhoods so that they might be in position to administer their own poverty program, own welfare, their own education systems, and their own—if they so voted—police and sanitation and fire protection for which they would proceed to pay out of their funds. They would then be able to hire their own people for their own neighborhood jobs and services. Their own teachers and communities would, if they desired, control their own schools. Their own union could rebuild their own slums. Black Power would be a political reality for Harlem and Bedford-Stuyvesant. Black people and, to the extent they desired, Puerto Rican people, could make separate but thoroughgoing attacks upon their economic problems, since direct neighborhood funding would be available to begin every variety of economic enterprise. Black militants interested in such communal forms of economic activity as running their own factories could begin to build economies, new unions and new trades in their neighborhoods.

Power to the neighborhoods would mean that any neighborhood could constitute itself on any principle, whether spiritual, emotional, economical, ideological or idealistic. Even prejudicial principles could serve as the base—if one were willing to pay. It could, for example, be established in the charter of the city-state that no principle of exclusion by race or religion would be tolerated in the neighborhoods unless each such neighborhood was willing to offer a stiff and proper premium for this desire in their taxes.

In reaction to this, each and every liberal, Negro and white, who would detest the relinquishment of the principle that no prejudice was allowed by law, might also consider the loss of the dream of integration as the greatest loss in the work of their lives. They would now be free to create neighborhoods which would incorporate on the very base of integration itself—Integration City might be the name of the first neighborhood to stand on the recapture of the old dream. Perhaps it might even exist where now is Stuyvesant Town.

On the other hand, people who wished anonymity or isolation from their neighbors could always choose large anonymous areas, neighborhoods only in name, or indeed could live in those undifferentiated parts of the city which chose no neighborhood for themselves at all. The critical point to conceive is that no neighborhood would come into existence because the mayoralty so dictated. To the extent that they had been conditioned for years by the notion that the government was

608

the only agency large enough and therefore effective enough to solve their problems, so to that extent would many people be reluctant to move to solutions which came from themselves.

To the degree, however, that we have lost faith in the power of the government to conduct our lives, so would the principle of power to the neighborhoods begin to thrive, so too would the first spiritual problem of the 20th century—alienation from the self—be given a tool by which to rediscover oneself.

In New York, which is to say, in the 20th century, one can never know whether the world is vastly more or less violent than it seems. Nor can we discover which actions in our lives are authentic or which belong to the art of the put-on. Conceive that society has come to the point where tolerance of others' ideas has no meaning unless there is benumbed acceptance of the fact that we must accept their lives. If there are young people who believe that human liberty is blockaded until they have the right to take off their clothes in the street—and more! and more!—make love on the hood of an automobile—there are others who think it is a sin against the eyes of the Lord to even contemplate the act in one's mind. Both could now begin to build communities on their separate faith—a spectrum which might run from Compulsory Free Love to Mandatory Attendance in Church on Sunday! Grant us to recognize that wherever there is a common desire among people vital enough to keep a community alive, then there must be also the presence of a clue that some kind of real life resides in the desire. Others may eventually discern how.

Contained beneath the surface of the notion is a recognition that the 20th century has lost its way—the religious do not know if they believe in God, or even if God is not dead; the materialist works through the gloomy evidence of socialism and bureaucracy; the traditionalist is hardly aware any longer of a battlefield where the past may be defended; the technician—if sensitive—must wonder if the world he fashions is evil, insane, or rational; the student rebellion stares into the philosophical gulf of such questions as the nature of culture and the students' responsibility to it; the blacks cannot be certain if they are fundamentally deprived, or a people of genius, or both. The answers are unknown because the questions all collide in the vast empty arena of the mass media where no price has ever to be paid for your opinion. So nobody can be certain of his value—one cannot even explore the validity of one's smallest belief. To wake up in New York with a new idea is to be plunged into impotence by noon, plunged into that baleful sense of boredom which hints of dread and future violence.

So the cry of Power to the Neighborhoods may yet be heard. For even as marriage reveals the balance between one's dream of pleasure and one's small real purchase upon it, even as marriage is the mirror of one's habits, and the immersion of the ego into the acid of the critic, so life in the kind of neighborhood which contains one's belief of a possible society is a form of marriage between one's social philosophy and one's private contract with the world. The need is deeper than we could expect, for we are modern, which is to say we can never locate our roots without a voyage of discovery.

Perhaps then it can be recognized that power to the neighborhoods is a most peculiar relocation of the old political directions. It speaks from the left across the divide to conservatism. Speaking from the left, it says that a city cannot survive unless the poor are recognized, until their problems are underlined as not directly of their own making; so their recovery must be based upon more than their own private efforts, must be based in fact upon their being capitalized by the city-state in order that the initial construction of their community economics, whether socialist or capitalist or both, can begin.

Yet with power in the neighborhoods, so also could there be on-the-job training in carpentry, stonemasonry, plumbing, plastering, electrical work and painting. With a pool of such newly skilled workers, paid by the neighborhood, the possibility is present to rebuild a slum area *room by room.*

Better! The occupant of an apartment who desires better housing could go to work himself on his own apartment, using neighborhood labor and funds, patching, plastering, painting, installing new wiring and plumbing—as the tenant made progress he could be given funds to continue, could own the pride of having improved his housing in part through his own efforts.

So power to these poor neighborhoods still speaks to conservative principles, for it recognizes that a man must have the opportunity to work out his own destiny, or he will never know the dimensions of himself, he will be alienated from any sense of whether he is acting for good or evil. It goes further. Power to all neighborhoods recognizes that we cannot work at our destiny without a context—that most specific neighborhood which welcomes or rejects our effort, and so gives a mirror to the value of our striving, and the distortion of our prejudice. Perhaps it even recognizes the deepest of conservative principles—that a man has a right to live his life in such a way that he may know if he is dying in a state of grace. Our lives, directed by abstract outside forces, have lost that possibility most of all. It is a notion on which to hit the campaign trail.

Which is where we go now—into the campaign: to talk in the days ahead of what power to the neighborhoods will mean. We will go down the steps of the position papers and talk of jobs and housing and welfare, of education, municipal unions and law and order, finance, the names of laws, the statistics of the budget, the problems of traffic and transportation. There will be a paucity of metaphor and a taste of stale saliva to the debates, for voters are hard-working people who trust the plain more than the poetic. How then can Mailer and Breslin, two writers with reputations notorious enough for four, ever hope to convince the voting hand of the electorate? What would they do if, miracle of political explosions, they were to win?

Well, they might cry like Mario Procaccino, for they would never have a good time again; but they would serve, they would learn on the job, they would conduct their education in public. They would be obliged to. And indeed the supposition could remain that they might even do well, better than the men before them. How else could they have the confidence to run? They might either have supposed that the Lord was not dead but behind them or they must have felt such guilt about the years of their lives that only the long running duties of office could satisfy the list of their dues.

As for the fact that they were literary men—that might be the first asset of all. They would know how to talk to the people—they would be forced to govern by the fine art of the voice. Exposed by their own confession as amateurs they might even attract the skill of the city to their service, for the community would be forced to swim in full recognition of the depth of the soup. And best of all, what a tentative confidence would reign in the eye of New York that her literary men, used to dealing with the proportions of worlds hitherto created only in the mind, might now have a sensitive nose for the balances and the battles, the tugs, the pushing, the heaves of that city whose declaration of new birth was implicit in the extraordinary fact that *him*, Mailer! and *him*, Breslin! had been voted in.

Sweet Sunday, dear friends, and take a chance. We are out on the lottery of the years.

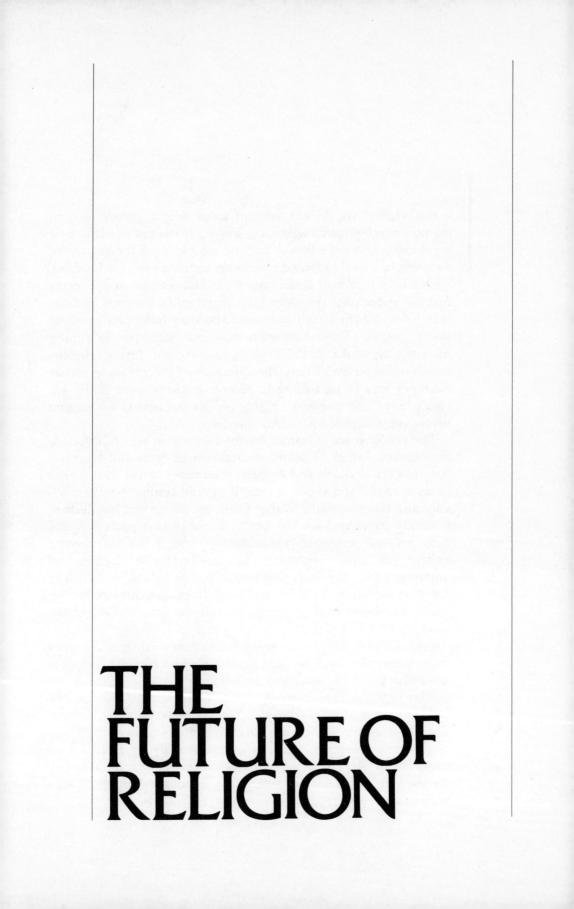

THE FUTURE OF RELIGION

n this section we do not attempt to present a survey of contemporary religious thought since any such attempt would at best be sketchy and superficial. Instead we focus on the search for meaning in a world reputedly become meaningless. God is dead, Nietzsche proclaimed at the end of the last century, and it seems that the subsequent Western faith in scientific progress and the search for objective truth have been less than fulfilling. Spiritual needs remain. These frequently manifest themselves in a quest for meaning, so that to Paul Tillich, for example, "being religious means asking passionately the question of the meaning of our existence and being willing to receive answers, even if the answers hurt." In one way or another, all the writers we present below are concerned with this question.

The predicament is framed by the two poems which introduce the section: Father Hopkins' declaration of faith and Matthew Arnold's cry of doubt and despair. Clarence Darrow then speaks as an agnostic and shows a clear if simple conflict between science and religion, while Walter Stace, an atheist and intellectual, is darkly concerned for the fate of morality in a godless world. But "godless" becomes "meaningless," and if nothing is more meaningful, more important, than anything else, then indeed anything goes. Precisely this notion is combatted by Tillich in the next selection; both he and John Robinson attempt to discover and define new meanings for religion and for God in our time.

Erich Fromm, too, is concerned with deeper values and a more meaningful life—what he calls psychospiritual renewal—but from a secular point of view, and he suggests that the erstwhile religious fight against idolatry is actually the same as the contemporary fight against alienation. The two selections by Eldridge Cleaver illustrate a sort of secular religion as well, partly skeptical, partly receptive. Cleaver is interestingly attracted by the character of Thomas Merton, whose journal shows, perhaps better than any of the other selections, the quality of life in tune with spirit.

Gerard Manley Hopkins (1844–1889)

GOD'S GRANDEUR

The world is charged with the grandeur of God.
  It will flame out, like shining from shook foil;
  It gathers to a greatness, like the ooze of oil
Crushed. Why do men then now not reck his rod?
Generations have trod, have trod, have trod;
  And all is seared with trade; bleared, smeared with toil;
  And wears man's smudge and shares man's smell: the soil
Is bare now, nor can foot feel, being shod.

And for all this, nature is never spent;
  There lives the dearest freshness deep down things;
And though the last lights off the black West went
  Oh, morning, at the brown brink eastward, springs—
Because the Holy Ghost over the bent
  World broods with warm breast and with ah! bright wings.

(1877)

Matthew Arnold (1822–1888)

DOVER BEACH

The sea is calm to-night.
The tide is full, the moon lies fair
Upon the straits;—on the French coast the light
Gleams and is gone; the cliffs of England stand
Glimmering and vast, out in the tranquil bay.
Come to the window, sweet is the night-air!
Only, from the long line of spray
Where the sea meets the moon-blanched land,
Listen! you hear the grating roar
Of pebbles which the waves draw back, and fling,
At their return, up the high strand,

Begin, and cease, and then again begin,
With tremulous cadence slow, and bring
The eternal note of sadness in.

Sophocles long ago
Heard it on the Ægean, and it brought
Into his mind the turbid ebb and flow,
Of human misery; we
Find also in the sound a thought,
Hearing it by this distant northern sea.

The Sea of Faith
Was once, too, at the full, and round earth's shore
Lay like the folds of a bright girdle furled.
But now I only hear
Its melancholy, long, withdrawing roar,
Retreating, to the breath
Of the night-wind, down the vast edges drear
And naked shingles of the world.

Ah, love, let us be true
To one another! for the world, which seems
To lie before us like a land of dreams,
So various, so beautiful, so new,
Hath really neither joy, nor love, nor light,
Nor certitude, nor peace, nor help for pain;
And we are here as on a darkling plain
Swept with confused alarms of struggle and flight,
Where ignorant armies clash by night.

(1867)

Clarence Darrow

Clarence Darrow is probably best known for his distinguished career in criminal law. Born in Ohio in 1857, he attended one year of law school at the University of Michigan, spent his second year in an attorney's office, and was admitted to the Ohio bar the third year, at the age of twenty-one. He soon left Ohio for Chicago and became the most sought-after and controversial

criminal lawyer of his time. His most famous cases include the
defense of the child-murderers Leopold and Loeb, for whom he
won a life sentence instead of the death penalty, and the Scopes
Trial in 1925—known as the Monkey Trial—which created a
national and international furor. Darrow, an outspoken agnostic,
defended John Scopes, a Dayton, Tennessee, science teacher who had
taught evolution and thus broken a state law prohibiting "the
teaching in public schools of any theories that deny the divine
creation of man as taught in the Bible." The prosecuting attorney
was William Jennings Bryan, a Fundamentalist. Darrow put
Bryan on the stand, cross-examined him regarding his Funda-
mentalist beliefs, and won what was considered a triumphant
victory, although Scopes was formally convicted and sentenced
to a nominal fine of $100. Bryan died five days later. The
reader may wish to keep this case in mind when reading the essay
we present below, reprinted here from Verdicts Out of Court
(ed. Arthur and Lila Weinberg, 1963). It was originally written
in 1929 for a symposium in which Darrow was joined by a rabbi,
a Protestant bishop, and a Catholic judge. Among Darrow's other
writings are two autobiographical books, Farmington *(1904) and*
The Story of My Life *(1932), and a number of socio-legal works,*
including Resist Not Evil *(1904),* Eye for an Eye *(1904), and*
Crime: Its Cause and Its Treatment *(1922).*

WHY I AM AN AGNOSTIC

An agnostic is a doubter. The word is generally applied to those who
doubt the verity of accepted religious creeds of faiths. Everyone is an
agnostic as to the beliefs or creeds they do not accept. Catholics are
agnostic to the Protestant creeds, and the Protestants are agnostic to the
Catholic creed. Anyone who thinks is an agnostic about something,
otherwise he must believe that he is possessed of all knowledge. And
the proper place for such a person is in the madhouse or the home for
the feeble-minded. In a popular way, in the western world, an agnostic
is one who doubts or disbelieves the main tenets of the Christian faith.

I would say that belief in at least three tenets is necessary to the
faith of a Christian: a belief in God, a belief in immortality, and a
belief in a supernatural book. Various Christian sects require much
more, but it is difficult to imagine that one could be a Christian, under
any intelligent meaning of the word, with less. Yet there are some

617

people who claim to be Christians who do not accept the literal interpretation of all the Bible, and who give more credence to some portions of the book than to others.

I am an agnostic as to the question of God. I think that it is impossible for the human mind to believe in an object or thing unless it can form a mental picture of such object or thing. Since man ceased to worship openly an anthropomorphic God and talked vaguely and not intelligently about some force in the universe, higher than man, that is responsible for the existence of man and the universe, he cannot be said to believe in God. One cannot believe in a force excepting as a force that pervades matter and is not an individual entity. To believe in a thing, an image of the thing must be stamped on the mind. If one is asked if he believes in such an animal as a camel, there immediately arises in his mind an image of the camel. This image has come from experience or knowledge of the animal gathered in some way or other. No such image comes, or can come, with the idea of a God who is described as a force.

Man has always speculated upon the origin of the universe, including himself. I feel, with Herbert Spencer, that whether the universe had an origin—and if it had—what the origin is will never be known by man. The Christian says that the universe could not make itself; that there must have been some higher power to call it into being. Christians have been obsessed for many years by Paley's argument that if a person passing through a desert should find a watch and examine its spring, its hands, its case and its crystal, he would at once be satisfied that some intelligent being capable of design had made the watch. No doubt this is true. No civilized man would question that someone made the watch. The reason he would not doubt it is because he is familiar with watches and other appliances made by man. The savage was once unfamiliar with a watch and would have had no idea upon the subject. There are plenty of crystals and rocks of natural formation that are as intricate as a watch, but even to intelligent man they carry no implication that some intelligent power must have made them. They carry no such implication because no one has any knowledge or experience of someone having made these natural objects which everywhere abound.

To say that God made the universe gives us no explanation of the beginning of things. If we are told that God made the universe, the question immediately arises: Who made God? Did he always exist, or was there some power back of that? Did he create matter out of nothing, or is his existence co-extensive with matter? The problem is still there. What is the origin of it all? If, on the other hand, one says that the universe was not made by God, that it always existed, he has the same difficulty to confront. To say that the universe was here last year, or millions of years ago, does not explain its origin. This is still a mystery. As to the question of the origin of things, man can only wonder and doubt and guess.

As to the existence of the soul, all people may either believe or disbelieve. Everyone knows the origin of the human being. They know that it came from a single cell in the body of the mother, and that the cell was one out of ten thousand in the mother's body. Before gestation the cell must have been fertilized by a spermatozoön from the body of the father. This was one out of perhaps a billion spermatozoa that was the capacity of the father. When the cell is fertilized a chemical process begins. The cell divides and multiplies and increases into millions of cells, and finally a child is born. Cells die and are born during the life of the individual until they finally drop apart, and this is death.

If there is a soul, what is it, and where did it come from, and where does it go? Can anyone who is guided by his reason possibly imagine a soul independent of a body, or the place of its residence, or the character of it, or anything concerning it? If man is justified in any belief or disbelief on any subject, he is warranted in the disbelief in a soul. Not one scrap of evidence exists to prove any such impossible thing.

Many Christians base the belief of a soul and God upon the Bible. Strictly speaking, there is no such book. To make the Bible, sixty-six books are bound into one volume. These books were written by many people at different times, and no one knows the time or the identity of any author. Some of the books were written by several authors at various times. These books contain all sorts of contradictory concepts of life and morals and the origin of things. Between the first and the last nearly a thousand years intervened, a longer time than has passed since the discovery of America by Columbus.

When I was a boy the theologicans used to assert that the proof of the divine inspiration of the Bible rested on miracles and prophecies. But a miracle means a violation of a natural law, and there can be no proof imagined that could be sufficient to show the violation of a natural law; even though proof seemed to show violation, it would only show that we were not acquainted with all natural laws. One believes in the truthfulness of a man because of his long experience with the man, and because the man has always told a consistent story. But no man has told so consistent a story as nature.

If one should say that the sun did not rise, to use the ordinary expression, on the day before, his hearer would not believe it, even though he had slept all day and knew that his informant was a man of the strictest veracity. He would not believe it because the story is inconsistent with the conduct of the sun in all the ages past.

Primitive and even civilized people have grown so accustomed to believing in miracles that they often attribute the simplest manifestations of nature to agencies of which they know nothing. They do this when the belief is utterly inconsistent with knowledge and logic. They believe in old miracles and new ones. Preachers pray for rain, knowing full well that no such prayer was ever answered. When a politician is sick, they pray for God to cure him, and the politician almost invariably dies. The modern clergyman who prays for rain and for the health of the politician is no more intelligent in this matter than the primitive man who saw a separate miracle in the rising and setting of the sun, in the birth of an individual, in the growth of a plant, in the stroke of lightning, in the flood, in every manifestation of nature and life.

As to prophecies, intelligent writers gave them up long ago. In all prophecies facts are made to suit the prophecy, or the prophecy was made after the facts, or the events have no relation to the prophecy. Weird and strange and unreasonable interpretations are used to explain simple statements, that a prophecy may be claimed.

Can any rational person believe that the Bible is anything but a human document? We now know pretty well where the various books came from, and about when they were written. We know that they were written by human beings who had no knowledge of science, little knowledge of life, and were influenced by the barbarous morality of primitive times, and were grossly ignorant of most things that men know today. For instance, Genesis says that God made the earth, and he made the sun to light the day and the moon to light the night, and in one clause disposes of the stars by saying that "he made the stars also." This was plainly written by someone who had no conception of the stars. Man, by the aid of his telescope, has looked out into the heavens and found stars whose diameter is as great as the distance between the earth and the sun. We now know that the universe is filled with stars and suns and planets and systems. Every new telescope looking further into the heavens only discovers more and more worlds and suns and systems in the endless reaches of space. The men who wrote Genesis believed, of course, that this tiny speck of mud that we call the earth was the center of the universe, the only world in space, and made for man, who was the only being worth considering. These men believed that the stars were only a little way above the earth, and were set in the firmament for man to look at, and for nothing else. Everyone today knows that this conception is not true.

The origin of the human race is not as blind a subject as it once was. Let alone God creating Adam out of hand, from the dust of the earth, does anyone believe that Eve was made from Adam's rib—that the snake walked and spoke in the Garden of Eden—that he tempted

Eve to persuade Adam to eat an apple, and that it is on that account that the whole human race was doomed to hell—that for four thousand years there was no chance for any human to be saved, though none of them had anything whatever to do with the temptation; and that finally men were saved only through God's son dying for them, and that unless human beings believed this silly, impossible and wicked story they were doomed to hell? Can anyone with intelligence really believe that a child born today should be doomed because the snake tempted Eve and Eve tempted Adam? To believe that is not God-worship; it is devil-worship.

Can anyone call this scheme of creation and damnation moral? It defies every principle of morality, as man conceives morality. Can anyone believe today that the whole world was destroyed by flood, save only Noah and his family and a male and female of each species of animal that entered the Ark? There are almost a million species of insects alone. How did Noah match these up and make sure of getting male and female to reproduce life in the world after the flood had spent its force? And why should all the lower animals have been destroyed? Were they included in the sinning of man? This is a story which could not beguile a fairly bright child of five years of age today.

Do intelligent people believe that the various languages spoken by man on earth came from the confusion of tongues at the Tower of Babel, some four thousand years ago? Human languages were dispersed all over the face of the earth long before that time. Evidences of civilizations are in existence now that were old long before the date that romancers fix for the building of the Tower, and even before the date claimed for the flood.

Do Christians believe that Joshua made the sun stand still, so that the day could be lengthened, that a battle might be finished? What kind of person wrote that story, and what did he know about astronomy? It is perfectly plain that the author thought that the earth was the center of the universe and stood still in the heavens, and that the sun either went around it or was pulled across its path each day, and that the stopping of the sun would lengthen the day. We know now that had the sun stopped when Joshua commanded it, and had it stood still until now, it would not have lengthened the day. We know that the day is determined by the rotation of the earth upon its axis, and not by the movement of the sun. Everyone knows that this story simply is not true, and not many even pretend to believe the childish fable.

What of the tale of Balaam's ass speaking to him, probably in Hebrew? Is it true, or is it a fable? Many asses have spoken, and doubtless some in Hebrew, but they have not been that breed of asses. Is salvation to depend on a belief in a monstrosity like this?

Above all the rest, would any human being today believe that a child was born without a father? Yet this story was not at all unreasonable in the ancient world; at least three or four miraculous births are recorded in the Bible, including John the Baptist and Samson. Immaculate conceptions were common in the Roman world at the time and at the place where Christianity really had its nativity. Women were taken to the temples to be inoculated of God so that their sons might be heroes, which meant, generally, wholesale butchers. Julius Caesar was a miraculous conception—indeed, they were common all over the world. How many miraculous-birth stories is a Christian now expected to believe?

In the days of the formation of the Christian religion, disease meant the possession of human beings by devils. Christ cured a sick man by casting out the devils, who ran into the swine, and the swine ran into the sea. Is there any question but what that was simply the attitude and belief of a primitive people? Does anyone believe that sickness means the possession of the body by devils, and that the devils must be cast out of the human being that he may be cured? Does anyone believe that a dead person can come to life? The miracles recorded in the Bible are not the only instances of dead men coming to life. All over the world one finds testimony of such miracles; miracles which no person is expected to believe, unless it is his kind of a miracle. Still at Lourdes today, and all over the present world, from New York to Los Angeles and up and down the lands, people believe in miraculous occurrences, and even in the return of the dead. Superstition is everywhere prevalent in the world. It has been so from the beginning, and most likely will be so unto the end.

The reasons for agnosticism are abundant and compelling. Fantastic and foolish and impossible consequences are freely claimed for the belief in religion. All the civilization of any period is put down as a result of religion. All the cruelty and error and ignorance of the period has no relation to religion. The truth is that the origin of what we call civilization is not due to religion but to skepticism. So long as men accepted miracles without question, so long as they believed in original sin and the road to salvation, so long as they believed in a hell where man would be kept for eternity on account of Eve, there was no reason whatever for civilization: life was short, and eternity was long, and the business of life was preparation for eternity.

When every event was a miracle, when there was no order or system or law, there was no occasion for studying any subject, or being interested in anything excepting a religion which took care of the soul. As man doubted the primitive conceptions about religion, and no longer accepted the literal, miraculous teachings of ancient books, he set himself to understand nature. We no longer cure disease by casting out devils. Since that time, men have studied the human body, have built hospitals and treated illness in a scientific way. Science is responsible for the building of railroads and bridges, of steamships, of telegraph lines, of cities, towns, large buildings and small, plumbing and sanitation, of the food supply, and the countless thousands of useful things that we now deem necessary to life. Without skepticism and doubt, none of these things could have been given to the world.

The fear of God is not the beginning of wisdom. The fear of God is the death of wisdom. Skepticism and doubt lead to study and investigation, and investigation is the beginning of wisdom.

The modern world is the child of doubt and inquiry, as the ancient world was the child of fear and faith.

W. T. Stace

Walter Terence Stace (1886–1967) was born in England and educated at Trinity College, Dublin University. He joined the British Civil Service in 1910 and served in Ceylon for twenty-two years. In 1932 he accepted a position teaching philosophy at Princeton University, where he taught until his retirement in 1955. His writings include The Philosophy of Hegel *(1924),* The Destiny of Western Man *(1942),* Religion and the Modern Mind *(1952),* The Teachings of the Mystics *(1961), and* Mysticism and Philosophy *(1961). The article we reprint below originally appeared in* The Atlantic Monthly, *September 1948.*

MAN AGAINST DARKNESS

[1]

The Catholic bishops of America recently issued a statement in which they said that the chaotic and bewildered state of the modern world is due to man's loss of faith, his abandonment of God and religion. For my part I believe in no religion at all. Yet I entirely agree with the bishops. It is no doubt an oversimplification to speak of *the* cause of so complex a state of affairs as the tortured condition of the world today. Its causes are doubtless multitudinous. Yet allowing for some element of oversimplification, I say that the bishops' assertion is substantially true.

M. Jean-Paul Sartre, the French existentialist philosopher, labels himself an atheist. Yet his views seem to me plainly to support the statement of the bishops. So long as there was believed to be a God in the sky, he says, men could regard him as the source of their moral ideals. The universe, created and governed by a fatherly God, was a friendly habitation for man. We could be sure that, however great the evil in the world, good in the end would triumph and the forces of evil would be routed. With the disappearance of God from the sky all this has changed. Since the world is not ruled by a spiritual being, but rather by blind forces, there cannot be any ideals, moral or otherwise, in the universe outside us. Our ideals, therefore, must proceed only from our own minds; they are our own inventions. Thus the world which surrounds us is nothing but an immense spiritual emptiness. It is a dead universe. We do not live in a universe which is on the side of our values. It is completely indifferent to them.

Years ago Mr. Bertrand Russell, in his essay *A Free Man's Worship*, said much the same thing.

> Such in outline, but even more purposeless, more void of meaning, is the world which Science presents for our belief. Amid such a world, if anywhere, our ideals henceforward must find a home. . . . Blind to good and evil, reckless of destruction, omnipotent matter rolls on its relentless way; for man, condemned today to lose his dearest, tomorrow himself to pass through the gate of darkness, it remains only to cherish, ere yet the blow falls, the lofty thoughts that ennoble his little day; . . . to worship at the shrine his own hands have built; . . . to sustain alone, a weary but unyielding Atlas, the world that his own ideals have fashioned despite the trampling march of unconscious power.

It is true that Mr. Russell's personal attitude to the disappearance of religion is quite different from either that of M. Sartre or the bishops or myself. The bishops think it a calamity. So do I. M. Sartre finds it "very distressing." And he berates as shallow the attitude of those who think that without God the world can go on just the same as before, as if nothing had happened. This creates for mankind, he thinks, a terrible crisis. And in this I agree with him. Mr. Russell, on the other hand, seems to believe that religion has done more harm than good in the world, and that its disappearance will be a blessing. But his picture of the world, and of the modern mind, is the same as that of M. Sartre. He stresses the *purposelessness* of the universe, the facts that man's ideals are his own creations, that the universe out-

624

side him in no way supports them, that man is alone and friendless in the world.

Mr. Russell notes that it is science which has produced this situation. There is no doubt that this is correct. But the way in which it has come about is not generally understood. There is a popular belief that some particular scientific discoveries or theories, such as the Darwinian theory of evolution, or the views of geologists about the age of the earth, or a series of such discoveries, have done the damage. It would be foolish to deny that these discoveries have had a great effect in undermining religious dogmas. But this account does not at all go to the root of the matter. Religion can probably outlive any scientific discoveries which could be made. It can accommodate itself to them. The root cause of the decay of faith has not been any particular discovery of science, but rather the general spirit of science and certain basic assumptions upon which modern science, from the seventeenth century onwards, has proceeded.

[II]

It was Galileo and Newton—notwithstanding that Newton himself was a deeply religious man—who destroyed the old comfortable picture of a friendly universe governed by spiritual values. And this was effected, not by Newton's discovery of the law of gravitation nor by any of Galileo's brilliant investigations, but by the general picture of the world which these men and others of their time made the basis of the science, not only of their own day, but of all succeeding generations down to the present. That is why the century immediately following Newton, the eighteenth century, was notoriously an age of religious skepticism. Skepticism did not have to wait for the discoveries of Darwin and the geologists in the nineteenth century. It flooded the world immediately after the age of the rise of science.

Neither the Copernican hypothesis nor any of Newton's or Galileo's particular discoveries were the real causes. Religious faith might well have accommodated itself to the new astronomy. The real turning point between the medieval age of faith and the modern age of unfaith came when the scientists of the seventeenth century turned their backs upon what used to be called "final causes." The final cause of a thing or event meant the purpose which it was supposed to serve in the universe, its cosmic purpose. What lay back of this was the presupposition that there is a cosmic order or plan and that everything which exists could in the last analysis be explained in terms of its place in this cosmic plan, that is, in terms of its purpose.

Plato and Aristotle believed this, and so did the whole medieval Christian world. For instance, if it were true that the sun and the moon were created and exist for the purpose of giving light to man, then this fact would explain why the sun and the moon exist. We might not be able to discover the purpose of everything, but everything must have a purpose. Belief in final causes thus amounted to a belief that the world is governed by purposes, presumably the purposes of some overruling mind. This belief was not the invention of Christianity. It was basic to the whole of Western civilization, whether in the ancient pagan world or in Christendom, from the time of Socrates to the rise of science in the seventeenth century.

The founders of modern science—for instance, Galileo, Kepler, and Newton—were mostly pious men who did not doubt God's purposes. Nevertheless they took the revolutionary step of consciously and deliberately expelling the idea of purpose as controlling nature from their new science of nature. They did this on the ground that inquiry into purposes is useless for what science aims at: namely, the prediction and control of events. To predict an eclipse, what you have to know is not its purpose but its causes. Hence science from the seventeenth century onwards became exclusively an inquiry into causes. The conception of purpose in the world was ignored and frowned on. This, though silent and almost unnoticed, was the greatest revolution in human history, far outweighing in importance any of the political revolutions whose thunder has reverberated through the world.

For it came about in this way that for the past three hundred years there has been growing up in men's minds, dominated as they are by science, a new imaginative picture of the world. The world, according to this new picture, is purposeless, senseless, meaningless. Nature is nothing but matter in motion. The motions of matter are governed, not by any purpose, but by blind forces and laws. Nature on this view, says Whitehead—to whose writings I am indebted in this part of my paper—is "merely the hurrying of material, endlessly, meaninglessly." You can draw a sharp line across the history of Europe dividing it into two epochs of very unequal length. The line passes through the lifetime of Galileo. European man before Galileo—whether ancient pagan or more recent Christian—thought of the world as controlled by plan and purpose. After Galileo European man thinks of it as utterly purposeless. This is the great revolution of which I spoke.

It is this which has killed religion. Religion could survive the discoveries that the sun, not the earth, is the center; that men are descended from simian ancestors; that the earth is hundreds of millions of years old. These discoveries may render out of date some of the details of older theological dogmas, may force their restatement in new intellectual frameworks. But they do not touch the essence of the religious vision itself, which is the faith that there is plan and purpose in the world, that the world is a moral order, that in the end all things are for the best. This faith may express itself through many different intellectual dogmas, those of Christianity, of Hinduism, of Islam. All and any of these intellectual dogmas may be destroyed without destroying the essential religious spirit. But that spirit cannot survive destruction of belief in a plan and purpose of the world, for that is the very heart of it. Religion can get on with any sort of astronomy, geology, biology, physics. But it cannot get on with a purposeless and meaningless universe.

If the scheme of things is purposeless and meaningless, then the life of man is purposeless and meaningless too. Everything is futile, all effort is in the end worthless. A man may, of course, still pursue disconnected ends, money, fame, art, science, and may gain pleasure from them. But his life is hollow at the center. Hence the dissatisfied, disillusioned, restless, spirit of modern man.

The picture of a meaningless world, and a meaningless human life, is, I think, the basic theme of much modern art and literature. Certainly it is the basic theme of modern philosophy. According to the most characteristic philosophies of the modern period from Hume in the eighteenth century to the so-called positivists of today, the world is just what it is, and that is the end of all inquiry. There is no reason for its being what it is. Everything might just as well have been quite different, and there would have been no reason for that either. When you have stated what things are, what things the world contains, there is nothing more which could be said, even by an omniscient being. To ask any question about *why* things are thus, or what purpose their being serves, is to ask a senseless question, because they serve no purpose at all. For instance, there is for modern philosophy no such thing as the ancient problem of evil. For this once famous question presupposes that pain and misery, though they seem so inexplicable and irrational to us, must ultimately subserve some rational purpose, must have their places in the cosmic plan. But this is nonsense. There is no such overruling rationality in the universe. Belief in the ultimate irrationality of everything is the quintessence of what is called the modern mind.

It is true that, parallel with these philosophies which are typical of the modern mind, preaching the meaninglessness of the world, there has run a line of idealistic philosophies whose contention is that the world is after all spiritual in nature and that moral ideals and values are inherent in its structure. But most of these idealisms were simply philosophical expressions of romanticism, which was itself no more than an unsuccessful counterattack of the religious against the scientific view of things. They perished, along with romanticism in literature and art, about the beginning of the present century, though of course they still have a few adherents.

627

At the bottom these idealistic systems of thought were rationalizations of man's wishful thinking. They were born of the refusal of men to admit the cosmic darkness. They were comforting illusions within the warm glow of which the more tender-minded intellectuals sought to shelter themselves from the icy winds of the universe. They lasted a little while. But they are shattered now, and we return once more to the vision of a purposeless world.

[III]

Along with the ruin of the religious vision there went the ruin of moral principles and indeed of all values. If there is a cosmic purpose, if there is in the nature of things a drive towards goodness, then our moral systems will derive their validity from this. But if our moral rules do not proceed from something outside us in the nature of the universe—whether we say it is God or simply the universe itself—then they must be our own inventions. Thus it came to be believed that moral rules must be merely an expression of our own likes and dislikes. But likes and dislikes are notoriously variable. What pleases one man, people, or culture displeases another. Therefore morals are wholly relative.

This obvious conclusion from the idea of a purposeless world made its appearance in Europe immediately after the rise of science, for instance in the philosophy of Hobbes. Hobbes saw at once that if there is no purpose in the world there are no values either. "Good and evil," he writes, "are names that signify our appetites and aversions; which in different tempers, customs, and doctrines of men are different. . . . Every man calleth that which pleaseth him, good; and that which displeaseth him, evil."

This doctrine of the relativity of morals, though it has recently received an impetus from the studies of anthropologists, was thus really implicit in the whole scientific mentality. It is disastrous for morals because it destroys their entire traditional foundation. That is why philosophers who see the danger signals, from the time at least of Kant, have been trying to give to morals a new foundation, that is, a secular or nonreligious foundation. This attempt may very well be intellectually successful. Such a foundation, independent of the religious view of the world, might well be found. But the question is whether it can ever be a *practical* success, that is, whether apart from its logical validity and its influence with intellectuals, it can ever replace among the masses of men the lost religious foundation. On that question hangs perhaps the future of civilization. But meanwhile disaster is overtaking us.

The widespread belief in "ethical relativity" among philosophers, psychologists, ethnologists, and sociologists is the theoretical counterpart of the repudiation of principle which we see all around us, especially in international affairs, the field in which morals have always had the weakest foothold. No one any longer effectively believes in moral principles except as the private prejudices either of individual men or of nations or cultures. This is the inevitable consequence of the doctrine of ethical relativity, which in turn is the inevitable consequence of believing in a purposeless world.

Another characteristic of our spiritual state is loss of belief in the freedom of the will. This also is a fruit of the scientific spirit, though not of any particular scientific discovery. Science has been built up on the basis of determinism, which is the belief that every event is completely determined by a chain of causes and is therefore theoretically predictable beforehand. It is true that recent physics seems to challenge this. But so far as its practical consequences are concerned, the damage has long ago been done. A man's actions, it was argued, are as much events in the natural world as is an eclipse of the sun. It follows that men's actions are as theoretically predictable as an eclipse. But if it is certain now that John Smith will murder Joseph Jones at 2.15 P.M. on January 1, 1963, what possible meaning can it have to say that when that time comes John Smith will be *free* to choose whether he will commit the murder or not? And if he is not free, how can he be held responsible?

It is true that the whole of this argument can be shown by a competent philosopher to be a tissue of fallacies—or at least I claim that it can. But the point is that the analysis required to show this is much too subtle to be understood by the average entirely unphilosophical man. Because of this, the argument against free will is generally swallowed whole by the unphilosophical. Hence the thought that man is not free, that he is the helpless plaything of forces over which he has no control, has deeply penetrated the modern mind. We hear of economic determinism, cultural determinism, historical determinism. We are not responsible for what we do because our glands control us, or because we are the products of environment or heredity. Not moral self-control, but the doctor, the psychiatrist, the educationist, must save us from doing evil. Pills and injections in the future are to do what Christ and the prophets have failed to do. Of course I do not mean to deny that doctors and educationists can and must help. And I do not mean in any way to belittle their efforts. But I do wish to draw attention to the weakening of moral controls, the greater or less repudiation of personal responsibility which, in the popular thinking of the day, result from these tendencies of thought.

[IV]

What, then, is to be done? Where are we to look for salvation from the evils of our time? All the remedies I have seen suggested so far are, in my opinion, useless. Let us look at some of them.

Philosophers and intellectuals generally can, I believe, genuinely do something to help. But it is extremely little. What philosophers can do is to show that neither the relativity of morals nor the denial of free will really follows from the grounds which have been supposed to support them. They can also try to discover a genuine secular basis for morals to replace the religious basis which has disappeared. Some of us are trying to do these things. But in the first place philosophers unfortunately are not agreed about these matters, and their disputes are utterly confusing to the non-philosophers. And in the second place their influence is practically negligible because their analyses necessarily take place on a level on which the masses are totally unable to follow them.

The bishops, of course, propose as remedy a return to belief in God and in the doctrines of the Christian religion. Others think that a new religion is what is needed. Those who make these proposals fail to realize that the crisis in man's spiritual condition is something unique in history for which there is no sort of analogy in the past. They are thinking perhaps of the collapse of the ancient Greek and Roman religions. The vacuum then created was easily filled by Christianity, and it might have been filled by Mithraism if Christianity had not appeared. By analogy they think that Christianity might now be replaced by a new religion, or even that Christianity itself, if revivified, might bring back health to men's lives.

But I believe that there is no analogy at all between our present state and that of the European peoples at the time of the fall of paganism. Men had at that time lost their belief only in particular dogmas, particular embodiments of the religious view of the world. It had no doubt become incredible that Zeus and the other gods were living on the top of Mount Olympus. You could go to the top and find no trace of them. But the imaginative picture of a world governed by purpose, a world driving towards the good—which is the inner spirit of religion—had at that time received no serious shock. It had merely to re-embody itself in new dogmas, those of Christianity or some other religion. Religion itself was not dead in the world, only a particular form of it.

But now the situation is quite different. It is not merely that particular dogmas, like that of the virgin birth, are unacceptable to the modern mind. That is true, but it constitutes a very superficial diagnosis of the present situation of religion. Modern skepticism is of a wholly different order from that of the intellectuals of the ancient world. It has attacked and destroyed not merely the outward forms of the religious spirit, its particularized dogmas, but the very essence of that spirit itself, belief in a meaningful and purposeful world. For the founding of a new religion a new Jesus Christ or Buddha would have to appear, in itself a most unlikely event and one for which in any case we cannot afford to sit and wait. But even if a new prophet and a new religion did appear, we may predict that they would fail in the modern world. No one for long would believe in them, for modern men have lost the vision, basic to all religion, of an ordered plan and purpose of the world. They have before their minds the picture of a purposeless universe, and such a world-picture must be fatal to any religion at all, not merely to Christianity.

We must not be misled by occasional appearances of a revival of the religious spirit. Men, we are told, in their disgust and disillusionment at the emptiness of their lives, are turning once more to religion, or are searching for a new message. It may be so. We must expect such wistful yearnings of the spirit. We must expect men to wish back again the light that is gone, and to try to bring it back. But however they may wish and try, the light will not shine again,—not at least in the civilization to which we belong.

Another remedy commonly proposed is that we should turn to science itself, or the scientific spirit, for our salvation. Mr. Russell and Professor Dewey both make this proposal, though in somewhat different ways. Professor Dewey seems to believe that discoveries in sociology, the application of scientific method to social and political problems, will rescue us. This seems to me to be utterly naïve. It is not likely that science, which is basically the cause of our spiritual troubles, is likely also to produce the cure for them. Also it lies in the nature of science that, though it can teach us the best means for achieving our ends, it can never tell us what ends to pursue. It cannot give us any ideals. And our trouble is about ideals and ends, not about the means for reaching them.

[V]

No civilization can live without ideals, or to put it in another way, without a firm faith in moral ideas. Our ideals and moral ideas have in the past been rooted in religion. But the religious basis of our ideals has been undermined, and the superstructure of ideals is plainly tottering. None of the commonly suggested remedies on examination seems likely to succeed. It would therefore look as if the early death of our civilization were inevitable.

Of course we know that it is perfectly possible for individual men, very highly educated men, philosophers, scientists, intellectuals in general, to live moral lives without any religious convictions. But the question is whether a whole civilization, a whole family of peoples, composed almost entirely of relatively uneducated men and women, can do this.

It follows, of course, that if we could make the vast majority of men as highly educated as the very few are now, we might save the situation. And we are already moving slowly in that direction through the techniques of mass education. But the critical question seems to concern the time-lag. Perhaps in a few hundred years most of the population will, at the present rate, be sufficiently highly educated and civilized to combine high ideals with an absence of religion. But long before we reach any such stage, the collapse of our civilization may have come about. How are we to live through the intervening period?

I am sure that the first thing we have to do is to face the truth, however bleak it may be, and then next we have to learn to live with it. Let me say a word about each of these two points. What I am urging as regards the first is complete honesty. Those who wish to resurrect Christian dogmas are not, of course, consciously dishonest. But they have that kind of unconscious dishonesty which consists in lulling oneself with opiates and dreams. Those who talk of a new religion are merely hoping for a new opiate. Both alike refuse to face the truth that there is, in the universe outside man, no spirituality, no regard for values, no friend in the sky, no help or comfort for man of any sort. To be perfectly honest in the admission of this fact, not to seek shelter in new or old illusions, not to indulge in wishful dreams about this matter, this is the first thing we shall have to do.

I do not urge this course out of any special regard for the sanctity of truth in the abstract. It is not self-evident to me that truth is the supreme value to which all else must be sacrificed. Might not the discoverer of a truth which would be fatal to mankind be justified in suppressing it, even in teaching men a falsehood? Is truth more valuable than goodness and beauty and happiness? To think so is to invent yet another absolute, another religious delusion in which Truth with a capital T is substituted for God. The reason why we must now boldly and honestly face the truth that the universe is nonspiritual and indifferent to goodness, beauty, happiness, or truth is not that it would be wicked to suppress it, but simply that it is too late to do so, so that in the end we cannot do anything else but face it. Yet we stand on the brink, dreading the icy plunge. We need courage. We need honesty.

Now about the other point, the necessity of learning to live with the truth. This means learning to live virtuously and happily, or at least

632

contentedly, without illusions. And this is going to be extremely difficult because what we have not begun dimly to perceive is that human life in the past, or at least human happiness, has almost wholly depended upon illusions. It has been said that man lives by truth, and that the truth will make us free. Nearly the opposite seems to me to be the case. Mankind has managed to live only by means of lies, and the truth may very well destroy us. If one were a Bergsonian one might believe that nature deliberately puts illusions into our souls in order to induce us to go on living.

The illusions by which men have lived seem to be of two kinds. First, there is what one may perhaps call the Great Illusion—I mean the religious illusion that the universe is moral and good, that it follows a wise and noble plan, that it is gradually generating some supreme value, that goodness is bound to triumph in it. Secondly, there is a whole host of minor illusions on which human happiness nourishes itself. How much of human happiness notoriously comes from the illusions of the lover about his beloved? Then again we work and strive because of the illusions connected with fame, glory, power, or money. Banners of all kinds, flags, emblems, insignia, ceremonials, and rituals are invariably symbols of some illusion or other. The British Empire, the connection between mother country and dominions, is partly kept going by illusions surrounding the notion of kingship. Or think of the vast amount of human happiness which is derived from the illusion of supposing that if some nonsense syllable, such as "sir" or "count" or "lord" is pronounced in conjunction with our names, we belong to a superior order of people.

There is plenty of evidence that human happiness is almost wholly based upon illusions of one kind or another. But the scientific spirit, or the spirit of truth, is the enemy of illusions and therefore the enemy of human happiness. That is why it is going to be so difficult to live with the truth.

There is no reason why we should have to give up the host of minor illusions which render life supportable. There is no reason why the lover should be scientific about the loved one. Even the illusions of fame and glory may persist. But without the Great Illusion, the illusion of a good, kindly, and purposeful universe, we shall *have* to learn to live. And to ask this is really no more than to ask that we become genuinely civilized beings and not merely sham civilized beings.

I can best explain the difference by a reminiscence. I remember a fellow student in my college days, an ardent Christian, who told me that if he did not believe in a future life, in heaven and hell, he would rape, murder, steal, and be a drunkard. That is what I call being a sham civilized being. On the other hand, not only could a Huxley, a John Stuart Mill, a David Hume, live great and fine lives without any religion, but a great many others of us, quite obscure persons, can at least live decent lives without it.

To be genuinely civilized means to be able to walk straightly and to live honorably without the props and crutches of one or another of the childish dreams which have so far supported men. That such a life is likely to be ecstatically happy I will not claim. But that it can be lived in quiet content, accepting resignedly what cannot be helped, not expecting the impossible, and thankful for small mercies, this I would maintain. That it would be difficult for men in general to learn this lesson I do not deny. But that it will be impossible I would not admit since so many have learned it already.

Man has not yet grown up. He is not adult. Like a child he cries for the moon and lives in a world of fantasies. And the race as a whole has perhaps reached the great crisis of its life. Can it grow up as a race in the same sense as individual men grow up? Can man put away childish things and adolescent dreams? Can he grasp the real world as it actually is, stark and bleak, without its romantic or religious halo, and still retain his ideals, striving for great ends and noble achievements? If he can, all may yet be well. If he cannot, he will probably sink back into the savagery and brutality from which he came, taking a humble place once more among the lower animals.

Paul Tillich

A profound and compassionate thinker and one of the great contemporary theologians, Paul Tillich (1886–1965) was born and educated in Germany and was well on his way to a distinguished academic career when he was dismissed from his post as Professor of Philosophy at the University of Frankfurt because of his outspoken criticism of the Nazi movement. In 1933, at the age of forty-seven, he emigrated to the United States at the invitation of Union Theological Seminary in New York, where he taught until 1954. That year he was appointed to the Divinity School Faculty at Harvard, and in 1962 he was named the first Duveen Professor of Theology at the University of Chicago. His books include The Shaking of the Foundations *(1948) and* The New Being *(1955), two volumes of sermons;* The Protestant Era *(1948);* The Courage to Be *(1952);* Dynamics of Faith *(1957); and* Ultimate Concern: Tillich in Dialogue *(ed. D. M. Brown,*

1965), based on tape recordings made during a seminar in the spring of 1964.

Paul Tillich thought of God not as a Being, but as our ultimate concern, the ultimate personal depth and ground of all being. It is this "lost" dimension of depth that he discusses here in an essay first printed in the June 14, 1958, Saturday Evening Post.

THE LOST DIMENSION IN RELIGION

Every observer of our Western civilization is aware of the fact that something has happened to religion. It especially strikes the observer of the American scene. Everywhere he finds symptoms of what one has called religious revival, or more modestly, the revival of interest in religion. He finds them in the churches with their rapidly increasing membership. He finds them in the mushroomlike growth of sects. He finds them on college campuses and in the theological faculties of universities. Most conspicuously, he finds them in the tremendous success of men like Billy Graham and Norman Vincent Peale, who attract masses of people Sunday after Sunday, meeting after meeting. The facts cannot be denied, but how should they be interpreted? It is my intention to show that these facts must be seen as expressions of the predicament of Western man in the second half of the twentieth century. But I would even go a step further. I believe that the predicament of man in our period gives us also an important insight into the predicament of man generally—at all times and in all parts of the earth.

There are many analyses of man and society in our time. Most of them show important traits in the picture, but few of them succeed in giving a general key to our present situation. Although it is not easy to find such a key, I shall attempt it and, in so doing, will make an assertion which may be somewhat mystifying at first hearing. The decisive element in the predicament of Western man in our period is his loss of the dimension of depth. Of course, "dimension of depth" is a metaphor. It is taken from the spatial realm and applied to man's spiritual life. What does it mean?

It means that man has lost an answer to the question: What is the meaning of life? Where do we come from, where do we go to? What shall we do, what should we become in the short stretch between birth and death? Such questions are not answered or even asked if the "dimension of depth" is lost. And this is precisely what has happened to man in our period of history. He has lost the courage to ask such questions with an infinite seriousness—as former generations did—and he has lost the courage to receive answers to these questions, wherever they may come from.

I suggest that we call the dimension of depth the religious dimension in man's nature. Being religious means asking passionately the question of the meaning of our existence and being willing to receive answers, even if the answers hurt. Such an idea of religion makes religion universally human, but it certainly differs from what is usually called religion. It does not describe religion as the belief in the existence of gods or one God, and as a set of activities and institutions for the sake of relating oneself to these beings in thought, devotion and obedience. No one can deny that the religions which have appeared in history are religions in this sense. Nevertheless, religion in its innermost nature is more than religion in this narrower sense. It is the state of being concerned about one's own being and being universally.

There are many people who are ultimately concerned in this way who feel far removed, however, from religion in the narrower sense, and therefore from every historical religion. It often happens that such people take the question of the meaning of their life infinitely seriously and reject any historical religion just for this reason. They feel that the concrete religions fail to express their profound concern adequately. They are religious while rejecting the religions. It is this experience which forces us to distinguish the meaning of religion as living in the dimension of depth from particular expressions of one's ultimate concern in the symbols and institutions of a concrete religion. If we now turn to the concrete analysis of the religious situation of our time, it is obvious that our key must be the basic meaning of religion and not any particular religion, not even Christianity. What does this key disclose about the predicament of man in our period?

If we define religion as the state of being grasped by an infinite concern we must say: Man in our time has lost such infinite concern. And the resurgence of religion is nothing but a desperate and mostly futile attempt to regain what has been lost.

How did the dimension of depth become lost? Like any important event, it has many causes, but certainly not the one which one hears often mentioned from ministers' pulpits and evangelists' platforms, namely that a widespread impiety of modern man is responsible. Modern man is neither more pious nor more impious than man in any other period. The loss of the dimension of depth is caused by the relation of man to his world and to himself in our period, the period in which nature is being subjected scientifically and technically to the control of man. In this period, life in the dimension of depth

636

is replaced by life in the horizontal dimension. The driving forces of the industrial society of which we are a part go ahead horizontally and not vertically. In popular terms this is expressed in phrases like "better and better," "bigger and bigger," "more and more." One should not disparage the feeling which lies behind such speech. Man is right in feeling that he is able to know and transform the world he encounters without a foreseeable limit. He can go ahead in all directions without a definite boundary.

A most expressive symbol of this attitude of going ahead in the horizontal dimension is the breaking through of the space which is controlled by the gravitational power of the earth into the world-space. It is interesting that one calls this world-space simply "space" and speaks, for instance, of space travel, as if every trip were not travel into space. Perhaps one feels that the true nature of space has been discovered only through our entering into indefinite world-space. In any case, the predominance of the horizontal dimension over the dimension of depth has been immensely increased by the opening up of the space beyond the space of the earth.

If we now ask what does man do and seek if he goes ahead in the horizontal dimension, the answer is difficult. Sometimes one is inclined to say that the mere movement ahead without an end, the intoxication with speeding forward without limits, is what satisfies him. But this answer is by no means sufficient. For on his way into space and time man changes the world he encounters. And the changes made by him change himself. He transforms everything he encounters into a tool; and in doing so he himself becomes a tool. But if he asks, a tool for what, there is no answer.

One does not need to look far beyond everyone's daily experience in order to find examples to describe this predicament. Indeed our daily life in office and home, in cars and airplanes, at parties and conferences, while reading magazines and watching television, while looking at advertisements and hearing radio, are in themselves continuous examples of a life which has lost the dimension of depth. It runs ahead, every moment is filled with something which must be done or seen or said or planned. But no one can experience depth without stopping and becoming aware of himself. Only if he has moments in which he does not care about what comes next can he experience the meaning of this moment here and now and ask himself about the meaning of his life. As long as the preliminary, transitory concerns are not silenced, no matter how interesting and valuable and important they may be, the voice of the ultimate concern cannot be heard. This is the deepest root of the loss of the dimension of depth in our period —the loss of religion in its basic and universal meaning.

If the dimension of depth is lost, the symbols in which life in this

637

dimension has expressed itself must also disappear. I am speaking of the great symbols of the historical religions in our Western world, of Judaism and Christianity. The reason that the religious symbols became lost is not primarily scientific criticism, but it is a complete misunderstanding of their meaning; and only because of this misunderstanding was scientific critique able, and even justified, in attacking them. The first step toward the non-religion of the Western world was made by religion itself. When it defended its great symbols, not as symbols, but as literal stories, it had already lost the battle. In doing so the theologians (and today many religious laymen) helped to transfer the powerful expressions of the dimension of depth into objects or happenings on the horizontal plane. There the symbols lose their power and meaning and become an easy prey to physical, biological and historical attack.

If the symbol of creation which points to the divine ground of everything is transferred to the horizontal plane, it becomes a story of events in a removed past for which there is no evidence, but which contradicts every piece of scientific evidence. If the symbol of the Fall of Man, which points to the tragic estrangement of man and his world from their true being is transferred to the horizontal plane, it becomes a story of a human couple a few thousand years ago in what is now present-day Iraq. One of the most profound psychological descriptions of the general human predicament becomes an absurdity on the horizontal plane. If the symbols of the Saviour and the salvation through Him which point to the healing power in history and personal life are transferred to the horizontal plane, they become stories of a half-divine being coming from a heavenly place and returning to it. Obviously, in this form, they have no meaning whatsoever for people whose view of the universe is determined by scientific astronomy.

If the idea of God (and the symbols applied to Him) which expresses man's ultimate concern is transferred to the horizontal plane, God becomes a being among others whose existence or nonexistence is a matter of inquiry. Nothing, perhaps, is more symptomatic of the loss of the dimension of depth than the permanent discussion about the existence or nonexistence of God—a discussion in which both sides are equally wrong, because the discussion itself is wrong and possible only after the loss of the dimension of depth.

When in this way man has deprived himself of the dimension of depth and the symbols expressing it, he then becomes a part of the horizontal plane. He loses his self and becomes a thing among things. He becomes an element in the process of manipulated production and manipulated consumption. This is now a matter of public knowledge. We have become aware of the degree to which everyone in our social structure is managed, even if one knows it and even if one belongs himself to the managing group. The influence of the gang mentality on adolescents, of the corporation's demands on the executives, of the conditioning of everyone by public communication, by propaganda and advertising under the guidance of motivation research, et cetera, have all been described in many books and articles.

Under these pressures, man can hardly escape the fate of becoming a thing among the things he produces, a bundle of conditioned reflexes without a free, deciding and responsible self. The immense mechanism, set up by man to produce objects for his use, transforms man himself into an object used by the same mechanism of production and consumption.

But man has not ceased to be man. He resists this fate anxiously, desperately, courageously. He asks the question, for what? And he realizes that there is no answer. He becomes aware of the emptiness which is covered by the continuous movement ahead and the production of means for ends which become means again without an ultimate end. Without knowing what has happened to him, he feels that he has lost the meaning of life, the dimension of depth.

Out of this awareness the religious question arises and religious answers are received or rejected. Therefore, in order to describe the contemporary attitude toward religion, we must first point to the places where the awareness of the predicament of Western man in our period is most sharply expressed. These places are the great art, literature and, partly, at least, the philosophy of our time. It is both the subject matter and the style of these creations which show the passionate and often tragic struggle about the meaning of life in a period in which man has lost the dimension of depth. This art, literature, philosophy is not religious in the narrower sense of the word; but it asks the religious question more radically and more profoundly than most directly religious expressions of our time.

It is the religious question which is asked when the novelist describes a man who tries in vain to reach the only place which could solve the problem of his life, or a man who disintegrates under the memory of a guilt which persecutes him, or a man who never had a real self and is pushed by his fate without resistance to death, or a man who experiences a profound disgust of everything he encounters.

It is the religious question which is asked when the poet opens up the horror and the fascination of the demonic regions of his soul, or if he leads us into the deserts and empty places of our being, or if he shows the physical and moral mud under the surface of life, or if he sings the song of transitoriness, giving words to the ever-present anxiety of our hearts.

It is the religious question which is asked when the playwright shows

639

the illusion of a life in a ridiculous symbol, or if he lets the emptiness of a life's work end in self-destruction, or if he confronts us with the inescapable bondage to mutual hate and guilt, or if he leads us into the dark cellar of lost hopes and slow disintegration.

It is the religious question which is asked when the painter breaks the visible surface into pieces, then reunites them into a great picture which has little similarity with the world at which we normally look, but which expresses our anxiety and our courage to face reality.

It is the religious question which is asked when the architect, in creating office buildings or churches, removes the trimmings taken over from past styles because they cannot be considered an honest expression of our own period. He prefers the seeming poverty of a purpose-determined style to the deceptive richness of imitated styles of the past. He knows that he gives no final answer, but he does give an honest answer.

The philosophy of our time shows the same hiddenly religious traits. It is divided into two main schools of thought, the analytic and the existentialist. The former tries to analyze logical and linguistic forms which are always used and which underlie all scientific research. One may compare them with the painters who dissolve the natural forms of bodies into cubes, planes and lines; or with those architects who want the structural "bones" of their buildings to be conspicuously visible and not hidden by covering features. This self-restriction produces the almost monastic poverty and seriousness of this philosophy. It is religious—without any contact with religion in its method—by exercising the humility of "learned ignorance."

In contrast to this school the existentialist philosophers have much to say about the problems of human existence. They bring into rational concepts what the writers and poets, the painters and architects, are expressing in their particular material. What they express is the human predicament in time and space, in anxiety and guilt and the feeling of meaninglessness. From Pascal in the seventeenth century to Heidegger and Sartre in our time, philosophers have emphasized the contrast between human dignity and human misery. And by doing so, they have raised the religious question. Some have tried to answer the question they have asked. But if they did so, they turned back to past traditions and offered to our time that which does not fit our time. Is it possible for our time to receive answers which are born out of our time?

Answers given today are in danger of strengthening the present situation and with it the questions to which they are supposed to be the answers. This refers to some of the previously mentioned major representatives of the so-called resurgence of religion, as for instance the evangelist Billy Graham and the counseling and healing minister, Norman Vincent Peale. Against the validity of the answers given by the former, one must say that, in spite of his personal integrity, his propagandistic methods and his primitive theological fundamentalism fall short of what is needed to give an answer to the religious question of our period. In spite of all his seriousness, he does not take the radical questions of our period seriously.

The effect that Norman Peale has on large groups of people is rooted in the fact that he confirms the situation which he is supposed to help overcome. He heals people with the purpose of making them fit again for the demands of the competitive and conformist society in which we are living. He helps them to become adapted to the situation which is characterized by the loss of the dimension of depth. Therefore, his advice is valid on this level; but it is the validity of this level that is the true religious question of our time. And this question he neither raises nor answers.

In many cases the increase of church membership and interest in religious activities does not mean much more than the religious consecration of a state of things in which the religious dimension has been lost. It is the desire to participate in activities which are socially strongly approved and give internal and a certain amount of external security. This is not necessarily bad, but it certainly is not an answer to the religious question of our period.

Is there an answer? There is always an answer, but the answer may not be available to us. We may be too deeply steeped in the predicament out of which the question arises to be able to answer it. To acknowledge this is certainly a better way toward a real answer than to bar the way to it by deceptive answers. And it may be that in this attitude the real answer (within available limits) is given. The real answer to the question of how to regain the dimension of depth is not given by increased church membership or church attendance, nor by conversion or healing experiences. But it is given by the awareness that we have lost the decisive dimension of life, the dimension of depth, and that there is no easy way of getting it back. Such awareness is in itself a state of being grasped by that which is symbolized in the term, dimension of depth. He who realizes that he is separated from the ultimate source of meaning shows by this realization that he is not only separated but also reunited. And this is just our situation. What we need above all—and partly have—is the radical realization of our predicament, without trying to cover it up by secular or religious ideologies. The revival of religious interest would be a creative power in our culture if it would develop into a movement of search for the lost dimension of depth.

This does not mean that the traditional religious symbols should be dismissed. They certainly have lost their meaning in the literalistic form into which they have been distorted, thus producing the critical reaction against them. But they have not lost their genuine meaning, namely, of answering the question which is implied in man's very existence in powerful, revealing and saving symbols. If the resurgence of religion would produce a new understanding of the symbols of the past and their relevance for our situation, instead of premature and deceptive answers, it would become a creative factor in our culture and a saving factor for many who live in estrangement, anxiety and despair. The religious answer has always the character of "in spite of." In spite of the loss of dimension of depth, its power is present, and most present in those who are aware of the loss and are striving to regain it with ultimate seriousness.

John A. T. Robinson

John A. T. Robinson was born in England in 1919 and educated at Cambridge University (Doctor of Philosophy, 1946; Doctor of Divinity, 1968). He was admitted to the Church of England as deacon in 1945 and became a priest in 1946. He established his reputation as a New Testament scholar while Fellow and Dean of Clare College, Cambridge, from 1951–1959 and has been a visiting professor at Harvard Union Theological Seminary and Cornell. He was Bishop of Woolwich from 1959 to 1969 and is presently Assistant Bishop of Southwater and Fellow and Dean of Trinity College, Cambridge. In 1963, Dr. Robinson touched off an international debate between radical and traditional interpreters of Christianity with the publication of a book, Honest to God, *in which he challenges the traditional image of God as a supernatural Person. The book brings together in popular form a number of radical ideas current in modern theology, especially those of Dietrich Bonhoeffer, the German pastor hanged by the Nazis, and of Paul Tillich.*

We print below the article in the London Observer *for March 17, 1963, in which Dr. Robinson explains the circumstances leading to publication of* Honest to God. *The principal statements in the ensuing controversy have been collected by*

David L. Edwards in The Honest to God Debate *(1963).*
Among Dr. Robinson's more recent works are Christian Morals
Today *(1964),* But That I Can't Believe *(1967), and*
Exploration into God *(1967).*

OUR IMAGE OF GOD MUST GO

Few people realise that we are in the middle of one of the most exciting theological ferments of the century. Some theologians have
sensed this for years; but now, quite suddenly, new ideas about God
and religion, many of them with disturbing revolutionary implications,
are breaking surface.

If Christianity is to survive it must be relevant to modern secular
man, not just to the dwindling number of the religious. But the
supernaturalist framework within which traditionally it has been
preached is making this increasingly impossible. Men can no longer
credit the existence of "gods," or of a God as a supernatural Person,
such as religion has always posited.

Not infrequently, as I watch or listen to a broadcast discussion between a Christian and a humanist, I catch myself realising that most
of my sympathies are on the humanist's side. This is not in the least
because my faith or commitment is in doubt, but because I instinctively share with him his inability to accept the "religious frame"
within which alone that faith is being offered to him. I feel that as
a secular man he is *right* to rebel against it, and I am increasingly
uncomfortable that "orthodoxy" should be identified with it, when it
is simply an out-moded view of the world.

The new ideas were first put on record by a German pastor in a
Nazi prison in 1944: "Our whole 1,900-year-old Christian preaching
and theology rests upon the 'religious premise' of man. What we call
Christianity has always been a pattern—perhaps a true pattern—of
religion. But if one day it becomes apparent that this *a priori* 'premise'
simply does not exist, but was an historical and temporary form of
human self-expression, i.e., if we reach the stage of being radically
without religion—and I think this is more or less the case already—
what does that mean for 'Christianity'?

"It means that the linchpin is removed from the whole structure of our
Christianity to date."

Those words were written on April 30, 1944. It is a date that may
yet prove a turning-point in the history of Christianity. For on it

Dietrich Bonhoeffer first broached the subject of "religionless Christianity" in a smuggled correspondence with his friend Eberhard Bethge, who subsequently edited his "Letters and Papers from Prison."

Bonhoeffer was a Lutheran pastor of very traditional upbringing. Had he lived, he would now be in his late fifties. From 1933–35 he was in charge of the German congregation in Forest Hill, South London —where the church, rebuilt out of British war-damage money, is now dedicated to his name. In the inner circle of the German Resistance, he was privy to the plot on Hitler's life, and within a year of penning that letter he had been hanged by the S.S., on the eve of liberation by the Americans.

When his letters were first published—a bare 10 years ago—one felt at once that the Church was not ready for what Bonhoeffer was saying. Indeed, it might properly be understood only 100 years hence. But it seemed one of those trickles that must one day split rocks.

The speed with which his ideas have become current coin, is not, I think, the result solely of the quickening pace of communication and change. It is the result of one of those mysteries of human history whereby, apparently without interconnection, similar ideas start bubbling up all over the place at the same time. Without this, I suspect, Bonhoeffer might have remained a voice in the wilderness for decades, like Kierkegaard a century earlier.

Perhaps at this point I may be personal. A year ago I was laid up for three months with a slipped disc. I determined to use the opportunity to allow their head to ideas that had been submerged by pressure of work for some time past. Over the years convictions had been gathering—from my reading and experience—which I knew I couldn't with integrity ignore, however disturbing they might seem.

But I wrote my book shut up in my room. What has astonished me since is the way in which within the last six months similar ideas have broken surface in articles and conversations in the most unlikely places —as far apart as Africa and Texas. However inarticulate one may be, one detects an immediate glance of recognition and what the editor of *Prism* has called "an almost audible gasp of relief" when these things are said openly.

It is not easy to put one's finger on the common factor. I suppose it is *the glad acceptance of secularisation as a God-given fact.* For we of our generation are secular men. And our question, as Christians, is: How can Christ be Lord of a genuinely secular world?

Hitherto, says Bonhoeffer, Christianity has been based on the premise that man is naturally religious: and it has been presented as the best and highest religion. The corollary has been that to the non-religious it has nothing to say. A person had to become religious first—to have,

644

or be induced to have, a religious sense of sin or need for God: then Christ could come to him as the answer.

Modern man has opted for a secular world: he has become increasingly non-religious. The Churches have deplored this as the great defection from God, and the more they write it off, the more this movement has seen itself as anti-Christian.

But, claims Bonhoeffer boldly, the period of religion is over. Man is growing out of it: he is "coming of age." By that he doesn't mean that he is getting better (a prisoner of the Gestapo had few illusions about human nature), but that for good or for ill he is putting the religious world-view behind him as childish and pre-scientific.

Bonhoeffer would accept Freud's analysis of the God of religion as a projection. Till now man has felt the need for a God as a child feels the need for his father. He must be "there" to explain the universe, to protect him in his loneliness, to fill the gaps in his science, to provide the sanction for his morality.

But now man is discovering that he can manage quite happily by himself. He finds no necessity to bring God into his science, his morals, his political speeches. Only in the private world of the individual's psychological need and insecurity—in that last corner of "the sardine-tin of life"—is room apparently left for the God who has been elbowed out of every other sphere. And so the religious evangelist works on men to coerce them at their weakest point into feeling that they cannot get on without the tutelage of God.

But "God is teaching us that we must live as men who can get along very well without him." And this, says Bonhoeffer, is the God Jesus shows us, the God who refuses to be a *Deus ex machina*, who allows himself to be edged out of the world on to the Cross. Our God is the God who forsakes us—only to meet with us on the Emmaus road, if we are really prepared to abandon him as a long-stop and find him not at the boundaries of life where human powers fail, but at the centre, in the secular, as "the 'beyond' in our midst."

Another way of putting this is to say that our whole mental image of God must undergo a revolution. This is nothing new in Christianity. The men of the Bible thought of God as "up there," seated upon a throne in a localised heaven above the earth, and it was this God to whom Jesus "ascended."

But with the development of scientific knowledge, the image of the God "up there" made it harder rather than easier to believe. And so, very boldly, Christians discarded it. I say very boldly, for in order to do so they had to go against the literal language of the Bible.

For it they substituted another mental image—of a God "out there," metaphysically if not literally. Somewhere beyond this universe was a Being, a centre of personal will and purpose, who created it and who sustains it, who loves it and who "visited" it in Jesus Christ. But I need not go on, for this is "our" God. Theism means being convinced that this Being exists: atheism means denying that he does.

But I suspect we have reached the point where this mental image of God is also more of a hindrance than a help. There are many who feel instinctively that the space-age has put paid to belief in God. The theologian may properly think them naïve. But what they are rebelling against is this image of a Being out beyond the range of the farthest rocket and the probe of the largest telescope. They no longer find such an entity credible.

To the religious, the idea of a supreme Being out there may seem as necessary for their thinking as was once the idea of a Being up there. They can hardly even picture God without it. If there wasn't really someone "there," then the atheists would be right.

But any image can become an idol: and I believe that Christians must go through the agonising process in this generation of detaching themselves from this idol. For to twentieth-century man the "old man in the sky" and the whole supernaturalist scheme seem as fanciful as the man in the moon.

Sir Julian Huxley has spent much time in his deeply moving book, "Religion Without Revelation," and in subsequent articles in this paper, dismantling this construction. He constantly echoes Bonhoeffer's sentiments, and I heartily agree with him when he says, "The sense of spiritual relief which comes from rejecting the idea of God as a super-human being is enormous."

For the real question of belief is not the *existence* of God, as *a* person. For God *is* ultimate reality (that's what we mean by the word), and ultimate reality must exist. The only question is what ultimate reality is like. And the Christian affirmation is that reality ultimately, deep down, in the last analysis, is *personal:* the world, incredible as it may seem, is built in such a way that in the end personal values will out.

Professor Bondi, commenting in the B.B.C. television programme, "The Cosmologists," on Sir James Jeans's assertion that "God is a great mathematician," stated quite correctly that what he should have said is "Mathematics is God." Reality, in other words, can finally be reduced to mathematical formulae. What the Christian says is that in, with and under these regularities, and giving ultimate significance to them, is the yet deeper reliability of an utterly personal Love.

That, in the world of the H-bomb, is a desperate act of faith. On purely humanistic grounds I could have no basis for believing it as more than wishful thinking. Huxley ends his book with the words "My faith is in the possibilities of man." It is significant that he was able to reissue it in 1957 without even a mention of the possibility, not to say probability, that there might not, within his frame of reference, be any prospects for humanity at all.

The belief that personality is of ultimate significance is for me frankly incredible *unless* what we see in Jesus of Nazareth is a window through the surface of things into the very ground of our being. That is why, in traditional categories, the survival of Christianity turned upon the assertion that he was "of one substance with the Father." For unless the substance, the being, of things deep down *is* Love, of the quality disclosed in the life, death and resurrection of Jesus Christ, then we could have no confidence in affirming that reality at its very deepest level is personal. And that is what is meant by asserting that *God* is personal.

This has nothing necessarily to do with positing the existence of a Person, an almighty Individual, "up there" or "out there." Indeed, as Paul Tillich, the great American theologian, also from Germany, has said: "The protest of atheism against such a highest person is correct."

Tillich has shown that it is just as possible to speak of God in terms of "depth" as of "height." Such language is equally symbolic. But it may speak more "profoundly" to modern man brought up on "depth psychology." Indeed, I believe that this transposition can bring fresh meaning to much traditional religious symbolism. Tillich talks of what is most deeply true about us and for us, and goes on:—

"That depth is what the word God means. And if that word has not much meaning for you, translate it, and speak of the depths of your life, of the source of your being, of your ultimate concern, of what you take seriously without any reservation. Perhaps, in order to do so, you must forget everything traditional you have learned about God, perhaps even that word itself. For if you know that God means depth, you know much about him. You cannot then call yourself an atheist or unbeliever. For you cannot think or say: Life has no depth! Life itself is shallow. Being itself is surface only. If you could say this in complete seriousness, you would be an atheist, but otherwise you are not."

Those words from his "Shaking of the Foundations" (now published as a Pelican [Book]) had a strangely moving effect on me when I first read them 14 years ago. They spoke of God with a new and indestructible relevance, which made the traditional language about a God that came in from outside both remote and artificial. And yet they preserved his "profound" mystery and transcendence.

The ultimate Christian conviction is that at the heart of things there is "nothing, in death or life . . . in the world as it is or the world as it shall be, in the forces of the universe, in heights or depths— nothing in all creation that can separate us from the love of God in

Christ Jesus our Lord." That I believe passionately. As for the rest, as for the images of God, whether metal or mental, I am prepared to be an agnostic with the agnostics, even an atheist with the atheists.

Indeed, though we shall not of course be able to do it, I can understand those who urge that we should give up using the word "God" for a generation, so impregnated has it become with a way of thinking we may have to discard if the Gospel is to signify anything.

I am well aware that what I have said involves radical reformulations for the Church in almost every field—of doctrine, worship, ethics and evangelism. This is a dangerous process, but immensely exhilarating: and the exciting thing is that it is not being forced upon the Church from outside but is welling up from within.

Erich Fromm

This is the last part of Chapter 5, "Steps to the Humanization of Technological Society," in Erich Fromm's The Revolution of Hope *(1968). For information about Fromm and his writings, see page 470.*

TOWARD RADICAL HUMANISM

We have argued throughout this book that the system Man does not function properly if only his material needs are satisfied, thus guaranteeing his physiological survival, but not those needs and faculties which are specifically human—love, tenderness, reason, joy, etc.

Indeed, inasmuch as he is also an animal, man needs first to satisfy his material wants; but his history is a record of the search for and expression of his trans-survival needs, such as in painting and sculpture, in myth and drama, in music and dance. Religion was almost the only system which incorporated these aspects of human existence.

With the growth of the "new science," religion in its traditional forms became less and less effective, and there appeared the danger that the values which in Europe were anchored in the theistic frame of reference would be lost. Dostoevski expressed this fear in his famous statement: "If there is no God, everything is possible." In the eighteenth and nineteenth centuries, a number of people saw the necessity for creating an equivalent to what religion stood for in the past. Robespierre tried to create an artificial new religion and necessarily failed because his background of enlightened materialism and idolatrous worship of posterity did not permit him to see the basic elements which would have been needed for founding a new religion, even if it could have been done. Similarly, Comte thought of a new religion and his positivism made it equally impossible to arrive at a satisfactory answer. In many ways, Marx's socialism in the nineteenth century was the most important popular religious movement—though it was formulated in secular terms.

Dostoevski's prognosis of the breakdown of all ethical values if the belief in God ceased was only partly fulfilled. Those ethical values of modern society which are generally accepted by law and custom, such as respect for property, for individual life, and other principles, remained intact. But those human values which go beyond the requirements of our social order did, indeed, lose their influence and weight. But Dostoevski was wrong in another and more important sense. Developments during the last ten, and especially the past five, years all over Europe and in America have shown a very strong trend toward the deeper values of the humanistic tradition. This new quest for a meaningful life did not arise only among small and isolated groups, but became a whole movement in countries of entirely different social and political structures, as well as within the Catholic and Protestant churches. What is common to the believers and the non-believers in this new movement is the conviction that concepts are only secondary to deeds and human attitudes.

A Hassidic story might exemplify this point. The adherent of a Hassidic master is asked, "Why do you go to hear the master? Is it in order to hear his words of wisdom?" The answer is, "Oh, no, I go to see how he ties his shoelaces." The point hardly needs an explanation. What matters in a person is not the set of ideas or opinions which he accepts, because he has been exposed to them since childhood or because they are conventional patterns of thought, but the character, attitude, the visceral root of his ideas and convictions. The Great Dialogue is based on the idea that shared concern and experience are more important than shared concepts. This does not mean that the various groups referred to here have abandoned their own concepts or ideas or hold that they are not important. But they have all come to the conviction that their shared concern, their shared experience, their shared action causes them to have much more in common than what separates them by their unshared concepts. Abbé Pire has expressed it in a very simple and forceful way: "What matters today is

649

not the difference between those who believe and those who do not believe, but the difference between those who care and those who don't."

This new attitude toward life can be expressed more specifically in the following principles: Man's development requires his capacity to transcend the narrow prison of his ego, his greed, his selfishness, his separation from his fellow man, and, hence, his basic loneliness. This transcendence is the condition for being open and related to the world, vulnerable, and yet with an experience of identity and integrity; of man's capacity to enjoy all that is alive, to pour out his faculties into the world around him, to be "interested"; in brief, to *be* rather than to *have* and to *use* are consequences of the step to overcome greed and egomania.[1]

From an entirely different standpoint, the principle shared by all radical humanists is that of negating and combating idolatry in every form and shape—idolatry, in the prophetic sense of worshiping the work of one's own hands and hence making man subservient to things, and in this process becoming a thing himself. The idols against which the Old Testament prophets fought were idols in stone or wood, or trees or hills; the idols of our day are leaders, institutions, especially the State, the nation, production, law and order, and every man-made thing. Whether or not one believes in God is a question secondary to whether or not one denies idols. The concept of alienation is the same as the Biblical concept of idolatry. It is man's submission to the things of his creation and to the circumstances of his doing. Whatever may divide believers and nonbelievers, there is something which unites them if they are true to their common tradition, and that is the common fight against idolatry and the deep conviction that no thing and no institution must ever take the place of God or, as a nonbeliever may prefer to say, of that empty place which is reserved for the No-thing.

A third aspect shared by the radical humanists is the conviction that there is a hierarchy of values in which those of the lower orders follow from the highest value, and that these values are binding and compelling principles for the practice of life—individual and social. There may be differences in the radicalism with regard to the affirmation of these values in the practice of one's life, just as there are in Christianity or in Buddhism among those who lead the monastic life and those who do not. But all these differences are relatively unimportant beside the principle that there are certain values which cannot be compromised.

---

[1] It is well known that the principle outlined here is the basic one shared by Buddhist and Judeo-Christian thought. It is interesting that a Marxist philosopher, Adam Schaff, in his *Society and the Individual*, speaks of overcoming egotism as the basic principle of Marxist ethics.

I submit that if people would truly accept the Ten Commandments or the Buddhist Eightfold Path as the effective principles to guide their lives, a dramatic change in our whole culture would take place. There is no need at this point to argue about details of the values which need to be practiced, for what matters is to gather those who accept the principle of *practice* rather than of *submission to an ideology.*

Another common principle is the solidarity of all men and the loyalty to life and to humanity which must always take precedence over the loyalty to any particular group. In fact, even this way of putting it is not correct. Any true love for another person has a particular quality: for I love in that person not only the person but humanity itself, or, as a Christian or Jewish believer would say: God. In the same way, if I love my country, this love is at the same time a love for man and mankind; and if it is not that, it is an attachment based on one's incapacity for independence and, in the last analysis, another manifestation of idolatry.

The crucial question is how these new-old principles can become effective. Those inside religion hope that they can transform their religion into the full practice of humanism, but many of them know that while this may prove to be true for some sectors of the population, there are others who for obvious reasons cannot accept the theistic concepts and rituals so closely interwoven with them that it is almost impossible to separate the two. What hope is there for that part of the population which cannot even enter the ranks of the living Church?

Can a new religion be founded which has no premises such as those in Revelation, or any kind of mythology?

Obviously religions are manifestations of the spirit within the concrete, historical process and the specific, social, and cultural circumstances of any given society. One cannot found a religion by putting together principles. Even the "nonreligion" of Buddhism cannot simply be made acceptable to the Western world, although it has no premises in conflict with rational and realistic thought and is basically free from all mythology.[2] Religions are usually founded by rare and charismatic

---

[2] It has been emphasized by an important Czechoslovak philosopher, Fišer, in his significant and profound work on Buddhism (to be published) that Buddhism, aside from Marxism, is the only philosophy in history which has immediately seized the mind of the masses and as a philosophical system has developed into what in the West would be called a religion. But he also states that one cannot duplicate Buddhism and accept it in its existing form as a new religion for industrial society. This also holds true for Zen Buddhism, which is the most highly sophisticated, anti-ideological, rational, psychospiritual system I know and which developed all the forms of a "nonreligious" religion. It is not accidental that Zen Buddhism has aroused keen interest among intellectuals and especially among young people, and given rise to the hope that it could have a deep influence on the Western world. I believe its ideas can have that influence, yet it would have to undergo new and unpredictable forms of transformation to become the equivalent of a religion in the West.

personalities of extraordinary genius. Such a personality has not appeared yet on today's horizon, although there is no reason to assume that he has not been born. But in the meantime we cannot wait for a new Moses or a new Buddha; we have to make do with what we have, and perhaps at this moment of history this is all to the good because the new religious leader might too quickly be transformed into a new idol and his religion might be transformed into idolatry before it had a chance to penetrate the hearts and minds of men.

Are we then left with nothing but some general principles and values?

I do not believe so. If the constructive forces within industrial society which are choked by a deadening bureaucracy, by artificial consumption, and manipulated boredom are released by a new mood of hope, by the social and cultural transformations discussed in this book, if the individual regains his confidence in himself, and if people make contact with each other in spontaneous and genuine group life, new forms of psychospiritual practices will emerge and grow which might be unified eventually in a total and socially acceptable system. Here, as well as with reference to many of the other points we have discussed, all depends on the courage of the individual to be fully alive and to seek solutions to the problem of his existence without waiting for the bureaucrats or the concepts to give him the answers.

It can even be hoped that certain forms of rituals become widely and meaningfully accepted. We see the beginnings of this, for instance, in songs like "We Shall Overcome," which are living rituals, not just songs. A ritual like that of common silence as it has been practiced by the Friends as the center of their religious service could become acceptable to large groups of people; it could become a custom that every meeting of significance begins or ends with five or fifteen minutes of common silence given to meditation and concentration. It is not too far-fetched an idea to suggest that, instead of prayers or patriotic formulae, classes in schools and special occasions in universities could be introduced by a period of common silence.

We also have shared symbols, such as the dove and the outline of a human figure as symbols of peace and respect for man.

There is no point in speculating about further details of possible common rituals and symbols outside of church life, because they will grow naturally once the soil is prepared. I might add that in the field of art and music there are innumerable possibilities for the creation of new ritual and symbolic expressions.[3]

Whatever new psychospiritual systems may arise, they will not be

---

[3] It is interesting to note that Albert Schweitzer Colleges have organized a week of conferences in 1969 on the theme "Roads to a Revitalization of Religion Through the Arts."

"fighting" religion, although they will be a challenge to those in the various religions who have made an ideology of religious teaching and an idol of God. Those who worship the "living God" will have no difficulty in sensing that they have more in common with the "unbelievers" than they have in what separates them; they will have a deep sense of solidarity with those who do not worship idols and who try to do what the believers call "God's will."

I expect that to many the hope expressed here for new manifestations of man's psychospiritual needs are too vague to form the basis of hope that such a development will happen. Those who want certainty and proof before they can take any hope seriously are right in reacting negatively. But those who believe in the reality of the yet unborn will have more trust that man will find new forms of expressing vital needs, even though at this moment there is only a dove with an olive branch indicating the end of the flood.

Eldridge Cleaver

Eldridge Cleaver was born in Arkansas in 1935 and grew up in Phoenix and in the Watts section of Los Angeles. He early became a petty criminal and completed high school in Soledad prison while serving a two-and-one-half-year sentence for possession of marijuana. On leaving Soledad, and impelled by motives of racial revenge, he became a rapist. In a year he was back in prison, serving a sentence of two to fourteen years for "assault with intent to murder." In San Quentin and Folsom prisons he began to read, became a Black Muslim minister, and then followed the dissident doctrines of Malcolm X. Cleaver began to write in prison and attracted the attention and sympathy of Beverly Axelrod, a San Francisco attorney, and of the editors of Ramparts *magazine.* Ramparts *published one of his essays (against James Baldwin) in June 1966, and through the agency of these friends he was paroled in December.*

Shortly thereafter Cleaver met Huey P. Newton and Bobby Seale in San Francisco and with them he founded the Black Panther party, becoming its Minister of Information. The party devoted itself to a militant defense of the rights of blacks. Among its tactics was a close surveillance of police activities in black neighborhoods, which resulted in a series of violent confrontations. On

April 5, 1968, the day after the Martin Luther King assassina-
tion, an exchange of gunfire with the Oakland police resulted in the
death of Panther Bobby Hutton and the wounding of Cleaver.
Cleaver's parole was revoked and he was sent back to prison.
He was released two months later on a writ of habeas corpus, the
judge finding that the unarmed Cleaver had not violated the terms
of his parole. Cleaver had time to become the Peace and Freedom
party candidate for President of the United States, receiving 30,000
votes nationally, before his release was revoked by a higher court.
Rather than return to prison, he fled first to Cuba, then to Algeria,
where at this writing he resides. Cleaver's powerful book of auto-
biographical and social essays, Soul on Ice *(1968), is the source*
of the following pieces. His Post-Prison Writings and Speeches
was published in 1969.

A RELIGIOUS CONVERSION, MORE OR LESS

Folsom Prison,
September 10, 1965

Once I was a Catholic. I was baptized, made my first Communion, my Confirmation, and I wore a Cross with Jesus on it around my neck. I prayed at night, said my Rosary, went to Confession, and said all the Hail Marys and Our Fathers to which I was sentenced by the priest. Hopelessly enamored of sin myself, yet appalled by the sins of others, I longed for Judgment Day and a trial before a jury of my peers—this was my only chance to escape the flames which I could feel already licking at my feet. I was in a California Youth Authority institution at the time, having transgressed the laws of man—God did not indict me that time; if He did, it was a secret indictment, for I was never informed of any charges brought against me. The reason I became a Catholic was that the rule of the institution held that every Sunday each inmate had to attend the church of his choice. I chose the Catholic Church because all the Negroes and Mexicans went there. The whites went to the Protestant chapel. Had I been a fool enough to go to the Protestant chapel, one black face in a sea of white, and with guerrilla warfare going on between us, I might have ended up a Christian martyr—St. Eldridge the Stupe.

It all ended one day when, at a catechism class, the priest asked if anyone present understood the mystery of the Holy Trinity. I had

654

been studying my lessons diligently and knew by heart what I'd been taught. Up shot my hand, my heart throbbing with piety (pride) for this chance to demonstrate my knowledge of the Word. To my great shock and embarrassment, the Father announced, and it sounded like a thunderclap, that I was lying, that no one, not even the Pope, understood the Godhead, and why else did I think they called it the *mystery* of the Holy Trinity? I saw in a flash, stung to the quick by the jeers of my fellow catechumens, that I had been used, that the Father had been lying in wait for the chance to drop that thunderbolt, in order to drive home the point that the Holy Trinity was not to be taken lightly.

I had intended to explain the Trinity with an analogy to 3-in-1 oil, so it was probably just as well.

"THE CHRIST" AND HIS TEACHINGS

Folsom Prison,
September 10, 1965

My first awareness of Thomas Merton came in San Quentin, back in (I believe) 1959–60. During that time, a saint walked the earth in the person of one Chris Lovdjieff. He was a teacher at San Quentin and guru to all who came to him. What did he teach? Everything. It is easier just to say he taught Lovdjieff and let it go at that. He himself claimed to be sort of a disciple of Alan W. Watts, whom he used to bring over to Q to lecture us now and then on Hinduism, Zen Buddhism, and on the ways the peoples of Asia view the universe. I never understood how "The Christ" (as I used to call Lovdjieff, to his great sorrow and pain) could sit at Watts' feet, because he always seemed to me more warm, more human, and possessed of greater wisdom than Watts displayed either in his lectures or his books. It may be that I received this impression from having been exposed more to Lovdjieff than to Watts. Yet there was something about Watts that reminded me of a slick advertisement for a labor-saving device, aimed at the American housewife, out of the center page of *Life* magazine; while Lovdjieff's central quality seemed to be pain, suffering, and a peculiar strength based on his understanding of his own helplessness, weakness, and need. Under Lovdjieff I studied world history, Oriental philosophy, Occidental philosophy, comparative religion, and economics. I could not tell one class from the other—neither could the other students and neither, I believe, could Lovdjieff. It was all Lovdjieff.

The walls of his classrooms were covered with cardboard placards which bore quotations from the world's great thinkers. There were quotes from Japanese, Eskimos, Africans, Hopi Indians, Peruvians, Voltaire, Confucius, Lao-tse, Jesus Christ, Moses, Mohammed, Buddha, Rabbi Hillel, Plato, Aristotle, Marx, Lenin, Mao Tse-tung, Zoroaster— and Thomas Merton, among others. Once Lovdjieff gave a lecture on Merton, reading from his works and trying to put the man's life and work in context. He seemed desperately to want us to respect Merton's vocation and choice of the contemplative life. It was an uphill battle because a prison is in many ways like a monastery. The convicts in Lovdjieff's class hated prison. We were appalled that a free man would voluntarily enter prison—or a monastery. Let me say it right out: we thought Merton was some kind of nut. We thought the same thing about Lovdjieff. My secret disgust was that in many ways I was nothing but a monk, and how I loathed that view of myself!

I was mystified by Merton and I could not believe in his passionate defense of monkhood. I distrusted Lovdjieff on the subject of Thomas Merton. My mind heard a special pleading in his voice. In his ardent defense of Merton, Lovdjieff seemed to be defending himself, even trying to convince himself. One day Lovdjieff confided to us that he had tried to be a monk but couldn't make it. He made it, all right, without even realizing it. San Quentin was his monastery. He busied himself about the prison as though he had a special calling to minister to the prisoners. He was there day and night and on Saturdays, without fail. The officials would sometimes have to send a guard to his class to make him stop teaching, so the inmates could be locked up for the night. He was horror-stricken that they could make such a demand of him. Reluctantly, he'd sit down heavily in his seat, burdened by defeat, and tell us to go to our cells. Part of the power we gave him was that we would never leave his class unless he himself dismissed us. If a guard came and told us to leave, he got only cold stares; we would not move until Lovdjieff gave the word. He got a secret kick out of this little victory over his tormentors. If, as happened once, he was unable to make it to the prison because his car had a blowout, he'd be full of apologies and pain next day.

Lovdjieff had extracted from me my word that I would some day read Merton for myself—he did not insist upon any particular time, just "some day." Easy enough. I gave my promise. In 1963, when I was transferred from San Quentin to Folsom for being an agitator, they put me in solitary confinement. The officials did not deem it wise, at that time, to allow me to circulate among the general inmate population. I had evolved a crash program which I would immediately activate whenever I was placed in solitary: stock up on books and read, read, read; do calisthenics and forget about the rest of the world. I had learned the waste and futility of worry. (Years ago, I had stopped being one of those convicts who take a little calendar and mark off each day.) When I asked for books to read in this particular hole, a trustee brought me a list from which to make selections. On the list I was delighted to see Merton's *The Seven Storey Mountain*, his auto-biography. I thought of Lovdjieff. Here was a chance to fulfill my promise.

I was tortured by that book because Merton's suffering, in his quest for God, seemed all in vain to me. At the time, I was a Black Muslim chained in the bottom of a pit by the Devil. Did I expect Allah to tear down the walls and set me free? To me, the language and symbols of religion were nothing but weapons of war. I had no other purpose for them. All the gods are dead except the god of war. I wished that Merton had stated in secular terms the reasons he withdrew from the political, economic, military, and social system into which he was born, seeking refuge in a monastery.

Despite my rejection of Merton's theistic world view, I could not keep him out of the room. He shouldered his way through the door. Wel-come, Brother Merton. I gave him a bear hug. Most impressive of all to me was Merton's description of New York's black ghetto—Har-lem. I liked it so much I copied out the heart of it in longhand. Later, after getting out of solitary, I used to keep this passage in mind when delivering Black Muslim lectures to other prisoners. Here is an excerpt:

Here in this huge, dark, steaming slum, hundreds of thousands of Negroes are herded together like cattle, most of them with nothing to eat and nothing to do. All the sense and imagination and sensibilities and emotions and sorrows and desires and hopes and ideas of a race with vivid feelings and deep emotional reactions are forced in upon themselves, bound inward by an iron ring of frustration: the prejudice that hems them in with its four insurmountable walls. In this huge cauldron, inestimable natural gifts, wisdom, love, music, science, poetry are stamped down and left to boil with the dregs of an elementally corrupted nature, and thousands upon thousands of souls are destroyed by vice and misery and degradation, obliterated, wiped out, washed from the register of the living, dehumanized.

What has not been devoured, in your dark furnace, Harlem, by mariju-ana, by gin, by insanity, hysteria, syphilis?

For a while, whenever I felt myself softening, relaxing, I had only to read that passage to become once more a rigid flame of indignation. It had precisely the same effect on me that Elijah Muhammad's writings used to have, or the words of Malcolm X, or the words of any spokes-man of the oppressed in any land. I vibrate sympathetically to any protest against tyranny.

But I want to tell more about Lovdjieff—The Christ.

Chris Lovdjieff had a profound mind and an ecumenical education. I got the impression that the carnage of World War II, particularly the scientific, systematic approach to genocide of the Nazi regime, had been a traumatic experience from which it was impossible for him to recover. It was as if he had seen or experienced something which had changed him forever, sickened his soul, overwhelmed him with sympathy and love for all mankind. He hated all restraints upon the human mind, the human spirit, all blind believing, all dogmatic assertion. He questioned everything.

I was never sure of just what was driving him. That he was driven there could be no doubt. There was a sense of unreality about him. It seemed that he moved about in a mist. The atmosphere he created was like the mystic spell of Khalil Gibran's poetry. He seemed always to be listening to distant music, or silent voices, or to be talking in a whisper to himself. He loved silence and said that it should only be broken for important communications, and he would expel students from his classes for distracting the others by chatting idly in the back rows. In his classes he was a dictator. He enforced certain rules which brooked no deviation--no smoking in his classroom at any time, before class, during class, at recess, or even when school was out; no talking in Lovdjieff's class unless it was pertinent to the subject at hand; no eating or chewing gum in his classroom; no profanity. Simple rules, perhaps, but in San Quentin they were visionary, adventurous, audacious. The Christ enforced them strictly. The other teachers and the guards wondered how he got away with it. We students wondered why we enthusiastically submitted to it. The Christ would look surprised, as if he did not understand, if you asked him about it. If one of the other teachers forgot and came into Lovdjieff's classroom smoking, he was sent hopping. The same went for prison guards. I can still see the shocked expression of a substitute teacher who, coming into Lovdjieff's room during recess smoking a pipe, was told: "Leave this room!"

When you came to Lovdjieff's classes, you came to learn. If you betrayed other motives, "Get out of here this minute!"—without malice but without equivocation. He was a magnet, an institution. He worked indefatigably. His day started when the school bell rang at 8 A.M. Often he would forego lunch to interview a few students and help them along with their schoolwork or personal problems. He never ceased complaining because the officials refused to allow him to eat lunch in the mess hall with the prisoners. Had they given him a cell he would have taken it. After lunch, he'd teach until 3 P.M. When night school convened at 6 P.M., The Christ would be there, beaming, radiating, and he'd teach passionately until 10 P.M. Then, reluctantly, he'd go home to suffer in exile until school opened next day. On

Saturdays he'd be there bright and early to teach—Lovdjieff. He would have come on Sundays too, only the officials put their foot down and refused to hear of it. The Christ settled for a Sunday evening radio program of two hours which he taped for broadcast to the prisoners.

His classes were works of art. He made ancient history contemporary by evoking the total environment—intellectual, social, political, economic—of an era. He breathed life into the shattered ruins of the past. Students sat entranced while The Christ performed, his silver-rimmed glasses reflecting the light in eye-twinkling flashes.

He dressed like a college boy, betraying a penchant for simple sweaters and plain slacks of no particular distinction. He burned incense in his classroom when he lectured on religion, to evoke a certain mood. He was drawn to those students who seemed most impossible to teach—old men who had been illiterate all their lives and set in their ways. Lovdjieff didn't believe that anyone or anything in the universe was "set in its ways." Those students who were intelligent and quickest to learn he seemed reluctant to bother with, almost as if to say, pointing at the illiterates and speaking to the bright ones: "Go away. Leave me. You don't need me. These others do."

Jesus wept. Lovdjieff would weep over a tragic event that had taken place ten thousand years ago in some forgotten byway in the Fertile Crescent. Once he was lecturing on the ancient Hebrews. He was angry with them for choosing to settle along the trade routes between Egypt and Mesopotamia. He showed how, over the centuries, time and time again, these people had been invaded, slaughtered, driven out, captured, but always to return.

"What is it that keeps pulling them back to this spot!" he exclaimed. He lost his breath. His face crumbled, and he broke down and wept. "Why do they insist on living in the middle of that—that [for once, I thought meanly, The Christ couldn't find a word] that—that—Freeway! They have to sit down in the center of the Freeway! That's all it is—look!" He pointed out the trade routes on the map behind his desk, then he sat down and cried uncontrollably for several minutes.

Another time, he brought tape-recorded selections from Thomas Wolfe's *Look Homeward Angel*. The Christ wept all through the tape.

The Christ could weep over a line of poetry, over a single image in a poem, over the beauty of a poem's music, over the fact that man can talk, read, write, walk, reproduce, die, eat, eliminate—over the fact that a chicken can lay an egg.

Once he lectured us all week on Love. He quoted what poets had said of Love, what novelists had said of Love, what playwrights had said of Love. He played tapes of Ashley Montagu on Love. Over the

659

weekend, each student was to write an essay on his own conception of Love, mindful to have been influenced by what he had been listening to all week long. In my essay I explained that I did not love white people. I quoted Malcolm X:

How can I love the man who raped my mother, killed my father, enslaved my ancestors, dropped atomic bombs on Japan, killed off the Indians and keeps me cooped up in the slums? I'd rather be tied up in a sack and tossed into the Harlem River first.

Lovdjieff refused to grade my paper. He returned it to me. I protested that he was being narrow-minded and dogmatic in not understanding why I did not love white people simply because he himself was white. He told me to talk with him after class.

"How can you do this to me?" he asked.

"I've only written the way I feel," I said.

Instead of answering, he cried.

"Jesus wept," I told him and walked out.

Two days later, he returned my essay—ungraded. There were instead spots on it which I realized to be his tears.

Although Lovdjieff's popularity among the prisoners continued to soar and the waiting lists for his classes grew longer and longer, prison authorities banned his radio program. Then they stopped him from coming in on Saturdays. Then they stopped him from teaching night school. Then they took away his pass and barred him from San Quentin.

I must say that this man has not been adequately described. Certain things I hold back on purpose, others I don't know how to say. Until I began writing this, I did not know that I had a vivid memory of him. But now I can close my eyes and relive many scenes in which he goes into his act.

Thomas Merton

Thomas Merton (1915–1968) grew up and studied in France, England, and the United States and received a Master's degree from Columbia in 1939. By this time he had begun the long spiritual climb of the mount of Purgatory recounted in his autobiography, The Seven Storey Mountain *(1948). He joined a Young Communist group, worked at a settlement house in Harlem, converted from the Anglican to the Roman Catholic church, and in 1941 became a Trappist (Cistercian) Monk. He made solemn vows in 1947 and was ordained a priest in 1949. Merton's role in the Abbey of Gethsemani, Kentucky, was in some ways an ambiguous one. He was an accomplished poet and essayist. The literary fame brought on by the publication of his autobiography perpetuated the demand that he continue to provide spiritual guidance for a wide audience. At the same time he had a taste for solitude so deep as to make him a hermit even in his own monastery. The present essay, from the 1967* Hudson Review, *beautifully and ironically catches the interplay of Merton's worlds. Among his more than thirty volumes are* Selected Poems *(1959),* Gandhi on Non-Violence *(1965),* Conjectures of a Guilty Bystander *(1966), and* Zen and the Birds of Appetite *(1968).*

DAY OF A STRANGER

The hills are blue and hot. There is a brown, dusty field in the bottom of the valley. I hear a machine, a bird, a clock. The clouds are high and enormous. Through them the inevitable jet plane passes: this time probably full of passengers from Miami to Chicago. What passengers? This I have no need to decide. They are out of my world, up there, busy sitting in their small, isolated, arbitrary lounge that does not even seem to be moving—the lounge that somehow unaccountably picked them up off the earth in Florida to suspend them for a while with timeless cocktails and then let them down in Illinois. The suspension of modern life in contemplation that *gets you somewhere!*

There are also other worlds above me. Other jets will pass over, with other contemplations and other modalities of intentness.

I have seen the SAC plane, with the bomb in it, fly low over me and I have looked up out of the woods directly at the closed bay of the metal bird with a scientific egg in its breast! A womb easily and mechanically opened! I do not consider this technological mother to be the friend of anything I believe in. However, like everyone else, I live in the shadow of the apocalyptic cherub. I am surveyed by it, impersonally. Its number recognizes my number. Are these numbers preparing at some moment to coincide in the benevolent mind of a computer? This does not concern me, for I live in the woods as a reminder that I am free not to be a number.

There is, in fact, a choice.

*

In an age where there is much talk about "being yourself" I reserve to myself the right to forget about being myself, since in any case there is very little chance of my being anybody else. Rather it seems to me that when one is too intent on "being himself" he runs the risk of impersonating a shadow.

Yet I cannot pride myself on special freedom, simply because I am living in the woods. I am accused of living in the woods like Thoreau instead of living in the desert like St. John the Baptist. All I can answer is that I am not living "like anybody." Or "unlike anybody." We all live somehow or other, and that's that. It is a compelling necessity for me to be free to embrace the necessity of my own nature.

I exist under trees. I walk in the woods out of necessity. I am both a prisoner and an escaped prisoner. I cannot tell you why, born in France, my journey ended here in Kentucky. I have considered going further, but it is not practical. It makes no difference. Do I have a "day"? Do I spend my "day" in a "place"? I know there are trees here. I know there are birds here. I know the birds in fact very well, for there are precise pairs of birds (two each of fifteen or twenty species) living in the immediate area of my cabin. I share this particular place with them: we form an ecological balance. This harmony gives the idea of "place" a new configuration.

As to the crows, they form part of a different pattern. They are vociferous and self-justifying, like humans. They are not two, they are many. They fight each other and the other birds, in a constant state of war.

*

There is a mental ecology, too, a living balance of spirits in this corner of the woods. There is room here for many other songs besides those of birds. Of Vallejo for instance. Or Rilke, or René Char, Montale, Zukofsky, Ungaretti, Edwin Muir, Quasimodo or some Greeks. Or the dry, disconcerting voice of Nicanor Parra, the poet of the sneeze. Here is also Chuang Tzu whose climate is perhaps most the climate of this silent corner of woods. A climate in which there is no need for explanations. Here is the reassuring companionship of many silent Tzu's and Fu's; Kung Tzu, Lao Tzu, Meng Tzu. Tu Fu. And Hui Neng. And Chao-Chu. And the drawings of Sengai. And a big graceful scroll from Suzuki. Here also is a Syrian hermit called Philoxenus. An Algerian cenobite called Camus. Here is heard the clanging prose of Tertullian, with the dry catarrh of Sartre. Here the voluble dissonances of Auden, with the golden sounds of John of Salisbury. Here is the deep vegetation of that more ancient forest in which the angry birds, Isaias and Jeremias, sing. Here should be, and are, feminine voices from Angela of Foligno to Flannery O'Connor, Theresa of Avila, Juliana of Norwich, and, more personally and warmly still, Raissa Maritain. It is good to choose the voices that will be heard in these woods, but they also choose themselves, and send themselves here to be present in this silence. In any case there is no lack of voices.

*

The hermit life is cool. It is a life of low definition in which there is little to decide, in which there are few transactions or none, in which there are no packages delivered. In which I do not bundle up packages and deliver them to myself. It is not intense. There is no give and take of questions and answers, problems and solutions. Problems begin down the hill. Over there under the water tower are the solutions. Here there are woods, foxes. Here there is no need for dark glasses. "Here" does not even warm itself up with references to "there." It is just a "here" for which there is no "there." The hermit life is that cool.

The monastic life as a whole is a hot medium. Hot with words like "must," "ought" and "should." Communities are devoted to high definition projects: "making it all clear!" The clearer it gets the clearer it has to be made. It branches out. You have to keep clearing the branches. The more branches you cut back the more branches grow. For one you cut you get three more. On the end of each branch there is a big bushy question mark. People are running all around with packages of meaning. Each is very anxious to know whether all the others have received the latest messages. Has someone else received a message that he has not received? Will they be willing to pass it on to him? Will he understand it when it is passed on? Will he have to argue about it? Will he be expected to clear his throat and stand up and say "Well the way I look at it St. Benedict said . . . ?" Saint Benedict saw that the best thing to do with the monastic life was to cool it but today everybody is heating it up. Maybe to cool it you have to be a hermit. But then they will keep thinking that *you* have got a special message. When they find out you haven't. . . . Well, that's their worry, not mine.

*

This is not a hermitage—it is a house. ("Who was that hermitage I seen you with last night? . . .") What I wear is pants. What I do is live. How I pray is breathe. Who said Zen? Wash out your mouth if you said Zen. If you see a meditation going by, shoot it. Who said "Love?" Love is in the movies. The spiritual life is something that people worry about when they are so busy with something else they think they ought to be spiritual. Spiritual life is guilt. Up here

663

in the woods is seen the New Testament: that is to say, the wind comes through the trees and you breathe it. Is it supposed to be clear? I am not inviting anybody to try it. Or suggesting that one day the message will come saying NOW. That is none of my business.

*

I am out of bed at two-fifteen in the morning, when the night is darkest and most silent. Perhaps this is due to some ailment or other. I find myself in the primordial lostness of night, solitude, forest, peace, a mind awake in the dark, looking for a light, not totally reconciled to being out of bed. A light appears, and in the light an ikon. There is now in the large darkness a small room of radiance with psalms in it. The psalms grow up silently by themselves without effort like plants in this light which is favorable to them. The plants hold themselves up on stems which have a single consistency, that of mercy, or rather great mercy. *Magna misericordia.* In the formlessness of night and silence a word then pronounces itself: Mercy. It is surrounded by other words of lesser consequence: "destroy iniquity" "Wash me" "purify" "I know my iniquity." *Peccavi.* Concepts without interest in the world of business, war, politics, culture, etc. Concepts also often without serious interest to ecclesiastics.

Other words: Blood. Guile. Anger. The way that is not good. The way of blood, guile, anger, war.

Out there the hills in the dark lie southward. The way over the hill is blood, guile, dark, anger, death: Selma, Birmingham, Mississippi. Nearer than these, the atomic city, from which each day a freight car of fissionable material is brought to be laid carefully beside the gold in the underground vault which is at the heart of this nation.

"Their mouth is the opening of the grave; their tongues are set in motion by lies; their heart is void."

Blood, lies, fire, hate, the opening of the grave, void. Mercy, great mercy.

The birds begin to wake. It will soon be dawn. In an hour or two the towns will wake, and men will enjoy everywhere the great luminous smiles of production and business.

*

—Why live in the woods?
—Well, you have to live somewhere.
—Do you get lonely?
—Yes, sometimes.
—Are you mad at people?
—No.
—Are you mad at the monastery?
—No.

—What do you think about the future of monasticism?
—Nothing. I don't think about it.
—Is it true that your bad back is due to Yoga?
—No.
—Is it true that you are practicing Zen in secret?
—Pardon me, I don't speak English.

*

All monks, as is well known, are unmarried, and hermits more un-married than the rest of them. Not that I have anything against women. I see no reason why a man can't love God and a woman at the same time. If God was going to regard women with a jealous eye, why did he go and make them in the first place? There is a lot of talk about a married clergy. Interesting. So far there has not been a great deal said about married hermits. Well, anyway, I have the place full of ikons of the Holy Virgin.

One might say I had decided to marry the silence of the forest. The sweet dark warmth of the whole world will have to be my wife. Out of the heart of that dark warmth comes the secret that is heard only in silence, but it is the root of all the secrets that are whispered by all the lovers in their beds all over the world. So perhaps I have an obligation to preserve the stillness, the silence, the poverty, the virginal point of pure nothingness which is at the center of all other loves. I attempt to cultivate this plant without comment in the middle of the night and water it with psalms and prophecies in silence. It be-comes the most rare of all the trees in the garden, at once the pri-mordial paradise tree, the *axis mundi*, the cosmic axle, and the Cross. *Nulla silva talem profert.* There is only one such tree. It cannot be multiplied. It is not interesting.

*

It is necessary for me to see the first point of light which begins to be dawn. It is necessary to be present alone at the resurrection of Day, in the blank silence when the sun appears. In this completely neutral instant I receive from the Eastern woods, the tall oaks, the one word "DAY," which is never the same. It is never spoken in any known language.

*

Sermon to the birds: "Esteemed friends, birds of noble lineage, I have no message to you except this: be what you are: be *birds*. Thus you will be your own sermon to yourselves!"

Reply: "Even this is one sermon too many!"

*

Rituals. Washing out the coffee pot in the rain bucket. Approaching the outhouse with circumspection on account of the king snake who likes to curl up on one of the beams inside. Addressing the possible king snake in the outhouse and informing him that he should not be there. Asking the formal ritual question that is asked at this time every morning: "Are you in there, you bastard?"

*

More rituals: Spray bedroom (cockroaches and mosquitoes). Close all the windows on South side (heat). Leave windows open on north and east sides (cool). Leave windows open on west side until maybe June when it gets very hot on all sides. Pull down shades. Get water bottle. Rosary. Watch. Library book to be returned.

It is time to visit the human race.

*

I start out under the pines. The valley is already hot. Machines out there in the bottoms, perhaps planting corn. Fragrance of the woods. Cool west wind under the oaks. Here is the place on the path where I killed a copperhead. There is the place where I saw the fox run daintily and carefully for cover carrying a rabbit in his mouth. And there is the cement cross that, for no reason, the novices rescued from the corner of a destroyed wall and put up in the woods: people imagine someone is buried there. It is just a cross. Why should there not be a cement cross by itself in the middle of the woods?

A squirrel is kidding around somewhere overhead in midair. Tree to tree. The coquetry of flight.

I come out into the open over the hot hollow and the old sheep barn. Over there is the monastery, bugging with windows, humming with action.

The long yellow side of the monastery faces the sun on a sharp rise with fruit trees and beehives. This is without question one of the least interesting buildings on the face of the earth. However, in spite of the most earnest efforts to deprive it of all character and keep it ugly, it is surpassed in this respect by the vast majority of other monasteries. It is so completely plain that it ends, in spite of itself, by being at least simple. A lamentable failure of religious architecture —to come so close to non-entity and yet not fully succeed! I climb sweating into the novitiate, and put down my water bottle on the cement floor. The bell is ringing. I have duties, obligations, since here I am a monk. When I have accomplished these, I return to the woods where I am nobody. In the choir are the young monks, patient, serene, with very clear eyes, then, reflective, gentle, confused. Today perhaps I tell them of Eliot's *Little Gidding,* analyzing the first movement of the poem ("Midwinter spring in its own season"). They will listen with attention thinking some other person is talking to them about some other poem.

*

Chanting the *alleluia* in the second mode: strength and solidity of the

Latin, seriousness of the second mode, built on the *Re* as though on a sacrament, a presence. One keeps returning to the *re* as to an inevitable center. *Sol-Re, Fa-Re, Sol-Re, Do-Re.* Many other notes in between, but suddenly one hears only the one note. *Consonantia:* all notes, in their perfect distinctness, are yet blended in one. (Through a curious oversight Gregorian chant has continued to be sung in this monastery. But not for long.)

*

In the refectory is read a message of the Pope, denouncing war, denouncing the bombing of civilians, reprisals on civilians, killing of hostages, torturing of prisoners (all in Vietnam). Do the people of this country realize who the Pope is talking about? They have by now become so solidly convinced that the Pope never denounces anybody but Communists that they have long since ceased to listen. The monks seem to know. The voice of the reader trembles.

*

In the heat of noon I return with the water bottle freshly filled, through the cornfield, past the barn under the oaks, up the hill, under the pines, to the hot cabin. Larks rise out of the long grass singing. A bumblebee hums under the wide shady eaves.

I sit in the cool back room, where words cease to resound, where all meanings are absorbed in the *consonantia* of heat, fragrant pine, quiet wind, bird song and one central tonic note that is unheard and unuttered. This is no longer a time of obligations. In the silence of the afternoon all is present and all is inscrutable in one central tonic note to which every other sound ascends or descends, to which every other meaning aspires, in order to find its true fulfillment. To ask when the note will sound is to lose the afternoon: it has already sounded, and all things now hum with the resonance of its sounding.

*

I sweep. I spread a blanket out in the sun. I cut grass behind the cabin. I write in the heat of the afternoon. Soon I will bring the blanket in again and make the bed. The sun is over-clouded. The day declines. Perhaps there will be rain. A bell rings in the monastery. A devout Cistercian tractor growls in the valley. Soon I will cut bread, eat supper, say psalms, sit in the back room as the sun sets, as the birds sing outside the window, as night descends on the valley. I become surrounded once again by all the silent Tzu's and Fu's (men without office and without obligation). The birds draw closer to their nests. I sit on the cool straw mat on the floor, considering the bed in which I will presently sleep alone under the ikon of the Nativity.

Meanwhile the metal cherub of the apocalypse passes over me in the clouds, treasuring its egg and its message.

THE
FUNCTION
OF ART

itizens have been telling artists what to do at least since Plato's day and artists have responded variously, sometimes with a sublime incoherence but occasionally with that resonant authority that is theirs alone. The fact that most essays in this section are by artists—one painter and four writers—gives the artists more than their usual share of representation in the debate on the function of art. The other two essays are given over to the philosopher and the political leader, each of whom perpetuates Plato's function in his own way. What all have in common, however, is the conviction that art is important.

Mrs. Langer's magisterial opening essay stresses the role of art in the rendering of imagination and feeling, of subjective reality. Henri Matisse, the painter, with deceptively artless simplicity, writes "notes" on painting that imply an aesthetic related to Mrs. Langer's. But the remaining selections deal equally with the question raised by the interview with Albert Camus: What can the artist do in the world of today? George Orwell justifies the art that has political purpose. Mao Tse-tung—concerned with criteria in art and literary criticism—demands the "unity of politics and art" and specifically asks the artist to "expose all dark forces which endanger the people and to extol all the revolutionary struggles of the people." Eudora Welty disagrees, quietly but emphatically. "The novelist and the crusader," she writes, "both have their own place—in the novel and the editorial respectively, equally valid whether or not the two happen to be in agreement." She distinguishes the novelist, and in a larger context the writer and the artist, by his personal vision and personal voice, both inevitably informed by an individual imagination. The reader will readily be able to relate the last two essays, by LeRoi Jones, to the ideas of the foregoing writers, and also to each other. In the first, Jones affirms that art "must be produced from the legitimate emotional resources of the soul in the world" and thus rejects both cultivated imitation and blueprinted reform. The second essay, written two years later, is far more radical in content as well as in style. It calls not for a symbolic representation of reality but for reality itself, for a "theatre of assault," for "actual explosions and actual brutality."

We conclude the section with a small anthology of poems in which the reader may test Matisse's remark "that the best explanation an artist can give of his aims and ability is afforded by his work."

Susanne K. Langer

Originally a lecture delivered at Syracuse University, this essay was first published in Aesthetic Form and Education *(ed. M. F. Andrews, 1958). It later appeared as Chapter 5 in Mrs. Langer's* Philosophical Sketches *(1962), and it is this text which we reprint below. For information about the author and her writings, see page 63.*

THE CULTURAL IMPORTANCE OF ART

Every culture develops some kind of art as surely as it develops language. Some primitive cultures have no real mythology or religion, but all have some art—dance, song, design (sometimes only on tools or on the human body). Dance, above all, seems to be the oldest elaborated art.

The ancient ubiquitous character of art contrasts sharply with the prevalent idea that art is a luxury product of civilization, a cultural frill, a piece of social veneer.

It fits better with the conviction held by most artists, that art is the epitome of human life, the truest record of insight and feeling, and that the strongest military or economic society without art is poor in comparison with the most primitive tribe of savage painters, dancers, or idol carvers. Wherever a society has really achieved culture (in the ethnological sense, not the popular sense of "social form") it has begotten art, not late in its career, but at the very inception of it.

Art is, indeed, the spearhead of human development, social and individual. The vulgarization of art is the surest symptom of ethnic decline. The growth of a new art or even a great and radically new style always bespeaks a young and vigorous mind, whether collective or single.

What sort of thing is art, that it should play such a leading role in human development? It is not an intellectual pursuit, but is necessary to intellectual life; it is not religion, but grows up with religion, serves it, and in large measure determines it.

We cannot enter here on a long discussion of what has been claimed as the essence of art, the true nature of art, or its defining function; in a single lecture dealing with one aspect of art, namely its cultural influence, I can only give you by way of preamble my own definition of art, with categorical brevity. This does not mean that I set up this definition in a categorical spirit, but only that we have no time to debate it; so you are asked to accept it as an assumption underlying these reflections.

Art, in the sense here intended—that is, the generic term subsuming painting, sculpture, architecture, music, dance, literature, drama, and film—may be defined as the practice of creating perceptible forms expressive of human feeling. I say "perceptible" rather than "sensuous" forms because some works of art are given to imagination rather than to the outward senses. A novel, for instance, usually is read silently with the eye, but is not made for vision, as a painting is; and though sound plays a vital part in poetry, words even in poetry are not essentially sonorous structures like music. Dance requires to be seen, but its appeal is to deeper centers of sensation. The difference between dance and mobile sculpture makes this immediately apparent. But all works of art are purely perceptible forms that seem to embody some sort of feeling.

"Feeling" as I am using it here covers much more than it does in the technical vocabulary of psychology, where it denotes only pleasure and displeasure, or even in the shifting limits of ordinary discourse, where it sometimes means sensation (as when one says a paralyzed limb has no feeling in it), sometimes sensibility (as we speak of hurting someone's feelings), sometimes emotion (e.g., as a situation is said to harrow your feelings, or to evoke tender feeling), or a directed emotional attitude (we say we feel strongly *about* something), or even our general mental or physical condition, feeling well or ill, blue, or a bit above ourselves. As I use the word, in defining art as the creation of perceptible forms expressive of human feeling, it takes in all those meanings; it applies to everything that may be felt.

Another word in the definition that might be questioned is "creation." I think it is justified, not pretentious, as perhaps it sounds, but that issue is slightly beside the point here; so let us shelve it. If anyone prefers to speak of the "making" or "construction" of expressive forms, that will do here just as well.

What does have to be understood is the meaning of "form," and more particularly "expressive form"; for that involves the very nature of art and therefore the question of its cultural importance.

The word "form" has several current uses; most of them have some relation to the sense in which I am using it here, though a few, such as "a form to be filled in for tax purposes" or "a mere matter of form," are fairly remote, being quite specialized. Since we are speaking of art, it might be good to point out that the meaning of stylistic pattern —"the sonata form," "the sonnet form"—is not the one I am assuming here.

I am using the word in a simpler sense, which it has when you say, on a foggy night, that you see dimly moving forms in the mist; one of them emerges clearly, and is the form of a man. The trees are gigantic forms; the rills of rain trace sinuous forms on the windowpane. The rills are not fixed things; they are forms of motion. When you watch gnats weaving in the air, or flocks of birds wheeling overhead, you see dynamic forms—forms made by motion.

It is in this sense of an apparition given to our perception that a work of art is a form. It may be a permanent form like a building or a vase or a picture, or a transient, dynamic form like a melody or a dance, or even a form given to imagination, like the passage of purely imaginary, apparent events that constitutes a literary work. But it is always a perceptible, self-identical whole; like a natural being, it has a character of organic unity, self-sufficiency, individual reality. And it is thus, as an appearance, that a work of art is good or bad or perhaps only rather poor—as an appearance, not as a comment on things beyond it in the world, or as a reminder of them.

This, then, is what I mean by "form"; but what is meant by calling such forms "expressive of human feeling"? How do apparitions "express" anything—feeling or anything else? First of all, let us ask just what is meant here by "express," what sort of "expression" we are talking about.

The word "expression" has two principal meanings. In one sense it means self-expression—giving vent to our feelings. In this sense it refers to a symptom of what we feel. Self-expression is a spontaneous reaction to an actual, present situation, an event, the company we are in, things people say, or what the weather does to us; it bespeaks the physical and mental state we are in and the emotions that stir us.

In another sense, however, "expression" means the presentation of an idea, usually by the proper and apt use of words. But a device for presenting an idea is what we call a symbol, not a symptom. Thus a word is a symbol, and so is a meaningful combination of words.

A sentence, which is a special combination of words, expresses the idea of some state of affairs, real or imagined. Sentences are complicated symbols. Language will formulate new ideas as well as communicate old ones, so that all people know a lot of things that they have merely heard or read about. Symbolic expression, therefore, extends our knowledge beyond the scope of our actual experience.

If an idea is clearly conveyed by means of symbols we say it is well expressed. A person may work for a long time to give his statement the best possible form, to find the exact words for what he means to say, and to carry his account or his argument most directly from one point to another. But a discourse so worked out is certainly not a spontaneous reaction. Giving expression to an idea is obviously a different thing from giving expression to feelings. You do not say of a man in a rage that his anger is well expressed. The symptoms just are what they are; there is no critical standard for symptoms. If, on the other hand, the angry man tries to tell you what he is fuming about, he will have to collect himself, curtail his emotional expression, and find words to express his ideas. For to tell a story coherently involves "expression" in quite a different sense: this sort of expression is not "self-expression," but may be called "conceptual expression."

Language, of course, is our prime instrument of conceptual expression. The things we can say are in effect the things we can think. Words are the terms of our thinking as well as the terms in which we present our thoughts, because they present the objects of thought to the thinker himself. Before language communicates ideas, it gives them form, makes them clear, and in fact makes them what they are. Whatever has a name is an object for thought. Without words, sense experience is only a flow of impressions, as subjective as our feelings; words make it objective, and carve it up into *things* and *facts* that we can note, remember, and think about. Language gives outward experience its form, and makes it definite and clear.

There is, however, an important part of reality that is quite inaccessible to the formative influence of language: that is the realm of so-called "inner experience," the life of feeling and emotion. The reason why language is so powerless here is not, as many people suppose, that feeling and emotion are irrational; on the contrary, they seem irrational because language does not help to make them conceivable, and most people cannot conceive anything without the logical scaffolding of words. The unfitness of language to convey subjective experience is a somewhat technical subject, easier for logicians to understand than for artists; but the gist of it is that the form of language does not reflect the natural form of feeling, so that we cannot shape any extensive concepts of feeling with the help of ordinary, discursive language. Therefore the words whereby we refer to feeling only name very general kinds of inner experience—excitement, calm, joy, sorrow, love, hate, and so on. But there is no language to describe just how one joy differs, sometimes radically, from another. The real nature of feeling is something language as such—as discursive symbolism—cannot render.

For this reason, the phenomena of feeling and emotion are usually treated by philosophers as irrational. The only pattern discursive thought can find in them is the pattern of outward events that occasion them. There are different degrees of fear, but they are thought of as so many degrees of the same simple feeling.

But human feeling is a fabric, not a vague mass. It has an intricate dynamic pattern, possible combinations and new emergent phenomena. It is a pattern of organically interdependent and interdetermined tensions and resolutions, a pattern of almost infinitely complex activation and cadence. To it belongs the whole gamut of our sensibility—the sense of straining thought, all mental attitude and motor set. Those are the deeper reaches that underlie the surface waves of our emotion, and make human life a life of feeling instead of an unconscious metabolic existence interrupted by feelings.

It is, I think, this dynamic pattern that finds its formal expression in the arts. The expressiveness of art is like that of a symbol, not that of an emotional symptom; it is as a formulation of feeling for our conception that a work of art is properly said to be expressive. It may serve somebody's need of self-expression besides, but that is not what makes it good or bad art. In a special sense one may call a work of art a symbol of feeling, for, like a symbol, it formulates our ideas of inward experience, as discourse formulates our ideas of things and facts in the outside world. A work of art differs from a genuine symbol—that is, a symbol in the full and usual sense—in that it does not point beyond itself to something else. Its realization to feeling is a rather special one that we cannot undertake to analyze here; in effect, the feeling it expresses appears to be directly given with it—as the sense of a true metaphor, or the value of a religious myth—and is not separable from its expression. We speak of the feeling *of*, or the feeling *in*, a work of art, not the feeling it means. And we speak truly; a work of art presents something like a direct vision of vitality, emotion, subjective reality.

The primary function of art is to objectify feeling so that we can contemplate and understand it. It is the formulation of so-called "inward experience," the "inner life," that is impossible to achieve by discursive thought, because its forms are incommensurable with the forms of language and all its derivatives (e.g., mathematics, symbolic logic). Art objectifies the sentience and desire, self-consciousness and world-consciousness, emotions and moods, that are generally regarded as irrational because words cannot give us clear ideas of them. But the premise tacitly assumed in such a judgment—namely, that anything language cannot express is formless and irrational—seems to me to be an error. I believe the life of feeling is not irrational; its logical forms are merely very different from the structures of discourse. But they are so much like the dynamic forms of art that art is their natural symbol. Through plastic works, music, fiction, dance, or dramatic forms we can conceive what vitality and emotion feel like.

This brings us, at last, to the question of the cultural importance of the arts. Why is art so apt to be the vanguard of cultural advance, as it was in Egypt, in Greece, in Christian Europe (think of Gregorian music and Gothic architecture), in Renaissance Italy—not to speculate about ancient cavemen, whose art is all that we know of them? One thinks of culture as economic increase, social organization, the gradual ascendancy of rational thinking and scientific control of nature over superstitious imagination and magical practices. But art is not practical; it is neither philosophy nor science; it is not religion, morality, or even social comment (as many drama critics take comedy to be). What does it contribute to culture that could be of major importance?

It merely presents forms—sometimes intangible forms—to imagination. Its direct appeal is to that faculty, or function, that Lord Bacon considered the chief stumbling block in the way of reason, and that enlightened writers like Stuart Chase never tire of condemning as the source of all nonsense and bizarre erroneous beliefs. And so it is; but it is also the source of all insight and true beliefs. Imagination is probably the oldest mental trait that is typically human—older than discursive reason; it is probably the common source of dream, reason, religion, and all true general observation. It is this primitive human power—imagination—that engenders the arts and is in turn directly affected by their products.

Somewhere at the animalian starting line of human evolution lie the beginnings of that supreme instrument of the mind—language. We think of it as a device for communication among the members of a society. But communication is only one, and perhaps not even the first, of its functions. The first thing it does is to break up what William James called the "blooming, buzzing confusion" of sense perception into units and groups, events and chains of events—things and relations, causes and effects. All these patterns are imposed on our experience by language. We think, as we speak, in terms of objects and their relations.

But the process of breaking up our sense experience in this way, making reality conceivable, memorable, sometimes even predictable, is a process of imagination. Primitive conception is imagination. Language and imagination grow up together in a reciprocal tutelage.

What discursive symbolism—language in its literal use—does for our awareness of things about us and our own relation to them, the arts do for our awareness of subjective reality, feeling and emotion; they give form to inward experiences and thus make them conceivable. The only way we can really envisage vital movement, the stirring and growth and passage of emotion, and ultimately the whole direct sense of human life, is in artistic terms. A musical person thinks of emotions musically. They cannot be discursively talked about above a very general level. But they may nonetheless be known—objectively set forth, publicly known—and there is nothing necessarily confused or formless about emotions.

676

As soon as the natural forms of subjective experience are abstracted to the point of symbolic presentation, we can use those forms to imagine feeling and understand its nature. Self-knowledge, insight into all phases of life and mind, springs from artistic imagination. That is the cognitive value of the arts.

But their influence on human life goes deeper than the intellectual level. As language actually gives form to our sense experience, grouping our impressions around those things which have names, and fitting sensations to the qualities that have adjectival names, and so on, the arts we live with—our picture books and stories and the music we hear—actually form our emotive experience. Every generation has its styles of feeling. One age shudders and blushes and faints, another swaggers, still another is godlike in a universal indifference. These styles in actual emotion are not insincere. They are largely unconscious —determined by many social causes, but *shaped* by artists, usually popular artists of the screen, the jukebox, the shop window, and the picture magazine. (That, rather than incitement to crime, is my objection to the comics.) Irwin Edman remarks in one of his books that our emotions are largely Shakespeare's poetry.

This influence of art on life gives us an indication of why a period of efflorescence in the arts is apt to lead a cultural advance: it formulates a new way of feeling, and that is the beginning of a cultural age. It suggests another matter for reflection, too—that a wide neglect of artistic education is a neglect in the education of feeling. Most people are so imbued with the idea that feeling is a formless, total organic excitement in men as in animals that the idea of educating feeling, developing its scope and quality, seems odd to them, if not absurd. It is really, I think, at the very heart of personal education.

There is one other function of the arts that benefits not so much the advance of culture as its stabilization—an influence on individual lives. This function is the converse and complement of the objectification of feeling, the driving force of creation in art: it is the education of vision that we receive in seeing, hearing, reading works of art—the development of the artist's eye, that assimilates ordinary sights (or sounds, motions, or events) to inward vision, and lends expressiveness and emotional import to the world. Wherever art takes a motif from actuality—a flowering branch, a bit of landscape, a historic event, or a personal memory, any model or theme from life—it transforms it into a piece of imagination, and imbues its image with artistic vitality. The result is an impregnation of ordinary reality with the significance of created form. This is the subjectification of nature that makes reality itself a symbol of life and feeling.

The arts objectify subjective reality, and subjectify outward experience of nature. Art education is the education of feeling, and a society that neglects it gives itself up to formless emotion. Bad art is corruption of feeling. This is a large factor in the irrationalism which dictators and demagogues exploit.

Henri Matisse

One of the most notable twentieth-century painters, Matisse was born in France in 1869. He first studied under Adolphe Bougereau, whom he found too academic; he then studied under Gustave Moreau, spending a great deal of time copying paintings of old masters at the Louvre. When he discovered the impressionists, he changed radically, joined the new school, and became one of its most memorable representatives. His first successful original painting, "Dinner Table," was exhibited in 1897 and in the next years Matisse painted a whole series of what have since been called masterpieces. He has also done some sculpting, worked with lithographs and etchings, illustrated many books, and designed two ballet sets—one for Diaghilev. In 1943 he left Paris for Vence, a small village in the hills behind Nice; he continued to work, and also designed the chapel of the Rosary for the Dominican nuns there. Matisse died in Nice in 1954 at the age of eighty-five. "Notes of a Painter" was originally published in La Grande Revue, *Paris, on December 25, 1908. We have taken our text from the English translation, by Margaret Scolari Barr, which was published first in* Henri-Matisse *(The Museum of Modern Art, 1931) and later in* Matisse: His Art and His Public, *by Alfred H. Barr, Jr. (1951). We have omitted the paragraph headings added by the editor.*

NOTES OF A PAINTER

A painter who addresses the public not in order to present his works but to reveal some of his ideas on the art of painting exposes himself to several dangers. In the first place, I know that some people like to think of painting as dependent upon literature and therefore like to see in it not general ideas suited to pictorial art, but rather specifically literary ideas. I fear, therefore, that the painter who risks himself in the field of the literary man may be regarded with disapproval; in any case, I myself am fully convinced that the best explanation an artist can give of his aims and ability is afforded by his work.

However, such painters as Signac, Desvallières, Denis, Blanche, Guérin, Bernard etc. have written on such matters in various periodicals. In my turn I shall endeavor to make clear my pictorial intentions and aspirations without worrying about the writing.

One of the dangers which appears to me immediately is that of contradicting myself. I feel very strongly the bond between my old works and my recent ones. But I do not think the way I thought yesterday. My fundamental thoughts have not changed but have evolved and my modes of expression have followed my thoughts. I do not repudiate any of my paintings but I would not paint one of them in the same way had I to do it again. My destination is always the same but I work out a different route to get there.

If I mention the name of this or that artist it will be to point out how our manners differ so that it may seem that I do not appreciate his work. Thus I may be accused of injustice towards painters whose efforts and aims I best understand, or whose accomplishments I most appreciate. I shall use them as examples not to establish my superiority over them but to show clearly through what they have done, what I am attempting to do.

What I am after, above all, is expression. Sometimes it has been conceded that I have a certain technical ability but that, my ambition being limited, I am unable to proceed beyond a purely visual satisfaction such as can be procured from the mere sight of a picture. But the purpose of a painter must not be conceived as separate from his pictorial means, and these pictorial means must be the more complete (I do not mean complicated) the deeper is his thought. I am unable to distinguish between the feeling I have for life and my way of expressing it.

Expression to my way of thinking does not consist of the passion mirrored upon a human face or betrayed by a violent gesture. The whole arrangement of my picture is expressive. The place occupied by figures or objects, the empty spaces around them, the proportions, everything plays a part. Composition is the art of arranging in a decorative manner the various elements at the painter's disposal for the expression of his feelings. In a picture every part will be visible and will play the rôle conferred upon it, be it principal or secondary. All that is not useful in the picture is detrimental. A work of art must be harmonious in its entirety; for superfluous details would, in the mind of the beholder, encroach upon the essential elements.

Composition, the aim of which is expression, alters itself according to the surface to be covered. If I take a sheet of paper of given dimensions I will jot down a drawing which will have a necessary relation to its format—I would not repeat this drawing on another sheet of different dimensions, for instance on a rectangular sheet if the first one happened to be square. And if I had to repeat it on a sheet of the same shape but ten times larger I would not limit myself to enlarging it: a drawing must have a power of expansion which can bring to life the space which surrounds it. An artist who wants to transpose a composition onto a larger canvas must conceive it over again in order to preserve its expression; he must alter its character and not just fill in the squares into which he has divided his canvas.

Both harmonies and dissonances of color can produce very pleasurable effects. Often when I settle down to work I begin by noting my immediate and superficial color sensations. Some years ago this first result was often enough for me—but today if I were satisfied with this my picture would remain incomplete. I would have put down the passing sensations of a moment; they would not completely define my feelings and the next day I might not recognize what they meant. I want to reach that state of condensation of sensations which constitutes a picture. Perhaps I might be satisfied momentarily with a work finished at one sitting but I would soon get bored looking at it; therefore, I prefer to continue working on it so that later I may recognize it as a work of my mind. There was a time when I never left my paintings hanging on the wall because they reminded me of moments of nervous excitement and I did not like to see them again when I was quiet. Nowadays I try to put serenity into my pictures and work at them until I feel that I have succeeded.

Supposing I want to paint the body of a woman: first of all I endow it with grace and charm but I know that something more than that is necessary. I try to condense the meaning of this body by drawing its essential lines. The charm will then become less apparent at first glance but in the long run it will begin to emanate from the new image. This image at the same time will be enriched by a wider meaning, a more comprehensively human one, while the charm, being less apparent, will not be its only characteristic. It will be merely one element in the general conception of the figure.

Charm, lightness, crispness—all these are passing sensations. I have a canvas on which the colors are still fresh and I begin work on it again. The colors will probably grow heavier—the freshness of the original tones will give way to greater solidity, an improvement to my mind, but less seductive to the eye.

The impressionist painters, Monet, Sisley especially, had delicate, vibrating sensations; as a result their canvases are all alike. The word "impressionism" perfectly characterizes their intentions for they register fleeting impressions. This term, however, cannot be used with reference to more recent painters who avoid the first impression and consider it deceptive. A rapid rendering of a landscape represents only one moment of its appearance. I prefer, by insisting upon its essentials, to discover its more enduring character and content, even at the risk of sacrificing some of its pleasing qualities.

Underneath this succession of moments which constitutes the superficial existence of things animate and inanimate and which is continually obscuring and transforming them, it is yet possible to search for a truer, more essential character which the artist will seize so that he may give to reality a more lasting interpretation. When we go into the XVII and XVIII century sculpture rooms in the Louvre and look for instance at a Puget, we realize that the expression is forced and exaggerated in a very disquieting way. Then, again, if we go to the Luxembourg the attitude in which the painters seize their models is always the one in which the muscular development will be shown to greatest advantage. But movement thus interpreted corresponds to nothing in nature and if we catch a motion of this kind by a snapshot the image thus captured will remind us of nothing that we have seen. Indication of motion has meaning for us only if we do not isolate any one sensation of movement from the preceding and from the following one.

There are two ways of expressing things; one is to show them crudely, the other is to evoke them artistically. In abandoning the literal representation of movement it is possible to reach towards a higher ideal of beauty. Look at an Egyptian statue: it looks rigid to us; however, we feel in it the image of a body capable of movement and which despite its stiffness is animated. The Greeks too are calm; a man hurling a discus will be shown in the moment in which he gathers his strength before the effort or else, if he is shown in the most violent and precarious position implied by his action, the sculptor will have abridged and condensed it so that balance is re-established, thereby suggesting a feeling of duration. Movement in itself is unstable and is not suited to something durable like a statue unless the artist has consciously realized the entire action of which he represents only a moment.

It is necessary for me to define the character of the object or of the body that I wish to paint. In order to do this I study certain salient points very carefully: if I put a black dot on a sheet of white paper the dot will be visible no matter how far I stand away from it—it is a clear notation; but beside this dot I place another one, and then a third. Already there is confusion. In order that the first dot may maintain its value I must enlarge it as I proceed putting other marks on the paper.

If upon a white canvas I jot down some sensations of blue, of green, of red—every new brushstroke diminishes the importance of the preceding ones. Suppose I set out to paint an interior: I have before me a cupboard; it gives me a sensation of bright red—and I put down a red which satisfies me; immediately a relation is established between this red and the white of the canvas. If I put a green near the red, if I paint in a yellow floor, there must still be between this green, this yellow and the white of the canvas a relation that will be satisfactory to me. But these several tones mutually weaken one another. It is necessary, therefore, that the various elements that I use be so balanced that they do not destroy one another. To do this I must organize my ideas; the relation between tones must be so established that they will sustain one another. A new combination of colors will succeed the first one and will give more completely my interpretation. I am forced to transpose until finally my picture may seem completely changed when, after successive modifications, the red has succeeded the green as the dominant color. I cannot copy nature in a servile way, I must interpret nature and submit it to the spirit of the picture—when I have found the relationship of all the tones the result must be a living harmony of tones, a harmony not unlike that of a musical composition.

For me all is in the conception—I must have a clear vision of the whole composition from the very beginning. I could mention the name of a great sculptor who produces some admirable pieces but for him a composition is nothing but the grouping of fragments and the result is a confusion of expression. Look instead at one of Cézanne's pictures: all is so well arranged in them that no matter how many figures are represented and no matter at what distance you stand, you will be able always to distinguish each figure clearly and you will always know which limb belongs to which body. If in the picture there is order and clarity it means that this same order and clarity existed in the mind of the painter and that the painter was conscious of their necessity. Limbs may cross, may mingle, but still in the eyes of the beholder they will remain attached to the right body. All confusion will have disappeared.

The chief aim of color should be to serve expression as well as possible. I put down my colors without a preconceived plan. If at the first step and perhaps without my being conscious of it one tone has particularly pleased me, more often than not when the picture is finished I will notice that I have respected this tone while I have progressively altered and transformed the others. I discover the quality of colors in a purely instinctive way. To paint an autumn landscape I will not try to remember what colors suit this season, I will only be inspired by the sensation that the season gives me; the icy clearness of the sour blue sky will express the season just as well as the tonalities of the leaves. My sensation itself may vary, the autumn may be soft and warm like a protracted summer or quite cool with a cold sky and lemon yellow trees that give a chilly impression and announce winter.

My choice of colors does not rest on any scientific theory; it is based on observation, on feeling, on the very nature of each experience. Inspired by certain pages of Delacroix, Signac is preoccupied by complementary colors and the theoretical knowledge of them will lead him to use a certain tone in a certain place. I, on the other hand, merely try to find a color that will fit my sensation. There is an impelling proportion of tones that can induce me to change the shape of a figure or to transform my composition. Until I have achieved this proportion in all the parts of the composition I strive towards it and keep on working. Then a moment comes when every part has found its definite relationship and from then on it would be impossible for me to add a stroke to my picture without having to paint it all over again. As a matter of fact, I think that the theory of complementary colors is not absolute. In studying the paintings of artists whose knowledge of colors depends only upon instinct and sensibility and on a consistency of their sensations, it would be possible to define certain laws of color and so repudiate the limitations of the accepted color theory.

What interests me most is neither still life nor landscape but the human figure. It is through it that I best succeed in expressing the nearly religious feeling that I have towards life. I do not insist upon the details of the face. I do not care to repeat them with anatomical exactness. Though I happen to have an Italian model whose appearance at first suggests nothing but a purely animal existence yet I succeed in picking out among the lines of his face those which suggest that deep gravity which persists in every human being. A work of art must carry in itself its complete significance and impose it upon the beholder even before he can identify the subject matter. When I see the Giotto frescoes at Padua I do not trouble to recognize which scene of the life of Christ I have before me but I perceive instantly the sentiment which radiates from it and which is instinct in the composition in every line and color. The title will only serve to confirm my impression.

What I dream of is an art of balance, of purity and serenity devoid of troubling or depressing subject matter, an art which might be for every mental worker, be he business man or writer, like an appeasing influence, like a mental soother, something like a good armchair in which to rest from physical fatigue.

Often a discussion arises upon the value of different processes, and their relation to different temperaments. A distinction is made between artists who work directly from nature and those who work purely from their imagination. I think neither of these methods should be preferred to the exclusion of the other. Often both are used in turn by the same man; sometimes he needs tangible objects to provide him with sensations and thus excite his creative power; at other times when his pictorial sensations are already present in his mind he needs contact with reality before he can organize them into a picture. However, I think that one can judge of the vitality and power of an artist when after having received impressions from nature he is able to organize his sensations to return in the same mood on different days, voluntarily to continue receiving these impressions (whether nature appears the same or not); this power proves he is sufficiently master of himself to subject himself to discipline.

The simplest means are those which enable an artist to express himself best. If he fears the obvious he cannot avoid it by strange representations, bizarre drawing, eccentric color. His expression must derive inevitably from his temperament. He must sincerely believe that he has only painted what he has seen. I like Chardin's way of expressing it: "I put on color until it resembles (is a good likeness)," or Cézanne: "I want to secure a likeness," or Rodin: "Copy nature!" or Leonardo: "He who can copy can do (create)." Those who work in an affected style, deliberately turning their backs on nature, are in error—an artist must recognize that when he uses his reason his picture is an artifice and that when he paints he must feel that he is copying nature—and even when he consciously departs from nature he must do it with the conviction that it is only the better to interpret her.

Some will object perhaps that a painter should have some other outlook upon painting and that I have only uttered platitudes. To this I shall answer that there are no new truths. The rôle of the artist, like that of the scholar, consists in penetrating truths as well known to him as to others but which will take on for him a new aspect and so enable him to master them in their deepest significance. Thus if the aviators were to explain to us the researches which led to their leaving earth and rising in the air they would be merely confirming very elementary principles of physics neglected by less successful inventors.

An artist has always something to learn when he is given information about himself—and I am glad now to have learned which is my weak point. M. Peladan in the "Revue Hébdomadaire" reproaches a certain number of painters, amongst whom I think I should place myself, for calling themselves "Fauves" (wild beasts) and yet dressing like everyone else so that they are no more noticeable than the floor walkers in a department store. Does genius count for so little? In the same article this excellent writer pretends that I do not paint honestly and I feel that I should perhaps be annoyed though I admit that he restricts his statement by adding, "I mean honestly with respect to the Ideal and the Rules." The trouble is that he does not mention where these rules are—I am willing to admit that they exist but were it possible to learn them what sublime artists we would have!

Rules have no existence outside of individuals: otherwise Racine would be no greater genius than a good professor. Any of us can repeat a fine sentence but few can also penetrate the meaning. I have no doubt that from a study of the works of Raphael or Titian a more complete set of rules can be drawn than from the works of Manet or Renoir but the rules followed by Manet and Renoir were suited to their artistic temperaments and I happen to prefer the smallest of their paintings to all the work of those who have merely imitated the "Venus of Urbino" or the "Madonna of the Goldfinch." Such painters are of no value to anyone because, whether we want to or not, we belong to our time and we share in its opinions, preferences and delusions. All artists bear the imprint of their time but the great artists are those in which this stamp is most deeply impressed. Our epoch for instance is better represented by Courbet than by Flandrin, by Rodin better than by Fremiet. Whether we want to or not between our period and ourselves an indissoluble bond is established and M. Peladan himself cannot escape it. The aestheticians of the future may perhaps use his books as evidence if they get it in their heads to prove that no one of our time understood a thing about the art of Leonardo da Vinci.

George Orwell

This essay is taken from Orwell's collection, Such, Such Were The Joys *(1953). For further information about the author and his writings, see page 79.*

WHY I WRITE

From a very early age, perhaps the age of five or six, I knew that when I grew up I should be a writer. Between the ages of about seventeen and twenty-four I tried to abandon this idea, but I did so with the consciousness that I was outraging my true nature and that sooner or later I should have to settle down and write books.

I was the middle child of three, but there was a gap of five years on either side, and I barely saw my father before I was eight. For this and other reasons I was somewhat lonely, and I soon developed disagreeable mannerisms which made me unpopular throughout my schooldays. I had the lonely child's habit of making up stories and holding conversations with imaginary persons, and I think from the very start my literary ambitions were mixed up with the feeling of being isolated and undervalued. I knew that I had a facility with words and a power of facing unpleasant facts, and I felt that this created a sort of private world in which I could get my own back for my failure in everyday life. Nevertheless the volume of serious—*i.e.* seriously intended—writing which I produced all through my childhood and boyhood would not amount to half a dozen pages. I wrote my first poem at the age of four or five, my mother taking it down to dictation. I cannot remember anything about it except that it was about a tiger and the tiger had "chair-like teeth"—a good enough phrase, but I fancy the poem was a plagiarism of Blake's "Tiger, Tiger." At eleven, when the war of 1914–18 broke out, I wrote a patriotic poem which was printed in the local newspaper, as was another, two years later, on the death of Kitchener. From time to time, when I was a bit older, I wrote bad and usually unfinished "nature poems" in the Georgian style. I also, about twice, attempted a short story which was a ghastly failure. That was the total of the would-be serious work that I actually set down on paper during all those years.

However, throughout this time I did in a sense engage in literary activities. To begin with there was the made-to-order stuff which I produced quickly, easily and without much pleasure to myself. Apart from school work, I wrote *vers d'occasion*, semi-comic poems which I could turn out at what now seems to me astonishing speed—at fourteen I wrote a whole rhyming play, in imitation of Aristophanes, in about a week—and helped to edit school magazines, both printed and in manuscript. These magazines were the most pitiful burlesque stuff that you could imagine, and I took far less trouble with them than I now would with the cheapest journalism. But side by side with all this, for fifteen years or more, I was carrying out a literary exercise of a quite different kind: this was the making up of a continuous "story" about myself, a sort of diary existing only in the mind. I believe this is a common habit of children and adolescents. As a very small child I used to imagine that I was, say, Robin Hood, and picture myself as the hero of thrilling adventures, but quite soon my "story" ceased to be narcissistic in a crude way and became more and more a mere description of what I was doing and the things I saw. For minutes at a time this kind of thing would be running through my head: "He pushed the door open and entered the room. A yellow beam of sunlight, filtering through the muslin curtains, slanted on to the table, where a matchbox, half open, lay beside the inkpot. With his right hand in his pocket he moved across to the window. Down in the street a tortoiseshell cat was chasing a dead leaf," etc., etc. This habit continued till I was about twenty-five, right through my non-literary years. Although I had to search, and did search, for the right words, I seemed to be making this descriptive effort almost against my will, under a kind of compulsion from outside. The "story" must, I suppose, have reflected the styles of the various writers I admired at different ages, but so far as I remember it always had the same meticulous descriptive quality.

When I was about sixteen I suddenly discovered the joy of mere words, *i.e.* the sounds and associations of words. The lines from *Paradise Lost*—

So hee with difficulty and labour hard
Moved on: with difficulty and labour hee,

which do not now seem to me so very wonderful, sent shivers down my backbone; and the spelling "hee" for "he" was an added pleasure. As for the need to describe things, I knew all about it already. So it is clear what kind of books I wanted to write, in so far as I could be said to want to write books at that time. I wanted to write enormous naturalistic novels with unhappy endings, full of detailed descriptions and arresting similes, and also full of purple passages in which words were used partly for the sake of their sound. And in fact my first completed novel, *Burmese Days*, which I wrote when I was thirty but projected much earlier, is rather that kind of book.

I give all this background information because I do not think one can assess a writer's motives without knowing something of his early development. His subject matter will be determined by the age he lives in—at least this is true in tumultuous, revolutionary ages like our own—but before he ever begins to write he will have acquired an emotional attitude from which he will never completely escape. It is his job, no doubt, to discipline his temperament and avoid getting stuck at some immature stage, or in some perverse mood: but if he escapes from his early influences altogether, he will have killed his impulse to write. Putting aside the need to earn a living, I think there are four great motives for writing, at any rate for writing prose. They exist in different degrees in every writer, and in any one writer the proportions will vary from time to time, according to the atmosphere in which he is living. They are:

(1) Sheer egoism. Desire to seem clever, to be talked about, to be

GEORGE ORWELL

remembered after death, to get your own back on grownups who snubbed you in childhood, etc., etc. It is humbug to pretend that this is not a motive, and a strong one. Writers share this characteristic with scientists, artists, politicians, lawyers, soldiers, successful business-men—in short, with the whole top crust of humanity. The great mass of human beings are not acutely selfish. After the age of about thirty they abandon individual ambition—in many cases, indeed, they almost abandon the sense of being individuals at all—and live chiefly for others, or are simply smothered under drudgery. But there is also the minor-ity of gifted, wilful people who are determined to live their own lives to the end, and writers belong in this class. Serious writers, I should say, are on the whole more vain and self-centered than journalists, though less interested in money.

(2) Esthetic enthusiasm. Perception of beauty in the external world, or, on the other hand, in words and their right arrangement. Pleasure in the impact of one sound on another, in the firmness of good prose or the rhythm of a good story. Desire to share an experience which one feels is valuable and ought not to be missed. The esthetic motive is very feeble in a lot of writers, but even a pamphleteer or a writer of textbooks will have pet words and phrases which appeal to him for non-utilitarian reasons; or he may feel strongly about typography, width of margins, etc. Above the level of a railway guide, no book is quite free from esthetic considerations.

(3) Historical impulse. Desire to see things as they are, to find out true facts and store them up for the use of posterity.

(4) Political purpose—using the word "political" in the widest possible sense. Desire to push the world in a certain direction, to alter other people's idea of the kind of society that they should strive after. Once again, no book is genuinely free from political bias. The opinion that art should have nothing to do with politics is itself a political attitude.

It can be seen how these various impulses must war against one another, and how they must fluctuate from person to person and from time to time. By nature—taking your "nature" to be the state you have attained when you are first adult—I am a person in whom the first three motives would outweigh the fourth. In a peaceful age I might have written ornate or merely descriptive books, and might have remained almost unaware of my political loyalties. As it is I have been forced into becoming a sort of pamphleteer. First I spent five years in an unsuitable profession (the Indian Imperial Police, in Burma), and then I underwent poverty and the sense of failure. This increased my natural hatred of authority and made me for the first time fully aware of the existence of the working classes, and the job in Burma had given me some understanding of the nature of imperialism: but these experiences were not enough to give me an accurate political orientation. Then came Hitler, the Spanish civil war, etc. By the end of 1935, I had still failed to reach a firm decision. I remember a little poem that I wrote at that date, expressing my dilemma:

A happy vicar I might have been
Two hundred years ago,
To preach upon eternal doom
And watch my walnuts grow;

But born, alas, in an evil time,
I missed that pleasant haven,
For the hair has grown on my upper lip
And the clergy are all clean-shaven.

And later still the times were good,
We were so easy to please,
We rocked our troubled thoughts to sleep
On the bosoms of the trees.

All ignorant we dared to own
The joys we now dissemble;
The greenfinch on the apple bough
Could make my enemies tremble.

But girls' bellies and apricots,
Roach in a shaded stream,
Horses, ducks in flight at dawn,
All these are a dream.

It is forbidden to dream again;
We maim our joys or hide them;
Horses are made of chromium steel
And little fat men shall ride them.

I am the worm who never turned,
The eunuch without a harem;
Between the priest and the commissar
I walk like Eugene Aram;

And the commissar is telling my fortune
While the radio plays,
But the priest has promised an Austin Seven,
For Duggie always pays.

I dreamed I dwelt in marble halls,
And woke to find it true;
I wasn't born for an age like this;
Was Smith? Was Jones? Were you?

The Spanish war and other events in 1936–7 turned the scale and thereafter I knew where I stood. Every line of serious work that I have written since 1936 has been written, directly or indirectly, *against* totalitarianism and *for* democratic socialism, as I understand it. It seems to me nonsense, in a period like our own, to think that one can avoid writing of such subjects. Everyone writes of them in one guise or another. It is simply a question of which side one takes and what approach one follows. And the more one is conscious of one's political bias, the more chance one has of acting politically without sacrificing one's esthetic and intellectual integrity.

What I have most wanted to do throughout the past ten years is to make political writing into an art. My starting point is always a feeling of partisanship, a sense of injustice. When I sit down to write a book, I do not say to myself, "I am going to produce a work of art." I write it because there is some lie that I want to expose, some fact to which I want to draw attention, and my initial concern is to get a hearing. But I could not do the work of writing a book, or even a long magazine article, if it were not also an esthetic experience. Anyone who cares to examine my work will see that even when it is downright propaganda it contains much that a full-time politician would consider irrelevant. I am not able, and I do not want, completely to abandon the world-view that I acquired in childhood. So long as I remain alive and well I shall continue to feel strongly about prose style, to love the surface of the earth, and to take a pleasure in solid objects and scraps of useless information. It is no use trying to suppress that side of myself. The job is to reconcile my ingrained likes and dislikes with the essentially public, nonindividual activities that this age forces on all of us.

It is not easy. It raises problems of construction and of language, and it raises in a new way the problem of truthfulness. Let me give just one example of the cruder kind of difficulty that arises. My book about the Spanish civil war, *Homage to Catalonia,* is, of course, a frankly political book, but in the main it is written with a certain detachment and regard for form. I did try very hard in it to tell the whole truth without violating my literary instincts. But among other things it contains a long chapter, full of newspaper quotations and the like, defending the Trotskyists who were accused of plotting with Franco. Clearly such a chapter, which after a year or two would lose its interest for any ordinary reader, must ruin the book. A critic whom I respect read me a lecture about it. "Why did you put in all that stuff?" he said. "You've turned what might have been a good book into journalism." What he said was true, but I could not have done otherwise. I happened to know, what very few people in England had been allowed to know, that innocent men were being falsely accused. If I had not been angry about that I should never have written the book.

In one form or another this problem comes up again. The problem of language is subtler and would take too long to discuss. I will only say that of late years I have tried to write less picturesquely and more exactly. In any case I find that by the time you have perfected any style of writing, you have always outgrown it. *Animal Farm* was the first book in which I tried, with full consciousness of what I was doing, to fuse political purpose and artistic purpose into one whole. I have not written a novel for seven years, but I hope to write another fairly soon. It is bound to be a failure, every book is a failure, but I do know with some clarity what kind of book I want to write.

Looking back through the last page or two, I see that I have made it appear as though my motives in writing were wholly public-spirited. I don't want to leave that as the final impression. All writers are vain, selfish and lazy, and at the very bottom of their motives there lies a mystery. Writing a book is a horrible, exhausting struggle, like a long bout of some painful illness. One would never undertake such a thing if one were not driven on by some demon whom one can neither resist nor understand. For all one knows that demon is simply the same instinct that makes a baby squall for attention. And yet it is also true that one can write nothing readable unless one constantly struggles to efface one's own personality. Good prose is like a window pane. I cannot say with certainty which of my motives are the strongest, but I know which of them deserve to be followed. And looking back through my work, I see that it is invariably where I lacked a *political* purpose that I wrote lifeless books and was betrayed into purple passages, sentences without meaning, decorative adjectives and humbug generally.

[1947]

Albert Camus

Albert Camus, regarded by many as the conscience of his age, was killed in an automobile accident in France at the age of forty-six. Born in Algeria in 1913, he spent his childhood in extreme poverty. The Wrong Side and the Right Side *(1937) is a moving record of those years. While he was working his way through the University of Algeria, he became interested in the*

theater, and for a few years managed, acted, and wrote for a
theatrical company. He then worked as a journalist, first for
Alger Républicain, *later in France for* Paris Soir. *In 1942 he*
joined the French Resistance movement; he edited and wrote many
articles—then unsigned—for the underground newspaper Combat.
After the liberation he began to devote full time to his writing.

Camus' reputation was soon solidly established, his fame
became international, and in 1957 he was awarded the Nobel
Prize for literature. The Committee cited his "clearsighted
earnestness" which "illuminates the problem of the human
conscience of our time." Some of his most influential expository
writing will be found in The Myth of Sisyphus *(1942),* The
Rebel *(1951), and* Resistance, Rebellion, and Death *(1960).*
His three novels, The Stranger *(1942),* The Plague *(1947),* The
Fall *(1956), and* Exile and the Kingdom *(1957), a book of*
short stories, express his philosophical ideas in fictional terms. At
least two pieces by Camus have been translated into English under
the title The Artist and His Time. *We present below a section*
of the 1953 piece printed in The Myth of Sisyphus and Other
Essays, *translated by Justin O'Brien (1955).*

WHAT CAN THE ARTIST DO IN THE WORLD OF TODAY?

He is not asked either to write about co-operatives or, conversely, to
lull to sleep in himself the sufferings endured by others throughout
history. And since you have asked me to speak personally, I am going
to do so as simply as I can. Considered as artists, we perhaps have
no need to interfere in the affairs of the world. But considered as men,
yes. The miner who is exploited or shot down, the slaves in the
camps, those in the colonies, the legions of persecuted throughout the
world—they need all those who can speak to communicate their silence
and to keep in touch with them. I have not written, day after day,
fighting articles and texts, I have not taken part in the common struggles because I desire the world to be covered with Greek statues and
masterpieces. The man who has such a desire does exist in me.
Except that he has something better to do in trying to instill life into
the creatures of his imagination. But from my first articles to my
latest book I have written so much, and perhaps too much, only
because I cannot keep from being drawn toward everyday life, toward
those, whoever they may be, who are humiliated and debased. They

need to hope, and if all keep silent or if they are given a choice between two kinds of humiliation, they will be forever deprived of hope and we with them. It seems to me impossible to endure that idea, nor can he who cannot endure it lie down to sleep in his tower. Not through virtue, as you see, but through a sort of almost organic intolerance, which you feel or do not feel. Indeed, I see many who fail to feel it, but I cannot envy their sleep.

This does not mean, however, that we must sacrifice our artist's nature to some social preaching or other. I have said elsewhere why the artist was more than ever necessary. But if we intervene as men, that experience will have an effect upon our language. And if we are not artists in our language first of all, what sort of artists are we? Even if, militants in our lives, we speak in our works of deserts and of selfish love, the mere fact that our lives are militant causes a special tone of voice to people with men that desert and that love. I shall certainly not choose the moment when we are beginning to leave nihilism behind to stupidly deny the values of creation in favor of the values of humanity, or vice versa. In my mind neither one is ever separated from the other and I measure the greatness of an artist (Molière, Tolstoy, Melville) by the balance he managed to maintain between the two. Today, under the pressure of events, we are obliged to transport that tension into our lives likewise. This is why so many artists, bending under the burden, take refuge in the ivory tower or, conversely, in the social church. But as for me, I see in both choices a like act of resignation. We must simultaneously serve suffering and beauty. The long patience, the strength, the secret cunning such service calls for are the virtues that establish the very renascence we need.

One word more. This undertaking, I know, cannot be accomplished without dangers and bitterness. We must accept the dangers: the era of chairbound artists is over. But we must reject the bitterness. One of the temptations of the artist is to believe himself solitary, and in truth he hears this shouted at him with a certain base delight. But this is not true. He stands in the midst of all, in the same rank, neither higher nor lower, with all those who are working and struggling. His very vocation, in the face of oppression, is to open the prisons and to give a voice to the sorrows and joys of all. This is where art, against its enemies, justifies itself by proving precisely that it is no one's enemy. By itself art could probably not produce the renascence which implies justice and liberty. But without it, that renascence would be without forms and, consequently, would be nothing. Without culture, and the relative freedom it implies, society, even when perfect, is but a jungle. This is why any authentic creation is a gift to the future.

(1953)

Mao Tse-tung

Mao Tse-tung is the Chairman of the Communist Party of the People's Republic of China and is widely regarded to be the ideological leader of the communist world. He was born in 1893 to a family of peasant origin. He attended teacher's college at Changsha, graduated in 1918, then held a variety of jobs: normal-school teacher, political organizer, editor, and library assistant at Peking University, where he read Karl Marx and deepened his own ideas of a communist revolution based on the Chinese peasantry. He was one of the twelve founding members of the Party in 1921.

With many political and military vicissitudes, Mao made his way to the head of a movement which successively wrested China from provincial warlords, Japanese invaders, and, between 1946 and 1949, from its erstwhile ally, the Kuomintang under President Chiang Kai-shek. Mao's regime has had moments of relative liberalism, but has been most characterized by severe repression of dissidents, as in the "Red Guard" cultural revolution of 1962. His theories are now considered infallible by masses of communist Chinese, who regard him as a "living Buddha."

His most important statements on art and literature were made in two talks at a forum held at Yenan, his headquarters, in 1942. At the time, the Communists were allied with the Kuomintang in a war against the invading Japanese. Mao was just instituting a "rectification" program, designed to tighten party discipline and get rid of undesirable elements. We print below a section from the second of his talks, as found in the fourth volume of his Selected Works *(1954–1961). Writings of related interest appear in* Mao Tse-tung on Art and Literature *(1960), the* Mao Tse-tung Anthology *(ed. Anne Fremantle, 1962), and* Mao and the Chinese Revolution, *with thirty-seven of Mao's poems (ed. Michael Bullock, 1965).*

FROM TALKS AT THE YENAN FORUM ON ART AND LITERATURE

One of the principal methods of struggle in the artistic and literary sphere is art and literary criticism. It should be developed and, as many comrades have rightly pointed out, our work in this respect was quite inadequate in the past. Art and literary criticism presents a complex problem which requires much study of a special kind. Here I shall stress only the basic problem of criteria in criticism. I shall also comment briefly on certain other problems and incorrect views brought up by some comrades.

There are two criteria in art and literary criticism: political and artistic. According to the political criterion, all works are good that facilitate unity and resistance to Japan, that encourage the masses to be of one heart and one mind and that oppose retrogression and promote progress; on the other hand, all works are bad that undermine unity and resistance to Japan, that sow dissension and discord among the masses and that oppose progress and drag the people back. And how can we tell the good from the bad here—by the motive (subjective intention) or by the effect (social practice)? Idealists stress motive and ignore effect, while mechanical materialists stress effect and ignore motive; in contradistinction from either, we dialectical materialists insist on the unity of motive and effect. The motive of serving the masses is inseparable from the effect of winning their approval, and we must unite the two. The motive of serving the individual or a small clique is not good, nor is the motive of serving the masses good if it does not lead to a result that is welcomed by the masses and confers benefit on them. In examining the subjective intention of an artist, *i.e.* whether his motive is correct and good, we do not look at his declaration but at the effect his activities (mainly his works) produce on society and the masses. Social practice and its effect are the criteria for examining the subjective intention or the motive. We reject sectarianism in our art and literary criticism and, under the general principle of unity and resistance to Japan, we must tolerate all artistic and literary works expressing every kind of political attitude. But at the same time we must firmly uphold our principles in our criticism, and adhere to our standpoint and severely criticise and repudiate all artistic and literary works containing views against the nation, the sciences, the people and communism, because such works, in motive as well as in effect, are detrimental to unity and the resistance to Japan. According to the artistic criterion, all works are good or comparatively good that are relatively high in artistic quality; and bad or comparatively bad that are relatively low in artistic quality. Of course, this distinction also depends on social effect. As there is hardly an artist who does not consider his own work excellent, our criticism ought to permit the free competition of all varieties of artistic works; but it is entirely necessary for us to pass correct judgments on them according to the criteria of the science of art, so that we can gradually raise the art of a lower level to a higher level, and to change the art which does not meet the requirements of the struggle of the broad masses into art that does meet them.

695

There is thus the political criterion as well as the artistic criterion. How are the two related? Politics is not the equivalent of art, nor is a general world outlook equivalent to the method of artistic creation and criticism. We believe there is neither an abstract and absolutely unchangeable political criterion, nor an abstract and absolutely unchangeable artistic criterion, for every class in a class society has its own political and artistic criteria. But all classes in all class societies place the political criterion first and the artistic criterion second. The bourgeoisie always rejects proletarian artistic and literary works, no matter how great their artistic achievement. As for the proletariat, they must treat the art and literature of the past according to their attitude towards the people and whether they are progressive in the light of history. Some things which are basically reactionary from the political point of view may yet be artistically good. But the more artistic such a work may be, the greater harm will it do to the people, and the more reason for us to reject it. The contradiction between reactionary political content and artistic form is a common characteristic of the art and literature of all exploiting classes in their decline. What we demand is unity of politics and art, of content and form, and of the revolutionary political content and the highest possible degree of perfection in artistic form. Works of art, however politically progressive, are powerless if they lack artistic quality. Therefore we are equally opposed to works with wrong political approaches and to the tendency towards so-called "poster and slogan style" which is correct only in political approach but lacks artistic power. We must carry on a two-front struggle in art and literature.

Both tendencies can be found in the ideologies of many of our comrades. Those comrades who tend to neglect artistic quality should pay attention to its improvement. But as I see it, the political side is more of a problem at present. Some comrades lack elementary political knowledge and consequently all kinds of muddled ideas arise. Let me give a few instances found in Yenan.

"The theory of human nature." Is there such a thing as human nature? Of course there is. But there is only human nature in the concrete, no human nature in the abstract. In a class society there is only human nature that bears the stamp of a class, but no human nature transcending classes. We uphold the human nature of the proletariat and of the great masses of the people, while the landlord and bourgeois classes uphold the nature of their own classes as if— though they do not say so outright—it were the only kind of human nature. The human nature boosted by certain petty-bourgeois intellectuals is also divorced from or opposed to that of the great masses of the people; what they call human nature is in substance nothing but bourgeois individualism, and consequently in their eyes proletarian human nature is contrary to their human nature. This is the "theory of human nature" advocated by some people in Yenan as the so-called basis of their theory of art and literature, which is utterly mistaken.

"The fundamental point of departure for art and literature is love, the love of mankind." Now love may serve as a point of departure, but there is still a more basic one. Love is a concept, a product of objective practice. Fundamentally, we do not start from a concept but from objective practice. Our artists and writers who come from the intelligentsia love the proletariat because social life has made them feel that they share the same fate with the proletariat. We hate Japanese imperialism because the Japanese imperialists oppress us. There is no love or hatred in the world that has not its cause. As to the so-called "love of mankind", there has been no such all-embracing love since humanity was divided into classes. All the ruling classes in the past liked to advocate it, and many so-called sages and wise men also did the same, but nobody has ever really practised it, for it is impracticable in a class society. Genuine love of mankind will be born only when class distinctions have been eliminated throughout the world. The classes have caused the division of society into many opposites and as soon as they are eliminated there will be love of all mankind, but not now. We cannot love our enemies, we cannot love social evils, and our aim is to exterminate them. How can our artists and writers fail to understand such a common sense matter?

"Art and literature have always described the bright as well as the dark side of things impartially, on a fifty-fifty basis." This statement contains a number of muddled ideas. Art and literature have not always done so. Many petty-bourgeois writers have never found the bright side and their works are devoted to exposing the dark side, the so-called "literature of exposure"; there are even works which specialise in propagating pessimism and misanthropy. On the other hand, Soviet literature during the period of socialist reconstruction portrays mainly the bright side. It also describes shortcomings in work and villainous characters, but such descriptions serve only to bring out the brightness of the whole picture, and not on a "compensating basis". Bourgeois writers of reactionary periods portray the revolutionary masses as ruffians and describe the bourgeois as saints, thus reversing the so-called bright and dark sides. Only truly revolutionary artists and writers can correctly solve the problem whether to praise or to expose. All dark forces which endanger the masses of the people must be exposed while all revolutionary struggles of the masses must be praised—this is the basic task of all revolutionary artists and writers.

"The task of art and literature has always been to expose." This

697

sort of argument, like the one mentioned above, arises from the lack of knowledge of the science of history. We have already shown that the task of art and literature does not consist solely in exposure. For the revolutionary artists and writers the objects to be exposed can never be the masses of the people, but only the aggressors, exploiters and oppressors and their evil aftermath brought to the people. The people have their shortcomings too, but these are to be overcome by means of criticism and self-criticism within the ranks of the people themselves, and to carry on such criticism and self-criticism is also one of the most important tasks of art and literature. However, we should not call that "exposing the people". As for the people, our problem is basically one of how to educate them and raise their level. Only counter-revolutionary artists and writers describe the people as "born fools" and the revolutionary masses as "tyrannical mobs".

"This is still a period of the essay, and the style should still be that of Lu Hsun." Living under the rule of the dark forces, deprived of freedom of speech, Lu Hsun had to fight by means of burning satire and freezing irony cast in essay form, and in this he was entirely correct. We too must hold up to sharp ridicule the fascists, the Chinese reactionaries and everything endangering the people; but in our border region of Shensi-Kansu-Ningsia and the anti-Japanese base areas in the enemy's rear, where revolutionary artists and writers are given full freedom and democracy and only counter-revolutionaries are deprived of them, essays must not be written simply in the same style as Lu Hsun's. Here we can shout at the top of our voice, and need not resort to obscure and veiled expressions which would tax the understanding of the broad masses of the people. In dealing with the people themselves and not the enemies of the people, Lu Hsun even in his "essay period" did not mock or attack the revolutionary masses and the revolutionary parties, and his style was also entirely different from that employed in his essays on the enemy. We have already said that we must criticise the shortcomings of the people, but be sure that we criticise from the standpoint of the people and out of a whole-hearted eagerness to defend and educate them. If we treat our comrades like enemies, then we are taking the standpoint of the enemy. Are we then to give up satire altogether? No. Satire is always necessary. But there are all kinds of satire; the kind for our enemies, the kind for our allies and the kind for our own ranks—each of them assumes a different attitude. We are not opposed to satire as a whole, but we must not abuse it.

"I am not given to praise and eulogy; works which extol the bright side of things are not necessarily great, nor are works which depict the dark side necessarily poor." If you are a bourgeois artist or writer, you will extol not the proletariat but the bourgeoisie, and if you are a proletarian artist or writer, you will extol not the bourgeoisie but the proletariat and the working people: you must do one or the other. Those works which extol the bright side of the bourgeoisie are not necessarily great while those which depict its dark side are not necessarily poor, and those works which extol the bright side of the proletariat are not necessarily poor, while those works which depict the so-called "dark side" of the proletariat are certainly poor—are these not facts recorded in the history of art and literature? Why should we not extol the people, the creator of the history of the human world? Why should we not extol the proletariat, the Communist Party, the New Democracy and socialism? Of course, there are persons who have no enthusiasm for the people's cause and stand aloof, looking with cold indifference on the struggle and the victory of the proletariat and its vanguard; and they only take pleasure in singing endless praises of themselves, plus perhaps a few persons in their own coterie. Such petty-bourgeois individualists are naturally unwilling to praise the meritorious deeds of the revolutionary masses or to heighten their courage in struggle and confidence in victory. Such people are the black sheep in the revolutionary ranks and the revolutionary masses have indeed no use for such "singers".

"It is not a matter of standpoint; the standpoint is correct, the intention good, and the ideas are all right, but the expression is faulty and produces a bad effect." I have already spoken about the dialectical materialistic view of motive and effect, and now I want to ask: Is the question of effect not one of standpoint? A person who, in doing a job, minds only the motive and pays no regard to the effect, is very much like a doctor who hands out prescriptions and does not care how many patients may die of them. Suppose, again, a political party keeps on making pronouncements while paying not the least attention to carrying them out. We may well ask, is such a standpoint correct? Are such intentions good? Of course, a person is liable to mistakes in estimating the result of an action before it is taken; but are his intentions really good if he adheres to the same old rut even when facts prove that it leads to bad results? In judging a party or a doctor, we must look at the practice and the effect, and the same applies in judging an artist or a writer. One who has a truly good intention must take the effect into consideration by summing up experiences and studying methods or, in the case of creative work, the means of expression. One who has a truly good intention must criticise with the utmost candour his own shortcomings and mistakes in work, and make up his mind to correct them. That is why the Communists have adopted the method of self-criticism. Only such a standpoint is the correct one. At the same time it is only through such a process of practice carried out conscientiously and responsibly that we can gradually understand what the correct point of view is and have a firm grasp of it. If we refuse to do this in practice, then we are really ignorant of the correct point of view, despite our conceited assertion to the contrary.

"To call on us to study Marxism may again lead us to take the repetition of dialectical materialist formulas for literary creation, and this will stifle our creative impulse." We study Marxism in order to apply the dialectical materialist and historical materialist viewpoint in our observation of the world, society and art and literature, and not in order to write philosophical discourses in our works of art and literature. Marxism embraces realism in artistic and literary creation but cannot replace it, just as it embraces atomics and electronics in physics but cannot replace them. Empty, cut-and-dried dogmas and formulas will certainly destroy our creative impulse; moreover, they first of all destroy Marxism. Dogmatic "Marxism" is not Marxist but anti-Marxist. But will Marxism not destroy any creative impulse? It will; it will certainly destroy the creative impulse that is feudal, bourgeois, petty-bourgeois, liberal, individualistic, nihilistic, art-for-art's-sake, aristocratic, decadent or pessimistic, and any creative impulse that is not of the people and of the proletariat. As far as the artists and writers of the proletariat are concerned, ought not these kinds of impulse to be done away with? I think they ought; they should be utterly destroyed, and while they are being destroyed, new things can be built up.

Eudora Welty

Eudora Welty is a versatile and distinctive Southern writer.
Born in Jackson, Mississippi, in 1909, she attended Mississippi
State College for Women, received her Bachelor's degree from the
University of Wisconsin, and did graduate work at the Columbia
University School of Advertising. Among her many honors
are the O'Henry Award (1942 and 1943), the William Dean
Howells Medal (1955), and The Creative Arts Medal for Fiction
from Brandeis University (1966). Her fiction, noted for its poetic
literary quality and its humor, includes four collections of short
stories, beginning with A Curtain of Green *(1941); and the*

novels Delta Wedding *(1946)*, The Ponder Heart *(1954)*, *and* Losing Battles *(1970)*. *The essay we present here is from* The Atlantic Monthly, *October 1965.*

MUST THE NOVELIST CRUSADE?

Not too long ago I read in some respectable press that Faulkner would have to be reassessed because he was "after all, only a white Mississippian." For this reason, it was felt, readers could no longer rely on him for knowing what he was writing about in his life's work of novels and stories, laid in what he called "my country."

Remembering how Faulkner for most of his life wrote in all but isolation from critical understanding, ignored impartially by North and South, with only a handful of critics in forty years who were able to "assess" him, we might smile at this journalist as at a boy let out of school. Or there may have been an instinct to smash the superior, the good, that is endurable enough to go on offering itself. But I feel in these words and others like them the agonizing of our times. I think they come of an honest and understandable zeal to allot every writer his chance to better the world or go to his grave reproached for the mess it is in. And here, it seems to me, the heart of fiction's real reliability has been struck at—and not for the first time by the noble hand of the crusader.

It would not be surprising if the critic I quote had gained his knowledge of the South from the books of the author he repudiates. At any rate, a reply to him exists there. Full evidence as to whether any writer, alive or dead, can be believed is always at hand in one place: any page of his work. The color of his skin would modify it just about as much as would the binding of his book. Integrity can be neither lost nor concealed nor faked nor quenched nor artificially come by nor outlived, nor, I believe, in the long run denied. Integrity is no greater and no less today than it was yesterday and will be tomorrow. It stands outside time.

The novelist and the crusader who writes both have their own place —in the novel and the editorial respectively, equally valid whether or not the two happen to be in agreement. In my own view, writing fiction places the novelist and the crusader on opposite sides. But they are not the sides of right and wrong. Honesty is not at stake here and is not questioned; the only thing at stake is the proper use of words for the proper ends. And a mighty thing it is.

Because the printed page is where the writer's work is to be seen, it may be natural for people who do not normally read fiction to confuse novels with journalism or speeches. The very using of words has these well-intentioned people confused about the novelist's purpose.

The writing of a novel is taking life as it already exists, not to report it but to make an object, toward the end that the finished work might contain this life inside it, and offer it to the reader. The essence will not be, of course, the same thing as the raw material; it is not even of the same family of things. The novel is something that never was before and will not be again. For the mind of one person, its writer, is in it too. What distinguishes it above all from the raw material, and what distinguishes it from journalism, is that inherent in the novel is the possibility of a shared act of the imagination between its writer and its reader.

"All right, Eudora Welty, what are you going to do about it? Sit down there with your mouth shut?", asked a stranger over long distance in one of the midnight calls that I suppose have waked most writers in the South from time to time. It is part of the same question, Are fiction writers on call to be crusaders? For us in the South who are fiction writers, is writing a novel *something we can do about it?*

It can be said at once, I should think, that we are all agreed upon the most important point: that morality as shown through human relationships is the whole heart of fiction, and the serious writer has never lived who dealt with anything else.

And yet, the zeal to reform, which quite properly inspires the editorial, has never done fiction much good. The exception occurs when it can rise to the intensity of satire, where it finds a better home in the poem or the drama. Large helpings of naïveté and self-esteem, which serve to refresh the crusader, only encumber the novelist. How unfair it is that when a novel is to be written, it is never enough to have our hearts in the right place! But good will all by itself can no more get a good novel written than it can paint in watercolor or sing Mozart.

Nevertheless, let us suppose that we feel we might help if we were to write a crusading novel. What will our problems be?

Before anything else, speed. The crusader's message is prompted by crisis; it has to be delivered on time. Suppose John Steinbeck had only now finished *The Grapes of Wrath?* The ordinary novelist has only one message: "I submit that this is one way we are." This can wait. When we think of Ibsen, we see that causes themselves may in time be forgotten, their championship no longer needed; it is Ibsen's passion that keeps the plays alive.

Next, we as the crusader-novelist shall find awkward to use the very weapon we count on most: the generality. On fiction's pages, generalities clank when wielded, and hit with equal force at the little and the big, at the merely suspect and the really dangerous. They make too much noise for us to hear what people might be trying to say. They are fatal to tenderness and are in themselves nonconductors of any real, however modest, discovery of the writer's own heart. This discovery is the best hope of the ordinary novelist, and to make it he begins not with the generality but with the particular in front of his eyes, which he is able to examine.

Taking a particular situation existing in his world, and what he feels about it in his own breast and what he can make of it in his own head, he constructs on paper, little by little, an equivalent of it. Literally it may correspond to a high degree or to none at all; emotionally it corresponds as closely as he can make it. Observation and the inner truth of that observation as he perceives it, the two being tested one against the other: to him this is what the writing of a novel is.

We, the crusader-novelist, having started with our generality, must end with a generality; they had better be the same. In the place of climax, we can deliver a judgment. How can the plot seem disappointing when it is a lovely argument spread out? It is because fiction is stone-deaf to argument.

The ordinary novelist does not argue; he hopes to show, to disclose. His persuasions are all toward allowing his reader to see and hear something for himself. He knows another bad thing about arguments: they carry the menace of neatness into fiction. Indeed, what we as the crusader-novelist are scared of most is confusion.

Great fiction, we very much fear, abounds in what makes for confusion; it generates it, being on a scale which copies life, which it confronts. It is very seldom neat, is given to sprawling and escaping from bounds, is capable of contradicting itself, and is not impervious to humor. There is absolutely everything in great fiction but a clear answer. Humanity itself seems to matter more to the novelist than what humanity thinks it can prove.

When a novelist writes of man's experience, what else is he to draw on but the life around him? And yet the life around him, on the surface, can be used to show anything, absolutely anything, as readers know. The novelist's real task and real responsibility lie in the way he uses it.

Situation itself always exists; it is whatever life is up to here and now, it is the living and present moment. It is transient, and it fluctuates. Using the situation, the writer populates his novel with characters invented to express it in their terms.

It is important that it be in their terms. We cannot in fiction set people to acting mechanically or carrying placards to make their sentiments plain. People are not Right and Wrong, Good and Bad, Black and White personified; flesh and blood and the sense of comedy object. Fiction writers cannot be tempted to make the mistake of looking at people in the generality—that is to say, of seeing people as not at all *like us*. If human beings are to be comprehended as real, then they have to be treated as real, with minds, hearts, memories, habits, hopes, with passions and capacities like ours. This is why novelists begin the study of people from within.

The first act of insight is to throw away the labels. In fiction, while we do not necessarily write about ourselves, we write out of ourselves, using ourselves; what we learn from, what we are sensitive to, what we feel strongly about—these become our characters and go to make our plots. Characters in fiction are conceived from within, and they have, accordingly, their own interior life; they are individuals every time. The character we care about in a novel we may not approve of or agree with—that's beside the point. But he has got to seem alive. Then and only then, when we read, we experience or surmise things about life itself that are deeper and more lasting and less destructive to understanding than approval or disapproval.

The novelist's work is highly organized, but I should say it is organized around anything but logic. Just as characters are not labels but are made from the inside out and grow into their own life, so does a plot have a living principle on which it hangs together and gradually earns its shape. A plot is a thousand times more unsettling than an argument, which may be answered. It is not a pattern imposed; it is inward emotion acted out. It is arbitrary, indeed, but not artificial. It is possibly so odd that it might be called a vision, but it is organic to its material: it is a working vision, then.

A writer works *through* what is around him if he wishes to get to what he is after—no kind of proof, but simply an essence. In practice he will do anything at all with his material: shape it, strain it to the breaking point, double it up, or use it backwards; he will balk at nothing—see *The Sound and the Fury*—to reach that heart and core. But even in a good cause he does not falsify it. The material itself receives deep ultimate respect: it has given rise to the vision of it, which in turn has determined what the novel shall be.

The ordinary novelist, who can never make a perfect thing, can with every novel try again. But if we write a novel to prove something, one novel will settle it, for why prove a thing more than once? And what then is to keep all novels by all right-thinking persons from being pretty much alike? Or exactly alike? There would be little reason for present writers to keep on, no reason for the new writers to start. There's no way to know, but we might guess that the reason

the young write no fiction behind the Iron Curtain is the obvious fact
that to be acceptable there, all novels must conform, and so must be
alike, hence valueless. If the personal vision can be made to order,
then we should lose, writer and reader alike, our own gift for perceiving, seeing through the fabric of everyday to what to each pair
of eyes on earth is a unique thing. We'd accept life exactly like
everybody else, and so, of course, be content with it. We should not
even miss our vanished novelists. And if life ever became not worth
writing fiction about, that, I believe, would be the first sign that it
wasn't worth living.

With a blueprint to work with instead of a vision, there is a good
deal that we as the crusader-novelist must be at pains to leave out.
Unavoidably, I think, we shall leave out one of the greatest things.
This is the mystery in life. Our blueprint for sanity and of solution
for trouble leaves out the dark. (This is odd, because surely it was
the dark that first troubled us.) We leave out the wonder because
with wonder it is impossible to argue, much less to settle. The ordinary novelist thinks it had better be recognized. Reckless as this may
make him, he believes the insoluble is part of his material too.

The novelist works neither to correct nor to condone, not at all to
comfort, but to make what's told alive. He assumes at the start an
enlightenment in his reader equal to his own, for they are hopefully
on the point of taking off together from that base into the rather different world of the imagination.

It's not only the fact that this world is bigger and that fewer con-
strictions apply that may daunt us as crusaders. But the imagination
itself is the problem. It is capable of saying everything but no. In
our literature what has traveled the longest way through time is the
great affirmative soul of Chaucer. The novel itself always affirms, it
seems to me, by the nature of itself. It says what people are like.
It doesn't, and doesn't know how to, describe what they are *not* like,
and it would waste its time if it told us what we ought to be like,
since we already know that, don't we? But we may not know nearly
so well what we are as when a novel of power reveals this to us.
For the first time we may, as we read, see ourselves in our own situation, in some curious way reflected. By whatever way the novelist
accomplishes it—there are many ways—truth is borne in on us in all
its great weight and angelic lightness, and accepted as home truth.

Passing judgment on his fellows, which is trying enough for anybody, is frustrating for an author. It is hardly the way to make the
discoveries about living that he must have hoped for when he began
to write. If he does not pass judgment, does this mean he has no
conscience? Of course he has a conscience; it is, like his temperament,
his own, and he is one hundred percent answerable to it, whether it

705

is convenient or not. What matters is that a writer is committed to his own moral principles. If he is, when we read him we cannot help but be aware of what these are. Certainly the characters of his novel and the plot they move in are their ultimate reflections. But these convictions are implicit; they are deep down; they are the rock on which the whole structure of more than that novel rests.

Indeed, we are more aware of his moral convictions through a novel than any flat statement of belief from him could make us. We are aware in that part of our mind that tells us truths about ourselves. Yet it is only by way of the imagination—the novelist's to ours—that such private neighborhoods are reached.

There is still to mention what I think will give us, as the crusader-novelist, the hardest time: our voice will not be our own. The crusader's voice is the voice of the crowd and must rise louder all the time, for there is, of course, the other side to be drowned out. Worse, the voices of most crowds sound alike. Worse still, the voice that seeks to do other than communicate when it makes a noise has something brutal about it; it is no longer using words as words but as something to brandish, with which to threaten, brag, or condemn. The noise is the simple assertion of self, the great, mindless, general self. And for all its volume it is ephemeral. Only meaning lasts. Nothing was ever learned in a crowd, from a crowd, or by addressing or trying to please a crowd. Even to deplore, yelling is out of place. To deplore a thing as hideous as the murder of the three civil rights workers demands the quiet in which to absorb it. Enormities can be lessened, cheapened, just as good and delicate things can be. We can and will cheapen all feeling by letting it go savage or parading in it.

Writing fiction is an interior affair. Novels and stories always will be put down little by little out of personal feeling and personal beliefs arrived at alone and at firsthand over a period of time as time is needed. To go outside and beat the drum is only to interrupt, interrupt, and so finally to forget and to lose. Fiction has, and must keep, a private address. For life is *lived* in a private place; where it means anything is inside the mind and heart. Fiction has always shown life where it is lived, and good fiction, or so I have faith, will continue to do this.

A Passage to India is an old novel now. It is an intensely moral novel. It deals with race prejudice. Mr. Forster, not by preaching at us, while being passionately concerned, makes us know his points unforgettably as often as we read it. And does he not bring in the dark! The points are good forty years after their day *because of the splendor of the novel.* What a lesser novelist's harangues would have buried by now, his imagination still reveals. Revelation of even the strongest forces is delicate work.

Indeed, great fiction shows us not how to conduct our behavior but

how to feel. Eventually, it may show us how to face our feelings and
face our actions and to have new inklings about what they mean. A
good novel of any year can initiate us into our own new experience.

From the working point of view of the serious writer of fiction,
nothing has changed today but the externals. They are important externals; we may have developed an increased awareness of them, which
is certainly to the good; we have at least the same capacity as ever
for understanding, the same eyes and ears, same hearts to feel, same
minds to agonize or remember or to try to put things together, see
things in proportion with. While the raw material of our fiction is
changing dramatically—as indeed it is changing everywhere—we are
the same instruments of perceiving that we ever were. I should not
trust us if we were not. And we do not know what is to be made out
of experience at any time until the personal quotient has been added.
To convey what we see around us, whatever it is, so as to let it speak
for itself according to our lights is the same challenge it ever was,
not a different one, not a greater one, only perhaps made harder by
the times. Now as ever we must keep writing from what we know;
and we must really know it.

No matter how fast society around us changes, what remains is that
there is a relationship in progress between ourselves and other people;
this was the case when the world seemed stable, too. There are relationships of the blood, of the passions and the affections, of thought
and spirit and deed. There is the relationship between the races.
How can one kind of relationship be set apart from the others? Like
the great root system of an old and long-established growing plant,
they are all tangled up together; to separate them you would have to
cleave the plant itself from top to bottom.

What must the Southern writer of fiction do today? Shall he do
anything different from what he has always done?

There have already been giant events, some of them wrenchingly
painful and humiliating. And now there is added the atmosphere of
hate. We in the South are a hated people these days; we were hated
first for actual and particular reasons, and now we may be hated still
more in some vast unparticularized way. I believe there must be such
a thing as sentimental hate. Our people hate back.

I think the worst of it is we are getting stuck in it. We are like
trapped flies with our feet not in honey but in venom. It's not love
that is the gluey emotion; it's hate. As far as writing goes, which is
as far as living goes, this is a devastating emotion. It could kill us.
This hate seems in part shame for self, in part self-justification, in
part panic that life is really changing.

Fury at ourselves and hurt pride, anger aroused too often, outrage at being hated need not obscure forever the sore spots we Southerners know better than our detractors. For some of us have shown bad hearts. As in the case of our better qualities, we are locally blessed with an understanding and intimate knowledge of our faults that our worst detractors cannot match, and have been in a less relentless day far more relentless, more eloquent, too, than they have yet learned to be.

I do not presume to speak for my fellow Southern writers, a group of individuals if there ever was one. Yet I would like to point something out: in the rest of the country people seem suddenly aware now of what Southern fiction writers have been writing about in various ways for a great long time. We do not need reminding of what our subject is. It is humankind, and we are all part of it. When we write about people, black or white, in the South or anywhere, if our stories are worth the reading, we are writing about everybody.

In the South, we who are now at work may not learn to write it before we learn, or learn again, to live it—our full life in the South within its context, in its relation to the rest of the world. "Only connect," Forster's ever wise and gentle and daring words, could be said to us in our homeland quite literally at this moment. And while the Southern writer goes on portraying his South, which I think nobody else can do and which I believe he must do, then if his work is done well enough, it will reflect a larger mankind as it has done before.

And so finally I think we need to write with love. Not in self-defense, not in hate, not in the mood of instruction, not in rebuttal, in any kind of militance, or in apology, but with love. Not in exorcisement, either, for this is to make the reader bear a thing for you.

Neither do I speak of writing forgivingly; out of love you can write with straight fury. It is the *source* of the understanding that I speak of; it's this that determines its nature and its reach.

We are told that Turgenev's nostalgic, profoundly reflective, sensuously alive stories that grew out of his memories of early years reached the Czar and were given some credit by him when he felt moved to free the serfs in Russia. Had Turgenev set out to write inflammatory tracts instead of the sum of all he knew, could express, of life learned at firsthand, how much less of his mind and heart with their commitments, all implicit, would have filled his stories! But he might be one of us now, so directly are we touched, with 113 years gone by since they were first published.

Indifference would indeed be corrupting to the fiction writer, indifference to any part of man's plight. Passion is the chief ingredient of good fiction. It flames right out of sympathy for the human condition and goes into all great writing. (And of course passion and the temper are different things; writing in the heat of passion can be done with extremely good temper.) But to distort a work of passion for the sake of a cause is to cheat, and the end, far from justifying the means, is fairly sure to be lost with it. Then the novel will have been not the work of imagination, at once passionate and objective, made by a man struggling in solitude with something of his own to say, but a piece of catering.

To cater to is not to love and not to serve well either. We do need to bring to our writing, over and over again, all the abundance we possess. To be able, to be ready, to enter into the minds and hearts of our own people, all of them, to comprehend them (us) and then to make characters and plots in stories that in honesty and with honesty reveal them (ourselves) to us, in whatever situation we live through in our own times: this is the continuing job, and it's no harder now than it ever was, I suppose. Every writer, like everybody else, thinks he's living through the crisis of the ages. To write honestly and with all our powers is the least we can do, and the most.

Time, though it can make happenings and trappings out of date, cannot do much to change the realities apprehended by the imagination. History will change in Mississippi, and the hope is that it will change in a beneficial direction and with a merciful speed, and above all bring insight, understanding. But when William Faulkner's novels come to be pictures of a society that is no more, they will still be good and still be authentic because of what went into them from the man himself. Mankind still tries the same things and suffers the same falls, climbs up to try again, and novels are as true at one time as at another. Love and hate, hope and despair, justice and injustice, compassion and prejudice, truth-telling and lying work in all men; their story can be told in whatever skin they are wearing and in whatever year the writer can put them down.

Faulkner is not receding from us. Indeed, his work, though it can't increase in itself, increases us. His work throws light on the past and on today as it becomes the past—the day in its journey. This being so, it informs the future too.

What is written in the South from now on is going to be taken into account by Faulkner's work; I mean the remark literally. Once Faulkner had written, we could never unknow what he told us and showed us. And his work will do the same thing tomorrow. We inherit from him, while we can get fresh and firsthand news of ourselves from his work at any time.

A source of illumination is not dated by what passes along under its ray, is not qualified or disqualified by the nature of the traffic. When the light of Faulkner's work will be discovering things to us no more, it will be discovering *us*. Even we shall lie enfolded in perspective one day: what we hoped along with what we did, what we didn't do, and not only what we were but what we missed being, what others yet to come might dare to be. For we *are* our own crusade. Before ever we write, we are. Instead of our judging Faulkner, he will be revealing us in books to later minds.

LeRoi Jones

LeRoi Jones, poet, playwright, and black activist, was born in
Newark, N. J., in 1934. He graduated from Howard University
(1954), served in the U. S. Air Force, did graduate work at
Columbia, then taught there and at The New School while pursuing
a literary career. He coedited some underground journals,
published a few slim volumes of verse, and wrote plays. The
Dutchman *(1964), a play about the murder of a quiet black*
youth by a vicious white girl, had a long run, was judged the best
Off-Broadway play of the year, and made him widely known.
He was a Guggenheim Fellow in 1965–1966. Meanwhile his
moderate, liberal views of both literature and race problems
had been giving way to radicalism and separatism. He founded
the Black Arts Repertory Theatre in Harlem in 1965 and in
1968 the Black Community Defense and Development Organization,
based in Newark. The latter is a Muslim sect of which Jones has
become minister. Its members take African names, wear African
clothes, and devote themselves to black political and social causes.
"Let the whites work out their own salvation," Jones has said.
He has continued to write prolifically. Among his better-known
writings are the plays The Toilet *(1964) and* A Black Mass
(1966); The System of Dante's Hell, *an autobiographical novel*
(1965); Blues People: Negro Music in White America *(1963);*
Tales *(1967); and* Black Magic *(poems, 1968). Some of his*
essays have been collected in Home: Social Essays *(1966), and*
from this volume we print the following two pieces. The first is an
address given in March 1962 at the American Society for
African Culture. The second, sharply reflecting the change in
Jones' aesthetic philosophy, was written in 1964. "Home," to
Jones, means getting back to his natal blackness. He writes in the
title essay: "Having been taught that art was 'what white men
710

did,' I almost became one. . . . But my tendency, body and
mind, is to make it. To get there, from anywhere, going wherever,
always. By the time this book appears, I will be even blacker."

THE MYTH OF A "NEGRO LITERATURE"

The mediocrity of what has been called "Negro Literature" is one of
the most loosely held secrets of American culture. From Phyllis
Wheatley to Charles Chesnutt, to the present generation of American
Negro writers, the only recognizable accretion of tradition readily
attributable to the black producer of a formal literature in this country, with a few notable exceptions, has been of an almost agonizing
mediocrity. In most other fields of "high art" in America, with the
same few notable exceptions, the Negro contribution has been, when
one existed at all, one of impressive mediocrity. Only in music, and
most notably in blues, jazz, and spirituals, i.e., "Negro Music," has
there been a significantly profound contribution by American Negroes.

There are a great many reasons for the spectacular vapidity of the
American Negro's accomplishment in other formal, serious art forms—
social, economic, political, etc.—but one of the most persistent and
aggravating reasons for the absence of achievement among serious
Negro artists, except in Negro music, is that in most cases the Negroes
who found themselves in a position to pursue some art, especially the
art of literature, have been members of the Negro middle class, a
group that has always gone out of its way to cultivate *any* mediocrity,
as long as that mediocrity was guaranteed to prove to America, and
recently to the world at large, that they were not really who they
were, *i.e.*, Negroes. Negro music alone, because it drew its strengths
and beauties out of the depth of the black man's soul, and because to
a large extent its traditions could be carried on by the lowest classes
of Negroes, has been able to survive the constant and willful dilutions
of the black middle class. Blues and jazz have been the only consistent exhibitors of "Negritude" in formal American culture simply because the bearers of its tradition maintained their essential identities
as Negroes; in no other art (and I will persist in calling Negro music,
Art) has this been possible. Phyllis Wheatley and her pleasant imitations of 18th century English poetry are far and, finally, ludicrous
departures from the huge black voices that splintered southern nights
with their *hollers, chants, arwhoolies,* and *ballits.* The embarrassing and

711

inverted paternalism of Charles Chesnutt and his "refined Afro-American" heroes are far cries from the richness and profundity of the blues. And it is impossible to mention the achievements of the Negro in any area of artistic endeavor with as much significance as in spirituals, blues and jazz. There has never been an equivalent to Duke Ellington or Louis Armstrong in Negro writing, and even the best of contemporary literature written by Negroes cannot yet be compared to the fantastic beauty of the music of Charlie Parker.

American Negro music from its inception moved logically and powerfully out of a fusion between African musical tradition and the American experience. It was, and continues to be, a natural, yet highly stylized and personal version of the Negro's life in America. It is, indeed, a chronicler of the Negro's movement, from African slave to American slave, from Freedman to Citizen. And the literature of the blues is a much more profound contribution to Western culture than any other literary contribution made by American Negroes. Moreover, it is only recently that formal literature written by American Negroes has begun to approach the literary standards of its model, *i.e.*, the literature of the white middle class. And only Jean Toomer, Richard Wright, Ralph Ellison, and James Baldwin have managed to bring off examples of writing, in this genre, that could succeed in passing themselves off as "serious" writing, in the sense that, say, the work of Somerset Maugham is "serious" writing. That is, serious, if one has never read Herman Melville or James Joyce. And it is part of the tragic naïveté of the middle class (brow) writer, that he has not.

Literature, for the Negro writer, was always an example of "culture." Not in the sense of the more impressive philosophical characteristics of a particular social group, but in the narrow sense of "cultivation" or "sophistication" by an individual within that group. The Negro artist, because of his middle-class background, carried the artificial social burden as the "best and most intelligent" of Negroes, and usually entered into the "serious" arts to exhibit his familiarity with the social graces, *i.e.*, as a method or means of displaying his participation in the "serious" aspects of American culture. To be a writer was to be "cultivated," in the stunted bourgeois sense of the word. It was also to be a "quality" black man. It had nothing to do with the investigation of the human soul. It was, and is, a social preoccupation rather than an aesthetic one. A rather daring way of status seeking. The cultivated Negro leaving those ineffectual philanthropies, Negro colleges, looked at literature merely as another way of gaining prestige in the white world for the Negro middle class. And the literary and artistic models were always those that could be socially acceptable to the white middle class, which automatically limited them to the most spiritually debilitated imitations of literature available. Negro music, to the middle class, black and white, was never socially acceptable. It was shunned by blacks ambitious of "waking up white," as low and degrading. It was shunned by their white models simply because it was produced by blacks. As one of my professors at Howard University protested one day, "It's amazing how much bad taste the blues display." Suffice it to say, it is in part exactly this "bad taste" that has continued to keep Negro music as vital as it is. The abandonment of one's local (*i.e.,* place or group) emotional attachments in favor of the abstract emotional response of what is called "the general public" (which is notoriously white and middle class) has always been the great diluter of any Negro culture. "You're acting like a nigger," was the standard disparagement. I remember being chastised severely for daring to eat a piece of watermelon on the Howard campus. "Do you realize you're sitting near the highway?" is what the man said, "This is the capstone of Negro education." And it is too, in the sense that it teaches the Negro how to make out in the white society, using the agonizing overcompensation of pretending he's also white. James Baldwin's play, *The Amen Corner,* when it appeared at the Howard Players theatre, "set the speech department back ten years," an English professor groaned to me. The play depicted the lives of poor Negroes running a store-front church. Any reference to the Negro-ness of the American Negro has always been frowned upon by the black middle class in their frenzied dash toward the precipice of the American mainstream.

High art, first of all, must reflect the experiences of the human being, the emotional predicament of the man, as he exists, in the defined world of his being. It must be produced from the legitimate emotional resources of the soul in the world. It can *never* be produced by evading these resources or pretending that they do not exist. It can never be produced by appropriating the withered emotional responses of some strictly social idea of humanity. High art, and by this I mean any art that would attempt to describe or characterize some portion of the profound meaningfulness of human life with any finality or truth, cannot be based on the superficialities of human existence. It must issue from *real* categories of human activity, *truthful* accounts of human life, and not fancied accounts of the attainment of cultural privilege by some willingly preposterous apologists for one social "order" or another. Most of the formal literature produced by Negroes in America has never fulfilled these conditions. And aside from Negro music, it is only in the "popular traditions" of the so-called lower class Negro that these conditions are fulfilled as a basis for human life. And it is because of this "separation" between Negro life (as an emotional experience) and Negro art, that, say, Jack Johnson or Ray Robinson is a larger cultural hero than any Negro writer. It

713

is because of this separation, even evasion, of the emotional experience of Negro life, that Jack Johnson is a more moderate political symbol than most Negro writers. Johnson's life, as proposed, certainly, by his career, reflects much more accurately the symbolic yearnings for singular values among the great masses of Negroes than any black novelist has yet managed to convey. Where is the Negro-ness of a literature written in imitation of the meanest of social intelligences to be found in American culture, *i.e.*, the white middle class? How can it even begin to express the emotional predicament of black Western man? Such a literature, even if its "characters" *are* black, takes on the emotional barrenness of its model, and the blackness of the characters is like the blackness of Al Jolson, an unconvincing device. It is like using black checkers instead of white. They are still checkers.

The development of the Negro's music was, as I said, direct and instinctive. It was the one vector out of African culture impossible to eradicate completely. The appearance of blues as a native *American* music signified in many ways the appearance of American Negroes where once there were African Negroes. The emotional fabric of the music was colored by the emergence of an American Negro culture. It signified that culture's strength and vitality. In the evolution of form in Negro music it is possible to see not only the evolution of the Negro as a cultural and social element of American culture, but also the evolution of that culture itself. The "Coon Shout" proposed one version of the American Negro—and of America; Ornette Coleman proposes another. But the point is that both these versions are accurate and informed with a legitimacy of emotional concern nowhere available in what is called "Negro Literature," and certainly not in the middlebrow literature of the white American.

The artifacts of African art and sculpture were consciously eradicated by slavery. Any African art that based its validity on the production of an artifact, *i.e.*, some *material* manifestation such as a wooden statue or a woven cloth, had little chance of survival. It was only the more "abstract" aspects of African culture that could continue to exist in slave America. Africanisms still persist in the music, religion, and popular cultural traditions of American Negroes. However, it is not an African art American Negroes are responsible for, but an American one. The traditions of Africa must be utilized within the culture of the American Negro where they *actually* exist, and not because of a defensive rationalization about the *worth* of one's ancestors or an attempt to capitalize on the recent eminence of the "new" African nations. Africanisms do exist in Negro culture, but they have been so translated and transmuted by the American experience that they have become integral parts of that experience.

The American Negro has a definable and legitimate historical tradition, no matter how painful, in America, but it is the only place such a tradition exists, simply because America is the only place the American Negro exists. He is, as William Carlos Williams said, "A pure product of America." The paradox of the Negro experience in America is that it is a separate experience, but inseparable from the complete fabric of American life. The history of Western culture begins for the Negro with the importation of the slaves. It is almost as if all Western history before that must be strictly a learned concept. It is only the American experience that can be a persistent cultural catalyst for the Negro. In a sense, history for the Negro, before America, must remain an emotional abstraction. The cultural memory of Africa informs the Negro's life in America, but it is impossible to separate it from its American transformation. Thus, the Negro writer if he wanted to tap his legitimate cultural tradition should have done it by utilizing the entire spectrum of the American experience from the point of view of the emotional history of the black man in this country: as its victim and its chronicler. The soul of such a man, as it exists outside the boundaries of commercial diversion or artificial social pretense. But without a deep commitment to cultural relevance and intellectual purity this was impossible. The Negro as a writer, was always a social object, whether glorifying the concept of white superiority, as a great many early Negro writers did, or in crying out against it, as exemplified by the stock "protest" literature of the thirties. He never moved into the position where he could propose his own symbols, erect his own personal myths, as any great literature must. Negro writing was always "after the fact," *i.e.*, based on known social concepts within the structure of bourgeois idealistic projections of "their" America, and an emotional climate that never really existed.

The most successful fiction of most Negro writing is in its emotional content. The Negro protest novelist postures, and invents a protest quite amenable with the tradition of bourgeois American life. He never reaches the central core of the America which *can* cause such protest. The intellectual traditions of the white middle class prevent such exposure of reality, and the black imitators reflect this. The Negro writer on Negro life in America postures, and invents a Negro life, and an America to contain it. And even most of those who tried to rebel against that *invented* America were trapped because they had lost all touch with the reality of their experience within the *real* America, either because of the hidden emotional allegiance to the white middle class, or because they did not realize where the reality of their experience lay. When the serious Negro writer disdained the "middlebrow" model, as is the case with a few contemporary black American writers, he usually rushed headlong into the groves of the Academy, perhaps the most insidious and clever dispenser of middlebrow standards of excellence under the guise of "recognizable tradition." That such recognizable tradition is necessary goes without saying, but even from the great philosophies of Europe a contemporary usage must be established. No poetry has come out of England of major importance for forty years, yet there are would-be Negro poets who reject the gaudy excellence of 20th century American poetry in favor of disembowelled Academic models of second-rate English poetry, with the notion that somehow it is the only way poetry should be written. It would be better if such a poet listened to Bessie Smith sing *Gimme A Pigfoot*, or listened to the tragic verse of a Billie Holiday, than be content to imperfectly imitate the bad poetry of the ruined minds of Europe. And again, it is this striving for *respectability* that has it so. For an American, black or white, to say that some hideous imitation of Alexander Pope means more to him, emotionally, than the blues of Ray Charles or Lightnin' Hopkins, it would be required for him to have completely disappeared into the American Academy's vision of a Europeanized and colonial American culture, or to be lying. In the end, the same emotional sterility results. It is somehow much more tragic for the black man.

A Negro literature, to be a legitimate product of the Negro experience in America, must get at that experience in exactly the terms America has proposed for it, in its most ruthless identity. Negro reaction to America is as deep a part of America as the root causes of that reaction, and it is impossible to accurately describe that reaction in terms of the American middle class; because for them, the Negro has never really existed, never been glimpsed in anything even approaching the complete reality of his humanity. The Negro writer has to go from where he actually is, completely outside of that conscious white myopia. That the Negro does exist is the point, and as an element of American culture he is completely misunderstood by Americans. The middlebrow, commercial Negro writer assures the white American that, in fact, he doesn't exist, and that if he does, he does so within the perfectly predictable fingerpainting of white bourgeois sentiment and understanding. Nothing could be further from the truth. The Creoles of New Orleans resisted "Negro" music for a time as raw and raucous, because they thought they had found a place within the white society which would preclude their being Negroes. But they were unsuccessful in their attempts to "disappear" because the whites themselves reminded them that they were still, for all their assimilation, "just coons." And this seems to me an extremely important idea, since it is precisely this bitter insistence that has kept what can be called "Negro Culture" a brilliant amalgam of diverse influences. There was always a border beyond which the Negro could not go, whether musically or socially. There was always a possible limitation to any dilution or excess of cultural or spiritual reference. The Negro could not ever become white and that was his strength; at some point, always, he could not participate in the dominant tenor of the white man's culture, yet he came to understand that culture as well as the white man. It was at this juncture that he had to make use of other resources, whether African, sub-cultural, or hermetic. And it was this boundary, this no-man's-land, that provided the logic and beauty of his music. And this is the only way for the Negro artist to provide his version of America—from that no-man's-land outside the mainstream. A no-man's-land, a black country, completely invisible to white America, but so essentially part of it as to stain its whole being an ominous gray. Were there really a Negro literature, now it could flower. At this point when the whole of Western society might go up in flames, the Negro remains an integral part of that society, but continually outside it, a figure like Melville's Bartleby. He is an American, capable of identifying emotionally with the fantastic cultural ingredients of this society, but he is also, forever, outside that culture, an invisible strength within it, an observer. If there is ever a Negro literature, it must disengage itself from the weak, heinous elements of the culture that spawned it, and use its very existence as evidence of a more profound America. But as long as the Negro writer contents himself with the imitation of the useless ugly inelegance of the stunted middle-class mind, academic or popular, and refuses to look around him and "tell it like it is"—preferring the false prestige of the black bourgeoisie or the deceitful "acceptance" of *buy and sell* America, something never included in the legitimate cultural tradition of "his people"—he will be a failure, and what is worse, not even a significant failure. Just another dead American.

THE REVOLUTIONARY THEATRE

The Revolutionary Theatre should force change; it should be change. (All their faces turned into the lights and you work on them black nigger magic, and cleanse them at having seen the ugliness. And if the beautiful see themselves, they will love themselves.) We are preaching virtue again, but by that to mean NOW, toward what seems the most constructive use of the world.

The Revolutionary Theatre must EXPOSE! Show up the insides of these humans, look into black skulls. White men will cower before

717

this theatre because it hates them. Because they themselves have been trained to hate. The Revolutionary Theatre must hate them for hating. For presuming with their technology to deny the supremacy of the Spirit. They will all die because of this.

The Revolutionary Theatre must teach them their deaths. It must crack their faces open to the mad cries of the poor. It must teach them about silence and the truths lodged there. It must kill any God anyone names except Common Sense. The Revolutionary Theatre should flush the fags and murders out of Lincoln's face.

It should stagger through our universe correcting, insulting, preaching, spitting craziness—but a craziness taught to us in our most rational moments. People must be taught to trust true scientists (knowers, diggers, oddballs) and that the holiness of life is the constant possibility of widening the consciousness. And they must be incited to strike back against *any* agency that attempts to prevent this widening.

The Revolutionary Theatre must Accuse and Attack anything that can be accused and attacked. It must Accuse and Attack because it is a theatre of Victims. It looks at the sky with the victims' eyes, and moves the victims to look at the strength in their minds and their bodies.

Clay, in *Dutchman*, Ray in *The Toilet*, Walker in *The Slave*, are all victims. In the Western sense they could be heroes. But the Revolutionary Theatre, even if it is Western, must be anti-Western. It must show horrible coming attractions of *The Crumbling of the West*. Even as Artaud designed *The Conquest of Mexico*, so we must design *The Conquest of White Eye*, and show the missionaries and wiggly Liberals dying under blasts of concrete. For sound effects, wild screams of joy, from all the peoples of the world.

The Revolutionary Theatre must take dreams and give them a reality. It must isolate the ritual and historical cycles of reality. But it must be food for all those who need food, and daring propaganda for the beauty of the Human Mind. It is a political theatre, a weapon to help in the slaughter of these dim-witted fatbellied white guys who somehow believe that the rest of the world is here for them to slobber on.

This should be a theatre of World Spirit. Where the spirit can be shown to be the most competent force in the world. Force. Spirit. Feeling. The language will be anybody's, but tightened by the poet's backbone. And even the language must show what the facts are in this consciousness epic, what's happening. We will talk about the world, and the preciseness with which we are able to summon the world will be our art. Art is method. And art, "like any ashtray or senator," remains in the world. Wittgenstein said ethics and aesthetics are one. I believe this. So the Broadway theatre is a theatre of reaction whose ethics, like its aesthetics, reflect the spiritual values of this unholy society, which sends young crackers all over the world blowing off colored people's heads. (In some of these flippy Southern towns they even shoot up the immigrants' Favorite Son, be it Michael Schwerner or JFKennedy.)

The Revolutionary Theatre is shaped by the world, and moves to reshape the world, using as its force the natural force and perpetual vibrations of the mind in the world. We are history and desire, what we are, and what any experience can make us.

It is a social theatre, but all theatre is social theatre. But we will change the drawing rooms into places where real things can be said about a real world, or into smoky rooms where the destruction of Washington can be plotted. The Revolutionary Theatre must function like an incendiary pencil planted in Curtis Lemay's cap. So that when the final curtain goes down brains are splattered over the seats and the floor, and bleeding nuns must wire SOS's to Belgians with gold teeth.

Our theatre will show victims so that their brothers in the audience will be better able to understand that they are the brothers of victims, and that they themselves are victims if they are blood brothers. And what we show must cause the blood to rush, so that pre-revolutionary temperaments will be bathed in this blood, and it will cause their deepest souls to move, and they will find themselves tensed and clenched, even ready to die, at what the soul has been taught. We will scream and cry, murder, run through the streets in agony, if it means some soul will be moved, moved to actual life understanding of what the world is, and what it ought to be. We are preaching virtue and feeling, and a natural sense of the self in the world. All men live in the world, and the world ought to be a place for them to live.

What is called the imagination (from image, magi, magic, magician, etc.) is a practical vector from the soul. It stores all data, and can be called on to solve all our "problems." The imagination is the projection of ourselves past our sense of ourselves as "things." Imagination (Image) is all possibility, because from the image, the initial circumscribed energy, any use (idea) is possible. And so begins that image's use in the world. Possibility is what moves us.

The popular white man's theatre like the popular white man's novel shows tired white lives, and the problems of eating white sugar, or else it herds bigcaboosed blondes onto huge stages in rhinestones and makes believe they are dancing or singing. WHITE BUSINESSMEN OF THE WORLD, DO YOU WANT TO SEE PEOPLE REALLY DANCING AND SINGING??? ALL OF YOU GO UP TO HARLEM AND GET YOURSELF KILLED. THERE WILL BE DANCING AND

SINGING, THEN, FOR REAL!! (In *The Slave*, Walker Vessels, the black revolutionary, wears an armband, which is the insignia of the attacking army—a big red-lipped minstrel, grinning like crazy.)

The liberal white man's objection to the theatre of the revolution (if he is "hip" enough) will be on aesthetic grounds. Most white Western artists do not need to be "political," since usually, whether they know it or not, they are in complete sympathy with the most repressive social forces in the world today. There are more junior birdmen fascists running around the West today disguised as Artists than there are disguised as fascists. (But then, that word, *Fascist*, and with it, *Fascism*, has been made obsolete by the words *America*, and *Americanism*.) The American Artist usually turns out to be just a super-Bourgeois, because, finally, all he has to show for his sojourn through the world is "better taste" than the Bourgeois—many times not even that.

Americans will hate the Revolutionary Theatre because it will be out to destroy them and whatever they believe is real. American cops will try to close the theatres where such nakedness of the human spirit is paraded. American producers will say the revolutionary plays are filth, usually because they will treat human life as if it were actually happening. American directors will say that the white guys in the plays are too abstract and cowardly ("don't get me wrong . . . I mean aesthetically . . .") and they will be right.

The force we want is of twenty million spooks storming America with furious cries and unstoppable weapons. We want actual explosions and actual brutality: AN EPIC IS CRUMBLING and we must give it the space and hugeness of its actual demise. The Revolutionary Theatre, which is now peopled with victims, will soon begin to be peopled with new kinds of heroes—not the weak Hamlets debating whether or not they are ready to die for what's on their minds, but men and women (and minds) digging out from under a thousand years of "high art" and weak-faced dalliance. We must make an art that will function so as to call down the actual wrath of world spirit. We are witch doctors and assassins, but we will open a place for the true scientists to expand our consciousness. This is a theatre of assault. The play that will split the heavens for us will be called THE DE-STRUCTION OF AMERICA. The heroes will be Crazy Horse, Denmark Vesey, Patrice Lumumba, and not history, not memory, not sad sentimental groping for a warmth in our despair; these will be new men, new heroes, and their enemies most of you who are reading this.

Seven Poems on Art

JOHN KEATS (1795–1821)

ODE ON A GRECIAN URN

I

Thou still unravish'd bride of quietness,
　Thou foster-child of silence and slow time,
Sylvan historian, who canst thus express
　A flowery tale more sweetly than our rhyme:
What leaf-fring'd legend haunts about thy shape
　Of deities or mortals, or of both,
　　In Tempe or the dales of Arcady?
What men or gods are these?　What maidens loth?
　What mad pursuit?　What struggle to escape?
　　What pipes and timbrels?　What wild ecstasy?

II

Heard melodies are sweet, but those unheard
　Are sweeter; therefore, ye soft pipes, play on;
Not to the sensual ear, but, more endear'd,
　Pipe to the spirit ditties of no tone:
Fair youth, beneath the trees, thou canst not leave
　Thy song, nor ever can those trees be bare;
　　Bold Lover, never, never canst thou kiss
Though winning near the goal—yet, do not grieve;
　She cannot fade, though thou hast not thy bliss,
　　For ever wilt thou love, and she be fair!

III

Ah, happy, happy boughs! that cannot shed
　Your leaves, nor ever bid the Spring adieu;
And, happy melodist, unwearied,
　For ever piping songs for ever new;
More happy love! more happy, happy love!
　For ever warm and still to be enjoy'd,
　　For ever panting, and for ever young;
All breathing human passion far above,

That leaves a heart high-sorrowful and cloy'd,
   A burning forehead, and a parching tongue.

IV

Who are these coming to the sacrifice?
   To what green altar, O mysterious priest,
Lead'st thou that heifer lowing at the skies,
   And all her silken flanks with garlands dressed?
What little town by river or sea shore,
   Or mountain-built with peaceful citadel,
      Is emptied of this folk, this pious morn?
And, little town, thy streets for evermore
   Will silent be; and not a soul to tell
      Why thou art desolate, can e'er return.

V

O Attic shape! Fair attitude! with brede
   Of marble men and maidens overwrought
With forest branches and the trodden weed;
   Thou, silent form, dost tease us out of thought
As doth eternity: Cold Pastoral!
   When old age shall this generation waste,
      Thou shalt remain, in midst of other woe
Than ours, a friend to man, to whom thou say'st,
   'Beauty is truth, truth beauty,'—that is all
      Ye know on earth, and all ye need to know.

                                                  (1819)

WILLIAM BUTLER YEATS (1865-1939)

SAILING TO BYZANTIUM
   I

That is no country for old men. The young
In one another's arms, birds in the trees
—Those dying generations—at their song,
The salmon-falls, the mackerel-crowded seas,
Fish, flesh, or fowl, commend all summer long

Whatever is begotten, born, and dies.
Caught in that sensual music all neglect
Monuments of unaging intellect.

II

An aged man is but a paltry thing,
A tattered coat upon a stick, unless
Soul clap its hands and sing, and louder sing
For every tatter in its mortal dress,
Nor is there singing school but studying
Monuments of its own magnificence;
And therefore I have sailed the seas and come
To the holy city of Byzantium.

III

O sages standing in God's holy fire
As in the gold mosaic of a wall,
Come from the holy fire, perne in a gyre,
And be the singing-masters of my soul.
Consume my heart away; sick with desire
And fastened to a dying animal
It knows not what it is; and gather me
Into the artifice of eternity.

IV

Once out of nature I shall never take
My bodily form from any natural thing,
But such a form as Grecian goldsmiths make
Of hammered gold and gold enamelling
To keep a drowsy Emperor awake;
Or set upon a golden bough to sing
To lords and ladies of Byzantium
Of what is past, or passing, or to come.

(1928)

ROBERT FROST (1874-1963)

FOR ONCE, THEN, SOMETHING

Others taunt me with having knelt at well-curbs
Always wrong to the light, so never seeing
Deeper down in the well than where the water
Gives me back in a shining surface picture
Me myself in the summer heaven, godlike,
Looking out of a wreath of fern and cloud puffs.
Once, when trying with chin against a well-curb,
I discerned, as I thought, beyond the picture,
Through the picture, a something white, uncertain,
Something more of the depths—and then I lost it.
Water came to rebuke the too clear water.
One drop fell from a fern, and lo, a ripple
Shook whatever it was lay there at bottom,
Blurred it, blotted it out. What was that whiteness?
Truth? A pebble of quartz? For once, then, something.

(1923)

MARIANNE MOORE (1887-)

POETRY

I, too, dislike it: there are things that are important beyond all this fiddle.
    Reading it, however, with a perfect contempt for it, one discovers in
        it after all, a place for the genuine.
            Hands that can grasp, eyes
            that can dilate, hair that can rise
                if it must, these things are important not because a

high-sounding interpretation can be put upon them but because they are
        useful. When they become so derivative as to become unintelligible,
        the same thing may be said for all of us, that we
            do not admire what
            we cannot understand: the bat
                holding on upside down or in quest of something to

724

eat, elephants pushing, a wild horse taking a roll, a tireless wolf under
    a tree, the immovable critic twitching his skin like a horse that
        feels a flea, the base-
  ball fan, the statistician—
      nor is it valid
        to discriminate against 'business documents and

school-books'; all these phenomena are important. One must make
    a distinction
    however: when dragged into prominence by half poets, the result
      is not poetry,
  nor till the poets among us can be
    'literalists of
    the imagination'—above
      insolence and triviality and can present

for inspection, 'imaginary gardens with real toads in them', shall
      we have
  it. In the meantime, if you demand on the one hand,
  the raw material of poetry in
    all its rawness and
    that which is on the other hand
      genuine, you are interested in poetry.

                                          (1921)

W. H. AUDEN (1907-)

SEPTEMBER 1, 1939

I sit in one of the dives
On Fifty-Second Street
Uncertain and afraid
As the clever hopes expire
Of a low dishonest decade:
Waves of anger and fear
Circulate over the bright
And darkened lands of the earth,
Obsessing our private lives;
The unmentionable odour of death
Offends the September night.

Accurate scholarship can
Unearth the whole offence
From Luther until now
That has driven a culture mad,
Find what occurred at Linz,
What huge imago made
A psychopathic god:
I and the public know
What all schoolchildren learn,
Those to whom evil is done
Do evil in return.

Exiled Thucydides knew
All that a speech can say
About Democracy,
And what dictators do,
The elderly rubbish they talk
To an apathetic grave;
Analysed all in his book,
The enlightenment driven away,
The habit-forming pain,
Mismanagement and grief:
We must suffer them all again.

Into this neutral air
Where blind skyscrapers use
Their full height to proclaim
The strength of Collective Man,
Each language pours its vain
Competitive excuse:
But who can live for long
In an euphoric dream;
Out of the mirror they stare,
Imperialism's face
And the international wrong.

Faces along the bar
Cling to their average day:
The lights must never go out,
The music must always play,
All the conventions conspire
To make this fort assume
The furniture of home;

Lest we should see where we are,
Lost in a haunted wood,
Children afraid of the night
Who have never been happy or good.

The windiest militant trash
Important Persons shout
It is not so crude as our wish:
What mad Nijinsky wrote
About Diaghilev
Is true of the normal heart;
For the error bred in the bone
Of each woman and each man
Craves what it cannot have,
Not universal love
But to be loved alone.

From the conservative dark
Into the ethical life
The dense commuters come,
Repeating their morning vow;
"I *will* be true to the wife,
I'll concentrate more on my work,"
And helpless governors wake
To resume their compulsory game:
Who can release them now,
Who can reach the deaf,
Who can speak for the dumb?

All I have is a voice
To undo the folded lie,
The romantic lie in the brain
Of the sensual man-in-the-street
And the lie of Authority
Whose buildings grope the sky:
There is no such thing as the State
And no one exists alone;
Hunger allows no choice
To the citizen or the police;
We must love one another or die.

Defenceless under the night
Our world in stupor lies;

Yet dotted everywhere,
Ironic points of light
Flash out wherever the Just
Exchange their messages:
May I, composed like them
Of Eros and of dust,
Beleaguered by the same
Negation and despair,
Show an affirming flame.

(1940)

DYLAN THOMAS (1914–1953)

IN MY CRAFT OR SULLEN ART

In my craft or sullen art
Exercised in the still night
When only the moon rages
And the lovers lie abed
With all their griefs in their arms,
I labour by singing light
Not for ambition or bread
Or the strut and trade of charms
On the ivory stages
But for the common wages
Of their most secret heart.
Not for the proud man apart
From the raging moon I write
On these spindrift pages
Nor for the towering dead
With their nightingales and psalms
But for the lovers, their arms
Round the griefs of the ages,
Who pay no praise or wages
Nor heed my craft or art.

(1945)

728

ARCHIBALD MACLEISH (1892–)

ARS POETICA

A poem should be palpable and mute
As a globed fruit,

Dumb
As old medallions to the thumb,

Silent as the sleeve-worn stone
Of casement ledges where the moss has grown—

A poem should be wordless
As the flight of birds.
*

A poem should be motionless in time
As the moon climbs,

Leaving, as the moon releases
Twig by twig the night-entangled trees,

Leaving, as the moon behind the winter leaves,
Memory by memory the mind—

A poem should be motionless in time
As the moon climbs.
*

A poem should be equal to:
Not true.

For all the history of grief
An empty doorway and a maple leaf.

For love
The leaning grasses and two lights above the sea—

A poem should not mean
But be.

(1926)

ON THE
STANDARDS
OF
JUDGMENT

ow do we judge what is good or bad in art or taste or behavior? The question is difficult, and frequently we simply evade it. In a society devoted like ours to equality and individualism, there seems indeed to be something offensive and snobbish—positively undemocratic or "elitist"—in the idea of standards. "Live and let live," is the popular answer. "I like what I like; and furthermore, nobody is going to tell me what to approve or disapprove." But one may be tolerant of the tastes and preferences of others and still be committed, for himself, to a view of life that implies the existence of standards. Against the old saying, "de gustibus non disputandum est"—"There's no disputing about tastes"—there stand the ideas of good and bad taste, good and bad art, better and worse judgment.

Each of the authors in this section (and, by implication, some of those in the previous section) suggest that there are indeed valid standards of judgment. Barbara Tuchman's essay is a peppery assault on the failure to insist on standards that comes from our lack of confidence in our own judgment. Her remarks cover many areas and show how closely questions of taste are related to "moral leadership" and to the largest matters of public policy. Thurber's story is in part a satire on this relationship. It assumes a certain sophistication of taste in the reader and offers, in Jack ("Pal") Smurch, a minor masterpiece in the portraiture of vulgarity. At the same time the story explores some of the possible hypocrisies in arbitrarily genteel standards of public conduct.

The essays by Richard Gilman and Marya Mannes deal with criticism in the arts. Gilman, a professional critic accustomed to the application of traditional, Western, humanistic standards to literature, concludes nevertheless that "white critics have not the right to make judgments on a certain kind of black writing." His argument may be compared to the more simple one of Mao Tse-tung in the preceding section, that standards of judgment in art and literature are completely dominated by social class. Marya Mannes comes out directly for absolute standards in the arts, and suggests how one may begin to acquire an appreciation of form, craftsmanship, and creativity. "In creating, the artist commits himself; in appreciating, you have a commitment of your own." It is on this note—and with her last sentence—that we are pleased to end this collection.

Barbara W. Tuchman

*Barbara Tuchman (born 1912) is one of America's distinguished
journalists and historians. A graduate of Radcliffe College in
1933, she soon became a staff writer and foreign correspondent
for* The Nation *and in 1937 was reporting the Spanish Civil
War from Madrid. She has been a correspondent for* The New
Statesman, *editor for the Office of War Information, and con-
tributor to many magazines, including* Foreign Affairs, The New
Republic, *and* The Christian Science Monitor. *In 1963
Mrs. Tuchman was awarded the Pulitzer Prize for* The Guns of
August, *her account of the origins of World War I. Among
her other books are* Bible and Sword *(1956) and* The Proud
Tower *(1966). We print below an address by Mrs. Tuchman
to The American Association for Higher Education, published in*
In Search of Leaders *(ed. G. Kerry Smith, 1967).*

THE MISSING ELEMENT: MORAL COURAGE

What I want to say is concerned less with leadership than with its
absence, that is, with the evasion of leadership. Not in the physical
sense, for we have, if anything, a superabundance of leaders—hundreds
of Pied Pipers, or would-be Pied Pipers, running about, ready and
anxious to lead the population. They are scurrying around, collecting
consensus, gathering as wide an acceptance as possible. But what
they are *not* doing, very notably, is standing still and saying, "*This* is
what I believe. This I will do and that I will not do. This is my code
of behavior and that is outside it. This is excellent and that is trash."
There is an abdication of moral leadership in the sense of a general
unwillingness to state standards.

Of all the ills that our poor criticized, analyzed, sociologized society
is heir to, the focal one, it seems to me, from which so much of our
uneasiness and confusion derive is the absence of standards. We are
too unsure of ourselves to assert them, to stick by them, or if necessary,
in the case of persons who occupy positions of authority, to impose
them. We seem to be afflicted by a widespread and eroding reluctance
to take any stand on any values, moral, behavioral, or aesthetic.

Everyone is afraid to call anything wrong, or vulgar, or fraudulent,
or just bad taste or bad manners. Congress, for example, pussyfooted

for months (following years of apathy) before taking action on a member convicted by the courts of illegalities; and when they finally got around to unseating him, one suspects they did it for the wrong motives. In 1922, in England, a man called Horatio Bottomley, a rather flamboyant character and popular demagogue—very similar in type, by the way, to Adam Clayton Powell, with similarly elastic financial ethics— who founded a paper called *John Bull* and got himself elected to Parliament, was found guilty of misappropriating the funds which his readers subscribed to victory bonds and other causes promoted by his paper. The day after the verdict, he was expelled from the House of Commons, with no fuss and very little debate, except for a few friendly farewells, as he was rather an engaging fellow. But no member thought the House had any other course to consider: out he went. I do not suggest that this represents a difference between British and American morality; the difference is in the *times*.

Our time is one of disillusion in our species and a resulting lack of self-confidence—for good historical reasons. Man's recent record has not been reassuring. After engaging in the Great War with all its mud and blood and ravaged ground, its disease, destruction, and death, we allowed ourselves a bare twenty years before going at it all over again. And the second time was accompanied by an episode of man's inhumanity to man of such enormity that its implications for all of us have not yet, I think, been fully measured. A historian has recently stated that for such a phenomenon as the planned and nearly accomplished extermination of a people to take place, one of three preconditions necessary was public indifference.

Since then the human species has been busy overbreeding, polluting the air, destroying the balance of nature, and bungling in a variety of directions so that it is no wonder we have begun to doubt man's capacity for good judgment. It is hardly surprising that the self-confidence of the nineteenth century and its belief in human progress has been dissipated. "Every great civilization," said Secretary Gardner last year, "has been characterized by confidence in itself." At mid-twentieth century, the supply is low. As a result, we tend to shy away from all judgments. We hesitate to label anything wrong, and therefore hesitate to require the individual to bear moral responsibility for his acts.

We have become afraid to fix blame. Murderers and rapists and muggers and persons who beat up old men and engage in other forms of assault are not guilty; society is guilty; society has wronged them; society beats its breast and says *mea culpa*—it is our fault, not the wrongdoer's. The wrongdoer, poor fellow, could not help himself.

I find this very puzzling because I always ask myself, in these cases, what about the many neighbors of the wrongdoer, equally poor, equally disadvantaged, equally sufferers from society's neglect, who nevertheless maintain certain standards of social behavior, who do *not* commit crimes, who do not murder for money or rape for kicks. How does it happen that they know the difference between right and wrong, and how long will they abide by the difference if the leaders and opinion-makers and pacesetters continue to shy away from bringing home responsibility to the delinquent?

Admittedly, the reluctance to condemn stems partly from a worthy instinct—*tout comprendre, c'est tout pardonner*—and from a rejection of what was often the hypocrisy of Victorian moral standards. True, there was a large component of hypocrisy in nineteenth-century morality. Since the advent of Freud, we know more, we understand more about human behavior, we are more reluctant to cast the first stone—to condemn—which is a good thing; but the pendulum has swung to the point where we are now afraid to place moral responsibility at all. Society, that large amorphous, nonspecific scapegoat, must carry the burden for each of us, relieving us of guilt. We have become so indoctrinated by the terrors lurking in the dark corridors of the guilt complex that guilt has acquired a very bad name. Yet a little guilt is not a dangerous thing; it has a certain social utility.

When it comes to guilt, a respected writer—respected in some circles —has told us, as her considered verdict on the Nazi program, that evil is banal—a word that means something so ordinary that you are not bothered by it; the dictionary definition is "commonplace and hack-neyed." Somehow that conclusion does not seem adequate or even apt. *Of course*, evil is commonplace; *of course* we all partake of it. Does that mean that we must withhold disapproval, and that when evil appears in dangerous degree or vicious form we must not con-demn but only understand? That may be very Christian in intent, but in reality it is an escape from the necessity of exercising judgment —which exercise, I believe, is a prime function of leadership.

What it requires is courage—just a little, not very much—the courage to be independent and stand up for the standard of values one believes in. That kind of courage is the quality most conspicuously missing, I think, in current life. I don't mean the courage to protest and walk around with picket signs or boo Secretary McNamara which, though it may stem from the right instinct, is a group thing that does not require any very stout spirit. I did it myself for Sacco and Vanzetti when I was about twelve and picketed in some now forgotten labor dispute when I was a freshman and even got arrested. There is nothing to that; if you don't do that sort of thing when you are eighteen, then there is something wrong with you. I mean, rather, a kind of lonely moral courage, the quality that attracted me to that odd character, Czar Reed, and to Lord Salisbury, neither of whom cared a rap for the

735

opinion of the public or would have altered his conduct a hair to adapt to it. It is the quality someone said of Lord Palmerston was his "you-be-damnedness." That is the mood we need a little more of.

Standards of taste, as well as morality, need continued reaffirmation to stay alive, as liberty needs eternal vigilance. To recognize and to proclaim the difference between the good and the shoddy, the true and the fake, as well as between right and wrong, or what we believe at a given time to be right and wrong, is the obligation, I think, of persons who presume to lead, or are thrust into leadership, or hold positions of authority. That includes—whether they asked for it or not—all educators and even, I regret to say, writers.

For educators it has become increasingly the habit in the difficult circumstances of college administration today to find out what the students want in the matter of curriculum and deportment and then give it to them. This seems to me another form of abdication, another example of the prevailing reluctance to state a standard and expect, not to say require, performance in accord with it. The permissiveness, the yielding of decision to the student, does not—from what I can tell —promote responsibility in the young so much as uneasiness and a kind of anger at *not* being told what is expected of them, a resentment of their elders' unwillingness to take a position. Recently a student psychiatric patient of the Harvard Health Services was quoted by the director, Dr. Dana Farnsworth, as complaining, "My parents never tell me what to do. They never stop me from doing anything." That is the unheard wail, I think, extended beyond parents to the general absence of a guiding, reassuring pattern, which is behind much of society's current uneasiness.

It is human nature to want patterns and standards and a structure of behavior. A pattern to conform to is a kind of shelter. You see it in kindergarten and primary school, at least in those schools where the children when leaving the classroom are required to fall into line. When the teacher gives the signal, they fall in with alacrity; they know where they belong and they instinctively like to *be* where they belong. They like the feeling of being in line.

Most people need a structure, not only to fall into but to fall out of. The rebel with a cause is better off than the one without. At least he knows what he is "agin." He is not lost. He does not suffer from an identity crisis. It occurs to me that much of the student protest now may be a testing of authority, a search for that line to fall out of, and when it isn't there students become angrier because they feel more lost, more abandoned than ever. In the late turmoil at Berkeley, at least as regards the filthy speech demonstration, there was a missed opportunity, I think (however great my respect for Clark Kerr) for a hearty, emphatic, and unmistakable "No!" backed up by sanctions.

Why? Because the act, even if intended as a demonstration of principle, was in this case, like any indecent exposure, simply offensive, and what is offensive to the greater part of society is anti-social, and what is anti-social, so long as we live in social groups and not each of us on his own island, must be curtailed, like Peeping Toms or obscene telephone calls, as a public nuisance. The issue is really not complicated or difficult but, if we would only look at it with more self-confidence, quite simple.

So, it seems to me, is the problem of the CIA.[1] You will say that in this case people have taken a stand, opinion-makers have worked themselves into a moral frenzy. Indeed they have, but over a false issue. The CIA is not, after all, the Viet Cong or the Schutzstaffel in blackshirts. Its initials do not stand for Criminal Indiscretions of America. It is an arm of the American government, our elected, representative government (whatever may be one's feelings toward that body at the moment). Virtually every government in the world subsidizes youth groups, especially in their international relations, not to mention in athletic competitions. (I do not know if the CIA is subsidizing our Equestrian Team, but I know personally a number of people who would be only too delighted if it were.) The difficulty here is simply that the support was clandestine in the first place and not the proper job of the CIA in the second. An intelligence agency should be restricted to the gathering of intelligence and not extend itself into operations. In armies the two functions are distinct: intelligence is G2 and operations is G3. If our government could manage its functions with a little more precision and perform openly those functions that are perfectly respectable, there would be no issue. The recent excitement only shows how easily we succumb when reliable patterns or codes of conduct are absent, to a confusion of values.

A similar confusion exists, I think, with regard to the omnipresent pornography that surrounds us like smog. A year ago the organization of my own profession, the Authors League, filed a brief *amicus curiae* in the appeal of Ralph Ginzburg, the publisher of a periodical called *Eros* and other items, who had been convicted of disseminating obscenity through the mails. The League's action was taken on the issue of censorship to which all good liberals automatically respond like Pavlov's dogs. Since at this stage in our culture pornography has so far gotten the upper hand that to do battle in its behalf against the dragon Censorship is rather like doing battle today against the bustle in behalf of short skirts, and since I believe that the proliferation of pornography in its sadistic forms is a greater social danger at the moment than

---

[1] The Central Intelligence Agency was discovered to be giving secret financial support to the National Student Association—eds.

censorship, and since Mr. Ginzburg was not an author anyway but a commercial promoter, I raised an objection, as a member of the Council, to the Authors League's spending its funds in the Ginzburg case. I was, of course, outvoted; in fact, there was no vote. Everyone around the table just sat and looked at me in cold disapproval. Later, after my objection was printed in the *Bulletin*, at my request, two distinguished authors wrote privately to me to express their agreement but did not go so far as to say so publicly.

Thereafter, when the Supreme Court upheld Mr. Ginzburg's conviction, everyone in the intellectual community raised a hullaballoo about censorship advancing upon us like some sort of Frankenstein's monster. This seems to me another case of getting excited about the wrong thing. The cause of pornography is *not* the same as the cause of free speech. There *is* a difference. Ralph Ginzburg is *not* Theodore Dreiser and this is not the 1920's. If one looks around at the movies, especially the movie advertisements, and the novels and the pulp magazines glorifying perversion and the paperbacks that make de Sade available to school children, one does not get the impression that in the 1960's we are being stifled in the Puritan grip of Anthony Comstock. Here again, leaders—in this case authors and critics—seem too unsure of values or too afraid of being unpopular to stand up and assert the perfectly obvious difference between smut and free speech, or to say "Such and such is offensive and can be harmful." Happily, there are signs of awakening. In a *Times* review of a book called *On Iniquity* by Pamela Hansford Johnson, which related pornography to the Moors murders in England, the reviewer concluded that "this may be the opening of a discussion that must come, the opening shot."

In the realm of art, no less important than morals, the abdication of judgment is almost a disease. Last fall when the Lincoln Center opened its glittering new opera house with a glittering new opera on the tragedy of Antony and Cleopatra, the curtain rose on a gaudy crowd engaged in energetic revels around a gold box in the shape of a pyramid, up whose sides (conveniently fitted with toe-holds, I suppose) several sinuous and reasonably nude slave girls were chased by lecherous guards left over from "Aida." When these preliminaries quieted down, the front of the gold box suddenly dropped open, and guess who was inside? No, it was not Cleopatra, it was Antony, looking, I thought, rather bewildered. What he was doing inside the box was never made clear. Thereafter everything happened—and in crescendos of gold and spangles and sequins, silks and gauzes, feathers, fans, jewels, brocades, and such a quantity of glitter that one began to laugh, thinking that the spectacle was intended as a parody of the old Shubert revue. But no, this was the Metropolitan Opera in the vaunted splendor of its most publicized opening since the Hippodrome. I gather it was Mr. Bing's idea of giving the first night customers a fine splash. What he achieved was simply vulgarity, as at least some reviewers had the courage to say next day. Now, I cannot believe that Mr. Bing and his colleagues do not know the difference between honest artistry in stage design and pretentious ostentation. If they know better, why do they allow themselves to do worse? As leaders in their field of endeavor, they should have been setting standards of beauty and creative design, not debasing them.

One finds the same peculiarities in the visual arts. Non-art, as its practitioners describe it—the blob school, the all-black canvasses, the paper cutouts and Campbell soup tins and plastic hamburgers and pieces of old carpet—is treated as art, not only by dealers whose motive is understandable (they have discovered that shock value sells); not only by a gullible pseudocultural section of the public who are not interested in art but in being "in" and wouldn't, to quote an old joke, know a Renoir from a Jaguar; but also, which I find mystifying, by the museums and the critics. I am sure they know the difference between the genuine and the hoax. But not trusting their own judgment, they seem afraid to say no to anything, for fear, I suppose, of making a mistake and turning down what may be next decade's Matisse.

For the museums to exhibit the plastic hamburgers and twists of scrap iron is one thing, but for them to *buy* them for their permanent collection puts an imprimatur on what is fraudulent. Museum curators, too, are leaders who have an obligation to distinguish—I will not say the good from the bad in art because that is an elusive and subjective matter dependent on the eye of the time—but at least honest expression from phony. Most of what fills the galleries on Madison Avenue is simply stuff designed to take advantage of current fads and does not come from an artist's vision or an honest creative impulse. The dealers know it; the critics know it; the purveyors themselves know it; the public suspects it; but no one dares say it because that would be committing oneself to a standard of values and even, heaven forbid, exposing oneself to being called square.

In the fairy story, it required a child to cry out that the Emperor was naked. Let us not leave that task to the children. It should be the task of leaders to recognize and state the truth as they see it. It is their task not to be afraid of absolutes.

If the educated man is not willing to express standards, if he cannot show that he has them and applies them, what then is education for? Its purpose, I take it, is to form the civilized man, whom I would define as the person capable of the informed exercise of judgment, taste, and values. If at maturity he is not willing to express judgment on matters of policy or taste or morals, if at fifty he does not believe that he has acquired more wisdom and informed experience than is possessed by the student at twenty, then he is saying in effect that education has been a failure.

James Thurber

James Thurber (1894–1961), one of the greatest of American
humorists, grew up in Columbus, Ohio, and for a time attended
Ohio State University. After World War I he worked as a
reporter in Columbus, Chicago, Paris, and New York, and in
1926 began the long and famous association with The New
Yorker *chronicled in* The Years with Ross *(1959). Thurber*
was a prolific essayist, cartoonist, and writer of plays, short
stories, and children's books. It would be impossible to summarize
justly here his first-rate achievements in all of these media. A
few of his best-known volumes are Is Sex Necessary? *(with E. B.*
White, 1929), My Life and Hard Times *(1933),* Fables for
Our Time *(1940), and* The Thurber Carnival *(1945).*

The story we present here, from the collection The Middle-
Aged Man on the Flying Trapeze *(1935), exemplifies both*
the edge and the geniality of Thurber's wit, his astonishing feeling
for imagery, at once economical and expressive, and his subtle
management of point-of-view. It was first printed in 1931 in
The New Yorker, *for readers who still remembered vividly the*
national celebration on the return of Charles A. Lindbergh
from his solo flight across the Atlantic in 1927. Younger readers
will recognize the 1969 moon landing as a comparable event.
The question we pose is whether they continue to recognize and
accept the system of values on which Thurber's satire and humor
depend.

THE GREATEST MAN IN THE WORLD

Looking back on it now, from the vantage point of 1940, one can only marvel that it hadn't happened long before it did. The United States of America had been, ever since Kitty Hawk, blindly constructing the elaborate petard by which, sooner or later, it must be hoist. It was inevitable that some day there would come roaring out of the skies a national hero of insufficient intelligence, background, and character successfully to endure the mounting orgies of glory prepared for aviators who stayed up a long time or flew a great distance. Both Lindbergh and Byrd, fortunately for national decorum and international amity, had been gentlemen; so had our other famous aviators. They wore their laurels gracefully, withstood the awful weather of publicity, married excellent women, usually of fine family, and quietly retired to private life and the enjoyment of their varying fortunes. No untoward incidents, on a worldwide scale, marred the perfection of their conduct on the perilous heights of fame. The exception to the rule was, however, bound to occur and it did, in July, 1937, when Jack ("Pal") Smurch, erstwhile mechanic's helper in a small garage in Westfield, Iowa, flew a second-hand, single-motored Bresthaven Dragon-Fly III monoplane all the way around the world, without stopping.

Never before in the history of aviation had such a flight as Smurch's ever been dreamed of. No one had even taken seriously the weird floating auxiliary gas tanks, invention of the mad New Hampshire professor of astronomy, Dr. Charles Lewis Gresham, upon which Smurch placed full reliance. When the garage worker, a slightly built, surly, unprepossessing young man of twenty-two, appeared at Roosevelt Field early in July, 1937, slowly chewing a great quid of scrap tobacco, and announced "Nobody ain't seen no flyin' yet," the newspapers touched briefly and satirically upon his projected twenty-five-thousand-mile flight. Aëronautical and automotive experts dismissed the idea curtly, implying that it was a hoax, a publicity stunt. The rusty, battered, second-hand plane wouldn't go. The Gresham auxiliary tanks wouldn't work. It was simply a cheap joke.

Smurch, however, after calling on a girl in Brooklyn who worked in the flap-folding department of a large paper-box factory, a girl whom he later described as his "sweet patootie," climbed nonchalantly into his ridiculous plane at dawn of the memorable seventh of July, 1937, spit a curve of tobacco juice into the still air, and took off, carrying with him only a gallon of bootleg gin and six pounds of salami.

When the garage boy thundered out over the ocean the papers were forced to record, in all seriousness, that a mad, unknown young man— his name was variously misspelled—had actually set out upon a preposterous attempt to span the world in a rickety, one-engined contraption, trusting to the long-distance refuelling device of a crazy schoolmaster. When, nine days later, without having stopped once, the tiny plane appeared above San Francisco Bay, headed for New York, spluttering and choking, to be sure, but still magnificently and miraculously aloft, the headlines, which long since had crowded everything else off the front page—even the shooting of the Governor of Illinois by the Vileti gang—swelled to unprecedented size, and the news stories began to run to twenty-five and thirty columns. It was noticeable, however, that the accounts of the epoch-making flight touched rather lightly upon the aviator himself. This was not because facts about the hero as a man were too meagre, but because they were too complete.

Reporters, who had been rushed out to Iowa when Smurch's plane was first sighted over the little French coast town of Serly-le-Mer, to dig up the story of the great man's life, had promptly discovered that the story of his life could not be printed. His mother, a sullen short-order cook in a shack restaurant on the edge of a tourists' camping ground near Westfield, met all inquiries as to her son with an angry "Ah, the hell with him; I hope he drowns." His father appeared to be in jail somewhere for stealing spotlights and laprobes from tourists' automobiles; his young brother, a weak-minded lad, had but recently escaped from the Preston, Iowa, Reformatory and was already wanted in several Western towns for the theft of money-order blanks from post offices. These alarming discoveries were still piling up at the very time that Pal Smurch, the greatest hero of the twentieth century, blear-eyed, dead for sleep, half-starved, was piloting his crazy junk-heap high above the region in which the lamentable story of his private life was being unearthed, headed for New York and a greater glory than any man of his time had ever known.

The necessity for printing some account in the papers of the young man's career and personality had led to a remarkable predicament. It was of course impossible to reveal the facts, for a tremendous popular feeling in favor of the young hero had sprung up, like a grass fire, when he was halfway across Europe on his flight around the globe. He was, therefore, described as a modest chap, taciturn, blond, popular with his friends, popular with girls. The only available snapshot of Smurch, taken at the wheel of a phony automobile in a cheap photo studio at an amusement park, was touched up so that the little vulgarian looked quite handsome. His twisted leer was smoothed into a pleasant smile. The truth was, in this way, kept from the youth's ecstatic compatriots; they did not dream that the Smurch family was despised and feared by its neighbors in the obscure Iowa town, nor that the hero himself, because of numerous unsavory exploits, had come to be regarded in Westfield as a nuisance and a menace. He had, the reporters discovered, once knifed the principal of his high school—not mortally, to be sure, but he had knifed him; and on another occasion, surprised in the act of stealing an altarcloth from a church, he had bashed the sacristan over the head with a pot of Easter lilies; for each of these offences he had served a sentence in the reformatory.

Inwardly, the authorities, both in New York and in Washington, prayed that an understanding Providence might, however awful such a thing seemed, bring disaster to the rusty, battered plane and its illustrious pilot, whose unheard-of flight had aroused the civilized world to hosannas of hysterical praise. The authorities were convinced that the character of the renowned aviator was such that the limelight of adulation was bound to reveal him, to all the world, as a congenital hooligan mentally and morally unequipped to cope with his own prodigious fame. "I trust," said the Secretary of State, at one of many secret Cabinet meetings called to consider the national dilemma, "I trust that his mother's prayer will be answered," by which he referred to Mrs. Emma Smurch's wish that her son might be drowned. It was, however, too late for that—Smurch had leaped the Atlantic and then the Pacific as if they were millponds. At three minutes after two o'clock on the afternoon of July 17, 1937, the garage boy brought his idiotic plane into Roosevelt Field for a perfect three-point landing.

It had, of course, been out of the question to arrange a modest little reception for the greatest flier in the history of the world. He was received at Roosevelt Field with such elaborate and pretentious ceremonies as rocked the world. Fortunately, however, the worn and spent hero promptly swooned, had to be removed bodily from his plane, and was spirited from the field without having opened his mouth once. Thus he did not jeopardize the dignity of this first reception, a reception illumined by the presence of the Secretaries of War and the Navy, Mayor Michael J. Moriarity of New York, the Premier of Canada, Governors Fanniman, Groves, McFeely, and Critchfield, and a brilliant array of European diplomats. Smurch did not, in fact, come to in time to take part in the gigantic hullabaloo arranged at City Hall for the next day. He was rushed to a secluded nursing home and confined in bed. It was nine days before he was able to get up, or to be more exact, before he was permitted to get up. Meanwhile the greatest minds in the country, in solemn assembly, had arranged a secret conference of city, state, and government officials, which Smurch was to attend for the purpose of being instructed in the ethics and behavior of heroism.

On the day that the little mechanic was finally allowed to get up and dress and, for the first time in two weeks, took a great chew of tobacco, he was permitted to receive the newspapermen—this by way of testing him out. Smurch did not wait for questions. "Youse guys," he said—and the *Times* man winced—"youse guys can tell the cock-eyed world dat I put it over on Lindbergh, see? Yeh—an' made an ass o' them two frogs." The "two frogs" was a reference to a pair of gallant French fliers who, in attempting a flight only halfway round the world, had, two weeks before, unhappily been lost at sea. The *Times* man was bold enough, at this point, to sketch out for Smurch the accepted formula for interviews in cases of this kind; he explained that there should be no arrogant statements belittling the achievements of other heroes, particularly heroes of foreign nations. "Ah, the hell with that," said Smurch. "I did it, see? I did it, an' I'm talkin' about it." And he did talk about it.

None of this extraordinary interview was, of course, printed. On the contrary, the newspapers, already under the disciplined direction of a secret directorate created for the occasion and composed of states-men and editors, gave out to a panting and restless world that "Jacky," as he had been arbitrarily nicknamed, would consent to say only that he was very happy and that anyone could have done what he did. "My achievement has been, I fear, slightly exaggerated," the *Times* man's article had him protest, with a modest smile. These newspaper stories were kept from the hero, a restriction which did not serve to abate the rising malevolence of his temper. The situation was, indeed, extremely grave, for Pal Smurch was, as he kept insisting, "rarin' to go." He could not much longer be kept from a nation clamorous to lionize him. It was the most desperate crisis the United States of America had faced since the sinking of the *Lusitania*.

On the afternoon of the twenty-seventh of July, Smurch was spirited away to a conference-room in which were gathered mayors, governors, government officials, behaviorist psychologists, and editors. He gave them each a limp, moist paw and a brief unlovely grin. "Hah ya?" he said. When Smurch was seated, the Mayor of New York arose and, with obvious pessimism, attempted to explain what he must say and how he must act when presented to the world, ending his talk with a high tribute to the hero's courage and integrity. The Mayor was followed by Governor Fanniman of New York, who, after a touch-ing declaration of faith, introduced Cameron Spottiswood, Second Secretary of the American Embassy in Paris, the gentleman selected to coach Smurch in the amenities of public ceremonies. Sitting in a chair, with a soiled yellow tie in his hand and his shirt open at the throat, unshaved, smoking a rolled cigarette, Jack Smurch listened with a leer on his lips. "I get ya, I get ya," he cut in, nastily. "Ya want me to act like a softy, huh? Ya want me to act like that — — baby-face Lindbergh, huh? Well, nuts to that, see?" Everyone took in his breath sharply; it was a sigh and a hiss. "Mr. Lindbergh," began a

United States Senator, purple with rage, "and Mr. Byrd—" Smurch, who was paring his nails with a jackknife, cut in again. "Byrd!" he exclaimed. "Aw, fa God's sake, *dat* big—" Somebody shut off his blasphemies with a sharp word. A newcomer had entered the room. Everyone stood up, except Smurch, who, still busy with his nails, did not even glance up. "Mr. Smurch," said someone, sternly, "the President of the United States!" It had been thought that the presence of the Chief Executive might have a chastening effect upon the young hero, and the former had been, thanks to the remarkable coöperation of the press, secretly brought to the obscure conference-room.

A great, painful silence fell. Smurch looked up, waved a hand at the President. "How ya comin'?" he asked, and began rolling a fresh cigarette. The silence deepened. Someone coughed in a strained way. "Geez, it's hot, ain't it?" said Smurch. He loosened two more shirt buttons, revealing a hairy chest and the tattooed word "Sadie" enclosed in a stencilled heart. The great and important men in the room, faced by the most serious crisis in recent American history, exchanged worried frowns. Nobody seemed to know how to proceed. "Come awn, come awn," said Smurch. "Let's get the hell out of here! When do I start cuttin' in on de parties, huh? And what's they goin' to be *in* it?" He rubbed a thumb and forefinger together meaningly. "Money!" exclaimed a state senator, shocked, pale. "Yeh, money," said Pal, flipping his cigarette out of a window. "An' big money." He began rolling a fresh cigarette. "Big money," he repeated, frowning over the rice paper. He tilted back in his chair, and leered at each gentleman, separately, the leer of an animal that knows its power, the leer of a leopard loose in a bird-and-dog shop. "Aw fa God's sake, let's get some place where it's cooler," he said. "I been cooped up plenty for three weeks!"

Smurch stood up and walked over to an open window, where he stood staring down into the street, nine floors below. The faint shouting of newsboys floated up to him. He made out his name. "Hot dog!" he cried, grinning, ecstatic. He leaned out over the sill. "You tell 'em, babies!" he shouted down. "Hot diggity dog!" In the tense little knot of men standing behind him, a quick, mad impulse flared up. An unspoken word of appeal, of command, seemed to ring through the room. Yet it was deadly silent. Charles K. L. Brand, secretary to the Mayor of New York City, happened to be standing nearest Smurch; he looked inquiringly at the President of the United States. The President, pale, grim, nodded shortly. Brand, a tall, powerfully built man, once a tackle at Rutgers, stepped forward, seized the greatest man in the world by his left shoulder and the seat of his pants, and pushed him out the window.

"My God, he's fallen out the window!" cried a quick-witted editor.

"Get me out of here!" cried the President. Several men sprang to his side and he was hurriedly escorted out of a door toward a side-entrance of the building. The editor of the Associated Press took charge, being used to such things. Crisply he ordered certain men to leave, others to stay; quickly he outlined a story which all the papers were to agree on, sent two men to the street to handle that end of the tragedy, commanded a Senator to sob and two Congressmen to go to pieces nervously. In a word, he skillfully set the stage for the gigantic task that was to follow, the task of breaking to a grief-stricken world the sad story of the untimely, accidental death of its most illustrious and spectacular figure.

The funeral was, as you know, the most elaborate, the finest, the solemnest, and the saddest ever held in the United States of America. The monument in Arlington Cemetery, with its clean white shaft of marble and the simple device of a tiny plane carved on its base, is a place for pilgrims, in deep reverence, to visit. The nations of the world paid lofty tributes to little Jacky Smurch, America's greatest hero. At a given hour there were two minutes of silence throughout the nation. Even the inhabitants of the small, bewildered town of Westfield, Iowa, observed this touching ceremony; agents of the Department of Justice saw to that. One of them was especially assigned to stand grimly in the doorway of a little shack restaurant on the edge of the tourists' camping ground just outside the town. There, under his stern scrutiny, Mrs. Emma Smurch bowed her head above two hamburger steaks sizzling on her grill—bowed her head and turned away, so that the Secret Service man could not see the twisted, strangely familiar, leer on her lips.

Richard Gilman

Richard Gilman was born in New York City in 1925. He served for three years in the Marine Corps, then graduated in 1947 from the University of Wisconsin. He became a free-lance writer, then an editor, critic, and teacher. He has been drama critic of Newsweek *and* Commonweal, *literary editor of* The New Republic, *has taught at Columbia, Stanford, and the Salzburg Seminar, and is now Professor of Drama and Criticism at the Yale Drama School. In 1967 Grinnell College awarded him an*

honorary Doctorate of Humane Letters. The present essay, a
review of Eldridge Cleaver's Soul on Ice, *first appeared in*
The New Republic *for March 9, 1968; it is reprinted here from*
the author's collection, The Confusion of Realms *(1969). In*
a companion piece, "Black Writing and White Criticism,"
Mr. Gilman answers objections to his review by insisting that
"we can no longer talk to black people, or they to us, in the
traditional humanistic ways."

WHITE STANDARDS AND BLACK WRITING

There is a growing body of black writing which is not to be thought
of simply as writing by blacks. It is not something susceptible of
being democratized and assimilated in the same way that writing by
Jews has been. The movement there was, very roughly, from Jewish
writing to Jewish-American writing to writing by authors "who happen to be Jews." But the new black writing I am talking about isn't
the work of authors who *happen* to be black; it doesn't make up the
kind of movement within a broader culture by which minorities, such
as the Jews or the Southerners in our own society, contribute from
their special cast of mind and imagination and their particular historical and psychic backgrounds something "universal," increments to the
literary or intellectual traditions.

These black writers I am speaking of take their blackness not as a
starting point for literature or thought and not as a marshaling ground
for a position in the parade of national images and forms, but as absolute theme and necessity. They make philosophies and fantasias out
of their color, use it as weapon and seat of judgment, as strategy and
outcry, source of possible rebirth, data for a future existence and
agency of revolutionary change. For such men and women, to write is
an almost literal means of survival and attack, a means—more radically
than we have known it—to *be,* and their writing owes more, consciously
at least, to the embattled historical moment in which black Americans
find themselves than to what is ordinarily thought of as literary expression or the ongoing elaboration of ideas.

That universality is not among the incentives and preoccupations of
this writing is something that makes for its particular, if sometimes
provisional, strength. A book like *The Autobiography of Malcolm X,*
the type and highest achievement of the genre (if we have to call it

that), forges its own special value and importance partly through its adamant specificity, its inapplicability as a model for many kinds of existence. Its way of looking at the world, its formulation of experience, is not the potential possession—even by imaginative appropriation —of us all; hard, local, intransigent, alien, it remains in some sense unassimilable for those of us who aren't black. And that is why it has become, to an even greater degree than novels like *Native Son* and *Invisible Man,* the special pride and inspiriting book of so many black Americans.

Malcolm's literacy, his capacity to write the book at all, were of course formed by what we have to call white traditions, but the book was not a contribution to those traditions, not another *Education of Henry Adams* or *Apologia Pro Vita Sua,* documents of the white normative Western consciousness and spirit, which blacks in America today have begun to repudiate in ways that are as yet clumsy, painful and confused. The point is that most Western intellectual autobiographies, apart from the writings of revolutionaries in whom the life was subordinate to the action in the world, have been luxury documents. Rising out of an already assured stock of consciousness and technical means, building on a civilization which had thrown up many precedents and models for the extension of the self into memorial and apologetic literature—writing which *takes for granted* the worth, dignity and substantial being of the individual, his right to talk about himself in public—such books could only have provided Malcolm with certain technical or organizational principles of procedure. As for spiritual models, could he have learned from *Up from Slavery,* that book which so many black Americans so fiercely repudiate today as much for its having been written in the borrowed, deferential spirit of imitation of Western sagas of the self as for its explicit Uncle Tomism?

There was a central element of dishonesty in white liberal reactions to Malcolm's book. It should have alarmed them far more radically than it did. But by praising Malcolm for his candor, his "power" or his "salutary indictment of our society," by making a literary compatriot of him, the white cultured community effectively blunted the really unsettling fact about his book: that it was not written for us, it was written for blacks. It is not talking about the human condition (that Western idea which from the battle line looks like a luxury product) but about the condition of black people; it is not, moreover, anything less—although it is other things as well—than a myth of blacks to live by now, as we have our myths of so many kinds.

The black man doesn't feel the way whites do, nor does he think as whites do—at the point, that is, when feeling and thought have moved beyond pure physical sensation or problems in mathematics.

"Prick me and I bleed," Shylock rightly said, but the difference begins when the attitude to the blood is in question: black suffering is not of the same kind as ours. Under the great flawless arc of the Greco-Roman and Judeo-Christian traditions we have implicitly believed that all men experience essentially the same things, that birth, love, pain, self, death, are universals; they are in fact what we mean by universal values in literature and consciousness. But the black man has found it almost impossible in America to experience the universal as such; this power, after all, is conferred upon the individual, or rather confirmed for him, by his membership in the community of men. Imagine how it must be to know that you have not the right to feel that your birth, your pain, your joy or your death are proper, natural elements of the human universe, but are, as it were, interlopers, unsanctioned realities, to be experienced on sufferance and without communal acknowledgment.

"We shall have our manhood. We shall have it or the earth will be leveled by our attempts to gain it." So writes Eldridge Cleaver in his book, *Soul on Ice*, a collection of letters, essays, reflections and reports from his life which go to make up a spiritual and intellectual autobiography that stands at the exact resonant center of the new black writing I have been referring to. Cleaver's book is in the tradition—that just-formed current—of Malcolm X's, and the latter is its mentor in the fullest sense. Unsparing, unaccommodating, tough and lyrical by turns, foolish at times, unconvincing in many of its specific ideas but extraordinarily convincing in the energy and hard morale of its thinking, painful, aggressive and undaunted, *Soul on Ice* is a book for which we have to make room, but not on the shelves we have already built.

Cleaver was born in Arkansas in 1935, grew up in the black ghetto of Los Angeles and at eighteen was sent to prison for possessing marijuana. Since then he has spent most of his time in one or another California prison, being at present on parole from the institution at Soledad and living in the Bay area where, the dust jacket quotes him as saying, he works as a "full-time revolutionary in the struggle for black liberation in America." He is a staff writer for *Ramparts*, minister of information for the Black Panther Party for Self-Defense, and at work on a book about "the future direction of the black liberation movement."

The year he first went to prison was the year of the Supreme Court decision overthrowing school segregation, and Cleaver holds the two events in firm, unambiguous relationship. The decision moved him into thought for the first time: "I began to form a concept of what it meant to be black in white America." As his intellect sought materials, he turned to the great white revolutionaries—Marx, Tom Paine,

Lenin, Bakunin, Nechayev (most of whom he must have read in periods outside prison)—and later to Negro writers like Richard Wright, W. E. B. Du Bois and, of course, with enormous impact on him, Malcolm X. The last stages of his education seem to have been his reading of white writers like Mailer, Burroughs and Ginsberg, who put him in touch with certain energies and approaches which he badly needed to escape provincialism.

He started to write a few years ago, he says, "to save myself." For from being jailed for possessing pot he had passed to true criminal status. Agonized, furious, blind with vengefulness, he had embarked, after completing his first sentence, on a deliberate career as a rapist, first with black women as victims—"in the black ghetto where dark and vicious deeds appear not as aberrations or deviations from the norm, but as part of the sufficiency of the Evil of a day"—and then with whites. "I had gone astray—astray not so much from the white man's law as from being human, civilized . . ."

This struggle, to be human and civilized without submitting one-self to the *whiteness* of those words, and above all without submitting to fear of the law which embodies them, is at the heart of much pas-sionate activity among blacks in America today. It was Malcolm X's struggle: in that change of heart and mind he underwent before his death, and which was the immediate cause of his death, Malcolm worked himself free of racism, out of the trap of being merely opposed, of being, therefore, fixed in the reduced identity of the opponent. "I have, so to speak," Cleaver writes, "washed my hands in the blood of the martyr, Malcolm X, whose retreat from the precipice of madness created new room for others to turn about in, and I am now caught up in that tiny space, attempting a maneuver of my own."

That tiny space: from one perspective it is the space between absolute hatred and repudiation of all whites and Uncle Tomism, from another, wider one the murderously curtailed room any one of us has to remain human and yet to *make something happen*, to change things. For Cleaver, the "maneuver" he carries out is an effort at grace, complexity and faithfulness. It is to *be* black, with no concessions, no adaptations to white expectations, but at the same time to hold back from excess; it is to be able to invent myths and intellectual schemes for containing black experience and providing for a black future, but at the same time to distinguish in the white-controlled present whatever has remained human and might recommend itself as ally.

Cleaver finds the ally among young whites, whose "prostrate souls and tumultuous consciences" are evidence to him of the great split in this country of which the racial war is only one, if major, constituent. "There is in America today," he writes, "a generation of white youth that is truly worthy of a black man's respect," "a rare event" in our "foul history." They are a generation which has lost its heroes, and Cleaver has no hesitation in asserting that the new heroes are black or yellow or Latin, in any case never Anglo-Saxon: Mao, Castro, Che Guevara, Martin Luther King, Ho Chi Minh, Stokely Carmichael, Malcolm. (In the several years since he wrote this, his list of heroes has been reduced by time's erosion of ideality—Nasser, Ben Bella and Kwame Nkrumah have of course lost their revolutionary credentials— but the general truth holds up.)

Yet having made his acknowledgments to white revolutionary youth and having distinguished, as it is crucial to do, the fact that the political conflict in this country is "deeper than race," Cleaver keeps going back to race as his theme and arena. As a self-described "ofay-watcher," he has his eye on a hundred manifestations of American ugliness or depravity or dishonesty, but he is not a social critic for *our* sake: his is a Negro perspective, sight issuing from the "furious psychic stance of the Negro today," and in its victories of understanding, its blindness and incompletions, its clean or inchoate energies, its internal motives and justifications, his writing remains in some profound sense not subject to correction or emendation or, most centrally, approval or rejection by those of us who are not black.

I know this is likely to be misunderstood. We have all considered the chief thing we should be working toward is that state of disinterestedness, of "higher" truth and independent valuation, which would allow us, white and black, to see each other's minds and bodies free of the distortions of race, to recognize each other's gifts and deficiencies as gifts and deficiencies, to be able to quarrel as the members of an (ideal) family do and not as embattled tribes. We want to be able to say without self-consciousness or inverted snobbery that such and such a Negro is a bastard or a lousy writer.

But we are nowhere near that stage and in some ways we are moving farther from it as polarization increases. And my point has been that it would be better for all of us if we recognized that in the present phase of interracial existence in America moral and intellectual "truths" have not the same reality for blacks and whites, and that even to write is, for many blacks, a particular act within the fact of their Negritude, not the independent universal "luxury" work we at least partly and ideally conceive it to be.

Here is Cleaver on a social manifestation of what I am talking about:

One thing that judges, policemen and administrators never seem to have understood, and for which they certainly do not make any allowances, is that Negro convicts, basically, rather than see themselves as criminals and perpetrators of misdeeds, look upon themselves as prisoners of war, the victims of a vicious, dog-eat-dog social system that is so heinous as to cancel out their own malefactions: in the jungle there is no right and wrong.

751

To turn from this to intellectual creation is to indicate how I myself, a "judge" who passes on writing, must take something into account. Cleaver's book devotes a great deal of space to his elaboration of a structure of thought, a legend really, about the nature of sexuality in America today. Some of it is grand, old-fashioned Lawrentian and Maileresque mythmaking:

This is the eternal and unwavering motivation of the male and female hemispheres, of man and woman, to transcend the Primeval Mitosis and achieve supreme identity in the Apocalyptic fusion.

Some of it is a Marxist-oriented analysis which ends by creating certain large controlling figures with which to account for experience. These are the white man, the Omnipotent Administrator, the white woman, the Ultrafeminine, the black man, the Supermasculine Menial; and the black woman, the Subfeminine Amazon. Sexually each has been forced into a role, as a result of his or her position in the society, and this frozen typology is what we have to battle against.

I find it unsatisfying intellectually, schematic and unsubtle most of the time. I don't want to hear again that the white man has been cut off from his body or that the black male has been forced back into his, that the black penis is more alive or the white woman's sexuality is artificial and contrived. Yet I don't want to condemn it, and I am not sure I know how to acknowledge it without seeming patronizing. For Cleaver has composed a myth to try to account for certain realities, black realities more than white ones: the fascination of black men with white standards of female beauty, the painfulness of having one's sexuality imprisoned within class or racial lines, the refusal of the society to credit the black man with a mind, the split between black men and women.

He knows what he is talking *from*, if not fully what he is talking *about*, and it is not my right to compare his thinking with other "classic" ways of grappling with sexual experience and drama; it isn't my right to draw him into the Western academy and subject his findings to the scrutiny of the tradition. A myth, moreover, is not really analyzable and certainly not something which one can call untrue.

But Cleaver gets me off the hook, I think, by providing me with a very beautiful section to quote, a letter "To All Black Women, From All Black Men," in which ideas are subordinated to intense feeling and in which the myth's unassailable usefulness is there to see. In it he addresses the black woman as "Queen-Mother-Daughter of Africa, Sister of My Soul, Black Bride of My Passion, My Eternal Love," and begs forgiveness for having abandoned her and allowed her to lose her sense of womanness. The last lines of the letter, and the book, make up an enormously impressive fusion of Cleaver's various revo-

752

lutionary strands, his assertion of a black reality, his hunger for sexual fullness and the reintegration of the self, his political critique and program and sense of a devastated society in need of resurrection:

Black woman, without asking how, just say that we survived our forced march and travail through the Valley of Slavery, Suffering and Death—there, that Valley there beneath us hidden by that drifting mist. Ah, what sights and sounds and pain lie beneath that mist. And we had thought that our hard climb out of that cruel valley led to some cool, green and peaceful, sunlit place—but it's all jungle here, a wild and savage wilderness that's overrun with ruins.
But put on your crown, my Queen, and we will build a New City on these ruins.

The passage is not addressed to me, and though I have called it beautiful and impressive and so on, that is out of the habit of the judge-critic, and I don't wish to continue in this strange and very contemporary form of injustice, that of sanctioning black thought from the standpoint of white criteria. I will go on judging and elucidating novels and plays and poetry by blacks according to what general powers I possess, but the kind of *black writing* I have been talking about, the act of creation of the self in the face of that self's historic denial by our society, seems to me to be at this point beyond my right to intrude on.

Marya Mannes

Marya Mannes, a talented and spirited journalist, is the daughter of two musicians and the niece of Walter Damrosch, the famous symphony conductor. She was born in 1904 in New York and was educated privately there. She worked as feature editor of Vogue *until World War II, then served three years in the Office of War Information. After a brief resumption of feature editing for* Glamour *(1946), she published a novel,* Message from a Stranger *(1948), and in 1952 she became a staff writer for* The Reporter. *She has lectured frequently, written plays, appeared on radio, had her own television program, and in 1970 began doing theater reviews for* The New York Times. *She has received many honors and awards, especially for her pungent and critical magazine essays on American art, morals, and culture. Some of these have been published in the*

collections More in Anger *(1958),* The New York I Know
(1961), and But Will It Sell? *(1964), from which we take the*
present essay.

HOW DO YOU KNOW IT'S GOOD?

Suppose there were no critics to tell us how to react to a picture, a
play, or a new composition of music. Suppose we wandered innocent
as the dawn into an art exhibition of unsigned paintings. By what
standards, by what values would we decide whether they were good or
bad, talented or untalented, successes or failures? How can we ever
know that what we think is right?

For the last fifteen or twenty years the fashion in criticism or appreciation of the arts has been to deny the existence of any valid criteria
and to make the words "good" or "bad" irrelevant, immaterial, and
inapplicable. There is no such thing, we are told, as a set of standards,
first acquired through experience and knowledge and later imposed on
the subject under discussion. This has been a popular approach, for
it relieves the critic of the responsibility of judgment and the public
of the necessity of knowledge. It pleases those resentful of disciplines,
it flatters the empty-minded by calling them open-minded, it comforts
the confused. Under the banner of democracy and the kind of equality
which our forefathers did *not* mean, it says, in effect, "Who are you to
tell us what is good or bad?" This is the same cry used so long and
so effectively by the producers of mass media who insist that it is the
public, not they, who decides what it wants to hear and see, and that
for a critic to say that *this* program is bad and *this* program is good
is purely a reflection of personal taste. Nobody recently has expressed
this philosophy more succinctly than Dr. Frank Stanton, the highly
intelligent president of CBS television. At a hearing before the
Federal Communications Commission, this phrase escaped him under
questioning: "One man's mediocrity is another man's good program."

There is no better way of saying "No values are absolute." There
is another important aspect to this philosophy of *laissez faire:* It is the
fear, in all observers of all forms of art, of guessing wrong. This fear
is well come by, for who has not heard of the contemporary outcries
against artists who later were called great? Every age has its arbiters
who do not grow with their times, who cannot tell evolution from
revolution or the difference between frivolous faddism, amateurish
754

experimentation, and profound and necessary change. Who wants to be caught *flagrante delicto* with an error of judgment as serious as this? It is far safer, and certainly easier, to look at a picture or a play or a poem and to say "This is hard to understand, but it may be good," or simply to welcome it as a new form. The word "new" —in our country especially—has magical connotations. What is new must be good; what is old is probably bad. And if a critic can describe the new in language that nobody can understand, he's safer still. If he has mastered the art of saying nothing with exquisite complexity, nobody can quote him later as saying anything.

But all these, I maintain, are forms of abdication from the responsibility of judgment. In creating, the artist commits himself; in appreciating, you have a commitment of your own. For after all, it is the audience which makes the arts. A climate of appreciation is essential to its flowering, and the higher the expectations of the public, the better the performance of the artist. Conversely, only a public ill-served by its critics could have accepted as art and as literature so much in these last years that has been neither. If anything goes, everything goes; and at the bottom of the junkpile lie the discarded standards too.

But what are these standards? How do you get them? How do you know they're the right ones? How can you make a clear pattern out of so many intangibles, including that greatest one, the very private I?

Well for one thing, it's fairly obvious that the more you read and see and hear, the more equipped you'll be to practice that art of association which is at the basis of all understanding and judgment. The more you live and the more you look, the more aware you are of a consistent pattern—as universal as the stars, as the tides, as breathing, as night and day—underlying everything. I would call this pattern and this rhythm an order. Not order—*an* order. Within it exists an incredible diversity of forms. Without it lies chaos. I would further call this order—this incredible diversity held within one pattern—health. And I would call chaos—the wild cells of destruction—sickness. It is in the end up to you to distinguish between the diversity that is health and the chaos that is sickness, and you can't do this without a process of association that can link a bar of Mozart with the corner of a Vermeer painting, or a Stravinsky score with a Picasso abstraction; or that can relate an aggressive act with a Franz Kline painting and a fit of coughing with a John Cage composition.

There is no accident in the fact that certain expressions of art live for all time and that others die with the moment, and although you may not always define the reasons, you can ask the questions. What does an artist say that is timeless; how does he say it? How much is fashion, how much is merely reflection? Why is Sir Walter Scott so hard to read now, and Jane Austen not? Why is baroque right for one age and too effulgent for another?

Can a standard of craftsmanship apply to art of all ages, or does each have its own, and different, definitions? You may have been aware, inadvertently, that craftsmanship has become a dirty word these years because, again, it implies standards—something done well or done badly. The result of this convenient avoidance is a plentitude of actors who can't project their voices, singers who can't phrase their songs, poets who can't communicate emotion, and writers who have no vocabulary—not to speak of painters who can't draw. The dogma now is that craftsmanship gets in the way of expression. You can do better if you don't know *how* you do it, let alone *what* you're doing.

I think it is time you helped reverse this trend by trying to rediscover craft: the command of the chosen instrument, whether it is a brush, a word, or a voice. When you begin to detect the difference between freedom and sloppiness, between serious experimentation and ego-therapy, between skill and slickness, between strength and violence, you are on your way to separating the sheep from the goats, a form of segregation denied us for quite a while. All you need to restore it is a small bundle of standards and a Geiger counter that detects fraud, and we might begin our tour of the arts in an area where both are urgently needed: contemporary painting.

I don't know what's worse: to have to look at acres of bad art to find the little good, or to read what the critics say about it all. In no other field of expression has so much double-talk flourished, so much confusion prevailed, and so much nonsense been circulated: further evidence of the close interdependence between the arts and the critical climate they inhabit. It will be my pleasure to share with you some of this double-talk so typical of our times.

Item one: preface for a catalogue of an abstract painter:

"Time-bound meditation experiencing a life; sincere with plastic piety at the threshold of hallowed arcana; a striving for pure ideation giving shape to inner drive; formalized patterns where neural balances reach a fiction." End of quote. Know what this artist paints like now?

Item two: a review in the *Art News*:

". . . a weird and disparate assortment of material, but the monstrosity which bloomed into his most recent cancer of aggregations is present in some form everywhere. . . ." Then, later, "A gluttony of things and processes terminated by a glorious constipation."

Item three, same magazine, review of an artist who welds automobile fragments into abstract shapes:

"Each fragment . . . is made an extreme of human exasperation, torn at and fought all the way, and has its rightness of form as if by accident. *Any technique that requires order or discipline would just be the human ego.* No, these must be egoless, uncontrolled, undesigned and different enough to give you a bang—fifty miles an hour around a telephone pole. . . ."

"Any technique that requires order or discipline would just be the human ego." What does he mean—"just be"? What are they really talking about? Is this journalism? Is it criticism? Or is it that other convenient abdication from standards of performance and judgment practiced by so many artists and critics that they, like certain writers who deal only in sickness and depravity, "reflect the chaos about them"? Again, whose chaos? Whose depravity?

I had always thought that the prime function of art was to create order *out* of chaos—again, not the order of neatness or rigidity or convention or artifice, but the order of clarity by which one will and one vision could draw the essential truth out of apparent confusion. I still do. It is not enough to use parts of a car to convey the brutality of the machine. This is as slavishly representative, and just as easy, as arranging dried flowers under glass to convey nature.

Speaking of which, i.e., the use of real materials (burlap, old gloves, bottletops) in lieu of pigment, this is what one critic had to say about an exhibition of Assemblage at the Museum of Modern Art last year:

"Spotted throughout the show are indisputable works of art, accounting for a quarter or even a half of the total display. But the remainder are works of non-art, anti-art, and art substitutes that are the aesthetic counterparts of the social deficiencies that land people in the clink on charges of vagrancy. These aesthetic bankrupts . . . have no legitimate ideological roof over their heads and not the price of a square intellectual meal, much less a spiritual sandwich, in their pockets."

I quote these words of John Canaday of *The New York Times* as an example of the kind of criticism which puts responsibility to an intelligent public above popularity with an intellectual coterie. Canaday has the courage to say what he thinks and the capacity to say it clearly: two qualities notably absent from his profession.

Next to art, I would say that appreciation and evaluation in the field of music is the most difficult. For it is rarely possible to judge a new composition at one hearing only. What seems confusing or fragmented at first might well become clear and organic a third time. Or it might not. The only salvation here for the listener is, again, an instinct born of experience and association which allows him to separate intent from accident, design from experimentation, and pretense from conviction. Much of contemporary music is, like its sister art, merely a reflection of the composer's own fragmentation: an absorption in self and symbols at the expense of communication with others. The artist, in short, says to the public: If you don't understand this, it's because you're dumb.

757

I maintain that you are not. You may have to go part way or even halfway to meet the artist, but if you must go the whole way, it's his fault, not yours. Hold fast to that. And remember it too when you read new poetry, that estranged sister of music.

"A multitude of causes, unknown to former times, are now acting with a combined force to blunt the discriminating powers of the mind, and, unfitting it for all voluntary exertion, to reduce it to a state of almost savage torpor. The most effective of these causes are the great national events which are daily taking place and the increasing accumulation of men in cities, where the uniformity of their occupations produces a craving for extraordinary incident, which the rapid communication of intelligence hourly gratifies. To this tendency of life and manners, the literature and theatrical exhibitions of the country have conformed themselves."

This startlingly applicable comment was written in the year 1800 by William Wordsworth in the preface to his "Lyrical Ballads"; and it has been cited by Edwin Muir in his recently published book "The Estate of Poetry." Muir states that poetry's effective range and influence have diminished alarmingly in the modern world. He believes in the inherent and indestructible qualities of the human mind and the great and permanent objects that act upon it, and suggests that the audience will increase when "poetry loses what obscurity is left in it by attempting greater themes, for great themes have to be stated clearly." If you keep that firmly in mind and resist, in Muir's words, "the vast dissemination of secondary objects that isolate us from the natural world," you have gone a long way toward equipping yourself for the examination of any work of art.

When you come to theatre, in this extremely hasty tour of the arts, you can approach it on two different levels. You can bring to it anticipation and innocence, giving yourself up, as it were, to the life on the stage and reacting to it emotionally, if the play is good, or listlessly, if the play is boring; a part of the audience organism that expresses its favor by silence or laughter and its disfavor by coughing and rustling. Or you can bring to it certain critical faculties that may heighten, rather than diminish, your enjoyment.

You can ask yourselves whether the actors are truly in their parts or merely projecting themselves; whether the scenery helps or hurts the mood; whether the playwright is honest with himself, his characters, and you. Somewhere along the line you can learn to distinguish between the true creative act and the false arbitrary gesture; between fresh observation and stale cliché; between the avant-garde play that is pretentious drivel and the avant-garde play that finds new ways to say old truths.

Purpose and craftsmanship—end and means—these are the keys to your judgment in all the arts. What is this painter trying to say when he slashes a broad band of black across a white canvas and lets the edges dribble down? Is it a statement of violence? Is it a self-portrait? If it is *one* of these, has he made you believe it? Or is this a gesture of the ego or a form of therapy? If it shocks you, what does it shock you into?

And what of this tight little painting of bright flowers in a vase? Is the painter saying anything new about flowers? Is it different from a million other canvases of flowers? Has it any life, any meaning, beyond its statement? Is there any pleasure in its forms or texture? The question is not whether a thing is abstract or representational, whether it is "modern" or conventional. The question, inexorably, is whether it is good. And this is a decision which only you, on the basis of instinct, experience, and association, can make for yourself. It takes independence and courage. It involves, moreover, the risk of wrong decision and the humility, after the passage of time, of recognizing it as such. As we grow and change and learn, our attitudes can change too, and what we once thought obscure or "difficult" can later emerge as coherent and illuminating. Entrenched prejudices, obdurate opinions are as sterile as no opinions at all.

Yet standards there are, timeless as the universe itself. And when you have committed yourself to them, you have acquired a passport to that elusive but immutable realm of truth. Keep it with you in the forests of bewilderment. And never be afraid to speak up.

Author and Title Index

America the Unimagining, 170

American Crisis, The [section introduction], 143

American Scholar, The, 42

Anatomy of Academic Discontent, The, 416

Anonymity, 572

Apocalypse, 55

ARNOLD, MATTHEW, 615

Ars Poetica [poem], 729

Arts of Selling, The, 127

AUDEN, W. H., 469, 725

BALDWIN, JAMES, 199, 251

Ballot or the Bullet, The, 346

BENEDICT, RUTH, 213

BETTELHEIM, BRUNO, 415

Bill of Rights, The, 295

BOSMAJIAN, HAIG A., 116

BROWN, NORMAN O., 54

BRUSTEIN, ROBERT, 445

By Way of Conclusion, 282

CAMUS, ALBERT, 691

Case for Professionalism, The, 445

Case for the White Southerner, The, 242

Centering as Dialogue, 34

CHIAROMONTE, NICOLA, 394

Chicago [poem], 545

Chorus of Priests [poem], 3

Civil Disobedience, 310

CLARK, KENNETH B., 591

CLEAVER, ELDRIDGE, 653, 655

COLES, ROBERT, 227

COMMAGER, HENRY STEELE, 193

Commencement Address, 451

COX, HARVEY, 572

Crito, The, 305

Cry of the Ghetto, The, 592

Cultural Importance of Art, The, 671

CUMMINGS, E. E., 4

DARROW, CLARENCE, 616

Day of a Stranger, 661

Declaration of Independence, 291

Democracy in America, 147

DEMOTT, BENJAMIN, 169

DE TOCQUEVILLE, ALEXIS, 146

DIDION, JOAN, 178

Disappearing City, The, 547

Dissent—1968 Style, 363

Dissent and Civil Disobedience [section introduction], 289

Dover Beach, 615

EMERSON, RALPH WALDO, 42

ESFANDIARY, F. M., 515

FANON, FRANTZ, 281

Fate of the City, The [section introduction], 543

Fire Next Time, The, 200

For Once, Then, Something, 724

FROMM, ERICH, 470, 648

FROST, ROBERT, 724

Function of Art, The [section introduction], 669

Future of Religion, The [section introduction], 613

General Survey of the Subject, 162

GILMAN, RICHARD, 746

GINSBERG, ALLEN, 107, 145

God's Grandeur [poem], 615

GOLDING, WILLIAM, 5

Grand Academy of Lagado, The, 522

Greatest Man in the World, The, 740

GREVILLE, FULKE, LORD BROOKE, 3

GRISWOLD, ERWIN N., 363

Historian Looks at Our Political Morality, A, 194

Historical Roots of Our Ecologic Crisis, The, 487

HOFSTADTER, RICHARD, 450

HOLT, JOHN, 111, 399

HOPKINS, GERARD MANLEY, 615

How City Planners Hurt Cities, 567

How Do You Know It's Good?, 754

HUXLEY, ALDOUS, 27, 127

I Hear America Singing [poem], 145

In My Craft or Sullen Art [poem], 728

Inaugural Address, 166

Indispensable Opposition, The, 298

Introduction to Herbert Kohl's *Teaching the Unteachable*, 112

JACOBS, JANE, 556, 567

JACOBS, PAUL, 134

JACOBSON, DAN, 552

JEFFERSON, THOMAS, 291

JONES, LEROI, 5, 710, 717

KEATS, JOHN, 721

KENNEDY, JOHN FITZGERALD, 166

KING, MARTIN LUTHER, JR., 328

KUNEN, JAMES SIMON, 381

LANGER, SUSANNE K., 63, 671

Language of White Racism, The, 116

LAQUEUR, WALTER, 428

Last Ditch, The, 227

Letter from Berkeley, 399

Letter from Birmingham Jail, 331

Letter from Rome, 394

Letter to Secretary McNamara, A, 108

LIPPMANN, WALTER, 297

Lost Dimension in Religion, The, 635

MACLEISH, ARCHIBALD, 729

MAILER, NORMAN, 599

MALCOLM X, 345

Man Against Darkness, 623

MANNES, MARYA, 753

Marrakech, 222

MATISSE, HENRI, 678

MERTON, THOMAS, 660

Missing Element: Moral Courage, The, 733

Moon Landing [poem], 469

MOORE, MARIANNE, 724

MORGAN, PERRY, 242

Morning of the Day They Did It, The [story], 529

Most Cheerful Graveyard in the World, The, 135

MUMFORD, LEWIS, 546

Must the Novelist Crusade?, 701

My Negro Problem—and Ours, 269

Mystical West Puzzles the Practical East, The, 516

Myth of a "Negro Literature," The, 711

Myth of Objective Consciousness, The, 498

Notes of a Native Son, 251

Notes of a Painter, 678

O Rotten Gotham, 581

Objectivity Unlimited, 500

Ode on a Grecian Urn [poem], 721

Of the Principal Source of Belief Among Democratic Nations, 147

On the Standards of Judgment [section introduction], 731

On Various Kinds of Thinking, 13

ORWELL, GEORGE, 79, 215, 222, 685

Our Image of God Must Go, 643

PLATO, 304

PODHORETZ, NORMAN, 269

Poetry [poem], 724

Politics and the English Language, 79

Prince of Creation, The, 63

Propaganda Under a Dictatorship, 28

Public Statement by Eight Alabama Clergymen, 329

Race and Racism [section introduction], 211

Racism: The *ism* of the Modern World, 213

Reflections on Youth Movements, 429

Religious Conversion, More or Less, A, 654

Revolutionary Theatre, The, 717

RICHARDS, MARY CAROLINE, 33

Right Use of Language, The [section introduction], 61

ROBINSON, JAMES HARVEY, 12

ROBINSON, JOHN A. T., 642

ROSZAK, THEODORE, 497, 500

Sailing to Byzantium [poem], 722

SANDBURG, CARL, 545

September 1, 1939 [poem], 725

Severed Tendon, The, 553

Shooting an Elephant, 215

since feeling is first [poem], 4

Some Dreamers of the Golden Dream, 179

STACE, W. T., 623

Strawberry Statement, The, 381

Student and the University, The [section introduction], 379

Supermarket in California, A [poem], 145

SWIFT, JONATHAN, 521

Talks at the Yenan Forum on Art and Literature, 694

Technology and Human Values [section introduction], 467

"The Christ" and His Teachings, 655

Thinking and Feeling [section introduction], 1

Thinking as a Hobby, 6

THOMAS, DYLAN, 728

THOREAU, HENRY DAVID, 309

THURBER, JAMES, 740

TILLICH, PAUL, 634

Toward Radical Humanism, 648

TSE-TUNG, MAO, 694

TUCHMAN, BARBARA, 733

Ultimate Terms in Contemporary Rhetoric, 91

University Research at Livermore and Los Alamos, 457

Violence in the City Streets, 557

WEAVER, RICHARD M., 90

WELTY, EUDORA, 700

WETHERILL, GEORGE W., 456

What Can the Artist Do in the World of Today?, 692

What Sort of Despotism Democratic Nations Have to Fear, 157

Where Are We Now and Where Are We Headed?, 471

WHITE, E. B., 529

WHITE, LYNN, JR., 486

White Standards and Black Writing, 747

WHITMAN, WALT, 145

Why Are We in New York?, 600

Why I Am an Agnostic, 617

Why I Write, 685

Why the Americans Are More Addicted to Practical Than to Theoretical Science, 151

WOLFE, TOM, 581

YEATS, WILLIAM BUTLER, 722

Young Soul [poem], 5

Rhetorical Index

We indicate below selections that well illustrate some genres, topics, and procedures traditionally discussed in rhetorical study. The listing is meant to be suggestive, not inclusive; many essays employ more than one rhetorical procedure, and many refuse to fit neatly into any traditional genre. What we mean by "plain style" is that described by George Orwell in "Politics and the English Language" (pp. 89–90).

GENRES (EXCLUDING THE ESSAY)

FICTION

Jonathan Swift, The Grand Academy of Lagado, 522

E. B. White, The Morning of the Day They Did It, 529

James Thurber, The Greatest Man in the World, 740

JOURNALS

James Simon Kunen, from The Strawberry Statement, 381

Eldridge Cleaver, A Religious Conversion, More or Less, 654; "The Christ" and His Teachings, 655

Thomas Merton, Day of a Stranger, 661

LETTERS (SOMEWHAT PUBLIC)

Allen Ginsberg, A Letter to Secretary McNamara, 108

Martin Luther King, Jr., Letter from Birmingham Jail, 331

POEMS

Fulke Greville, Lord Brooke, Chorus of Priests, 3

E. E. Cummings, since feeling is first, 4

LeRoi Jones, Young Soul, 5

Walt Whitman, I Hear America Singing, 145

Allen Ginsberg, A Supermarket in California, 145

W. H. Auden, Moon Landing, 469

Carl Sandburg, Chicago, 545

Gerard Manley Hopkins, God's Grandeur, 615

Matthew Arnold, Dover Beach, 615

John Keats, Ode on a Grecian Urn, 721

William Butler Yeats, Sailing to Byzantium, 722

Robert Frost, For Once, Then, Something, 724

Marianne Moore, Poetry, 724

W. H. Auden, September 1, 1939, 725

Dylan Thomas, In My Craft or Sullen Art, 728

Archibald MacLeish, Ars Poetica, 729

PUBLIC DOCUMENTS

Declaration of Independence, 291

The Bill of Rights, 295

SPEECHES AND TALK

Ralph Waldo Emerson, The American Scholar, 42

Norman O. Brown, Apocalypse, 55

John Fitzgerald Kennedy, Inaugural Address, 166

Malcolm X, The Ballot or the Bullet (taped), 346

Erwin N. Griswold, Dissent—1968 Style, 363

Richard Hofstadter, Commencement Address, 451

Kenneth B. Clark, The Cry of the Ghetto (from taped interviews), 592

Albert Camus, What Can the Artist Do in the World of Today?, 692

Mao Tse-tung, from Talks at the Yenan Forum on Art and Literature, 694

Barbara W. Tuchman, The Missing Element: Moral Courage, 733

TOPICS

LANGUAGE STUDY

George Orwell, Politics and the English Language, 79

Richard M. Weaver, Ultimate Terms in Contemporary Rhetoric, 91

Haig A. Bosmajian, The Language of White Racism, 116

Theodore Roszak, Objectivity Unlimited, 500

STYLE AND TONE
The Distinctive Style

Susanne K. Langer, The Prince of Creation, 63

Benjamin DeMott, America the Unimagining, 170

Martin Luther King, Jr., Letter from Birmingham Jail, 331

Malcolm X, The Ballot or the Bullet, 346

Tom Wolfe, O Rotten Gotham, 581

Kenneth B. Clark, The Cry of the Ghetto, 592

LeRoi Jones, The Revolutionary Theatre, 717

See also entries under The Personal Note

The Personal Note

Mary Caroline Richards, Centering as Dialogue, 34

Ralph Waldo Emerson, The American Scholar, 42

Norman O. Brown, Apocalypse, 55

Allen Ginsberg, A Letter to Secretary McNamara, 108

Robert Coles, The Last Ditch, 227

James Baldwin, Notes of a Native Son, 251

Norman Podhoretz, My Negro Problem—and Ours, 269

Frantz Fanon, By Way of Conclusion, 282

Henry David Thoreau, Civil Disobedience, 310

James Simon Kunen, from *The Strawberry Statement*, 381

John Holt, Letter from Berkeley, 399

George W. Wetherill, University Research at Livermore and Los Alamos, 457

Eldridge Cleaver, A Religious Conversion, More or Less, 654; "The Christ" and His Teachings, 655

Thomas Merton, Day of a Stranger, 661

George Orwell, Why I Write, 685

Albert Camus, What Can the Artist Do in the World of Today?, 692

Richard Gilman, White Standards and Black Writing, 747

The Plain Style

George Orwell, Politics and the English Language, 79

Joan Didion, Some Dreamers of the Golden Dream, 179

James Baldwin, from *The Fire Next Time*, 200

George Orwell, Shooting an Elephant, 215

George Orwell, Marrakech, 222

James Baldwin, Notes of a Native Son, 251

Norman Podhoretz, My Negro Problem—and Ours, 269

Jonathan Swift, The Grand Academy of Lagado, 522

E. B. White, The Morning of the Day They Did It, 529

Dan Jacobson, The Severed Tendon, 553

James Thurber, The Greatest Man in the World, 740

USE OF RESEARCH MATERIALS

Haig A. Bosmajian, The Language of White Racism, 116

Erwin N. Griswold, Dissent—1968 Style, 363

Theodore Roszak, Objectivity Unlimited, 500

Harvey Cox, Anonymity, 572

Tom Wolfe, O Rotten Gotham, 581

John A. T. Robinson, Our Image of God Must Go, 643

PROCEDURES

CONTESTING ARGUMENT

Perry Morgan, The Case for the White Southerner, 242

Walter Lippmann, The Indispensable Opposition, 298

Plato, from *The Crito*, 305

Henry David Thoreau, Civil Disobedience, 310

Martin Luther King, Jr., Letter from Birmingham Jail, 331

Erwin N. Griswold, Dissent—1968 Style, 363

Bruno Bettelheim, The Anatomy of Academic Discontent, 416

Robert Brustein, The Case for Professionalism, 445

George W. Wetherill, University Research at Livermore and Los Alamos, 457

Theodore Roszak, Objectivity Unlimited, 500

F. M. Esfandiary, The Mystical West Puzzles the Practical East, 516

Jane Jacobs, How City Planners Hurt Cities, 567

Norman Mailer, Why Are We in New York?, 600

Clarence Darrow, Why I Am an Agnostic, 617

Paul Tillich, The Lost Dimension in Religion, 635

Mao Tse-tung, from Talks at the Yenan Forum on Art and Literature, 694

Eudora Welty, Must the Novelist Crusade?, 701

LeRoi Jones, The Myth of a "Negro Literature," 711

Richard Gilman, White Standards and Black Writing, 747

DEFINITION

William Golding, Thinking as a Hobby (thinking), 6

James Harvey Robinson, On Various Kinds of Thinking (thinking), 13

Susanne K. Langer, The Prince of Creation (symbolism), 63

Aldous Huxley, The Arts of Selling (propaganda), 127

Ruth Benedict, Racism: The *ism* of the Modern World (racism), 213

Theodore Roszak, from *The Myth of Objective Consciousness* (expertise), 498

Tom Wolfe, O Rotten Gotham (behavioral sink), 581

Eudora Welty, Must the Novelist Crusade? (the novel), 701

DESCRIPTION

William Golding, Thinking as a Hobby, 6

Paul Jacobs, The Most Cheerful Graveyard in the World, 135

Joan Didion, Some Dreamers of the Golden Dream, 179

George Orwell, Marrakech, 222

Dan Jacobson, The Severed Tendon, 553

Jane Jacobs, Violence in the City Streets, 557

Thomas Merton, Day of a Stranger, 661

EXPOSITION OF IDEAS

James Harvey Robinson, On Various Kinds of Thinking, 13

Aldous Huxley, The Arts of Selling, 127

Alexis de Tocqueville, from *Democracy in America*, 147

Henry Steele Commager, A Historian Looks at Our Political Morality, 194

Susanne K. Langer, The Prince of Creation, 63

Ruth Benedict, Racism: The *ism* of the Modern World, 213

Walter Laqueur, Reflections on Youth Movements, 429

Richard Hofstadter, Commencement Address, 451

Lynn White, Jr., The Historical Roots of Our Ecologic Crisis, 487

Harvey Cox, Anonymity, 572

Susanne K. Langer, The Cultural Importance of Art, 671

See also entries under Contesting Argument

NARRATION

Joan Didion, Some Dreamers of the Golden Dream, 179

George Orwell, Shooting an Elephant, 215

James Baldwin, Notes of a Native Son, 251

Norman Podhoretz, My Negro Problem—and Ours, 269

James Simon Kunen, from *The Strawberry Statement*, 381

John Holt, Letter from Berkeley, 399

Jonathan Swift, The Grand Academy of Lagado, 522

E. B. White, The Morning of the Day They Did It, 529

Eldridge Cleaver, A Religious Conversion, More or Less, 654

Thomas Merton, Day of a Stranger, 661

James Thurber, The Greatest Man in the World, 740

SATIRE

Paul Jacobs, The Most Cheerful Graveyard in the World, 135

Jonathan Swift, The Grand Academy of Lagado, 522

E. B. White, The Morning of the Day They Did It, 529

James Thurber, The Greatest Man in the World, 740

ABOUT THE AUTHORS

CHARLES MUSCATINE is Professor of English at the University of California at Berkeley where he has taught since 1948. He received the Ph.D. from Yale University and has served as a Visiting Professor at Wesleyan University and the University of Washington. A distinguished medievalist, Professor Muscatine has received Fulbright and Guggenheim research fellowships, is the author of *Chaucer and the French Tradition* and *The Book of Geoffrey Chaucer*, and has published widely in professional journals. At Berkeley he has been chairman of the Committee on Freshman English, and of the Select Committee on Education.

MARLENE GRIFFITH is on the faculty of Laney College in Oakland, California, where she is a member and former chairman of the Department of English. She has also taught at Western College for Women, San Francisco State College, and the University of California at Berkeley. She received her B.A. from American International College in Springfield, Mass., and her M.A. from Berkeley. Since 1959 she has taught literature, expository and creative writing, and basic reading and writing courses. She has been a contributor to *College Composition and Communication, Twentieth Century Literature*, and *Modern Fiction Studies*.

A NOTE ON THE TYPE

The text of this book was set by means of modern photocomposition. The text type selected is ELEGANTE, the Linofilm counterpart of PALATINO. The display type is ZENITH, the Linofilm counterpart of OPTIMA. Both are contemporary creations of the German type designer, HERMANN ZAPF. Elegante is distinguished by broad letters and vigorous, inclined serifs typical of the work of a sixteenth century Italian master of writing. Zenith merges the clarity and expressiveness of the classic form with the simplicity and efficiency of linear sans-serif design. Both Elegante and Zenith reflect the early Venetian scripts influencing Zapf's creations.

This book was composed by Westcott & Thomson, Inc., Philadelphia, Pa., and printed and bound by H. Wolff Book Manufacturing Co., Inc., New York, N. Y. Random Collegiate Text paper supplied by Alan & Gray, New York, N. Y.

Typographic design by JACK RIBIK

Cover design by PETER RAUCH